ECONOMIC AND SOCIAL HISTORY OF BRITAIN

WEALTH AND WELFARE

ECONOMIC AND SOCIAL HISTORY OF BRITAIN

General Editor: Martin Daunton

ECONOMIC AND SOCIAL HISTORY OF BRITAIN

Wealth and Welfare

AN ECONOMIC AND SOCIAL HISTORY OF BRITAIN,
1851-1951

Martin Daunton

OXFORD
UNIVERSITY PRESS

OXFORD
UNIVERSITY PRESS

Great Clarendon Street, Oxford OX2 6DP

Oxford University Press is a department of the University of Oxford.
It furthers the University's objective of excellence in research, scholarship,
and education by publishing worldwide in

Oxford New York

Auckland Cape Town Dar es Salaam Hong Kong Karachi
Kuala Lumpur Madrid Melbourne Mexico City Nairobi
New Delhi Shanghai Taipei Toronto

With offices in

Argentina Austria Brazil Chile Czech Republic France Greece
Guatemala Hungary Italy Japan Poland Portugal Singapore
South Korea Switzerland Thailand Turkey Ukraine Vietnam

Oxford is a registered trade mark of Oxford University Press
in the UK and in certain other countries

Published in the United States
by Oxford University Press Inc., New York

© Martin Daunton 2007

British Library Cataloguing in Publication Data

Data available

Library of Congress Cataloging in Publication Data

Data available

Typeset by Laserwords Private Limited, Chennai, India
Printed in Great Britain on acid-free paper by
Ashford Colour Press Limited, Gosport, Hampshire

ISBN 978–0–19–873209–9

In Memory
Ronald James Daunton
1919–2006

Martin Daunton is Professor of Economic History in the University of Cambridge and Master of Trinity Hall. He is currently President of the Royal Historical Society. His previous publications include *Progress and Poverty: An Economic and Social History of Britain, 1700-1850*, which is the previous volume in this series. He has also produced two volumes on the politics of taxation in Britain between 1799 and 1979, and edited the Cambridge Urban History of Britain, 1840–1950. His current research deals with the interplay between domestic and international economic policy since the Second World War, and the taxation of the British empire from the mid-nineteenth to mid-twentieth centuries.

GENERAL EDITOR'S PREFACE

The five volumes of the Economic and Social History of Britain series cover the millennium between the Norman Conquest and the opening of the twenty-first century. This was a period of immense change in Britain's economy and society, of central importance to wider transformations in the history of the world. Until the late eighteenth century, the balance between natural resources and population was finely drawn, with the limits of sustainability reached first in the early fourteenth and again in the early seventeenth centuries. But by the end of the eighteenth century, the population at last exceeded its earlier peak without a collapse into misery and death—and from the mid-nineteenth century both population and welfare moved to new levels. Britain pioneered a fundamental transformation of economic and social life, surpassing by the eighteenth century the levels of urbanization found in other European countries, shifting workers from the land in unprecedented numbers, and developing a highly sophisticated commercial society. Britain was also central to the emergence of a global economy, culminating in the free trade, liberal empire of the second half of the nineteenth century, which was followed by deglobalization in the 1920s and 1930s, and a tentative reconstruction of a global economy after 1945 under American leadership, before the resurgence of globalization in the last quarter of the twentieth century. The economic and social history of Britain is about much more than the insular history of a small European island.

The series takes a distinctive approach to the subject. Its focus is the economy viewed as a social and cultural phenomenon. It does not approach economic history as the application of modern economic theories to the past, but sees the economy through meanings, social relations, and power. Economists make assumptions about *homo economicus* or rational economic man, even when they admit that rationality is bounded. Equally, economists assume that collective action is extremely difficult to achieve as each person pursues individual self-interest to the point that it may be self-defeating by destroying natural resources, or by allowing population to rise above the ability of the land to sustain it. By contrast, this series seeks to understand how men and women tried to make sense of what it meant to live within a market economy. It seeks to understand the nature of economic life from the perspectives of contemporaries, through an appreciation of cultural meanings, social practices, economic thinking, and political action.

The authors of the five volumes turn to social, political, and cultural history in order to understand how choice was actually driven, how and why collective action was achieved, and how population and resources were balanced. Economic history should work with cultural and social history in helping us to understand the meaning of economic relations. How, for example, were trust and reputation constructed to mitigate the risks of market exchange? Similarly, economic history should work with political history to appreciate the role of political action in distributing scarce resources and limiting the self-defeating pursuit of self-interest. And economic history should ally with intellectual history in order to elucidate the shifting understandings of political thinkers, social critics, and economists about market exchange and its implications for human relations.

This book is obviously dependent on the work of many scholars, and my debt is clear from the bibliography at the end of each chapter. The notes are kept to a minimum, covering specific information or points of interpretation. All works cited in the notes can be found in the Further Reading for each chapter; place of publication is London unless otherwise stated.

Martin Daunton

CONTENTS

LIST OF FIGURES

LIST OF TABLES

ACKNOWLEDGEMENTS

The origins of this book are to be found in the late 1980s, when I was approached by Robert Faber to write a single volume on the period 1700 to 1914. It soon became clear that a single volume was not feasible, and the first part appeared as *Progress and Poverty*, with the idea that a second volume would be extended up to 1950. The appearance of the book has been delayed for various reasons—not least because I had the pleasure of working with Robert Faber on the Oxford Dictionary of National Biography but also because I wrote another two books on the politics of British taxation. I am very grateful to all the editors at Oxford University Press who were sympathetic and understanding—as well as firm—during the long gestation of this book. I would especially thank Tony Morris and Matthew Cotton.

During the writing of the book, I moved from University College London to the University of Cambridge. The students who sat through my lectures in London and Cambridge will recognize much of what follows, and they have been a sympathetic and critical audience. The influence of colleagues at both institutions will be apparent, especially my colleagues at Cambridge with whom I teach the paper on British economic history since 1870 and run the seminar in modern economic history. Above all, Simon Szreter has been a source of ideas and stimulation. The intrusions of university politics and other chores mean that I have been heavily dependent on a number of people for assistance in bringing the book to completion. In particular, I would thank: Ginny Swepson for assistance with editing as well as ordering my life at Trinity Hall with efficiency and humour; Ben Griffin, Binoy Kampmark and Adrian Lashmore-Davies for checking footnotes; and Ruth Willats for invaluable assistance in editing. At the Press, Jackie Pritchard saw the book through production with care and efficiency. Once more, the index has been produced by Auriol Griffith-Jones to her customarily high standards.

I dedicated *Progress and Poverty* to Claire, who has lived with this companion volume for too long, and provided support and frequent encouragement to finish. I dedicate *Wealth and Welfare* to my father, who died shortly after I submitted the manuscript to the Press. He had always encouraged me as a historian, and many of the themes in this volume touch on his own life.

Martin Daunton
Trinity Hall
July 2006

CHAPTER I

The Nation's Wealth and the People's Welfare

In 1852, George Graham, William Farr, and Horace Mann reflected on the population tables of the census of 1851. They were full of pride and optimism in what they found. Since the first census of 1801, the population of Great Britain had increased by 10 million—which nearly equalled the increase 'in all preceding ages'. At the same time, the population was concentrated into new industrial towns at ever greater densities. The question they pondered was whether this population could be 'profitably employed'.[1] Many economists, not many years previously, doubted that they could, fearing that the growth of population would result in a decline in economic welfare as predicted by T. R. Malthus. The possibilities of economic growth seemed to be extremely limited.

The Possibilities of Growth

In the early nineteenth century, the world of T. R. Malthus still had some relevance. As he argued in his *Essay on Population* in 1797, population could grow rapidly in geometric progression (2, 4, 8, 16) and outstrip the ability of the land to provide more food, gained by hard-won advances in arithmetic progression (2, 4, 6, 8). The race between the hare of population and the tortoise of food supply might lead to the disaster of a positive check of famine and disease; much better was the pursuit of prudence and forethought to impose a 'preventive' check on population growth. In Malthus' words, it was better to put the hare to sleep and to allow the tortoise to catch up. In the moral world of the reverend Mr Malthus, prudence meant celibacy and delayed marriage rather than sexual practices which 'polluted' the marital bed. He attacked social policies which threatened prudential restraint, criticizing the poor law for offering relief to families with children which did more harm than good. What was the point of giving relief to the poor, so weakening their moral restraint, producing more children, and leading to higher food prices which made everyone worse off?[2]

David Ricardo approached the matter in a somewhat different manner. He argued that an increase in population would drive agricultural production to inferior, marginal land with lower yields. The price of corn would 'rise with the difficulty of producing the last portions of it' on inferior land, on which the farmer would receive only the ordinary rate of profit. On superior land, where costs did not increase in line with the price of corn, the farmer's profit margin widened. Since he was receiving more than the ordinary rate of profit, other capitalists were encouraged to compete for the land, and the landlord was able to raise the level of rent. The result was that the farmer's profit fell and the return to the landlord rose. Ricardo defined the gap between the cost of production and the price of corn as the Economic Rent: it was the difference between production on inferior and superior land, and it was appropriated by the landlord. Ricardo expected that an increase in population pushed production to marginal land so that prices rose and imposed strain upon the standard of living of the population, which fell back to subsistence level. Rent took a larger share of the income of the country at the expense of capital, and profits fell to a minimum which was barely sufficient to induce saving. There was little prospect of an increase in the rate of profit, for a rise in the amount of capital and labour produced a shift to inferior land with a declining yield. Ricardian economics assumed that the economy was closed and finite, in thrall to the laws of diminishing returns on marginal land.[3] Any increase in the welfare of the population as a whole was constrained, and most of the benefit would go to a small group of landowners.

As recently as 1848, John Stuart Mill's *Principles of Political Economy* accepted that growth would cease and a 'stationary state' set in. 'The expansion of capital would soon reach its ultimate boundary', remarked J. S. Mill in his *Principles*, 'if the boundary itself did not continually open and leave more space.' In a country such as Britain, where there had long been a large annual increase in capital, and where there were no reserves of fertile land, 'the rate of profit is habitually within . . . a hand's breadth of the minimum, and the country therefore on the very verge of the stationary state'. Welfare was therefore constrained. Although Mill was an official of the East India Co., he gave little role to the reserves of land in the subcontinent or the New World. At most, the downward tendency of profit could be checked. The waste of capital in rash speculation or its export to other countries would reduce the supply of funds and keep up the rate of return; and he suggested that cheap food from abroad would maintain profits by allowing the payment of lower wages. He assumed that population would rise and he did not expect cheap food imports to produce any significant gains in the standard of living. Improvements in production might maintain profits, yet Mill was still sceptical about the ability to escape the onset of a 'stationary economy'. Inventions led to cheaper goods, so producing an improvement in the standard of living of the workers, and encouraging them to 'people up to the improvement in their condition'. Money wages would fall;

profits would consequently rise; more capital would be accumulated; and profits would be eroded. Mill remained pessimistic about the possibility of inventions and improvements in production leading to higher growth and permanent gains; their role was merely 'in some degree to widen the interval which has to be passed before arriving at the stationary state'.[4] Mill was content to accept this outcome, for he believed that the 'stationary state' could reach a reasonable standard of living, where people could spend their time on better tasks than the mere pursuit of material gain.

Others took a less sanguine view, developing Ricardo's insight to suggest that the result would be conflict between classes over resources, above all Friedrich Engels in *The Condition of the Working Class in England in 1844* and Karl Marx and Engels in the *Communist Manifesto*. Engels and Marx were schooled in German dialectical thought, and saw that the situation set out by the classical economists was unstable. Ricardo's depersonalized factors of production might form the basis of class warfare and the demise of capitalism. To Marx and Engels, the landowners and their claims to Rent were no longer the crucial issue. In their view, the industrial bourgeoisie in receipt of profits had defeated feudalism, and conflict was now between the industrial bourgeoisie and the proletariat. The industrialists were making large profits, expropriating the surplus value of the goods produced by the workers above their subsistence needs. The welfare of most of the population might therefore decline, and the result was a potential crisis of capitalism. The erosion of wages and immiseration of the workers might lead to revolt; or a glut of capital without any means of investment would create an inner contradiction in capitalism, a failure of profitable outlets for the value expropriated from labour. Engels anticipated a revolution soon after he published *The Condition of the Working Class*. It did not occur, and looking back in 1914, Lenin suggested that one reason was the expansion of the empire as an outlet for surplus capital, and the use of the proceeds of imperialism to secure prosperity and stability at home.[5]

In reality, Malthusian disaster was avoided in England, Wales, and Scotland, unlike in Ireland with the horrors of the potato famine of 1846. Britain achieved a higher level of per capita income than any other country in the world by 1851, despite the pressure of population growth. The population of Britain continued to rise in the first half of the nineteenth century, without the positive check of disease as in the early fourteenth or seventeenth centuries, or in Ireland in the 1840s; and without a collapse in the welfare of the people. British agriculture managed to increase its output by extending the margin of cultivation and raising productivity through changes in organization and the development of new techniques. Above all, the resources of British agriculture were supplemented by both the greater use of mineral fuel and inputs from the colonies. As Kenneth Pomeranz remarks, 'without the dual boons of coal and colonies, Britain would have faced an ecological impasse with no apparent internal solution'.[6] The restraints of the Malthusian system rested on an 'organic economy': the reliance upon water or wind to operate mills, or upon human and animal power to work machinery, meant that the available amount of energy was strictly limited. It was a flow, determined by the short-term vagaries of the weather or by the availability of food to sustain men and beasts. Since the supply of resources could not easily be augmented, marginal costs would soon increase.

These restraints were loosened by the gradual replacement of wood by coal as a fuel, so releasing more land for food crops. By the early nineteenth century, steam engines were also starting to replace horses as motive power, so releasing land from fodder crops and supplementing water and wind power to increase energy inputs. In 1815, the output of coal in Britain was 22.6 million metric tons, and in continental Europe only 3.0 to 3.5 million metric tons. Britain had a considerable advantage over other economies, for it was possible to inject large amounts of energy into the economy as a stock rather than flow. The output of coal in 1815 was equivalent to the energy produced from about 15 million acres of land, even on a conservative estimate; in 1867, Britain's total arable land amounted to 17 million acres. Clearly, the output of coal marked a major difference from earlier periods of demographic crisis, as did the contribution of the colonies and countries brought into the orbit of Britain's economic power. Raw cotton from Egypt, India, and above all the southern United States provided inputs into the Lancashire cotton textile industry on a scale beyond the possibilities of production of domestic flax and wool. New sources of wool were available from the Cape and Australia, allowing the Yorkshire woollen textile industry to expand far beyond the resources of British flocks. Cane sugar from the Caribbean and Mauritius became an important supply of calories, exceeding the yield of potatoes—a highly productive crop—by fourfold. Timber was imported from North America as well as from the Baltic. By 1830, these four commodities were equivalent to about 25 to 30 million acres of British land.[7]

Much of this addition to Britain's acreage came from the dispossession of indigenous peoples in North America and Australasia, and from the transformation of production in Asia. The success of Britain relied not only on its commercial acumen and entrepreneurial dynamism, but also on the fiscal-military state in extracting resources from the rest of the world. Britain's ability to escape from the Malthusian trap rested not only on coal, but on the ability of the Royal Navy to seize islands in the Caribbean and to transport convicts to Australia; the achievement of the East India Co. as a military and revenue-extracting body; and the use of naval power to open the market in China. In some cases, production involved white settlers and family farms, but in many cases the commodities came from plantations, operated by slaves or other forms of unfree labour.[8]

By the 1850s, the proportion of the workforce engaged in high-productivity sectors was sufficient to influence the growth rate of the economy as a whole. In 1831, only about 10 per cent of adult men in England were employed in manufacturing, both in factories and in the putting-out trades based in workshops which supplied distant markets. Many more men—32 per cent—were employed in retail and handicraft trades supplying local markets. As E. A. Wrigley has pointed out, productivity growth by means of specialization—Adam Smith's principle of the division of labour—was difficult beyond a certain point. After 1831, the proportion of men engaged in factories using powered machinery started to rise, moving beyond the possibilities of the division of labour and allowing output to move ahead of population growth.[9]

Britain's economic success in 1851 also rested on the existence of social and legal institutions, a culture of commerce and credit, which had developed since the late seventeenth century. In order for areas of the country and individual households to specialize in one commodity, they needed to be confident that they could sell their own output and buy other goods. This condition required a sophisticated system of credit, which moved away from a local, personal assessment of reputation. The emergence of much longer-distance, impersonal credit implied greater levels of risk, and the need to develop legal and social practices to mitigate the dangers of failure—whether through the law of bankruptcy, the development of insurance, or the emergence of specialist bankers and brokers who could assess the 'reputation' of paper instruments such as bills of exchange. The creation of these institutional and cultural underpinnings of a highly commercialized society took a long time and was not easily replicated: the process had gone furthest in the Netherlands and in Britain. British society was able to deal with the conditions of risk and insecurity in business life, gaining a considerable advantage in sectors such as insurance and banking. Further, the British state had a high level of acceptance and legitimacy, so that there was less risk of financial crisis which hit other European countries, and the credit of the British state was high so that it could borrow on easy terms.[10]

Graham, Farr, and Mann had probably not heard of Engels or Marx; they were surely aware of the writings of the English classical economists. But they came to a very different and more optimistic view of the future of the British economy. The wealth of the nation could rise to new levels, benefiting the welfare of the entire population. Labour had been divided into specialized trades, and industry organized in towns so that production was rising faster than the population. They were confident of the beneficial moral effects of the growth of towns, arguing that mental activity was increased 'as the aggregation in towns brings them oftener into combination and collision'. Of course, the growth of towns and the rise in their density threatened disease and death, but they were optimistic that a solution could be found: 'extensive sanitary arrangements, and all the appliances of physical as well as of social science, are necessary to preserve the national vigour of the population, and to develop the inexhaustible resources of the English race.'[11]

Farr and his colleagues were far from being disinterested observers, for they had a particular view of economic growth and of their role as men of science in ensuring that the towns were healthy and well organized. Nevertheless, their comments indicate a shift in sentiment and in economic thinking that provides the theme of this book. In the previous volume in this series, *Progress and Poverty*, the theme was the race between the tortoise of food supply and the hare of population that set limits to the wealth of the nation and shaped the distribution of the welfare of the people. In *Wealth and Welfare*, the crucial issue is how the welfare benefits of greater national wealth should be distributed. The change in emphasis from the gloom of Malthus and Ricardo was reflected in another great event of 1851—the Great Exhibition. This celebration of industry and trade in the Crystal Palace in Hyde Park is, by now, a cliché in British history—the symbol of Britain's supremacy as the 'workshop of the world', the first industrial nation, and—as the census of 1851 indicated—the first urban nation. In fact, the Great Exhibition was much more interesting than the cliché allows, for it was not only a symbol of success and British dominance. It also indicated the difficulties, tensions, and ambiguities in the process of industrialization. Farr and his colleagues were presenting one view of Britain's economy and society; to others, the growth of large towns and industry implied dangerous imbalance and collapse into moral disorder. In 1851, the Conservatives had not yet reconciled themselves entirely to free trade, and feared that the result might be a distortion of the balance of the economy between agriculture and industry, and a corruption of politics by the vested interests of the towns.[12]

The origins of the exhibition lay in the concern of the Royal Society of Arts concerns about the failures of technical education and design—could it be that the goods celebrated by the census were of poor quality and in bad taste? The question was: what should be the nature of a mass consumption society? The issue troubled the Royal Commissioners appointed to run the exhibition. The Commissioners included Richard Cobden, the leader of the Anti-Corn Law League, as well as Sir Robert Peel and William Gladstone who had been so important as Prime Minister and President of the Board of Trade in reducing tariffs and repealing the corn laws. But there were also opponents of free trade such as William Thompson, who wished to retain protection of the shipping industry, and Philip Pusey, the founder of the Royal Agricultural Society. The Commission represented the Royal Academy (for artists), the Royal Society (for scientists), the Institution of Civil Engineers, the Geological Society, the Royal Asiatic Society; its members included the president of the Manchester Chamber of Commerce. Under their general guidance, the organizers secured 100,000 exhibits, obtained donations and a guarantee fund from private individuals, and built the Crystal Palace. An appeal was made to everyone in a triumph of inclusive voluntarism that was so characteristic of the mid-Victorian political economy of free trade liberalism. Over 300 local committees were created to collect subscriptions and exhibits, and to encourage visitors. The exhibition opened to great acclaim on May Day 1851.

The exhibition was more than a metropolitan event; it was national and inclusive, a celebration of British commercial and economic success rather than a divisive celebration of free trade. The rhetoric of the exhibition stressed that it symbolized a free people, a triumph of entrepreneurs and initiative rather than of an all-powerful state. Organizers of local committees were told to emphasize four reasons for supporting the exhibition: it would benefit the entire economy, both industry and agriculture; it would benefit all classes, whether producers, distributors, or consumers, workers or capitalists; it would promote peace; and it had the support of the monarchy. What might have been a divisive celebration of free trade became a non-partisan national event, a vision of harmony, unity, co-operation, and inclusion. It was part of the process by which a deeply contentious economic policy and massive changes in the organization of society became 'natural', a source of British identity and political culture. Workers were no longer threats to the social and political order as in the Chartist protests of the 1830s and 1840s; they were energetic producers and participants in a new world of goods. The pursuit of wealth could increase the welfare of everyone and make goods available to all. The exhibition 'promulgated an image of industrialization that was inclusive rather than exclusive',[13] an approach found also in attitudes towards the tax system and to the regulation of utilities. The government wished to reduce duties and to control gas tariffs and passenger fares in order to make goods and services readily available to everyone. The exhibition showed the benefits of technology, of hard work, and of consuming with taste and discrimination, to the development of the welfare of the British people.

Of course, there were tensions. Commentators such as Ruskin were nostalgic for destroyed craftsmanship and quality; others showed pride in quantity and cheapness. Was value expressed in the labour embodied in the good—or in what the market would bear? Everyone could be invited under one roof, to admire industrial production and consumption—but only within a properly hierarchical social order, with discriminations of entry charges and times of attendance. Locating the exhibition in the fashionable West End of London, and inviting all to attend so soon after the crises of Chartism, symbolized the fact that society could safely enjoy the common blessings of commercial success. For the first time, a national railway system provided cheap excursions to bring thousands to London. Samuel Wilberforce, the Evangelical Christian and crusader against slavery, felt that the exhibition 'sets forth in its true light the dignity of the working classes—and it tends to make other people feel the dignity which attaches to the producers of these things'. Radical ex-Chartists could point out with justice that the exhibition did not display exploitation of labour such as sweated tailors or shoemakers.[14] But to most observers, the exhibition was a symbol of social integration and cohesion within a hierarchical social order, a sign that the benefits of economic growth were widely available and not the preserve of a minority. The Great Exhibition marked the point at which the bulk of the population could start to share in the benefits of industrialization. The fears of a 'stationary state' or a collapse of capitalism had some substance in the early nineteenth century when the standard of living of most people was restrained. In the second half of the nineteenth century, the standard of living of the British people started to rise to new levels.

Distribution and Growth

By the 1850s, economic growth was for the first time breaking through the barriers of the Malthusian world: how should benefits be distributed? In any society, there is a trade-off between growth and welfare, between the need for incentives to stimulate wealth and the concern that inequality might threaten the welfare of the bulk of the population, with serious consequences for social stability and peace. The question was absolutely fundamental to British society between 1851 and 1951. In 1853, the budget of William Gladstone laid down the basis of the mid-Victorian social contract based on the rejection of redistributive taxation, which was widely accepted as socially just. After the Second World War, the Labour Chancellor Hugh Dalton—himself the author of a book on equality—stressed the virtues of a highly redistributive fiscal system and the shortcomings of pursuing personal gain in the market. The exact balance between equality and efficiency or growth was a matter of practical politics with the development of mass democracy and the need to compete for markets. It was also debated by leading economists and political philosophers.

The dominant mid-Victorian view of the balance between growth and equality was expressed in John Stuart Mill's *Principles* of 1848. 'I do not see how you can', he remarked, 'either with justice or policy, tax a person more heavily because he earns more, or because, after having earned more, he saves more. I do not think you can lay a tax upon energy, or industry, or prudence.' Large incomes were a reward for industry and enterprise; what Mill did accept was a graduated tax on inherited wealth on the grounds that inheritance undermined the active industry and prudence of the recipient. Taxation should be based on 'proportionality'—the state should take the same proportion of the income of all classes and interests in society.[15] Gladstone's budget of 1853 followed much the same line. Taxation should be neutral between classes in order to challenge the radical critique that it distributed money from the poor or enterprising to landowners or rentiers. It should not distribute from rich to poor, or land to industry, which would create bitter conflict between classes. In any case, redistribution would be harmful for everyone in society by undermining economic growth. The income of the rich led to savings, and hence to investment and employment for the poor who should be encouraged to be self-reliant, developing their own welfare and savings. The role of the state was to allow everyone to share in the benefits of economic growth and material abundance, by removing barriers to trade, reducing taxes on consumption, and ensuring that the new ventures in rail, gas, and water did not charge exploitative prices. By such means, the state would be seen as even-handed and fair, and the social order as just and beneficial.

Mill's political philosophy was developed and extended in the next generation by Henry Sidgwick, Alfred Marshall, and A. C. Pigou. At the heart of Sidgwick's philosophy was the issue of whether there were any grounds for demonstrating that altruism and a concern for the welfare of others was superior to egoism and the pursuit of self-interest. Sidgwick admitted that equality would, on the face of things, increase happiness, but he was concerned that it might also mean a loss of welfare, much as in Malthus' critique of the poor law. If the poor had more money, they might be tempted into idleness and to have more children; meanwhile, the rich would have less to save and the efficiency of capital would fall. The average income would support a larger population, and welfare would suffer as a result of redistribution and equality. In other words, the pursuit of altruism might be harmful to the welfare of others.[16] Marshall was more confident that economic man was altruistic, and in his *Principles of Economics* of 1890 he provided the cornerstone of marginal or neo-classical economics, with its notion that the satisfaction from each additional or marginal item fell.[17] His successor at Cambridge, A. C. Pigou, applied marginal economics to welfare. His *Wealth and Welfare* (1912) and its elaboration in *The Economics of Welfare* (1920) offered another way of addressing Sidgwick's dilemma of altruism versus egoism by asking how to maintain the balance between the 'national dividend' and transfer payments to the poor. His reasoning rested on two propositions: economic welfare would increase if the national dividend rose without the poor becoming worse off; and economic welfare would also increase if the poor became better off without the national dividend falling. The task of the welfare economist was to establish whether these conditions were met. The national dividend would be at its maximum when the marginal net product was equal in all activities—that is, the employment of one more worker in making cotton cloth would lead to the same net benefit as one more worker in hairdressing. In order to ensure an equal marginal net product in all uses, it was necessary to control monopolies and remove impediments to the free movement of capital and labour. It was also necessary to redistribute to the poor at the expense of the rich. A loss of income by the rich would leave their efficiency virtually unchanged; an increase in consumption by the poor would produce a higher rate of return. There was one condition: the poor must invest efficiently in themselves. Could they be trusted to do so, and not to spend their additional money on idleness and dissipation? Pigou felt that the poor needed to be controlled and directed; and that social spending would not produce a higher rate of return if invested in the elderly and defective rather than in sound children and normal men of middle life. Redistribution would lead to efficiency, provided it was complemented by a degree of coercion or regulation—precisely the loss of liberty feared by 'new Liberals' who wished instead to remove the material impediments which prevented men and women from taking charge of their own lives. To new Liberals such as L. T. Hobhouse, the plight of the poor removed their chances of taking charge of their own lives; if the state could remove structural impediments, their characters could blossom. Coercion would merely create another constraint on their sense of autonomy and self-esteem.[18]

Of course, many old Liberals and Conservatives continued to support the basic propositions of Mill and Gladstone, that wealth and high income offered incentives and provided the basis for savings, investment, and growth. These assumptions were challenged by John Maynard Keynes in the 1930s. He stressed the inability of effective demand to utilize all available resources. One way of boosting effective demand was to redistribute money to the poor, who had a higher propensity to consume; another was to smooth the depression through deficit finance. To Keynes, the incomes of the rich were not needed to produce more savings and hence investment and employment, as assumed by Gladstone. Rather, a high level of demand and a prosperous economy would stimulate investment and lead to a demand for savings. In the absence of effective demand, savings would not be used and would reduce consumption.[19]

Although Pigou differed fundamentally from Keynes's approach to the depression of the 1930s, he did have a considerable impact on two of the leading figures in the creation of the post-war welfare state: William Beveridge and Hugh Dalton. In the opinion of Jose Harris, Beveridge's thinking was 'permeated' by the ideas of Pigou.[20] Dalton studied economics in Cambridge, going on to produce a study of *Some Aspects of the Inequality of Incomes in Modern Communities* (1920). In this book, he developed Pigou's ideas to provide support for socialism. Inequalities of income, he argued, meant that 'the less urgent needs of the rich are satisfied, while the more urgent needs of the poor are left unsatisfied'. In his budgets of 1945–7, he pursued a consciously redistributive policy a world away from Gladstone.[21]

The Labour party was committed to equality on grounds of both efficiency and ethics. The threat to liberty did not come from the drive to equality and its undermining of incentives and enterprise. On the contrary, the real threat to liberty came from the chaos of capitalism which led to war, fascism, or communism. In 1930, H. J. Laski reflected that 'It is when the economy of a society begins to contract that liberty is in danger.' In Laski's opinion, liberty 'implies power to expand, the choice by the individual of his own way of life without imposed prohibitions from without'. A necessary condition of choice and liberty was equality, which 'is such an organization of opportunity that no man's personality suffers frustration to the private benefit of others'. Without economic equality, consent was not likely to operate; in the absence of consent, social peace was not possible. 'An unequal society always lives in fear, and with a sense of impending disaster in its heart . . . men will not accept the state as the appointed conscience of the nation unless they conceive themselves to possess a full share of its benefits.'[22] Equality was central to Labour's vision; personal incentives through high profits and incomes were destructive and unmerited, creating waste, inefficiency, and speculation. Indeed, the experience of full employment after the war suggested that equality was economically rational in ending depression created by low levels of demand. The disagreement between Labour politicians was over priorities and means rather than a commitment to equality. Some felt that public ownership and planning were prerequisites; others believed that a redistribution of material rewards through taxation was sufficient; and others stressed a more qualitative vision of socialist fellowship.[23]

Whether or not Pigou's own formulation met with agreement, *Wealth and Welfare* posed the crucial issue of British economic and social history in the new world of growth after 1851: where should the balance be struck between the national dividend and transfers to the poorer members of society? By 1951, many economists and politicians felt that Labour had skewed the balance too far towards transfer payments at the expense of the national dividend. But it would be a rash politician who suggested a return to the levels of inequality of 1851 or, for that matter, 1939. The context for debates over the proper balance between growth and distribution had shifted, and not only as a result of changes in economic analysis and political philosophy. The franchise was extended, and there was a different relationship between votes and income levels. Gladstone was well aware that most voters in 1853 were paying income tax, so he could confidently expect them to vote for cheap government which would reduce their own burdens. What would happen if the majority of voters fell below the threshold of income tax; and if the median voter received less than the median income? They might demand redistributive taxation, placing the costs of social welfare policies on the better-off members of society—a possibility that seemed very real by the First World War. The issue was not only one of redistributive taxation and social transfers; it was also about the extent to which economic policy should be determined by considerations of domestic stability or international competitiveness.

Decline and the British Economy: Reality or Misnomer?

From a vantage point of the early nineteenth century, the second half of the nineteenth century appears as a remarkable period of growth and prosperity, when the shackles of the 'stationary state' were broken. From a vantage point of the early twentieth century, 1851 seemed a golden age of British superiority now under threat from the emergence of Germany and the United States as major industrial powers. It was only to be expected that Britain's dominant industrial position was challenged. Other countries—above all Belgium, Germany, and the United States—developed their own coal reserves and eroded Britain's advantage in the supply of energy. Similarly, British access to the cheap resources of the rest of the world—sugar, coffee, tobacco from the Americas, tea from Asia, grain and meat from the temperate settler economies, and raw materials such as rubber and copper from around the world—were available to other industrial economies by global free trade and cheap steam transport.

When economic historians started to analyse the period, many took their cue from the concern about competition with the United States and Germany at the turn of the nineteenth and twentieth centuries. These fears of prospective decline in the 1890s and 1900s meshed with the obsession of British economists and politicians from the 1960s with the fact that post-war British growth rates were lower than in many other European countries. Historical analysis of the later nineteenth century was informed by debates over modernizing the British economy in the 1960s, 1970s, and 1980s, for the seeds of problems were located in this period. Perhaps British entrepreneurs were inadequate, in thrall to an anti-industrial culture of the rural elite, more anxious to be gentlemen than profit-maximizing businessmen.[24] Perhaps institutional structures helped to mitigate risk and create social stability, at the expense of entrenching union power in the workplace and hindering productivity growth.[25] Perhaps the state frustrated economic growth by pursuing policies favourable to financiers at the expense of productive industry, and neglecting technical education and economic modernization.[26]

These historical debates reflected contemporary concerns about the modernization of the British economy in the 1960s and 1970s, and so distorted understanding of the later nineteenth and early twentieth centuries. Approaching the second half of the nineteenth century and first half of the twentieth century from the standpoint of the earlier nineteenth century gives a different perspective: a successful escape from the limits of the Malthusian world. The emphasis on decline diverted attention from more interesting questions. How were the welfare benefits of economic growth distributed and what were the implications of the choices for British society and its ability to sustain growth? What was the nature of the British state: was it in thrall to the financiers of the City who extracted income at the expense of industry and its workforce—or were financiers concerned with the needs of industry and technology, with the state neutral between interests and classes? Should British culture be read as dominated by an anti-industrial ethos of rural nostalgia and aristocratic contempt which threatened economic growth, or was British culture pluralistic and at ease with change?

Indeed, it might be argued that the British economy was remarkably successful and competitive in comparison with the rest of Europe throughout the period, and that the real puzzle is less the supposed decline of Britain than the divergence of the United States from the levels of productivity in manufacturing of both Britain and Germany. A comparison with Britain's main European rival—Germany—suggests at once that the notion of decline has limited relevance. As the figures in Table 1.1 indicate, Germany did not overtake the United Kingdom in GDP per capita until the 1960s. On this measure, the British economy was more efficient and producing a higher level of welfare than Germany throughout the period covered by this book. An explanation of the higher levels of British GDP per capita emerges if the two economies are divided into agriculture, industry, and services (Table 1.2).

Britain had a very clear lead in productivity in agriculture and in services. In the case of agriculture, Germany was in a worse comparative position in 1950 than in 1871—and the large size of the German agricultural sector meant that the overall level of productivity in Germany was held down compared to Britain (see Table 1.3). The British economy was highly efficient and modern in terms of the allocation of

TABLE 1.1. *Gross domestic product per capita, UK and Germany, 1820–1973*

	UK	Germany
1820	100	63.3
1870	100	58.6
1913	100	76.2
1929	100	82.5
1938	100	85.7
1950	100	62.5
1973	100	109.7

Source: Broadberry, 'Anglo-German productivity differences', 248.

TABLE 1.2. *German and UK labour productivity level by selected sectors, 1871–1950 (UK=100)*

	1871	1891	1911	1929	1935	1950
Agriculture	55.7	53.7	67.3	56.9	57.2	41.2
Manufacturing	92.6	94.0	119.3	104.7	102.0	96.0
Utilities	31.3	64.2	103.8	158.6	144.0	120.6
Transport/communications	96.8	147.5	216.9	151.2	132.4	122.0
Distribution/finance	70.7	45.9	52.5	50.3	54.3	50.7
Professional/personal services	89.7	77.0	76.3	99.8	105.6	94.2
All sectors	60.8	60.7	75.5	73.0	75.7	74.4

Source: Broadberry, 'Anglo-German productivity differences', 251.

TABLE 1.3. *Sectoral shares of employment, UK, USA, and Germany, 1870–1950 (%)*

United Kingdom	1871	1911	1930	1950
Agriculture	22.2	11.8	7.6	5.1
Manufacturing	33.5	32.1	31.7	34.9
Distribution/finance/services	27.0	32.3	35.2	31.7
United States	1870	1910	1930	1950
Agriculture	50.0	32.0	20.9	11.0
Manufacturing	17.3	22.2	21.3	25.0
Distribution/finance/services	18.3	26.2	33.1	40.0
Germany	1875	1913	1935	1950
Agriculture	49.5	34.5	29.9	24.3
Manufacturing	24.7	29.5	30.0	31.4
Distribution/finance/services	16.0	19.5	22.3	21.1

Source: Broadberry, *Productivity Race*, 64.

its resources: little was done to maintain employment in agriculture compared with Germany, where the state took steps to sustain a small-scale, inefficient form of agriculture. The agricultural sector in Britain was relatively small and efficient, and its success in releasing labour meant that two other sectors were unusually large in 1851: manufacturing and services.

The British lead over Germany widened in distribution and finance, with more or less parity in personal and professional services from the 1930s. Indeed, some historians have gone so far as to argue that Britain was always much better at services than at manufacturing, and that it was more rational to concentrate on the former than the latter.[27] Deindustrialization and the growth of the service economy—and especially the City of London—may therefore be a rational use of resources. Other historians have taken a somewhat different view, arguing that the strong record of the service industries positively harmed industry. An influential interpretation of the British economy assumes that the great landowners and financiers of the City of London moved together in the later nineteenth century, creating a new social elite of 'gentlemanly capitalists'. They shared a common education and culture, often intermarrying, and dominating the upper reaches of the British state, including the Bank of England and the Treasury which defined their interests as 'national' rather than a special, sectional interest. Further, these gentlemanly capitalists dominated imperial expansion. By contrast, the industrialists were excluded and their interests seen as sectional.[28]

The argument developed in this book dissents from such an interpretation, suggesting that industry was not ignored or opposed to the interests of finance, which should be redefined as much more than the international financiers of the City of London. The service sector was much more than the City of London and international finance, for major ventures emerged in the domestic economy and helped to cope with the insecurities and risks of life in a highly commercialized and urban society. Financial institutions are often criticized for harming the welfare of the British people by failing to invest at home, without paying attention to this contribution to social security. Although some historians argue that domestic banks did not respond to the needs of industry, the British banking system had the merit of stability compared with many other countries. Furthermore, the development of a sophisticated financial sector meant that the state was able to borrow on reasonable terms: the larger local authorities turned to the London market to fund investment in the infrastructure; and the central government was able to borrow on cheaper rates than its counterparts elsewhere in Europe. Rather than stressing the supposed failures of the British financial system to meet domestic needs, attention should be paid to the positive features of stability and flexibility, and its contribution to reducing risk and improving welfare. The service economy included many other sectors where Britain was in the forefront, such as sport and seaside resorts, catering for the needs of an urban, industrial society.

Moral and cultural responses to credit and consumption continued to inform political debate. Could working-class families be trusted with credit, and how should their debts be treated? How were middle-class housewives, using their husbands' credit, to be viewed? And how should consumers be protected from adulterated or poor-quality goods? How to define the consumer interest provides a theme across the period, from the world of free trade as a way of supplying a cheap loaf and 'free breakfast table', to debates over consumer issues within the post-war Labour government. Did consumers need representation in the nationalized industries or was state ownership in itself a guarantee that the public could not be exploited? Did competition between private firms result in waste or inefficiency, or spread the benefits of consumer choice?

In manufacturing industry, Germany pulled ahead of Britain in the years leading up to the First World War, achieving a higher level of productivity before converging between the wars, with Britain gaining a slight advantage after the Second World War. In the case of manufacturing, German labour productivity reached British levels by 1899 and secured a sizeable advantage by 1913. The lead was then lost, and Britain and Germany were on more or less equal terms in manufacturing up to 1950. German industry regained its previous advantage only in the 1960s and opened up a sizeable advantage of 49 per cent by 1977. For the period covered by this book, the story is of German and British comparability, and of a growing lag behind America from the end of the nineteenth century (see Table 1.4).[29] Whatever the explanation for the gap, it was not peculiar to Britain and any simple notion of 'decline' is problematic.

TABLE I.4. *Manufacturing output per person employed, USA/UK and Germany/UK, 1899–1989 (UK = 100)*

	USA/UK	Germany/UK
1899	194.8	99.0
1913	212.9	119.0
1929	249.9	104.7
1937	208.3	96.0
1950	262.6	96.0
1958	250.0	111.1
1977	229.6	148.6
1989	177.0	105.1

Source: Broadberry, 'Manufacturing and the convergence hypothesis', 774.

The clearest and most consistent divergence was in transport and utilities, where Britain fell far behind German levels of productivity. A wide gap emerged in utilities, transport, and communications which were increasingly important sectors of the economy. Investment in these 'network industries' was central to resolving the problems of urban health noted by Farr and his colleagues—trams and trains took people to the suburbs; gas, water, drains, and electricity created a better urban and domestic environment to limit disease. The 'network' industries had a number of distinctive features. They required large lump-sum investments before any income could be secured—unlike many manufacturing industries where growth was often dependent on ploughing back profits—and they were run by joint-stock companies. Usually, they relied on authority granted by the state to purchase land or secure rights of passage—to excavate the roadway for pipes and cables, or to demolish property to build railway lines. Furthermore, they often had monopoly power over the consumer, so posing the danger that joint-stock companies might behave irresponsibly. The welfare implications were of great significance. Consumers could not realistically provide these services for themselves or select another supplier, and the power of the water or gas company to set charges was, in effect, a right to impose a tax. These features of the network industries meant that the state was involved in regulating the ability of private concerns to exploit the public. The nature of state control over utilities, transport, and communications might be counter-productive, leading to inefficiency and preventing the full exploitation of economies of scale. Arguably, British performance in this important sector of the economy was less than satisfactory, reflecting some of the difficulties of striking a balance between the protection of the consumer and the creation of efficiency.

This sectoral breakdown indicates where weaknesses were to be found in the British economy—and equally where shortcomings might be found in Germany.

Narratives of decline miss the more important point: how to understand the distinctive shape and institutional or cultural patterns of the British economy in comparative perspective for each major sector. Here is the theme of Part I, where the various sectors of the British economy are anatomized.

Global versus Insular Capitalism

The role of the service sector in international trade and finance points to another major theme: the rise and fall of globalization, which is discussed in Part II. The period from 1850 to 1914 marks the great age of globalization. Trade barriers were lower and Britain, the world's greatest trading power, maintained an open market. At the same time, Britain exported capital on an unprecedented scale, both to its imperial possessions and to areas of recent settlement beyond its formal control. There were few barriers to the migration of labour from low- to high-wage areas, and large numbers of migrants left Europe for the temperate areas of white settlement in the United States, Canada, Argentina, and Australia. As a result, wage levels were pushed up in Britain and constrained across the Atlantic, leading to a convergence in welfare within the Atlantic economy.[30] Although the slave trade ended in the first half of the nineteenth century, a new pattern of indentured labour emerged with large movements of people from India and China to work in the cane fields of the Caribbean or the mines of South Africa. Meanwhile, the world's monetary system was increasingly integrated on the basis of the gold standard and the pound sterling, with London as the major financial centre of the world. The decade before the First World War was the apogee of globalization, and Britain was the dominant power within this liberal world economy.

The global economy of the late nineteenth and early twentieth centuries combined free trade, fixed exchange rates in the form of the gold standard, and a high level of capital mobility. These three policies gave priority to Britain's international economic position, and hence limited the ability of the government and the Bank of England to adopt economic policies explicitly directed to maintaining domestic employment and stability. Here was the 'inconsistent quartet': an active domestic monetary policy was ruled out by the need to preserve a fixed exchange rate, capital mobility, and free trade; any variation in interest rates was determined by international considerations.[31] These policy choices pose a vital question for understanding the period from the Great Exhibition to the First World War: was the pursuit of international or 'cosmopolitan' economic interests beneficial to particular interests (and above all the City) at the expense of the welfare of the bulk of the population? For much of the second half of the nineteenth century the combination of free trade, stable money, and capital movements was seen by most people as beneficial to the welfare of the British people, guaranteeing cheap food, rising real wages, and buoyant export markets. Cosmopolitan policies or globalization could, it seemed, lead to welfare gains.

At the end of the nineteenth century, these assumptions faced challenge from a number of directions. The free movement of people, money, and goods could be seen as a cultural threat, a solvent of national identity and independence. The campaign for tariff reform or imperial preference launched by Joseph Chamberlain in 1903 argued that Britain was facing growing competition from Germany and the United States with their protected, large home markets: the answer should be to convert the British empire into a trade bloc behind tariff walls. In the opinion of tariff reformers, the welfare of the British people would be improved as a result of steady work in stable markets, with cheap food still coming from the farmers of the empire. Tariff reform was defeated in 1906 and 1910, and free trade persisted up to 1914—but the political context was changing. Although progressive Liberals and Labour remained loyal to free trade, it was on certain conditions. They no longer assumed that free trade in itself would improve the welfare of the British people if it implied low wages at home to secure export markets, or if goods were being exported as a result of a lack of demand at home. A cosmopolitan economic policy should only be pursued on condition that it did not reflect a misallocation of income and wealth at home.[32]

Despite these pressures, up to the First World War the Liberal government and its Labour allies accepted that free trade offered consumers cheap food and that the gold standard kept prices low which resulted in higher real wages. Domestic opposition to the cosmopolitan, liberal world economy was held in check by a more or less credible commitment to international mechanisms, and above all to the gold standard, which limited the national governments' ability to accede to domestic pressure. Globalization was reversed in the inter-war period. Domestic opposition to the global economy mounted, and it proved more difficult to ignore the pressures for prioritizing domestic welfare over the dictates of the international economy. Domestic stability and employment were starting to take precedence over fixed exchange rates, free trade, and capital mobility—all of which were abandoned in 1931/2.[33]

Deglobalization between the wars created particularly acute problems for the staple industries of coal, cotton, shipbuilding, engineering (so reliant on export markets), for the City of London (so committed to capital exports and international finance), and for politicians and civil servants (whose assumptions about a liberal world order were challenged). The question in the 1930s was whether Britain's welfare was better served by 'insular capitalism' or an imperial customs union rather than by the open global economy of the second half of the nineteenth century. In the 1850s, Richard Cobden had no doubt that free trade and the pursuit of comparative advantage would lead to prosperity and peace. By the 1930s, even J. M. Keynes—a committed free trader in earlier decades—feared that a liberal world economy was threatening Britain's prosperity and culture; national welfare and identity might be better preserved by national economic policies.[34] At Bretton Woods, he negotiated the post-war economic order with the United States, trying to strike a balance between the American attempt to restore a liberal trading system, and his own realization that open markets and convertibility were beyond Britain's capacity at the end of the war. The global economy was remade at the end of the Second World War, by combining elements of the late nineteenth century and the 1930s so that the restoration of the world economy should not threaten the pursuit of domestic stability and welfare. Although the Americans wished to restore multilateral trade, in practice the reduction of trade barriers was slow and the British government was able to cling to imperial preference and import controls. A regime of fixed exchange rates was created, with a degree of flexibility to prevent serious domestic disruption. The pursuit of a liberal world economy was tempered by the needs of domestic welfare. By balancing domestic and international considerations, the dangers of insular capitalism and depression could be avoided.

Poverty, Population, and Prosperity

In the early nineteenth century, Malthus was concerned about the harmful effects of population growth on welfare. Despite the confidence of the authors of the census report of 1851 that the curse of Malthus had been overcome, population issues remained important throughout the period. Indeed, a Royal Commission on Population was appointed in 1944. Its concern was not that population was outstripping the resources of the country; rather, its appointment arose from a widespread belief in the 1930s that parenthood had gone out of fashion. Keynes feared that the Malthusian devil had been tamed, only for another to emerge: low population growth made recovery from depression difficult, for excess capacity was not taken up so quickly. The Commission agreed that births were below replacement rates, and argued that a stable or falling population would mean more elderly people, and fewer productive workers, with a mounting burden of pensions. Flexibility would be reduced, for new trades would find it more difficult to recruit workers. The Commission pointed to further undesirable consequences. First, the sources of suitable immigrants were limited, as was the ability of Britain to absorb people from different races and religions. Second, the outflow of British migrants to the Commonwealth would fall and so reduce the growth of their economies. The Commission expressed alarm that the rate of population growth of 'oriental peoples' was meanwhile increasing, with serious consequences both for military security and for maintaining and extending western values. Not surprisingly, the Commission recommended support to mothers to boost the number of white Britons.[35]

The Royal Commission's report was merely one in a long line of reflections on the population of Britain triggered by the decline in the birth rate from the 1870s. As the standard of living started to improve, Malthus' model predicted that more people would marry at a younger age and any gains in welfare would soon be eroded unless the prudential restraint on marriage was very powerful. In fact, the birth rate started to drop from the 1870s and a new set of cultural expectations emerged so that prosperity was linked with a low birth rate. The decline in fertility varied between occupations, classes, and regions—and many worried observers feared that one result might be deterioration in the racial stock. By the late nineteenth century, many commentators no longer feared that a high birth rate would drive down the standard of living to subsistence levels. Instead, they feared that the low birth rate might be a threat to national prosperity and power, with too few people—or too few of the right sort—to preserve the empire and an efficient economy.

Malthus' population theories influenced Charles Darwin by suggesting that the battle for scarce resources led to the survival of the fittest. Darwin's biological theories could be turned back onto society, with a concern that social intervention allowed the survival of the unfit. Social Darwinists or 'eugenicists' drew alarming consequences from the drop in the birth rate, for they believed that the fall started amongst the most 'prudential', respectable, and intelligent members of society, so that the quality of the racial stock was declining. Malthus' alarm that the poor law led to excessive population might now be replaced by concern that social intervention was sustaining the unfit. Debates over social policy were therefore permeated with concerns about sexuality and reproduction. But the outcome in Britain was somewhat different from other countries where sterilization of the mentally unfit was adopted. In Britain, eugenics took a different turn, emphasizing the need to find intelligence wherever it existed through mental testing, and to overcome the social and environmental impediments to the full utilization of ability.

The relationship between economic growth and welfare is reflected in health and life expectancy. The connection was not always positive, for areas of most rapid economic growth and highest wages might experience low life expectation and high infant mortality as a result of insanitary conditions and industrial pollution. Engels's account of the squalid slums of Manchester in the 1840s was only one of many descriptions of appalling conditions in the great cities that resulted in high levels of mortality. Families had a choice: should they stay in rural districts with a high life expectation and a much better chance that their children would survive; or should they move to the growing towns with higher wages? From about 1870, death rates in the great cities started to fall, and by 1900 life expectancy at birth was close to the level found in rural areas. Economic growth and health were now in balance, and the welfare gains of living in cities were much clearer.

Historians have debated the reasons for the fall in the death rate and rise in life expectation. One possible explanation is that improvements in food and a higher standard of living provided resistance to disease, complemented by higher standards of accommodation. Other historians stress investment in social overhead capital in better sanitation and water supply, and the success of preventive medicine in controlling the spread of infectious disease. Changes in mortality might therefore depend upon a shift from a myopic concern for cheap government to a greater awareness of the long-term implications of low investment, sustained by changes in the availability of capital.

Up to 1850, a subsistence crisis or a serious drop in the standard of living was averted without as yet consistent increases in real incomes. In the second half of the nineteenth century, real wages rose to new levels. The adoption of powered machinery raised productivity. Meanwhile, an increase in food imports and a drop in prices hit British farmers and landowners, and resulted in a considerable gain in welfare for the bulk of the population. But the largest shift in the distribution of welfare between various groups of the British people came in the First World War. High levels of taxation and controls over profits, land rents, and house rents reduced the share of the national income received by capital. Meanwhile, labour gained at the end of the war; above all, unskilled workers narrowed their wage differential with skilled workers. Employed workers maintained these welfare gains between the wars. As Keynes realized, wages were 'sticky' in a downward direction and the attempt of employers and the government to reduce wages in order to make British goods competitive did not succeed. The result was a loss of welfare in other directions, for the First World War acted as a shock to the British economy, pushing it from equilibrium and leading to a high level of unemployment.

As the standard of living rose and the size of families fell, patterns of consumption changed. At the beginning of the period, most people bought basic necessities of food, clothing, and accommodation. Over time, more people were able to purchase consumer goods and to spend money on leisure. Consumption patterns varied between short-term gratification and prudential deferred gratification. Moralizing middle-class observers complained that the poor lacked prudence, using their money for immediate gratification, buying goods with expensive credit. Patterns of spending were related to moral assumptions which permeated attitudes to credit. Consumption was a crucial marker of status, defining identity and social position through clothing, interior decoration, and patterns of association. These differences cross-cut classes: working-class nonconformists avoided the temptations of alcohol and gambling; their Anglican or Catholic counterparts had fewer scruples. Nevertheless, there were class markers: the middle class had its pattern of sociability in new tennis or golf clubs; working men had clubs and societies for pigeon racing or brass bands. How far was the outcome two highly distinct cultures, each cohesive but not integrated with each other?[36] How far did increasing affluence and a commercialization of leisure lead to a blurring of these lines, through common enjoyment of radio programmes and Hollywood movies?

The welfare of the British people was also affected by changes in the occupational and social structure. In the second half of the nineteenth century, the shift of labour from agriculture to industry was largely complete; in the first half of the twentieth century, the proportion of workers in industry declined and the share of services increased. At the same time, industrial and service firms shifted towards larger, more bureaucratic concerns. These changes had welfare implications. The proportion of workers in casual employment declined as a result of government policies designed to create steadier work as well as labour shortages during the First World War. More workers started to expect stability of employment with career ladders and promotion. The emergence of more white-collar positions created opportunities for social mobility, at least for those with the necessary education and skills. Changes in the labour market affected the distribution of income in society, leading to a greater 'bunching' of incomes in the middle ranges than allowed for in Engels's and Marx's account of polarization between a prosperous bourgeoisie and a pauperized proletariat.

Policy

The debates over globalization and population were closely connected to economic and social policy. In Part IV, attention turns more directly to policy choices which posed the question of the priority to be given to the pursuit of economic growth or to the allocation of welfare. Would employment and decent wages be secured by protecting the British market from competition—or by allowing in cheap commodities to hold down the cost of living? Should the government offer incentives and profits to risk-takers who would invest and create work? Or would growth and prosperity be achieved through a policy of equality, a redistribution of income and wealth from the rich to the poor designed to create a stronger domestic market?

In 1850, few economists or politicians were willing to condone redistributive taxation, and large incomes were generally regarded as beneficial, offering incentives and providing a source for savings. Redistributive taxation would not only harm accumulation but also set class against class, so endangering social harmony. By 1909, attitudes were shifting and the first progressive income tax was introduced. The two world wars resulted in much higher levels of progressive taxation and an increase in the bargaining power of less-skilled workers. Income distribution became more equal, and the share of the national income received by labour rose in both world wars. By the end of the period, Labour Chancellors consciously pursued redistribution in an attempt to break down 'socially created' wealth in the hands of the rich. In their opinion, equality would create a sense of social integration, encouraging workers to be more efficient in a society that no longer exploited them. On this view, growth did not depend on incentives from high profits and incomes but justice and inclusion. Here were fundamental questions. Was spending on welfare at the expense of efficiency by driving up costs or a means of preserving human capital? Would social spending be better directed towards education to create an efficient workforce? Should the government respond to depression with public works, or would such a policy feather-bed inefficient producers? Should the government shape its policies by international considerations, giving priority to the external exchange rate over the domestic implications, or should it give priority to domestic concerns in shaping monetary and trade policy?

The standard of living is a matter not only of wage rates but also of social entitlements. Malthus feared that the old poor law undermined prudence and led to a counter-productive growth in the population. The poor law was reformed in 1834 in order to restrict relief in the hope that self-reliance would be encouraged. In fact, the attempt was only partially successful. Most beneficiaries of relief were not able-bodied adult men receiving grants in aid of their wages to support large families, as the authors of the Act assumed; they were the elderly, sick, or widows with children. Able-bodied men were more likely to seek relief because of high levels of unemployment during downturns of the trade cycle. The failure of a worker in the shipyards of the Tyne to get a job during a cyclical downturn or of a cotton mill hand to find employment in the 'cotton famine' of the American Civil War had nothing to do with their own willingness to work. Attitudes to state welfare started to shift, with a greater concern for preserving the efficiency of respectable workers, with harsher attitudes to those who did not seek self-sufficiency.

Of course, problems of social insecurity were not only a matter for the state. All industrial societies cover social risks of unemployment, sickness, old age, and death which are the lot of everyone and not just the poor. Demographic change affected the welfare system in many, complex ways. High levels of mortality meant a large number of marriages were broken by death, leaving single-parent families in straitened circumstances. On the other hand, an increase in life expectancy placed more strain on the finances of the poor law in order to support the elderly. The question was not whether action should be taken; it was by whom and on what terms. Should the state provide cover against social risk and, if so, should it be tax funded and cover the entire population, or rely on insurance contributions from particular segments of the population? Should employers make provision through company schemes for health care or pensions—and if so, which workers should be covered? Voluntary organizations might be self-directed through trade union cover against unemployment or friendly societies' sick pay and medical treatment. They might be other-directed through charities for every eventuality from the rescue of prostitutes and abandoned children, to infirmaries and care for the elderly. Social risk was covered by commercial bodies, both for the poor and the wealthy. Poor families insured against death to provide a respectable funeral; better-off families relied on life insurance policies to purchase annuities in retirement and to support dependants. The mix of insurance changed over time, and it should not be assumed that there was a self-evident progression towards a collective welfare state. Even if the proportion of welfare provided by the state did increase over time, the capacity created by previous institutional structure helped to shape the form of the state's response.

Since the sixteenth century, England was unusual in possessing a tax-funded poor law. Scotland took a different path, with a less generous poor law. Instead, Scotland had a system of parochial schools, with a higher level of literacy than in England. Economists now talk of investment in human capital, and consider it a major influence on economic growth. In comparison with other advanced economies, the level of public spending on education in England was low, and it might be wondered why, and with what consequences. Not only did the level of spending influence rates of growth; the form of education also influenced social mobility. Was the educational system designed to reinforce the existing social structure or to find able children and stimulate social mobility?

The theme of this book is the interconnection between economic growth and its welfare implications considering not only the performance and structure of the economy but also the way it was perceived and assessed in political culture and economic theory. It closes with the Festival of Britain, an expression of Labour's vision of society. It commemorated the centenary of the Great Exhibition and celebrated recovery from the disruptions of war and reconstruction. Much as the Great Exhibition symbolized the major transformations in British society in the middle of the nineteenth century, so the Festival of Britain indicated the tensions and dilemmas of the mid-twentieth century.

NOTES

1. *Census of Great Britain*: Report, George Graham, William Farr, and Horace Mann, 220–2.
2. Malthus, *Essay on Population*. The nature of these limits to growth is assessed in *Progress and Poverty*, ch. 1, especially 4–12.
3. Ricardo, *Principles*, 276.
4. Mill, *Principles*, 738, 743.
5. Engels, *Condition*; Marx and Engels, *Communist Manifesto*; Lenin, *Imperialism*.
6. Pomeranz, *Great Divergence*, 218.
7. Wrigley, *Continuity, Chance and Change*, 28, 29 n.; Pomeranz, *Great Divergence*, 218, 274–8.
8. On coal, see Wrigley, *Continuity, Chance and Change*, 29 n. Pomeranz, *Great Divergence*, 274–8, 218.
9. Wrigley, *Continuity, Chance and Change*, 83–6, 128–9.

10. Ibid. 102–3; Muldrew, *Economy of Obligation*; Stasavage, *Public Debt*; Clark, *Betting on Lives*.

11. *Census of Great Britain*, i. 221–2.

12. Gambles, *Protection and Politics*, 50–1, 57, 72, 78–9, 228-9; Daunton, *Progress and Poverty*, 4–8.

13. Auerbach, *Great Exhibition*, 94.

14. Ibid. 129.

15. Quoted in Daunton, *Trusting Leviathan*, 155–6; Mill, *Principles*, ch. 7.

16. Sidgwick, *Methods of Ethics*, 415–17.

17. Pearson, 'Economics and altruism', 35–6.

18. Pigou, *Wealth and Welfare*, especially ch. 9; Hobhouse, *Liberalism*, 158–9.

19. Keynes, *General Theory*.

20. Harris, 'Economic knowledge and British social policy', 392.

21. Pimlott, *Dalton*, 62–3; Dalton, *Some Aspects of the Inequality of Incomes*, 10.

22. Laski, *Liberty in the Modern State*, 15, 38–9, 48, 53, 186–7, 193, 194–5, quoted in Daunton, 'Payment and participation', 209–10.

23. Ellison, *Egalitarian Thought and Labour Politics*, 15–16, 21–7.

24. Coleman, 'Gentlemen and players'; Wiener, *English Culture and the Decline of the Industrial Spirit*; Barnett, *Audit of War*.

25. Lazonick, *Competitive Advantage on the Shop Floor*; Crafts and Broadberry, 'The postwar settlement'.

26. Cain and Hopkins, 'Gentlemanly capitalism, I and II'.

27. Lee, *British Economy*; Lee, 'The service sector'; Lee, 'Regional growth', 452; Rubinstein, *Men of Property*, 61.

28. Cain and Hopkins, 'Gentlemanly capitalism, I and II'.

29. Broadberry, 'Manufacturing and the convergence hypothesis', 776.

30. O'Rourke and Williamson, *Globalization and History*, 15, 273–7, 280–2.

31. Obstfeld and Taylor, *Global Capital Markets*, 29–31.

32. Trentmann, 'Wealth versus welfare'.

33. For example, James, *End of Globalization*.

34. Skidelsky, *John Maynard Keynes*, ii. 371–3, 476–7.

35. *Royal Commission on Population, Report*, 224–6, 227–8; Skidelsky, *John Maynard Keynes*, ii. 632.

36. McKibbin, *Classes and Cultures*, 527–8.

FURTHER READING

Auerbach, J. A., *The Great Exhibition of 1851: A Nation on Display* (New Haven, 1999)

Barnett, C., *The Audit of War: The Illusion and Reality of Britain as a Great Nation* (1986)

Broadberry, S. N., 'Manufacturing and the convergence hypothesis: what the long-run data show', *Journal of Economic History*, 53 (1993)

Broadberry, S. N., *The Productivity Race: British Manufacturing in International Perspective, 1850–1990* (Cambridge, 1997)

—— 'Anglo-German productivity differences 1870–1990: a sectoral analysis', *European Review of Economic History*, 1 (1997)

Cain, P. J., and Hopkins, A. G., 'Gentlemanly capitalism and British expansion overseas, I: The old colonial system, 1688-1850', *Economic History Review*, 39 (1986) and 'II: The new imperialism, 1850–1945', *Economic History Review*, 40 (1987)

Census of Great Britain, 1851: Population Tables, vol. i.

Clark, G., *Betting on Lives: The Culture of Life Insurance in England, 1695–1775* (Manchester, 1999)

Coleman, D., 'Gentleman and players', *Economic History Review*, 26 (1973)

Crafts, N. F. R., and Broadberry, S., 'The post-war settlement: not such a good bargain after all', *Business History*, 40 (1998)

Dalton, H., *Some Aspects of the Inequality of Incomes in Modern Communities* (1920)

Daunton, M., *Progress and Poverty: An Economic and Social History of Britain, 1700–1850* (Oxford, 1995)

—— *Trusting Leviathan: The Politics of Taxation in Britain, 1799–1914* (Cambridge, 2001)

—— 'Payment and participation: welfare and state formation in Britain, 1900–51', *Past and Present*, 150 (1996)

—— and Hilton, M. (eds.), *The Politics of Consumption: Material Culture and Citizenship in Europe and America* (Oxford, 2001)

Ellison, N., *Egalitarian Thought and Labour Politics: Retreating Visions* (1994)

Engels, F., *Condition of the Working Classes in England*, ed. with an introd. by D. McLellan (Oxford, 1993)

Gambles, A., *Protection and Politics: Conservative Economic Discourse, 1815–52* (Woodbridge, 1999)

Habakkuk, H. J., *American and British Technology in the Nineteenth Century: The Search for Labour Saving Inventions* (Cambridge, 1962)

Harris, J., 'Economic knowledge and British social policy', in M. O. Furner and B. Supple (eds.), *The State and Economic Knowledge: The American and British Experiences* (Cambridge, 1990)

Hobhouse, L. T., *Liberalism* (1911)

James, H., *The End of Globalization: Lessons from the Great Depression* (Cambridge, Mass., 2001)

Keynes, J. M., *The General Theory of Employment, Interest and Money* (1936)

Laski, H. J., *Liberty in the Modern State* (3rd edn., 1948; first published 1930)

Lazonick, W., *Competitive Advantage on the Shop Floor* (Cambridge, Mass., 1990)

Lee, C., *The British Economy since 1700: A Macroeconomic Perspective* (Cambridge, 1986)

—— 'Regional growth and structural change in Victorian Britain', *Economic History Review*, 34 (1981)

—— 'The service sector, regional specialisation and economic growth in the Victorian economy', *Journal of Historical Geography*, 10 (1984)

Lenin, V. I., *Imperialism, the Highest Stage of Capitalism*, introd. N. Lewis and J. Malone (1996)

McKibbin, R., *Classes and Cultures: England, 1918–1951* (Oxford, 1998)

Malthus, T. R., *An Essay on the Principle of Population* (1st edn., 1798), ed. E. A. Wrigley and D. Souden (1986)

Marshall, A., *Principles of Economics: An Introductory Volume* (1890)

Marx, K., and Engels, F., *Communist Manifesto*, introd. and notes G. Stedman Jones (2002)

Mill, J. S., *Principles of Political Economy*, in *The Collected Works of John Stuart Mill*, iii, ed. J. M. Robson (Toronto, 1965)

Muldrew, C., *The Economy of Obligation: The Culture of Credit and Social Relations in Early Modern England* (Basingstoke, 1998)

Obstfeld, M., and Taylor, A. M., *Global Capital Markets: Integration, Crisis and Growth* (Cambridge, 2004)

O'Rourke, K. H., and Williamson, J. G., *Globalization and History: The Evolution of a Nineteenth-Century Atlantic Economy* (Cambridge, Mass., 1999)

Pearson, H., 'Economics and altruism', in M. Daunton and F. Trentmann (eds.), *Worlds of Political Economy: Knowledge and Power in the Nineteenth and Twentieth Centuries* (Basingstoke, 2004)

Pigou, A. C., *Wealth and Welfare* (1912)

Pimlott, B., *Hugh Dalton* (1985)

Pomeranz, K., *The Great Divergence: China, Europe and the Making of the Modern World Economy* (Princeton, 2000)

Ricardo, D., *The Principles of Political Economy and Taxation*, ed. D. Winch, (1973)

Royal Commission on Population, Report (1949)

Rubinstein, W. D., *Men of Property: The Very Wealthy in Britain since the Industrial Revolution* (1981)

Sidgwick, H., *The Methods of Ethics* (1874)

Skidelsky, R., *John Maynard Keynes: A Biography*, 3 vols. (1983–2000)

Stasavage, D., *Public Debt and the Birth of the Democratic State: France and Great Britain, 1688–1789* (Cambridge, 2003)

Trentmann, F. 'Wealth versus welfare: the British left between free trade and national political economy before the First World War', *Historical Research*, 70 (1997)

Wiener, M., *English Culture and the Decline of the Industrial Spirit, 1850–1980* (Cambridge, 1981)

Wrigley, E. A., *Continuity, Chance and Change: The Character of the Industrial Revolution in England* (Cambridge, 1988)

PART I

....

THE ANATOMY OF THE BRITISH ECONOMY

....

CHAPTER 2

Agriculture and the Land

In 1845, the Home Secretary, Sir James Graham, wrote to his son expressing pessimism about his prospects as the owner of a 26,000-acre agricultural estate. Since 1819, he had spent £93,000 on improvements, had consolidated farms, and had improved the calibre of the tenancy. Although his income had increased from £17,946 in 1818 to £21,599 in 1845, his outgoings had also risen so that he had only £7,000 to maintain his standing as a leading politician. If he could sell the estate for £700,000 and pay off loans, he could expect to receive an income of almost £14,000 a year. Above all, the prospect of repeal of the corn laws filled him with gloom.[1]

The landed interest was protected by the corn laws: when the price of corn rose above a certain point imports were permitted, but when they fell the rate of duty was increased. The corn laws might appear as blatant class legislation to benefit agricultural producers against urban consumers, yet they had a justification in terms of public policy designed to generate the food supply of Britain's growing population. This concern was at the heart of political stability and economic policy. To many leading politicians, a domestic agriculture with stable prices and reasonable profits was the best way of feeding the people. But the politics of food was changing and the corn laws were fiercely criticized.

Despite his misgivings, Graham supported repeal in 1846. Furthermore, he did not sell the estate; nor did his son. Repeal did not immediately undermine the prosperity of the aristocrats and gentry, and the expectation that they would be displaced by industrialists active in the Anti-Corn Law League was disappointed. Rather, it was the League that disappeared. Britain continued to be ruled by a landed elite for at least a generation, and the tenurial structure survived up to the First World War.

British agriculture had a tripartite system. At the bottom were landless labourers. Few had any rights to gleaning or commons by 1850—and the extent to which they had been dispossessed became a subject of heated historical debate and political controversy around the turn of the century.[2] There were few small owner-occupying farmers; most of the land was managed by substantial tenant farmers who provided livestock and machinery. In the eighteenth century, some farmers held land on long leases with a relatively modest annual rent and periodic 'fines' as lives fell in or the lease was renewed, but by 1850, the majority of farms were held on 'rack' rents, that is annual tenancies with a full market rent paid in cash, and tenants had lost many of their rights. Most of the land was owned by aristocratic and gentry estates, and the holdings of the Church and charitable foundations. Contemporaries were divided on the benefits and drawbacks of the system. Had the great landowners accumulated their estates through the misuse of political power and the creation of legal impediments to a free market in land, so dispossessing yeomen farmers and independent peasants? Should the land be restored to the people? Did the tenurial system allow great landowners to pass the risks of agriculture on to their tenants who paid their rent regardless of circumstances? Or did the division of responsibility lead to efficiency, freeing farmers from the need to find capital to buy land, so that they could concentrate on the provision of animals, fertilizers, and machinery? Was the British tenurial system a model of efficiency or a pathological deformation? The question was pondered by foreign observers and within Britain as part of the radical critique of 'landlordism', by the Chartists in the 1840s, by the Irish Land League, and by the new Liberals before the First World War. If the tenurial system rested on the abuse of power, then the land had been 'stolen' from the people by the dissolution of the monasteries, by the appropriation of clan lands in Scotland, by the dispossession of the Irish, and by parliamentary enclosure. Doubts on the efficiency of the tripartite system mounted at the end of the century, among both radicals and some Conservatives who saw the benefits of owner-occupying farmers as a 'bulwark' to defend property.[3]

When Hippolyte Taine, the French writer, reported in 1872 on a visit to the House of Lords, he did not comment on the standard of debate or the majesty of the building. What impressed him was the phenomenal wealth of its members drawn from the landed aristocracy. Here, it seemed to Taine, was the wealthiest ruling class in Europe which was still able to overwhelm the fortunes of even the most successful industrialist. By contrast, Karl Marx, writing in 1852, believed that Cobden and the free traders formed 'the official representatives of modern English society', who would carry through 'the complete annihilation of Old England as an aristocratic country'. Cobden himself was more doubtful. Rather than the bourgeois triumph he desired, 'feudalism is every day more and more in the ascendant'.[4] How was this remarkable degree of continuity achieved? The answer for the period 1846–73 is simple: agriculture remained profitable and productive during the era of 'high farming'.

High Farming and Prosperity, 1846–1873

The repeal of the corn laws, according to the Anti-Corn Law League, would lead to the import of cheap cereals, undercutting British producers and reducing the price of bread. Wheat imports did increase from 7.5 per cent of the consumption of wheat in England and Wales in 1843–6 to 19.5 per cent in 1847–8, and 40.1 per cent in 1860–8,[5] yet produced only a modest fall in prices. The sharp decline in corn prices only came in the 1870s, with the most serious decline in the 1880s (Fig. 2.1). The conjunction of increasing imports and a modest fall in prices until the 1880s is explained by the rise of prices in the exporting countries. Britain's major source of supply in the 1840s and 1850s was the Baltic provinces of Russia and Prussia, where average price stood at 31s. 9d. a quarter between 1828 and 1841, considerably below the price in England and Wales (58s. 10d.). The corn laws at this stage were keeping a glut of cheap European wheat off the British market. By 1849–59, the price differential was eroded, less because of British demand than the increase in European population. Prices in Prussia stood at 44s. 6d. a quarter, in comparison with 52s. 6d. in England and Wales; the difference was largely accounted for by the costs of transport and insurance.[6]

The real threat to British agriculture came when sources of supply shifted to the United States and transport costs fell. The United States was the largest supplier of wheat by 1861, a position lost as a result of the Civil War. In the 1870s and 1880s, American imports moved to a new level, producing a fundamental transformation in market conditions in Britain. Although American farmers turned to their home market at the end of the nineteenth century, the fall in supplies from the USA was compensated by other areas of new settlement. In Russia, production expanded; Canada, Argentina, and Australia increased their share; and India emerged as a major exporter (see Table 2.1). The British farmer now faced an entirely new market environment, and the threat of the repeal of the corn laws was realized. By the 1880s, 'high farming' had been swept away by American wheat.

TABLE 2.1. *Wheat imports into the UK, 1847–1930 (000 cwt)*

	Russia	Germany	USA	Canada	India	Australia	Argentina
1847	3,654	2,125[a]	1,837	385	—	—	—
1861	4,513	6,270	10,867	2,381	—	—	—
1870	10,269	3,348	12,372	2,838	—	—	—
1880	2,880	1,599	36,191	3,888	3,229	4,246	—
1890	19,389	1,101	17,201	1,128	9,112	3,058	2,810
1900	4,478	1,828	32,588	6,338	6	3,788	18,524
1910	28,942	—	10,949	16,449	17,917	13,748	15,132
1920	2	—	45,422	10,189	20	19,971	30,831
1930	18,717	—	21,036	26,179	3,342	12,733	15,189

Note: The figures are based on port of origin, except 1910 which is based on the country of consignment
[a] This figure refers to Prussia.
Source: Mitchell and Deane, *Abstract of British Historical Statistics*, 100–2.

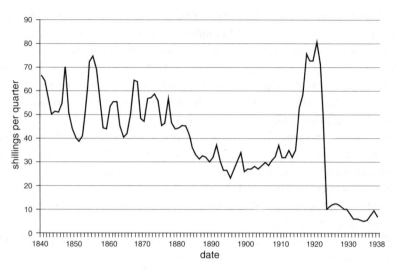

Fig. 2.1. Average price of wheat per quarter, UK, 1840–1938
Source: Mitchell and Deane, *Abstract*, 488–9.

In 1846, a golden age of farming seemed implausible to opponents of repeal, who anticipated distortion of the economy, an overthrow of the social order, and a debasement of politics by selfish urban interests. They argued that the result would be over-dependence on industry, exposure to international trade, and the growth of unhealthy towns. In response, the Anti-Corn Law League attacked the selfishness of farmers and landowners who used political power to maintain their profits. Peel felt that the repeal of the corn laws was necessary, for autarky was no longer feasible. Rather than holding back a deluge of corn, the problem was a shortage of grain and the high price of food imports. An open market would provide foreign producers with the assurance of a constant demand, so encouraging them to produce more for British consumers. To Peel, repeal of the corn laws was a measure of prudence and survival. A continuation of the corn laws in the changed circumstances of tighter supply would call the position of the landowner into question. It was one thing to introduce the corn laws to protect agriculture from lower prices after the Napoleonic wars; it was quite another to retain them when their continuation threatened hardship. Repeal was politically expedient if landowners were not to be accused of a blatant use of state power in the service of a vested interest. Peel was confident that the economic consequences of repeal would not be disastrous in the changed supply conditions of the 1840s. British farmers should, he believed, move to a more productive system of agriculture, based on high yields and profits summarized in the phrase 'high farming'. The repeal of the corn laws was the stick; the introduction of cheap government loans for field drainage in the Public Money

Drainage Act of 1846 was the carrot. Certainly, Peel's strategy was not to replace one class by another so much as to *perpetuate* the status of the landed interest.

The correct response to the coming of free trade in corn, it seemed to many contemporaries, was to apply greater amounts of capital to the land, so raising efficiency and making British agriculture more competitive. Since the dominance of the landed interest and the profitability of agriculture could no longer rest on high prices, it should rely on high production. On such a view, the repeal of the corn laws was less a sign of surrender to the industrial middle class than a mark of its ability to opt for economic adaptability. Repeal, remarked Sir James Caird, 'saved us from the insurrections that rapidly spread on the Continent, changing dynasties and unsettling Governments' and was therefore not to be regretted. Scientific rationality should be applied to farming, in order to improve seeds, raise standards of animal nutrition and breeding, gain greater knowledge of soils, and make more extensive use of steam power. Farmers should, at the same time, show a greater sensitivity to market trends. Although the price of wheat was the same as at the beginning of the century, the price of meat, dairy products, and wool had doubled. Here was an opportunity for farmers.[7]

The initial response of consumers to the fall in the price of wheat was to switch from the 'lesser grains'. In 1801, 66.4 per cent of the population of England and Wales, and 10 per cent of Scotland, ate wheaten bread. The proportion increased to 88 and 44 per cent respectively in 1850, and 97 and 84 per cent in 1900.[8] The next stage was to switch from a diet based on carbohydrates to one with a high content of protein. The result was a 'second agricultural revolution' as farming ceased to be a closed system in which the fertility of the soil rested on the farm's own resources. It was a system of mixed farming based on 'high feeding' of animals, with the land under constant tillage and highly fertilized to produce more crops and to raise the number of stock on the farm. Inputs of manure and fertilizers were large, and resources were supplemented by outside supplies of feedstuffs (oil-cake) and fertilizer (guano and nitrates). The advantage of mixed farming was that the proportion of cereal or livestock could be varied in response to changing prices.

'High farming' was far from a universal panacea. The wet soils of the clay districts had a shorter growing season and the costs of traction were high. It was difficult

TABLE 2.2. *Relative price movements of wheat and beef, 1851–80 (1865–74 = 100), England*

	1851/5	1861/5	1876/80
Wheat	103	87	87
Beef	77	87	103

Source: Collins and Jones, 'Sectoral advance', 79.

to grow fodder crops for winter feed of livestock, so limiting the amount of manure which could be applied to the corn fields in order to raise yields. Farmers and landlords were caught in a trap, which was expressed with great economy in Buckinghamshire in 1855: 'No food, no stock; no stock, no dung; no dung, no corn.'[9] The situation on light soils was different. There was an upward spiral of productivity based on more feed, more stock, more dung, more fodder, more grain. On the lighter soils, it was possible to respond by piecemeal adjustments, whereas clay lands could only compete by the installation of drainage. Mixed farming spread only slowly onto the clay soils, and the drainage loans offered by Peel were a sop to discontented landowners rather than an economically significant intervention. Only about 20 per cent of land was drained by 1873, and success was limited to more easily worked clays.[10] Many of the claims for high farming were a desperate attempt to follow the example of the light soils, and success was less striking than its advocates hoped. A more attractive response, particularly in the north, was to switch to pastoralism. This response was encouraged by the higher wages in the north, for permanent grass required less labour. The second agricultural revolution was, therefore, a regional phenomenon.

'High farming' depended on the investment of tenant farmers in stock, machinery, and soil improvement. The Settled Estates Acts of 1856–64 allowed landowners to charge the costs of improvements to estates under settlements, and the Public Drainage Act was amended so that private companies could offer loans with preference over other creditors. As a result, insurance companies invested in 'high farming'. Whether this investment paid depended on when it was made and where. Drainage at £2 / £5 per acre in the 1840s might pay for itself by the onset of depression, whereas an investment at £7 per acre in the early 1870s would not be recouped in higher rents. Indeed, the benefit was more likely to go to the tenant farmer for rents were not increased in proportion to the outlay, so that drainage was a form of subsidy to farmers.[11] Investment in high farming might also hamper adjustment in the subsequent depression, for the burden of servicing the debt prevented landowners from raising further money in response to the collapse of cereal prices which was a vital prop of the mixed farming system. Hence investment in 'high farming' might lead to an over capitalized system which was incapable of adjusting. In some cases investment in high farming did help, for areas previously devoted to cereals adopted mixed farming, which was a step in the right direction when grain prices collapsed.[12] In general, mixed farming was relatively successful until the 1870s because it could adjust to movements in the price of cereals relative to livestock. The economics of the system were called into doubt when cereal prices collapsed. 'High farming' made less sense when the manure produced by 'high feeding' of livestock was of little value as an input for the growing of cereals. The fall in the price of corn also meant that it was more sensible to use wheat to feed the cattle.

TABLE 2.3. *Structure of landownership in England, 1873: percentage of land held by owners of various sizes*

Great owners (10,000 acres and above)	24
Greater gentry (3,000–10,000 acres)	17
Squirearchy (1,000–3,000 acres)	12.4
Smaller owners (under 1,000 acres)	38.5
Of whom greater yeomen (300–1,000 acres)	14
Lesser yeomen (100–300 acres)	12.5
Under 100 acres	12
Of whom small owner-occupiers 10	

Source: Thompson, *English Landed Society*, 32, 114, 115, 117.

High farming required a greater input of resources and so had implications for farmers' relationship with the landlords. Tenants often co-operated with landowners in making permanent investments in drainage and buildings, with the landowner supplying the materials and the farmer the labour. Even in the absence of such collaboration, 'high farming' required the farmer to purchase greater quantities of fertilizers and increase the number of livestock. The declining profitability of specialist corn growers and the higher profitability of mixed farming produced a shift in the structure of the farming community towards more substantial farms with a larger capital to meet the costs of high farming. Farms of less than 300 acres declined and farms of 300–1,000 acres became more important. The bulk of these farmers were tenants, paying rent to landlords who were themselves more concentrated than ever (see Table 2.3).[13]

The great landed families of Britain were a self-confident elite in the second and third quarters of the nineteenth century. In the eighteenth and early nineteenth centuries, the needs of the state for war finance led to close functional ties with the City, and in some cases to marriage between aristocratic sons and the daughters of great financiers. Gentry families also apprenticed their younger sons to merchants. By the second quarter of the nineteenth century, the state had less need for loans so that these links were less strong. At the same time, the prosperity of agriculture and the expansion of rent rolls meant that fewer aristocratic families needed marriage alliances with finance and commerce. W. D. Rubinstein suggests that the landed aristocracy was 'increasingly becoming a caste-like and socially isolated group'.[14] In his view, it was not only that they held aloof from marriage outside their own circles; new men of wealth could not buy into the ranks of great landowners.

Whether or not aristocrats had a distaste for new men of wealth, they were avid in their pursuit of all forms of profit from their estates. Many aristocratic fortunes drew on non-agricultural sources, sharing in the benefits of an industrial and urban society. The earl of Leicester was the only peer mentioned by Taine to depend almost entirely upon agricultural income from his Holkham estate in Norfolk. Of the other peers mentioned, the Bedford family owned Bloomsbury, as well as mineral rights in Devon; the Devonshire family was heavily involved in the industrial town of Barrow-in-Furness and the seaside resort of Eastbourne; Buccleuch invested in Barrow; Sutherland derived income from the Potteries; Westminster owned a large section of west London; Northumberland received mineral royalties in the north-east; the Butes owned a large part of the south Wales coalfield as well as being ground landlords in Cardiff; and the Lonsdales were heavily involved in industry in Cumbria, as was the Dudley family in the Black Country. They combined aristocratic culture and industrial vigour, exploiting the resources of their estates in whatever way was most profitable.

Were these great landed families in reality caste-like? Could new men of wealth enter the ranks of the great landowners? One name mentioned by Taine stands apart: Baron Overstone. His was not an old aristocratic title, for Samuel Jones Loyd was raised to the peerage in 1850. In 1816, the future Baron Overstone became a partner in the family bank of Jones, Loyd and Co. Between 1817 and 1848, he received an income of £563,000 from the bank, and inherited the fortunes of both of his uncles and of his father. On receiving his title, he retired from business and until his death in 1883 lived as a rentier. Between 1823 and 1883, his net purchases of land amounted to £3,033,553, or 72 per cent of his total investments.[15] Rubinstein argues that Overstone was exceptional, but his claim rests on a highly restrictive definition of entry into the landed elite. He takes a high threshold of 2,000 acres, whereas most newcomers would only aspire to join the gentry. The amount of land was fixed and was often held off the market by strict settlement. The number of fortunes was expanding, and it was not easy to acquire an estate of 2,000 acres. In any case, it was possible to be accepted into gentry (or even aristocratic) society with a smaller estate, for income from non-agricultural sources allowed a landed lifestyle to be maintained with few acres. Further, he considers the experience of the first generation of *nouveaux riches* - the men who made the wealth - rather than the second and third generations who inherited their fortunes. On a more realistic measure, most 'new wealth' moved into land within one or two generations.[16]

Far from a closed, caste-like landed elite, F. M. L. Thompson observes an apparently inexorable march of large business fortunes into the countryside. Of course, long-established landowners might still hold aloof from marriage with the daughters of new men, but entry to the landed class was by no means closed. Between 1809 and 1879, forty millionaires died with fortunes from industry, finance, and commerce of whom thirty-two founded landed families. They included the Rothschilds (bankers), Brasseys (railway contractors), and Crawshays (industrialists in iron and coal). Similarly, twenty-one of twenty-five millionaires who died between

1880 and 1893 created landed estates, including Overstone. By no means all followed Overstone's example and abandoned other activities for the lure of the House of Lords. Where retreat from business did occur, it was more likely to be in the second or third generation.[17]

The explanation was not necessarily a desire to surrender to a dominant aristocratic or gentry culture. Land purchase might be a highly rational decision, providing a means of supporting family members. Indeed, businesses were *more* likely to survive where the family bought land. Between 1809 and 1860, forty-six half-millionaires died, of whom eleven were landless and whose heirs did not purchase land. In no case did the business survive. By contrast, fifteen of the sixteen men who bought land in their lifetimes continued in business, and five had sons who were significant businessmen. Land was a hedge against risk, a means of securing social status and reputation, and making contacts which could be used for the benefit of the firm and the regional industrial economy. Indeed, 'the combination of business wealth and landed estate . . . [was] the indispensable recipe for continued business success at the highest level'. Members of this 'aristocratic bourgeoisie' combined aspects of both social groupings. The landed aristocracy tried to maintain the integrity of their landed estates; the 'new men of wealth' were more likely to follow the middle-class practice of partible inheritance. In some cases, a landed estate was part of a wider family strategy for the wealthy business elite. At a time when limited liability was rare, land protected the family against the hazards of trade. The landed estate could establish a dynasty based on the eldest son; and the firm could survive on the basis of meritocratic selection from the younger sons or wider kin. The aspiration to found a landed family was compatible with continuing the family firm and might even be a positive help.[18]

The flow of new money into land did not result in any fundamental change in the highly concentrated pattern of ownership of land, or in the tripartite tenurial structure of landlords, tenant farmers, and landless labourers. However, the increased capital needs of 'high farming' might cause problems for the agrarian system. Tenants needed more capital but could not borrow against the security of ownership of land, or even the certainty of a continuing tenancy. The division of responsibilities between the owner of the land and the tenant farmer could be viewed in two ways. On the one hand, it might be seen as co-operative with the landlord providing fixed capital beyond the capability of the tenant. On the other hand, the relationship could be seen as exploitative, with the tenant supporting a superstructure of gentry and aristocratic society which battened upon production, and created inflexibilities in response to economic pressures.

The debate between these two perceptions became a subject of political concern after the repeal of the corn laws, focusing in particular on the issue of 'tenant right' or compensation to departing tenants for any 'unexhausted improvements'. A common law ruling in 1803 established that whatever was put into the soil passed into the soil, and therefore belonged entirely to the landowner. Consequently, a farmer who applied fertilizers with a lifespan of several years had no common law right to recompense for his investment in 'unexhausted improvements' when he left the land. One solution was the development of 'tenant right', which required an incoming tenant to compensate his predecessor for any unexhausted improvements, creating a form of dual ownership of the soil and offering the tenant security for his investment. From 1847, James Caird, an advocate of high farming, pressed for legislation to extend tenant right to the whole of England and Wales. Does this provide evidence of a conflict of interests between tenants and landowners who were more eager to maintain dominance than to improve agricultural efficiency by giving farmers greater independence and a share in the land? Landowners were probably sensible to oppose the extension of tenant right on the grounds of economic efficiency, for it might overcompensate an outgoing tenant, and oblige the new tenant to find a large lump sum. The ruling of 1803 did not prevent owners and tenants from negotiating private contracts, and landowners favoured freedom of contract in preference to national legislation and 'rights' which would reduce flexibility by imposing rigid schedules for various improvements. In 1875, Parliament reaffirmed private contract.[19]

In 1863, *Punch* published a cartoon which expressed one view of 'high farming': a gloomy agricultural labourer stands in front of his dilapidated cottage, leaning on the wall of a new pigsty. 'Ah!', he comments to the pigs, 'I'd like to be cared vor half as well as thee be!'[20] Yet the cartoon failed to specify *where* the unfortunate worker was living. In his survey of agriculture in England and Wales in 1850–1, Caird emphasized that the standard of living of farm workers varied widely. The division was not simply between the predominantly corn-growing districts of the east and south and mixed farming in the midlands and west. There was a more important consideration: 'the proximity of manufacturing and mining enterprise'. The midlands and west had a similar pattern of production, yet weekly wages varied between 8s. 6d. in Devon and 12s. in Cheshire. Similarly, in east and south, the weekly wage varied between 11s. in Northumberland and 7s. 6d. in Cambridgeshire. There was also a wide range of expenditure on the poor rate. In the mixed farming districts, the annual expenditure per capita on poor relief was 7s. $0\frac{1}{2}d.$ in Devon and 3s. 8d. in Cheshire; and in the eastern corn districts the figure stood at 5s. $7\frac{1}{2}d.$ in Northumberland and 9s $1\frac{1}{4}d.$ in Cambridgeshire.[21] The southern and western counties were cursed with surplus population, which resulted in low wages and low productivity. The level of nutrition was inadequate to maintain efficient work, and farmers who were faced with surplus labour opted to employ more workers than were strictly needed. Their concern was to create work rather than to use labour more efficiently, and the result was underemployment. In the south, productivity was held down by low wage levels; in the north, farmers paid higher wages and achieved superior productivity without sacrificing profit.[22]

The nature of employment also varied. 'Service in husbandry' was the norm in the early modern period: adolescents left home to work for farmers on annual contracts, living with the family so that payment was mainly in food and lodging. Employment as a servant was a stage in the lifecycle. Service meant a higher age of marriage, and an opportunity to save before setting up as an independent farmer or craftsman. By the nineteenth century, farmers were increasingly employing day labourers, with the expectation that they and their children would remain labourers. Nevertheless, service in various forms did survive into the second half of the nineteenth century.

The boundary of these different labour systems did not entirely follow the division between high- and low-wage counties. Devon and Cambridgeshire were both low-wage counties, yet the proportion of hired hands who were servants in husbandry in 1851 was respectively about half and below 10 per cent.[23] In Cambridgeshire, cereal farming required temporary workers to cover the peak of the harvest. Where farms were large and rural crafts of little importance, service in husbandry had less role as a balancing device. Substantial farmers were less likely to put their children out as servants and more likely to employ landless labourers. Service survived in Devon because farms were small and livestock rearing required permanent workers who often needed to be on hand at all hours. The tenant in Devon, as Caird remarked, was 'at once a dairy farmer, a breeder or feeder of cattle, of sheep, and of pigs, and a grower of corn and of cider'.[24] Servants in husbandry permitted small farmers to balance their labour needs, allowing them to shed children who were surplus to requirements in order to join families of other small or medium farmers where there were 'gaps' in the household economy. In the north-eastern lowlands of Scotland a variant of service in husbandry arose from the complementarity of large and small farms. Large farmers hired unmarried male servants for a year; they were lodged either in a 'bothy' where they were given provisions, or in a 'farm-kitchen' where meals were provided. This system rested on the survival of small farmers who supplied the large farmers with two vital inputs: lean cattle for fattening and labour. The male servants were usually the sons of crofters and small farmers, adjusting the labour supply of the family croft or small farm before returning to a small holding.[25]

The nature of the regional labour market was another important influence. Where labour was in short supply, service, in the form of long contracts of a year, was attractive because it provided a constant and assured supply of labour. Where population growth was rapid, day labour could be hired as required. Hence in Lancashire and Cheshire, rapid industrialization obliged farmers to hire unmarried male servants in order to guarantee a labour supply over the year. In other cases - above all the south-eastern lowlands of Scotland and north-east England - farmers relied on 'cottars' or 'hinds'. The 'hind' entered into an agreement at the annual hiring to work for the coming year in return for a rent-free house, coal, corn, the right to grass and straw for a cow, permission to keep a pig and to plant potatoes, and a small cash payment. Usually, he agreed to supply a woman 'bondager' or 'strong sufficient labourer' - in most cases his wife or daughter - who was paid a daily rate. The farmer could rely on the labour of the hind over the year, and could vary the amount of work supplied by the bondager according to the seasonal demand for labour. The cottar or hind system was a rational response to the circumstances, for demand for industrial labour on Tyneside and Clydeside meant that the north-east and the Scottish lowlands were not marked by a glut of labour as in the south of England.[26]

Labour systems affected and influenced the poor law. The Scottish poor law did not offer support to able-bodied men, so that surplus labourers were forced to migrate, thereby maintaining a rough balance between the supply and demand of labour. By contrast, in arable districts of England, the poor law supported a 'reserve army' of workers. Many areas of England, especially the cereal-growing areas of the south, had a labour surplus, and farmers had to choose between employing the poor and maintaining them through poor relief. Despite the new poor law of 1834, the practice survived with only minor changes to the 1860s. Farmers used the workhouse as a reservoir for unemployed surplus labour in winter, whose release onto the labour market was controlled by the parish. One method was the 'ticket' issued to applicants for relief: they sought work and farmers entered on the ticket the work offered or refused. Farmers realized that an offer of work would keep down the poor rate, and preferred to pay a low wage for even a small marginal product in preference to poor relief which offered no benefit. Similarly, the labourer knew that the alternative to accepting a job at a low wage was poor relief. The system therefore contributed to employment of more agricultural workers than could be justified on economic grounds. Further, it dampened the incentive to migrate, for underemployed workers became captives of the system.[27]

The system survived as long as entitlement to welfare was determined by individual parishes. Although parishes were brought together in unions in 1834, rates were still set for the individual parish with an incentive to minimize the demands of the poor. Caird suggested that one result was a mosaic of 'open' and 'close' parishes. In close parishes, a dominant landowner could restrict the number of families with a 'settlement' entitling them to poor relief. Labour was then recruited from an 'open' parish where fragmented ownership reduced the ability of better-off ratepayers to restrict the number of residents. Rates certainly varied: in Norfolk in 1861, the lowest poor rate was $\frac{3}{4}d.$ and the highest 6s. $5\frac{3}{4}d.$ in the pound. Caird's attack on 'close' villages was part of a wider criticism of the law of settlements which, critics claimed, prevented the operation of a free labour market. Caird believed that a free market would solve the problem of rural poverty, rather as labour exchanges were intended to solve the difficulty of casual labour in the docks after 1910. But there might be other explanations for rural poverty and labour surpluses than the operation of social policy. A surplus might arise because a parish was in an area of declining industry. A deficit might exist because a parish was in an area of recent enclosure or reclamation, or because a landlord lacked interest in his estate or wished to avoid unprofitable investment in accommodation. In any event, the Union Chargeability Act of 1865 ended the incentive to create 'close' parishes, for rates now applied to the entire union so that a 'close' parish could no longer escape the costs of maintaining the poor in an 'open' parish within the same union.[28]

Although *Punch* had reason to complain of the conditions of the agricultural labourer in 1863, the countryside was at least peaceable. Was the explanation that agricultural workers were despondent and repressed; or that conditions showed a marked improvement? High farming did not mean a reduction in the number of agricultural workers, for it remained labour intensive and the agricultural workforce reached its absolute peak in the 1840s. 'Green crops require more manual labour than corn', commented Caird, 'and even an increase of grass combined with green crops would probably not diminish the demand for labour.'[29] From 1851, the rural population started a slow fall in absolute as well as relative terms, and 'high farming' witnessed the beginning of modest improvement in the conditions of the agricultural labourer. Better housing and social facilities were provided. Wages started to increase, and farmers in the south slowly came to the view that low wages created an inefficient workforce. But improvement should not be overstated. The weekly wage in Northumberland in 1850 was 11s., or 29.4 per cent above the rate of 8s. 6d. in Norfolk. In 1892, the weekly wage in Northumberland was 17s. or 41.7 per cent above the rate of 12s. in Norfolk.[30] Although the agricultural labourer in the south experienced an unprecedented improvement in his wages, it is doubtful whether he and his family escaped from the old order of a low-productivity economy.

The extent of technical change was slight. Until 1870, most work was still intensive hand labour, with a wide seasonal variation. Farmers in the south used two methods of meeting the demands of the harvest before 1870. One was to make fairly simple improvements to hand tools.[31] The second was a change in the use of seasonal labour. Men from pastoral areas, where the peak demand for labour was in haymaking earlier in the year, moved to cereal areas. In the corn districts, gangs of harvesters worked on several harvests by moving from earlier harvests in the south to the north, or from light to heavy soil, or lowland to hills. More significant was migration from small farms. Such seasonal migration offered 'an efficient allocation of resources at a stage of economic development when mechanization was neither technically possible nor always socially desirable and when labour, properly distributed, was a cheap and flexible factor of production'.[32]

Pressure on the agricultural labour supply was intensified by rural migration. The rural population fell as a proportion of the entire population in the eighteenth and early nineteenth centuries, releasing large numbers of people to work in industry and the services. The first signs of an *absolute* reduction in rural population appeared in a few areas in the 1840s, and started to bite in the 1850s and 1860s. In East Anglia the population rose in all fifty-six registration districts between 1831 and 1841; four experienced a fall between 1841 and 1851; thirty-eight between 1851 and 1861; and thirty-two between 1861 and 1871. Most of the migrants were young men and women, so that farmers became more dependent on youths and men aged 55 and above. Men aged 20 to 54 were under-represented, with serious consequences for the future growth of the rural population. Agricultural labourers continued to have large families, but there were fewer within the fertile age groups. A reduction in the permanent workforce and a curtailment of seasonal migration pushed farmers towards mechanization, particularly in the high-wage districts. Threshing was the first process to be mechanized, and farmers adopted horse-drawn mowers, reapers, horse rakes, and eventually binders. The result was to throw more work on a smaller, permanent workforce.[33]

In retrospect, the age of high farming was a golden age of high rents, decent profits, burgeoning markets, with imports at such a level that prices failed to break. The disaster predicted by the supporters of the corn laws had not arrived; and the optimism of the proponents of repeal had been justified. Support for free trade, as for the gold standard, had become a central prop of the social contract of the Victorian state. What would happen after 1873 as imports started to increase and prices started a long downward trend?

Agricultural Depression and the Limits of Adjustment, 1873–1914

The influx of cheap cereals from the United States and other areas of recent settlement had serious consequences, leading R. E. Prothero to claim that agriculture was 'plunged indeed into the abyss'.[34] How responsive was agriculture to the new market situation? After all, falling cereal prices also offered opportunities. Consumers could shift from bread to meat and dairy products, and cheap grain reduced the costs of animal feed. The tenurial system was now placed under a new strain. Would large landowners provide the funds for reinvestment and structural change, or did squire and parson impose rigidities and high costs through their demands for rents and tithes?

Not all sectors of agriculture were equally hit by foreign competition. The fall in prices in the last quarter of the nineteenth century concentrated on cereals and on wool, which faced competition from Australia and New Zealand. Other prices were less affected. The improved standard of living of the urban consumer in the later nineteenth century created a more buoyant demand for meat, milk, vegetables, and fruit. These sectors were not completely free from foreign competition. The dairy sector faced increased competition from Danish and Dutch butter and cheese, and output fell by about 40 per cent from the 1860s to 1914. Milk was less labour intensive and the trade was insulated against competition, so that milk prices fell only slightly and output quadrupled. Although imports of meat did rise, livestock prices fell less than for cereals. Farmers had an incentive to abandon 'high farming' of livestock and to put arable land under permanent grass with the great advantage of saving about three workers for every 100 acres (see Tables 2.4 and 2.5 and Fig.2.2).

Despite the fall in prices and profits, workers were in a stronger position—a point given dramatic expression by the emergence of Joseph Arch's National Agricultural Labourers' Union in 1872 and the 'Revolt of the Field'. The NALU had 86,214 members by 1874, and there were a further 49,000 members in local unions in Lincolnshire, Kent, and Sussex. The 'revolt' was triggered by an improvement of

TABLE 2.4. *Product distribution of UK agriculture, 1870–1913 (%)*

	1870	1895	1909/13
Crops	47.2	35.5	28.6
Wheat	12.7	2.3	4.0
Livestock	52.8	64.5	71.4
Cattle	10.9	13.8	20.2
Pigs	8.1	13.9	11.4
Milk	19.2	19.4	18.0

Source: Turner, 'Agricultural output, income and productivity' 299.

TABLE 2.5. *Crop utilization of acreage in Britain, 1867–96 (000s)*

	1867		1880		1896	
	Acres	%	Acres	%	Acres	%
Cereals	9,284	33.3	8.875	27.5	7,417	22.6
Of which wheat	(3,368)	(12.1)	(2,909)	(9.0)	(1,694)	(5.2)
Root and green crop	3,498	12.5	3,486	10.8	3,26	19.9
Fallow	923	3.3	813	2.5	432	1.3
Temporary grass	3,003	10.8	4,434	13.7	4,596	14.0
Permanent grass	11,136	39.9	14,427	44.7	16,727	51.0
Other	64	0.2	247	0.8	351	1.1
Total	27,908	100.0	32,282	100.0	32,784	100.0

Source: Turner, 'Agricultural output, income and productivity'.

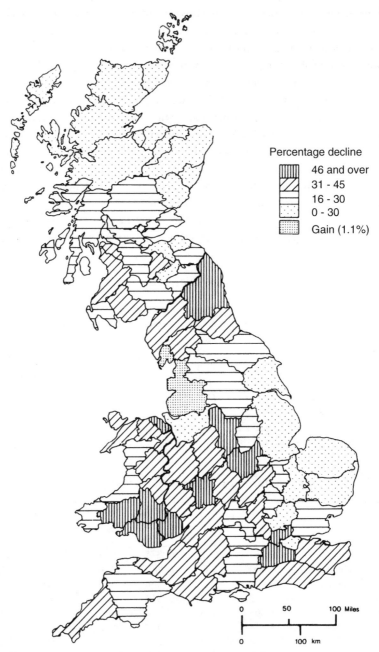

Percentage decline

▥	46 and over
▨	31 - 45
▤	16 - 30
⋰	0 - 30
▦	Gain (1.1%)

FIG. 2.2. Decline in the corn acreage of Great Britain, 1870–1914
Source: Lawton and Pooley, *Britain 1740–1950*, 154.

real wages before the formation of the union, and a feeling that the gains were by no means adequate. But it was more than a campaign for higher wages; it was a protest against the assumption that the labourer was 'a social pariah'. They were challenging the dominance of society by the farmers and gentry. In Kent, the union attempted to undermine the employers' control over religion and charity by creating a union friendly society and seeking some say within the Church. The power of the unions weakened after the early 1870s, and there was a backlash from the employers in 1878/9: by 1889, the NALU was down to 4,254 members and disbanded in 1896.[35] Nevertheless, the period of agricultural depression was one of marked improvements in the standard of living of agricultural workers: real wages rose by about 25 per cent between 1873 and 1896. Farm workers were the one class within agriculture to witness an improvement in their standard of living, gaining at the expense of landlords' rent and farmers' profit (see Table 2.6), yet the gap with workers in industry did not close and the regional disparity remained. At the same time, labour systems based on long hirings were challenged, as farm workers attached less value to the promise of security. In the 1860s, Northumbrian and Scottish hinds resisted the obligation to provide a bondager, and resentment against the limited diet of oats and potatoes mounted as falling prices reduced the real value of payment in kind. By the 1890s, the balance between payment in kind and cash had shifted, and the requirement to provide a bondager was dropped. In the north-east of Scotland, the relation between small and large farms altered and large farmers now obtained lean cattle from Ireland rather than from small farmers in the region. Meanwhile, the south of England started to shift to higher-productivity, better-paid labour.

Although cereal farmers were more seriously affected, not everyone within the livestock sector benefited from the more buoyant market for meat. Farmers fattening stock in the lowland districts had the advantage of lower prices for grain, and rents fell more in these districts which traditionally relied upon arable farming. Breeders in the highlands did less well, for they did not benefit from cheaper grain and rents fell less. Market gardening and fruit farms in the vale of Evesham and Kent also expanded. There was, therefore, some scope for diversification, with animal products rising

TABLE 2.6. *Distribution of farm income, 1871–1914, UK, (%)*

	Rent	Occupiers' capital	Labour
1871/75	26.9	14.5	58.6
1891/95	20.5	12.3	67.2
1911/14	18.5	14.8	66.8

Source: Turner, 'Agricultural output, income and productivity', 271.

from 58.6 per cent of the gross output of United Kingdom agriculture in 1870–6 to 71.5 per cent by 1904–10, and a shift from arable crops to grass (see Tables 2.4 and 2.5).[36] The sense of depression arose from the decline in rural industry, which led to a feeling of loss in the countryside, as much as from the difficulties of agriculture.[37]

Turner suggests that the greatest gains in productivity came during the depression, as farmers traded one factor against another to buy their way out. His calculation of agricultural output in England and Wales shows a fall at current prices from £145m in 1872–4 to £110m in 1895–7, a decline of 24 per cent compared with a fall in the weighted price index of 32 per cent.[38] In other words, physical output increased but the income of farmers and landlords fell, especially of landlords who were forced to cut rents (Table 2.6). Arguably, the response of farmers to changing market conditions was less marked than it might have been. British farmers lost about half the high-value markets for butter, bacon, and eggs, and failed to adopt new technology for the factory production of butter and cheese. The Danes captured the British market for pig meat whereas in Britain holdings of pigs fell (Table 2.7). Britain did less well than other 'open' economies such as Denmark which took advantage of the British market. Perhaps Britain's distinctive tripartite tenure was now a barrier to adjustment, and the agricultural system lacked flexibility. Liberal politicians could portray the landowners as parasites, denying their demand for protection; to the Liberals, the corn laws meant the 'hungry forties' and free trade meant a high standard of living for consumers. They stressed instead the need to tax the great landowners and to restore a prosperous class of owner-occupying farmers.

The flexibility of the system of mixed farming over forty years reduced the incentive for change, not least because most farmers lacked adequate accounts to measure the profitability of each component of their business. Farmers assumed they could compete in the cultivation of cereals by shifting to barley for brewing,

TABLE 2.7. *Home and foreign supplies of agricultural produce, Britain, 1905–10 (%)*

	Home produced	Net imports from British-controlled areas	Net imports from foreign countries
Food normally produced in Britain			
	48.4	18.7	32.9
Including food not normally produced in Britain			
	43.3	17.7	39.0
Wheat	20.0	27.9	52.1
Meat	52.0	17.0	31.0
Dairy	47.6	21.6	30.8

Source: Turner, 'Agricultural output, income and productivity', 225.

and by adopting the reaping machine and thresher. But the scope for change was limited. Mechanization was hampered by small and irregular sized fields. Many landowners were reluctant to pump more money into their fields, given the low returns on drainage as rents started to fall. Many farmers could not afford the cost of a shift into livestock production, given that a considerable amount of investment by both landowner and farmer was tied up in 'high farming'.[39] The financial cost of conversion was linked to the political question of the tenant's ability to provide security for loans. Political opponents of the gentry and aristocracy claimed that the uncompetitiveness of British agriculture arose from the demands on farmers to pay for the luxury of parson and squire, unlike their counterparts in the United States or Argentina. On this view, British farmers' problem was that rent levels and land prices were higher than in other countries, determined by the need to support the hierarchy of British agrarian society.[40]

How widespread and realistic were such criticisms? Would landowners and farmers close ranks as a united agricultural interest in response to the threat of foreign competition, or would farmers see their solution through resisting their landowners' demands for rent and the Church's imposition of tithes? The campaign for 'tenant right' was revived and took a more militant turn with the Farmers' Alliance of 1879. A fissure seemed to be opening. On one account, landowners opposed tenants' rights and dual ownership in land to retain political and social dominance over the rural community and entrepreneurial farmers turned from their landlords to the state for legal security for improvements. In the opinion of one historian, the Agricultural Holdings Act of 1883 meant that 'the injunctions of the state superseded the paternalism of the squire'. But was there really such a deep divide? Although the Liberals gained forty-three rural seats in 1880, this was less a sign of a 'farmers' revolt' than a return of old Whig seats lost in 1874.[41] England - and even Wales and Scotland—were not Ireland, where bitter hostility to English landowners exploded in the land wars. The Irish Land Act of 1881 offered Irish tenants the three Fs - fair rent, fixity of tenure, and free sale of improvements, which entailed the creation of Land Courts and, in effect, a form of dual ownership. Rather than providing a precedent, the Irish agitation and legislation tended to *weaken* support for the Alliance. Might the Alliance's demand for one F (free sale of improvements) lead to the other two, with the threat of outside bodies intervening in the determination of rents? Most English farmers were opposed to such an outcome. The Agricultural Holdings Act of 1883 did not mark a severance of the bonds between landlord and tenant so much as a drawing together after a period of strain. English farmers did not want radical change; they were more concerned about the general condition of agriculture.

Animosity was more apparent in Wales and Scotland. English tenant farmers were more or less at one with their landlords; Welsh farmers were not, and defined themselves as a different kind of society rather than as part of a hierarchy stretching up from the lower gentry to the great landed magnates. As a result, freehold farming started to emerge in Wales from the late nineteenth century, in part because landowners were more inclined to sell in the face of hostility from Welsh-speaking nonconformists. Aristocratic and gentry families received less deference, and paternalism was more contested. In 1913, two-thirds of Welsh farmers wished to buy, reflecting not so much land-hunger as a desire to create an autonomous Welsh culture.[42] In the case of Scotland, the Crofters' Act of 1886 offered protection against landlords seeking to impose absolute property rights. In Ireland and Scotland, land tenure had been 'reformed' on English lines in the course of the eighteenth and nineteenth centuries. In the 1880s, attitudes were shifting in the face of social protest, and in the light of new historical interest in ancient Celtic forms of land tenure and social organization, based on the clan and the township.[43] In the case of England, the use of history was somewhat less radical, but could be used to justify rights to commons and to footpaths, as well as showing how state power had been used to erode the position of yeomen farmers and peasants, and might therefore in turn be used to erode the power of the landowners.

The economic case against the gentry, aristocracy, and Church did not convince everyone. The division between tenant farmer and landlord offered an advantage, for farmers did not need to find capital for their land. The real issue is whether British landowners received a rate of return above the market rate, and whether they passed the risks of falling prices to their tenants. Annual tenancies and rack rents gave a huge advantage to landlords when prices rose: they could increase rents, and farmers lacked the security of tenure offered in the past by long leases or customary tenure. The system meant that most risks fell on the farmer, who had to pay his rent regardless of poor weather or disease. In practice, most landlords were careful not to exploit their power, both to ensure that good tenants remained on the estate and to maintain a reputation for caring, paternal ownership. But what would happen as prices started their downward slide? Most landowners offered remissions on the rent due, and also periodically reassessed rent levels. On the duke of Bedford's arable estates, the rent per acre fell by 24.3 per cent between 1872–4 and 1890–2; in Cheshire, where dairying was more prosperous, the reduction was in the order of 10 or 12 per cent. The fall in capital values was even more striking. The Plush Manor estate in Dorset was bought for £28,000 in 1879 and a further £12,600 was spent on improvements, yet in 1897 it was valued at £17,000–18,000. In the era of 'high farming', agricultural estates were sold for 30 to 40 times the annual rent; by the 1890s, the price was 20 to 25 times the rent, which had itself fallen - and it was doubtful that a buyer could be found.[44] Not surprisingly, many landowners were disinclined to make further investments in restructuring agriculture.

Traditionally, landlords provided the greater part of the capital needed to respond to changed economic circumstances. However, the general response in the last quarter of the nineteenth century was to invest *outside* their estates. As a result, agriculture became less responsive to changing market conditions. Investment did not stop, and some landlords spent money in order to readjust agriculture on their estates - with doubtful benefit for themselves and the economy in general. One way of interpreting this continued investment is to say that landlords were subsidizing farmers, so keeping them on the land and committing resources to a low-productivity sector.[45] However, this point pales into insignificance compared with France or Germany where the agricultural sector was much larger and much less productive—and preserved by protective policies. The tripartite tenurial structure of British agriculture meant that people left the land in unprecedented numbers in the eighteenth and nineteenth centuries, releasing labour for industry and the services. Above all, agriculture was not protected. British farmers did not have the political clout of their counterparts in continental Europe, and were unlikely to obtain tariffs to stem the flow of cheap food consumed by the much larger urban population. At most, Conservative governments were able to reduce the burden of local rates on agricultural land. There were too few agricultural voters, for all the survival of landowners as members of the political elite. At the end of the nineteenth century, the countryside was not so much an active political force as a screen onto which urban residents projected their desires.

Criticism of the landed aristocrats might be rephrased. Rather than imposing high rents on farmers to sustain the social hierarchy of the countryside at the expense of competitiveness, they continued to invest against their own economic interests in order to maintain the social structure of tenant farming. Denmark and New Zealand, which took a large part of the British market in pig meat, lamb, and dairy products, rested on freehold farmers who invested their own funds and developed co-operative dairies and marketing. Freehold or peasant farmers in Denmark and the Netherlands co-operated in the provision of creameries, dairies, and marketing associations, raising funds to invest in processing and marketing on the security of their equity in land. In Britain, landowners traditionally provided much of the fixed investment, and tenants did not have the means or the incentive to introduce major structural change. In the past, the tenurial system of British agriculture allowed a flexible response to change; it was now becoming a source of rigidity. Perhaps a more rapid retreat of the landed gentry and aristocracy might have allowed a greater shift in the composition of agricultural output. Equally, it might have brought British agriculture crashing into ruins.

After about 1880, the attraction of land purchase was in decline, both on economic grounds and as a symbol of social status. The peerage started to include a number of industrialists who did not own landed estates, and the House of Lords slowly started to become divorced from landownership.[46] It was no longer necessary or desirable for new peers to give up 'trade' like Lord Overstone. Although the attractions of joining landed society continued and were even democratized as land fell in price, the purchase of a large estate was no longer necessary. More and more middle-class families purchased or built residences in the country with a small amount of land which did not provide sufficient income to support the house. The country house became the house in the country.

It is precisely at this point that some historians claim to see a 'gentry counter-revolution' against industry linked with the concept of 'gentlemanly capitalism'. Such a view offers only a partial understanding of the cultural role of the countryside, less as atavistic nostalgia than a new form of consumption. Although this account of British economic development has been influential, it misses many significant features by creating false divisions in the place of a more subtle and complex picture of British culture and economy.

In the late nineteenth-century depression, old landed families shifted towards other, non-landed, sources of income, often beyond their own estates. In the past, the Bedfords, Butes, and Devonshires exploited their estates, whether copper and coal mines, suburbia, docks, or seaside resorts. Now attitudes changed and they sold their estates in order to diversify portfolios. The fall in rental income in the last quarter of the nineteenth century hit the income of landowners, particularly in the arable farming districts. For example, the net income of the earl of Leicester from his Holkham estate more than halved.[47] There must have been alarm amidst the laughter at the opening of Oscar Wilde's The Importance of Being Earnest in 1895, when Lady Bracknell remarked that 'Land has ceased to be either a pleasure or a profit. It gives one position and prevents one from keeping it up. That's all that can be said about land.' Fortunate landowners were able to escape from Lady Bracknell's paradox: they could have land and wealth, both position and the means to maintain it. 'The super-rich were becoming rentiers,' remarks David Cannadine. 'Their style of life might have remained landed in its mode of expenditure; but it was increasingly plutocratic in terms of its sources of income'.[48]

Success was more likely when the landowner possessed non-agricultural sources of income on his estate from urban ground rents or mineral royalties. But it was also possible to remain amongst the richest families without non-agricultural income. The second earl of Leicester is a case in point. Until 1870, his investments followed a traditional pattern of exploiting the potential of his landed estate, which led him to place modest sums in local railways and corn exchanges. The change after 1870 is striking, for he made large investments in domestic and Indian railways. By the time of his death in 1909, he had £977,000 in non-landed property. Diversification was possible because the second earl had cleared his debts before the onset of depression, so that he could face the decline in rents with relative equanimity.[49] Others were less well placed, even when they possessed a large non-agricultural income, for the burden of debt and unwise investments could impose strains upon even the most fortunate estates. When the seventh duke of Devonshire inherited in 1858, he had a total mortgage debt of almost £1m. Although his net income was a massive £115,000, interest charges and annuities took £60,000, and the balance could not cover inheritance and succession duties and election expenses. By the late 1860s and early 1870s, the situation had improved: rents rose, as did income from dividends, largely as a result of the seventh duke's investment in railways and in shipbuilding and steel, especially at Barrow-in-Furness. But his strategy was flawed, for the investment was financed by incurring new debts on the security of the agricultural estate. When the economy of Barrow slumped, resources were used to shore up the investment. Agricultural rents started to fall, the cost of servicing the debt rose, and by 1887 the surplus after the payment of interest and annuities was a mere £12,067. Transformation was difficult during the agricultural depression, and the eighth duke faced a serious situation when he inherited in 1891. His response was a massive shift in the structure of assets. He pulled out of Barrow and sold large amounts of land. The debt was reduced and the surplus was invested in British, colonial, and American government bonds and foreign railway shares. By the First World War, about 30 per cent of the income of the duke of Devonshire came from dividends - no longer from investments linked to the exploitation of the estate but from a wide portfolio of shares obtained from selling land.[50]

The sale of land accelerated at the end of the century. As prices fell in the last quarter of the nineteenth century, the potential supply outstripped demand and some landowners could not sell their estates, turning instead to dispose of paintings to the new rich of America. As land prices reached bottom and rents slightly recovered, many aristocrats and gentry seized their opportunity and disposed of land. 'The apparently stable Edwardian society', F. M. L. Thompson remarks, 'had in fact resolved upon a social revolution, the liquidation of the landed interest.'[51] Whether land sales meant the destruction of the aristocracy as a class is another matter. Aristocrats such as Leicester and Devonshire redirected their interests away from landed estates, whether primarily agricultural or more widely based upon mineral royalties and urban development. They became more involved with the operation of the Stock Exchange and international finance, though never dominating its operations as they had once controlled county society. In the case of Leicester, the relationship was at arm's length; in other cases, it could lead to active participation or intermarriage. A web of connections developed between the leading financiers and members of the aristocracy. The families of bankers such as the Grenfells, Mills, and Barings became interlocked by marriages, and were further linked to the families of the earls of Harewood and Grey. Members of banking families moved into the heart of the establishment. Evelyn Baring, first Earl Cromer, served as consul-general in Egypt and Finance Minister of India rather than working in the family bank. The result, Youssef Cassis suggests, 'was the formation of a renewed elite which added the financial power of the City to the prestige of the old aristocracy'.[52] A new plutocracy emerged, offering boundless amusement to the old elite to scoff at the pretensions of the *nouveaux riches*.[53] The outcome was, in the opinion of some historians, a fusion between the City and the aristocracy, and the domination of the state by policies beneficial to international finance and harmful to domestic industry.[54] However, the formulation of policy and the interplay of interests was much more complex. What *did* occur was a process of differentiation within the old landed families, leading to a more fragmented social group.

Radicals at the time had a more cynical explanation for the huge estates of the aristocracy and their survival into the later nineteenth century. They believed that the aristocracy used political power to preserve their holdings. Radicals attacked the laws of settlement, inheritance, and conveyance which were seen as artificial props of an exploitative class, allowing them to rig the market for urban development, forcing up the price of houses, factories, and mineral rights, and permitting them to obtain an unearned increment at the expense of the rest of society. Radicals interpreted aristocratic involvement in industry and urban development as essentially parasitical, a drain on productive enterprise. The increase in the value of mineral rights or of urban land was viewed as an unearned increment, appropriated by the aristocrats. The classical economists argued that the development of industry and towns hit a strictly limited supply of land, resulting in increased Rent. Since wages were determined by the logic of Malthusian theory, any increase led to a higher birth rate, placing pressure on the supply of food and leading to higher prices and lower real wages. The outcome, on this logic, was a failure of growth beyond a certain point. The experience of economic growth and a rising standard of living from about 1850 blunted the critique. But the ideas re-emerged in the 1880s, in particular through the writings of Henry George.[55] In his view, the economy was growing as a result of the efforts of industrialists, builders, workers, yet the benefit went to the landowners. The 'unearned increment' should therefore be taxed—a process starting with graduated death duties in 1894, and continuing with the 'Liberal land campaign' prior to the First World War. Landowners were under growing attack from Liberals for misappropriating their estates from the public during the Reformation and parliamentary enclosures, 'stealing' land intended for charitable purposes, and destroying common rights and a prosperous yeomanry. Campaigns were mounted to tax landowners, and also to preserve commons and footpaths—demands with a radical, anti-aristocratic edge which could also move into a more conservative attempt to preserve the countryside. Landowners countered that they were aiding rather than hindering the process of development, providing building plots at low prices, investing in the urban infrastructure of drains and roads, and reducing the capital needs of small builders through the use of leases. The Bute estate had the financial resources to make large-scale investment in the docks at Cardiff which helped to open up the south Wales coalfield; and they provided the infrastructure for building development.[56] How landowners were perceived depended on political ideology and cultural identities. Liberal politicians placed the blame for poor urban housing on the urban ground landlords, so creating an alliance with Welsh and Irish farmers. Such an approach helped the Liberals to counter any suggestion that the fundamental divide was between capital and labour. But to many small builders and traders, the landowners were not exploitative parasites so much as fellow property owners.

The cultural and political meanings of the land were contested, and involved much more than denigration of industry and the adulation of rural and aristocratic values stressed by some historians. Frank Trentmann points to a form of anti-modern romanticism offering an escape from urban materialism. In his view, it consisted of two strands: a non-partisan movement of ramblers and collectors of folk songs; and a more fundamentalist group wishing to break with urban and commercial society.[57] Similarly, Martin Wiener argues that, despite the decline of agricultural rents and land values, cultural developments in the late nineteenth century 'entrenched premodern elements within the new society, and gave legitimacy to antimodern elements'. Hence a conception of 'Englishness' emerged which virtually excluded industrialists: bourgeois culture was 'gentrified', leading to a dampening of economic endeavour as businessmen shunned entrepreneurship for the more socially accepted role of the gentleman. Industry suffered from a political system which was 'permeated by the values of the gentry counter-revolution against industry.'[58]

But such interpretations are at best partial and at worst misleadingly so. The purchase of land and cultural assimilation could allow the industrialists of the north and midlands to forge closer ties with the traditional ruling class at the level of the region, as part of a process by which their leverage and influence were increased. Sir Alfred Hickman, the millionaire Wolverhampton steel manufacturer, built a house in the country and rode with the Albrighton Hunt, mixing with the rural grandees and entertaining at his town house in London. Yet he retained an interest in the civic affairs of Wolverhampton, using his regional and national ties to foster its economy. 'The upper middle class adopted a more confident approach to the landed elite', remarks Rick Trainor, ' . . . the limited and reciprocal convergence of lifestyle and attitudes which occurred was as much a sign of middle-class strength as weakness.' The relationship between landed and industrial society was on the terms of industry as much as of land, and the continued political role of aristocrats in the Black Country after 1850 rested on deference to businessmen and the professional middle class. Gentrification was a limited process in which the landed aristocracy and gentry preserved some influence while the industrialists increased their power.[59]

The argument that industry was succumbing to an anti-industrial gentry culture rests on a limited view of culture and identity. In the nineteenth century, romantic notions of the landscape were moderated by the belief that nature was created for the service of humanity by a beneficent deity.[60] The result was far more complex than a divide between aristocrats and industrialists, for cultural ambivalence ran throughout society. Again, admiration of medieval art and the construction of Gothic buildings do not imply that industry was held in contempt; they might equally emulate the burgher culture of Flemish or north Italian towns or reflect the desire of industrialists and merchants to express a distinctive historical identity for themselves and their region, a claim to importance alongside other visions of the British past. York could claim its proud Roman and Christian history; similarly, Bradford and Leeds needed to stake their own claims as centres of industry and freedom.[61]

Indeed, the chronology was probably the reverse of Wiener's account. He suggests that prior to 1870, British culture was predominantly modern, industrial, anti-historical, and anti-aristocratic, before turning to the cultural embrace of heritage and rural myth. But Peter Mandler's analysis of the place of the country house in English culture suggests a different evolution. In the early nineteenth century, the Palladian country house was often viewed as alien and exclusive, and older medieval and Tudor houses were given greater value as symbols of harmony and inclusiveness. From the 1880s, attitudes shifted, as criticism of aristocrats made appreciation of country houses politically doubtful. In Mandler's words, 'there was a counter-revolution of values in attitudes to heritage, but it was one that questioned the relevance of the national past and devalued the contributions of the aristocracy'. And how is the 'new romanticism' to be interpreted, as expressed by bodies such as the Commons Preservation Society (1865), Society for the Preservation of Ancient Buildings (1877), National Footpaths Preservation Society (1884), National Trust (1894), Folk Song Society (1898), and English Folk Dance Society (1911)? They aimed to preserve open spaces and access to the land, to protect old churches and barns, and to record the customs of the countryside. Their concern was with vernacular buildings and landscapes rather than the parks and houses of the elite which were signs of exploitation and loss. Although a few pioneers such as William Morris and other 'arts and crafts' designers moved to the Cotswolds, the market for their goods was amongst the prosperous residents of suburbia. The preservationist societies gave cultural value to a non- or even anti-aristocratic society, asserting the virtues of authenticity over artifice, the superiority of the village wood turner (as reinterpreted by the arts and crafts movement) over Chippendale. In any event, their members were a small minority, opposing both the aristocratic culture of the old elite and the rapid development of commercial leisure and a new form of mass culture. The preservationists complained that economic progress was given priority over heritage, yet many historians have taken their protest as evidence that anti-modernism dominated culture. Historians who see a turn away from modernity towards tradition have mistaken the protests of a minority troubled by mass culture for the sentiments of the majority who enjoyed the music halls and also a walk in the country.[62]

One way of making change and modernity acceptable and unthreatening was to place it within a long, continuous tradition. A climate of political stability made history a means of negotiating change and accepting different notions of the future. Continuity made more sense than in France and Germany. In Britain, it was possible to come to terms with the new and modern through a strong sense of historical continuities. There was not a deep divide between a monarchist and republican tradition as in France, which produced two competing pantheons of historical heroes and villains, and two literary canons. In Britain, they could be brought together in a single pantheon or literary canon, in the pages of the *Dictionary of National Biography*, on the walls of the National Portrait Gallery, in the selections of Palgrave's *Golden Treasury* of English verse, and in history paintings and statues. It was an organic notion of the national past—a notion expressed by James Murray's new English dictionary, which rested on the organic nature of English as a language, with the liberty to use and speak it as one wished. Stefan Collini's point is surely correct, that the dominant relationship with the English past was a 'repository of treasures which all members of a united nation can enjoy as part of their uniquely glorious heritage'. There was a myth of continuity and longevity which could heal and absorb conflicts, an emphasis on English culture without martyrs and shrines—a culture of incorporation, toleration, diversity, and organic change.[63] Rather than suggesting a counter-revolution against industrial capitalism or modernity, the culture of late Victorian and Edwardian Britain should be seen as responsive to change. Indeed, acceptance of the modern seemed less threatening than in Germany where any new development was tested to see if it was in accord with national *Kultur*. The modern was more likely to be disruptive and to be politicized than in Britain with its emphasis on a culture of flexibility and pluralism.[64] Rather than turning back to rural nostalgia in flight from the future and the modern, British narratives of modernity were informed by a stronger sense of continuity than in many other countries. The absence of a sense of crisis or rupture should not be taken as an indication of failure to come to terms with economic, social, and intellectual change and of a retreat into nostalgia. On the contrary, it reflected the easy acceptance of change as an expression of a tolerant, adaptable national character and culture.

The Liberal land campaign was concerned to encourage development of the land, making it cheaper so that it could be combined with capital and labour in the service of economic growth. On the other hand, many Liberals believed in the redemptive power of the countryside—and argued that natural beauty should be more widely available. In a sense, the countryside was emptied of its autonomous political importance, which it still retained in most other European countries. Instead, it became a resource for town dwellers: 'the rural idyll was essentially an accretion to urban life rather than a substitute for it', providing 'a source of unity and a comforting expression of stability'. Arcadian and picturesque images of the countryside did not imply a rejection of towns for, in Crossick's phrase, 'only a truly urban Britain could really invent the countryside'.[65]

World War to World War

The debate over free trade and tariff reform was central to the vision of Britain's future in the Edwardian period. Joseph Chamberlain looked to the empire as a market for British goods; he wished to exclude foreign manufactures and food, but to allow in imperial raw materials and foodstuffs without controls or protective duties. The Liberal proponents of free trade countered that tariff reform or imperial preference was merely a device to ease the introduction of full-blown agricultural protection, a return to the corn laws. In the view of many members of the Liberal party, what was needed was a tax on landowners rather than a tax on food. The moral superiority of free trade remained an important theme, yet the Liberal government that won the elections of 1906 and 1910 on a platform of free trade embarked on a naval race with Germany, rejecting the animosity of Gladstone to huge naval programmes which had led to his final resignation as Prime Minister in 1893. In 1914, the naval race culminated in war with Germany.

The link between free trade and the naval race was not a coincidence. In the event of war would Britain be starved into submission if it could not obtain imports? Might supply lines be disrupted or trade routes across the Atlantic threatened? British officials and politicians soon realized that Germany was in an equally exposed position. Although Germany was less reliant on imports of grain it was still importing considerable quantities of foods and raw materials. Strategists at the Admiralty pressed for a dual policy, which was accepted by the Committee of Imperial Defence in 1909. First, Britain should ensure its own food supplies through close links across the Atlantic and with the dominions. These societies could ally in a common sense of 'whiteness' against Britain's colonies in Asia. Second was a naval blockade of Germany. The Admiralty argued that the threat of a blockade would deter Germany from action—and if it did not, would soon result in Germany's defeat. The approach was adopted, despite opposition from the War Office and some naval officers, as British strategic policy. Free trade and the naval race seemed contradictory in the mind-set of Cobdenite Liberals; to the strategists of the Admiralty and leading Liberal politicians in the pre-war government, they were mutually dependent.[66]

Matters did not work out entirely as anticipated. The German government was concerned that Britain's superior fiscal system would allow it to build more battleships.[67] The German high command realized that it could not win a long war, and so planned a swift victory over France as in the Franco-Prussian War. Their plans failed, and Germany fought the long war that its generals feared they could not win. Neither did Britain fight the war anticipated by the naval strategists: it was very soon committed to a land war with a mass army. As many British men rushed to enlist, a mass army was available from the start of the war—and the links with the dominions led to a similar pattern in Canada, New Zealand, and Australia. These men were soon needed to support the French army in blocking the German land campaign. By 1917, the Germans turned to a new strategy: why not strike at Britain's food supplies by submarine warfare? The decision made sense, even though it would bring the United States into the war. Food supply and politics were at the very heart of the First World War, leading to the extension of an essentially European conflict into a global war.[68]

In the words of Avner Offer, the First World War was 'not only a war of steel and gold, but a war of bread and potatoes'. The German army was not defeated decisively on the battlefield but difficulties with the food supply 'played a decisive role in the unravelling of the German war effort'. Although the blockade took a lot longer than the Admiralty expected, it did play a considerable role in the armistice, and was maintained to force the Germans to sign the peace treaty in 1919. The task facing Germany was virtually impossible as a result of the blockade. The civilian population and the army did not starve, but they were frequently hungry, cold, and miserable. The response of the authorities did not help. Periods of deprivation, insufficient food to maintain body weight, the need to resort to the black market for between a fifth and a third of food, glaring inequalities in the availability of food, and changes in diet, all contributed to a loss of military and civilian morale. The failures of administration and co-ordination undermined the authority of the German state and led to deep social divisions and political crisis—as well as anger at the allies for retaining the blockade after the armistice. In the case of Britain, the provision of food was much more successful and the authorities seemed more responsive and effective in creating a basic fairness: social tensions were less divisive and disabling. Even at its worst in 1917, the calorie content of the average British diet was only 4 per cent below the pre-war level. Britain's victory was not so much the result of superior military forces on the battlefields as its ability to feed and maintain its population.[69]

Estimates made at the time by the Food (War) Committee of the Royal Society indicated the heavy reliance of Britain on imported food: the proportion of calories supplied by British farmers was 42 per cent in total. In fact, reliance on imports was higher, for imported feed and fertilizers were major inputs.[70] British dependence on imports was at once a threat and an opportunity. The threat came from the vulnerability of supplies in the U-boat campaign, as well as financial constraints. The government therefore attempted to increase domestic production, by rolling back the changes of the last quarter of the nineteenth century and turning grassland over to crops. However, the availability of imports from the rest of the world also offered an opportunity: Britain's access to foreign and imperial food reduced pressures on labour supply created by the demands of the munitions industry and armed services. At the outbreak of the war, little if anything was done to protect the supply of labour and materials from the demands of the military. Agricultural workers were only 'protected' from military service from the middle of 1917; farm horses were commandeered by the army, and fertilizers and machinery were difficult to obtain. How could the conflicting needs for scarce resources be balanced, not least when the U-boats threatened food imports?

Many commentators pointed to the success of British farmers in increasing their output and shifting from livestock to arable crops. As many agriculturalists and nutritionists realized, an acre of land would feed more people if the produce went straight to humans rather than being fed to livestock. In 1914, British agriculture was dominated by livestock, with a high proportion of land under permanent grass or rough grazing.[71] Here is one possible explanation for the success of British agriculture: the ability to plough up grassland. But examination of the data suggests that conversion to arable was not the major factor.

Until the end of 1916, the government took little direct action, merely advising that farmers should turn grass over to cereals without offering any positive inducements. Did the initial failure to impose controls on agriculture lead to serious difficulties?

TABLE 2.8. *Farmland in Britain by use, 1914 (%)*

	England	Wales	Scotland
Permanent grass	57.7	50.0	31.1
Rotation grass/clover	9.4	34.3	31.2
Grain	22.3	11.8	24.8
Other arable	8.1	3.6	12.5
Miscellaneous	1.1	0.1	0.2
Fallow	1.4	0.2	0.2
Total	100.0	100.0	100.0
Notional addition			
Rough grazing	10.0	48.6	191.1

Source: Dewey, *British Agriculture*, 11.

Official figures suggested a considerable reduction in the workforce by the end of 1916. More recent calculations indicate that the loss was around 11 per cent by the end of 1916, or 9 per cent when account is taken of the use of children and women—a serious though not disabling reduction. Although the number of farm horses initially fell, the army soon turned to other sources so that the number of horses in farming recovered by the end of 1916, and was supplemented by tractors. The supply of fertilizers and feed dropped by about 20 per cent and 10 per cent respectively, without seriously affecting output. Overall, there was little change in agriculture in the first two years of the war: the area under arable crops rose by 4 per cent in the harvest of 1915, and then fell by 3 per cent in 1916.[72] At this point, the President of the Board of Agriculture started to argue for a more interventionist policy, an approach supported by a departmental committee chaired by Alfred Milner. The Milner Committee suggested that farmers should have a guaranteed minimum price for wheat for four years, with the government making a 'deficiency' payment of the difference between the guaranteed price and the actual price received.[73] Of course, the advocates of ploughing could point to the superior output of calories from crops—but there was a much wider and worrying implication for the Liberal shibboleth of free trade. Did the policy have overtones of the corn laws? The deficiency payments avoided the danger of protection, for the consumer would still pay the world price for food; the farmer would receive the difference between this price and the guaranteed price from general tax revenue. However, the Milner Committee challenged the principle of comparative advantage at the heart of free trade ideology, arguing that the policy of conversion to crops should continue after the war.

The recommendations of the Committee were not immediately accepted by Asquith's administration, which continued its policy of advice and encouragement through the War Agricultural Committees, but became government policy in December 1916 when Milner himself joined the War Cabinet and R. E. Prothero took over at the Board of Agriculture. The new policy was encapsulated in the Corn Production Act 1917. There was now a conscious policy of ploughing land, with compliance enforced through County Agricultural Executive Committees reporting to the Food Production Department, backed by guaranteed prices and deficiency payments to farmers over a period of six years. Farm workers would receive minimum wages of 25s. a week, and agricultural rents were controlled during the period of guaranteed prices to ensure that landlords did not appropriate the benefits. A Food Controller was appointed at the end of 1916 to take charge of distribution. Of course, the policy of ploughing could only work if farmers had labour, so that agriculture was protected from the army, and soldiers, women, and prisoners of war were put to work in the fields. The labour position was not serious: over the war, the demand for agricultural labour probably rose by about 5 per cent and the supply dropped by 4 per cent, so that the overall shortage in 1918 was 9 per cent compared with pre-war levels.[74] The increase in tillage came mainly in 1918. The average tillage area in Britain in 1909–13 was 10.46m acres, in 1916 only 10.23m, and in 1918 12.36m which was back at the level of the mid–1880s. Considerable potential still remained, as indicated by experience in the Second World War when the tillage area reached 13.71m acres in 1944.[75]

How successful was the policy of increasing agricultural production? Despite shortages of resources, the output of British agriculture was only 2 per cent below pre-war levels in 1916; somewhat surprisingly, the fall in output was more serious during the period of control when shortages of feedstuffs hit livestock and milk production to a greater extent than the increase in cereals and potatoes. In 1918, the output of British agriculture was 7 per cent below 1909–13.[76] Of course, the output of agriculture is not the same as the number of calories consumed, and here success was greater. Unlike in Germany, the food supply remained adequate: William Beveridge's figures indicated that the calories consumed by the average man were 3 per cent higher in 1915 than in 1909–13, and then fell to 3 per cent below in 1918, a modest reduction which did not threaten the war effort. In terms of the calorific content, home production fell from 41 per cent of the food supply of the UK in 1909–13 to 38 per cent in 1916 and then rose to 47 per cent in 1918. The rise was not particularly impressive, and in large part was not due to changes in agricultural production.[77]

The appointment of the Food Controller at the end of 1916 allowed a more efficient use of available supplies, and considerable economies were possible. Above all, a higher proportion of wheat could be consumed by people. Before the war, about 70 per cent of wheat was extracted to make white flour, with the remaining 30 per cent used for animal feed. During the war, the level of extraction was increased to 90 per cent, so increasing calories for human consumption without the need for major changes in agriculture. The policy on breadstuffs was more important than the ploughing policy.[78] The development of policies to manage food supply within Britain and in international markets was crucial. The main achievement was the maintenance of food distribution with the growth of an efficient system from the level of individual cities up to inter-allied co-operation, rather than the efforts of domestic agriculture.

Although free trade survived the war, the success of these government interventions did mark a shift in the discourse of economic policy. Before the war, free trade was seen as the major defence of the consumer against exploitation. During the war, the rhetorical emphasis shifted from the cheap, white loaf to issues of purity and nutrition. The white loaf was no longer a patriotic symbol; eating brown bread was now a duty rather than a symbol of inferiority. State intervention was needed to raise nutritional standards. Above all, pure milk was necessary for health, and could only be secured through state inspection and, possibly, ownership. In 1918, the Ministry of Food took control of the wholesale milk trade, and there was considerable concern that the retail trade was falling into the hands of trusts such as United Dairies. The government established a Consumers' Council in 1918 to advise on issues of food supply, bringing together representatives from the co-operative movement, trade unions, and other organized working-class consumers. Free trade and the free market were no longer so clearly guarantees of the interest of the consumer. Controls should be retained as the best way of protecting consumers. Against this view, the co-operative movement argued for decontrol in the belief that its own activities could counter trusts. Divisions meant that at the end of 1920, the Council resigned and decontrol was imposed. The co-operative movement went on to expand its interests in the milk trade, supplying about a quarter of the national market by the Second World War. But the weight of opinion in the Labour and Liberal parties was turning towards political control and regulation. Consumer interests moved from free trade and cheapness to trade regulation and fair prices.[79]

The wartime attempts to increase domestic agricultural production led some politicians and commentators to argue for a continued drive to self-sufficiency. At the end of the war, a Royal Commission was appointed to consider the economic prospects of agriculture. In 1919, a bare majority of twelve members proposed that price guarantees be maintained for a further four years; a minority of eleven argued against 'embarking on a policy involving the expenditure of public money in diverting agriculture into uneconomic fields'.[80] In 1920, the majority appeared to have won: the Agriculture Act continued guarantees for wheat and oats without a time limit. Their victory was short-lived for in 1921 the government dropped price guarantees, leaving farmers with a bitter sense of abandonment and betrayal.

During the 1920s, British farmers were left to face foreign competition, with the single major exception of a subsidy for the cultivation of sugar beet which was introduced in 1924. Farmers responded by shifting back to grass, livestock, and dairying. British agriculture was seriously hit by the fall in world prices after 1929, not least as other European countries moved towards protection and left Britain as one of the few open markets. When imperial preference was introduced in the 1930s, agriculture derived little benefit. Although the Ottawa agreement imposed duties on foreign wheat, imports from the empire remained duty free, so that unlike most farmers in continental Europe, British farmers were not sheltered. Imports merely shifted from foreign to imperial sources of supply.[81] Clearly, the political calculation in Britain differed from many other European countries where governments faced powerful agricultural interests. In Britain, the government needed to help the farmer without driving up prices.

The solution was to rationalize or co-ordinate production, and to return to deficiency grants as during the First World War. In 1931, the Labour government's

Agricultural Marketing Act gave power to a 'substantial' majority of producers in any commodity to introduce a mandatory marketing scheme with minimum and maximum prices. Since the Act did not control imports, little could be done to prevent them from dropping below the minimum. In 1933, imports could be controlled and marketing schemes were soon introduced for milk, potatoes, and bacon. The aim was to balance the interests of farmers and consumers and to co-ordinate distribution. In the case of cereals, guaranteed prices and deficiency grants were reintroduced. The consumer had the benefit of cheap flour and bread; the farmer secured a decent income through a subsidy financed by a levy on all flour. In other words, the producer of foreign grain was paying to preserve British farmers, and the glut on world markets meant that the incidence of the subsidy fell on farmers in the major exporting areas. The policies adopted in Britain meant that food prices were low for domestic consumers.

The emergence of marketing schemes connects with another major change in British agriculture: the reduction in the power of the landed aristocracy. The war marked a fundamental change in the position of landowners and a major shift in the distribution of income. In 1909–13, landowners took 27 per cent of the income of agriculture, falling to 12 per cent in 1918. Although Lloyd George abandoned land taxes at the end of the war, the ambitions of his 'land campaign' were achieved by rent controls and death duties. Although agriculture prices rose two- or threefold during the war, rents were controlled; at the end of the war, rents rose, but usually only by about 15 per cent before falling again. At the same time, landowners had to pay for jointures, mortgages, and death duties which severely eroded their income. Although capital values also fell sharply, many landowners saw little option except to sell. In the years immediately before and after the war, about a quarter of the land of England and a third of Wales and Scotland was sold. In 1924, one MP pointed to 'a silent social revolution in progress . . . . We are, unless I mistake it, witnessing in England the gradual disappearance of the old landed classes.' Perhaps worst hit were the small gentry, who were less able to dispose of parts of their estates. Landowners not only retreated from their agricultural estates; they also disposed of urban and mineral estates. Works of art were sacrificed; London town houses were sold and in many cases demolished; even country houses were abandoned. The political power of the landed elite declined, and they lost their grip over the Church, armed forces, and law, surviving only at Court and in the Foreign Office, and in dignified ceremonial positions at home and the colonies. Meanwhile, farmers' share of agricultural income rose from 42 to 64 per cent between 1909–13 are 1918, and the proportion of holdings occupied by their owners in England rose from 13 per cent in 1909 to 37 per cent in 1927.[82]

The countryside moved from being the site of political tensions to a site for consumption and leisure. The retreat of the aristocracy was complemented by a wider appreciation of the aesthetic of the arts and crafts movement, with its stress on the domesticity of the cottage and the farmhouse, a search for tranquillity and homeliness in country churchyards and villages, amongst dry-stone walls and quick-set hedges. The great country houses were not part of this aesthetic, and their destruction was likely to be welcomed. The ideal of the arts and crafts ethos was the Tudor yeoman, not the Whig grandee in a Palladian pile who had destroyed the old order. As Mandler remarks, 'these images resonated because they caught the tone of England's peculiar, conservative modernity between the wars . . . . The countryside became a playground and an imaginative space in which urban society could reconstruct itself on new lines.'[83]

The creators of the arts and crafts ethos were concerned that in the process, the very things they so admired were being destroyed by trippers, billboards, teashops, and trinkets; their admiration for vernacular architecture was debased by mock Tudor houses in suburbia and horse brasses in roadside public houses. The fear of unplanned sprawl and commercialization was encapsulated in the title of Clough Williams-Ellis's book of 1928: *England and the Octopus*. How was the countryside to be saved? One response was to re-evaluate the aristocratic estates and country houses as protectors of the countryside and orderly development of towns, which was expressed in the decision of the National Trust to introduce a scheme to preserve country houses in 1936. But this was still a minority view.[84] A more significant approach was what may be called 'planning preservation'. When the Council for the Preservation of Rural England was established in 1926, it was not just a celebration of the English village. One of its creators was Patrick Abercrombie, the town planner. His vision of modernity in new towns such as Stevenage or Harlow was of a piece with his attitude to the countryside: the resources of Britain should be planned and disciplined to create order and beauty. The CPRE was opposed to sprawl and ribbon development, to unsightly telephone and electricity cables—not to planned towns carefully placed in the countryside, or to disciplined electricity pylons. The problem was *laissez-faire*; the preservationists and planners would offer discipline and aesthetic design. Abercrombie argued that the only control in the past came from the great landlords; the break-up of their estates threatened the despoliation of the countryside. The solution was for the state to take over the role of the aristocrat, managing the nation as one great estate.

The National Trust would preserve the country, but its actions were not enough: the state needed to develop new towns, designate national parks, and protect lowland areas of scenic beauty. The vision was implemented by the Labour government after the war. In 1946, Hugh Dalton argued in his budget speech for the preservation of the natural beauty of England as the nation's memorial to those who died. As Minister of Town and Country Planning, he established the first national parks and pressed ahead with new towns. Abercrombie's and Dalton's approach shared some of Stanley Baldwin's rhetoric of the inter-war period. He stressed that the English were essentially countrymen in order to write class and industrial conflict out of the story. It was a clever piece of political rhetoric which has misled some historians into assuming that an anti-industrial culture was in the ascendant. But while Baldwin talked of the smell of wood smoke, the sight of the plough-team, or roses around the cottage door, in reality, he did little. As Matless points out, his vision was of an evasive and quiet little England. The preservationist planners wanted an assertive, progressive, modern England.[85] England's landscape needed to be designed, in the same way that its economy needed to be planned. It should also be enjoyed. In order to make the landscape available to the public, the public needed to be taught how to behave and what to see. From 1934, the Shell county guides developed a new genre of 'motoring pastoralism', indicating that the car and petrol companies were celebrating rather than destroying the countryside.[86] The Youth Hostels Association was formed in 1930, the Ramblers' Association in 1935—bodies which had a particular expectation of how to enjoy the countryside which was often anti-aristocratic in their demands for access to the land.

Proponents of an organic rural life opposed the modern city, planner preservationists, and wartime drives for production. To writers such as Rolfe Gardiner, a founder of the Kinship in Husbandry of 1941, inorganic farming was short term and exploitative, a symbol of what was wrong with England under the rule of bureaucrats and managers. These 'organicists' saw a mystical link with the soil, connecting the land with the people, and opposing financial capitalism and rootlessness. Their attitude was connected with wider issues: international debt and artificial fertilizers were both exploitative and destructive; society grew from the soil, and so should the state and political authority. Their vision was not enjoyment of the country—it was one of work on the land, eating fresh, local whole-food, and breeding fit people away from the contamination of the city. The dangers of this rhetoric were apparent in Germany, where blood and soil came together in anti-Semitism and racial ideology. By no means all 'organicists' became fascists, despite their close links. Although Gardiner took a group of morris dancers to the Berlin Olympics and in 1939 visited the German Minister of Agriculture and pioneer of organic farming, he rejected racial ideology, and felt that the Nazis distorted organic ideas, pursuing war through industrial materialism, stressing blood at the expense of soil.[87]

During the war and post-war reconstruction, the planner preservationists were in the ascendant. Agricultural production and food distribution would be crucial to success: the countryside was used as a symbol of what Britain was fighting to preserve, but it had also to be modernized and made productive. In 1936, the government established a department to prepare wartime food policies, which was replaced by the Ministry of Food at the outbreak of war. The county committees created during the First World War were reinstated and arable farming was expanded. Food imports accounted for 70 per cent of Britain's pre-war consumption, and declined much more sharply than in the First World War, dropping from 22m tons before the war to 11–12m tons a year in 1942–4. The increase in arable acreage was also greater than in the First World War, expanding from 12m acres in 1939 to 18m in 1945. Grain production rose by 81 per cent between 1939 and 1943, and meat production fell by 36 per cent. In terms of calories, the contribution of domestic production rose from 30 per cent before the war to 40 per cent in 1943/4—less than during the First World War. The size of the labour force remained stable (Table 2.9) and, in view of the expansion of machinery during the war, total factor productivity in agriculture actually fell. The great success was in providing calories: the calorific content of output rose, as did the number of calories produced per worker.[88]

As in the First World War, the real success was in bringing imports into Britain, and then ensuring that food was distributed as fairly as possible. Marketing schemes and deficiency grants were suspended. Instead, farmers received fixed prices. By 1944, the government was able to suggest policies for the end of war, not least to offset the sense of betrayal and fear of a post-war slump which might lead to a loss of production. The government offered to guarantee the price of milk, cattle, and sheep to 1948, and to set the price of other products by an annual review in association with the National Union of Farmers. These guarantees were made permanent in the Agriculture Act of 1947: assured prices and guaranteed markets were offered to farmers to produce 'such part of the nation's food . . . as in the national interest it is desirable to produce in the United Kingdom', and at such prices as would offer 'proper remuneration and living conditions for farmers and workers in agriculture and an adequate return on capital'.[89] Of course, these words were open to interpretation: what part was desirable and what was a proper remuneration or an adequate return? The government was anxious to work with farmers to increase output, in response to the perception that the world would face shortages and the need to save foreign exchanges. The Labour government pressed for an increase in agricultural output by 50 per cent above the pre-war level by 1951/2—a target that was almost achieved. One result was to turn the Ministry of Agriculture, Food, and

TABLE 2.9. *Output, employment, and labour productivity in UK agriculture, 1939–44*

	Real value of net output	Calorific value of net output	Employment (standardized)	Real output per employee	Calories per employee
1939/40	104	110	99	105	111
1941/2	98	136	103	95	132
1943/4	115	191	108	106	177

Source: Broadberry and Howlett, 'UK', 63.

Fisheries into the defender of the producer. The interests of the consumer were to be protected in other ways. Rationing was continued and extended to bread in 1946; food prices were held down by subsidies. By 1951, food subsidies cost £465m a year; and schoolchildren received free school milk from 1946 as part of their entitlement to health. Labour was committed to 'real consumer choice', which meant rationing by need rather than by the purse. By the end of the Second World War, the consumers' interests were protected by entitlements and regulated prices rather than by free trade.[90]

By 1950 many voters were rejecting controls and rations. Food subsidies might be seen as a distortion of consumer choice rather than liberation from want, merely increasing taxes on the goods consumers wished to buy. The result might be a reduction in consumer satisfaction, and a misallocation of resources. Indeed, Labour policies could be seen as out of touch with affluence and consumer choice. The new Conservative government removed rationing and reduced food subsidies in stages. Above all, fixed prices were replaced by deficiency payments and a return to the marketing schemes of the 1930s.

The post-war Labour government marked the triumph of the planning preservationists. The drive to increase agricultural productivity was linked with the creation of 'green belts' to prevent sprawl; new towns were constructed; all development gains from land were appropriated by the state in 1947; national parks were created in 1949. The various preservationist bodies were able to hold together an alliance to prevent the destruction of the countryside. But the tensions were apparent. The scheme to acquire all development gains in 1947 proved flawed and was repealed; the powers of the national parks were modest; and the attempt to raise productivity proved destructive of hedgerows and wildlife.

NOTES

1. Spring, 'A great agricultural estate', 80, 81.
2. For example, Tawney, *Agrarian Problems*; Hammond and Hammond, *Village Labourer*; Johnson, *Disappearance of the Small Landowner*.
3. Thompson, 'Changing perceptions of land tenures in Britain'; O'Brien and Keyder, *Economic Growth in Britain and France*.
4. Cannadine, 'Landowner as millionaire, 77; Daunton, 'Gentlemanly capitalism', 119.
5. Fairlie, 'Corn laws and British wheat production', 103.
6. Fairlie, 'Nineteenth-century corn law', 572–3, 574; Fairlie, 'Corn laws and British wheat production', 106.
7. Caird, *English Agriculture*, ix–x, xiii, 483–5.
8. Collins, 'Dietary change and cereal consumption', 105, 114.
9. Quoted in Collins and Jones, 'Sectoral advance', 67.
10. Perry, 'High farming', 368; Phillips, *Underdraining of Farmland*.
11. Perry, 'High farming', 366–7.

12. Martins, *Great Estate at Work*, 156–7.

13. Data on farm size from Mingay, *Agrarian History of England and Wales*, vi, ii, 759–61.

14. Rubinstein, *Men of Property*, 219.

15. Michie, 'Income, expenditure and investment', 59–61, 66–7.

16. Thompson, 'Life after death' 53–5.

17. Ibid. 44–5; Thompson, 'Business and landed elites'.

18. Thompson, 'Life after death', 41, 47, 57–9; Rose, 'Diversification', 80–1, 88–9.

19. Caird, *English Agriculture*, pp. xxiv, 130–2, 506–7; Fisher, 'Landowners and English tenant right'; McQuiston, 'Tenant right'.

20. Armstrong, *Farmworkers*, 90.

21. Caird, *English Agriculture*, 511–14.

22. Hunt, 'Labour productivity', 285–90.

23. Kussmaul, *Servants in Husbandry*, 20, 171.

24. Caird, *English Agriculture*, 50.

25. Carter, *Farmlife in Northeast Scotland*, 109–10, 120.

26. On the lowlands, see Devine (ed.), *Farm Servants and Labour*, 1–3 (Devine, 'Service in the agricultural revolution'), 74–5 (Robson, 'The Border farm worker'), 104–6 (Devine, 'Women workers, 1850–1914'); on the north-east of England, Dunbabin, *Rural Discontent*, 155–7.

27. Digby, 'The labour market', 69–71.

28. Digby, *Pauper Palaces*, 89; Caird, *English Agriculture*, 517; Banks, 'Nineteenth-century scandal'.

29. Caird, *English Agriculture*, 487.

30. Jones, 'Agricultural labour market', 338.

31. Collins, 'Harvest technology', 455, 458, 460.

32. Collins, 'Migrant labour', 59.

33. Jones, 'Agricultural labour market', 322–38; Saville, *Rural Depopulation*, 53–9.

34. Quoted in Fletcher, 'Great depression', 417.

35. Dunbabin, *Rural Discontent*; Peacock, *Revolt of the Fields*; Arnold, 'Revolt of the field'.

36. Turner, *Agricultural output, income and productivity*, II, 2000–1.

37. Thompson in Mingay (ed.), *Victorian Countryside*, i. 115.

38. Turner 'Agricultural output, income and productivity,' 320, table 38.11.

39. Perry, *British Farming in the Great Depression*, 22.

40. Offer, *First World War*, 114, 117, 129.

41. Fisher, 'Farmers' Alliance'; McQuiston, 'Tenant right'.

42. Davies, 'End of the great estates', 209.

43. Dewey, 'Celtic agrarian legislation'.

44. Thompson, 'Rent of agricultural land', 595–602; Thompson, *English Landed Society*, 310–13, 317–18; Perry, *British Farming*, 75, 77.

45. O'Grada, 'British agriculture', 172.

46. See Pumphrey, 'Introduction of industrialists into the British peerage'.

47. Martins, *Great Estate at Work*, 60.

48. Cannadine, *Decline*, 135–6.

49. Martins, *Great Estate at Work*, 61–5, 267–9; Rubinstein, *Men of Wealth*, 199.

50. Cannadine, *Decline*, 124, 135, 407.
51. Thompson, *English Landed Society*, 326; Cannadine, *Decline*, ch. 3.
52. Cassis, 'Bankers in English society', 220–4, 229; Owen, *Cromer*.
53. Crook, *Rise of the Nouveaux Riches*.
54. Cain and Hopkins, 'Gentlemanly capitalism'.
55. George, *Progress and Poverty*.
56. Daunton, *Coal Metropolis*, chs. 2 and 5.
57. Trentmann, 'Civilisation and its discontents', 587–92, 603–9.
58. Wiener, *English Culture and the Decline of the Industrial Spirit*, 7–10, 97, 126, 158.
59. Trainor, 'Gentrification', 171, 196–7.
60. Mandler, 'Politics and English landscape', 461.
61. Dellheim, *Face of the Past*, 65–7, 120, 160–1; Gunn, 'The "failure" of the Victorian middle class', 29.
62. Mandler, *Fall and Rise of the Stately Home*, 106, 109–110; Mandler, 'Politics and English landscape', 461–2.
63. Collini, *Public Moralists*, 345–6.
64. Rieger, 'Envisioning the future'.
65. Crossick, 'Urbanisation, migration and Arcadian myths', 42–3, 67–71.
66. See Offer, *First World War*, 25, 155, 239, 242, 264, 305, 352–4, 402 and French, *British Strategy and War Aims*, 13–14.
67. Ferguson, 'Public finance', 143, 161–2.
68. Offer, *First World War*, 355–67.
69. Ibid. 1; see Bonzon and Davis, 'Feeding the cities', 308; Dewey, *British Agriculture*, 1.
70. Dewey, *British Agriculture*, 16.
71. Ibid. 13–14 and appendix D; Dewey, 'British farming profits', 384–5.
72. Dewey, *British Agriculture*, tables 7.2 and 7.3.
73. Ibid. 24–5.
74. Ibid. 141.
75. Ibid. 103, 202.
76. Ibid. 215.
77. Ibid. 220, 227.
78. Ibid. 226–7.
79. Trentmann, 'Bread, Milk', 154; Hilton, *Consumerism in Twentieth-Century Britain*, ch. 2.
80. Tracy, *Agriculture in Western Europe*, 152.
81. Ibid., 168.
82. Cannadine, *Decline*, 93, 94, 97, 98, 106, 111, 113, 119, 122, 126, 604; Dewey, *British Agriculture*, 236; Sturmey, 'Owner-farming in England and Wales, 1900–1950'.
83. Mandler, *Fall and Rise*, 226–7.
84. Ibid. 263.
85. Matless, *Landscape and Englishness*, 25–32.
86. Ibid. 64.
87. Ibid. 104, 119–30, 146–8.
88. Astor and Murray, *Agriculture*; Broadberry and Howlett, 'UK', 61–3; Tracy, *Agriculture in Western Europe*, 157–70.

89. Tracy, *Agriculture in Western Europe*, 254.

90. Trentmann, 'Bread, milk', 156–8.

FURTHER READING

Armstrong, W. A., *Farmworkers: A Social and Economic History, 1770–1980* (1988)

Arnold, R., 'The "revolt of the field" in Kent, 1872–79', *Past and Present*, 64 (1974)

Astor, Viscount, and Murray, K. A. H., *The Planning of Agriculture* (1933)

Banks, S. J., 'Nineteenth-century scandal or twentieth-century model? A new look at "open" and "close" parishes', *Economic History Review*, 41 (1988)

Beckett, J. V., *The Aristocracy in England, 1660–1914* (1986)

Bonzon, T., and Davis, B., 'Feeding the cities', in J. Winter and J.-L. Robert (eds), *Capital Cities at War: London, Paris, Berlin, 1914–1919* (Cambridge, 1997)

Broadberry, S., and Howlett, P., 'The UK: "Victory at all costs"', in M. Harrison (ed.), *The Economics of World War II: Six Great Powers in International Comparison* (Cambridge, 1998)

Brown, R., 'Cultivating a "green" image: oil companies and outdoor publicity in Britain and Europe, 1920–36', *Journal of European Economic History*, 22 (1993)

Caird, J., *English Agriculture in 1850–51* (1852; republished 1968 with an introduction by G. E. Mingay)

Cannadine, D., *Lords and Landlords: The Aristocracy and the Towns, 1774–1967* (1980)

—— 'The landowner as millionaire: the finances of the dukes of Devonshire, c.1800–c.1926', *Agricultural History Review*, 25 (1977)

—— 'Aristocratic indebtedness in the nineteenth century: the case reopened', *Economic History Review*, 30 (1977)

—— *The Decline and Fall of the British Aristocracy* (1990)

Carter, I., 'Social differentiation in the Aberdeenshire peasantry, 1696–1870', *Journal of Peasant Studies*, 5 (1977–8)

—— *Farmlife in Northeast Scotland, 1840–1914: The Poor Man's Country* (Edinburgh, 1979)

Cassis, Y., 'Bankers in English society in the late nineteenth century', *Economic History Review*, 38 (1985)

Collini, S., *Public Moralists: Political Thought and Intellectual Life in Britain, 1850–1930* (Oxford, 1991)

Collins, E. J. T., *The Agrarian History of England and Wales*, vii: *1850–1914* (Cambridge, 2000)

—— 'Dietary change and cereal consumption in Britain in the nineteenth century', *Agricultural History Review*, 23 (1975)

—— 'Harvest technology and labour supply in Britain, 1790–1870', *Economic History Review*, 22 (1969)

—— 'Migrant labour in British agriculture in the nineteenth century', *Economic History Review*, 29 (1976)

—— and Jones, E. L., 'Sectoral advance in English agriculture, 1850–80', *Agricultural History Review*, 15 (1967)

Crook, J. M., *The Rise of the Nouveaux Riches: Style and Status in Victorian and Edwardian Architecture* (1999)

Crossick, G., 'Urbanisation, migration and Arcadian myths in late Victorian Britain, 1875–1900', in H. G. Haupt and P. Marschalck (eds.), *Stadtische Bevolkerungsentwicklung in Deutschland im 19. Jahrhundert: Soziale und demographische Aspekte der Urbanisierung* (St Katharinen, 1994)

Daunton, M. J., 'Gentlemanly capitalism and British industry, 1820–1914', *Past and Present*, 122 (1989)

—— 'Inheritance and succession in the City of London in the nineteenth century', *Business History*, 30 (1988)

—— *Coal Metropolis: Cardiff, 1870–1914* (Leicester, 1977)

—— *Progress and Poverty: An Economic and Social History of Britain, 1700–1850* (Oxford, 1995)

David, P., 'The landscape and the machine', in P. David, *Technical Choice, Innovation and Economic Growth* (1975)

Davies, J., *Cardiff and the Marquesses of Bute* (1981)

—— 'The end of the great estates and the rise of freehold farming in Wales', *Welsh History Review*, 7 (1974)

Dellheim, C., *The Face of the Past: The Preservation of the Medieval Inheritance in Victorian England* (Cambridge, 1982)

Devine, T. (ed.), *Farm Servants and Labour in Lowland Scotland, 1770–1914* (Edinburgh, 1984)

Dewey, C., 'Celtic agrarian legislation and the Celtic revival: historicist implications of Gladstone's Irish and Scottish land acts, 1870–86', *Past and Present*, 64 (1974)

Dewey, P. E., *British Agriculture in the First World War* (1989)

—— 'Agricultural labour supply in England and Wales during the First World War', *Economic History Review*, 28 (1975)

—— 'British farming profits and government policy during the First World War', *Economic History Review*, 37 (1984)

Digby, A., 'The labour market and the continuity of social policy after 1834: the case of the eastern counties', *Economic History Review*, 28 (1975)

—— *Pauper Palaces* (1978)

Dunbabin, J. P. D., *Rural Discontent in Nineteenth-Century Britain* (1974)

—— 'The "revolt of the field": the agricultural labourers' movement in the 1870s', *Past and Present*, 26 (1963)

Fairlie, S., 'The corn laws and British wheat production, 1829–76', *Economic History Review*, 22 (1969)

—— 'The nineteenth-century corn law reconsidered', *Economic History Review*, 18 (1965)

Ferguson, N., 'Public finance and national security: the domestic origins of the First World War revisited', *Past and Present*, 142 (1994)

Fisher, J. R., 'The Farmers' Alliance: an agricultural protest movement of the 1880s', *Agricultural History Review*, 25 (1978)

—— 'Landowners and English tenant right, 1845–52', *Agricultural History Review*, 31 (1983)

Fletcher, T. W., 'The great depression of English agriculture, 1873–96', *Economic History Review*, 13 (1961)

French, D. W., *British Strategy and War Aims, 1914–16* (1986)

George, H., *Progress and Poverty: An Inquiry into the Causes of Industrial Depressions and of Increase of Want with Increase of Wealth: The Remedy* (1881)

Gunn, S., 'The "failure" of the Victorian middle class: a critique', in J. Wolff and J. Seed (eds.), *The Culture of Capital: Art, Power, and the Nineteenth-Century Middle Class* (1988)

Hammond, J., and Hammond, B., *The Village Labourer, 1760–1832: A Study in the Government of England before the Reform Bill* (1911)

Hilton, M., *Consumerism in Twentieth-Century Britain* (Cambridge, 2004)

Holderness, B. A., '"Open" and "close" parishes in England in the eighteenth and nineteenth centuries', *Agricultural History Review*, 20 (1972)

Hunt, E. H., 'Labour productivity in English agriculture, 1850–1914', *Economic History Review*, 20 (1967)

Johnson, A. H., *The Disappearance of the Small Landowner* (Oxford, 1909)

Jones, A. W., 'Glamorgan custom and tenant right', *Agricultural History Review*, 31 (1983)

Jones, E. L., 'English farming before and during the nineteenth century', *Economic History Review*, 15 (1962)

—— *The Development of English Agriculture, 1815–73* (1968)

—— 'The changing basis of English agricultural prosperity, 1853–73', *Agricultural History Review*, 10 (1962)

—— 'The agricultural labour market in England, 1793–1872', *Economic History Review*, 17 (1964)

Kussmaul, A., *Servants in Husbandry in Early Modern England* (1981)

McQuiston, J. R., 'Tenant right: farmer against landlord in Victorian England, 1847–83', *Agricultural History*, 47 (1973)

Mandler, P., 'Politics and the English landscape since the First World War', *Huntington Library Quarterly*, 55 (1992)

—— *The Fall and Rise of the Stately Home* (New Haven, 1997).

Marshall, A., *The Correspondence of Alfred Marshall*, ed. J. K. Whitaker, 3 vols. (Cambridge, 1996)

Martins, S. W., *A Great Estate at Work: The Holkham Estate and its Inhabitants in the Nineteenth Century* (1980)

Matless, D., *Landscape and Englishness* (1998)

Michie, R. C., 'Income, expenditure and investment of a Victorian millionaire: Lord Overstone, 1823–83', *Bulletin of the Institute of Historical Research*, 58 (1985)

Mill, J. S., *Principles of Political Economy with Some of their Applications in Social Philosophy*, 2 vols. (8th edn., 1878)

Mingay, G. E. (ed.), *The Victorian Countryside*, 2 vols. (1981)

—— (ed.), *The Agrarian History of England and Wales*, vi: *1750–1850* (Cambridge, 1981).

Mitchell, B. R., with the collaboration of P. Deane, *Abstract of British Historical Statistics* (Cambridge, 1962)

Moore, D. C., 'The corn laws and high farming', *Economic History Review*, 18 (1965)

Mutch, A., 'The mechanization of the harvest in south-west Lancashire, 1850–1914', *Agricultural History Review*, 29 (1981)

O'Brien, P. K., and Keyder, C., *Economic Growth in Britain and France, 1780–1914: Two Paths to the Twentieth Century* (1978)

Offer, A., *Property and Politics, 1870–1914: Landownership, Law, Ideology and Urban Development in England* (1981)

—— *The First World War: An Agrarian Interpretation* (Oxford, 1989)

O'Grada, C., 'Agricultural decline, 1860–1914', in R. Floud and D. McCloskey (eds.), *The Economic History of Britain since 1700*, ii, *1860 to the 1970s* (Cambridge, 1981)

—— 'The landlord and agricultural transformation, 1870–1900: a comment on Richard Perren's hypothesis', *Agricultural History Review*, 27 (1979)

Owen, R., *Lord Cromer: Victorian Imperialist, Edwardian Proconsul* (Oxford, 2004)

Peacock, A., *The Revolt of the Fields in East Anglia* (1962)

Perkin, H., 'An open elite', *Journal of British Studies*, 24 (1985)

Perren, R., 'The landlord and agricultural transformation, 1870–1900', *Agricultural History Review*, 18 (1970)

Perry, C. R. 'In search of H. V. Morton: travel writing and cultural values in the first age of British democracy', *Twentieth Century British History*, 10 (1994)

Perry, P. J. 'High farming in Victorian Britain: the financial foundations', *Agricultural History*, 52 (1978)

—— *British Farming in the Great Depression, 1870–1914* (1974)

Petersen, C., *Bread and the British Economy c.1770–1870* (Aldershot, 1995)

Phillips, A. D. M. *Underdraining of Farmland in England during the Nineteenth Century* (Cambridge, 1989)

Pumphrey, R. E., 'The introduction of industrialists into the British peerage: a study in the adaptation of a social institution', *American Historical Review*, 65 (1959)

Reynolds, H., *The Law of the Land* (Ringwood, Victoria, 1987)

Rieger, B., 'Envisioning the future: British and German reactions to the Paris World Fair in 1900', in M. Daunton and B. Rieger (eds.), *Meanings of Modernity: Britain from the Late Victorian Era to World War II* (Oxford, 2001)

Robb, P., *Ancient Rights and Future Comfort: Bihar, the Bengal Tenancy Act of 1885, and British Rule in India* (Richmond, 1997)

Rose, M. B., 'Diversification of investment by the Greg family, 1800–1914', *Business History*, 31 (1979)

Rubinstein, W. D., 'New men of wealth and the purchase of land in nineteenth-century England', *Past and Present*, 92 (1981)

—— *Men of Property: The Very Wealthy in Britain since the Industrial Revolution* (1981)

Saville, J., *Rural Depopulation in England and Wales, 1851–1951* (1957)

Shepherd, J. A., 'East Yorkshire's agricultural labour force in the mid-nineteenth century', *Agricultural History Review*, 9 (1961)

Spring, D., 'A great agricultural estate: Netherby under Sir James Graham, 1820–45', *Agricultural History*, 29 (1955)

Stedman Jones, G., *Outcast London: A Study in the Relationship between Classes in Victorian Society* (Oxford, 1971)

Stone, L., and Stone, J. F. C., *An Open Elite? England, 1540–1880* (1984)

Sturgess, R. J., 'The agricultural revolution on the English clays', *Agricultural History Review*, 14 (1966)

Sturmey, S. G., 'Owner-farming in England and Wales, 1900–1950', reprinted in W. E. Minchinton (ed.), *Essays in Agrarian History*, ii (Newton Abbot, 1968)

Tawney, R. H., *Agrarian Problems in the Sixteenth Century* (1912)

Thompson, F. M. L., *English Landed Society in the Nineteenth Century* (1963)

—— 'The English great estate in the nineteenth century', *Contributions and Communications to the First International Conference of Economic History, Stockholm* (1960)

—— 'Land and politics in England in the nineteenth century', *Transactions of the Royal Historical Society*, 5th ser. 15 (1965)

—— 'Life after death: how successful nineteenth-century businessmen disposed of their fortunes', *Economic History Review*, 43 (1990)

—— 'The landed aristocracy and business elites in Victorian Britain', in Collection de l'École Française de Rome, 107, *Les Noblesses européennes au XIXe siécle* (1988)

—— 'The second agricultural revolution, 1815–80', *Economic History Review*, 21 (1968)

—— 'Agriculture since 1870', in E. Crittall (ed.), *Victoria County History*, iv: *Wiltshire* (1959)

—— 'Changing perceptions of land tenures in Britain, 1750–1914', in D. Winch and P. O'Brien (eds.), *The Political Economy of British Historical Experience, 1688–1914* (Oxford, 2002)

—— 'Business and the landed elites in the nineteenth century', in F. M. L. Thompson (ed.), *Landowners, Capitalists and Entrepreneurs* (Oxford, 1994)

—— *Gentrification and the Enterprise Culture: Britain 1780–1980* (Oxford, 2001)

Thompson, R. J., 'An inquiry into the rent of agricultural land in England and Wales in the nineteenth century', *Journal of the Royal Statistical Society*, 70 (1907)

Tracy, M., *Agriculture in Western Europe: Crisis and Adaptation since 1880* (1964)

Trainor, R., 'The gentrification of Victorian and Edwardian industrialists', in A. L. Beier, D. Cannadine, and J. H. Rosenheim (eds.), *The First Modern Society: Essays in English History in Honour of Lawrence Stone* (1990)

—— *Black Country Elites: The Exercise of Authority in an Industrial Area, 1830–1900* (Oxford, 1993)

Trentmann, F., 'Bread, milk and democracy: consumption and citizenship in twentieth-century Britain', in M. Daunton and M. Hilton (eds.), *The Politics of Consumption: Material Culture and Citizenship in Europe and America* (Oxford, 2001)

—— 'Civilization and its discontents: English neo-romanticism and the transformation of anti-modernism in twentieth-century western culture', *Journal of Contemporary History*, 29 (1994)

Trevelyan, G. M., *A Life in History* (1992)

Turner, M. E., 'Agricultural output, income and productivity', in E. J. T. Collins (ed.), *The Agrarian History of England and Wales*, vii: *1850–1914, Part I* (Cambridge, 2000)

Wiener, M. J., *English Culture and the Decline of the Industrial Spirit, 1850–1950* (1981)

Wilde, O., *The Importance of Being Earnest* (ed. 1969)

···

CHAPTER 3

Industry and the Urban Economy

In *Hard Times,* Charles Dickens presented a graphic picture of a northern industrial town as he imagined it in the early 1850s:

It was a town of red brick, or of brick that would have been red if the smoke and ashes had allowed it . . . It was a town of machinery and tall chimneys, out of which interminable serpents of smoke trailed themselves for ever and ever, and never got uncoiled. It had a black canal in it, and a river that ran purple with ill-smelling dye, and vast piles of building . . . where the piston of the steam-engine worked monotonously up and down, like the head of an elephant in a melancholy state of madness. It contained several large streets all very like one another, and many small streets still more like one another, inhabited by people equally like one another . . . to whom every day was the same as yesterday and tomorrow, and every year the counterpart of the last and the next.[1]

Here was the image of an urban economy where workers were reduced to cogs, their independence and individuality destroyed by industrial capitalism. It was not far removed from the picture of Manchester drawn by Engels a few years earlier, where he saw a wider and wider social gulf opening between factory masters and workers, paving the way for a social war between bourgeoisie and proletariat. Engels and Marx felt that social relationships in industrial towns were based on amoral markets, which 'left remaining no other nexus between man and man than naked self-interest, than callous "cash payment", in a war of all against all'.[2]

Alfred Marshall presented a very different picture in his *Principles of Economics* (1890) and *Industry and Trade* (1919). At the centre of his interpretation of Britain's industrial economy were two images: knowledge, and the organization of the industrial district and the individual firm. In his view, great benefits followed from the proximity of small firms engaged in the same industry in the same district—such as the cotton industry in Lancashire. Rather than the dreary and monotonous world imagined by Dickens, the result was energy and inventiveness:

so great are the advantages which people following the same skilled trade get from near neighbourhood to one another. . . . Good work is rightly appreciated, inventions and improvements in machinery, in processes and the general organization of the business have their merits promptly discussed.

Marshall argued that the wider urban or regional economy offered external benefits to small and medium firms without the costly internal management systems of large firms where bureaucracy would stifle change and creativity. On the other hand, Marshall was suspicious of joint-stock companies. John Stuart Mill, the leading proponent of classical economics and liberalism, had adopted the same line, fearing that joint-stock ownership allowed shareholders to distance themselves from actions which would be repellent to them as individual traders. Marshall went further, claiming that the division of ownership and control would be inefficient. Unlike individual owners, managers were more concerned with creating systems to monitor and control their workforce, an approach that 'is necessarily wasteful of effort, and hostile to elasticity'. The result was a loss of initiative, 'a tendency to ossification of the social organism . . . as the result of bureaucratic habits of shirking troublesome initiative'. He argued that economic growth depended on competition between firms of moderate size. The economies of scale would soon reach their limit, which was just as well, for 'small businesses are on the whole the educators of the initiative and versatility, which are the chief sources of progress'. Smaller firms would be flexible and responsive; they would work together within the industrial district rather than pursuing destructive competition. In his view, 'constructive co-operation' was found in Lancashire—the district where Dickens, Engels, and Marx saw brutal competition and the triumph of the cash nexus. In Marshall's account, a plethora of specialist firms secured all the benefits of concentration without the cumbersome organization of a large firm. Their associations supplied information, established a framework for contracts and arbitration, and helped to set wage rates without impinging on the individuality of each firm. In Marshall's world, competition and individuality were moderated by co-operation, and the benefits of scale were achieved through the associational life of the district. Economic growth rested on knowledge and organization.[3]

Marshall's picture of economic efficiency through 'externalities' connected with a normative view of how economic relations *ought* to be—a world of free trade based on harmony and an active associational life. To Dickens, as to Marx and Engels or Ruskin, the pursuit of material gain was destructive of human relationships, leading to an alienation of workers and a callous pursuit of profit. In Ruskin's view, the outcome was not the creation of wealth but its opposite—'illth'.[4] By contrast, Marshall was a committed free trader which he linked with a highly articulate expression of a particular economic culture of personal reputation, energy, and self-expression, a means of interpreting economic life and informing debates over policy. But did his account describe the economic life of industrial towns in the second half of the nineteenth century, and if it did, when did it become a source of inefficiency rather than dynamism?

Industrial Districts

Many historians have argued that Britain lacked a confident urban bourgeoisie so that the great industrial cities lost their leadership and civic culture was weak. Such a view connects with two other themes in the historical literature: the supposed ascendancy of 'gentlemanly capitalists' in London and the south over industrial capitalists in the north and midlands; and the onset of a 'gentry counter-revolution' against industry in the later nineteenth century.[5] However, these arguments miss the emergence of a powerful municipal culture and take a somewhat limited view of urban culture. It is more realistic to stress the confidence of great industrial cities with powerful municipal cultures and urban elites into the inter-war period.

During the last quarter of the nineteenth century, larger businessmen started to move into urban government—a phenomenon symbolized by Joseph Chamberlain. Until the election of Chamberlain and other major industrialists in the 1870s, Birmingham's council was dominated by small traders who failed to invest in public services. Chamberlain's three years as lord mayor marked a shift in policy, and municipal government became an active force for economic and social advancement. Large-scale investment was necessary for urban efficiency in a city dominated by small-scale production. Chamberlain took over the existing water and gas companies, and constructed expensive reservoirs in mid-Wales. Water was both an industrial input and a means of solving public health problems. By contrast, the municipal gas undertaking was profitable and the proceeds allowed higher public expenditure, including the creation of an art gallery and museum. The gallery—like most provincial art collections—purchased Pre-Raphaelite paintings. The medievalism of these canvases should not be read as a lurch into nostalgia. On the contrary, these paintings were dangerously modern compared with the old masters; they acted as symbols of difference rather than deference.[6] At the same time, Chamberlain embarked on a programme of slum clearance, constructing Corporation Street as a new commercial route from the station to the town hall. A new university was founded in 1900, its buildings a statement of urban assurance. The university taught engineering to assist local industry, and it had the first faculty of commerce in the country. The metaphor used by Chamberlain for his municipal ventures was telling: the city was presented as a great joint-stock company, with the inhabitants as shareholders receiving dividends in health and education.[7]

Birmingham was a striking example for it was consciously making up for lost ground. Many of the same processes may be seen at Glasgow, Leeds, Liverpool, or Newcastle-upon-Tyne. Civic universities emerged from the various learned societies where the middle class established their credentials and aspiring workers pursued self-improvement. Businessmen built art galleries, whether as a personal initiative, through a voluntary society, or in conjunction with the local authority. Ratepayers had the option of voting to provide revenues for libraries and museums. These new institutions might turn to the history of the area, and construct Gothic town halls with frescoes picturing the past. But these initiatives involved more than a rejection of urban culture. Although Pugin's medievalism opposed the horrors of the modern world (as he saw it), the point should not be extrapolated to all Gothic revivalism. Brash newcomers were expressing their pride in the region by linking their present with a particular view of the national story. Gothic forms could express the commercial power of the cities of the Low Countries such as Ghent or Ypres; equally, classical idioms could symbolize a new 'Athenian democracy'. Changing fashions and styles in art and architecture have their own dynamics and cannot simply be read as expressions of attitudes to industry and to modernity.

The importance of 'externalities' for industrial efficiency led to considerable investment in public works. The creation of an efficient urban economy was more than a matter of drains, gas, and trams; it also involved the creation of information systems and social networks. The process had a number of components. Middle-class membership of philharmonic or choral societies showed the culture and civilization of towns to which members of the local gentry and aristocracy might be co-opted. The Liverpool Philharmonic Society was created in 1840. Manchester followed in 1858 when Charles Hallé formed an orchestra to perform in the Free Trade Hall. Even in the absence of a professional symphony orchestra, towns developed an active public musical life. A similar pattern was found in the creation of zoological or botanic societies, naturalists' clubs and record societies, and in the emergence of voluntary associations to run hospitals or orphanages. Membership helped stabilize inter-class relations and define the middle class. Societies provided venues for socializing and for establishing a reputation for trustworthiness and responsibility, as well as exchanging information. The societies brought together industrialists with the professional middle class drawn from the local medical, legal, religious, and financial community, and might involve local aristocrats and gentry as patrons and presidents. Industrialists might also seek membership of organizations dominated by the local gentry, such as hunts; and they might purchase a country residence.[8]

In most towns, more formal and specialized institutions emerged to represent the economic concerns of the local trades—bodies such as the Manchester and Birmingham Chambers of Commerce, or the provincial exchanges for commodities such as coal (in Cardiff) and wool (in Bradford). They discussed political issues relating to the trade, whether the level of import duties in India or the desirability of social reform at home; they standardized contracts and arbitrated in disputes. These bodies often acted as 'nodes' for a wider regional economy, sometimes alongside industrial

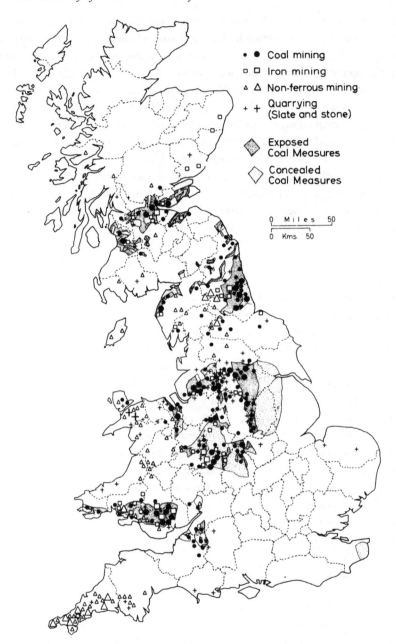

FIG. 3.1. (a) Employment in Great Britain in 1851: (a) mining industries, (b) metallurgical and engineering industries
Source: Lawton and Pooley, *Britain 1740–1950*, 171, 182, based on the map of A. Petermann in the Census of Great Britain, 1851.

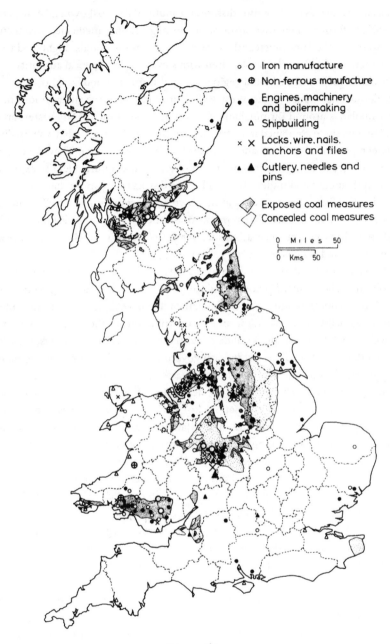

Fig. 3.1. (b).

associations such as the Monmouthshire and South Wales Coal-owners' Association. Specialists formed their own associations in engineering, medicine, architecture, and so on. In the later nineteenth century, these various strands might lead to the construction of technical schools, often with support from the local authority.

A cluster of towns around a regional capital formed an industrial district—the woollen textiles trades of the West Riding around Leeds, the metal trades of the west midlands around Birmingham, the cotton trades around Manchester, and so on. Usually, these combined industry, finance, and marketing, so that a sharp divide between provincial industry and southern finance is misleading. They developed a political voice to defend their economic interests, and a cultural identity expressing pride in their craft and trades. Above all, these districts were more than a collection of individual firms, for the trades in the town and region formed a 'self-reinforcing cluster'. As Geoffrey Tweedale remarks of Sheffield, its 'vast workshop of cutlery and steel firms was at once atomistic, yet at the same time closely interlocked; competitive and yet co-operative'.[9]

At what point did these industrial districts start to lose their dynamism and autonomy? The industrial elite started to distance itself from urban governance in the early twentieth century. For example, the Liberal welfare reforms of 1911 meant that industrialists were paying insurance contributions to the central government as well as poor rates to the localities; and the partial derating of industry in 1929 considerably weakened interest in local government. Furthermore, the regulations of wartime meant that national industrial associations had to negotiate with the central government. The impact of the depression of the 1920s on the old industrial districts also forced trade associations to work on a national basis, negotiating with central government for assistance. Many concerns were floated on the Stock Exchange after the war, losing their close connection with a particular family and its local networks. The headquarters of many large firms relocated to London. Town councils ceased to represent local industries, and were instead fought over by the lower middle class and Labour. But the character of industrial districts had not entirely disappeared by 1939. Much depended on the nature of the local economy. In Leicester and Nottingham relatively small concerns still possessed a dynamic local society and politics. In Birmingham and Coventry, motor manufacturers continued to rely on a range of specialist suppliers, even if finance was more likely to come from London.

Urban government continued to be dynamic in the inter-war period despite the retreat of industrialists. Urban authorities were involved in house construction and slum clearance; they operated transport services and utilities, schools, clinics, and hospitals. The retreat of industrialists allowed working-class voters to have more power. The Labour party built up support in working-class neighbourhoods, turning attention to the provision of municipal services and transforming the concept of an active civic culture. Above all, Herbert Morrison presented a vision of efficient urban services in London, providing high standards of transport, housing, and health services. Labour could present itself as a party of effective urban government rather than of trade union self-interest. But Labour also realized that its arena was national rather than local. The National Health Service was run centrally; gas and electricity came to be run by national bodies; and social services were increasingly financed from national taxes. Urban authorities could do little to generate efficient local industrial economies in the face of the depression of the 1920s and 1930s which sapped the confidence of firms and elites. Any solution to the problems of these districts rested on central government action.[10]

Marshall stressed the positive features of externalities but had little to say about urban diseconomies. Clustering people in towns and industrial districts might generate ideas but also led to pollution and disease. Life expectancy was low in the second quarter of the nineteenth century as a result of poor sanitation and overcrowding. Complex legal issues arose: the decision of a council to build a sewage plant might solve the problem of ill health in the city but pollute the river downstream. When county councils were created in 1888, they could establish new bodies to adjudicate between the different users of the river system, extending the definition of the urban district. Much more difficult to control was air pollution from chemical works, metal refining, and the chimneys of mills and workshops. A pall of smoke meant prosperity and also disease.

Industrial Productivity: Comparisons with Germany and the USA

To many historians, the world described by Marshall was not the cause of celebration. Rather, small firms and personal capitalism prevented a shift to mass production and large-scale managerial capitalism. Indeed, productivity in manufacturing in the United States was already double the level of Britain by 1870, widening to about two-and-a half times after the First World War (see Table 3.1). By focusing on the comparison with the United States, historians of British 'decline' explain the apparent shortcomings of British industry compared with the world's most productive industrial economy. All too often the result is to analyse British industry in terms of failures and shortcomings. The real puzzle is why the United States did so much better than both Britain and Germany, rather than why Britain's industrial economy experienced decline.

To some historians, the key divergence between Britain and Germany on the one hand and the United States on the other was between flexible production in the European economies and mass production in America. The distinction rests on the degree of standardization or customization of output, and the skill of the labour force. In mass production, standardized products are made with special-purpose machinery and an unskilled workforce; in flexible production, customized products are made with general-purpose machinery and a skilled workforce. On this view, British industry failed to move to mass production, remaining wedded to less efficient methods. British industrialists are criticized for using relatively cheap and abundant labour, failing to impose strict work discipline, and failing to adopt mechanical power.

Indeed, mechanization of one process might well encourage labour-intensive employment in other sectors. Lady Bell, writing of her husband's iron works, commented in 1908 that 'part of the absorbing interest of watching the manufacture of iron is that in this country, at any rate, it is all done by human hands, and not by machinery'.[11] Similarly, cotton cloth from factories in Lancashire was turned into clothing by seamstresses and tailors working at home or in small workshops. In Raphael Samuel's evocative account,

The industrial landscape would be seen to be full of diggings and pits as well as of tall factory chimneys. Smithies would sprout in the shadows of the furnaces, sweatshops in those of the looms. . . . There might be navvies digging sewers and paviours laying flags. On the building sites there would be a bustle of man-powered activity, with house-painters on ladders, and slaters nailing roofs. Carters would be loading and unloading horses, market women carrying baskets of produce on their heads; dockers balancing weights. The factories would be hot and steamy, with men stripped to the singlet, and juvenile runners in bare feet. At the lead works women would be carrying pots of poisonous metals on their heads, in the bleachers' shed they would be stitching yards of chlorined cloth, at a shoddy mill sorting rags. Instead of calling his picture 'machinery' the artist might prefer to name it 'toil'.[12]

Indeed, the construction of the Crystal Palace itself symbolized the combination of machinery and hand labour. Each part was adjusted on site by construction workers and the glass was hand made. Much the same applied to the goods on display in the Crystal Palace, for the individual parts of British manufactures were 'fitted' together by careful adjustments.

A contrast between British and American manufactures such as small arms, clocks, and locks was apparent to informed observers at the Great Exhibition. The differences were confirmed—and exaggerated—by the government reports of 1854 and 1855 which drew attention to the 'American system of manufactures'. The reports contrasted American machine production of standardized, small metal goods using interchangeable parts and British handicraft production of a wide range of parts which needed to be adjusted using manual skills, such as small metal goods in Birmingham. There was little mechanization or standardization, and the industrial structure was based upon a considerable number of small workshops. These depended on middlemen or 'factors' who co-ordinated production of specialized parts and organized finance and marketing. The industrial system of Birmingham relied on subcontracting, initially between the factor and small masters for producing parts in their own workshops. When the factor became a factory owner, he usually relied on 'internal subcontracting', paying the worker by the piece.[13]

Many historians assume that the failure to adopt the American system provides an explanation for the divergence between British and American industrial productivity. One of the most influential studies of the 1960s, H. J. Habakkuk's *American and British Technology in the Nineteenth Century*, provided a more systematic explanation of the divergence between American and British technology proposed by the reports of the 1850s. He accepted that the divergence existed and explained the choice of technology by the relative costs of factors of production, and especially of labour and capital. In the United States, he argued, the competing attraction of agriculture and the frontier set a high supply price for industrial labour and gave the American industrialist an incentive to substitute capital for labour, scrapping existing machinery and investing in more sophisticated equipment. The productivity of the workforce would therefore rise, and the increased efficiency of the new machinery meant that the productivity of capital would also be higher. The profit margin was maintained, and at the same time it was possible to reduce prices and to raise wages. The result was capital deepening. In Britain, abundant and cheap labour in agriculture meant that an industrialist did not encounter a fall in his profit by increasing production through existing technology. The marginal cost of labour was not likely to rise when he took on an additional worker, and there was no incentive to scrap existing machinery. Production was more likely to be increased by capital widening. Although capital was more abundant and cheaper in Britain than in America, Habakkuk argued that the important consideration was its cost relative to labour. The pattern of work noted by Florence Bell was therefore entirely rational, reflecting the optimal allocation of resources.[14]

Habakkuk's approach stimulated considerable debate, initially refining his argument. The first refinement applied to the supply of labour. Was it really the case that the United States suffered from a shortage of labour? Blacks in the south and immigrants from Europe were cheap and abundant. Perhaps the real difference was a shortage of skilled workers. Unskilled labour could be used just as 'wastefully' in America as in Britain; the major difference was that capital was used to replace scarce skilled men with semi-skilled machine minders.[15] The difference between the supply of labour in the United States and Europe was reinforced by social institutions and policy choices. In Britain and Germany, apprenticeship was commonplace; in the USA, more attention was paid to training managers, and in shifting skill to laboratories.[16] Furthermore, the ability to weaken unions and challenge workers' control rested on the political compromises struck between labour and capital at the level of the state.

The second refinement extends Habakkuk's analysis from the relative cost of labour and capital by adding a third factor of production. In America, land and raw materials were cheaper than in Britain, and it was rational to substitute abundant natural resources for relatively expensive capital and labour. The abundance of land did not only increase the price of labour relative to capital: it also reduced the relative price of raw materials and energy. Steam technology is a case in point. In Britain, high-pressure engines were used, which were more expensive to build and saved on fuel; in America, low-pressure engines were more usual, which were cheaper to build and used more fuel. In the construction of railroads, American engineers frequently opted for steeper gradients than in Britain, which saved labour in construction and capital for tunnels and bridges, but required the use of more fuel. Generally, American workers had more power per head than in Britain. The difference is clear in the relative costs of one hour's labour and a kilowatt hour of electricity in Britain and the United States. If the ratio in the UK is taken as 100, the figure in the United States was 349.1 in 1924 and 430.9 in 1948; in other words, labour in the USA was over three times as expensive compared with energy as in the UK. Consequently, horsepower per worker in manufacturing was over double the level of the UK in the early twentieth century. In Germany, the cost of electricity relative to labour and horsepower per head were both very close to the British level. The development of technology therefore rested on the relative costs of *three* factors, and the contrast between Britain and America was not only in the adoption of skilled labour-saving inventions. American production technology was resource and machinery intensive, and saved on skilled workers; European production was intensive in the use of skilled labour and economized on natural resources and machinery.[17]

These refinements are important, but do not challenge the basic assumption that American industry was based on superior mass production. In the 1980s, some historians challenged the view that the American system was the model to follow, arguing that 'flexible specialization' had much to commend it. Their analysis rested in part on a preference for the type of society associated with small-scale concerns and in part on the realization that affluence entailed demand for more individual or personalized consumption as well as mass-produced washing machines or motor cars.[18] Policies designed to foster mass production were criticized for weakening the industrial networks sustaining many British industries in the nineteenth century.

In fact, the division between American mass production and European flexible production is misleading. Mass production was not adopted in all sectors even within the United States: the choice depended on the type of good and the market. A better way of considering the choice of technology is to distinguish between three broad categories—routine, mass, and flexible—none of which is necessarily superior to the other, for each is appropriate to the nature of commodities and their markets. For highly complicated products mass production was not possible. In other cases, consumers preferred individuality and originality, and 'flexible specialization' allowed a swift response to customers and their needs. Routinized production was linked with stable markets and a narrow range of goods. It might entail producing in bulk with relatively simple technology and semi-skilled workers, with reasonably low costs of entry and fierce competition, such as beer or cigarettes. Mass or flow production involved a large throughput of goods with immense investment in technically complex plant, such as the motor assembly lines of Henry Ford or oil refining. Such firms were much less typical of American industry than Habakkuk assumed, and their success rested on specialist firms who supplied hugely expensive, technically sophisticated plant, built to order or in small batches.[19] There was, therefore, no single model of industrial success, and goods in all industrial economies were produced by a variety of techniques. The question is whether British industrialists ignored real opportunities to move into mass or routinized production; or whether the productivity gap arose from lower levels of efficiency across the board, regardless of the system of production.

Speciality production remained important in the United States as in Britain, in the form of custom production by small concerns, or batch production of a small number of items in huge plants. The author of the British government report on American small-arms production in 1855 did not realize that costs were *higher* with standardization than with traditional methods, and that the technique arose only because the government was willing to cover the considerable development costs. The inception of the 'American system' owed more to the demands of the Ordnance Department of the US government for interchangeable parts on the battlefield than to economic considerations. The diffusion of the technique to commercial goods such as sewing machines was not easy, and at least until the 1880s rested upon marketing and the ability to sell at high prices at the top of the market rather than on the full application of interchangeability and a reduction in costs and prices. The breakthrough came in 1913 when Henry Ford adopted assembly lines with mass production at the lowest cost. But Ford soon found that mass production of a narrow product range was a dead-end, for consumers preferred product differentiation and frequent changes of model. Ford's definition of mass production gave way to 'flexible' mass production.[20] The specialized production techniques of Birmingham should not be dismissed as mere conservatism, for they allowed a flexible response to a varied market. The American system *was* adopted by the British government in a new factory at Enfield to produce rifles for the British army, where a standardized design was highly desirable. However, the small workshops of Birmingham or Coventry could easily adapt to make parts for bicycles or motor cars, which were assembled from parts produced by smaller firms throughout the midlands—much as the shipyards on the Tyne and Clyde drew on the specialist skills of engineering firms in the area.

Although America opened up a gap across the board, it was much less in some industries than others (see Table 3.1). In industries where mass production was

TABLE 3.1. *Comparative US/UK labour productivity by sector,*
1907–50 (UK = 100)

	1907/09	1929/30	1950
Cotton	151	194	249
Shipbuilding	95	154	111
Seed crushing	77	131	n.a.
Tobacco	108	134	251
Motor vehicles/cars	435	725	466
Total manufacturing	209	263	273

Source: Broadberry, *Productivity Race*, 29–30.

difficult to adopt, Britain retained a better productivity record than the United States. In shipbuilding, for example, the yards on the Tyne and Clyde were better able to meet the demand for individualized vessels than their American competitors, and Britain remained competitive in specialist steels for armaments and large forgings for gun barrels or electricity plants. British firms also moved to mass production of homogeneous products without any noticeable lag. Craft production was inappropriate in sectors such as brewing, seed crushing, flour milling, or cigarette manufacture. The cotton industry stood somewhere between the two: despite Marshall's belief in the efficiency of 'externalities', the small, specialized firms of Lancashire were somewhat behind their American counterparts.[21] The productivity lag was greatest in industries where British firms failed to adopt American techniques of mass production, such as in motor vehicles where American motor manufacturers had an astonishing productivity lead of more than sevenfold in 1929–30.

What needs to be explained is an American lead in all forms of production, and a massive divergence in mass production industries, rather than just a failure to adopt mass production. The answer is by no means clear. One possibility is that the endowment of resources and the nature of institutional structures created 'technological lock-in'.[22] As we have seen, American workers had more energy per head than their British counterparts which would affect productivity in all sectors. Further, the amount of effort each worker was willing to expend in producing goods differed. The bargain struck by industrialists and labour in the mid- and late nineteenth century institutionalized the form of internal subcontract found in Birmingham, leaving a large amount of control on the shop floor. Consequently, British employers had much less ability to control the level of effort than their counterparts in America. Even if one employer or industrial sector wished to impose more control on the shop floor, they were constrained by the wider political system. At the very time that industrialists wished to adopt 'American' technology or systems of control over work in the later nineteenth century, the role of unions was sustained

TABLE 3.2. *Labour force unionization, UK, USA, and Germany, 1892–1950*

	Whole economy			Manufacturing	
	UK	USA	Germany	UK	USA
1892/97/91	9.4	1.8	1.5	13.0	4.3
1911/10/10	15.4	5.9	10.8	18.6	8.6
1921/20/25	33.0	11.5	20.3	48.5	18.1
1938/40	25.7	14.2	—	31.1	23.6
1950/53/50	39.3	24.8	26.8	47.0	42.0

Source: Broadberry, *Productivity Race*, 145–7.

by the state. Unions were accepted in Britain and usually did not operate to raise productivity. Rather, they adopted an adversarial attitude, viewing the division between wages and profits as a zero-sum game in which a higher return for the capitalist was assumed to be at the expense of the workers. The issue was not only the contrast in levels of unionization (see Table 3.2). More significantly, the nature of bargaining and the form of production institutions on the shop floor had wide implications; it affected the ability of employers in *all* sectors to control the level of effort and secure high rates of work.[23]

The adoption of more efficient technology or systems of control was also constrained by the reduction in competition from abroad and at home between the wars. Britain had an open economy in the second half of the nineteenth century, but introduced protection in the 1930s. Unlike Germany and the United States, tariffs were retained after the Second World War so that British industrialists did not face the threat of foreign competition (Table 3.3). At the same time, competition between British firms was reduced by an increase in the level of concentration and

TABLE 3.3. *Tariffs: ratio of duties to total imports, UK, USA, and Germany, 1850–1950*

	UK	USA		Germany
1850	21.7	24.5		
1910	4.5	21.1		7.4
1929	9.7	13.5		8.2
1938	24.1	15.5		33.4
1945	38.2	9.3	(1948)	31.3
1950	31.2	6.0		5.4

Source: Broadberry, *Productivity Race*, 139, 140, 141.

TABLE 3.4. *Percentage of net output taken by the largest 100 firms in manufacturing, 1909–58*

	1909	1935	1958
United Kingdom	16	24	32
United States	22	26	30

Median size of plant in manufacturing, 1925–39 (employees)

Britain	300
Germany	140
United States	330

Source: Broadberry, *Productivity Race*, 131, 136.

the introduction of price controls. The share of net output controlled by the largest manufacturers caught up with the United States, and the median size of plant was little different from the United States and larger than in Germany (Table 3.4). These figures might be read as a sign of efficiency achieved by economies of scale; in reality the emergence of larger concerns was linked with price-fixing agreements and cartels. During the 1920s and 1930s, the British economy was marked by high levels of concentration, large plant size, widespread collusion, and high levels of protection. After the war, the return to a liberal trade regime was slower than in Germany and the United States, and internal competition was limited. As we shall see, the government took little action to encourage competition. The outcome was a 'low-effort equilibrium': workers secured reasonable wages and employers earned decent profits without too much effort, a state of affairs that was sustainable so long as they were safe from competition from abroad or the threat from aggressive competitors at home.[24]

Comparative industrial performance involves more than a contrast between mass production and flexible specialization. All industrial economies had various forms of production appropriate to particular commodities and markets. Although the divergence between American and British productivity was greatest in sectors such as motor production, a gap opened in other sectors as well, albeit later and to a lesser extent. The general divergence, as well as the particularly marked gap in some sectors, can probably be explained by levels of energy input, by the 'effort bargain', and by patterns of competition. Other factors have not yet been sufficiently investigated as a result of historians' obsession with mass production. Could factory layouts, the flow of materials through the production process, and the efficiency of managers in ensuring continuity of production have a role?[25] More research is needed before we can satisfactorily explain the divergence between Britain—and Germany—and the United States.

Production Institutions and Labour Relations

Most British industrial firms relied on institutions outside the firm to set wages and conditions. The Lancashire cotton industry used a system of 'internal subcontracting'. In the opinion of some historians, industrialists in Lancashire consciously embarked on a policy of 'divide and rule' to impose control by creating a group of 'labour aristocrats' over the rank-and-file workers. Here was Lenin's answer to the failure of the revolution predicted by Marx and Engels: the upper reaches of the proletariat were 'bribed' with high wages, and turned into the 'non-commissioned officers' of the bourgeoisie.[26] According to this argument, the upper grade of workers in cotton spinning played a crucial role, but did their status and authority emerge from a cynical ploy of the employers to create allies or did it rest on their own assertion of power?

In cotton spinning, a pair of mule spindles was operated by three male workers: a minder, the big piecer, and the little piecer. The mill-owner paid the minder according to output from his mules, and left the minder to divide the proceeds between the workers. The minder was, in effect, an internal subcontractor. Wage differentials widened over the later nineteenth century. By 1906, a pair of mules in Oldham earned on average 75*s*. 2*d*. a week, of which the minder retained 41*s*. 10*d*. and paid 19*s*. 4*d*. to the big piecer and 14*s*. to the little piecer. The minder–piecer distinction was peculiar to Lancashire, and had no technical justification: other countries had different systems of employment on identical machines. In the United States, mule spinning relied on top-down hierarchical control of female spinners by male supervisors, assisted by a mechanic. In Scotland, the joiner–minder system was adopted: two adults were paid a moderate wage and were assisted by one boy. How, then, did the minders prevent a decline into semi-skilled factory hands and their replacement by women, and why did employers in Lancashire not set out to win control and impose 'top-down' control?[27]

Historians who follow Lenin's approach argue that the minder–piecer system was created as a means of controlling the workforce and resolving the problems of class relations. Management was made easier: the minders had little reason to oppose any increase in the intensity of work since they were able to capture most of the benefit. They imposed discipline, so the argument runs, reducing the need for management by the owners. In reality, the minder–piecer system was not a cynical attempt by employers to divide the workforce and to intensify work. When fully mechanized mule spindles were adopted in the 1830s, the employers were anxious to destroy the power of male workers in the system of semi-mechanized production, and to utilize cheaper female labour. Their ambition failed. The cotton industry was moving from depression into boom, and industrialists had to decide whether to seize the immediate opportunities or engage in a costly struggle with the workers. They took the first course, and the minder–piecer division therefore emerged against the intention of industrialists.

Crucially, the relation between effort and earnings was set by the workers as much as by the mill-owners: employers could not influence the effort bargain directly, but only through varying the piece rate and hoping that the workers responded.

The organization of work was entrenched in institutions. The boom in the cotton industry in the mid-nineteenth century predisposed mill-owners to favour conciliation, and from 1853 agreements were reached to regulate wages which embedded the minder–piecer system. By 1885, 95 per cent of minders were members of unions and piecers were excluded. In Britain, political acceptance of unions helped to reinforce craft control, unlike in the United States where labour turnover was higher, so creating an incentive for skill-saving technology. The unions in Lancashire mill towns negotiated 'spinning lists', setting down the rates to be paid for different types of yarn and speeds of spinning, with strict limits on the timing and extent of changes. It became very difficult to change the pattern of employment, for the social relations of the workplace were enmeshed with the institutions of collective bargaining and as the industry was highly fragmented, it was difficult for one mill-owner to impose his will. These boards helped maintain industrial order by enforcing awards and wage contracts, and preventing strikes. The trend towards formalization and institutionalization was indicated by the Labour Department of the Board of Trade in 1910, when it found that there were 1,696 collective agreements covering 2.4 m workers out of a total occupied male workforce of 12.9 m in 1911.[28] Collective agreements were a means of reducing the impact of competition and market pressures without taking control of the effort bargain on the shop floor. Change became very difficult, and many employers were content to maintain a system which minimized managerial tasks.

The internal subcontract survived in cotton spinning into the inter-war period. The social organization of work allowed mill-owners to squeeze the most out of the existing technology and erected barriers to the adoption of the new technology which would destroy the entrenched institutions of labour control. Managers did not introduce more co-ordinated, planned organization; indeed, the emphasis on 'rationalization' between the wars served to maintain the existing system rather than to invest in new plant. Persistence with the minder–piecer structure in these new circumstances of shrinking output had serious consequences for the workers. When output was expanding, big piecers could expect promotion to minder; as production declined, their prospects were seriously harmed.[29]

Despite Marshall's confidence, the external institutions of the industrial districts could become a barrier to change. Production institutions could be in tension with production technologies and so limit the employers' freedom of action.[30] Whether industrialists could—or should—change the production technology or reform production institutions raises a number of issues. Were they conservative, ignoring the possibilities of change, or were they trapped by a vertically disintegrated structure and by a political system which made it extremely difficult to overturn the existing pattern of work? The second possibility has considerable force, for the bargaining system and union structure persisted until the 1980s, limiting the employers' ability to control the effort bargain or to make a fundamental change. Decisions were informed not only by the allocation of resources; they were constrained by the structure of industry and the nature of institutions. Although a higher level of productivity may have been possible with a rejection of the minder–piecer divide in mule spinning and a shift to ring spinning, a single entrepreneur did not have the ability to overturn the established order.

The crucial factor is the effort bargain: who determined how much effort the workers would expend? As we saw, the spinners controlled the duration and intensity of effort. Although they had some incentive to secure more work from the minders, they were anxious not to undermine their own position. On the whole, British workers did not see themselves as co-operating with employers to raise effort and productivity; rather, they assumed employers sought higher profits at their expense. The attitude reflected a deeply ingrained cultural system. Each class created its own institutions. They created social cohesion *within* each group, but did not overlap and integrate. Unions were accepted and resented encroachment in their control of the workplace. As one commentator noted, the attitude of British workers was defeatist: they wished to stay within their class, and to defend their position from change.[31] Labour relations rested on adversarial bargaining: unions were accepted, but workers defined their interests against the employers.

In Britain, craft control inhibited effort-saving technology, and employers were reluctant or unable to break the system and move to managerial control. In the United States, control was removed from the shop floor by investing in management structures and technology. The process entailed more than merely a destruction of unions and the imposition of tight labour discipline through 'scientific management'; it also involved the promise of stable employment and a share in productivity gains. In Britain, industrialists did not face serious constraints in the supply of craft labour; the state's attitude towards trade unions made the task of employers much more difficult; and the structure of the market made high throughput production systems less appealing. These factors were mutually reinforcing. Such arguments subvert Marshall's analysis: craft control in proprietary firms becomes a source of weakness.[32]

Many features of the production institutions in cotton and other staple industries were carried over into newer industrial sectors. The key, according to Wayne Lewchuk, was less the relative cost of factors of production than 'the difference in the ability of British and American employers to convert labour time into labour effort'.[33] The production institutions inherited from the late nineteenth century and the existing effort bargain prevented the full use of new methods of production. When British motor manufacturers started to use mass production techniques, they were not able to shift the production institutions. In the United States, Ford increased the amount of effort through systematic control of the workplace in return for good wages. In Britain, employers were less successful in controlling effort norms and imposing authority on the shop floor.

The motor industry emerged from engineering, where labour relations rested on the bargain struck between the employers and the Amalgamated Society of Engineers. This system was challenged in 1896, when British employers established the Engineering Employers' Federation and attempted to impose more control on the shop floor by 'locking out' members of the ASE in 1897/8—a strategy it repeated in 1922.[34] The EEF consciously pursued an American strategy of seizing direct control and seemed to have defeated the union in 1898 when a disputes procedure was imposed which survived until 1971. However, a new effort bargain was not achieved and the engineering employers failed to appreciate the reasons for American success. The EEF argued that wages should be cut on the new machines, unlike in the United States where acceptance of the new technology was encouraged by maintaining wages and raising the level of effort. The EEF was less powerful than its victory suggested, for it was a fragile coalition, only able to mobilize in exceptional circumstances. Its actions in confronting the union were also constrained by the government. The agreement of 1898 accepted collective bargaining over wages in return for the union's recognition of managerial power in other areas; and insisted that any dispute be referred to a regional and national system of arbitration between employers and union. In effect, the settlement entrenched the existing social organization of production. Divisions within the EEF and government suspicion of aggression against labour limited the challenge to unions. In any case, the employers preferred low supervision methods. In most sectors, employers relied on traditional techniques of work and were reluctant to take full control over the work process. Consequently, the ASE and its successor, the Amalgamated Engineering Union, were able to reassert their position as soon as the labour market and political context allowed. When new machinery was introduced, workers resisted attempts to increase the level of effort and employers turned to 'payment by results'. Consequently, shop-floor workers continued to determine the amount of effort, rather as in cotton.[35]

During the First World War, the state imposed a compromise between labour and capital in the 'Treasury agreement' by which less-skilled men and women were allowed to work on machine tools, with existing working practices to be reinstated after the war. However, most employers remained conservative, with little confidence that dilution would be effective. Each firm wished to retain skilled labour, which gave power to the unions at a time of labour shortage. Furthermore, the state was generally supportive of organized labour given Labour representation in the coalition government, and the need for consent. British employers did not adopt

American scientific management on the return to peace: instead, most relied on 'incentive payments' (a higher payment as output rose) to encourage greater effort. The decision whether or not to work faster remained in the hands of employees, and manufacturers failed to gain control over the speed of machinery. Production institutions constrained their freedom to act, complemented by the feeling of many employers and politicians that labour relations were more important than tighter control and productivity. British industrialists did not accept that high wages would increase effort, and the attitudes of workers suggested that they might be right. Many workers assumed that high wages from increased effort would be temporary, before industrialists cut piece rates. Why make the additional effort, only to end up working harder for the same income? The attitude of the EEF did nothing to counter this. As Lewchuk remarks, 'In the end, the EEF strategy doomed British engineering to a low wage/low effort equilibrium.'[36]

Why did the employers act as they did? British motor manufacturers were not forced into their choice of production institutions by powerful unions; on the contrary, unions were weak. Labour relations were shaped by the wider institutional system and political structures, and by the market. The market for motor cars in the United States was radically different from other countries. There were seven Americans per motor car in 1924, compared with 78 residents per motor car in the UK, 470 in Germany, and 108 in France. By 1935, the gap had narrowed to 5.7 Americans per motor car, 29 in UK, 84 in Germany, and 26 in France (see Table 3.5 for output). The British industry was doing well in European terms, but manufacturers were aware of demand constraints. In the late 1920s, British motor manufacturers assumed that the market was largely confined to incomes of more than £400 p.a. and that it was close to saturation. They believed that demand was price-inelastic. In the 1930s, they competed by stressing reliability, economy, and product differentiation rather than price. Their decision made business sense, for the middle-class market could still expand and Britain had an advantage over Europe in higher incomes and the availability of hire purchase. British manufacturers had little

TABLE 3.5. *Output of motor cars USA, UK, France, and Germany, 1924–37 (000)*

	USA	UK	France	Germany
1924	3185.9	116.6	145.0	n.a.
1929	4587.4	179.2	211.0	51.9
1933	1560.6	220.1	159.0	84.6
1937	3929.2	379.3	177.0	264.4

Source: Bowden, 'Demand and supply constraints', 244.

incentive to reduce their prices and shift to mass ownership.[37] The strategy worked in the 1930s, for mass unemployment meant that workers could not exploit their opportunities; and protection meant that profits were maintained. After the Second World War, full employment gave the workers more power, and managers turned to shop stewards rather than to direct control. The system was only viable so long as British producers were protected from foreign competition; when import duties were reduced, they could no longer obtain a decent profit and pay reasonable wages.

Trade Unions and Labour Relations

Why did British employers and the state adopt a distinctive pattern of production institutions? Their choice rested on three factors. The first was voluntarism: labour relations were not enforced by contractual obligation. The second was adversarialism: interests were seen as divergent, with a zero-sum approach where any gain by one party is assumed to mean a loss for the other party; agreements could therefore be breached whenever an opportunity arose.[38] The third factor might seem to contradict the first two: unions were increasingly recognized by the state and employers. Above all, the Trade Disputes Act of 1906 enshrined the first two variables: unions were given extraordinary legal powers, allowing them to break agreements with their employers without legal redress.

By 1850, trade unions had scarcely made an impact on the British economy. Unions of the 1850s were small and pragmatic. In the Webbs' terminology, 'new model unions', found in skilled trades such as engineering, were exclusive: they limited entry; they were able to control wage rates through restricting the labour supply; they had high subscriptions to provide welfare benefits; and were usually accepted by their employers. The Webbs were right to highlight the characteristics of these unions, but their neat argument breaks down for large, stable unions were also found in other sectors and had different characteristics. The most unionized sectors of the economy were cotton and coal, where 'closure' of the labour market was much less secure than in engineering. In the Lancashire cotton industry, the Spinners' Union was accepted by the employers as part of the management system. Like the ASE, union membership was restricted; unlike the new model unions, it did not offer welfare benefits and concentrated on negotiating wages. By contrast, the Weavers' Union was open to everyone and the unskilled were the first to organize.[39]

In coal mining, acceptance of unions only started in the 1870s, above all in Northumberland and Durham. Disagreements were resolved by a hierarchy of committees from the pit, to district and county, with decisions formally recorded. Similarly, the general wage rate and the conditions of work were formally negotiated. However, unions were not welcomed in south Wales. The context was different, for the union exploited the division between two groups of coal-owners. Iron producers were facing serious competition and shifted their coal output into the expanding export trade; they paid lower wages than new concerns in the export market. The union took advantage of the situation by striking against one group and allowing the other to seize market share. Before long, both groups of owners opted to unite against the union. In 1875, the coal-owners' association imposed a sliding scale fixing wages by the price of coal which would, in theory, prevent disputes and unite capital and labour in the prosperity of the trade. In practice, the exact terms of the sliding scale could be a source of deep dissension, and it could be biased against the workers—a realization that led to its demise in south Wales in 1910 and the emergence of a more militant form of union. Generally, miners were the most organized and the most militant workers with the exception of the east midlands where the employers remained anti-union into the inter-war period.[40]

Much of the underlying growth of unionization in the later nineteenth century came from a steady increase in employment in the most unionized sectors. In mining, for example, the workforce doubled between 1888 and 1910, and the level of unionization also rose from 19 per cent to 60 per cent. There was also spasmodic expansion into previously non-unionized sectors. One wave took place in the early 1870s when casual and unskilled workers organized for the first time, taking advantage of the boom of the early 1870s, with membership of unions affiliated to the TUC increasing from 256,000 in 1872 to 1,192,000 in 1874. When the boom broke, membership fell back to 558,000 in 1876 and many unions disappeared. The pattern was repeated in the late 1880s. A third wave of organization came just before the First World War: membership of all unions increased from 2.6 m in 1910 to 4.1 m in 1913. The periods of high union membership were also marked by a high level of working days lost due to strike activity.[41]

The Webbs suggested that the growth in membership came as a result of the growth of 'new unions'. However, their appearance explains the sudden peaks rather than the underlying trend. These unions were inclusive, for their bargaining position depended upon organizing as many potential members as possible. Their subscriptions were necessarily low, so welfare benefits could not be offered; and they were not recognized by the employers. Leaders of unions such as the dockers were likely to turn to the state, both for the provision of welfare and for support for recognition. Employers had little reason to recognize the bargaining rights of the union, for their interest was in retaining an open, unorganized labour market with the ability to hire and fire according to the movement of ships and goods. When the Dockers' Union went on strike or was 'locked out' by the employers, it turned to violent picketing in order to secure some closure of the labour market—so justifying the employers' belief that unions were destructive. The weakness of the Dockers' Union and other unskilled unions led them into alliances with other work groups who were usually themselves unrecognized, so leading to sympathetic strikes. Hence a dispute in the shipping industry might spill over into a strike of dock workers who refused to load ships in solidarity with the sailors. The dispute might then escalate to involve railway workers whose union was similarly rejected by the companies. The railway workers might refuse to carry goods to the docks in solidarity with the waterfront workers—and they might expect the same solidarity in return. Sympathetic action might spread to the coal miners who could refuse to produce coal for export. These alliances were later formalized in the Transport Workers' Federation and Triple Alliance shortly before the First World War. Consequently, the organization of unskilled workers on the waterfront led to alarm that labour unrest was being extended to affect trades not directly involved in the initial dispute.[42]

The question facing politicians and civil servants in the last quarter of the nineteenth century was whether the pattern of the ASE, with its welfare benefits and apprenticeship schemes, should be extended by encouraging employers on the waterfront and railways to accept unions; or whether the rights of the employers should be protected against sympathetic strikes and the demand for collective bargaining. In cotton and engineering, unions could be incorporated into the system of management; the employers on the waterfront and in other casual trades, as well as the railway companies, had no such incentive, and remained firmly opposed to unions. The railways had an alternative pattern of labour control based on strict managerial control resting on pensions, promotion hierarchies, and uniforms, and the docks relied on an open labour market. In Britain, such anti-union sentiment was marginalized and most politicians and officials assumed that unions were desirable, a source of order and stability. By contrast, tn the United States, many employers were sceptical of the value of unions and formal institutions for wage bargaining, and relied instead on open shops or strong internal systems of management.[43] Similarly, trade unions were not welcomed by German employers and the state.

The explanation is to be found in part in the nature of the British state and parties, and in part in the nature of work relations and industrial technology. In the opinion of Ross McKibbin, the British state absented itself from conflicts of capital and labour, preferring to establish a neutral framework resting on voluntarism. Any attempt to impose a legal or punitive framework on labour relations would challenge the stability of the state. The stress on fairness constrained workers who accepted the legitimacy of political institutions. Some historians are sceptical, arguing that the courts and the law were biased, willing to find unions guilty of civil conspiracy; and claiming that the British state was ready to use power, sending in the metropolitan police or troops to reinforce the local constabulary.[44] The argument has some plausibility in the 1850s when master–servant law was unequal between workers and their employers, but as we will see discrepancies were lessened or removed in the later nineteenth century. Despite the fact that courts were becoming fairer towards employees, workers were nevertheless disinclined to turn to them. The key was predictability rather than systematic bias: except in compensation cases, the decision turned on the interpretation of custom or vague concepts such as implied contract. Consequently, unions preferred voluntarism.[45]

In any case, constraints worked both ways, for the state was also disinclined to use force. Engels realized that rulers limited their ability to use coercion as it contradicted their rhetoric and exposed them to political hostility. The limits on the use of force were tight, with troops or the metropolitan police only sent into a strike area when public order was breaking down. Neither were the unions controlled by incorporation into institutions on the terms of employers. An agreement between union leaders and employers did not turn the leaders into tools of the owners in imposing discipline: it could maintain their power on the shop floor.[46] As we noted in the Lancashire cotton industry, acceptance of unions and their role in managing the workforce arose *despite* the wishes of the employers, who only subsequently opted to work with the unions. The perception of both workers and their employers was that British workmen were independent and assertive of their rights as 'free-born Englishmen'. Hence unions and employers accepted that their interests were not identical, and their approach was adversarial. But conflict was carried on without the state supporting employers; on the contrary, the attitude of the state was that disputes would be less damaging if employers recognized their opponents and bargained with them.

The British state allowed unions a greater freedom of action than in other industrial countries. At the start of the period, their activities were limited by the power of suing unions for breach of contract and the threat of criminal conspiracy in restraint of trade. The Masters and Servants Act of 1867 clarified the position by limiting criminality to 'aggravated cases' of conspiracy; it also laid down penalties for breach of contract. In the 1860s, the role of unions and their legal standing came into sharp focus as a result of the 'Sheffield outrages' of 1866, when union members used arson and violence to intimidate non-unionists. The TUC countered that the attacks were the work of a few misguided individuals and that the solution was to *increase* the rights and privileges of unions. Although the minority report of the Royal Commission on Trade Unions appointed in 1867 sympathized with this view, the majority report took a different line, stressing that the common law was identical with classical political economy. The labour market could exhibit the same virtues of free trade through the efficient use of resources only if artificial combination were prevented. These different perceptions were contested, with the balance of opinion moving towards the minority's view as a result of evidence on the actual operation of unions, historical arguments against classical political economy which stressed the 'feudal' roots of the law, and the realization that workers were criminalized for actions which were not criminal if carried out by others. Consequently, legislation in the 1870s decriminalized restraint of trade, protected union funds, limited the scope of criminal conspiracy, legalized peaceful picketing, and removed criminal sanctions in cases of breach of contract, except in public utilities. The legislation reflected a cross-party agreement, for it was largely drafted by Gladstone's ministry and passed by Disraeli's. To contemporaries, it marked the victory of freedom of contract for unions as for any other person in society.[47]

A problem remained, for unions could still be charged with *civil* conspiracy. Employers might seek an injunction to stop a strike that was harming their interests; it was less clear whether unions could be made to pay damages. Were collective agreements and union rules binding, and was notice needed before a strike started? Could a union or employer simply break an agreement without penalty? If the agreement was binding, were unions responsible for the actions of their members and liable to be sued? In theory, unions were unincorporated corporations with no legal personality and so were immune. However, the courts came to the view that by acting as if they were incorporated, unions left themselves open to be sued. There was also the issue of picketing. Peaceful picketing was lawful from 1875, but effective picketing on the waterfront often led to violence. The law on these points was somewhat confused. Although politicians and civil servants were moving in the direction of collective bargaining and recognition, the courts were raising complex issues on the legal status of unions. Why, after all, should unions not have the same legal responsibilities as any other corporation and be bound by contract?[48]

The extension of legal protection and the removal of disabilities are easily explained by the feeling of many politicians and social commentators that unions were a source of stability. Most commentators accepted that unions could not push wages higher than the market could bear. As Marshall remarked, 'the power of Unions to raise general wages by direct means is never great; it is never sufficient to contend successfully with the general economic forces of the age, when their drift is against a rise in wages.'[49] Further, the unions seemed to represent the most conscientious and hard-working men. Membership was a sign of responsibility and self-improvement. Trade unions prevented constant, small, 'unofficial' disputes. Sir Benjamin Browne spoke for the iron and coal trades of the north-east when he remarked in 1906 that unions 'stop far more disputes than they make'. Perhaps the clearest expression of these views was the report of the Royal Commission on Labour of 1891–4. It accepted that labour relations were most peaceable where unions were recognized. Disruption was therefore a temporary phenomenon and collective bargaining should be extended to a greater section of the workforce. One outcome was the creation of the Labour Department of the Board of Trade whose officials—most notably Herbert Llewellyn Smith and George Askwith—acted as missionaries on behalf of collective agreements. When a national rail strike was threatened in 1907, the President of the Board of Trade (David Lloyd George) and

Askwith pressed the companies to introduce a Board of Conciliation to resolve disputes. Similarly, the government's attempt to decasualize the waterfront rested on co-operation with the unions.[50]

Granting exceptional legal privileges to trade unions, liberating them from the penalties of breach of contract, is less easily explained. Why was recognition not linked with legal obligations and duties? The crucial measure was the Trade Disputes Act of 1906 which followed the Taff Vale Decision. In 1900, the workers of the Taff Vale Railway Co. went on strike without giving proper notice. The question put to the courts was whether the union was liable to pay damages. The answer was not clear, but eventually the company won its case in the highest court, and the union paid £23,000 in damages and costs. Unions were alarmed and their concern led in 1900 to the creation of the Labour Representation Committee to campaign for reform. The law was in a state of uncertainty, and the trade unions wished to return to their unincorporated status without liability to be sued. In 1903, the government set up a Royal Commission on Trade Disputes and Trade Combinations to consider the issue. The Lord Chancellor argued that parliament had deliberately left unions in an anomalous position in 1871 and 1875, and judges were wrong to remove the anomaly. However, legal immunity, with the consequent ability of unions to inflict damages without any right of redress, was not supported by the majority report of the Royal Commission which felt that powerful bodies capable of inflicting financial loss should not be immune. The view was supported by the Webbs who argued for compulsory arbitration before any strike or lockout, an approach introduced in New Zealand in 1896 and Australia in 1904 but opposed by powerful British unions which resented limits to their action. The Liberal government initially accepted the view of the Royal Commission. However, the proposal was defeated in the Commons, and the Act of 1906 gave unions complete immunity. The unions could break any agreement without fear of legal action—a position held by no one else except the crown.[51]

The explanation was in part that politicians feared that judges had too much power in interpreting the intentions of the union executive through the law of agency; they might find against unions and open up still more disputes. One solution was to revise the law of agency but the Prime Minister favoured the easier option of granting complete legal immunity. The solution seemed sensible, given the assumption that trade unions prevented conflict and promoted harmony. The leader of the Conservatives, Arthur Balfour, agreed:

There is no party which does not recognize to the full all that trade unions have done, the gap which they have filled in the social organization and the impossibilities of carrying on organized labour except by an institution formed upon their model. Undoubtedly, trade disputes in this country have been carried on with a wisdom and a moderation on both sides which cannot be paralleled in another industrial country.[52]

In effect, agreements between unions and employers were not contracts: they could be broken by either side if they saw an advantage, so that agreements had no legal force, and rested on the mutual understanding of both sides—a positive advantage in the opinion of supporters of the Act who believed that industrial relations would be more stable if based on strong associations with exceptional privileges used in a trustworthy manner. Bargaining was both voluntaristic and adversarial. Hindsight suggested that this pattern was the worst of both worlds. British employers did not opt for tight managerial control as in America; neither were workers convinced that their interests and the employers' were identical. Agreements were not legally enforceable or compulsory; and unions did not see their interests as being symmetrical with their employers. The two sides were disinclined to co-operate. The contrast with the United States is marked: there unions were much weaker, but the workers were offered higher wages; when unions were recognized under the Wagner and Taft–Hartley Acts of 1935 and 1947, it was on condition that agreements could not be broken. The British system of industrial relations was highly distinctive—and the main features survived to 1951 and beyond.

Union membership doubled between 1906 and 1914, and doubled again by 1920. The unions were more militant and in a much stronger bargaining position as a result of wartime labour shortages. Wages increased and working hours fell, with serious effects on the performance of the British economy. In 1920, the miners were demanding a 'national wage' which would, in effect, have prevented the restoration of the coal industry to private hands, and they threatened to call out the Triple Alliance in support of their demands. However, the leaders of the railwaymen and dockers had accepted arbitration. Soon after, the railwaymen reconsidered and called out their members with the result that the government immediately reached a settlement with the miners. When the post-war boom broke, the government and employers had every reason to expect that wages would fall; the unions had every reason to think that the gains gave them a fairer share of the national income. In 1921, the pits were returned to their owners who attempted to reduce wages; the miners again went on strike, and a few days later the railwaymen and dockers were called out in common defence of wages. But joint action did not last. The miners refused an offer of negotiations which their allies felt they should have accepted; on 'Black Friday' (15 April 1921) the railwaymen and dockers called off their action.

Black Friday seemed to be a defeat for the unions. However, wages proved 'sticky' and the demise of the Triple Alliance was compensated by the emergence of the Trades Union Congress as a more effective co-ordinating body with the creation of its General Council in 1920. The humiliation of Black Friday could not be allowed to be repeated: joint sympathetic action was to be defensive and concerned with wages. The aim was to force the government to intervene to resolve the initial dispute and not to raise any wider constitutional issue. In 1925, the coal-owners demanded a cut in wages and increase in hours, which prompted the General Council to urge all unionists to support the miners and to consider plans for imposing an embargo on coal. Before the notice given by the coal-owners to their workers expired, the government intervened and agreed to pay a subsidy to the coal industry. The subsidy was portrayed by some Conservatives as a response to an unconstitutional threat. The unions, Churchill complained, were using the 'exceptional immunities' of 1906 in order to pursue 'far-reaching political and economic aims', threatening to cut off a vital supply as a political weapon.[53] The unions were bemused: in their opinion they were merely defending the wages of the miners. The TUC felt that their action in urging the government to grant a subsidy was legitimate; that it was backed by the threat to block supplies was no departure from the Act of 1906. The government disagreed, and when the general strike started in 1926 could easily portray it as unconstitutional—an excellent piece of rhetoric.[54]

The subsidy was due to expire on 30 April 1926, and the government prepared for a showdown. The unions were less active and hopes were pinned on the government's inquiry into the industry as the basis of a negotiated solution. In fact, the inquiry proposed a wage cut and the government refused to pursue the plans for reorganization. The miners were locked out and the TUC had little alternative except to call a general strike. On this occasion, the government was prepared and the strike soon ended. Much as the TUC protested that it was only a sympathetic strike, the government could easily portray it as a constitutional threat. The general strike was called off without achieving its aim: the government refused to continue the subsidy to the coal industry, so that the owners had no alternative except to impose a wage cut. After nine months, the miners accepted defeat.

Did the general strike mark a turning point? It was a symptom of the shift from international to domestic considerations in economic policy. The gold standard was

TABLE 3.6. *British trade union membership and strikes, 1920–39*

	Membership (000)	Days lost through stoppages (000)
1920	8,348	26,568
1921	6,633	85,872
1925	5,506	7,952
1926	5,219	162,233
1927	4,919	1,174
1933	4,389	1,072
1938	6,053	1,334

Source: British Labour Statistics 1886–1968 and *Abstract of Labour Statistics 21, 1919–33*; Mitchell and Deane, *Abstract*, 68, 72.

no longer allowed to dictate economic policy to the same extent as before 1914 or as had been expected in 1925. Furthermore, the government did not use its apparent victory to undo the legislation of 1906. The government used the rhetoric of unconstitutionality, but did not pursue the point. As Baldwin put it in 1926, 'there should be no attack on unions: There can be no greater disaster than that there should be anarchy in the trade union world. It would be impossible in our highly organized and highly developed system of industry, to carry on unless you had organizations which could speak for and bind the parties on both sides.' The strategy seemed to work, for in the 1930s, trade disputes dropped to a very low level and the general secretary of the TUC and the head of the huge Imperial Chemical Industries entered into talks to build an understanding. The so-called Mond–Turner conferences had their origin even before the strike, and continued with the encouragement of Baldwin. Nothing practical came of the talks, but they were a symptom of the desire to re-establish political stability.[55]

Joint Stock, Monopolies, and Morals

In Marshall's account of the urban-industrial economy, personal reputation was crucial, and he feared that impersonal, joint-stock companies would become bureaucratic and inflexible. Many commentators in the previous fifty or so years were concerned that joint-stock companies with limited liability would lower moral responsibility and encourage destructive speculation. Investment was desirable; speculation was reprehensible. Entrepreneurial initiative was to be applauded; fraud and acquisitiveness were to be condemned. Many Victorian businessmen and political economists were concerned to reconcile morality with the market. *The Economist* was confident that commerce was intrinsically moral. Not everyone went that far. The point of commercial life, Samuel Smiles argued, was to rise above its moral dangers, for 'if there were no temptations, there would be no training in self-control, and but little merit in virtue'. Similarly, Herbert Spencer was more than an advocate of individualism and the survival of the fittest. He believed that society was evolving from egoism to altruism but feared that 'trade is essentially corrupt' as a result of 'the *indiscriminate respect paid to wealth'*. Urban, industrial society should not collapse into an atomistic pursuit of self-interest, a war of all against all; it should be moral and co-operative.[56]

Such moral concerns posed the question of what criteria should be used to distinguish legitimate and illegitimate behaviour, and how to impose moral checks on the economy.[57] Unlimited liability meant that illegitimate or speculative behaviour would be punished through personal insolvency. But the Evangelical link between illegitimate trade and punishment was severed by the adoption of limited liability in 1856: speculation could now create profits without punishment. If the threat of financial ruin and retribution did not suffice, what did? Were the norms of Evangelical morality internalized by businessmen, regardless of limited liability? Was there a widespread acceptance of altruism being as important as self-interest, or were these Evangelical and altruistic ideas confined to a small number of preachers and writers with little impact on the behaviour of most businessmen? Paul Johnson argues that commercial norms became dominant, so that speculation and even fraud were tolerated. Rather than commerce being civilized by Evangelicalism or altruism, Johnson argues that 'the morality of Mammon . . . was exported to and enthroned in the wider world of law and politics'.[58] Of course, business scandals are easily found, and some involved leading politicians. But Johnson's argument is too one-sided, ignoring very real concerns about the culture of a market society that informed politicians and judges.

Suspicion of joint-stock companies and speculation was widespread in early and mid-Victorian Britain, and not only among Evangelicals. Might joint-stock companies threaten commercial morality by weakening any sense of personal responsibility? Whereas partnerships rested on character and reputation, corporations rested on a more casual relationship. Shareholders did not have the same close identity with the company, lacking personal involvement with the morality of its activities. Companies might lead to speculation and gambling through playing the stock market; they might exploit the public through monopolies, or by behaving irresponsibly. Shareholders themselves might be exploited, seduced by deceitful directors who drew lucrative salaries or manipulated share prices. Companies might rest on mere show and display rather than real worth. Such fears posed the question of how these new corporate forms should be treated in order to prevent their subverting moral order and economic stability. Family firms and partnerships could not operate railways or utilities with their large demands for capital. On what terms should the privilege of joint stock be granted, and how should companies be controlled? How should claims on companies' profits be adjudicated between directors, shareholders, customers, and workers? The issue was less one of Evangelical morality than of distributive justice and the power of companies over owners and the public.

In the first half of the nineteenth century, joint stock was a closely guarded privilege. In 1844, the right to create a joint-stock company was granted by the state either by application to the Board of Trade or to parliament, as yet without limited liability. The motivation was to prevent fraud, for in the early 1840s, the railway mania and insurance scams were assisted by the companies' unincorporated status. Granting joint-stock status had much in common with Sir Robert Peel's imposition of strict monetary policy in the Bank Charter Act of 1844. This Act was not a narrowly technical economic policy, for it had a moral dimension: to remove the temptation to speculate created by monetary laxity, and to ensure that those who gambled faced retribution.[59] Similarly, free trade had a moral justification as a policy to purge the state of corruption and self-interest, and to benefit consumers with cheap food. By formalizing the status of joint-stock companies, they might be forced into respectability. Of course, the argument could be reversed: companies with a more secure legal status might be better able to exploit unsuspecting and naive investors.

Despite these concerns, joint-stock status was liberalized in 1855–6. Liberalization complemented free trade and freedom of contract: denial of joint-stock status would restrict trade, and the government was not competent to judge between moral and immoral, efficient and fraudulent companies. Companies were seen as agents of technical progress and investment. The legislation was consistent with the reform of tariffs and the state. In the same way that tariffs offered opportunities for corruption and the pursuit of self-interest, so did discretion in the award of joint-stock status; free trade and a more routine granting of corporate status purged the state of favouritism and corruption. The aim was to create stability and responsible behaviour: creditors would need to consider the assets of the company and the reputation of directors rather than rely on the unlimited liability of shareholders, so cutting off supplies of unsound money which fuelled speculation.[60]

Between 1856 and 1865, 4,839 companies were registered, with the largest numbers in gas and water (469) and in coal, iron, lead, and copper mines (633). By contrast, there were only twenty in woollen textiles and 157 in cotton. In manufacturing industry and trade, family and firm remained closely connected, fundamentally affecting the operation of the business. Over his career, a partner moved from an initial stage of indebtedness when loans were incurred and drawings out of the firm were low, to a point where loans were repaid and larger drawings were possible. Men in their fifties gradually moved from active involvement to unearned rentier income, making larger drawings out of the firm to provide for sons who were not involved in the business, or to give marriage settlements to daughters. When a partner retired or died, equity was taken out of the business in order to escape from the risks of unlimited liability, and to provide for his heirs. These heavy cash withdrawals, and the need to buy out the equity, could impose immense strain on the firm. The remaining partners had to find money to buy out the share, and they faced the difficult task of finding a successor from within the family, their social networks, or able employees. Succession and inheritance were not always handled with care, and the boundaries between family and firm were often blurred to the detriment of both. If assets were kept in the firm, the family might suffer from business failure; and if incompetent family members ran the firm, the business might face difficulties. In a joint-stock company, it was easier to dispose of shares or to recruit a salaried manager. Manufacturing concerns only started to take up joint-stock form on any scale from the 1890s. One motivation was to float companies for the owners to extract value by selling shares at inflated prices, which happened in the late 1890s, in the post-war boom, and again in the late 1920s. Another was to convert family firms or partnerships into private limited companies. But larger concerns also needed to turn to joint-stock organization to separate ownership from control. The number of domestic manufacturing and distribution companies quoted on the London Stock Exchange rose from 569 in 1907 to 719 in 1924 and 1,712 in 1939. A market was emerging in ownership rights so that poorly performing companies were liable to takeover or intervention.[61]

The separation between ownership and control, and between trader and customer, posed serious questions for the morality of business. The repeal of the corn laws and free trade offered cheap food, but what if the flour or bread was adulterated? Should they be monitored by public officials, or should the principle of *caveat emptor* apply? Of course, a customer could only beware if the adulteration were detectable and if there were alternative suppliers. As Mill pointed out, it was one thing to remove custom from a baker who charged excessive prices or supplied poor bread; it was quite another thing with gas and water, where the consumer was powerless and joint-stock companies could exploit him, unconstrained by the sense of personal responsibility of family firms and partnerships. The monopoly powers of the East India Co. or the protection of West Indies sugar planters had ended; might not the new monopolists of the local gas concern simply take their place? Tariffs on raw materials might be abolished, only to place producers at the mercy of companies able to charge high prices for other vital commodities. Mill was concerned that the utility companies were not accountable: in theory, shareholders had power over the directors of companies, but in practice their input was minimal. There were serious dangers, for Mill pointed out that 'a government which concedes such monopoly unreservedly to a private company does much the same thing as if it allowed an individual or an association to levy any tax they chose for their own benefit, on all the malt produced in the country, or on all the cotton imported into it'. What was needed was strict regulation, or even to take the concerns into public ownership. As Mill saw it, any 'delegated management' was likely to be 'jobbing, careless and ineffective' compared with personal management by the owner, whose own reputation was at stake. Despite the dangers that a powerful state bureaucracy would keep citizens in a childlike condition, Mill felt that the threat posed by company control of gas and water was still more serious. Public ownership might therefore have its origins in individualism rather than in socialism. The contention that the 'morality of Mammon' was exported to the wider world misses these debates and concerns.[62]

The railway and utility companies could not operate unless they were granted power against the property rights of other parties. Parliament granted power to the companies, and regulated them to prevent abuse of their position. The politics of natural monopolies were formulated in the same way as the politics of taxation: electors and their representatives needed to pay close attention to the spending and taxing powers of the government; and consumers of gas and water needed to pay close attention to the ability of companies to 'tax' through their charges for essential services. In both cases, the 'franchise' should be carefully devised to provide effective controls. The politics of joint-stock companies did not end with making limited liability more easily available, for the rights of various stakeholders continued to be in tension. Companies operated in the public sphere and were intrinsically political entities; their performance reflected their response to the interplay of different stakeholders. What power should directors have over the company; how accountable should they be to shareholders? Would the shareholders have large denomination shares and form an oligarchy; or would shares have low denominations and allow a more democratic franchise? Might consumers use their political voice to demand more or less stringent regulation; might they form an alliance with the shareholders against the directors, or join with the directors against the threat of consumers and workers to their profits and dividends? The directors needed to mobilize to oppose controls which threatened the dividend paid to shareholders, perhaps by presenting themselves as the guardians of managerial efficiency against the corrupting power of political authority. Workers might secure political voice, demanding protection of their welfare and safety, and even nationalization of the industry. The politics of joint-stock companies were complex, and varied between sectors.[63]

Gas, water, railways, trams, telegraphs, telephones, electricity needed large-scale investment and entry costs were high. Competition meant costly duplication of water and gas pipes. Where competing companies did exist, firms had an incentive to use predatory pricing. The greater the volume of gas or water supplied, the lower the unit cost: the fixed costs of plant would be spread over a greater volume and variable costs were not high. The largest firm was therefore likely to become the sole supplier. Equally, monopoly meant the company had little reason to charge low prices or to become more efficient, for there was little fear of entry by a new competitor. Consequently, parliament's initial strategy of relying on competition to protect the consumer was soon abandoned: large-scale concerns were more efficient, and policy should focus on protecting the consumer from an abuse of monopoly power. The matter was controversial and contested. The fixed assets in the network industries greatly exceeded manufacturing industry (see Table 3.7), and inefficiency would have considerable ramifications for the rest of the economy. High freight rates would impose costs on manufacturers; expensive electricity would delay the redesign of production and slow down the uptake of new consumer goods; failure to provide cheap water or urban transport would create public health problems, as well as reducing the efficiency of the urban economy. Productivity in the utility industries fell behind both Germany and the United States, and there is a prima facie case that the system of regulation led to inefficiencies.

TABLE 3.7. *Distribution of fixed assets in network industries and manufacturing, 1850–1930 (% of UK total)*

	Network industries	Manufacturing
1850	17.9	13.5
1900	23.0	13.6
1930	30.5	16.0

Source: Foreman-Peck and Millward, *Public and Private Ownership*, 3.

The politics of joint stock was played out in the utilities of gas, water, and electricity, with different outcomes. The purely local market of the gas industry meant that a 'subscribers' democracy' had more chance of success, provided that shares were open to anyone. Consumers also had considerable power, for the market was closely allied to the local government franchise. But which consumers were to have priority? Mill-owners and shopkeepers with high usage claimed preferential terms; domestic consumers resented their apparent 'subsidy'. A crucial issue was who controlled the companies with their power to 'tax' the consumer. Ownership of shares gave dividends and votes in running the company: the company's 'electorate' was self-electing if shares were offered to existing shareholders who could 'tax' the public with higher charges. Most early gas Acts imposed a maximum price, which was often too high as technical change reduced costs. One solution was to insist that all shares should be offered to the public in an 'auction', so that any consumer had the opportunity to secure a vote. The 'model clauses' of 1847 imposed a maximum dividend, and empowered any two 'gas ratepayers' to apply to the courts for an accountant to report on the concern and, if necessary, to order a reduction in the price. But these clauses left loopholes. A limit on dividends did not necessarily result in lower prices, for companies could expand the capital on which the profit was calculated and issue new shares to existing owners. They had an incentive to 'water' the capital in order to pay more profits rather than to use the plant efficiently.

The gas companies were exposed to the threat of 'confiscation', for the overlap between consumers and the local electorate meant that the local authorities could present themselves as the protectors of the consumer interest. In London, public bodies pressed for a new form of regulation: a sliding scale allowing dividends to rise only if the price of gas fell and vice versa. The sliding scale would provide an incentive for efficiency, encouraging firms to adopt new technology and increase productivity which would allow them both to pay a decent dividend and to charge low prices. In 1875, a sliding scale was adopted in one London gas bill. The measure appealed to some companies and it was welcomed by the Board of Trade. At the same time, companies were obliged to offer shares for auction to the public at the highest price, so removing the 'closed' franchise. By 1900, the sliding scale system applied to half the companies.

Meanwhile, the politics of the gas industry changed as the municipal electorate and the composition of gas consumers widened. In many cities, the outcome was public ownership by municipal authorities. Usually, they kept prices at the same level and diverted the profits from private shareholders to public revenues. By 1907, local authorities were responsible for 33 per cent of the net output of gas. Municipalization was facilitated where the company's area was more or less coterminous with the local authority; difficulties arose if a number of authorities were involved. By the inter-war period, falling profits led to a greater interest in economies of scale and in regionalization, and some private concerns came together in holding companies, often without operational integration. The Gas Regulation Act of 1920 allowed neighbouring local authorities to merge their systems, but the independence of local authorities meant that progress was slow and only five joint ventures were created. In 1948, local initiative was replaced by national ownership.[64]

The regulation of gas only partially provided the framework for the new technology of electricity. The Electric Lighting Act 1882 gave each local authority the right to sanction a company in its area or to generate electricity itself, and to set a maximum price. Most importantly, the local authority had the right to purchase the private company after twenty-one years (raised to forty-two years in 1888). Rather than adopting the sliding scale principle, the Act followed the approach of the Railways Act of 1844 and, more immediately, the Tramways Act of 1870 which allowed local authorities to purchase tramways after twenty-one years at their 'then value'. The terms of the Act of 1882 created two potential difficulties, of time horizon and geography. Would private companies invest, knowing that they might be appropriated by a local authority at 'then value'? Certainly, the development of electricity was initially slower in Britain than in the USA, but not only because of the purchase clause. In Britain, electricity had to compete with an efficient gas industry; and the geography of local authorities led to technical inefficiencies. In the gas industry, distribution was difficult over long distances; in the case of electricity, local authority areas were too small for efficiency as the economies of scale rose. In London, for example, there were sixty-five suppliers and seventy generating plants in 1913, with forty-nine different supply systems, ten frequencies, and twenty-four voltage levels. Although the Select Committee of 1898 accepted that technological change meant that powers should be given over a wider area, local authorities resisted change. In most towns, the local authorities themselves provided electricity: in 1907, 64 per cent of electricity was generated by public concerns, above all in urban centres. Usually, private concerns supplied the surrounding area under local authority sanction. The political boundaries made no technical sense, frustrating the creation of interconnected systems and economies of scale, and the division between private and public concerns led to mutual distrust.[65]

After the First World War, the government made a conscious attempt to adjust the discrepancy between the economics of generation and political boundaries. During the war, an inquiry concluded that the 600 existing concerns had developed on the wrong lines both technically and commercially; it recommended sixteen electricity districts to centralize generation, with distribution remaining in the hands of existing bodies. The fundamental problem was: who should own the plant? One committee advised that existing plant should be bought by district electricity boards. A second committee recommended national ownership, with a dissenting memorandum in favour of private enterprise. Not surprisingly, the Electricity (Supply) Act 1919 was weak and ineffective, and a more radical solution was implemented in 1926. Existing undertakings would keep control of electricity generation and a Central Electricity Board would purchase power from them, using the most efficient plant to cover the baseload and least efficient to meet peak demand. Power would then be distributed to the consumer by existing concerns. The Board would plan new capacity and construct a grid under the control of technical experts. The compromise resolved conflict between municipal and private generators, and created an interconnected system. In 1914, a ton of coal generated 44.3 units of electricity; by 1939 the level had risen to 1,566 units. Costs of supplying electricity to the grid fell from 1.098*d.* per unit in 1923 to 0.34*d.* in 1939. But there was no authority to amalgamate existing undertakings or to prevent local authorities from creating new franchises. A committee was set up to review the situation in 1935 and soon came to the conclusion that it was 'chaotic' with many different voltages and wide variations in costs of distribution. The committee recommended reducing the number of undertakings to about 250. As in gas, there was a realization that neither the market nor local authorities would solve the problem, and the situation might even deteriorate if the local authorities used their powers of purchase under the 1888 Act. Opinion moved from persuasion towards the use of compulsion. Pre-war doubts and delays gave way to action in 1948: generation was nationalized, and distribution was in the hands of regional electricity boards.[66]

Regulation was needed to protect consumers. The result was reasonably successful in electricity where technical experts had a clear sense of what was needed but was less successful in gas, where co-ordination scarcely made any progress between the wars. In both industries, the regulation of private concerns was unsatisfactory. By the inter-war period, Marshall's world was in retreat: the publication of *Industry and Trade* in 1919 was a despairing response to mergers and amalgamations to improve efficiency and to create a more 'rational' industrial structure. Much the same sense of structural change also started to affect manufacturing industry. At the turn of the nineteenth and twentieth centuries, a wave of mergers and company flotations affected a number of industrial sectors, and the process was carried further as a result of the war and post-war boom. Economic culture was moving from a commitment to family ownership, partnerships, or private companies. Many small firms survived in 'light' industries providing everything from furniture to hosiery, and they might still remain part of urban networks, but they were increasingly seen as an outmoded form of organization.

Cartelization and Competition

In 1851, the major structural shift from agriculture to industry was largely complete: 42.9 per cent of employment was in manufacturing, mining, and building, with only a modest increase in 1911 when 46.4 per cent of employment was in these sectors, the highest level ever reached in British history.[67] Most structural change up to 1911 was *within* industrial employment. In 1831, the census differentiated between employment in manufacturing for distant markets and handicrafts or retail trades producing goods for local markets, where productivity was lower and stable. In 1831, only about 10 per cent of adult male workers in England and Wales were employed in manufacturing compared with 32 per cent in handicrafts and retail trades. From 1831—and even more from 1851—employment in manufacturing grew.[68] The industrial structure in 1851 had two poles, one based on small-scale concerns, the other on large-scale production with unskilled and semi-skilled workers (Table 3.8). The difference is apparent in data for Scottish towns (Table 3.9). After 1851, more workers moved into manufacturing, and especially higher-productivity trades with a greater use of powered machinery. The largest sector of industrial

TABLE 3.8. *Percentage of employers with different numbers of male employees, England and Wales, 1851*

	No men or not stated	1 or 2	3–9	10–19	20–49	50–99	100+
Cotton	28.9	4.9	10.4	7.4	12.9	10.3	24.6
Engine and machine maker	19.1	18.2	35.2	10.8	8.6	4.8	4.1
Shoes	41.4	34.1	20.6	2.5	1.0	0.2	0.2
Building	8.0	11.5	42.6	19.4	13.8	3.1	1.4

Source: Census of Great Britain 1851: Population Tables, I, cclxxvi–cclxxix.

TABLE 3.9. *Industry in nine leading burghs in Scotland, 1851*

No. of workers	Percentage of employers	Percentage of employees	
1 or 2	29.9	2.5	
3 to 9	42.9	12.0	24.5
10 to 19	12.5	10.0	
20 to 49	8.4	14.3	
50 to 99	3.8	11.6	25.9
100 to 349	2.5	23.3	
350 and above	0.7	26.1	

Source: Rodger, 'Concentration and fragmentation', 188.

employment in 1851 was textiles, followed by clothing. Mechanization of the 'lesser' textile trades meant that their share of employment fell. By contrast, two sectors increased their employment: metals, engineering, and shipbuilding rose from 6.1 per cent of employment in 1851 to 10.5 per cent in 1911; and mining and quarrying from 4.2 to 6.6 per cent. The declining sectors had lower productivity and value added per worker. Although the benefits of moving labour from agriculture to industry were largely exhausted by 1851, there were still gains from a structural shift within industry.[69]

The perception of most commentators in the first half of the twentieth century was that Britain was lagging behind both Germany and the USA in pursuit of the economies of scale. In reality, the scale of British firms was similar. Although the very largest British concerns were in the service sector, 91 of the largest 125 concerns in Britain in 1907 produced goods. In Germany, the largest concerns were state owned, with only one non-state enterprise in the list of the largest German firms. Even in the USA, the picture was similar to Britain with the exception of a few large companies.[70] Between the wars, the level of concentration rose, and cartels or agreements to fix prices and output became commonplace (see Table 3.10). The rise in the level of concentration was, in part, a response to the changing composition of industrial output. In the cotton industry, cutlery, and small metal goods, for example, entry was relatively easy by purchasing raw materials on credit, engaging workers with the requisite skills from the external labour market, and hiring space in a mill with machinery on credit from specialist producers of machinery. The situation was very different in the motor industry or in chemicals and artificial fibres, where large-scale 'lumpy' investment was needed, with considerable expertise in designing plant and marketing large volumes of output. The process started before 1914 in sectors with large economies of scale as a result of high throughput. W. D. and H. O. Wills acquired exclusive control of a

TABLE 3.10. *Share of the largest 100 firms in manufacturing net output in UK, 1907–70 (%)*

1907	15	1935	23
1919	17	1939	22
1921	21	1953	26
1930	26	1970	40

Source: Hannah, *Rise of the Corporate Economy*, 180.

machine to produce cigarettes, and developed a range of branded cigarettes which gave it 55 per cent of the UK market by 1901. The crucial factor was control of a specialized machine technology, supported by patents, allied to the development of national marketing and branding. Where demand could be standardized and extended to a wider spectrum of the population, not least with the improvement in the standard of living after 1873, long production runs became viable in commodities such as soap and cleaning products where Lever Brothers created national brands. The production of artificial fibres was dominated from the outset by Courtaulds whose overseas competitors had similarly monopolistic positions in their own markets.[71]

Mergers and the growth of large firms were also influenced by access to capital. In Germany, bankers sat on the boards of the firms and industrialists turned to them for long-term capital. Consequently, interlocking directors could co-ordinate output and prices. In the United States, some of the largest mergers were sponsored by financiers. In Britain, capital was more readily available and the power of bankers and financiers was less marked. A number of specialist firms emerged to assist in the flotation of large companies. In these cases, the directors were often the former partners who retained large holdings.[72] In the 1890s, a wave of mergers (see Table 3.11) arose from speculative motives: company promoters saw an opportunity to float companies on the Stock Exchange, luring unsuspecting outsiders to buy shares and leaving profits both for the existing owners and for the promoter. The notorious promoter E. T. Hooley floated a number of companies in this way, including Dunlop Co.

TABLE 3.11. *Number of firm disappearances by merger, UK manufacturing industry, 1880–1949*

1880–9	207	1920–9	1,884
1890–9	769	1930–9	1,414
1900–9	659	1940–9	778

source: Hannah, *Rise of the Corporate Economy*, 178.

His motivation was purely short-term speculative gain. Dunlop prospered with the emergence of motor cars but faced continued problems as a result of the failure of its chairman to distinguish between his family and company interests. In 1913, he appointed the speculator James White as financial adviser to the company, and his activities in share manipulation at the end of the war brought the company close to collapse.[73] Most mergers were in periods of rapidly rising share prices and financial considerations played a major role. Between 1888 and 1914, an average of around sixty-seven firms a year disappeared through mergers; between 1898 and 1900, 650 firms disappeared in 198 mergers.[74] Whether the result was efficiency may be doubted. The Calico Printers' Association, for example, brought together fifty-nine firms in 1899 with eighty-four directors of whom eight were managing directors; the firm was seriously overcapitalized and its board meetings chaotic. Neither were the large firms in the more modern and dynamic sectors. Of the fifty-two largest companies in Britain in 1905, eighteen were in brewing and distilling and ten in textiles, whereas in the USA in 1907 only one firm was found in each sector. In Britain, only nine of the largest companies were in iron, steel, and metals; in the USA, there were twenty-three.[75]

The level of concentration was more than a matter of capital requirements and economies of scale, for firms acted to prevent destructive competition within a fragmented business structure. Competing concerns might control some of their costs to reduce the margin of uncertainty. In some sectors, firms attempted to form cartels to set prices or determine output in order to create stability and high profits. The problem was that one firm might break ranks, stealing market share by exceeding the quota or undercutting prices. In Britain, cartels were inherently unstable. On the other hand, price-fixing agreements were not illegal as in the United States. British firms were left in an ambivalent position. In Germany, enforceable cartels removed the motivation for firms to merge; in the United States, firms were encouraged to merge because cartels were illegal.[76] In Britain, price-fixing agreements were periodically attempted and mergers might follow, not necessarily to achieve economies of scale and technical efficiency but rather to secure market control within a single concern. This was a feature of the depressed industries of the inter-war period.

After the First World War, attitudes to industrial organization changed: a preference for small, competitive firms gave way to a widespread belief in the virtues of scale and 'rationalization'. During the war, government controls over materials, and the need to take direct control over key sectors, or to foster developments in the arms industries, led to a greater concern for planning and co-ordination. Industrialists needed to negotiate with the government over the allocation of scarce resources and the control of industry; as a result, trade associations became more powerful and the first national organization—the Federation of British Industries—was created. At the end of the war, the government had to decide how to return industry to private control. In the coal industry, a Royal Commission was appointed to advise—and surprisingly recommended nationalization. The proposal was not adopted, but rationalization was embraced. As the management expert Lyndall Urwick remarked in 1930, 'The rapid development of the idea of rationalization has given rise to amalgamations at a speed and to a degree which is altogether novel'. Urwick had a vested interest in selling his consulting services, but similar views were expressed by Harold Macmillan. In his words, 'some form of conscious social direction will have to supplement the old system under which the regulation of our economy was entrusted to the method of trial and error in response to the price indicator'. Planning seemed scientific and rational, an alternative to the use of the free market. But who was to undertake the planning, and on what criteria? It could mean socialism or that power should pass to industrialists to manage the economy. In practice, the rationalization movement might mean little more than price-fixing cartels, with a reduction in the level of competition at home and abroad.[77]

The shift was partly ideological, a major change in political culture away from the virtues of Mill and Marshall to the benefits of organization. Of course, the old world had its adherents and there were reasons for scepticism given the poor performance of many large companies. But the case for larger concerns was generally accepted, on the grounds that they would provide research laboratories and secure economies of scale. British business consciously imitated foreign examples. Indeed, some American firms entered the British market. In other cases, the response was through competition with large foreign rivals. Mergers in the German chemical industry culminated in the creation of IG Farben in 1925, and British firms felt that their own future depended on their reaction to this new power. The four largest British concerns, Nobel, Brunner Mond, British Dyestuffs Corporation, and United Alkali, merged in 1926 to form Imperial Chemical Industries. The choice of name reflected the belief that the empire offered industry its best chance of a prosperous future. ICI would rely on its 'natural' markets in the empire, and Du Pont and IG Farben would be left with the USA and Europe respectively. Rationalization at home was part of a wider process of international cartels or market agreements.[78]

Efficiency was to be found in new systems of management rather than competition. Lever Brothers was rescued from over-expansion in the post-war boom and the impact of the slump by D'Arcy Cooper. He replaced Lever's autocracy with order and a new class of professional management. At Dunlop, survival depended on a new type of businessman. Frederic De Paula was brought in as chief accountant. He created an integrated system of budgetary control and financial reporting.[79] At ICI, Mond created a new managerial ethos. Managers were socialized in a club on the lines of an officers' mess or college, and were selected and trained more systematically. New structures were put in place, with a gradual development of divisional systems under a functionally specialized head office, and clerical workforces became more important. Before the First World War, about 8 per cent of manufacturing employees were in 'overheads'. By 1935, the figure was 15.1 per cent, and by 1948 19.7 per cent. The worst problems of multi-firm mergers in the late nineteenth century were avoided. In the 1880s, the average number of firms per merger was 19.6, but the number had fallen to 6.9 in the 1930s.[80] Most inter-war mergers were small and firms paced acquisitions so that they could be absorbed. The problems of management were also reduced by telephones and the adoption of office equipment to mechanize accounting, and by the development of new specialisms such as the Institute of Cost and Works Accountants or the Purchasing Officers' Association.

The government and courts condoned the growth of larger concerns. At the end of the war, the Committee on Commercial and Industrial Policy felt that trusts should be constrained merely by publicity, and stressed the benefits of combination. Although outcry against excessive war profits did lead to political action in the Profiteering Act of 1919, it had very little impact. The Act served to contain political pressure; it had no real power, and the attempt to secure greater authority with the Trade Monopolies Bill of 1920 came to nothing. The Cabinet was torn between the need to placate public hostility and the sentiment of industrialists. It was initially concerned not to alienate labour, but as prices started to fall, changed its emphasis to bolster firms. The Profiteering Act came to an end in 1921 and no further action was taken against trusts and mergers. The report of the Balfour Committee on large-scale production concluded that no immediate action was needed.[81] Generally, the benefits of amalgamation were accepted both on the left and on the right.

The government was therefore reluctant to intervene to maintain competition. Should it give positive encouragement to reorganization? The issue arose in a particularly stark way in the depressed staple industries. How to deal with the problems of low prices and profits, allied with high levels of indebtedness, posed serious difficulties. Some outside agency was needed to reorganize steel, cotton, shipping and shipbuilding, coal, and other sectors. The banks and City were involved, for they loaned money to companies in the boom of 1919–20. The banks abandoned their traditionally cautious approach to overdrafts, which rose to 42 per cent of bank assets in 1920. Difficulties emerged with the onset of depression. At the same time, the organization of a number of industries was deeply politicized. When the government rejected the Royal Commission's recommendation to nationalize the coal industry and opted to return the firms to private hands, the miners felt betrayed. The future of the industry was highly political, for miners and the Labour party felt that the solution was nationalization and any decision on policy would necessarily involve discussion with the workers. Banks had little role in the coal industry: they had not made loans on any scale and preferred to avoid the political difficulties of the industry. In cotton and steel, labour had a much smaller role than the banks and

Bank of England, which aimed to reorganize the industries and to keep the state at arm's length. The political economy of the depressed industries therefore differed.

Bankers were not directly involved in the management of industry before the First World War, and were wary of intervening. One response was to nurse firms through the depression by increasing their overdrafts, in the hope that they would be repaid when the economy recovered. But it was soon clear that more drastic action was needed. The outcome was not a fusion of finance and industry; the banks and City were unwilling to become directly involved in the affairs of firms, and preferred to create a general framework for rationalization. Steven Tolliday points out that the approach adopted by Montagu Norman at the Bank of England assumed that the banks were a sort of neutral national interest group.[82] The Bank of England would intervene to encourage firms to merge; it did not believe that reorganization required central direction from anyone except industry itself. The Bank of England formed the Lancashire Cotton Corporation in 1928 in order to sustain indebted and often inefficient firms, hence supporting the Lancashire banks which had lent them so much money in the post-war boom. The Lancashire Cotton Corporation sponsored private reorganization, acquiring seventy companies in 1929 and a further twenty-six in 1930—a task beyond the ability of managers. Norman's main desire was to preserve the financial stability of banks and in this he was successful. The cotton industry remained troubled by surplus capacity, and the industry realized that the solution was not amalgamation but a reduction in the number of spindles. The trade association pressed for government support for a scheme to scrap machines which was introduced in 1936: a compulsory levy was imposed on the industry, and the Spindles Board bought and scrapped 6 million spindles. The problem was that firms were diverting money into schemes to destroy capacity rather than allowing inefficient firms to fail and using funds to invest in efficiency.[83] In the case of steel, the rationalization schemes proposed by the Securities Management Trust and Bankers' Industrial Development Corporation were economically sensible, but their implementation depended on the willingness of steel firms to co-operate. The internal divisions and fragmentation of the industry between sectors and regions meant that the British Iron and Steel Federation was the forum for the defence of existing interests rather than rationalization which would have torn it apart.[84]

The government welcomed the Bank's lead in the rationalization of steel and cotton in the 1920s, for it avoided the political dangers of forcing industrialists into mergers. Industry preferred to be left to resolve its own difficulties, without government intervention. When Labour came to power in 1929, Horace Wilson was appointed as the government's industrial adviser, but his role was to stimulate discussion and use moral persuasion. Similarly, the National government preferred to encourage discussion. Most Conservative politicians looked to industrial self-regulation or self-government, with the state creating the conditions for effective associations. As Tolliday points out, industrial self-government rested on a self-denying ordinance: 'the government opted to confer legal privileges and protection on the organized producers already established in crisis-ridden industries.' The aim, as he remarks, 'was industrial autonomy under the umbrella of the state'.[85]

In terms of modernization or efficiency, the actions of the state were probably counter-productive. A good example is the coal industry where the government sponsored cartels to prevent price cuts and to remove the downward pressure on wages. Labour made up about 75 per cent of total costs, and mine-owners had every reason to cut wages. Indeed, miners were the only major group of workers to experience a fall in real wages in the 1920s. But would further cuts be politically possible, and would they solve the basic problem of the industry? The Coal Mines Act of 1930 aimed to increase prices. The Act was largely a response to the pressures on the welfare of mining communities, and reflected the demands of the Miners' Union rather than the coal-owners' association. 'Excessive' competition was controlled in order to stabilize the conditions of workers rather than to modernize the industry. The scheme imposed production quotas for each coalfield, which were then allocated to individual pits regardless of their efficiency or costs. A modern pit with low costs would pay a fine if it exceeded its quota, even if it could produce more coal at a low marginal cost; old, inefficient pits which did not meet their quota would receive a subsidy. The government established the framework, and left the setting of prices and quotas to 'autonomous self-regulation' by committees drawn from the industry. The result was to reinforce the existing structure of the industry, keeping inefficient pits in operation and raising prices to maintain wages and profits at the expense of the consumer. The state stimulated the organization of corporate groups; by bolstering their autonomy, state power was itself diminished in the face of large oligopolies and powerful institutions.[86]

These criticisms could be read in a number of ways. One response would be to say that the market should have been left to drive inefficient firms into bankruptcy rather than propping up ailing sectors on grounds of social cohesion and political stability. Another would be to argue that the government or the banks should have taken a more active role, shifting power away from industrialists to create a modern, planned economy. However, the concern of the banks with their own financial stability—and hence of the economy as a whole—is understandable. A further response was to give more power to business itself to plan the economy. Why did the government reject these options and cling to its policy of industrial self-government? At the time, it was concerned by the social consequences of allowing industries to fail with devastating consequences for south Wales, the north of England, and central Scotland. In the 1930s, the government was moving to a policy of 'economic nationalism' or industrial self-sufficiency. Industrial self-government had the advantage of preventing the state from being too involved in battles between different private interests. Direct involvement in the affairs of individual firms was highly unusual: one of the few exceptions was the merger between the Cunard and White Star shipping lines in 1934, and the subsidy for the construction of new liners, a policy with clear strategic motivations. Generally, the government allowed industrial associations to set prices and control competition behind tariff walls. The low level of internal and external competition characterized the British economy for the next thirty or more years, and helped to sustain the low-effort bargain.

Conclusion

The history of industry and the urban economy involves far more than a narrow business history of the performance of individual firms in response to the conditions of supply and demand. Their resources and their markets were not given; they were shaped by political processes and choices. The relative price of capital and labour reflected the assumptions of politicians, civil servants, economists, and social commentators towards trade unions and labour relations. Political and cultural preferences helped to determine the effort bargain. Similarly, the market was deeply cultural and political, reflecting policy choices on the protection of consumers and the priority to be given to their interests over shareholders and workers. Manufacturers and the directors of network industries did not make purely economic choices, for they needed to think about political strategies to balance the different voices. The choices had economic consequences for good or ill. The regulatory regime might be appropriate at one time but could become a hindrance. Much the same applied to the production institutions of industries where the bargain between workers and employers could 'freeze' technical change. Many of the production institutions of the later nineteenth century continued into the twentieth century. But there were also clear shifts around the First World War. The commitment to small firms and proprietary capitalism gave way to a greater stress on the efficiencies to be derived from scale and managerial capitalism. Again, the change was political and cultural, marking a shift from the political and economic culture of free trade to restraint of competition and control over the economy. The consumer would no longer be protected by free trade, and the interests of the producer, in coal or cotton, had greater weight. Competition was re-evaluated not as beneficial but wasteful, and small firms not as responsible but as ineffective. Marshall's ideals were in retreat in the face of a victorious ideology of scale and bureaucratic management.

NOTES

1. Dickens, *Hard Times*, 22.
2. Engels, *Condition*; Marx and Engels, *Communist Manifesto*, 222–3.

3. These comments of Marshall come from *Principles*, 138–9, 271, 279–80, 283–5, 304; *Industry and Trade*, 249, 324–5, 577–8, 582–4, 590, 605–8; Pigou (ed.), *Memorials*, 249. His arguments on Lancashire are supported by Leunig, 'British industrial success', III.

4. Ruskin, *Unto this Last*, 126.

5. Thompson, 'Town and city' and *Rise of Respectable Society*, 360–1; Cain and Hopkins, 'Gentlemanly capitalism', 2–3; and Wiener, *English Culture*, 27–40.

6. Macleod, *Art and the Middle Class*.

7. Jones, 'Public pursuit of private profit?'; Hennock, *Fit and Proper Persons*.

8. Dellheim, *Face of the Past*, 16–19, 167–75; Morris, *Class, Sect and Party*; Biagini, 'Liberalism and direct democracy'.

9. Tweedale, *Steel City*, 54.

10. Savage and Miles, *Remaking*, 68–9; Daunton (ed.), *Cambridge Urban History*, iii. 54–5, 278–86, 339, 389, 416–19, 583–92, 676.

11. Bell, *At the Works*, 38.

12. Quoted in Samuel, 'Workshop of the world', 58–9.

13. Rosenberg (ed.), *American System*; Fox, 'Industrial relations'; Ames and Rosenberg, 'Enfield arsenal' 825, 828.

14. Habakkuk, *American and British Technology*, 138–9.

15. Harley, 'Skilled labor'; on the use of labour in American industry, see Brody, *Steelworkers*; Montgomery, *Fall of the House of Labor*; Montgomery, *Workers' Control*.

16. Edgerton and Horrocks, 'British industrial research and development'.

17. Rosenberg, *Technology and American Economic Growth*, 64–6; Halsey, 'Choice between high-pressure and low-pressure steam power'; Broadberry, *Productivity Race*, 101, 109; Harley 'Skilled labor'; Broadberry, *Productivity Race*; Broadberry, 'Manufacturing and the convergence hypothesis'.

18. Sabel and Zeitlin, 'Historical alternatives'.

19. For an excellent overview, see Scranton, *Endless Novelty*.

20. Hounsell. *From the American System to Mass Production*, 294–7.

21. Tweedale, *Steel City*; Tweedale, *Sheffield Steel and America*; but see Leunig, 'British industrial success', which argues for superior productivity in Lancashire cotton.

22. Broadberry, *Productivity Race*, 83–4, 98, 102.

23. Broadberry and Crafts, 'British economic policy', 76; McKibbin, *Ideologies*, ch. 1; Zeitlin, 'Triumph of adversarial bargaining'.

24. Broadberry, *Productivity Race*, 9.

25. Tiratsoo, 'Materials handling'; Booth, 'Manufacturing failure hypothesis'.

26. Lenin, *Imperialism*, 174–5; Foster, *Class Struggle*, 203.

27. Lazonick, *Competitive Advantage*, 78–95; Jewkes and Gray, *Wages and Labour*, 30, 31.

28. Labour Department of the Board of Trade; Price, *Masters, Unions and Men*; Odber, 'Origins of industrial peace'; Lazonick, *Competitive Advantage*; Rose, *Firms, Networks and Business Values*; White, *Limits of Trade Union Militancy*.

29. Lazonick, *Competitive Advantage*, ch. 6.

30. Ibid. 184–212; Lewchuck, *American Technology and the British Vehicle Industry*, ch. 9.

31. McKibbin, *Ideologies*, 165, 166.

32. Lazonick, *Competitive Advantage;* on the weakening of craft control in the USA see Montgomery, *Workers' Control*; Montgomery, *Fall of the House of Labor*; Brody, *Steelworkers*.

33. Lewchuk, *American Technology and the British Vehicle Industry*, 2.

34. Ibid., 70; Floud, *Machine Tool Industry*, 27, 64.

35. Zeitlin, 'Internal politics'; 'Labour strategies'; 'Between flexibility'; Lewchuk, *American Technology and the British Vehicle Industry*, 160–1; Reid, 'Employers' strategies'.

36. Reid, 'Dilution'; Lewchuk, *American Technology and the British Vehicle Industry*, 110.

37. Tolliday, 'Management and labour'; Tolliday, 'Failure of mass production unionism'; Tolliday, 'Ford and "Fordism" '; Bowden, 'Demand and supply constraints'.

38. Zeitlin, 'Triumph of adversarial bargaining', 405–6.

39. Webb and Webb, *Trade Unionism*, 199–200 and, for a critical assessment, Duffy, 'New unionism'; Turner, *Trade Union Growth*, 45, 50, 108.

40. Williams, 'The south Wales sliding scale'; Williams, 'Coalowners of south Wales'; Morris and Williams, *South Wales Coal Industry*; Church, *Coal Industry*; Daunton, 'Down the pit'; Waller, *Dukeries Transformed*.

41. Mitchell and Deane, *Abstract*, 68, 71, 72.

42. Lovell, *Stevedores and Dockers*; Daunton, 'Inter-union relations'.

43. Furner, 'Knowing capitalism'; Brody, *Steelworkers*; Montgomery, *Fall of the House of Labor*; Harris, *Right to Manage*.

44. McKibbin, *Ideologies* ch. 1; for an alternative view, Johnson, 'Class law' 147–9; Phelps Brown, *Origins of Trade Union Power*; Townsend, *Making the Peace*; Gatrell, 'Policeman state'; Davidson, *Whitehall and the Labour Problem*; Price, *Masters, Unions and Men*.

45. Steinmetz, 'Was there a de-juridification of individual employment relations in Britain?'

46. Engels, introduction of 1895 to Marx, *The Class Struggles in France 1848 to 1850* 41; Zeitlin, 'From labour history', 169–76.

47. Phelps Brown, *Origins of Trade Union Power*, 29; McKibbin, *Ideologies* 28; Curthoys, *Governments, Labour and the Law*.

48. Phelps Brown, *Origins of Trade Union Power*, 36

49. Marshall, cited in Phelps Brown, *Origins of Trade Union Power*, 27.

50. Phelps Brown, *Origins of Trade Union Power*, 27, 28, 31; Royal Commission on Labour 1894, 25–8, 97–103, 112–13.

51. Phelps Brown, *Origins of Trade Union Power*, 39, 40.

52. Ibid. 46

53. Quoted ibid. 86.

54. Fox, *History and Heritage*, 329–30.

55. Phelps Brown, *Origins of Trade Union Power*; Fox, *History and Heritage*, 327–36; for a less sanguine account, Phillips, *General Strike*, 270–9, 288–95.

56. Quoted in Searle, *Morality and the Market*, 21, 46, 98.

57. Ibid. 274.

58. Hilton, *Age of Atonement*, ch. 4; Collini, *Public Moralists*, 62; Taylor, 'Commercial fraud and public men'; Johnson, 'Civilizing Mammon', 304–6, 314, 316–19.

59. Hilton, *Age of Atonement*, 224.

60. Based on Taylor, *Creating Capitalism* chs. 4, 5, and epilogue.

61. Morris, 'Middle class and the property cycle'; Morgan and Moss, '"Wealthy and titled persons"'; Shannon, 'First five thousand limited companies', 422; Hannah, *Rise of the Corporate Economy*, 61.

62. Alborn, *Conceiving Companies*, 51–2; Mill, *Public Agency v Trading Companies*, 434; Mill, *Principles*, ch. XI of book IV.

63. See Alborn, *Conceiving Companies*.

64. Daunton, 'The material politics of natural monopoly'; Matthews, 'Laissez-faire and the London gas industry'; Chatterton, 'State control of public utilities'; Millward and Ward, 'From private to public ownership of gas undertakings'; Millward, 'Market behaviour of local utilities'; Foreman-Peck and Millward, *Public and Private Ownership*, 124–33; Wilson, 'Motives for gas nationalization'.

65. Hughes, *Networks of Power*; Hannah, 'Public policy and the advent of large-scale technology'.

66. Hannah, *Electricity before Nationalisation*, 147; Chick, 'The political economy of nationalization'.

67. Ashworth, *Economic History*, 9, 76–80.

68. Wrigley, *Continuity, Chance and Change*, 84–6.

69. Ashworth, *Economic History*, 79–100.

70. Wardley, 'Emergence of big business', 92, 98, 100.

71. Alford, *W. D. and H. O. Wills*; Wilson, *Unilever*; Coleman, *Courtaulds*.

72. Payne, 'Emergence', 522; Church, *Coal Industry*, iii, 133–46.

73. Armstrong, 'Hooley'; Jones, 'Dunlop'; *ODNB* entries on E. T. Hooley, A. P. Du Cros, James White.

74. Hannah, *Rise of the Corporate Economy*, 21.

75. Payne, 'Emergence', 528, 539–41.

76. Lamoreaux, *Great Merger Movement*; Nussbaum, 'Cartels and syndicates'.

77. Hannah, *Rise of the Corporate Economy*, 27, 28, 31; *ODNB* on Urwick.

78. Reader, *Imperial Chemical Industries*, i. 464 and ii. 7.

79. *ODNB* entries on De Paula and Cooper.

80. Hannah, *Rise of the Corporate Economy*, 72, 82–5.

81. Ibid. 37, 46.

82. Tolliday, *Business, Banking and Politics*, 269.

83. Hannah, *Rise of the Corporate Economy*; Bamberg, 'Rationalisation of the British cotton industry'.

84. Tolliday, *Business, Banking and Politics*, 336.

85. Ibid. 341, 336.

86. Supple, 'Political economy of demoralization'; Supple, *Coal Industry*, iv: *1913–1946*, ch. 7, 297; Tolliday, *Business, Banking and Politics*, 339, 342.

FURTHER READING

Alborn, T., *Conceiving Companies: Joint-Stock Politics in Victorian England* (1998)

Alford, B. W. E., *W. D. and H. O. Wills and the Development of the UK Tobacco Industry 1786–1965* (1973)

Ames, E., and Rosenberg, N., 'The Enfield arsenal in theory and history', *Economic Journal*, 78 (1968)

Armstrong, J., 'Hooley and the Bovril Company', *Business History*, 28 (1986)

Ashworth, W., *An Economic History of England, 1870–1939* (1960)

—— 'Changes in the industrial structure', *Yorkshire Bulletin of Economic and Social* Research, 17 (1965)

Bamberg, J. H., 'The rationalisation of the British cotton industry in the interwar years', *Textile History*, 19 (1988)

Bell, F., *At the Works* (1908)

Biagini, E. F., 'Liberalism and direct democracy: John Stuart Mill and the model of ancient Athens', in E. F. Biagini (ed.), *Citizenship and Community: Liberals, Radicals and Collective Identities in the British Isles 1865–1931* (Cambridge, 1996)

Booth, A., 'The manufacturing failure hypothesis and the performance of British industry during the long boom', *Economic History Review*, 56 (2003)

Bowden, S. M., 'Demand and supply constraints in the interwar UK car industry: did the manufacturers get it right?', *Business History*, 33 (1991)

Broadberry, S. N., *The Productivity Race: British Manufacturing in International Perspective, 1850–1990* (Cambridge, 1997)

—— 'Manufacturing and the convergence hypothesis: what the long-run data show', *Journal of Economic History*, 53 (1993)

—— and Crafts, N. F. R., 'British economic policy and industrial performance in the early postwar period', *Business History*, 38 (1996)

Brody, D., *Steelworkers in America* (Cambridge, Mass., 1960)

Byatt, I. C. R., *The British Electrical Industry, 1875–1914: The Economic Returns of a New Technology* (Oxford, 1979)

Cain, P. J., and Hopkins, A. G., 'Gentlemanly capitalism and British expansion overseas, II: new imperialism, 1850–1945', *Economic History Review*, 39 (1986)

Cassis, Y., *Big Business: The European Experience in the Twentieth Century* (Oxford, 1997)

Chandler, A. D., *Strategy and Structure: Chapters in the History of the Industrial Enterprise* (Cambridge, Mass., 1962)

—— *Scale and Scope: The Dynamics of Industrial Capitalism* (Cambridge, Mass., 1990)

Chapman, S. J., 'Some theoretical objectives to sliding-scales', *Economic Journal*, 13 (1903)

Chatterton, D. A., 'State control of public utilities in the nineteenth century: the London gas industry', *Business History*, 14 (1972)

Chick, M., 'The political economy of nationalization: the electricity industry', in R. Millward and J. Singleton (eds.), *The Political Economy of Nationalisation in Britain, 1920–1950* (Cambridge, 1995).

Church, R. A., *The History of the British Coal Industry*, i: *1830–1913, Victorian Pre-Eminence* (Oxford, 1986)

Clegg, H. A., Fox, A., and Thompson, A. F., *A History of British Trade Unions since 1889*, i: *1889–1910* (Oxford, 1964)

Coleman, D. C., *Courtaulds: An Economic and Social History*, ii: *Rayon* (Oxford, 1969)

Collini, S., *Public Moralists: Political Thought and Intellectual Life in Britain, 1850–1930* (Oxford, 1991)

Curthoys, M., *Governments, Labour and the Law in Mid-Victorian Britain: The Trade Union Legislation of the 1870s* (Oxford, 2004)

Daunton, M. J. (ed.), *The Cambridge Urban History of Britain*, iii: *1840–1950* (Cambridge, 2000)

—— 'Down the pit: work in the Great Northern and South Wales coalfields, 1870–1914', *Economic History Review*, 34 (1981)

—— 'Jack ashore: seamen in Cardiff before 1914', *Welsh History Review*, 9 (1978)

—— 'The material politics of natural monopoly: consuming gas in Victorian Britain', in M. Daunton and M. Hilton (eds.), *The Politics of Consumption* (Oxford, 2000)

—— 'Inter-union relations on the waterfront: Cardiff 1880–1914', *International Review of Social History*, 22 (1877)

Davidson, R., *Whitehall and the Labour Problem in Late-Victorian and Edwardian Britain* (Beckenham, 1985)

Dellheim, C., *The Face of the Past: The Preservation of the Medieval Inheritance in Victorian England* (Cambridge, 1982)

Dickens, C., *Hard Times* (1854; Everyman edn. 1907)

Dobbin, F., *Forging Industrial Policy: The United States, Britain and France in the Railway Age* (Cambridge, 1994)

Drummond, D., *Crewe: Railway Town, Company and People 1840–1914* (Aldershot, 1984)

Duffy, A. E. P., 'New unionism in Britain, 1889–90: a reappraisal', *Economic History Review*, 14 (1961)

Edgerton, D., *Warfare State: Britain, 1920–1970* (Cambridge, 2006)

—— and Horrocks, S., 'British industrial research and development before 1914', *Economic History Review*, 47 (1984)

Engels, F., *Condition of the Working Class in England*, ed. W. O. Henderson and W. H. Chaloner (Oxford, 1958)

Evans, E. W., *The Miners of South Wales* (Cardiff, 1961)

Farnie, D. A., *The English Cotton Industry and the World Market, 1815–96* (1979)

Floud, R., *The British Machine Tool Industry, 1850–1914* (Cambridge, 1976)

Foreman-Peck, J., and Millward, R., *Public and Private Ownership of British Industry, 1820–1914* (Oxford, 1994)

Foster, J., *Class Struggle and the Industrial Revolution: Early Capitalism in Three English Towns* (1974)

Fox, A., *History and Heritage: The Social Origins of the British Industrial Relations System* (1985)

—— 'Industrial relations in nineteenth-century Birmingham', *Oxford Economic Papers*, 7 (1955)

Furner, M. O., 'Knowing capitalism: public investigation and the labour question in the long progressive era', in M. O. Furner and B. Supple (eds.), *The State and Economic Knowledge: The American and British Experiences* (Cambridge, 1990)

Gattrell, V., 'Policeman state', in F. M. L. Thompson (ed.), *The Cambridge Social History of Britain, 1750–1950* (Cambridge, 1990)

Gospel, H. F., *Markets, Firms and the Management of Labour in Modern Britain* (Cambridge, 1992)

Habakkuk, H. J., *American and British Technology in the Nineteenth Century: The Search for Labour Saving Inventions* (Cambridge, 1962)

Halsey, H. I., 'The choice between high-pressure and low-pressure steam power in America in the early nineteenth century', *Journal of Economic History*, 41 (1981)

Hannah, L., 'Mergers in British manufacturing industry, 1880–1918', *Oxford Economic Papers*, NS 26 (1974)

—— *The Rise of the Corporate Economy* (2nd edn., 1983)

—— *Electricity before Nationalisation: A Study of the Development of the Electricity Supply Industry in Britain to 1948* (1979)

—— 'Public policy and the advent of large-scale technology: the case of electricity supply in the USA, Germany and Britain', in N. Horn and J. Kocka (eds.), *Law and the Formation of the Big Enterprise in the Nineteenth and Early Twentieth Centuries* (Göttingen, 1979)

Harley, C. K., 'Skilled labor and the choice of technique in Edwardian industry', *Explorations in Economic History*, 11 (1974)

Harris, H. J., *The Right to Manage: Industrial Relations Policies of American Business in the 1940s* (Madison, 1982)

Harrison, R. (ed.), *Independent Collier: The Coal Miner as Archetypal Proletarian Reconsidered* (Hassocks, 1978)

Hennock, E. P., *Fit and Proper Persons: Ideal and Reality in Nineteenth Century Urban Government* (1973)

Hilton, B., *The Age of Atonement: The Influence of Evangelicalism on Social and Economic Thought 1785–1865* (Oxford, 1988)

Hounsell, D., *From the American System to Mass Production, 1830–1932: The Development of Manufacturing Technology in the United States* (1984).

Hughes, T. P., *Networks of Power: Electrification in Western Society, 1880–1930* (Baltimore, 1983)

Jeffreys, M., and Jeffreys, J. B., 'The wages, hours and trade customs of the skilled engineers in 1861', *Economic History Review*, 17 (1947)

Jewkes, J. and Gray, E. M., *Wages and Labour in the Lancashire Cotton Spinning Industry* (Manchester, 1935)

Johnson, P. 'Class law in Victorian England', *Past and Present*, 141 (1993)

—— 'Civilizing Mammon: laws, morals and the City in nineteenth-century England', in P. Burke, B. Harrison, and Slack, P. (eds.), *Civil Histories: Essays Presented to Sir Keith Thomas* (Oxford, 2000)

Jones, G., 'The growth and performance of British multinationals before 1939: the case of Dunlop', *Economic History Review*, 37 (1984)

Jones, L., 'Public pursuit of private profit? Liberal businessmen and municipal politics in Birmingham, 1865–1900', *Business History*, 25 (1983)

Joyce, P., *Work, Society and Politics: The Culture of the Factory in Later Victorian England* (Brighton, 1980)

Kellett, J. R. *Impact of Railways on Victorian Cities* (1969)

Kingsford, F., *Victorian Railwaymen: The Emergence and Growth of Railway Labour 1830–70* (1970)

Lamoreaux, N., *The Great Merger Movement in American Business, 1895–1904* (1985)

Lazonick, W., *Competitive Advantage on the Shop Floor* (Cambridge, Mass., 1990)

Lazonick, W., 'Production relations, Labour productivity and choice of technique: British and US cotton spinning', *Journal of Economic History*, 41 (1981)

Lenin, V. I., *Imperialism: The Highest Stage of Capitalism*, (French edition, 1920, in *Selected Works*, 1969)

Leunig, T., 'A British industrial success: productivity in the Lancashire and New England cotton-spinning industries a century ago', *Economic History Review*, 56 (2003)

Lewchuk, W., *American Technology and the British Vehicle Industry* (Cambridge, 1987)

Lloyd-Jones, R., and Lewis, M. J., 'Business structure and political economy in Sheffield: the metal traders, 1880–1920', in C. Binfield et al. (eds.), *The History of the City of Sheffield, 1843–1993*, ii: *Society* (Sheffield, 1993)

Lloyd-Jones, R., and Lewis, M. J., *British Industrial Capitalism since the Industrial Revolution* (1998)

Lovell, J., *Stevedores and Dockers* (1969)

McKibbin, R., *The Ideologies of Class: Social Relations in Britain 1880–1950* (Oxford, 1990)

Macleod, D. S., *Art and the Victorian Middle Class: Money and the Making of Cultural Identity* (Cambridge, 1996)

Marshall, A., *Principles of Economics* (1890)

—— *Industry and Trade* (1919)

Marx, K., *The Class Struggles in France, 1848–50*, (Moscow edn. 1952)

—— and Engels, F., *The Communist Manifesto*, ed. G. Stedman Jones (2002)

Matthews, D., 'Laissez-faire and the London gas industry in the nineteenth century: another look', *Economic History Review*, 39 (1986)

Mill, J. S., *Public Agency v Trading Companies: The Economical and Administrative Principles of Water-Supply for the Metropolis* (1851), reprinted in *Collected Works of John Stuart Mill*, v: *Essays on Economics and Society*, ed. J. M. Robson (1967)

—— *Principles of Political Economy* (1848; last major revision 1865)

Millward, R., 'The market behaviour of local utilities in pre-World War I Britain: the case of gas', *Economic History Review*, 44 (1991)

—— and Ward, R., 'From private to public ownership of gas undertakings in England and Wales, 1851–1947: chronology, incidence and causes', *Business History*, 35 (1993)

Mitchell, B. R., with the assistance of P. Deane, *Abstract of British Historical Statistics* (Cambridge, 1962)

Montgomery, D., *The Fall of the House of Labor: The Workplace, the State and American Labor Activism, 1865–1925* (Cambridge, 1987)

—— *Workers' Control in America: Studies in the History of Work, Technology and Labor Struggles* (Cambridge, 1979)

Morgan, N. J., and Moss, M., ' "Wealthy and titled persons": the accumulation of riches in Victorian Britain: the case of Peter Denny', *Business History*, 31 (1989)

Morris, J. H., and Williams, L. J. *The South Wales Coal Industry, 1841–75* (Cardiff, 1958)

Morris, R. J., *Class, Sect and Party: The Making of the British Middle Class. Leeds, 1820–1850* (Manchester, 1990)

—— 'The middle class and the property cycle during the industrial revolution', in T. C. Smout (ed.), *The Search for Wealth and Stability* (1979)

Nussbaum, H., 'Cartels and syndicates in the process of transition from family to large-scale enterprises (Germany and Britain)', in Eighth International Economic History Congress, Budapest, 1982, B9, *From Family Firm to Professional Management: Structure and Performance of Business Enterprise* (1982)

Odber, A. J., 'The origins of industrial peace: the manufactured iron trade of the North of England', *Oxford Economic Papers*, NS 3 (1951)

Payne, P. L., 'The emergence of the large-scale company in Great Britain, 1870–1914', *Economic History Review*, 2nd ser. 20 (1967)

Phelps Brown, E. H., *The Origins of Trade Union Power* (Oxford, 1983)

Phillips, G., *The General Strike: The Politics of Industrial Conflict* (1976)

—— and Whiteside, N., *Casual Labour. The Unemployment Question in the Port Transport Industry, 1880–1970* (Oxford, 1985)

Pigou, A. C. (ed.), *Memorials of Alfred Marshall* (1925)

Pollard, S., *A History of Labour in Sheffield* (Liverpool, 1959)

Price, R., *Masters, Unions and Men: Work Control in Building and the Rise of Labour, 1830–1914* (Cambridge, 1980)

Reader, W. J., *Imperial Chemical Industries: A History*, i: *The Forerunners 1870–1926* (1970) and ii: *The First Quarter of a Century 1926–52* (1975)

Reid, A., 'Dilution, trade unionism and the state in Britain during the First World War', in S. Tolliday and J. Zeitlin (eds.), *Shop Floor Bargaining and the State: Historical and Comparative Perspectives* (Cambridge, 1985)

—— 'Employers' strategies and craft production: the British shipbuilding industry, 1870–1950', in S. Tolliday and J. Zeitlin (eds.), *The Power to Manage?* (1981)

Rodger, R., 'Concentration and fragmentation: capital, labour and the structure of mid-Victorian Scottish industry', *Journal of Urban History*, 14 (1988)

Rose, M. B., *Firms, Networks and Business Values: The British and American Cotton Industries since 1750* (Cambridge, 2000)

Rosenberg, N. (ed.), *The American System of Manufactures: The Report of the Committee on the Machinery of the United States 1855 and the Special Reports of George Wallis and Joseph Whitworth 1854* (Edinburgh, 1969)

—— *Technology and American Economic Growth* (New York, 1972)

Royal Commission on Labour, *Fifth and Final Report* (1894)

Ruskin, J., *Unto this Last: Four Essays on the First Principles of Political Economy* (1862; 1960 edn.)

Sabel, C., and Zeitlin, J., 'Historical alternatives to mass production: politics, markets and technology in nineteenth century industrialisation', *Past and Present*, 108 (1985)

Samuel, R., 'The workshop of the world: steam power and hand technology in mid-Victorian Britain', *History Workshop Journal*, 3 (1977)

—— (ed.), *Miners, Quarrymen and Saltworkers* (1977)

Savage, M., and Miles, A. *The Remaking of the British Working Class, 1840–1940* (1994)

Saville, J., 'Sleeping partnership and limited liability, 1850–56', *Economic History Review*, 8 (1955–6)

Scranton, P., *Endless Novelty: Speciality Production and American Industrialisation, 1865–1925* (Princeton, 1997)

Searle, G. R., *Morality and the Market in Victorian Britain* (Oxford, 1998)

Shannon, H. A., 'The first five thousand limited companies and their duration', *Economic History*, 2 (1930–3)

Steinmetz, W., 'Was there a de-juridification of individual employment relations in Britain?', in W. Steinmetz (ed.), *Private Law and Social Inequality in the Industrial Age* (Oxford, 2000)

Supple, B., 'The political economy of demoralization: the state and the coalmining industry in America and Britain between the wars', *Economic History Review*, 41 (1988)

Supple, B., *The History of the British Coal Industry*, iv: *1913–46: The Political Economy of Decline* (Oxford, 1987)

Taylor, J., 'Commercial fraud and public men in Victorian Britain', *Historical Research*, 78 (2005)

—— *Creating Capitalism: Joint-Stock Enterprise in British Politics and Culture, 1800–70* (Woodbridge, 2006)

Thompson, F. M. L., *The Rise of Respectable Society: A Social History of Victorian Britain 1830–1900* (1988)

—— 'Town and city', in F. M. L. Thompson (ed.), *The Cambridge Social History of Britain, 1750–1950*, i: *Regions and Communities* (Cambridge, 1990)

Tolliday, S., 'Management and labour in Britain, 1896–1939', in S. Tolliday and J. Zeitlin (eds.), *The Automobile Industry and its Workers: Between Fordism and Flexibility* (Cambridge, 1987)

—— 'The failure of mass production unionism in the motor industry, 1914–39', in C. Wrigley (ed.), *A History of British Industrial Relations*, iii: *1914–37* (Brighton, 1987).

Tolliday, S., 'Ford and "Fordism" in postwar Britain: enterprise management and the control of labour, 1937–87', in S. Tolliday and J. Zeitlin (eds.), *The Power to Manage?* (1981)

—— *Business, Banking and Politics: The Case of British Steel, 1918–39* (Cambridge, Mass., 1987)

Tomlinson, J., *Government and Enterprise since 1900: The Changing Problem of Efficiency* (Oxford, 1994)

Townsend, C., *Making the Peace: Public Order and Public Security in Modern Britain* (Oxford, 1993)

Trainor, R., *Black Country Elites: The Exercise of Authority in an Industrialized Area, 1830–1900* (Oxford, 1993)

—— , 'The gentrification of Victorian and Edwardian industrialists', in A. L. Baier, D. Cannadine, and J. M. Rosenheim (eds.), *The First Modern Society* (Cambridge, 1989)

Turner, H. A., *Trade Union Growth, Structure and Policy: A Comparative Study of the Cotton Unions* (1962)

Tweedale, G., *Steel City: Entrepreneurship, Strategy, and Technology in Sheffield, 1743–1993* (Oxford, 1995)

—— *Sheffield Steel and America: A Century of Commercial and Technological Interdependence, 1830–1930* (Cambridge, 1987)

Waller, B., *The Dukeries Transformed: The Social and Political Development of a Twentieth-Century Coalfield* (Oxford, 1983)

Warburton, W. H., *The History of Trade Union Organisation in the North Staffordshire Potteries* (1931)

Wardley, P., 'The emergence of big business: the largest corporate employers of labour in the UK, Germany and the US, c.1907', *Business History*, 41 (1999)

Webb, S., and Webb, B., *The History of Trade Unionism* (1901)

White, J. L., *The Limits of Trade Union Militancy: The Lancashire Textile Workers, 1910–14* (1978)

Wiener, M., *English Culture and the Decline of the Industrial Spirit, 1850–1980* (Cambridge, 1981)

Williams, J. H., 'The south Wales sliding scale, 1876–9: an experiment in industrial relations', *Manchester School*, 28 (1960)

—— 'The coalowners of south Wales, 1873–80: problems of unity', *Welsh History Review*, 8 (1976)

Wilson, C., *The History of Unilever: A Study in Economic Growth and Social Change*, 2 vols. (1954)

Wilson, J. F., 'The motives for gas nationalization: practicality or ideology?', in R. Millward and J. Singleton (eds.), *The Political Economy of Nationalisation in Britain, 1920–1950* (Cambridge, 1995)

Wrigley, E. A., Continuity, Chance and Change (Cambridge, 1988)

Zeitlin, J., 'From labour history to the history of industrial relations', *Economic History Review*, 40 (1987)

—— 'The internal politics of employer organization: the Engineering Employers' Federation, 1896–1939', in S. Tolliday and J. Zeitlin (eds.), *The Power to Manage? Employers and Industrial Relations in Comparative Historical Perspective* (1981)

—— 'The triumph of adversarial bargaining: industrial relations in British engineering, 1880–1939', *Politics and Society*, 18 (1990)

—— 'The labour strategies of British engineering employers, 1896–1922', in H. F. Gospel and C. R. Littler (eds.), *Managerial Strategy and Industrial Relations: An Historical and Comparative Survey* (1983)

—— 'Between flexibility and mass production: strategic ambiguity and selective adaptation in British engineering, 1840–1914', in C. Sabel and J. Zeitlin (eds.), *World of Possibilities: Flexibility and Mass Production in Western Industrialization* (Cambridge, 1997)

....

CHAPTER 4

The Service Economy

In 1966, Nicholas Kaldor posed a question which troubled politicians and economists at the time: why was the growth of the British economy so slow? His answer was that Britain had already passed through the major structural transition from agriculture to manufacturing and was experiencing a second structural change: a shift from manufacturing into services. The result, Kaldor argued, was slow growth, for he assumed that the service sector had lower productivity than manufacturing. In his opinion, faster economic growth could be achieved by moving labour back into manufacturing. His approach was adopted by James Callaghan, Labour's Chancellor of the Exchequer, who introduced a tax on employment in the service sector. The Conservatives derided the tax as a belief that the heavy industries of the past provided the real basis for the economy and argued that Labour was committed to a 'ludicrously old-fashioned view of the structure of our economy'. Industry now relied on an efficient banking, insurance, and distribution system.[1]

These two views informed debates over Britain's future—and over the interpretation of its past. The concern of Kaldor and other economists led them to search for the origins of decline from the late nineteenth century largely in the industrial sector. By contrast, much less was written about the service economy: when it was considered, it was often to explain the difficulties experienced by industry. Thus banks were criticized for neglecting the needs of domestic industry, and comparisons were drawn with the supposedly more supportive role of German and American banks. In 1910, J. A. Hobson divided the country into the consumers' south, where a rich class of rentiers and financiers enjoyed a leisured life, and a producers' north, where industrialists and workers produced real value. The division formed the basis of Peter Cain and A. G. Hopkins's notion of metropolitan 'gentlemanly capitalists' created by a fusion of land and finance in southern England. In Cain and Hopkins's interpretation, the middle class was divided and the financial sector largely looked to the empire rather than to the needs of industry.[2]

By the 1980s, the Thatcher government was taking a different view. The old industrial districts should be allowed to decay for the future was in the service sector, and most obviously the City. A number of historians pointed out that Britain had always been much more successful in the service sector than in manufacturing.[3] Manufacturing, it followed, could be allowed to wither away: the production of goods could move to areas of the world with low labour costs and Britain could concentrate on design, advertising, finance, and credit. By no means everyone was convinced. The expansion of service employment was not only in creative, highly paid jobs, but also in lowly paid, casual work; and the decline of industry in many northern cities led to poverty and social exclusion. In the opinion of Will Hutton the problems of industry could be explained by the short-termism of the City of London, its pursuit of quick profits rather than long-term investment and development.[4] On this view, gentlemanly capitalism and its indifference to industry applied to the 1980s as much as to the 1900s.

These debates provide the context for historical interpretations of the previous century or so. We need to focus on two issues. First, in comparative terms, British performance in many services was much better than in manufacturing. Whereas labour productivity in American manufacturing industry was more than double the British level by the end of the nineteenth century, the gap was still modest in distribution, finance, and government in 1950; only in transport and communications did the United States establish a lead on the same scale as in manufacturing. In Germany, labour productivity in distribution, finance, and government was still below Britain in 1950. However, Germany did secure a lead in transport and communications (see Table 4.1). Why was Britain relatively more successful in some parts of the service sector? The second issue is the rate of change in productivity. Since the end of the nineteenth century, the divergence in labour productivity in industry has been relatively stable. By contrast, the performance of the service sector in the United States and Germany improved relative to Britain. America's and Germany's superior performance in the economy as a whole is to be explained by two processes: moving workers from agriculture; and improving the relative performance in services.[5] Clearly, Kaldor's assumption that services did not experience major gains in productivity was incorrect.[6]

The service sector experienced significant change between 1850 and 1950. There was a shift from 'customized, low-volume, high-margin business organized on a network basis to modern business enterprise, characterized by standardized, high-volume, low-margin business and multiple operating units managed by a hierarchy of salaried executives'.[7] The rate of change varied between services. In some cases, customers preferred personal service in high-margin businesses, and economies of scale were inappropriate; in other cases, change would have been economically rational but was prevented by restraints on trade or measures to stop the growth of nationwide banking concerns (as in the USA) or monopolistic railways. Variations in the levels of labour productivity reflected the use of technologies to communicate

TABLE 4.1. *Comparative productivity levels, services, UK, USA, and Germany, 1869–1950 (UK = 100)*

	1869/71		1909/11		1935/7		1950	
	USA	Gmy	USA	Gmy	USA	Gmy	USA	Gmy
Transport/communications	110.0	96.8	217.4	216.9	283.4	132.4	348.4	122.0
Distribution	66.9	n.a.	120.0	52.5	119.8	54.3	135.2	50.7
Finance/services	64.1	89.7	77.9	76.3	96.1	105.6	111.5	94.2
Government	114.3	97.8	95.8	98.2	100.0	100.0	116.2	96.9

Source: Broadberry, 'How did the United States and Germany overtake Britain?', 378, 382.

and to process information, which in turn depended on a workforce with the appropriate education and attitudes.[8] Any explanation of variations in the comparative level and rate of change in labour productivity in the service sector should avoid assuming that a divide between industry and services was central to the poor performance of industry. Instead, we should consider the productivity record of the service sector itself.

In any case, gentlemanly capitalism and industry were far less distinct than Cain and Hopkins claim. The questions should be changed. Rather than stressing the failure of British banks to provide long-term finance to industry, we might ask whether British banks were successful in creating financial stability and providing credit for the purchase of goods. Although insurance companies placed a considerable part of their investments overseas, they were not ignoring the needs of domestic industrial society but providing security against the endemic risks of old age, illness, fire, or motoring accidents. It was not enough to produce goods: they had to be advertised, distributed, and sold, which relied on marketing and credit. The expansion of multiple shops in the food trades and the emergence of new consumer goods were intimately connected with overseas investment and the financial services of the City. Chain stores sold tea from India and meat from Argentina; pianos used African ivory for their keys; bicycles needed rubber from Malaya for their tyres; and electrical wiring could not work without copper from southern Africa. The investors and financiers of the City profited from their involvement in overseas investment and financial services, but their activities cannot be separated from the dynamics of the domestic, industrial economy. Further, investment at home and overseas was less clearly divided between north and south than is often assumed. Both individual and institutional investors wished to diversify their portfolios in order to reduce risk.

Transport and Communications

Both the United States and Germany had a marked lead over Britain in labour productivity in transport and communications by the First World War; here Britain fell behind its main competitors to a greater extent than in manufacturing industry (see Table 4.1.). The result was important not only for the efficiency of transport and communications, but also for the economy more generally. How is this poor performance to be explained?

The answer would not appear to be scale. Around 1907, 46.1 per cent of the employees of the 130 largest concerns in Britain were in transport and communications. The single largest employer in the country was the General Post Office with 199,178 workers; the next, a long way behind, was the London and North Eastern Railway with 84, 377. In terms of market value, the railways were dominant; the Post Office as a public enterprise does not appear in the lists. The Midland Railway had the highest market value in 1904/5, at £136.7 m; the largest industrial company, J. and P. Coats, was twelfth with a market value of £42.1 m. Railways were still amongst the largest concerns in 1934/5, but the gap had closed. In 1934/5, the London, Midland, and Scottish Railway had the largest market value of any concern in Britain, at £306.8 m, but Imperial Tobacco was second with a market value of £259.3 m. As we have noted, British companies were large by international standards, and railways were amongst the very largest.[9]

Of course, British railways might still be smaller than their counterparts in other countries, and government policy up to the First World War prevented amalgamations. However, the problem facing British railways was less a matter of scale than cost structure and the way that charges were determined. British railways faced high costs as a result of parliamentary procedures in authorizing their construction. The creation of a railway network led to an immediate problem: on what terms should they be allowed to acquire land? Any company could apply to parliament for a private Act, and competing lines were seen as desirable. In each case, parliament decided whether the benefit justified expropriation of land or demolition of buildings on the approach to stations. The companies were heavily dependent on lawyers to steer the private bills through parliament and to negotiate the purchase of land. Although the process was simplified in 1845, costs remained high. The result was a serious long-term problem: revenues and variable costs were comparable with other countries, but unregulated construction raised costs by 50 per cent around 1900.[10]

High construction costs affected the internal politics of the companies. The directors were heavily dependent on financiers for loans, and in the early years they had to give priority to paying interest to financiers over distributing dividends to disaffected shareholders. The rhetoric of parliamentary reform and taxation was easily applied to the railway companies, for the directors could be seen as analogous to unaccountable, unreformed politicians. Passengers and freighters—like taxpayers—were also concerned about the charges imposed by the companies. Rowland Hill, the creator of the penny post in 1840, complained that the greed of the companies undermined the finances of the postal service; he called for state control.[11] Parliament's response, in return for allowing the companies to acquire land, was to set fares and freight rates and the level of service. Who should establish these terms, on what basis, and how were the conditions to be policed? In 1840, the Railway Department of the Board of Trade was created to consider the terms of bills and to review the safety of new lines. The Department lacked authority, for it was not concerned with the planning of lines; nor could it require safety measures to be adopted until 1889. In 1844, Gladstone obliged the companies to provide a third-class service on every line at 1d. a mile at least once a day, so that the benefits of the new technology were spread to the workers. Furthermore, the state now had the right to purchase any new line after twenty-one years.

By the 1850s, directors were less dependent on financiers for loans and could pay more attention to shareholders who demanded efficiency from competent chairmen and managers, adopting a rhetoric similar to the demands for administrative reform in the civil service and government. Shareholders were also sympathetic to directors who protected their property from the demands of workers and from customers. Indeed, the case for nationalization was seriously considered by Gladstone, who contemplated using the purchase clause in the 1844 Act. However, the attempt to increase dividends to satisfy shareholders created other difficulties. In order to secure their support against government intervention in favour of the customers, the directors opted to borrow: by securing capital at a modest interest rate, they were able to pay their shareholders higher dividends. They faced a number of questions. Should companies cut wages to increase profit margins; could they secure traffic from other lines by rate discrimination in favour of large customers, or by refusing to carry through traffic from competing lines; or should they end competition and increase fares by merging or negotiating price fixing agreements? Strategy depended on parliamentary approval and could not please everyone. Generally, companies turned away from an initial strategy of mergers (often opposed by parliament) towards cartels and price fixing (often permitted by parliament). British policy took a distinctive form, refusing to sanction mergers or to encourage price competition, both of which threatened smaller concerns. Instead, it protected small firms by banning rate discrimination, and by encouraging cartels and price-fixing agreements.

Traders complained that they were being 'taxed' by unfair rates, and a Railway Commission was established in 1873 to hear complaints. The policy was only a partial success as far as the customers were concerned, for the Commission validated rate-fixing agreements. By 1888, agreements were positively encouraged and the Commission set about creating a national agreement on rates which was implemented in 1893. The companies misjudged their response, opting to raise their rates to the maximum permitted and failing to balance the interests of their customers and shareholders. The government responded with the Railway and Canal Traffic Act of 1894 which allowed complaints against any 'unreasonable' increase in rates. The Railway Commission's interpretation of the Act meant that rates were in effect pegged at a time of rising costs. Consequently, the railway companies' profitability was eroded less by the inefficiencies of managers than by the constraints imposed by parliament. The failure of the railways was political rather than operational.[12]

Pressure from customers for low fares and freight rates collided with two other interests: workers' demands for better wages and conditions; and shareholders' for higher dividends. These competing claims were not easily resolved. Working costs in the UK rose from 51 per cent of revenue in 1870–4 to 62 per cent in 1900–4. From 1896, the finances of railway companies sharply deteriorated as coal prices and wages rose, and the companies embarked on large-scale investment to increase their market share. Not surprisingly, the average return on ordinary shares fell sharply. Many shareholders sold their shares or complained about the directors' policies. Operation of the Act of 1894 prevented higher rates, so opposition to unions was understandable. Trade unions did not fit well with the semi-military discipline of the railways. Workers were strictly disciplined and loyalty to the company was achieved by welfare benefits, housing, promotion hierarchies, and the prospect of a pension. In the early twentieth century, railway workers were more militant, demanding higher wages which the companies could not afford. Here was the background to the hostility of the Taff Vale Railway Co. to their workers in 1900 which followed a shareholders' revolt against low dividends. Tensions intensified with a national railway strike in 1907 and mounting demands for nationalization. The companies were able to convince the government and traders that public ownership would lead to political corruption through rebates for favoured interests, and to high charges. [13]

The railway companies responded to their difficulties in the Edwardian period by attempting to reduce competition or seeking permission to merge. In 1907, Lloyd George apparently conceded the need for agreements or mergers in compensation for the Board of Conciliation imposed on the industry to deal with labour disputes. The Board of Trade reasoned that mergers would not only benefit the companies but also allow efficiency gains both to pay higher wages and charge lower rates. But the proposal soon ran into difficulties in the face of parliamentary opposition, for amalgamation alienated Liberal supporters of the free market and Labour advocates of nationalization. Workers went on strike in 1911 and remained discontented with their wages and conditions. The government responded by allowing the companies to increase freight rates to pay higher wages, so alienating traders. Furthermore, shareholders were unhappy about their low dividends. In 1913, the government appointed a Royal Commission to consider the problem, including the possibility of nationalization. The Commission indicated that change was needed, but the prospects of swift action were not high. The situation was fundamentally changed by the war.[14]

During the First World War, the railways were taken into government control. Management passed to the Railway Executive Committee and in return, the companies were promised compensation for loss of revenue and deferred repairs. At the end of the war, the benefits of co-ordination were stressed in contrast to the inefficiencies and waste of pre-war management, and Labour proposed nationalization. In 1918, the government appointed Eric Geddes, the former general manager of the North Eastern Railway, to reorganize transport. In 1919, he joined the government and proposed a new Ministry of Ways and Communications to control railways, canals, harbours, and road transport as part of a wider economic policy. The proposal was implemented in a more modest form by the Railways Act of 1921. When the companies were returned to their private owners in 1923, the pre-war ambitions of Lloyd George were realized through government action. The existing 120 companies were 'grouped' into four large companies and received considerably less compensation than anticipated. The government could also require them to standardize their equipment and adopt co-operative working. Prior to the return of the companies to private control, the unions secured full recognition, national pay scales, and an eight-hour day, and they retained most of their gains with the establishment of Wage Boards for collective bargaining. The companies were regulated by a new Rates Tribunal which set a target 'standard revenue' of 4 to 5 per cent of capital, with any excess divided between the companies and their customers. The companies had defined geographical regions which limited the opportunities for competition, and rate discrimination was banned. The new companies were, in other words, strictly regulated oligopolies; they were treated as public utilities rather than profitable concerns.

The Act of 1921 contributed to the problems. Some advocates hoped that the economies of scale from amalgamation would be sufficient to allow higher wages, lower charges, and a decent profit. Others were more sceptical, pointing out that economies needed large administration reorganization, and that there were diseconomies of scale from the loss of corporate identity. The sceptics had a point. Economies took some time to appear; meanwhile, the Act limited the freedom of the companies to take rational business decisions. The Rates Tribunal and Wages Board meant that the companies were not able to pursue their own business needs, and they were under pressure to behave as a public utility. The ban on rate discrimination meant that road hauliers were able to undercut the railways, especially for high-value, lighter commodities. The railways' largest customers were depressed industries, and the government was more concerned about their plight than the profitability of the railways. Many of the railway directors were linked with local industries and were more concerned with the needs of the regional economy than with their shareholders. The companies complained that wages were too high, but reductions were modest and difficult to achieve. Working costs continued to rise, reaching 81 per cent of revenue in 1934–8. Not surprisingly, the standard revenue envisaged by the Act was never achieved. Dividends were maintained by drawing on reserves and investment was low.[15]

The structure of the industry remained controversial. Were the existing companies too large, and would competition lead to improved service? Or should amalgamation be taken further? If consolidation was the answer, did this imply nationalization? The companies had no wish to return to the world prior to 1914, yet they were not satisfied with the Act of 1921. Might criticism of rationalization simply offer ammunition to the advocates of nationalization? One response was to concentrate on 'unfair' competition from the road hauliers. Tonnage carried by road rose from 11.3 per cent of the combined total of road and rail in 1927 to 35.3 per cent in 1935.

Consumers' expenditure on railway transport in the UK fell from £72.7 m in 1921 to £53.3 m in 1938, compared with an increase in spending on private motoring from £37 m to £117.4 m, and on buses and coaches from £33.3 m to £64.3 m.[16] The shift was in part a response to the benefits of road transport, but it also reflected policy choices. Road hauliers paid only part of the cost of roads and they paid no interest on the original capital. Nor were they affected by labour regulation.

Increasingly, the Act lost credibility and pressure for nationalization mounted. The report of the Royal Commission on Transport in 1931 accepted the case for a Public Transport Trust, a non-political body apart from the ministry; the minority report went further, arguing for nationalization of transport to co-ordinate both road and rail. When wages were cut on the railways in 1931, the unions pressed for nationalization. By 1937, even William Whitelaw, chairman of the LNER, accepted that shareholders would not oppose nationalization on fair terms. Renewed control during the Second World War meant that nationalization was inescapable, and a government report of 1940/1 recommended it. The case for co-ordination was generally accepted, and the process started with the nationalization of railways, in the hands of the British Railways Board in 1946. Road transport followed. Although Geddes's ambition for co-ordination seemed to be fulfilled, in reality transport policy remained unsystematic.[17]

The model was the London Passenger Transport Board, a public corporation outside direct ministerial control. Both the private underground lines and the bus companies had been reaching agreements or merging since the turn of the century. In 1933, they amalgamated, together with the London County Council trams, as a single authority. The new concern was largely based on the existing underground group, with continuity of management. Public ownership of transport facilities had long been a feature of British cities. Docks and harbours were often owned by public bodies, reflecting massive investment and their long-term or social returns. Indeed, the Port of London Authority of 1909 was a precursor of the corporate form of the LPTB: the financially precarious docks and wharves were transferred to a public corporation rather than to the LCC which was considered too powerful and politically partisan.

In many towns, tramways were taken over by local councils. The need to tear up streets for tram lines meant that a single operator was given authority with the dangers of monopoly power. The companies were regulated by the Tramways Act 1870: local authorities granted a company permission to operate for twenty-one years, with the right to purchase at 'then value' when the term expired. Here, it seemed to many commentators, was an explanation for the lag in the development of tramways in Britain. Horse-drawn trams came to Britain only after 1870. Electrification was also slow: in the USA, 84 per cent of lines were electrified by 1895 compared with only 6 per cent in Britain, rising to 38 per cent in 1902. The explanation was not only inappropriate regulation; the market also differed, for British cities grew rapidly before the new transport technology and the companies could not share in the profits from land unlike their counterparts in America. Conversion to electricity became feasible only when existing lines were fully depreciated and they could be rebuilt for heavier electric trams. This point was reached at the end of the century, coinciding with the building boom of the late 1890s. At the same time, many municipalities took over the companies, and their access to loans on favourable terms encouraged investment. By 1925, 73 per cent of mileage was in public hands, and electric trams allowed a large reduction in fares. Although some local authorities took over buses, effective control only started during the war when the government tried to limit the number of routes. When operators pressed for greater freedom from control they were opposed by larger companies who wished to limit competition. Independent Traffic Commissioners were created in 1930 with comprehensive licensing powers, so removing competition in bus services for the next fifty years—a common feature of the British economy at this time.[18]

The single largest concern in nineteenth-century Britain was a public body—the Post Office. Unlike later nationalized bodies that followed the model of the public corporation, the Post Office was a department of state under a minister and its employees were civil servants. Expansion started with the penny post of 1840 which was extended to cover the entire country and from 1898 the empire. Contracts were negotiated with the railway companies and subsidies were paid to steamships and airlines to carry mail overseas. The Post Office moved into financial services with postal orders from 1860, and the Post Office Savings Bank from 1861 to encourage thrift amongst the poor. In 1870, it took over telegraphs and in 1912 telephones. The Post Office was widely seen as efficient, but in the twentieth century it started to face problems with doubts that a highly centralized system could cope with the pressure of work. Reform was slow. Clement Attlee, Postmaster General in the Labour government of 1929–31, not surprisingly concluded that nationalised industries should not be run by civil servants under the Treasury and parliamentary control. The approach of the LPTB seemed much more appropriate.[19]

The telegraph system was nationalized in 1870 to create an integrated system for the entire country. The private telegraph companies were earning large profits and charging high rates for a poor service. Free enterprise was seen as wasteful and inefficient, creating an oligopoly which exploited the public and did not deliver the supposed merits of competition. There were three possible solutions: a regulated private monopoly; competition with the right to erect lines on public wayleaves; or nationalization. The third solution was adopted by both Conservative and Liberal administrations. The Post Office was at the height of its reputation, and its zealous and confident officials were eager for new opportunities. The policy had the blessing of the provincial press which was heavily dependent on telegraph companies for transmitting news; nationalization was welcomed as a way of escaping from existing contracts. Nationalization was widely expected to produce a profit for the government, lower charges, and deliver a better level of service. It would promote the flow of information and create a united nation. In the event, confidence in the Post Office was misplaced for the purchase price was excessive, workers were able to secure higher wages, and the press negotiated unduly generous terms. The telegraph system slumped into deficit.[20]

The rate of development of telephones in Britain was slower than in Germany and the United States. In 1910, there were 8.3 telephones per 1,000 population in the USA, but only 0.2 in the United Kingdom; in 1930, the figures were 16.3 and 4.1 respectively, and in 1950 28.4 and 10.2.[21] To some extent, the lag was rational, for Britain had a cheap and efficient postal service. But much of the explanation is to be found in the failures of regulation. The Post Office was involved from the first, for it had the right to lay wires along public wayleaves and the courts ruled in 1880 that its monopoly in the operation of telegraphs applied equally to telephones. The development of the private companies was therefore closely regulated by the Post Office. The initial response was to license private companies for twenty-one years in return for a royalty and with the right to purchase after fixed intervals. But the government and Post Office were inconsistent, shifting their policy with scant regard for efficiency. At one moment, the policy was to foster competition between private companies, at another between private companies and municipal operators, at another between the private companies and the Post Office, and on other occasions to seek co-operation between private companies and state-owned trunk lines. The motivation of the government was, in part, to force down the value of the private companies prior to nationalization; and the strategy of the private companies rested on maximizing their value. As the Post Office pointed out in 1911, the result was friction and divided responsibility. In the case of the telegraphs, the Post Office was seen as the saviour of an inadequate private system; in the case of telephones, the state produced a muddle. In the end, nationalization was the 'least expensive escape route', a solution accepted by both Conservative and Liberal administrations. In 1912, the telephone industry was nationalized in the hands of the Post Office and investment was constrained by Treasury control.[22]

Financial Services

In financial, professional, and personal services, the United States had a small advantage in productivity by the First World War, but fell below British productivity during the 1930s; after the Second World War, the USA overtook Britain by a relatively small margin (see Table 4.1). Britain remained more efficient than

Germany. A personal approach with high margins was necessary in the case of large transactions; for small transactions, a more impersonal and standardized approach was possible. In this mass market, Britain had large concerns such as the Prudential and the Post Office Savings Bank, and the growth of national branches in retail banking stood in marked contrast to the USA. British financial services were efficient and sophisticated, a corrective to a single narrative of 'decline' and to the supposed domination of financial services by 'gentlemanly capitalism'.

A frequent criticism of British banks was that they neglected domestic industry and concentrated on overseas loans. In this view, Britain had the most sophisticated financial centre in the world in the City of London yet ignored the needs of industrialists. In W. P. Kennedy's words, 'capital markets in the US and Germany, by making resources available to a large group of technologically progressive industries on a scale unequalled in Britain, account for much of the difference in the economic growth performance between these two countries and Britain'.[23] As noted earlier, the explanation has often been sought in the cultural assumptions of financiers who socialized with and married into the landed aristocracy. This point is linked with institutional and state structures: the Bank of England's Court was dominated by the leading international bankers to the exclusion of domestic bankers, and the Bank and Treasury were interconnected. Above all, British bankers are criticized for concentrating on short-term credit at the expense of long-term loans and an active role in restructuring firms. British industry, so the story continues, could not respond to the changing world economy, remaining trapped in small-scale proprietary capitalism with weak management hierarchies. The point has been made most forcefully by Michael Best and Jane Humphries. 'It was in its inability to become a dynamic force in the reorganization of basic industry that, in comparative and relative terms, the British financial system "failed".'[24] On this view, firms were forced to rely on a capital market through easily traded shares and debentures. The result, so the critics claim, was 'short-termism': investors could easily sell if profits and dividends were not maintained; and companies might face a takeover if share values dropped. Immediate profit was therefore given priority over long-term success.[25] Just how plausible is this critique?

The interpretation rests on a comparison between two approaches to banking and to the organization of industry. British 'transaction banking' made loans to industrial concerns without control over their management or organization; ownership was in the hands of families or partnerships, with changes depending on succession, failure, or sale. In the twentieth century, the growth of joint-stock companies meant that change in control or ownership rested on a market-based system of exchange of shares. In Germany, change in ownership and management was more dependent on 'organizational control' and 'relationship banking': bankers sat on the boards of industrial firms, forming interlocking directorships with the ability to reorganize industry and take a more long-term, strategic control. The German investment bankers are seen as positive forces in shaping the economy: 'it was they who very often mapped out a firm's path of growth, conceived far-sighted plans, decided on major technological and locational innovations, and arranged for mergers and capital increases.'[26]

The comparison has serious shortcomings. The first is that many German industrialists were delighted to escape from the hold of bankers after the First World War when inflation allowed them to repay loans. The link between bankers and industrialists might block entry to newcomers by directing funds to a small number of firms.[27] The second is that the connection between industry and banks might lead to financial instability. The low level of direct involvement of British banks contributed to the financial stability which was such a striking feature of Britain between the Great Exhibition and the Festival of Britain. Finally, Britain was not alone in failing to develop universal banks: a closer inspection of the practice in other European countries shows many similarities with the British pattern.[28]

Criticism of the financial sector focuses on the City of London, and above all the international financial houses. As far as most industrialists in the second half of the nineteenth century were concerned, these London merchant bankers were irrelevant; their contacts were local. British bankers had a clear rationale for their approach to industry, and they should not necessarily be criticized for failing to adopt the German approach. A major feature of British banking was a preference for highly liquid assets which could easily be converted into cash. The banks' preference connected with the nature of their liabilities: money held in current or short-term deposit accounts which could be repaid on demand or short notice. The growth of deposits in British banks reflected the highly commercial nature of British society and a rise in incomes, and was actively pursued by extending branch networks to 'tap' deposits. The issue was not a bias against industry or irrational risk aversion. The widespread use of bank accounts shaped the banks' lending policies: they needed a high proportion of cash and assets placed at short notice with other financial institutions in order to cover the deposits of thousands of individuals. The liquid assets of English and Welsh banks rose from 23 per cent in the mid-1860s to 42–3 per cent from 1892 to 1910. The banks responded to the financial crises of 1866 and 1878 by increasing their liquidity ratio so that they were less susceptible to panics. The other major influence was mergers, for the London-based banks were more liquid than provincial concerns and, over time, took a larger market share. Mergers contributed to the stability of the financial system, but also to the loss of local autonomy. In 1870, the largest ten banks were responsible for 32.8 per cent of deposits in England and Wales, growing to 64.7 per cent in 1910 and 96.6 per cent in 1920; the share of the largest five banks grew from 25.0 per cent to 43.0 per cent and 80.0 per cent. By contrast, Scottish banks did not consolidate, and their earlier lead over England in bank assets and notes per head narrowed. As Collins and Baker conclude, 'It was the English commercial banks' ability to retain a highly liquid loan portfolio and to minimize loss that helped create an extremely stable banking system in the decades before World War I.' [29]

The criticism of British banks for failing to lend to industry can be turned round by arguing that they were part of a highly monetized and commercial society. The banks faced a political task of balancing the claims of their shareholders, depositors, and borrowers. This was not always easy, and in some countries banks are seen as exploitative of borrowers and a threat to the business community. Hostility to 'money power' was common in the United States, Germany, and France. British banks were less likely to be seen as threats. The joint-stock banks changed from essentially local bodies in the early nineteenth century bringing together shareholders, depositors, and borrowers, to regional and national bodies drawing on a large number of depositors. The banks maintained widespread acceptance by stressing their modernity, efficiency, and probity, and at the same time offered good dividends. One reason for lack of hostility was that many more customers were depositors than borrowers. The reliance on the London money market as an outlet for deposits meant that a major source of profits came from outside the local community and, indeed, outside the country and so lacked political voice. The abundance of money from bankers seeking outlets for their funds on the London market contributed to the efficiency of the Stock Exchange which had abundant credit for its deals; and the active market in securities meant that the banks could purchase long-term bonds in the knowledge that they could sell in times of need. The domestic banks therefore formed part of the same financial system as the merchant banks in London, linking provinces and metropolis, industrial capitalism and gentlemanly capitalism. The domestic banks gathered the small deposits of a large number of middle-class families who needed liquidity and easy access to their money, and in turn loaned the money to discount houses and stockbrokers in London, aware that they could secure repayment at short notice. The arrangement helped to sustain the international economy, and offered benefits to the middle class of provincial towns. Meanwhile, shareholders received decent dividends with confidence in the safety of their investment.[30]

The banks did not ignore the needs of local industrialists. At the beginning of the period, many local banking concerns had overlapping directorships with industrialists and close ties with the rest of the business community. By the end of the nineteenth century, these links were weaker. As we have seen, many local banks were submerged in larger concerns under the control of London head office, and with stricter controls over the decisions of branch managers. Local managers did not make their decisions on the basis of personal reputation gleaned from their participation in the business community so much as financial information of a more impersonal nature. Banking became more professional. The Institute of Bankers was formed in 1879 and set examinations; banks developed promotion hierarchies for their staff, linked with movement around the country to prevent their 'capture' by local businessmen. Strict systems of internal controls and close monitoring of accounts were linked with local knowledge of the firm and the character of the partners and directors. Banks were well placed to 'screen' borrowers, assessing their creditworthiness and monitoring their performance. They had 'insider information' through access to bank accounts and could obtain confidential information when agreeing to a loan; they were also better able to assess the collateral. In other words, the banks dealt with problems of 'moral hazard' and 'adverse selection' much more effectively than individuals. The costs of gathering information and monitoring fell as banks increased in scale. The banks allowed depositors to obtain a better return on their assets: individuals with a need for liquidity would not lend to industrial concerns, whereas the banks could.[31]

The absence of long-term loans did not mean that banks neglected the needs of industry. Most industrialists were able to find long-term capital by calling on partners, family, and shareholders, and from ploughed-back profits. Even when these sources proved inadequate, most firms were able to secure long-term funds by issuing debentures, often on better terms than bank loans.[32] On the whole, industrialists did not feel constrained by the lending policies of the banks, and the comparison with Germany could be turned around by arguing that Britain had a greater availability of non-bank funds. Perhaps domestic banks ignored investment banking for the obvious reason that the financial system was more varied than in Germany.[33] Banks were only one source of external finance in Britain and the provision of investment capital was left to other sectors of a sophisticated market for financial services. When industrialists turned to the banks, it was mainly for short-term loans or overdrafts for working capital to pay wages, purchase raw materials, or provide credit to customers. Nevertheless, around a fifth of loans covered capital expenditure. The system was flexible. The banks often did not require collateral and might rely on personal guarantees. Although contemporary banking ideology stressed that loans should be short and self-liquidating, reality was more complex. Renewal was common and banks continued to lend to firms in distress, for strict vetting of loans and their short formal duration reduced risk. Collins and Baker found total losses on only 0.2 per cent of loans between 1860 and 1913. The banks did become more liquid up to the First World War, and were arguably less supportive of industry. Nevertheless, they provided flexible open credit for working costs and cash flow, and there were no bank failures after 1878. Regulation was unimportant in creating stability: the banks learned 'good behaviour' within the framework of the Bank Charter Act of 1844 and were left to their own devices.[34]

Criticism of the banks was a common theme in the 1920s and 1930s. Did British banks fail to address the problems of the declining staple industries, and neglect to provide funds to the new, expanding industries? In 1931, a government Committee on Finance and Industry (the Macmillan Committee) concluded that links between British firms and industry had never been as strong as in Germany, and recommended the creation of a specialist financial institution. Similar sentiments were expressed by *The Economist* and the Federation of British Industries. Bankers protested that solving industry's problems was not their task.

The British banks were disingenuous for they did intervene if they felt that businesses were badly run. Lloyds helped remove Thomas Lipton and William Lever from control of their firms; and the Midland Bank played an active role as a creditor of the Austin Motor Co. More generally, banks took a leading role in the 'rationalization' of cotton and steel. Here, the complaint of the critics is not that the banks failed to intervene but that they were merely concerned with minimizing their losses. The Bank of England was alarmed that the banks were exposed by their loans, and that the stability of the banking system might be compromised. Accordingly, the Bank encouraged mergers and established the Securities Management Trust and the Bankers' Industrial Development Co. to restructure industry. These bodies, so the critics argue, were less concerned with industrial efficiency than with reducing risk; once that aim was achieved, they retreated. The banks were, on this view, conservative and obstructive.

The criticisms are not entirely fair, and they rely on inappropriate comparisons with Germany. In the steel industry, the banks were constrained by industrialists who were able to play one bank off against another; the problem was internal divides within the industry as different firms and regions tried to secure an advantage. Why should banks be expected to solve the difficulties of industry when industrialists themselves were so divided? The banks had their own businesses to consider—above all, to ensure that their shareholders received dividends, their depositors retained confidence, and the financial system remained stable. Why should they be expected to reform industry which was not within their remit or expertise? The Macmillan Committee held up Germany as the model, without pondering whether Britain had developed a different financial system. Indeed, it might even be argued that the British system was more sophisticated and specialized. *The Economist* was well aware of this when it warned the Macmillan Committee not to attack the banks for failing to undertake the work of issuing houses, discount dealers, and foreign exchange dealers.

In Britain, domestic industrial issues of shares expanded in the 1920s and 1930s, and merchant banks such as Morgan Grenfell and Barings took an active role. At the same time, investment trusts expanded and insurance companies placed a larger proportion of their funds in industrial shares. These institutional investors helped to mitigate the risks of individuals; and the market operated as a clear signal on the performance of the companies. If the companies were not performing well and dividends fell, there was a strong incentive for shareholders, and above all institutional investors, to demand change. Companies were also exposed to potential mergers or takeovers so that industrial performance and restructuring were driven by market signals. The existence of information meant that firms could raise finance through marketable securities rather than bank loans; and these securities were readily traded, allowing restructuring of concerns through the transfer of their ownership rights. There was, as Duncan Ross remarks, a relatively efficient market for corporate control. The universal banks in Germany had a greater role as lenders and investors, with seats on boards; external finance was more likely to take the form of debt, without the ability to transfer securities and ownership rights. Restructuring was left to the banks. Clearly, the holders of debt have every reason to propose restructuring if their loans were threatened by industrial depression or poor performance. But would they be any less likely to take decisions to protect their own finances than British banks, and were the changes in structure any more effective? Indeed, German banks were more exposed to financial instability than their British counterparts as a result of their links with particular firms. The approach recommended by the Macmillan Committee might expose banks to higher risks, so threatening confidence and stability. Britain had a specialized and effective market-oriented financial system; it is not evident that the German organizational approach was superior.[35]

Central to Britain's financial system was the emergence of insurance. The institutions ranged from friendly societies offering protection against the risk of sickness to large life companies offering insurance against death, and eventually 'composite' concerns with a full range of policies. For members of the middle class, life insurance became very important. 'Whole' life insurance provided dependants with a lump sum, and might be used to purchase an annuity. Term or endowment policies paid out after a number of years; they might cover school fees, a dowry, or entry into business for a son, as well as an annuity on retirement. In 1853, Gladstone offered tax relief on life insurance premiums and life insurance became one of the major forms of tax-efficient saving for the middle class.

Starting a life insurance business was relatively simple. These concerns took two forms: commercial or proprietary companies; and mutuals. In theory, mutuals offered a better deal for there were no shareholders to satisfy; in practice, policy holders had little ability to monitor the managers. Despite competition, premiums did not fall; rather, policy holders looked to a share of the surplus through a 'bonus', so that life insurance became an investment opportunity. Since companies were not committed to the bonus in any one year, they had greater flexibility than a reduction in premium levels.

Some entrants were fraudulent and aggressive competition could lead to unsound practices and high costs. The debate over the morality of life insurance led to a Select Committee in 1853: should the government intervene to protect widows and orphans, or should free competition be allowed on the grounds that regulation would weaken 'private prudence and vigilance'? The Committee's proposals were modest: an investment of £10,000 in public funds and registration. In fact, little was done and the insurance industry largely put itself in order. Only with the collapse of the Albert Life Assurance Society in 1870 did the government pass the Life Assurance Companies Act which required new offices to deposit £20,000 and to publish standard accounts.[36]

In 1871, there were 101 life offices in the United Kingdom assuring a total of £292.6 m and holding funds of £87.8 m. By 1914, they were assuring £869.7 m and holding life funds of £390.1 m. Most growth was in endowment policies. In 1890, endowment policies amounted to 9.3 per cent of the sum assured and by 1913 to 39.0 per cent. Between 1886 and 1913, the sums assured grew by 2.8 per cent per annum. Life insurance continued to expand between the wars at a still faster rate: between 1922 and 1937, the sum assured grew by 4.3 per cent per annum. People were saving a larger share of their income. The market was encouraged by monthly instalment payments, the growth of salaried employment, and by rising incomes for those in work. Policies could be used for house purchase, school fees, and above all pensions. People were living longer and retiring at a fixed date; they needed security for old age. Insurance firms responded by developing a new branch of business from 1918: group life and insurance plans for the employees of particular companies, offering a fixed pension and death benefit. As the *Bankers' Magazine* commented, life offices were 'great investment trusts not only providing the people with protection against the financial loss resulting from death or old age but with the means of systematically investing their savings under expert guidance'. The point was even more apparent with the collapse of the Stock Market in 1929–32, and the government's commitment to low interest rates. The growth of the middle class, the development of suburbia, and the rise of retirement provided opportunities for insurance concerns.[37] 'Industrial insurance' for the working class developed from around 1850. The Prudential came to dominate this market: it was responsible for over half the premiums by 1905. The policies were for small amounts, designed to cover the cost of a funeral rather than to provide for dependants, and to accumulate a small endowment for children. Prudence and thrift were becoming more common as wages rose and the birth rate fell.[38]

Of course, insurance companies offered many other forms of cover. In 1914, fire was still the largest sector of insurance business and fire premiums rose sixfold from the early 1870s to the First World War when the market was close to saturation. The companies responded by looking for business overseas. Between 1871/2 and

1875/6, foreign fire premiums were 51.5 per cent of the total premiums of the Phoenix, rising to 80.1 per cent in 1911.[39] Accident insurance rose in importance as new risks emerged: livestock (1844); personal accident (1848); plate glass (1852); engineering (1858); public liability (1875); employers' liability (1880); burglary (1887); credit (1893); and motor vehicle (1896). Such developments were a response to the complexities of commercial society. In some cases, laws created explicit liability. The Employers' Liability Act of 1880 continued the common law principle that injury had to be shown to arise from the employer's negligence; even so, it was sensible to take out cover. In 1897, the Workmen's Compensation Act introduced 'no fault' compensation and industrialists grouped together to provide mutual indemnity against loss. Between 1920 and 1937, premiums against accidents rose by 67.6 per cent, above all for motor insurance. Profits were low, for motor premiums were held down by competition and accidents were frequent. Insurers did not assess the risks accurately, for they charged low premiums on small cars which had more accidents. From 1931, motor insurance was compulsory. In 1932, the companies introduced graduated no-claims bonuses, and in 1935 a system of rating districts by risk of accident.[40]

The aggressive search for new business meant that costs were high. The life offices advertised heavily and recruited solicitors and other professionals as agents. in return for a commission, as well as using their own salaried staff and local boards. Competition for business also drove up costs. One response was consolidation. By the early twentieth century, concerns were moving from specialization to become 'composites' offering a range of services. The share of the five largest life offices rose from 21 to 35 per cent between 1881 and 1914; in fire, the nine leading offices increased their share from 54 per cent in 1899 to 66 per cent in 1904. Large offices had an advantage in geographical spread and in their image. Firms realized that the public preferred to use one agent for all claims, and therefore tried to move into new lines. Although some firms grew by internal diversification, in many cases they acquired a going concern with expertise in a particular category of risk. Specialists were absorbed into existing concerns, and mergers took place between life and fire offices.[41] A new form of composite office emerged, with worldwide connections, responding to intense competition with aggressive mass marketing. The insurance companies developed divisional structures for each class of business, with branches around the country and overseas, answerable to a central executive—precisely the sort of organization British industrialists have been criticized for failing to develop.

How did the firms invest their premium income to cover their risks and provide bonuses to their customers and (in the companies) dividends to shareholders? In the early nineteenth century, they relied mainly on government securities; by the middle of the century, they turned to mortgages, loans to local authorities, debentures to private firms, and annuities. In the late nineteenth century, the range widened: mortgages and local authority loans declined in importance, and colonial and foreign government loans increased, as well as bonds, debentures, and even the preferred and ordinary shares of companies. Life funds shifted their investments in response to declining yields which threatened their profitability; it was rational to diversify in pursuit of higher yields. Once attitudes changed, the new pattern of investment continued when interest rates rose from 1900. As one actuary said, 'Events of recent years had taught actuaries that safety and immunity from loss were not to be obtained by simply investing in so-called gilt-edged securities, but rather that a wide field of investment should be adopted by distributing funds in a large number of varying interests all the world over'.[42] Overseas investment was an economically rational response by insurance companies competing in the market for life insurance for the British middle class. Unfortunately, foreign investments can only be distinguished in government securities and not in private investments (see Table 4.2), but Supple estimates that the share of overseas assets rose to 40 per cent by 1913.[43] Between the wars, the share of government securities also rose, from 1 per cent of the investment of companies with life business in 1913, to 32 per cent in 1920 in response to the war, then falling back to 16 per cent in 1938. Mortgages fell to about 10 per cent while ordinary stocks and shares rose from under 4 per cent in 1913 to 9 per cent in 1937. Although some companies adhered to a conservative policy, others adopted active management of investments and equities. An active market-oriented financial system was continuing to evolve.[44]

TABLE 4.2. *Investment by UK life offices, 1870 and 1913 (%)*

	1870	1913
Mortgages	49.8	22.6
UK local authorities		6.2
Indian and colonial municipal authorities	9.8	4.5
Foreign municipal securities		2.9
British govt securities	7.9	1.1
Indian and colonial govt securities	5.1	3.8
Foreign govt securities	1.2	4.9
Debentures and debenture stocks	10.0	26.3
Shares and stocks	3.0	9.8
Loans on life policies	5.1	5.8
Land, house property, ground rents	4.5	9.2
Life interests and reversions	1.6	2.3
Loans on personal security	1.7	0.5

Source: Supple, *Royal Exchange Assurance*, table 13.4.

Financial services involved much more than the merchant banks and stockbrokers of the City. In the 1930s, the merchant banks lost much of their international role as capital exports declined and the global world economy of the late nineteenth century went into retreat. Some concerns shifted their emphasis to the domestic economy, and it was only with the emergence of the Eurodollar market that the City started to regain its international role. Even in the international and cosmopolitan world before 1914, the City was not separated from the needs of the domestic economy: it was linked to industry through the provision of trade credit, investment in the infrastructure of developing countries, and the exploitation of their resources. Could the industries of Britain flourish without the availability of imported raw materials? Banks in the provinces were linked with the London money market, allowing an outlet for their funds and a decent return to their depositors and shareholders, and at the same time providing liquidity for dealers in stocks and bonds in London. The great insurance companies covered the risks of large numbers of individuals and concerns throughout the country, and invested the proceeds in a wide, diversified portfolio. The financial system was stable. The active market in stocks and shares, with the transfer of ownership rights, meant that inefficient management could be challenged by mergers and takeovers. Both central and local government were able to borrow on favourable terms in order to invest in welfare and warfare. Many commentators at the time and since believed that Britain invested too much overseas before 1914 at the expense of public spending on the social infrastructure and industry. But to write the history of financial services as one of failure is to miss the point that the British financial system reflected its particular institutional, economic, and political structures. Britain had a specialized and sophisticated market-oriented system dealing with the risks of a highly complex commercial society. Debates over the superiority or inferiority of national financial systems were part of the discourse of policy formation in all countries: the existence of a foreign exemplar was always a useful rhetorical ploy, and should not always be taken at face value.

Distribution and Retailing

The USA overtook British productivity in distribution by the First World War, by a margin of 20–35 per cent, and Britain retained a considerable advantage over Germany (Table 4.1). In comparative terms Britain was considerably more efficient in distribution than in manufacturing,

In 1850—and still in 1950—most shops in Britain were single outlets; in working-class districts small corner shops were often run by the wives of working men. In 1850, these small retailers were often producers of the goods they sold. Others purchased goods from manufacturers or wholesalers but undertook some processing. At the start of the period, many shopkeepers served an apprenticeship; by 1950, fewer had such skills, for they mainly dealt with branded and packaged goods. By far the largest part of retailing remained in the hands of small shopkeepers, usually run as a family business, but now mass production techniques had been applied to consumer goods. Consequently, the wholesaler became more important, and small producer-retailers lost ground.

Most shops remained single branches. Multiples were significant in grocery, meat, and footwear, and the most striking feature of retailing was the increasing number of small independent shopkeepers rather than the growth of chains. In 1950 the Census of Distribution found that proprietors of a single shop controlled 45 per cent of the market.[45] Small shopkeepers accepted a smaller return, compensated by the social rewards of independence and a sense of social mobility. Although multiples and department stores were used for more expensive purchases, customers relied on local shops for regular purchases. Storing goods was difficult before the development of domestic refrigerators and most consumers had to carry their purchases home.

How did small shopkeepers respond to competition, amongst themselves and from multiple shops? Unlike in continental Europe, they did not turn to the state for assistance for they tended to view the state as an imposition rather than a solution; they lacked corporate traditions such as the *tribunaux de commerce* of France and were loyal to liberal economic assumptions of non-intervention. Instead, they attempted to limit competition. Particularly in the inter-war period, retailers lost control over price setting, for the price of branded goods was fixed by the producers and individual shopkeepers could not undercut each other. 'Retail price maintenance' rose from 3 per cent of total consumers' expenditure in 1900 to 30 per cent in 1938 and 50 per cent in 1955—another sign of the limitation of competition in the inter-war period.[46] Competition was less in terms of price than of service. Only with the abolition of resale price maintenance in 1964 did large supermarkets start to erode the position of small shopkeepers.

In addition to fixed shops, itinerant traders remained commonplace. Although pedlars declined in the countryside, numbers rose in urban areas. They sold perishables as well as clothing, drapery, and haberdashery. Although historians have emphasized the department store as a symbol of modernity and mass consumption, many working-class women were brought into the expanding consumer market by the tallymen or 'Scotch drapers'. Many commentators were highly critical of their business practices, their fears compounded by the use of the county courts to enforce the payment of small debts which led to the imprisonment of men for the purchases of their (supposedly) irresponsible wives. From the point of view of the tallymen, the problem was how to deal with customers who secured goods on false information. In most large towns, credit traders established societies to share information and to assist in the collection of debt. The Manchester Guardian Society for the Protection of Trade, for example, set up a debt collection department in 1850, and specialist credit drapers' societies emerged to handle debt payments, distancing the individual trader from moralizing critics and from the hostility of customers. In reality, shopkeepers were greater users of the courts to enforce payment than itinerant traders, and the development of hire purchase by larger retailers inserted a new moral concern into the rise of a mass consumer society.[47] Itinerant traders declined in the twentieth century, but face-to-face sales within working-class neighbourhoods continued with the emergence of mail-order catalogues. Although mail order was only about 1 per cent of total retail sales by value in 1950, a number of large firms emerged, using spare-time agents. Mail-order retailers could use existing knowledge in order to sell goods on credit to working-class households with a minimal risk of bad debt.[48]

Although small shops still dominated in 1950, retailing changed. More goods were branded and marketed by their producers. These commodities were produced by large concerns and sustained by large-scale advertising. One of the most successful firms was Lever Brothers. In 1884, William Lever registered Sunlight soap and opened a factory in Warrington; the firm prospered, concentrating on soap and other oil-based products, entering the trade for raw materials and running plantations in West Africa. From 1919, it became a more diversified conglomerate.[49] W. D. and H. O. Wills dominated the trade in cheap, branded cigarettes. Initially, tobacco was sold loose, and cigarettes were under 0.5 per cent of total UK sales; by 1900, cigarettes accounted for 12 per cent of sales and between the wars for 60 per cent. Growth was phenomenal. By the inter-war period, market penetration had reached such a level that the choice was less between smoking or not, and more a matter of which brand was preferred. In 1901 the American Tobacco Co. moved into the British market and British producers responded by creating the Imperial Tobacco Co. Although the two firms called a truce, competition continued as other concerns such as Players entered the market. Mass advertising was needed to secure market share, with price cutting and the use of loyalty devices such as cigarette cards. Here was a new world of mass consumption and advertising, of highly efficient centralized production linked with sales through myriad small shops and kiosks.[50]

At the same time, Home and Colonial, Liptons, and Dewhurst built up national chains of shops selling groceries and meat, in some cases from their own farms, plantations, and processing or storage facilities. One of the most successful chains was created by Thomas Lipton, who started in Scotland before moving into the English provinces in the 1880s and to London in 1888. In time, he controlled the sources of supply, processed commodities, and supplied other retailers. His strategy was to purchase in bulk to reduce prices and to use heavy advertising. The increased need for capital meant that the firm went public in 1898, with control still in the hands of Lipton, but his personal failings were compounded by high fixed charges as a result of the overcapitalization of the business and the high valuation of goodwill. In 1927, Lipton's own shares were acquired by a Dutch company which merged the same year to form the Margarine Union. In 1929, the Margarine Union merged with Lever to form Unilever. The result was a single large firm which manufactured a wide range of branded products from soap to margarine.[51] Similar trends emerged in non-food trades. In menswear, Montague Burton owned 595 shops in 1939, supported by a large factory in Leeds which employed 10,500 people at its peak. In 1879, there were twenty-nine multiples with ten or more shops in Britain, a total of 978 branches. By 1920, the number had risen to 471 multiples with ten or more branches, a total of 24,713 branches; and by 1939 to 680 firms with 44,487 branches. By then, twelve retail firms had over 500 branches, and five over 1,000. By far the largest number of branches was in groceries, followed by meat, footwear, menswear, and chemists. A few national chains emerged such as Boots in toiletries and pharmaceuticals, or W. H. Smith in books and newspapers. Variety chain stores developed such as British Home Stores and Marks and Spencer. They concentrated on economies of scale in purchasing and in administration, using aggressive advertising, standardized techniques, cash sales, and low prices.[52]

Co-operative stores were also remarkably successful. The first opened at Rochdale in 1844. Stores were owned by members and run democratically. Members paid cash for their goods and received a 'dividend' each year. In 1862, there were 400 societies in Britain, rising to 1,455 in 1903. In 1863, the retail societies formed the Co-operative Wholesale Society, the sixth biggest concern in Britain in 1905. Initially, the movement was concentrated in the north and Scotland. By the later nineteenth century, the societies moved into such commodities as shoes, clothing, furniture, and expanded into the large-scale distribution of staple commodities such as milk. Between the wars, the societies expanded into the south and midlands. By 1939, membership reached the massive figure of 8.5 million. The societies were in a privileged position, for they were not liable to income tax and they expanded by re-investing their profits. The societies were successful in a purely business sense, offering unadulterated goods at reasonable prices and with the promise of the 'divi'. The co-operative movement may easily be portrayed as dull and reduced to an expression of material need for working-class members. But scant means are not necessarily a barrier to idealism. The co-operatives, for at least some members, were a model of moral consumption and part of their social life. Profits were used to provide recreational and educational facilities, and the co-operative movement engaged in political activities, not least through the Co-operative Women's Guild.[53]

Department stores emerged in the later nineteenth century. In 1914, there were between 175 and 225 stores, and in 1939 between 475 and 525.[54] Between the wars, many stores were integrated into national chains such as John Lewis, Debenhams, and United Drapery Stores. Although department stores were responsible for only a modest share of sales, they were significant cultural artefacts. Above all, gender was central to commercialization of city centres which were redefined as pleasurable

TABLE 4.3. *Distribution of retail sales by type of outlet, Britain, 1900–39 (%)*

	1900	1920	1939
Co-operatives	6.0–7.0	7.5–9.0	10.0–11.5
Department stores	1.0–2.0	3.0–4.0	4.5–5.5
Multiple shops	3.0–4.5	7.0–10.0	18.0–19.5
Others	86.5–90.0	77.0–82.5	63.5–67.5

Source: Jefferys, *Retail Trading*, 73.

spaces for bourgeois women. Shopping meant a day in town. As well as inspecting and buying goods, a day in town entailed lunch or tea, and a visit to a museum, theatre, or cinema. The practice was culturally ambivalent: was the woman a pleasure-seeker, seduced from domestic responsibilities by her longing for goods and the distractions of urban life? When William Whiteley's store opened in west London, small retailers argued that its lavish facilities would unleash uncontrollable female passions—not least when the store applied for a licence to sell alcohol in its restaurant in 1872. Of course, the small traders were using the claim that department stores fostered immoral behaviour as a way of protecting themselves. Whitley responded by arguing that women shoppers were rational and respectable, and that he was offering a safe, regulated environment, with doormen and shop walkers to 'police' entry, and catering, lavatories, and even reading rooms. Stores presented themselves as safe and emancipating places for women. Men had their clubs and public houses; department stores offered women an acceptable form of public femininity, complemented by coffee houses and restaurants such as Lyons corner-houses and Kardomah cafés.[55]

From Counting House to Office

The service sector contained some of the largest concerns in Britain, but data on labour productivity suggest that they were less efficient than their counterparts in the United States. In the case of transport and communications, the level of productivity was considerably higher in both the United States and Germany, with a greater discrepancy than in manufacturing. In finance services, British productivity was favourable compared with the United States and Germany, but their rate of change was high, so contributing to their catching up with or overtaking British productivity in the economy as a whole. In distribution, the British level of productivity was relatively favourable; again, the rate of change in the United States was high, though the gap with Germany widened. Clearly, the focus on British 'decline' compared with Germany has been exaggerated; what stands out is the similarity of the British and German industrial records compared with the much higher levels of productivity achieved in the United States, with Britain performing relatively well in some service sectors with the notable exception of transport and communications.

Stephen Broadberry argues that the emergence of high-volume, low-margin business in services was slower in Britain than in the United States. The change from the 'counting house' to office was linked with the diffusion of new systems of communication and storing data by means of telephones, typewriters, duplicators, filing systems, and calculators. The telephone allowed information to be sent over long distances at speed, which helped the operation of wholesalers or railway companies. It had less effect on the operation of high-volume business, where methods of storing and retrieving large amounts of data within the concern were much more important. In the counting house, information was laboriously written into ledgers in chronological order, so that retrieval was difficult. The use of typewriters and vertical files allowed data to be stored more flexibly. Similarly, adding machines, punch cards, and cash registers permitted larger amounts of data to be handled with speed and accuracy. These new machines were linked with an increase in the number of clerical workers, their specialization on particular tasks, and intensification of work under closer supervision. The recruitment of clerks became more impersonal. In the mid-Victorian period, clerks were relatively secure and differentiated from the urban working class. By the 1870s, their status was being eroded, above all by the entry of women who formed 20.2 per cent of the clerical workforce in Britain in 1911 and 58.8 per cent in 1951. Nevertheless, male clerks maintained their differential over manual workers until the late 1930s, and they had better security, conditions, and pensions, with the prospect of modest progress within large concerns—often at the expense of women who left on marriage.[56]

British firms were slower to adopt new office technology than their counterparts in the United States, and they failed to secure the same gains in productivity. In 1908, sales of typewriters in the UK were 0.5 per 1,000 population compared with 1.13 in the USA; in 1930, sales were 1.32 and 4.34; and in 1948, 1.74 and 7.76. The value of sales of cash registers, calculating machines, and other office machinery at constant 1929 prices was £28.3 per 1,000 population in the UK in 1930 compared with £128.9 in the USA; in 1948, the figures were £106.0 and £252.1. The slow adoption of office machinery was as striking as the divergence in mass production technology.[57] As in the case of industry, the adoption of new technology was slower where workers had power to resist change, or where weak competition meant that managers and workers could avoid the need to intensify work. Services were not susceptible to foreign competition in the same way as manufacturing, so that inefficient firms were more likely to survive. However, these points cannot entirely account for the slower pace of adoption of the modern office in Britain, for similar considerations applied in the USA.

The slow adoption of new technology was rational in some cases. In the Prudential, for example, mechanized processing of data was implemented over a long period between the 1870s and 1930s. Existing policies were updated using manual processes, at the same time as new policies were handled with the new technology. Similarly, the organization of business in the Post Office Savings Bank limited the room for new technology. In 1890, over 1,600 clerks were responsible for nearly 5 million accounts, with mechanization only starting in the 1920s. The POSB reduced the workload by using pre-printed standard letters. Calculation of interest was easy, for a new balance was not created every time money was deposited or withdrawn; the account was balanced at the end of the year, when interest was calculated in the nearest whole pound—a simple task for interest was fixed at 2.5 per cent (or exactly 0.5*d.* per pound). Delay in mechanization was therefore rational but there was also an element of conservatism. In 1903, the purchase of adding machines was rejected for no very good economic reason. Although an experiment in new forms of record keeping was recommended a few years later, action was delayed. After the war, the POSB opted for evolutionary change, an approach with many virtues. In the 1920s, the Dutch Post Office adopted punch cards in one massive operation, a change that proved disastrous; the POSB carefully assessed new methods though trials and parallel working, and ensured that the efficient parts of the existing system were preserved.[58] The railways had less reason for delay. The Railway Clearing House handled large numbers of payments between companies and was resistant to change. In 1920, calculating machines costing £600 would replace seventy men with six women at an annual saving of over £18,000. Nevertheless, change was halting.[59] One explanation was the slower development of elementary and above all secondary education, the lower investment in human capital, and the ability of clerks and managers to resist change with its threat of increased standardization and monitoring.[60]

The last three chapters have considered the performance of each sector of the British economy and the notion of 'decline' has been modified. The aim of the next chapter is to combine the three sectors in order to assess the overall rate of growth of the British economy between 1850 and 1950. Did its growth falter before 1914, or was the First World War the critical turning point? How successful was recovery between the wars, or was it delayed until after the Second World War?

NOTES

1. Daunton, *Just Taxes*, 299–300.
2. Hobson, 'General election of 1910'; Cain and Hopkins, *British Imperialism*.
3. Rubinstein, *Men of Property*; Lee, 'Regional growth' and 'Service sector'. See also Gemmell and Wardley, 'Contribution of services'.

4. Hutton, *The State We Are In*.

5. Broadberry, 'How did the United States and Germany overtake Britain?'; Broadberry and Ghosal, 'From counting house to the modern office'.

6. Matthews et al., *British Economic Growth*; Gemmell and Wardley, 'Contribution of services'.

7. Broadberry, 'How did the United States and Germany overtake Britain?', 376, 392–3, 400; Broadberry and Ghosal, 'From counting house to the modern office', 968.

8. Broadberry and Ghosal, 'From counting house to the modern office', 968–9.

9. Wardley, 'Emergence of big business', 92, 102; Wardley, 'Anatomy', 278, 279, 289–90.

10. Kellett, *Impact of Railways*; Kostal, *Law and English Railway Capitalism*, ch. 4; Foreman-Peck and Millward, *Public and Private Ownership of British Industry*, 96.

11. Daunton, *Royal Mail*, 27, 124–33.

12. Dobbin, *Forging Industrial Policy*; Alborn, *Conceiving Companies*; Cain, 'Traders versus railways'; Cain, 'Private enterprise or public utility?'; Gourvish, 'Performance of British railway management'; Irving, 'Profitability and performance'.

13. Gourvish, *Railways and the British Economy*, 42; Cain, 'Railway combination', 627, 628; Alderman, 'Railway companies and the growth of trade unionism'.

14. Alborn, *Conceiving Companies*, 253; Dobbin, *Forging Industrial Policy*, 200–3; Cain, 'Railway combination'.

15. Grieves, 'Sir Eric Geddes'; Crompton, 'Efficient and economical working?'

16. Scott, 'British railways', 106.

17. Crompton, 'Efficient and economical working?'; Crompton 'Railway companies and the nationalisation issue'; Gourvish, *British Railways*, 20.

18. Foreman-Peck and Millward, *Public and Private Ownership*, 166; Ward, 'Comparative historical geography of streetcar suburbs'; McKay, *Tramways and Trolleys*; Barker and Robbins, *London Transport*, ii; Warner, *Streetcar Suburbs*; Mulley, 'Background to bus regulation'.

19. Daunton, *Royal Mail*.

20. Perry, *Victorian Post Office*, chs. 4, 5.

21. Broadberry and Ghosal, 'From counting house to the modern office', 981.

22. Perry, *Victorian Post Office*, ch. 7.

23. Kennedy, *Industrial Structure*, 120.

24. Best and Humphries, 'The City and industrial decline', 236–7.

25. This is the short-termism argument of Hutton, *The State We Are In*.

26. Gerschenkron, *Economic Backwardness*, 137; Lazonick and O'Sullivan, 'Finance and industrial development, I and II'.

27. For this debate, Edwards and Ogilvie, 'Universal banks'; Fohlin, 'Rise of interlocking directorates'; Fohlin, 'Universal; banking'; Neuburger and Stokes, 'German banks and German growth'; Collins and Baker, *Commercial Banks*; Fremdling and Tilly, 'German banks, German growth'.

28. See Collins and Baker, *Commercial Banks*, 29; Collins, 'English bank development'.

29. Collins and Baker, *Commercial Banks*, 70–1, chs. 5 and 6; Capie and Rodrik-Bali, 'Concentration in British banking', 287; Checkland, *Scottish Banking*, 532–3.

30. Alborn, *Conceiving Companies*, ch. 6; Michie, *London and New York Stock Exchanges*.

31. Collins and Baker, *Commercial Banks* 48–53, ch. 8.

32. Watson, 'New issue market'; Watson, 'Banks and industrial finance'; Church, *British Coal Industry*, ch. 2.

33. See Collins and Baker, *Commercial Banks*, ch. 2; Sylla and Toniolo, *Patterns of European Industrialisation*, 1; James 'Causes', 72, 79; Balderston, 'German banking between the wars'.

34. Collins and Baker, *Commercial Banks*, chs. 9–12.

35. On the inter-war period, see Ross, 'Commercial banking'; Ross, 'Information'; Ross, 'Macmillan gap'; Ross, 'Banks and industry'; Ross, 'Unsatisfied fringe'; Balderston, 'German banking between the wars'; Bamberg, 'Rationalisation'; Cassis, 'Emergence'; Heim, 'Limits to intervention; Tolliday, *Business, Banking and Politics*; Garside and Greaves, 'Bank of England'.

36. Supple, *Royal Exchange Assurance*, 138–43.

37. Ibid. 220–1 433–7, 450–1; Trebilcock, *Phoenix Assurance*, 533–57; Butt, 'Life assurance in war and depression'.

38. Supple, *Royal Exchange Assurance,* 218–24.

39. Trebilcock, *Phoenix Assurance*, 103–12 and ch 5, ch 2, tables 2.1 and 2.3.

40. Supple, *Royal Exchange Assurance*, 431.

41. Ibid. 295–6, 299; Trebilcock, *Phoenix Assurance*, tables 5.3, 5.4.

42. Supple, Royal Exchange Assurance, 341, 346.

43. Ibid. 346.

44. Ibid. 427, chs. 10, 12 , 13, 18; Trebilcock, *Phoenix Assurance*, ch. 8.

45. Winstanley, *Shopkeepers' World*, 216–17.

46. Ibid. 220; Jefferys, *Retail Trading*, 54.

47. Finn, 'Scotch drapers', 90, 93; Benson, *Rise of Consumer Society*; Benson, *Penny Capitalists*; Rubin, 'From, packmen, tallymen and "perambulating Scotchmen" to Credit Drapers' Associations; Green, 'Street trading in London'.

48. Coopey, O'Connell, and Porter, *Mail Order Retailing*, 53.

49. Wilson, *Unilever*; Fieldhouse, *Unilever Overseas*.

50. Alford, *W. D. and H. O. Wills*, 171, ch. 11, 269; Hilton, *Smoking*, 94 and ch. 14.

51. Mathias, *Retailing Revolution*; Wilson, *History of Unilever*.

52. Sigsworth, *Montague Burton* Jefferys, Retail Trading.

53. Johnson, *Saving and Spending*, ch. 5; Gurney, *Co-operative Culture*; Jefferys, *Retail Trading*.

54. Jefferys, *Retail Trading*, 59.

55. Rappaport, *Shopping for Pleasure* and ' "Halls of temptation" '.

56. Lockwood, *Black Coated Worker*; Broadberry and Ghosal, 'From counting house to the modern office', 975–7.

57. Broadberry and Ghosal, 'From counting house to the modern office', 977–83.

58. Campbell-Kelly, 'Data-processing and technological change'.

59. Broadberry and Ghosal, 'From counting house to the modern office', 983–5; Campbell-Kelly, 'Large-scale data processing'; Campbell-Kelly, 'Data-processing and technological change'; Campbell-Kelly 'Railway clearing house'.
60. Broadberry and Ghosal, 'From counting house to the modern office', 985–93; Routh, *Occupation and Pay*, 4–5; Anderson, *Victorian Clerks*.

FURTHER READING

Alborn, T., 'Senses of belonging: the politics of working-class insurance in Britain, 1880-1914', *Journal of Modern History*, 73 (2001)
—— *Conceiving Companies: Joint-Stock Politics in Victorian England* (1998)
Alderman, G., 'The railway companies and the growth of trade unionism in the late nineteenth and early twentieth centuries', *Historical Journal*, 14 (1971)
Alford, B. W. E., *W. D. and H. O. Wills and the Development of the UK Tobacco Industry, 1786–1965* (1973)
Anderson, G., *Victorian Clerks* (Manchester, 1976)
Baker, M., and Collins, M., 'Financial crisis and structural change in English commercial bank assets, 1860–1913', *Explorations in Economic History* 36 (1999)
—— 'English industrial distress before 1914 and the response of the banks', *European Review of Economic History*, 3 (1999)
Balderston, T., 'German banking between the wars: the crisis of the credit banks', *Business History Review*, 65 (1991)
Bamberg, J., 'The rationalisation of the British cotton industry in the interwar years', *Textile History*, 19 (1988)
Barker, T. C., and Robbins, M., *A History of London Transport*, ii: *The Twentieth Century to 1970* (1974)
Benson, J., *Penny Capitalists: A Study of Nineteenth-Century Working-Class Entrepreneurs* (Dublin, 1983)
—— *The Rise of Consumer Society in Britain, 1880–1980* (1984)
Best, M. H., and Humphries, J., 'The City and industrial decline', in B. Elbaum and W. Lazonick (eds.) *The Decline of the British Economy* (Oxford, 1986)
Broadberry, S. N., 'How did the United States and Germany overtake Britain? A sectoral analysis of comparative productivity levels, 1870–1990', *Journal of Economic History*, 58 (1998)
—— and Ghosal, S., 'From counting house to the modern office: explaining Anglo-American productivity differences in services, 1870–1990', *Journal of Economic History*, 62 (2002)
Butt, J., 'Life assurance in war and depression: the Standard Life Assurance Company and its environment, 1914–39', in O. Westall (ed.), *The Historian and the Business of Insurance* (Manchester, 1984)
Cain, P. J., 'Traders versus railways: the genesis of the Railway and Canal Traffic Act of 1894', *Journal of Transport History*, NS 2 (1973)
—— 'Private enterprise or public utility? Output, pricing and investment in English and Welsh railways, 1870–1914', *Journal of Transport History*, 3rd ser. 1 (1980)
—— 'Railway combination and government, 1900–1914', *Economic History Review*, 25 (1972)

Cain, P. J., and Hopkins, A. G., *British Imperialism: Innovation and Expansion, 1688–1914* (1993)

—— and Hopkins, A. G., *British Imperialism: Crisis and Deconstruction, 1914-1990* (Harlow, 1993)

Campbell-Kelly, M., 'Data-processing and technological change: the Post Office Savings Bank, 1861–1930', *Technology and Culture*, 39 (1998)

—— 'The railway clearing house and Victorian data processing', in L. Bud-Frierman (ed.), *Information and Acumen* (1994)

Capie, F., and Collins, M., 'Banks, industry and finance, 1880–1914', *Business History*, 41 (1999)

—— and Rodrik-Bali, G., 'Concentration in British banking, 1870–1920', *Business History*, 24 (1982)

Cassis, Y., 'The emergence of a new financial institution: investment trusts in Britain, 1870–1939', in J. J. van Helten and Y. Cassis (eds.), *Capitalism in a Mature Economy: Financial Institutions, Capital Exports and British Industry, 1870–1914* (Aldershot, 1990)

—— *City Bankers, 1890–1914* (Cambridge, 1994)

Checkland, S. G., *Scottish Banking: A History, 1695–1873* (Glasgow, 1975)

Church, R., *The History of the British Coal Industry*, iii: *1830–1913: Victorian Pre-eminence* (Oxford, 1986)

Collins, M., *Banks and Industrial Finance in Britain, 1800–1939* (Cambridge, 1991)

—— 'The banking crisis of 1878', *Economic History Review*, 42 (1989)

—— 'English bank lending and the financial crisis of the 1870s', *Business History*, 32 (1990)

—— 'English bank development within a European context, 1870–1939', *Economic History Review*, 51 (1998)

—— and Baker, M., 'English commercial bank liquidity, 1860–1913', *Accounting, Business and Financial History*, 11 (2001)

—— —— 'Sectoral differences in English bank asset structures and the impact of mergers, 1860–1913', *Business History*, 43 (2001)

—— —— *Commercial Banks and Industrial Finance in England and Wales, 1860–1913* (Oxford, 2004)

Coopey, R., O'Connell, S., and Porter, D., *Mail Order Retailing in Britain: A Business and Social History* (Oxford, 2005)

Cottrell, P. L., *Industrial Finance, 1830–1914: The Finance and Organisation of English Manufacturing Industry* (1980)

Crompton, G. W., 'Efficient and economical working? The performance of the railway companies, 1923–33', *Business History*, 27 (1985)

—— 'The railway companies and the nationalization issue, 1920–50', in R. Millward and J. Singleton (eds.), *The Political Economy of Nationalisation in Britain, 1920–50* (Cambridge, 1995)

Crossick, G. J., 'Shopkeepers and the state in Britain, 1870–1914', in G. Crossick and H.-G. Haupt (eds.), *Shopkeepers and Master Artisans in Nineteenth-Century Europe* (1984)

Daunton, M. J., *Royal Mail: The Post Office since 1840* (1985)

—— *Just Taxes: The politics of Taxation in Britain, 1914–79* (Cambridge, 2002)

Dobbin, F., *Forging Industrial Policy: The United States, Britain and France in the Railway Age* (Cambridge, 1994)

Edwards, J., and Ogilvie, S., 'Universal banks and German industrialisation: a reappraisal', *Economic History Review*, 49 (1996)

Fieldhouse, D., *Unilever Overseas: The Anatomy of a Multinational, 1895–1965* (1978)

Finn, M. C., 'Scotch drapers and the politics of modernity: gender, class and national identity in the Victorian tally trade', in M. Daunton and M. Hilton (eds.), *The Politics of Consumption: Material Culture and Citizenship in Europe and America* (Oxford, 2001)

Fohlin, C., 'The rise of interlocking directorates in Imperial Germany', *Economic History Review*, 52 (1999)

—— 'Universal banking in pre-World War I Germany: model or myth?', *Explorations in Economic History*, 36 (1999)

—— 'The balancing act of German universal banks and English deposit banks, 1880–1913', *Business History*, 43 (2001)

Foreman-Peck, J., and Millward, R., *Pubic and Private Ownership of British Industry, 1820–1990* (Oxford, 1994)

Fremdling, R., and Tilly, R., 'German banks, German growth and econometric history', *Journal of Economic History*, 36 (1976)

Garside, W. R., and Greaves, J. I., 'The Bank of England and industrial intervention in interwar Britain', *Financial History Review*, 3 (1996)

Gemmell, N., and Wardley, P., 'The contribution of services to British economic growth, 1856–1913', *Explorations in Economic History*, 27 (1990)

Gerschenkron, A., *Economic Backwardness in Historical Perspective* (1962)

Gourvish, T. R., 'The performance of British railway management after 1860: the railways of Watkins and Forbes', *Business History*, 20 (1978)

—— *Railways and the British Economy, 1830–1914* (1980)

—— *British Railways 1948–73: A Business History* (Cambridge, 1986)

Green, D. R., 'Street trading in London: a case study of casual labour, 1830–1860', in J. Benson and G. Shaw (eds.), *The Retailing Industry*, i (1999)

Grieves, K., 'Sir Eric Geddes, Lloyd George and the transport problem, 1918–21', *Journal of Transport History*, 3rd ser. 13 (1992)

Gurney, P., *Co-operative Culture and the Politics of Consumption in England, 1870–1930* (Manchester, 1996)

Heim, C., 'Limits to intervention: the Bank of England and industrial diversification in the depressed areas', *Economic History Review*, 38 (1984)

Hilton, M., *Smoking in British Popular Culture 1800–2000* (Manchester, 2000)

Hobson, J. A., 'The general election: a sociological interpretation', *Sociological Review*, 3/2 (1910)

Hutton, W., *The State We Are In* (1995)

Irving, R. J., 'The profitability and performance of British railways, 1870–1914', *Economic History Review*, 31 (1978)

—— 'British railway investment and innovation, 1900–14: an analysis with special reference to the North Eastern and London and North-Western Railway Companies', *Business History*, 13 (1971)

James, H., 'The causes of the German banking crisis of 1931', *Economic History Review*, 37 (1984)

Jefferys, J. B., *Retail Trading in Britain 1850–1950: A Study of Trends in Retailing with Special Reference to the Development of Co-operative, Multiple Shop and Department Store Methods of Trading* (1954)

Jeremy, D., 'The hundred largest employers in the United Kingdom, in manufacturing and non-manufacturing industries, in 1907, 1935 and 1955', *Business History*, 33 (1990)

Johnson, P., *Saving and Spending: The Working-Class Economy in Britain, 1870–1939*, (Oxford, 1985)

Kellett, J. R. *Impact of Railways on Victorian Cities* (1969)

Kennedy, W. P., *Industrial Structure, Capital Markets and the Origins of British Economic Decline* (Cambridge, 1987)

Kostal, R. W., *Law and English Railway Capitalism, 1825–1875* (Oxford, 1994)

Kynaston, D., *The City of London: Goldon Years, 1890–1914* (1996)

—— *The City of London: Illusions of Gold, 1914–45* (1999)

Lazonick, W., and O'Sullivan, M., 'Finance and industrial development. Part I: the United States and the United Kingdom', *Financial History Review*, 4 (1997)

—— —— 'Finance and industrial development: evolution to market control. Part II: Japan and Germany', *Financial History Review*, 4 (1997)

Lee, C. H., 'Regional growth and structural change in Victorian Britain', *Economic History Review*, 34 (1981)

—— 'The service sector, regional specialisation and economic growth in the Victorian economy', *Journal of Historical Geography*, 10 (1984)

Lockwood, D., *The Black-Coated Worker: A Study in Class Consciousness* (1958)

Lloyd-Jones, R., and Lewis, M. J., *Raleigh and the British Bicycle Industry: An Economic and Business History, 1870–1960* (2000)

McKay, J., *Tramways and Trolleys: The Rise of Urban Mass Transport in Europe* (Princeton, 1976)

Mathias, P., *Retailing Revolution: A History of Multiple Retailing in the Food Trades Based upon the Allied Suppliers Group of Companies* (1967)

Matthews, R. C. O., Feinstein, C. H., and Odling-Smee, J. C., *British Economic Growth, 1856–1973* (Oxford, 1982)

Michie, R., *The London and New York Stock Exchanges, 1850–1914* (1987)

Mulley, C., 'The background to bus regulation in the 1930 Road Traffic Act: economic, political and personal influences', *Journal of Transport History*, 3rd ser. 4 (1983)

Neuburger, H. and Stokes, H., 'German banks and German growth: an empirical view', *Journal Economic History*, 34 (1974)

Newton, L., 'Regional bank–industry relations during the mid-nineteenth century: links between bankers and manufacturing in Sheffield, *c.*1850–*c.*1885', *Business History*, 38 (1996)

Perry, C. R., *The Victorian Post Office: The Growth of a Bureaucracy* (Woodbridge, 1992)

Rappaport, E. D., *Shopping for Pleasure: Women in the Making of London's West End* (Princeton, 2000)

—— ' "The halls of temptation": gender, politics and the construction of the department store in late Victorian London', *Journal of British Studies*, 35 (1996)

Ross, D. M., 'Banks and industry: some new perspectives on the interwar years', in J. J. van Helten and Y. Cassis (eds.), *Capitalism in a Mature Economy* (Aldershot, 1990)

—— 'Information, collateral and British bank lending in the 1930s', in Y. Cassis et al. (eds.), *The Evolution of Financial Institutions and Markets in Twentieth-Century Europe* (Aldershot, 1995)

—— 'Commercial banking in a market-oriented financial system: Britain between the wars', *Economic History Review*, 49 (1996)

Ross, D.M., 'The unsatisfied fringe in Britain, 1930s–1980s', *Business History*, 38 (1996)

—— 'The Macmillan gap and the British credit market in the 1930s', in P. L. Cottrell, A. Teichova, and T. Yuzova (eds.), *Finance and Industry in the Age of the Corporate Economy: Britain and Japan* (Leicester, 1996)

Routh, G., *Occupation and Pay in Great Britain, 1906–1979* (2nd edn., 1980)

Rubin, G., 'From packmen, tallymen and "perambulating Scotchmen" to Credit Drapers' Associations, c.1840–1914', *Business History*, 28 (1986)

Rubinstein, W. D., *Men of Property: The Very Wealthy in Britain since the Industrial Revolution* (1981)

Scott, P., 'British railways and the challenge from road haulage, 1919–39', *Twentieth Century British History*, 13 (2002)

Sheppard, D. K., *The Growth and Role of UK Financial Institutions, 1880–1962* (1971)

Sigsworth, E., *Montague Burton and the Clothing Trade, 1885–1952* (1990)

Supple, B., *The Royal Exchange Assurance: A History of British Insurance, 1720–1970* (Cambridge, 1970)

Sylla, R., and Toniolo, G. (eds.), *Patterns of European Industrialisation: The Nineteenth Century* (1991)

Taylor, J., *Creating Capitalism: Joint-Stock Enterprise in British Politics and Culture, 1800–1870* (Woodbridge, 2006)

Tilly, R., 'Mergers, external growth and finance in the development of large-scale enterprise in Germany, 1880–1913', *Journal of Economic History*, 42 (1982)

Tolliday, S., *Business, Banking and Politics: The Case of British Steel, 1918–1939* (Cambridge, Mass., 1987)

Trebilcock, C., *Phoenix Assurance and the Development of British Insurance*, ii: *The Era of the Insurance Giants, 1870–1984* (Cambridge, 1998)

Wale, J., 'What help have the banks given British industry? Some evidence on bank lending in the Midlands in the late nineteenth century', *Accounting, Business and Financial History*, 4 (1994)

Ward, D., 'A comparative historical geography of streetcar suburbs in Boston, Mass., and Leeds, England, 1850–1920', *Annals of the Association of American Geographers*, 54 (1964)

Wardley, P., 'The emergence of big business: the largest corporate employers of labour in the United Kingdom, Germany and the United States, c.1907', *Business History*, 41 (1999)

—— 'The anatomy of big business: aspects of corporate development in the twentieth century', *Business History*, 33 (1991)

Warner, S. B., *Streetcar Suburbs: The Process of Growth in Boston, 1870–1900* (Cambridge, Mass., 1962)

Watson, K., 'The new issue market as a source of finance for the UK brewing and iron and steel industries, 1870–1913', in Y. Cassis et al. (eds.), *The Evolution of Financial Institutions and Markets in Twentieth Century Europe* (Aldershot, 1995)

—— 'Banks and industrial finance: the experience of brewers, 1880–1913', *Economic History Review*, 49 (1996)

Williams, P. M., 'Public opinion and the railway rates question in 1886', *English Historical Review*, 67 (1952)

Wilson, C., *The History of Unilever: A Study in Economic Growth and Social Change* (1954)

—— *First with the News: The History of W. H. Smith, 1792–1972* (1985)

Wilson, J. F., *Ferranti and the British Electrical Industry, 1864–1930* (Manchester, 1988)

Winstanley, M. J., *The Shopkeeper's World, 1830–1914* (Manchester, 1983)

....

CHAPTER 5

The Growth of the British Economy

By the late 1950s, politicians were alarmed at Britain's poor growth record compared with other countries and their attention turned to competing cures for the 'sick man of Europe'. As Jim Tomlinson points out, 'declinism' became an ideology, an assertion that something should be done. By 1964, this had become the central issue of the general election.[1] Not surprisingly, the writings of economic historians on British performance in the previous hundred years were influenced by these debates. Their analysis was shaped by contemporary political debates over economic decline, and they drew on the past to refute or support policy proposals. Whatever their disagreements, most economic historians in the 1960s and 1970s agreed that 'declinism' provided the framework for understanding Britain's economic performance. To take one influential example: H. J. Habakkuk's *American and British Technology in the Nineteenth Century* provided an explanation for low British labour productivity compared with the United States. His work reflected the emergence of labour productivity as a concern of the government in the 1960s, offering a means of dealing with wage inflation, high costs, and uncompetitiveness. American mass production was held up as the model to pursue.[2]

Should we still be writing within a framework of decline? By the end of the twentieth century, comparisons with the economic miracles of Germany and Japan made little sense: their economies were growing slowly or not at all, and these erstwhile models of dynamism now seemed to be in need of reform. Indeed, in some quarters Britain was held up as a model of success. The context for thinking and writing about British economic growth has changed: the late nineteenth century can now be interpreted less as a period of decline and more as an era of globalization. The shift in emphasis meant that capital exports before 1914 were less likely to be analysed for their deleterious impact, and more likely to be viewed as an important element in the process of globalization. The growth of financial services in the City of London in the late nineteenth century might be seen less as a mark of a bias in state policy against industry, and more as a mark of dynamism within a prosperous world economy.

TABLE 5.1. *Comparative GDP per capita and per worker hour, UK, France, Germany, and USA, 1900–53*

	GDP per head	GDP per worker hour
1900		
United Kingdom	100	100
France	62	59
Germany	68	73
United States	89	105
1913		
United Kingdom	100	100
France	69	67
Germany	76	82
United States	105	120
1928/9		
United Kingdom	100	100
France	89	75
Germany	83	79
United States	132	136
1950–3		
United Kingdom	100	100
France	76	72
Germany	63	56
United States	140	161

Source: Booth, 'Manufacturing failure hypothesis', 24.

An emphasis on decline distorts our understanding of the century between the Great Exhibition and the Festival of Britain. In reality, decline was less intense and considerably later than implied by economic historians who were looking back from a vantage point of the economic malaise of the late 1950s and 1960s. Any 'decline' was relative rather than absolute, and only in comparison with the most rapidly growing industrial economies in the world—above all Germany and the United States. In 1870, Britain was still the most productive economy in the world with the highest GDP per head. Although soon overtaken by the United States, Britain remained more productive and with a higher per capita GDP than most other countries up to 1951 and beyond (see Table 5.1). As we have noted, Germany only passed British levels of productivity and per capita GDP in the 1960s. Germany's lead in industrial productivity before 1914 was narrow and not sustained between the wars; Britain had a considerable advantage in both agriculture and services.[3] Concentration on lower annual rates of growth in Britain obscures the fact that it was still the leader to be caught. The frame of reference could be changed: Britain should be placed with a group of other leading industrial countries whose income per capita was growing, with a widening divergence with what would now be called the developing world. Is it more important that Britain's economic growth fell somewhat behind Germany in the later nineteenth century, or that both Britain and Germany were opening up a gap with most of Africa and Asia? Should we concentrate on 'decline' in Britain compared with Germany rather than explaining the success of the west over the rest? In any event, modest variations between the advanced industrial countries were arguably of less significance than trends in the international economy. The concept of 'declinism' has distorted our understanding of modern British history—whether the influence of classics and rural nostalgia on entrepreneurial culture, or the dominance of finance over economic policy.

The pattern of British economic growth is reasonably clear and follows much the same trend as elsewhere. The figures in Table 5.2 have wide margins of error, but one irrefutable point stands out: a serious and disruptive decline in the rate of economic growth came with the First World War and its aftermath, when GDP *fell* by 0.1 per cent per annum, between two periods of similar peacetime growth. Clearly, the role of the First World War needs attention. By contrast, the Second World War and its aftermath proved much less disruptive of growth. Although Germany, France, and the United States followed much the same pattern, there were some deviations around the cycle. The First World War and its aftermath did not disrupt the economy of the United States; indeed, it captured British and German markets and benefited from war demand. Germany was even more seriously disrupted than Britain over the trans-war period. Where Britain did better than both Germany and the United States was in the depression of the 1930s, when it fell less and recovered more quickly. British policies and institutional structures may explain these variations but they cannot explain the cycle itself. Above all, the experience of the trans-war period of 1913–24 must be at the heart of our understanding of the growth of the British economy over the century covered by this book. How far was the economy able to recover after 1924, or did the war have a long-term effect on the equilibrium of the economy, locking it into unemployment and excess capacity? By contrast, any decline before the First World War fades into insignificance, despite the heated debate over the supposed failings of the late Victorian and Edwardian economy.

From the Great Exhibition to the First World War

Both the Great Exhibition and census of 1851 indicated that the economic difficulties of the second quarter of the nineteenth century were resolved, and that fears of a stationary state or immiseration could be forgotten. National income per capita was rising and most people could share in the benefits of industrialization. Table 5.2 indicates that growth in GDP per capita was at its peak from 1856 to 1873, before falling off in the 'great depression' of 1873-96 and perhaps even more from 1899. As

TABLE 5.2. *Growth of GDP and GDP per man-year in the UK and Great Britain and Northern Ireland, 1856–1951 (annual percentage growth rates)*

	United Kingdom		GB and N. Ireland	
	GDP	GDP per man-year	GDP	GDP per man-year
Peacetime phase				
1856–1873	2.2	1.3	2.4	1.2
1873–1913	1.8	0.9	2.0	0.9
Trans-war phase				
1913–24	−0.1	0.3	−0.1	0.3
Peacetime phase				
1924–37	2.2	1.0	2.2	1.0
Trans-war phase				
1937–51	1.8	1.0	1.8	1.0
Peacetime phase				
1951–73	2.8	2.4	2.8	2.4

Source: Matthews, Feinstein, and Odling-Smee, *British Economic Growth*, table 2.1, 22.

we shall see, these figures are contested but they do indicate why many economic historians agree that the Great Exhibition marked a turning point. To many, the mid-Victorian period was 'the upswing of the "golden years" of the Victorians', a period of very rapid growth and even euphoria, before the 'climacteric' or slowing down of the last quarter of the nineteenth century.[4] Are these historians right in their periodization?

Despite its reputation, growth in the mid-Victorian period was not uninterrupted. Depressions were very deep, especially in 1858 when the slump was on a par with the alarming downturns of the early nineteenth century. The rise in real wages was not consistent and uninterrupted. A modest improvement in real wages up to about 1853 was reversed, and the ground was only made up in the early 1860s with a rise to a new peak in 1865. Welfare gains might be less satisfactory when account is taken of unemployment, for there were some periods of intense depression, not least in the Lancashire cotton famine. Growth came in a number of intense booms, and the period could just as well be characterized as one of speculative sprees followed by crashes. Rather than a period of rising profits and uninterrupted entrepreneurial success, many sectors of the mid-Victorian economy experienced a squeeze on profits, with marked fluctuations in output and intense competition.[5] It was a period not only of Samuel Smiles's *Self Help* (1859) but also of deep concern that morals were subverted by a scramble for profits. Anthony Trollope's *The Way We Live Now* (1875) offered a particularly jaundiced view of the corrupting power of money; the theme was also common in the novels of Dickens and Thackeray.

TABLE 5.3. *Growth of trade and GDP, Britain, 1856–1961 (annual percentage growth rates)*

	Exports		Imports		GDP
	Goods/services	Goods	Goods/services	Goods	
1856–73	3.6	3.4	4.6	4.7	2.2
1873–1913	2.6	2.7	2.7	2.8	1.8
1913–24	−1.8	−2.3	1.4	1.0	−0.1
1924–37	−0.8	−1.1	1.7	1.6	2.2
1937–51	2.6	2.9	0.1	−0.8	1.8

Source: Matthews, Feinstein and Odling-Smee, *British Economic Growth*, table 14.1, 428.

Whatever their impact on morality and character, the intense investment booms of mid-Victorian Britain pushed ahead the completion of the railway network and the mechanization of large parts of industry. After 1850, mechanized factories became more significant than artisan or craft production, and steam power was transforming manufacturing industry.[6] Textiles and capital goods were exported on an unprecedented scale. Foreign trade was a major impetus to economic growth, especially in the export-led boom in the 1850s. As Table 5.3 indicates, 1856–73 was the period of fastest growth of exports—and imports—in the period. The mid-Victorian period also marked much higher expenditure on the basic infrastructure of an industrial-urban economy—transport and communications, housing, public buildings, sanitation, and water supplies. In all, three-quarters of gross domestic fixed capital formation went into these sectors. Productivity was not only a matter of investing in industrial plant: it was also a matter of providing gas lighting to extend the working hours of mills, constant supplies of water for washing and dyeing textiles, and improved transport within and between towns.

The mid-Victorian period was more consistent in price trends. Prices moved down from the late 1830s to a trough in the late 1840s, and then moved up in 1853–5, possibly in response to gold discoveries and the impact of the Crimean War. Prices stabilized in the mid-Victorian period, with a very slight fall from 1864 to 1870, and a marked rise from 1870 to 1873 (see Fig. 5.1). Prices then started to fall—a break in price trends that led many historians to speak of a 'great depression' lasting until 1896 when prices recovered. But how realistic is this notion of a 'great depression', and how plausible is the assumption that 1873–96 formed a distinct period? Certainly, many industrialists complained of competition and loss of profits, leading to the appointment of a Royal Commission on the Depression of Trade and Industry in 1883. But as Alfred Marshall pointed out, the evidence presented to the Commission showed that any depression was of a particular, and limited, kind. Output rose and living standards of the majority improved, despite the complaints of industrialists and agriculturalists of a depression in prices and profits. The Commission noted in its final

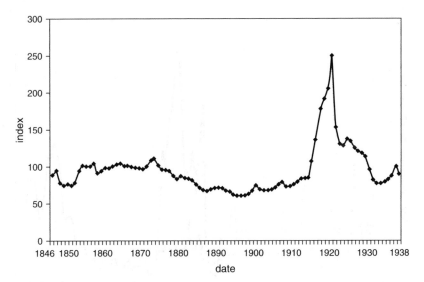

FIG. 5.1. Price index (Sauerbeck Statist), 1846–1938 (1867–77 100)
Source: Mitchell and Deane, *Abstract*, 474–5.

report that 'while the general production of wealth in the country has continuously increased, its distribution has been undergoing great changes'.[7] Essentially, the result benefited consumers and labourers. The value of agricultural produce fell, and the production of other commodities increased faster than demand. Consequently, the profits of farmers, landowners, and industrialists were squeezed. On the other hand, anyone with a fixed salary or income from fixed-interest investments stood to gain, as did most wage earners (see Chapter 12).

The period from 1873 to 1896 does have some relevance for price trends. Wholesale prices were more or less stable between the two peaks of the mid-1850s and early 1870s, and then started on a downward trend from 1873. Although the fall of prices faltered in the late 1880s, a further drop took prices to a trough in 1896. A modest rise then took prices back to the level of 1880 by the First World War (see Fig. 5.1). The explanation troubled contemporaries as well as more recent historians. The simplest explanation was the availability of gold: after the gold rushes in Australia and California, trade grew faster than the stock of money so that prices fell until the gold discoveries in South Africa from the 1880s and the Klondike in 1896. As Marshall realized, financial markets were becoming more efficient, which helped explain the paradox that prices were falling without shortages of money leading, as might be expected, to rising interest rates.[8]

Money was one influence, but not the only variable. Investment in opening up the world to trade contributed to the decline in prices. The production of most primary

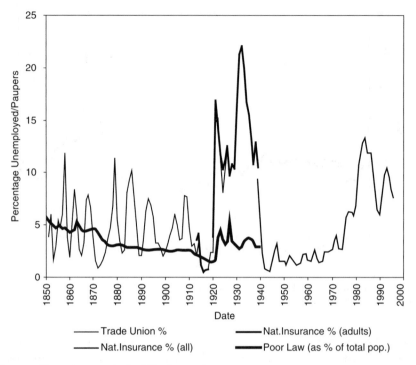

FIG. 5.2. Unemployment in the UK, 1851–1996
Source: Southall, 'The urban labour market', 625.

goods proceeds in spasms: high prices lead to investment, which takes some time to feed through into the market; prices then drop steeply as a result of oversupply, before demand catches up, prices rise, and the cycle is repeated. The period from the end of the American Civil War was remarkable for the extension of production throughout the world which contributed to a fall in prices. The application of powered machinery to manufacturing had similar effects in industry, both in Britain and increasingly in Europe and the United States. The Royal Commission pointed to a further influence: demand. Possibly, depression in the United States and Germany in the 1870s had some role in reducing demand, and arguably the movement of the terms of trade against primary producers affected their ability to purchase manufactures. Hence the expansion of supply might outstrip effective demand. For example, in the United States the extension of cultivation on the prairies meant low prices until a growing domestic market led to rising prices and falling exports from about 1900, forcing Britain to turn to new suppliers. The movement of prices reflected a combination of all these factors.

Although the dates 1873 and 1896 have some applicability to prices, many other trends do not readily fit these turning points. They are somewhat less relevant for trends in real wages. A more or less consistent rise may be dated from the 1860s; after a temporary reversal in 1866–7, real wages rose to 1876, and again from 1882 to 1900. Competition from other industrial countries was already apparent in 1870 and intensified after 1896. During the period, there were major booms in overseas investment as well as marked downturns. The fall in freight rates did not start until about 1880, and then continued up to the First World War. And the trend in the terms of trade changed, moving strongly in favour of Britain from the mid-1850s to 1873, turning against Britain to the early 1880s, and then moving back in Britain's favour up to the First World War.

If there was not a great depression, could there still be a break in the growth rate or a 'climacteric' in the later nineteenth century? The Report of the Royal Commission on the Depression of Trade argued that demand had fallen from its previously rapid rate of growth, and many later historians pointed to a similar deceleration in the rate of growth of output per head. In 1952, E. H. Phelps Brown and S. J. Handfield-Jones claimed that there was a break in the growth of income per head in the 1890s which they attributed to the working out of the technological innovations of the first industrial revolution, before the innovations of the second industrial revolution.[9] Critics responded that they mistimed the climacteric, which could more plausibly be placed in the 1870s.[10] This debate was followed by a deluge of articles seeking to explain 'decline' in the later nineteenth century. One theme was the supposed failure of British entrepreneurs to seize new opportunities and their inability to develop their own sense of identity.[11] This approach may be characterized as 'free-will pessimism': the economy was not fulfilling its potential; the problems were cultural and social; and could have been resolved if individuals had been more dynamic and profit seeking.

Other historians were unconvinced by the notion of a climacteric in the 1870s or the 1890s, and developed an optimistic alternative. They pointed to examples of entrepreneurial success, not least in consumer goods and distribution.[12] Neo-classical economists extended the argument from individuals to the economy as a whole. They assumed that the market was an efficient device for allocating resources, and that neither individual British entrepreneurs nor the British economy as a whole were failing. Even if the rate of growth in Britain was slower than other countries, industrialists could do very little to improve it, for they were constrained by the availability of resources and the nature of the market. Their choice of technique was influenced by the cost of labour and capital in each country, and the market for the particular commodity. Various studies of individual sectors provided rational explanations for the supposed inertia of British industrialists and investors in an optimistic account of the British economy. Hence British investors might have been rational to neglect investment in electricity, given competition from a well-established and efficient gas industry. Lancashire mill-owners were rescued from the charge of ignoring new forms of 'ring spinning' technology; they might have been rational in continuing to invest in the old technology of mule spinning which allowed them to use cheap raw cotton. The entrepreneur in late Victorian Britain, in the title of one highly influential article, was on his way from damnation to redemption.[13] More generally, McCloskey argued that available resources were fully employed and allocated rationally.[14]

These careful investigations provided a useful corrective, but undoubtedly went too far. McCloskey's approach was static, assuming that capital retained at home would have been invested into more of the same type of machinery or social overhead, and would produce a low rate of return. Other historians were doubtful. N. R. F. Crafts claimed higher domestic investment would have raised the ratio of capital to labour, and an increase in investment to the level of Germany might have produced a gain of 25 per cent in per capita consumption in 1911. Above all, Crafts argued that British industrial development has been characterized since the industrial revolution by a low level of investment in human capital—and attacks on poor technical education have been a persistent theme.[15]

The critique was taken a stage further by a group of historians who suggested that economic decisions were constrained by institutional rigidities. Such a view might be termed 'fatalistic pessimism': the economy was not growing at the optimal rate, and a solution was beyond the free will of individuals who were constrained in their actions. William Lazonick and his collaborators argued above all for the emergence of a system of industrial relations or 'production institutions' from the 1870s, based on craft control over the workplace and a low level of managerial authority. Essentially, the task of labour control was passed to the workers, at the cost of imposing constraints on changes in production technology. Ring spinning could not be adopted without breaking the pattern of labour relations and production institutions associated with mule spinning—and collective agreements and trade union structure were irretrievably linked with the nature of local and national politics. Although unions were accepted and institutionalized, they adopted an adversarial approach. Agreements were not binding; wages and profits were seen as opposed rather than a mutually beneficial reward for efficiency.[16] Similarly, the slow development of electricity or the telephone might be explained not only by the highly efficient gas industry or postal service, but by failings of regulation. Crafts, Leybourne, and Mills point out that, even if growth did not decline in the later nineteenth century, British institutions might still have prevented faster growth made possible by the second industrial revolution in other countries. In Crafts's view, these institutions reduced British productivity growth, with politicians unwilling to take the electoral risk of reforming them.[17] Obviously, such views could be used to justify trade union reform and privatization in the later twentieth century—another link between economic history and current politics.

TABLE 5.4. *Growth of labour, capital, total factor input, and total factor productivity, Britain, 1856–1951*

	Quality-adjusted labour	Capital	Contribution to TF(q)I of		TFI	TFP
			Quality-adj. labour	Capital		
1856–73	1.4	1.9	0.8	0.8	1.6	0.6
1873–1913	1.7	1.9	1.0	0.8	1.8	0.0
1913–24	−0.4	0.9	−0.3	0.4	0.1	−0.2
1924–37	2.1	1.8	1.5	0.5	2.0	0.2
1937–51	1.1	1.1	0.7	0.4	1.1	0.7

Source: Matthews, Feinstein, and Odling-Smee, *British Economic Growth*, table 16.2, 501.

When Matthews, Feinstein, and Odling-Smee produced their major statistical overview of British economic growth, their figures confirmed a decline in the rate of growth after 1873. Indeed, they suggested that the decline might have come mainly after 1899 (see Table 5.2).[18] But these figures have extremely large margins of error. Their approach relied on growth accounting, that is an attempt to divide the sources of growth between total factor inputs (the availability of more labour and more capital) and total factor productivity, a measure of the efficiency with which capital and labour were used (see Table 5.4). In their view, the explanation for the slower rate of economic growth was not found in a decline in the rate of growth of labour input, for population grew at a constant rate and both its educational attainment and age distribution were more favourable after 1873. Neither was there any decline in domestic capital accumulation. They concluded that the slowing of growth is to be explained by a decline in total factor productivity. More generally, they suggested that a fall in industrial profit rates in the 1870s and 1880s might have affected entrepreneurial responsiveness (see Table 5.5). After 1900, the stagnation of real wages led to a deterioration in industrial relations—and Matthews, Feinstein, and Odling-Smee suggested that the system of industrial relations might well have created a 'vicious circle between performance and remuneration'.[19] Another factor was demand deficiency, especially in 1873–90 (as a result of foreign competition) and 1899–1913 (as a result of a fall in house building after the boom of the late 1890s and a rise in world prices). If the view of Matthews, Feinstein, and Odling-Smee is correct, Britain was experiencing a climacteric before 1914 and in particular from 1899.

These figures are not without their problems, and the decline might be no more than a 'statistical artefact'.[20] GDP may be measured by income, expenditure, and output, each of which produced different results with wide margins of error. Matthews and his colleagues produced a compromise estimate from an average of the three, which is not necessarily a sensible procedure. The data were soon attacked. Solomou

TABLE 5.5. *Gross and net profits' share in trading income and rate, Britain, 1856–1951*

	Gross		Net	
	Share	Rate	Share	Rate
1856	35.6	13.2	32.7	15.6
1873	38.1	14.0	35.1	17.3
1913	33.8	11.8	29.8	14.9
1924	24.9	8.7	20.5	11.2
1937	27.0	10.6	23.0	14.2
1951	23.8	7.7	18.2	9.3

Source: Matthews, Feinstein, and Odling-Smee, *British Economic Growth*, tables 6.12 and 6.13, 186.

and Weale's alternative measure disaggregated the data and found similar levels of growth in 1874-89 and 1899–1913. Similarly, Crafts, Leybourne, and Mills concluded that growth was 'trend-stationary'. On their calculation, any slowing of trend growth was around 5 per cent, nowhere close to Feinstein, Matthews, and Odling-Smee's estimate. In the judgement of Crafts, Leybourne, and Mills, there was no climacteric.[21]

The most sensible conclusion is that confidence in the dating or even the existence of a climacteric is misplaced, and any slowing down after 1899 is better seen as a modest cyclical retardation. In any case, the debate over a climacteric in the later nineteenth century is curious in view of the much more striking fall in growth rates after 1913. The real problem arose in the trans-war period of 1913-24 when a transitory shock pushed the economy away from equilibrium and led to persistent unemployment and spare capacity.[22]

The Trans-war Period, 1913–1924

The massive impact of the First World War and post-war reconstruction is apparent in Table 5.2: GDP fell by 0.1 per cent per annum. The 'shock' of the war meant not only a loss of growth over those years, for it pushed the economy away from equilibrium, resulting in persistent unemployment and excess capacity right up to the Second World War (see Fig. 5.2). As Matthews, Feinstein, and Odling-Smee point out, 'the absolute fall in GDP across the war, not made good till the late 1920s, is one of the most spectacular features of recent British economic history'.[23] Indeed, the 'balanced estimates' of Solomou and Weale indicate that the depression of 1920–1 was even deeper and more persistent than Matthews, Feinstein, and Odling-Smee allow, with 'persistent adverse effects' on GDP throughout the inter-war period.[24]

The growth accounting technique used by Matthews, Feinstein, and Odling-Smee indicates that the explanation for lower growth is to be found in TFI with little change in TFP. In their view, the reduction in growth in 1913-24 was mainly the result of a drop in inputs of labour (Table 5.4). Population growth was reduced as a result of the war and the 1919 influenza epidemic. Further, hours of work were cut drastically, without a cut in wages.[25] At the end of the war, unionization was much higher, union members were highly militant, and they had a strong bargaining position in the post-war boom. Stephen Broadberry suggests that the unions pressed for a drastic cut in hours because shortages of goods and wartime controls led to frustrated demand, so that leisure was more desirable than income.[26] More plausibly, the reduction in hours should be placed in a longer chronology of occasional marked cuts in working hours; in any case, workers were anxious to secure higher wages and even, as in the case of coal, to nationalize the industry. The post-war boom was a period of startling change and opportunities. After the boom broke, Matthews, Feinstein, and Odling-Smee suggest that supply constraints were replaced by a low level of demand as the main explanation for low growth. The reduction in demand was mainly a result of a fall in foreign trade (see Chapter 6). Increased competition would doubtless have had an impact even in the absence of war, but the war speeded up the process of replacing British exports.[27]

The growth accounting techniques of Matthews, Feinstein, and Odling-Smee provide the 'proximate' causes of growth. But their approach does not explain why these variables changed. Indeed, we might take a somewhat different approach, suggesting that the main significance of the immediate post-war period was to knock the economy off balance. Again, the key is the operation of the labour market. The large reduction in hours was not linked with a cut in money wage—in many cases money wages actually increased ahead of inflation. Prices rose during the war and at the end of the war rose sharply as a result of a short-lived restocking boom and cost-push from higher wages. When prices started to fall from 1921, money wages did not fall in line, and British goods were uncompetitive.

The outcome has been a subject of dispute: was the gap between wages and productivity temporary or long term? On one view, the events of 1919-20 marked a permanent shift in the supply of labour, pushing the real wage index above labour productivity throughout the inter-war period.[28] Certainly, labour income rose by 10 per cent of GNP over the trans-war period (see Chapter 12). In the 1920s, redistribution from profits and property hit confidence and increased costs. The attempt to push down wages and labour costs in the 1920s did not succeed, both because of low levels of investment in new plant and the unwillingness of employers and the government to mount an attack on the British system of production institutions. Workers gained, provided they had a job: money wages did not fall in line with the retail price index and their real wage rose. However, a more relevant measure is the cost of labour compared with the proceeds from the sale of the final output, and on this measure the gap between productivity and wages was eliminated by 1922, and productivity rose ahead of real wages right up to 1938.[29] Even so, the transitory wage gap at the end of the war had long-term effects, in part through the damaging effects of policies adopted to remove the gap between wages and productivity, and to make British goods more competitive in international markets.

During the war and immediate post-war period, inflation in Britain was higher than in the United States. If the ratio of wholesale prices in the United Kingdom and United States was 100 in 1913, in May 1919 it was 109 and in December 1919 123.[30] High inflation in Britain meant that returning to gold at the parity of 1913 entailed a deflationary monetary policy and high real interest rates, in order to raise nominal exchange rates and depress prices to make British goods more competitive. The policy had its greatest economic impact in the early 1920s. The initial shock to aggregate supply as a result of the cut in hours at the end of the war was now extended by a shock to aggregate demand as a result of the fall in world trade and the adoption of a deflationary monetary policy.[31]

How far can the decision to prepare for the return to gold at the 1913 parity and overvaluation of sterling explain Britain's poor economic performance after the war? Solomou suggests that competitiveness and cyclical recovery in the 1920s demanded exchange rate depreciation, and that countries with depreciated nominal exchange rates had a long-run stimulus relative to their competitors. Just how much the pound was overvalued was a matter of controversy both at the time and more recently. Keynes suggested that the pound was overvalued by 10 per cent compared to the dollar at the time of return to gold in 1925, but this figure reflected his choice of price indices. Other data indicate anything from a 4 per cent undervaluation to a 17 per cent overvaluation. Of course, Britain traded with many other countries, so that the dollar exchange rate is a very partial guide. More meaningful estimates are weighted by the amount of trade with various trading partners—the real multilateral exchange rate. Various calculations of this rate show that sterling was still overvalued by at least 5 per cent and possibly as much as 25 per cent in 1925 (see Table 5.6).[32] However, the choice of 1913 as the base line might be misleading, for the pound was at a low point. In 1900, the real effective exchange rate was about 12 per cent higher, so reducing the case for overvaluation. Against this more optimistic conclusion, we should remember that 1925 is not necessarily a good benchmark, for the exchange rate had already been adjusted. The multilateral real effective exchange rate was more overvalued in 1920–1 than in 1925: taking January 1924 as 100, the real effective exchange rate in 1920 was 110.8 and in 1921 107.2, compared with 103.3 in 1925.[33] The overvaluation of the pound in the early 1920s did indeed have serious and long-lasting consequences.

International comparisons indicate that countries returning to gold at 1913 parities performed worse than countries opting for a lower parity. One estimate, based on

TABLE 5.6. *Multilateral real effective exchange rate for pound, 1924–30* (1913 = 100)

	Deflating by	
	Wholesale prices (trade weighted, 19 countries)	Retail prices (trade weighted, 16 countries)
1924	95.2	83.4
1925	94.8	79.6
1926	92.0	73.8
1927	97.3	81.5
1928	98.5	81.9
1929	101.3	84.9
1930	103.5	87.2

Note: Below 100 for overvaluation, above 100 for undervaluation.
Source: Redmond, 'Sterling overvaluation', table 3, 529.

an overvaluation of 11 per cent in 1925, shows a loss of 750,000 jobs through the impact of the exchange rate on the balance of trade.[34] This estimate does not provide the entire picture, for the damage started before 1925. The overvaluation of 1920-2 priced British goods out of foreign markets and allowed foreign firms to penetrate British markets. Once foreign firms had established their distribution networks and reputation, British goods would not easily replace them, until the introduction of protection in the 1930s.[35] Hence the import ratio increased in the early 1920s and stayed high. Neither does the calculation consider the impact of returning to the gold standard on the ability of the British government to adopt a discretionary monetary policy. From 1920, the British government adopted a deflationary or 'contractionary' monetary policy with high nominal and even higher real interest rates, and price deflation was higher than in France, Belgium, and Italy whose governments opted not to return to gold at the 1913 parity.[36]

The harmful effects of overvaluation and a deflationary monetary policy were reinforced by the behaviour of businessmen and bankers. In the immediate post-war period, a restocking boom led industrialists in export sectors to borrow. One of the worst affected sectors was shipping and shipbuilding, where second-hand and new ships changed hands for fantastic prices as freight rates soared after the war. But the shortage of tonnage was more apparent than real. The boom soon broke, leaving shipowners trapped in debt and shipbuilders starved of orders. The ensuing period of deflation left firms with a high burden of debt, which acted as a drain on their profitability as well as posing dangers for British banks. The debt–income ratio in the United Kingdom in 1913 was 1.6 and in 1929 had risen to 2.8; in France, the ratio fell from 2.8 before the war to 2.1 in 1929. Of course, a low debt–income ratio was not necessarily desirable in all circumstances, for the debt–income ratio was still lower in Germany, where hyperinflation wiped out loans and at the same time seriously weakened the financial system with dire consequences in the early 1930s.[37]

In the trans-war period, profits faced serious erosion both as a share of trading income and as a rate of return (see Table 5.5). The war marked a drop of about 10 percentage points in profits' share of trading income, and 3 percentage points fall in the rate of profit. Profits were squeezed by the rise in labour costs at the end of the war, but this was not the only explanation. Another was taxation of profits and income. Industrialists were aggrieved, complaining that their counterparts in Germany were less burdened as a result of the reduction of the national debt by inflation. The government was well aware of the issue, but argued that high taxes would eventually assist industrialists, for the money repaid to the holders of government bonds would be available for investment in industry.[38]

The shock of the trans-war period also led to an increase in the level of unemployment. Before the First World War, unemployment was around 4.5 per cent, with additional underemployment of casual workers. Casual work was in decline prior to the war, and did not return to anything like the same extent after the war. Instead, the level of unemployment rose and remained nearly 10 per cent from 1920 to the Second World War, with peaks in 1920–1 and 1929–32. This was high compared with other countries, and the transitory shock of the war had a longer-term impact which pushed the mean rate of unemployment to a higher level. In the 1930s, the level of unemployment in other countries increased more than in Britain and in some cases exceeded British rates (see Table 5.7).[39] As we shall see, some historians have concluded that Britain experienced rapid recovery in the 1930s. Although this is true in comparative terms, optimism should not be carried too far. The mean rate of unemployment remained higher than before the First World War, and the inter-war period as a whole was pushed away from equilibrium.

TABLE 5.7. *Average industrial and total unemployment rates in major industrial economies, 1921–38 (%)*

	Industrial unemployment		Total unemployment	
	1921–9	1930–8	1921–9	1930–8
France	3.8	10.2	—	—
Germany	9.2	21.8	4.0	8.8
UK	12.0	15.4	6.8	9.8
USA	7.7	26.1	4.9	18.2

Source: Solomou, *Themes*, 55.

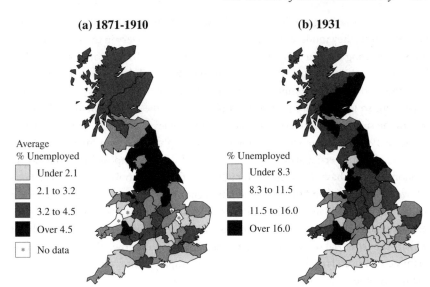

(a) 1871-1910

(b) 1931

Average
% Unemployed

Under 2.1
2.1 to 3.2
3.2 to 4.5
Over 4.5
* No data

% Unemployed

Under 8.3
8.3 to 11.5
11.5 to 16.0
Over 16.0

FIG. 5.3. Urban unemployment rates in the UK, (a) 1871–1910, (b) 1931
Source: Southall, 'The urban labour market', 626. Reproduced with permission of Humphrey Southall.

Slump and Recovery, 1924–1937

Between 1924 and 1937, British economic growth returned to pre-war levels, and Britain recovered more quickly than other countries from depression in the 1930s. In eleven of the fifteen leading industrial countries, growth was lower in the 1930s than in 1913–29; Britain was one of the few countries to do better in the 1930s. Indeed, during the cyclical recovery from 1932 to 1937 GDP grew at 4 per cent p.a.[40] In the 1960s, a number of historians, and above all H. W. Richardson, seized on strong recovery from a relatively mild depression to argue that the 1930s were a period of transformation and regeneration, laying the basis for the post-war economic miracle. In Richardson's view, Britain was escaping from the burden of the old staple industries of the nineteenth century with their declining export markets, and was moving to new commodities serving a prosperous domestic market. He claimed that 'the real pacesetters in the recovery were the new industries', a 'block' of industries that pushed the economy out of depression. He suggested that these new industries moved through stages, and that the timing of their movement from one stage to another affected the cycle. In his view, the new industries became a significant element in the American economy in the 1920s, so intensifying the boom. By the end of the 1920s, the market for new goods was saturated, and the new industries moved to maturity with lower rates of growth, so intensifying the downturn of the 1930s. By contrast, the new industries were still immature in Britain in the 1920s, moving to the stage of rapid growth and significant weight in the economy in the 1930s. Consequently, they moderated the slump and assisted recovery in the 1930s. Britain's unusually strong recovery is explained, in his opinion, less by economic policies than by structural shifts. Rather than stressing the continued depression of the north, Scotland, and Wales, he emphasized the prosperity of the midlands and south, and even went so far as to argue that unemployment in the 1930s should be seen as a sign of the success of recovery, an indication of high levels of productivity growth.[41]

In the 1970s, another view emerged—what might be termed 'market realism'. In 1979, a controversial article by Benjamin and Kochin proposed that the British economy could have been more rapidly transformed if only markets had been allowed to function, and the poor had not been misguidedly cocooned by generous social benefits. The date is significant: Mrs Thatcher came to power in the same year, dedicated to the imposition of market discipline. Benjamin and Kochin argued that welfare prevented labour markets from clearing, so slowing down the transformation of the economy and resulting in an increase in unemployment.[42] How much credence can be given to these two views?

The diversity of British economic experience was apparent to anyone in the 1930s (see Table 5.8). On the one hand, there was the industrial England of the nineteenth century. On the other, there was the new post-war England:

... of arterial and by-pass roads, of filling stations and factories ... You need money in this England, but you do not need much money ... You could almost accept Woolworths as its symbol. ... Years and years ago the democratic and enterprising Blackpool ... began all this. Modern England is rapidly Blackpooling itself.[43]

The question is how far England had become like Blackpool and Woolworths—or how far the images of the Jarrow hunger marches should stay uppermost in our mental image of the 1930s.

Most historians would now reject both the optimistic and 'market realist' interpretations of the 1930s. Unemployment remained high and cannot be dismissed as the product of exceptional productivity growth and a structural shift from labour- to capital-intensive industries. Any rise in productivity was more plausibly the result of removing the least efficient firms. Structural change was not exceptional, as Richardson proposes. The estimate of Matthews, Feinstein, and Odling-Smee indicates that structural change in manufacturing was twice as high between 1913 and 1924 as between 1900 and 1913, but then fell between 1924 and 1937.[44] Indeed, the case for the role of new industries in the recovery of the 1930s is highly dubious. Richardson fails to define the new industries, and he does not establish that they were a closely linked bloc moving through the various stages. His argument is tautological: new industries are assumed to be those growing most rapidly, and economic recovery is then explained by the high growth rate of the new industries. A more careful analysis would define the new industries by some characteristic other than growth, and then enquire into their growth rate and pattern. We might plausibly assume that the new industries were based on scientific and technical advances in sectors such as chemicals, electrical engineering, precision instruments, and motor vehicles. Yet when the economic performance of such industries is measured, the case for the transforming power of new industries is weak. Their growth was not significantly different, and some sectors (such as light electrical goods) were labour intensive. Neither were the new industries a clearly separate bloc: artificial fibres, for example, were used in the cotton industry.[45]

Nor can the high level of unemployment be explained by the frustration of regeneration by generous welfare benefits. Benjamin and Kochin's model has faced serious technical criticism for assuming that the labour market was in equilibrium and for ignoring sectoral and regional problems. Resources were persistently unemployed, and would have continued to be unemployed regardless of the provision of welfare. Data collected for *The New Survey of London* between 1929 and 1931 show that benefits had no effect on household heads, but that they might have some influence on other adult males who were a small proportion of the adult male workforce. Consequently, the overall effect was low.[46]

The finding is not surprising, for benefits were not particularly generous and the terms of the dole were demeaning. If unemployed men were not actively seeking work, the explanation may be found in factors other than the supposed generosity of benefits. Economists have suggested two alternative possibilities. The first is that the level of unemployment rose as a result of the declining employability of men suffering from long-term idleness who declined into apathy and fatalism. Their chances of re-employment were affected by the time out of work. Rather than reducing the level of long-term unemployment, a cut in benefits would merely have cut welfare still further. Crafts is surely right to suggest that the explanation for any 'voluntary' employment was not that the unemployed were manipulating the welfare system and staying out of work in order to enjoy leisure. Most heads of household had pride in their ability to support their families, which was lost by enforced idleness. Any choice to remain out of work was made under duress.[47] They were victims, not free agents; their leisure was a burden.

Persistent unemployment may more plausibly be explained by the 'shock' in the early 1920s of the reduction in hours of work and of a tight monetary policy. A small part of the rise in unemployment may be explained by demographic trends, for the proportion of the population of working age increased from 64 per cent before the war to 70 per cent 1924-37.[48] More significantly, the ending of the age of mass international migration meant that domestic unemployment could no longer be adjusted by people leaving Britain. Prior to 1914, British workers hit by a collapse of their trade were willing, even eager, to find a new life overseas. The American

TABLE 5.8. *Duration of unemployment, by region and by age (1938) (1932 and 1938)*

	Percentage of applicants unemployed 12 months or more	
	June 1932	Feb 1938
London	4.4	5.8
South-east	3.8	6.6
South-west	8.8	8.6
Midlands	14.6	15.9
North/north-west/north- east	19.6	25.0
Scotland	27.6	29.7
Wales	21.1	30.7

	Duration of male unemployment, GB, Feb. 1938	
	Percentage of claimants unemployed over 1 yr	Average duration of unemployment to date of claimants (weeks)
All	20.5	38.6
18–24	12.6	14.8
25–34	14.3	27.7
35–44	21.0	38.8
45–54	25.5	48.1
55–64	37.0	48.4

Source: Crafts, 'Long-term unemployment in Britain', 421–2.

government imposed restrictions on immigration from 1924, and higher levels of unemployment in the United States in the 1930s meant that migration was scarcely appealing. These demographic variables were considerably less important than strains in the international economy that hit Britain's export markets and created mass unemployment in export sectors. The result was a deficiency of demand, and the failure of home demand to absorb all of the resources. Changes in relative prices might well signal a need to transfer resources from old to new industries—but the low level of aggregate demand constrained the incentive to invest.[49]

Nevertheless, the depression *was* milder than in many other countries and recovery to 1937 was stronger. The explanation is to be found, in part, in the relative stability of domestic consumption. Although domestic consumption did not increase sufficiently to compensate for the loss of export demand and to transform the economy, neither did it collapse (see Table 5.9). The purchasing power of those in work increased. Unlike in other European countries, British farmers were not

TABLE 5.9. *Aggregate consumption, Britain, 1929–38, £m*

	Consumers' expenditure Current market prices	1929 prices
1929	4,062	4,062
1930	4,006	4,206
1931	3,865	4,290
1932	3,743	4,267
1933	3,751	4,329
1934	3,864	4,482
1935	3,995	4,554
1936	4,145	4,601
1937	4,356	4,661
1938	4,457	4.680

Source: Richardson, *Economic Recovery*, 103.

protected and consumers did not pay high prices for their food, so that more spending power could be released for consumer goods. The fall in the birth rate meant that family income was freed from support of children. Real wages rose; and welfare benefits for those out of work helped to stabilize demand. Taxation remained at the level of the First World War, and contributed to a redistribution of income from rich to poor. The shift in factor shares from capital to labour was preserved, and resulted in an increase in the propensity to consume.

Economic policy provides a further explanation. The adoption of protection and abandonment of the gold standard together amounted to a policy of economic nationalism on similar lines to many other countries. However, a number of peculiarities moderated the impact of the depression. In the first place, British governments in the 1930s had more freedom than their counterparts in adopting an active domestic monetary policy. The emphasis on financial stability and prudence in the 1920s resulted in deflation and overvaluation that constrained recovery up to 1929. More positively, Britain avoided high levels of inflation and maintained both the legitimacy of state finances and the security of the financial system. Consequently, British politicians could be more flexible in response to the slump. Generally, those countries devaluing soonest in the 1930s were those which overvalued in the 1920s, so 'buying' financial stability with room for greater discretion in the future. Thus the French government undervalued the franc in the early 1920s and suffered from inflation; in the 1930s, devaluation of the franc was rejected and growth was low. In Britain, overvaluation of the pound in the 1920s led to low growth and low inflation, and made devaluation more acceptable in the 1930s. By holding the pound below its earlier level, the depressed export industries were helped and the domestic

TABLE 5.10. *GDP growth rates of gold bloc and devaluers, 1932–7, and change in industrial production, 1929–36 (%)*

	Growth rate (% p.a.)
Gold bloc	
Belgium	1.86
France	1.51
Devaluers	
Germany	8.16
UK	4.18
USA	8.42 (1933–7)

Change in industrial production (%)	
Gold bloc	−13.9
Exchange control	−2.3
Sterling bloc	27.8
Other depreciators	27.1

Source: Solomou, *Themes*, 118–19.

market was protected from imports. By abandoning the rigidity of the gold standard, the British government could allow interest rates to fall and to expand the money supply.[50] The divergence in growth rates between different exchange rate regimes is clear in Table 5.10: devaluers did better than those remaining on gold. The initiators of devaluation benefited from early recovery, but they have also been condemned for 'beggar my neighbour' policies. As Eichengreen and Sachs point out, the criticism is not entirely fair. Protectionism necessarily leaves everyone worse off, whereas devaluation does lead to benefits of lower interest rates, higher domestic investment, and increased demand in the depreciating country. Of course, other countries lose, but the extent to which they are 'beggared' depends on the way the policy of devaluation was pursued as a corrective to price disparities or aggressively to secure market share. In the 1930s, the lack of co-ordination meant that it was harmful on balance; after 1944, devaluation was more carefully controlled in order to correct imbalances.[51]

How did monetary policy influence recovery? At least until 1935, banks did not increase advances to industry, so that the impact of lower interest rates was more likely to be through the stimulus to housing or to consumption. One of the most distinctive features of the 1930s was a housing boom. However, the influence of cheap money and housing should not be exaggerated. Building societies attracted more money in the 1920s, so that they were able to provide more loans even without cheap money. The fall in the cost of borrowing was not the only reason for the boom: at the same time, the income of those in work rose and building costs and land prices fell. Perhaps half of the rise in building may be explained by low interest rates; and the contribution of housing to the growth of GDP actually declined from 12.5 per cent between 1924 and 1929 to 8.7 per cent in 1932–3. House building was most important in the early stages of recovery, accounting for 17 per cent of the rise in GDP between 1932 and 1933.[52] Perhaps the greatest influence of cheap money was indirect: low interest rates and cheaper mortgage payments stimulated demand for consumer goods, and hence the recovery in manufacturing industry.[53] Indeed, manufacturing industry was much more important than housing, accounting for 35.6 per cent of growth in GDP between 1924 and 1929, and 46.6 per cent in 1932–3.[54]

In the early 1920s, overvaluation made British goods uncompetitive and allowed foreign suppliers to penetrate British markets. Abandoning gold and devaluing gave British exporters a competitive advantage, and increased the cost of imported goods. The shift in exchange rate policy was complemented by a move away from unilateral free trade to protection with the general tariff of 1932 (see Table 5.11 and Chapter 6). Exchange rates and tariffs worked together, giving domestic producers a gain in competitiveness. The combination of devaluation and protection meant that the import penetration of the early 1920s was now reversed and domestic producers took a larger share of the market (see Chapter 6). Did the policy lead to recovery? Capie is very sceptical. The two sectors contributing most to recovery were construction and iron and steel, and both received very low effective rates of protection. Clearly, there was no danger of competition from imported houses, and builders paid duties on inputs of timber and other materials. Consequently, the building industry was 'taxed' with an effective rate of protection of −7.2 per cent. Shipbuilding faced the same problem. Imperial preference did not create a customs union with a large free trade zone, and was more in the nature of a collection of agreements. On Capie's figures, the main result of imperial preference was to protect the motor car industry and to embitter the United States. Kitson and Solomou dissent and argue that protection was crucial to recovery. Industries that lacked protection in the

TABLE 5.11. *Average tariff levels of European countries, 1913–31*

	1913	1927	1931
Germany	16.7	20.4	40.7
France	23.6	23.0	38.0
Italy	24.8	27.8	48.3
UK	—	4.0	17.0

Source: Solomou, *Themes*, 133.

TABLE 5.12. *Output indices for the newly protected and non-newly protected manufacturing sectors, UK, 1929–35 (1935 = 100)*

	Newly protected	Non-newly protected
1924	83.22	76.13
1930	82.83	89.18
1935	100.00	100.00
Growth per annum (%)		
1924–30	−0.1	+2.7
1930–5	+3.8	+2.3

Source: Kitson and Solomou, *Protectionism and Economic Recovery*, 77.

1920s declined between 1924 and 1930; they grew by 3.8 per cent between 1930 and 1935 (see Table 5.12). Protection was linked with preference for the empire. Imports from foreign countries fell from 71 per cent in 1931 to 59.6 per cent in 1938; at the same time, exports to foreign countries fell from 56.3 to 50.1 per cent.[55] Britain, in common with many other countries, was creating a trading bloc in response to the collapse of multilateral trade. The strategy was arguably counter-productive, leading to a general decline in foreign trade and contributing to the lack of demand in the world economy. In the longer term, reliance on empire markets delayed diversification and integration with Europe. But in the shorter term, and given the general shift to trade blocs throughout the world, Britain had an advantage in the size of its imperial trade bloc.

Trans-Second World War, 1937–1951

Although the experience of the Second World War had some similarities with the First World War, there were also striking differences. Both wars led to the loss of assets and to deterioration in the balance of payments, to low investment, and increased government involvement in the economy. More striking was a marked difference between the two post-war periods: after the Second World War, growth continued without massive disruptions. The Second World War brought the unemployment of resources of the inter-war period to an end and created a new equilibrium. From 1951, growth accelerated and the developed world experienced a remarkable period of prosperity.

In 1939, the British economy had spare capacity that was brought into full use during the war. The long-term unemployed now returned to the labour market, and employment increased as more women moved into the labour market to fill the gaps left by the mobilization of men (see Table 5.13 and Fig. 5.2). The increase in labour

TABLE 5.13. *UK population and employment, 1939–45 (% of 1938)*

	Population	Employment inc. armed forces	Female civil employment	Armed forces
1939	100.6	104.1	104.9	111.1
1943	102.2	116.7	146.8	1,106.5
1945	103.1	113.0	136.2	1,187.5

Source: Broadberry and Howlett, 'The United Kingdom', 46.

TABLE 5.14. *UK GDP per employee, 1938 (%)*

1939	97.0
1943	108.8
1944	103.2

Source: Broadberry and Howlett, 'The United Kingdom', 46.

productivity per employee was modest, and most of the increase in output came as a result of an increase in employment (Table 5.14). In the early months of the war, the construction or conversion of plant, and the training of workers, meant that productivity gains were not to be expected; later, productivity improved as conditions stabilized. The government gave more attention to schemes to increase efficiency, though with only limited success. Not surprisingly, a large proportion of expenditure was directed away from consumption towards the war, with considerable net disinvestment in non-war sectors. In 1938, consumption amounted to 87.2 per cent of the UK's net national expenditure, with war spending accounting for 7.4 per cent and non-war investment for 5.4 per cent. At the peak of mobilization in 1943, consumption was down to 55.5 per cent of net national expenditure, with war spending up to 55.3 per cent and non-war investment at 10.8 per cent. Overall, net losses during the war amounted to 18.6 per cent of pre-war wealth.[56]

Unlike in the First World War, the government was much more conscious of the risks of inflation. It was more concerned to remove the 'inflationary gap' of excess spending through high taxation, supplemented by subsidies to food and essential goods to hold down prices. Although most accounts of the war emphasize the success of fiscal policy, recently historians have pointed to the potential impact of high taxation on incentives, and the distorting impact of subsidies on consumer preferences. The government also borrowed to finance the war, with low interest rates to reduce the cost of servicing the debt. The government took steps to encourage the private sector to hold long-term government debt in order to prevent inflationary pressure, by controlling other outlets through the Capital Issues Committee and restrictions on bank advances. As a result, the monetary supply increased modestly, with strict controls over banks to prevent inflationary pressures. Further, the government introduced rationing and controls. In spring 1945, rationing covered about a third of consumer spending and poses the question of whether consumers complied voluntarily, or were strictly monitored and policed.[57] Scarce resources were allocated by the government, not least through the 'manpower budget'—the allocation of labour to the armed forces, munitions, or civilian consumption. The total workforce rose from 17.8m in 1938 to a peak of 22.2m in 1943, with a fall in the share of all sectors except munitions and the armed forces up to 1943. In 1943, munitions and related industries formed the largest sector, with 23.6 per cent of employed workers in the UK. As munitions supply increased from the United States, more British workers were shifted to the armed forces. These two sectors accounted for over 40 per cent of the workforce from 1942.[58] The result was a decline in the production of consumer goods. The market no longer allocated resources by means of price signals; instead, scarce resources were allocated through centralized controls and planning.

Of course, there were serious problems in allocating resources by administrative decision, for different government departments were in conflict. Crucially, the price mechanism had to be replaced by detailed and reliable statistical data. Individual departments might attempt to limit the flow of information in order to protect their position or to manipulate data to their advantage, so a neutral body was needed to filter the data. Decision making was divided into two spheres. The first was the strategic sphere where military decisions were taken, by feeding information upwards from the various theatres of war to the service departments, with a final decision taken by the War Cabinet. Strategy was dominant, determining the allocation of resources to production. The decisions were then passed downwards from the War Cabinet to the production sphere where output was determined to meet the military needs, descending from the Defence Committee (Supply) to individual firms. The two spheres were linked through the War Cabinet Office, and the data on resouces produced by each department and industry were assessed by 'neutral' or expert bodies—the Central Statistical Office and the Economic Section. This system ensured that the flow of information was both full and free. Officials gradually moved from competition to co-operation. Resource allocation during the war was to have a longer-term impact, for ministers in the post-war Labour government were heavily involved and they drew on their wartime experiences in their peacetime plans. Physical planning seemed to work in allocating resources: what role remained for the price mechanism and market?

At the end of the First World War, the removal of controls led to a boom and slump; after the Second World War, controls were maintained and demand was more gradually released. Britain was also in a stronger position in export markets, for competitors were more seriously affected than during the First World War. The recovery of exports was assisted by the different attitude to exchange rates, for the international agreement at Bretton Woods in 1944 created a compromise between stability of exchange rates and their readjustment in response to economic difficulties. Unlike in the early 1920s, there was no worldwide slump or serious industrial unrest.[59] However, optimism should not be taken too far.

After 1951, Britain grew much less rapidly than other major European economies, though somewhat faster than the United States. One explanation is that the share of the workforce in industry was falling. Another was Britain's institutional structure and policy options. In the second half of the nineteenth century unions were accepted and given a powerful legal position, yet adopted an adversarial attitude to employers based on a belief that wages and profits were in opposition. The system survived between the wars, and after 1945 the Labour government secured the agreement of unions to a wage freeze designed to prevent inflation and to hold down costs, in return for dividend restraint. The policy continued into the 1950s, and resulted in a 'low-effort equilibrium'. Why should workers and industrialists make the effort to raise productivity if wages and profits were held down? This low-effort equilibrium was not threatened by competition from abroad or at home, for protectionism was not challenged, and price and output quotas survived. The exigencies of war and the ideology of Labour meant that competition was severely limited, so that poor management and low quality went unpunished. Reform was to prove difficult. Individual firms could not change the system of industrial relations which was part of a much wider social and political structure. For their part, politicians were disinclined to take actions with uncertain economic benefits; they were more concerned with re-election and hence short-term economic management.[60] The characteristics of the British economy of the late nineteenth and first half of the twentieth century were to linger on to the 1980s. Such an interpretation of economic growth is close to another political nostrum: the need for liberal market economics. Economic history continues to inform and to be shaped by debates over the current state of the British economy.

NOTES

1. Tomlinson, 'Inventing "decline" ', 732–3.
2. Habakkuk, *American and British Technology*; Tomlinson, 'British "productivity problem" ', 194.
3. Broadberry, *Productivity Race*, 31, 40–1.
4. For example, Hobsbawm, *Industry and Empire*, 296; Kindleberger, 'Foreign trade and economic growth', 10; Best, *Mid-Victorian Britain*, 1. Church, *Great Victorian Boom* still provides a useful overview.

5. Church, *Great Victorian Boom*, 55, 76–7.
6. Wrigley, *Continuity, Chance and Change*, 108–9.
7. Quoted in Court, *British Economic History*, 19.
8. Marshall quoted in Saul, *Myth*, 16.
9. Phelps Brown and Handfield-Jones, 'Climacteric of the 1890s', 282–3.
10. Coppock, 'Climacteric of the 1890s', 2.
11. An early statement was Aldcroft, 'Entrepreneur'; his approach was developed by Wiener, *English Culture* which was taken up by Conservative politicians in the 1980s.
12. Wilson, 'Economy and society'. See Ch. 4 for details.
13. McCloskey and Sandberg, 'From damnation to redemption'.
14. McCloskey, 'Did Victorian Britain fail?', 459.
15. Pollard, 'Capital exports', 495, 513; Crafts, 'Victorian Britain did fail', 536, 533; Crafts and Thomas, 'Comparative advantage', 643.
16. Elbaum and Lazonick (eds.), *Decline*, 2, 28; 19–21 Lazonick, *Competitive Advantage*, 177, 178, 184.
17. Crafts, Leybourne, and Mills, 'Climacteric', 115; Bean and Crafts, 'British economic growth', 145–7.
18. Matthews, Feinstein, and Odling-Smee, *British Economic Growth*, appendix L, 606–7 and Feinstein, Matthews, and Odling-Smee, 'Timing of the climacteric', 175.
19. Matthews, Feinstein, and Odling-Smee, *British Economic Growth*, 113–5.
20. Solomou, *Themes*, 7.
21. Solomou and Weale, 'Balanced estimates', 59, 61–2; Crafts, Leybourne, and Mills, 'Climacteric', 103, 113–15. See also Greasley, 'British economic growth', 417–18, 423, 429–31, 438–9.
22. Broadberry, 'Emergence of mass unemployment', 271; see also Broadberry, 'Aggregate supply in interwar Britain', 467–81; Solomou, *Themes*, 11; See also Crafts, Leybourne, and Mills, 'Climacteric' 105, 114–15.
23. Matthews, Feinstein, and Odling-Smee, *British Economic Growth*, 543.
24. Solomou and Weale, 'UK national income', 105–9.
25. Matthews, Feinstein, and Odling-Smee, *British Economic Growth*, 503; Dowie, '1919–20', 440.
26. Broadberry, 'Emergence of mass unemployment', 274–6.
27. Matthews, Feinstein, and Odling-Smee, *British Economic Growth*, 543–4.
28. Broadberry, *British Economy*, 81–3.
29. Solomou, *Themes*, 68.
30. Dowie, '1919–20', 447.
31. Broadberry, *British Economy*, 94.
32. Redmond, 'Sterling overvaluation', 523, 529. For an alternative estimate, see Matthews, 'Was sterling overvalued' and the doubts expressed about his calculations by Solomou, *Themes*, 38–9.
33. Solomou, *Themes*, 40 and fig. 2.5; Broadberry, *British Economy*, 121 and 'Emergence of mass unemployment', 279–81.
34. Moggridge, *British Monetary Policy*, 245–9; Broadberry, 'North European depression', 166–7.

35. Solomou, *Themes*, 47; Kitson and Solomou, *Protectionism and Economic Revival*, 51–3, 83.
36. Solomou, *Themes*, 35, 44–6, 48; Broadberry, 'North European depression', 166–7.
37. Solomou, *Themes*, 47.
38. Daunton, *Just Taxes*, 83–94.
39. These figures are open to dispute: see Garside, *British Unemployment*, 5, 8–14.
40. Solomou, *Themes*, 113–14.
41. Richardson, *Economic Recovery*, 82, 90–3, 96–9, 315–16; Richardson, 'Basis of economic recovery', 354, 361, 363; Richardson, 'New industries', 366; Richardson, 'Over-commitment', 240–2.
42. Benjamin and Kochin, 'Searching', 442, 464–7.
43. Priestley, *English Journey*, 400–2.
44. Broadberry, 'Unemployment in inter-war Britain', 463–4, 467, 483; Matthews, Feinstein, and Odling-Smee, *British Economic Growth*, table 9.1, 255.
45. Broadberry, 'Unemployment in inter-war Britain', 467–9; von Tunzelman, 'Structural change', 5, 34–5, 42, 46–7; Dowie, 'Growth', 103–7.
46. Collins, 'Unemployment in interwar Britain', 371, 374–5, 378; Crafts, 'Long-term unemployment in Britain', 427–31; Hatton, 'Unemployment benefits', 487–90, 502–4; Eichengreen, 'Unemployment', 602, 613–21.
47. Crafts, 'Long-term unemployment in Britain', 426, 431.
48. Solomou, *Themes*, 78. In Feinstein Matthews, and Odling-Smee's growth-accounting model, higher labour inputs contributed to growth in TFI: 'Timing of the climacteric', 178–9.
49. Broadberry, 'Unemployment in inter-war Britain', 465, 483.
50. Solomou, *Themes*, 49; Redmond, 'Indicator', 88.
51. Eichengreen and Sachs, 'Exchange rates'.
52. Humphries, 'Inter-war house building', 325–6, 329, 332, 334, 336, 342; Broadberry, 'Cheap money', 383; Kitson and Solomou, *Protectionism and Economic Recovery*, 91–2; Solomou, *Themes*, 126.
53. Bowden, 'Consumer durables revolution', 52.
54. Solomou, *Themes*, 126.
55. Ibid., 153; Kitson, Solomou, and Weale, 'Effective protection', 335.
56. Broadberry and Howlett, 'The United Kingdom', 47, 69.
57. Ibid. 54.
58. Ibid. 57–8.
59. Matthews, Feinstein, and Odling-Smee, *British Economic Growth*, 545–6.
60. Bean and Crafts, 'British economic growth', 153–4; Eichengreen, 'Institutions and economic growth', 43–6.

FURTHER READING

Aldcroft, D. H., 'The entrepreneur and the British economy, 1870–1914', *Economic History Review*, 17 (1964)

——— 'Technical progress and British enterprise, 1875–1914', *Business History*, 8 (1966)

Bean, C., and Crafts, N. F. R., 'British economic growth since 1945: relative economic decline . . . and renaissance?', in N. F. R. Crafts and G. Toniolo (eds.), *Economic Growth in Europe since 1945* (Cambridge, 1996)

Benjamin, D. K., and Kochin, L. A., 'Searching for an explanation of unemployment in interwar Britain', *Journal of Political Economy*, 87 (1979)

Best, G., *Mid-Victorian Britain* (1971)

Booth, A., 'The manufacturing failure hypothesis and the performance of British industry during the long boom', *Economic History Review*, 56 (2003)

—— Melling, J., and Dartmann, C., 'Institutions and economic growth: the politics of productivity in West Germany, Sweden and the United Kingdom, 1945–55', *Journal of Economic History*, 57 (1997)

Bowden, S., 'The consumer durables revolution in England, 1932–38: a regional analysis', *Explorations in Economic History*, 25 (1988)

—— and Turner, P., 'The demand for consumer durables in the United Kingdom in the interwar period', *Journal of Economic History*, 53 (1993)

Broadberry, S., *Productivity Race: British Manufacturing in International Perspective, 1850–1990* (Cambridge, 1997)

—— 'Unemployment in inter-war Britain: a disequilibrium approach', *Oxford Economic Papers*, 35 (1983)

—— 'The north European depression in the 1920s', *Scandinavian Economic History Review*, 32 (1984)

—— *The British Economy between the Wars: A Macroeconomic Survey* (Oxford, 1986)

—— 'Cheap money and the housing boom in interwar Britain: an econometric appraisal', *Manchester School*, 87 (1987)

—— 'The emergence of mass unemployment: explaining macroeconomic trends in Britain during the trans-World War I period', *Economic History Review*, 43 (1990)

—— 'Aggregate supply in interwar Britain', *Economic Journal*, 96 (1986)

—— and Crafts, N. F. R., 'The impact of the depression of the 1930s on the production potential of the United Kingdom', *European Economic Review*, 34 (1990)

—— and Howlett, P, 'The United Kingdom: "Victory at all costs"', in M. Harrison (ed.), *The Economics of World War II: Six Great Powers in International Comparison* (Cambridge, 1998)

Cagan, P., *Determinants and Effects of Changes in the Stock of Money, 1875–1960* (New York, 1965)

Church, R. A., *The Great Victorian Boom, 1850–1873* (1975)

Coleman, D., 'Gentlemen and players', *Economic History Review* (1973)

Collins, M., 'Unemployment in interwar Britain: still searching for an explanation', *Journal of Political Economy*, 90 (1982)

Coppock, D. J., 'The climacteric of the 1890s: a critical note', *Manchester School*, 24 (1956)

Court, W. H. B., *British Economic History, 1870–1914: Commentary and Documents* (Cambridge, 1965)

Crafts, N. F. R., 'Victorian Britain did fail', *Economic History Review*, 32 (1979)

—— 'Long-term unemployment in Britain in the 1930s', *Economic History Review*, 40 (1987)

Crafts, N. F. R., 'Long-term unemployment and the wage equation in Britain, 1925–39', *Economica*, 56 (1989)

—— Leybourne, S. J., and Mills, T. C., 'The climacteric in late Victorian Britain and France: a reappraisal of the evidence', *Journal of Applied Econometrics*, 4 (1989)

—— and Thomas, M., 'Comparative advantage in UK manufacturing trade, 1910–35', *Economic Journal*, 96 (1986)

—— and Toniolo, G., 'Post-war growth: an overview', in N. F. R. Crafts and G. Toniolo (eds.), *Economic Growth in Europe since 1945* (Cambridge, 1996)

Daunton, M., *Just Taxes: The Politics of Taxation in Britain, 1914–1979* (Cambridge, 2002)

Dowie, J., '1919–20 is in need of attention', *Economic History Review*, 28 (1975)

—— 'Growth in the inter-war period: some more arithmetic', *Economic History Review*, 21 (1968)

Eichengreen, B. J., 'Unemployment in interwar Britain: dole or doldrums?', *Oxford Economic Papers*, 39 (1987)

—— 'Institutions and economic growth: Europe after World War II', in N. F. R. Crafts and G. Toniolov (eds.), *Economic Growth in Europe since 1945* (Cambridge, 1996)

—— and Sachs, J. D., 'Exchange rates and economic recovery in the 1930s', *Journal of Economic History*, 45 (1985).

Elbaum, B., and Lazonick, W. (eds.), *The Decline of the British Economy* (Oxford, 1986)

Feinstein, C. H., Matthews, R. C. O., and Odling-Smee, J. C., 'The timing of the climacteric and its sectoral incidence in the UK, 1873–1913', in C. P. Kindleberger and G. diTella (eds.), *Economics in the Long View: Essays in Honour of W. W. Rostow*, vol. ii (1982)

Garside, W., *British Unemployment, 1919–1939: A Study in Public Policy* (Cambridge, 1990)

Glynn, S., and Booth, A., 'Unemployment in interwar Britain: a case for relearning the lessons of the 1930s?', *Economic History Review*, 36 (1983)

Greasley, D., 'British economic growth: the paradox of the 1880s and the timing of the climacteric', *Explorations in Economic History*, 23 (1986)

Habakkuk, H. J., *American and British Technology in the Nineteenth Century: The Search for Labour Saving Inventions* (Cambridge, 1962)

Hatton, T. J., 'Unemployment benefits and the macroeconomics of the interwar labour market: a further analysis', *Oxford Economic Papers*, 35 (1983)

Higgonet, R. P., 'Bank deposits in the UK, 1870–1914', *Quarterly Journal of Economics*, 71 (1957)

Hobsbawm, E. J., *Industry and Empire: An Economic History of Britain since 1750* (1968)

Howlett, P., 'New light through old windows: a new perspective on the British economy in the Second World War', *Journal of Contemporary History*, 28 (1993)

Humphries, J., 'Inter-war house building, cheap money and building societies: the housing boom revisited', *Business History*, 29 (1987)

Kindleberger, C. P., 'Foreign trade and economic growth; lessons from Britain and France, 1850–1913', *Economic History Review*, 14 (1961)

Kirby, M. W., 'Institutional rigidities and Britain's industrial decline', *Business History Review* 63 (1989)

—— 'Institutional rigidities and economic decline: reflections on the British experience', *Economic History Review*, 45 (1992)

Kitson, M., and Solomou, S., *Protectionism and Economic Revival: The British Interwar Economy* (Cambridge, 1990)

Kitson, M., and Weale, M. R., 'Effective protection and economic recovery in the United Kingdom during the 1930s', *Economic History Review*, 44 (1991)

Lazonick, W., *Competitive Advantage on the Shop Floor* (Cambridge Mass., 1990)

McCloskey, D. N, 'Did Victorian Britain fail?', *Economic History Review*, 23 (1970)

—— and Sandberg, L. G., 'From damnation to redemption: judgments on the late Victorian entrepreneur', *Explorations in Economic History* (1971)

Matthews, K. G. P., 'Was sterling overvalued in 1925?', *Economic History Review*, 39 (1986)

Matthews, R. C. O., Feinstein, C. H., and Odling-Smee, J. C., *British Economic Growth, 1856–1973* (Oxford, 1982)

Mercer, H., 'The Monopolies and Restrictive Practices Commission 1949–56: a study in regulatory failure', in G. Jones and M. Kirby (eds.), *Competitiveness and the State* (Manchester, 1991)

Mills, T. C., 'Are fluctuations in UK output transitory or permanent?', *Manchester School*, 59 (1991)

Moggridge, D. E., *British Monetary Policy, 1934–1951* (Cambridge, 1972)

Phelps Brown, E. H., and Handfield-Jones, S. J., 'The climacteric of the 1890s: a study in the expanding economy', *Oxford Economic Papers*, 4 (1952)

Phinney, J. T., 'Gold production and the price level', *Quarterly Journal of Economics*, 47 (1933)

Pollard, S., 'Capital exports, 1870–1914: harmful or beneficial?', *Economic History Review*, 38 (1985)

Priestley, J. B. *English Journey* (1934)

Redmond, J., 'An indicator of the effective exchange rate of the pound in the 1930s', *Economic History Review*, 33 (1980)

—— 'The sterling overvaluation in 1925: a multilateral approach', *Economic History Review*, 37 (1984)

Richardson, H. W., 'The new industries between the wars', *Oxford Economic Papers*, 13 (1961)

—— 'The basis of economic recovery in the 1930s: a review and a new interpretation', *Economic History Review*, 15 (1962)

—— *Economic Recovery in Britain, 1932–1939* (1967)

—— 'Over-commitment in Britain before 1930', *Oxford Economic Papers*, 17 (1965)

Rostow, W. W., *The British Economy of the Nineteenth Century* (Oxford, 1948)

Saul, S. B., *The Myth of the Great Depression, 1873–1896* (1969)

Solomou, S., *Themes in Macroeconomic History: The UK Economy, 1919–1939* (Cambridge, 1996)

—— and Weale, M., 'Balanced estimates of UK GDP, 1870–1913', *Explorations in Economic History*, 28 (1991)

—— —— 'UK national income 1920–38: the implications of balanced estimates', *Economic History Review*, 49 (1996)

Southall, H. 'The urban labour market', in M. Daunton (ed.), *The Cambridge Urban History of Britain*, iii: *1840–1950* (Cambridge, 2000)

Tomlinson, J., 'The British "productivity problem" in the 1960s', *Past and Present*, 175 (2002)

—— 'Inventing "decline": the falling behind of the British economy in the postwar years', *Economic History Review*, 49 (1996)

Von Tunzelmann, G. N., 'Structural change and leading sectors in British manufacturing', in C. P. Kindleberger and G. di Tella (eds.), *Economics in the Long View: Essays in Honor of W. W. Rostow*, ii (1982)

Wiener, M., *English Culture and the Decline of the Industrial Spirit, 1850–1980* (Cambridge, 1981)

Wilson, C., 'Economy and society in late Victorian Britain', *Economic History Review*, 18 (1965)

Wrigley, E. A., *Continuity, Chance and Change: The Character of the Industrial Revolution in England* (Cambridge, 1988)

PART II

....

GLOBALIZATION AND DEGLOBALIZATION

....

CHAPTER 6

Free Trade and Protectionism

'What an extraordinary episode in the economic progress of man that age was which came to an end in August 1914!', exclaimed Keynes from the very different world of the 1920s:

The inhabitant of London could order by telephone, sipping his morning tea in bed, the various products of the whole earth, in such quantity as he might see fit, and reasonably expect their early delivery upon his doorstep; he could at the same moment and by the same means adventure his wealth in the natural resources and new enterprises of any quarter of the world, and share, without exertion or even trouble, in their prospective fruits and advantages. . . . [He] could then proceed abroad to foreign quarters, without knowledge of their religion, language or customs, bearing coined wealth upon his person, and would consider himself greatly aggrieved and much surprised at the least interference.[1]

Here was a hymn of praise to the *pax Britannica* and global economy of the nineteenth and early twentieth centuries. Trade was free, the gold standard assured stability of exchanges, the Royal Navy kept the sea lanes open, the British merchant marine was the world's carrier, the City of London provided finance and insurance, the movement of capital and labour was unfettered by controls. The dream of Richard Cobden that the pursuit of comparative advantage would lead to economic prosperity and international harmony—had seemingly come to pass. The situation was very different by the end of the First World War, when Keynes was eulogizing a world under threat.

The process of globalization of the late nineteenth and early twentieth centuries gave way to deglobalization in the 1930s, when even Keynes accepted the case for national or 'insular' capitalism. Cobden had hoped free trade would link nations together in peace and harmony; Keynes similarly wished to create the conditions of peace, but he realized that different times required different policies. In the late nineteenth century, a combination of free trade, fixed exchange rates, and capital mobility seemed to underwrite economic growth at home and abroad. After the First World War, the situation was very different. In their attempt to return to the golden age of 1914, politicians appeared to sacrifice domestic prosperity to the gold standard and free trade, assuming that wages and costs should adjust to international exchanges. In the 1920s and 1930s, the threat to peace and prosperity came to be seen in the social tensions arising from economic collapse and mass unemployment. Keynes saw the dangers and he argued that international policies should adjust to domestic wages rather than the other way around. Free trade and international capital mobility were, he feared, likely to create 'strains and enmities': 'let goods be homespun whenever it is reasonably and conveniently possible; and, above all, let finance be primarily national.' He believed that economic nationalism would not lead to conflict, for 'If nations can learn to provide themselves with full employment by their domestic policy . . . there need be no important economic forces calculated to set the interest of one country against that of its neighbours.'[2] The ambition of his *General Theory of Employment, Interest and Money* was to re-establish the conditions for peace, by creating domestic prosperity in a period of deglobalization. During the war, he shifted his ground to urge the creation of a new set of institutions to resolve the tensions between domestic prosperity and the international economy. The theme of this chapter is the rise and fall of the assumption that free trade was the pillar of Britain's prosperity and welfare.

The Political Culture of Free Trade

In 1850, the political economy of free trade was still contested by Tory protectionists. In their view, production and consumption would not automatically balance, and the interests of domestic producers should be protected to achieve sustainable economic development. The solution to economic depression was to boost consumption by creating stable markets at home and in the colonies, not merely to protect agriculture but to support domestic production more generally. This was a plausible response to the problems of cyclical depression and poverty in the second quarter of the century—and was to reappear in a new guise in the depression of the 1930s. The protectionists rejected the assumptions of free traders. In their opinion, growth rested on a balance between production and consumption which would be thrown out of equilibrium by free trade. Free trade would sacrifice domestic producers to international competition, and so threaten a collapse of consumer demand. Protection, claimed G. C. Holland, supplied the 'broad basis of home consumption, on which the interests of all classes can alone permanently repose'. Protectionists justified their policy as socially inclusive, and they attacked free traders for creating economic and political imbalance. They believed that repeal of the corn laws marked the imposition of the narrowly self-interested view of urban manufacturers, the abandonment rather than the emergence of an impartial economic policy.[3]

TABLE 6.1. *Net customs revenue as a percentage of net import values, Britain and France, 1841–1900*

	Britain	France
1841–5	32.2	17.9
1861–5	11.5	5.9
1876–80	6.1	6.6
1896–1900	5.3	10.2

Source: Nye, 'Myth of free trade Britain', 26.

In 1852, the Conservatives accepted political realities and abandoned their opposition to free trade. As yet, free trade was less dogmatic than it was to become by the early twentieth century. In the 1850s, import duties could still be maintained for revenue purposes. Duties were only gradually reduced, and the British economy was probably *less* open than the French until the 1880s (see Table 6.1). In the 1850s, Cobden's vision of world peace flowing from trade was not shared by many leading Whig and Liberal politicians. In Palmerston's vision, diplomacy and, where necessary, force were needed to secure trade, as in the case of the opium wars in China in 1839–42 and 1856–60. In 1842, the treaty of Nanking opened five Chinese ports to British trade, as well as ceding Hong Kong to Britain. When the Chinese authorities searched a British-registered ship in 1856, the governor of Hong Kong retaliated by bombarding Canton. Palmerston, who was now Prime Minister, supported his action and won a general election on the issue. Military intervention resulted in a further eleven ports being opened to western merchants, and the use of opium was legalized. Protectionism might have been renounced in 1852, yet tension continued between the political economy of Cobden and Palmerston. Cobden's approach only moved to the ascendant in the 1860s, as a result of Gladstone's desire to reduce government expenditure and Cobden's own shift from unilateral free trade. Rather than adopting free trade and waiting for other countries to follow, Cobden now accepted the need for diplomacy. The Cobden–Chevalier treaty of 1860 marked the shift away from unilateral free trade to negotiated tariff reductions. The treaty offered the French a reduction in duties on silks, wines, and spirits, in return for the abolition of prohibitory duties on British goods, and a general reduction in duties to 25 per cent over five years. The French agreed to negotiate further treaties with other countries, and then to pass on the benefit to Britain through the 'most favoured nation' clause of the Cobden–Chevalier treaty. Other free traders criticized the treaty as an abandonment of pure, unilateral free trade principles. The Cobdenites defended themselves by pointing out that earlier bilateral treaties limited the tariff reductions to the two countries; by contrast, the new treaty offered the benefits to *all* countries. John Bright, Cobden's ally in the Anti-Corn Law League, explained that the treaty did not entail a retrograde policy of 'exclusive dealing and bargaining' between Britain and France: 'All that England has done in this case has been to carry out in practice, towards all the world, in respect of some remaining items of our tariff, that principle of free trade which we have so loudly professed.'[4]

The treaty offered an alternative to Palmerston's imperialism. Unlike Palmerston's concern with the empire, British welfare was to be linked with Europe—in part a response to the Indian Mutiny of 1857. Indeed, the self-governing dominions were using their new political freedoms to erect tariff barriers. Canada adopted a new tariff in 1859 and Victoria introduced new duties in 1866. The treaty would also create an *entente cordiale* at a time of strain in Anglo-French relations. As Gladstone remarked, 'there were only two alternatives, one of them the French treaty and the other war with France'.[5] By reducing revenue from tariffs, the treaty would help him to impose financial retrenchment after the expense of Palmerston's foreign policy and particularly the Crimean War.

In reality, British and continental European policies were somewhat divergent. British liberal ideology preferred an open market for goods from all countries on a non-discriminatory basis, and hostility to commercial diplomacy revived from the later 1860s. As Gladstone pointed out in 1871 when the treaty with France was due for renewal, 'is it not our safest course to fall back upon our old basis namely that the cause of freedom in commerce will, as a rule, be most effectively advanced by leaving each nation to consider the subject in the light of its interests alone'.[6] Further, Gladstone was concerned that negotiations would strengthen the claims of vested interests within Britain, as well as drawing British politicians into French domestic politics. Most other countries opted for bilateral agreements. After 1860, the British government reduced tariffs for *all* countries; and the French negotiated additional reciprocal deals with selected other countries. The result was a low-tariff zone in Europe, which 'arguably achieved its nearest approach to a liberal trading regime until after the Second World War'.[7] These bilateral agreements led to an attempt to create a European customs union in 1875—a precursor of the later European Common Market, and a departure from a single world of free trade favoured by British liberals. The scheme failed, the Anglo-French treaty was not renewed in 1877, and European tariffs started to move up in the 1870s. Commercial diplomacy was losing its appeal with the rise of Prussia and wars against Austria and France. Free trade within Europe was not a solution to militarism. The emergence of competing European imperialisms, with the attempt to create self-sustaining trade zones, called into question Britain's turn to Europe. 'Most favoured nation' agreements expired, tariffs were raised, and trade wars broke out. British officials and politicians held aloof, adopting a strict stance of unilateralism rather than using treaties to bargain for tariff reductions in Europe.[8]

The change in approach reflected the fact that Britain had little to offer in terms of further reductions in tariffs. At the end of the nineteenth century, the commitment to a completely open market meant that British officials were incapable of negotiating with trading partners to retain open markets for British goods. Treasury officials applied very strict tests to any change in British duties, which were to be 'neutral'. Tariffs should not 'distort' the allocation of resources or offer monopoly profits, so that they should ideally be limited to goods which were not produced at home. At the very least, an import duty should be offset by a countervailing excise duty on home production. Further, customs and excise duties should, as far as possible, be limited to 'luxuries' or voluntary consumption.

Of course, the emergence of higher tariffs in other countries could lead not to a rejection of commercial diplomacy and a firm commitment to unilateralism, but to a positive use of retaliation to force other countries to reconsider their protectionist policies. The emergence of 'fair trade' in the 1880s marked an initial attack on free trade, though it did not have any practical outcome. Alternatively, the empire could be converted into a British trading zone, offering a refuge from protected European markets. By the 1880s, British trade was increasingly turning towards Asia and Africa—a trend which divided free traders. Could free trade be combined with imperialism? Or were imperialism and free trade fundamentally opposed? In the later nineteenth century, no one seriously proposed erecting tariff barriers around the empire as a privileged British market. Free traders could agree that the empire should not become a commercial union and that an empire based on sentiment was more likely to last than an empire based on material interests. By 1896, Gladstone feared that 'the Cobdenian faith is in all points at a heavy discount—Peace, Retrenchment, Free Trade and all the rest of it, to my great grief I must confess'.[9] In fact, the challenge of Joseph Chamberlain's adumbration of imperial preference in 1903 revived free trade: the 'Cobdenian faith' was reborn and redefined. In Gladstone's heyday, free trade was defended as a moral and economic good, guaranteeing both the incorruptibility of government and prosperity. On both counts, free trade appealed to radicals and to working men. Free trade meant low government expenditure or retrenchment, which was welcomed as a way of containing militarism and 'waste' by aristocratic hangers-on. As yet, government spending was not linked with redistributive welfare schemes. Free trade also meant cheap food and a higher standard of living. As the new century opened, free trade and Cobdenism were liberated from retrenchment and *laissez-faire* and joined with state intervention in the provision of social welfare and an attack on landowners. In Europe, free trade had been an elitist policy of economic development in the mid-nineteenth century which was threatened by the emergence of democracy and nationalism at the end of the century. In Britain, it was consolidated by the extension of democracy as an anti-aristocratic policy of domestic prosperity and rational, incorrupt politics.

Defending Free Trade

Free trade was a central element in the political culture and political economy of late Victorian and Edwardian Britain. It implied much more than a simple belief in *laissez-faire*: it involved normative assumptions about the nature of society and economic relations, and its own distinctive approach to the issue of consumption. Free trade was more than a trade policy whose rise and fall is to be understood in terms of material interests, a simple calculation by each economic sector of whether free trade 'paid'.[10]

In response to the revival of protectionism after 1903, free traders argued that their policy had allowed an escape from the misery of the 'hungry forties'. An open world economy was the engine of prosperity, and the pursuit of individual interest was in the general interest. Free trade meant cheapness, so benefiting the consumer in comparison with the Rent-seeking monopolists of protectionism. Even the so-called 'dumping' of goods by foreign manufacturers at low prices was beneficial to the consumer and seen as coterminous with the public interest, a view expressed in the rhetoric of Robert Peel in the 1830s and 1840s. As Peel remarked in 1830, it was

one of the first duties of the legislature to do all in its power to excite a taste in the humbler classes of society for those comforts and those enjoyments . . . of civilized society, the desire for which, and the habitual possession of which, would form the best guarantee for their good conduct, and the best guarantee that the higher classes could have for the possession of their property and their power, as at present enjoyed.[11]

Peel pursued this policy with the introduction of the income tax in 1842 and the repeal of the corn laws in 1846. The Great Exhibition of 1851 was a symbol of the success of a policy designed to show that working-class families could now share in the enjoyment of goods, through reducing duties on imports, cutting excise taxes on domestic production, and regulating public utilities. E. H. Hamilton, a leading figure at the Treasury, summed up the sentiment: 'In the days of Protection, producers were more powerful than consumers. Nowadays consumers are more powerful and will remain so.'[12] As the progressive economist J. A. Hobson put it, 'Production divides, consumption unites.'[13]

Free trade also marked (in the opinion of its supporters) a delivery from political corruption and autocracy, replacing the special pleading of protectionism with a new purity of politics. Free trade would purge parliament of vested interests demanding preferential treatment by import duties, so that MPs could concentrate on the national well-being and the state's finances. Free trade was a prophylactic against monopoly power and corruption. It was about transparency. In this Liberal view of the world, free trade meant liberty and prosperity, protectionism implied autocracy and poverty. At the centenary of Cobden's birth in 1904, the future Liberal Prime Minister Henry Campbell-Bannerman expressed the stark choice facing Britain: 'One road . . . leads to Protection, to conscription, to the reducing of free institutions to a mere name . . .. And the other leads to consolidation of liberty and the development of equity at home.' It appealed beyond the Liberal Party. Robert Cecil, a Conservative opponent of Chamberlain, feared that protection would debase politics, driving out public-minded individuals and replacing them with unscrupulous demagogues.[14]

Free trade was not simply a cynical ploy to justify market capitalism to workers through the 'cheap loaf';[15] it was a moral statement about the nature of society. To Cobden, it was a policy for peace. Commerce was civilizing, spreading notions of reputation and integrity far removed from the culture of militarism and the aristocracy. Free trade entailed the removal of monopolistic privileges or protection, so creating an economy in which anyone could participate freely, profiting from hard work and prudence. Once freedom had been won from chartered monopolies, it should not be surrendered to new monopolies. Free trade did not mean complete freedom for the operation of economic forces; it entailed a world of family firms and partnerships where personal reputation was at stake, unlike in impersonal joint-stock companies where individuals could evade moral responsibility. Family firms and partnerships would compete, but also work together through an active associational life to provide marketing and commercial information, to arbitrate in disputes over contracts, to set wage rates, and to co-operate in charities to deal with the problems of urban life.

The debate over free trade was complicated by another concern—the fear that Britain was destined to follow the path of the Netherlands, ceasing to be a producer and becoming a rentier state, with a new threat of corruption by financiers and passive recipients of interest. Both protectionists and free traders expressed their concern. 'England', remarked one protectionist in 1899, 'is fast becoming [the world's] creditor, its mortgagee, its landlord.'[16] In his view, imperial preference offered a cure by creating a strong domestic, productive economy. Free traders were similarly alarmed. Geoffrey Drage complained in 1911 that Britain was ceasing to be an industrial exporting state devoted to free trade, and was changing into a 'Rentner Staat' with the London Stock Exchange at its centre. He denied that free trade was responsible for this harmful development, pointing out that the 'Rentner' were the main supporters of protection while industrialists were committed to free trade.[17] The rhetoric started to shift to denigrate rentiers as mere consumers in an effete, leisured south, and to praise free trade as the policy of active, energetic producers in the north. In Consumer's England, remarked J. A. Hobson, the well-to-do classes, from their numbers, wealth, leisure and influence, mould the external character of the civilization.... The Home Counties, the numerous seaside and other residential towns, the cathedral and university towns, and in general terms, the South, are full of well-to-do and leisured families, whose incomes [are] disassociated from any present exertion...[18]

And in Hobson's view the outcome was inimical to Producer's England, creating a cultural hostility to industry which was starved of capital by the flow of funds abroad. The moral high ground was shifting from consumers (now defined as an idle elite rather than the nation) to producers (as the active, enterprising class set against rentiers and landlords). Terms and identities were malleable.

Both sides of the debate agreed on the diagnosis. Where they differed was the cause and the cure. To some, free trade was the cause of the problem and tariffs the cure; to others, free trade was the antidote and demand for tariffs a symptom of the malaise. Drage and Hobson interpreted free trade as a policy supported by industry and production, and saw protection as a device to build up the empire to the benefit of the rentier class. One Liberal free trader, J. M. Robertson, believed protection would encourage parasitism: imports would be dearer, and more goods would have to be sold abroad; as a result, artisans would work longer hours, for lower wages, in order to buy dearer food. The only beneficiaries, he believed, would be landlords.[19] In the minds of many Liberals, free trade and the land question were combined as means of reducing the parasitism of non-productive land and the unearned increment of the rentier class.

The approach was taken furthest by Hobson. In his view, free trade might be distorted by an over-reliance on export markets as a result of the low level of domestic demand or underconsumption. This in turn led to over-saving by the rich, who exported their capital rather than investing at home. The failure of investment at home resulted in poverty and a threat to the productive economy, while the flow of interest payments to the rich from their overseas earnings led to imports of wasteful luxuries, and to the corruption of the state by financiers and the landed elite. To Hobson, imperialism was the cause of the weakness of the domestic economy, and protection based upon the empire would make things even worse. His aim was to create a strong national productive economy in combination with free trade, by means of two connected policies. The first was a deliberate attempt to kill off the rentier class and their socially created wealth by death duties and a high level of income tax on unearned income. The second was an improvement in working-class consumption through an attack on casual underemployment and the imposition of minimum wages. Hobson argued that free trade and an international economy would lead to prosperity and harmony, always provided that the distribution of resources at home was not pathological. Unlike older Liberals, he did not assume that individual self-interest coincided with that of society. Hobson and the new Liberals accepted that society was more than the sum of its parts. Wealth was created by society as much as by an individual, and the pursuit of one person's self-interest could impose costs on others. It was therefore legitimate for society to intervene to reform capitalism on a moral basis. Such a shift in Liberal ideology was at the basis of the welfare reforms of 1906 to 1914 (see Chapter 16). It was not a total rejection of individualism and an acceptance of collectivism, so much as a reinterpretation of Cobdenite liberalism in order to ensure that the pursuit of self-interest and wealth by some did not cause harm to society, and did not create poverty for others which reduced them to dependence. The intention was to create a society in which all members could be self-sufficient and independent. Hobson's support for free trade was therefore based on a rejection of another element of Victorian Liberalism: involvement in the global economy should not reflect a distorted income distribution and should be based on an equitable allocation of resources. Free trade alone could not guarantee the rights of the consumer.[20]

Many Liberals were suspicious of Hobson's policy of redistributive taxation. However, another strand within the Liberal party looked in a different direction. In rejecting Palmerstonian policies, the Gladstonian Liberal party had surrendered imperialism to Disraeli, and the Liberal Imperialists or 'Limps' now wished to reclaim it. One way was to support imperial federation which aimed to remove internal tariff barriers within the empire. The Imperial Federation League was established in 1884, with the ambition of securing the unity of the empire through the creation of a federal structure and a large free trade area. Rosebery, the Liberal Prime Minister in 1894–5 and doyen of the 'Limps', was the chairman of the League from 1886. This combination of economic nationalism and free trade appealed to sections of the City. Unlike a customs union which might harm commercial and financial interests, an imperial federation might increase business. Imperial conferences were held between 1887 and 1897, where measures were adopted to secure imperial unity through an imperial penny post and the extension of trustee status to colonial bonds by the Colonial Stock Act of 1900.[21] Joseph Chamberlain was to take these ideas further with his scheme for imperial preference which *did* aim at turning the empire into a customs union.

Chamberlain became Colonial Secretary in 1895, and the next year he proposed an imperial *Zollverein* which would not only create a free trade area within the empire but also erect a tariff against foreign goods. At the Imperial Conference of 1897, he obtained concessions from Canada to reduce duties on some British manufactures. During the Boer War, a temporary registration duty was placed on grain, and at the end of the war Chamberlain argued that it should be retained on foreign imports with colonial produce coming in duty free. He was defeated in Cabinet, and in 1903 resigned to launch his campaign to convert the Conservative party and the country to tariff reform. He proposed a duty of 10 or 20 per cent on imports, with preference for imperial goods. Free trade and Cobden's belief in comparative advantage had, in his view, failed. The growth in foreign industries might benefit middle-class consumers and those sending their capital overseas, at the expense of unemployment at home. Chamberlain's solution was to introduce tariffs in order to protect domestic industry from imports 'dumped' by foreigners whose own domestic markets were sheltered and who had low wages. Tariffs elsewhere allowed industries to develop, and the same strategy would work for Britain. 'Tariff Reform', according to the slogan of the movement, 'Means Work For All'. Full employment would benefit workers and wages would rise as a result of increased demand for labour and migration to prosperous colonies. The worst social problems of poverty would be removed, and the income from tariffs could be used to finance social reform. There was a similarity with the 'new Liberal' strategy of social reform and the fostering of a productive economy. But there the ways parted: Chamberlain saw the empire as the *solution* rather than the problem; and he wished to finance social reform by indirect taxes rather than redistributive income tax. Imperial preference offered a new way of balancing production and consumption, creating a strong domestic market supplemented by a prosperous imperial market. It would encourage production in order to counteract the 'cosmopolitan' interests of finance and services. Although a society based on finance and services might be prosperous, the example of the Netherlands showed that it would be unable to sustain its empire in the face of powerful American or European economies. Chamberlain believed that 'a system of preferential tariffs is the only system by which the Empire can be kept together', offering the basis for military and political union.[22]

Chamberlain saw tariff reform as a policy to appeal to the working class and industry rather than a narrowly sectional agricultural interest. His aim was not to appeal to the agricultural and landed interest which could no longer deliver enough votes to win a parliamentary election; it was to create mass support for a programme of social reform and imperial economic unity. After the extension of the franchise in 1884, the task facing politicians was to devise strategies to secure enough support in order to win elections, and Chamberlain saw the answer in a national strategy based on tariff reform and imperialism. Chamberlain did not convince all of his colleagues in the Conservative party, many of whom were wary of his demands for social reform and his populist campaigns for working-class votes. Balfour, the leader of the party and Prime Minister, attempted to hold them together by criticizing 'one-sided free trade' and suggesting that tariffs be offered as a bargaining ploy to reduce duties against British goods. This compromise marked a return to the principles of 1860; it was not accepted by either the advocates of tariff reform or dogmatic free traders.

Chamberlain's problem was that the Conservative party was easily portrayed as a landed interest by the Liberals who presented tariff reform as an attack on the 'cheap loaf'. Chamberlain denied the charge, for he assumed that the colonies would export primary products to Britain and purchase manufactures in return. Vincent Caillard, a leading tariff reformer, was honest enough to admit that imperial preference would do little to help British agriculture; he went on to argue that the colonies were 'great outlying counties' so that farmers in Sussex had no more reason to expect protection from Alberta than from Norfolk. His case hardly appealed to British farmers and landowners, and the campaign moved in the direction of the landed interest as a way of constructing support within the Conservative party, and so playing into the hands of Liberal free traders.

At the end of the nineteenth century, a sizeable group of industrialists started to question unilateral or 'pure' free trade. There was growing support for reciprocity or retaliation against other countries erecting trade barriers. Many chambers of commerce were alarmed. On the whole, they did not wish to impose tariff walls and to seal Britain off; they wanted to retaliate, using tariffs in an aggressive manner to keep the world economy as *open* as possible. In other words, unilateral free trade was dangerous. Did free trade mean a market open to *all* goods, even if that meant free entry for subsidized European sugar? In 1902, the British government signed the Brussels sugar convention against subsidized imports, marking a shift from free importation as a benefit to the consumer to a wider concern about the social costs of 'dumping'. Few businessmen wished to see *general* tariffs on imported goods; they wanted retaliation against *specific* goods. This option was closed by the polarization of debate between the two dogmas of rigid free trade and tariff reform. Any suggestion of negotiating seemed to compromise 'pure' free trade, paving the way to Chamberlain's programme of tariff reform. Consequently, a pragmatic use of tariffs was foreclosed, both as a source of revenue and as a tool to negotiate reciprocal trade agreements.[23]

The attempt to rally a new electoral coalition behind tariff reform failed, and the Conservatives lost the election of 1906. Now the Liberals were left with the problem of devising a free trade solution to social problems, and raising finance by means other than tariffs. They were forced in the direction of taxes on land and higher levels of income tax. Free trade had triumphed, but political support was now more fragile. Would middle-class voters accept that the price of free trade was redistributive taxation? Would Labour MPs support the Liberal government without further social reform? They might start to push definitions of free trade in the direction of greater redistribution of income and wealth. Domestic pressures were intruding into trade policy even before the First World War.

Sidney Pollard has argued that 'the tariff reform campaign was a manufacturers' campaign', so that the defeat of Chamberlain was a victory for the City and rentiers over productive industry.[24] But this claim is misleading. Hobson, Drage, and Robertson were not convinced that tariff reform was a producers' ideology;

they viewed it as a southern rentier ideology. The attitude of the City of London was by no means uniform. A survey of opinion in 1903 found that the Stock Exchange was almost entirely in favour of tariffs, as was the majority of shipowners. On the other side stood the bulk of bankers and finance houses, who argued that 'the position of London as the money centre of the world is entirely due to Free Trade'. The majority of import and export merchants opposed tariff reform, fearing a diminution of trade and loss of business. The colonial houses had a more sophisticated understanding of the problems of implementing Chamberlain's policy. He wanted free trade within the empire, so that tariffs imposed by the colonies would have to be removed, with a consequent threat to colonial industries. Since colonial tariffs were usually introduced to raise revenue, unpopular taxes would be needed. Neither, for that matter, was industry united in support of tariff reform. Industrialists were more inclined to support discriminatory or retaliatory tariffs than the grand designs of Chamberlain. Material interest might suggest a split between free trade export industries and industries catering for the home market which would favour protection, particularly those facing the incursion of foreign competition such as the midlands metal trades, glass, and chemicals. But the division of industries into two blocs was not hard and fast. Many industrialists straddled the divide so that it was difficult to predict how they would react. Caillard, a leading tariff reformer, was a City financier who was involved in the production of munitions and ships as a director of Vickers, with subordinate interests in public utilities and motor cars. W. T. Lewis, who was a leading protectionist and member of the Tariff Commission, was a major coal-owner as well as the managing director of the Bute Docks Co. which was the major export port in the country. These interests might suggest support for free trade. Yet he also had secondary interests in iron, steel, and tinplate, and the marquess of Bute, the owner of the docks, was a major aristocratic landowner who feared the impact of the Liberal land campaign.[25]

In any case, economic interests did not determine decisions, and party allegiance was not necessarily formed by attitudes to trade policy. Religious or cultural factors might lead to support for one party rather than another. An industrialist might have doubts on tariff reform, but still feel that the Liberal welfare reforms and high levels of direct taxation were a greater danger to industry than the abandonment of free trade.[26] Attitudes could also be shaped by culturally informed perceptions of the future development of the world economy, rather than by an immediate calculation of self-interest. An industrialist might accept that he was currently benefiting from free trade, but that the long-term trend was towards trade blocs. Equally, he might fear that trade blocs were a threat to political stability and that free trade should be maintained. Industrialists were more than mere calculators of immediate cost and benefit; they held views about the past and the future, about the nature of society and politics. It is far too simple to claim that the rejection of tariff reform indicated that productive industry lacked political muscle and that the City secured victory.

Despite their deep differences, free traders and protectionists shared important assumptions about the nature of the domestic industrial economy. The tariff reformers concentrated on the *external* problems of British industry created by open markets, and did not argue a case for internal reform. On the whole, they shared the free traders' belief in the virtues of small-scale competitive concerns owned by families and partnerships, and viewed cartels or combinations as inflexible and inefficient. They assumed that firms in Germany, France, and the United States were eroding British markets as a result of their 'unfair' business practices. The problem was not considered to be the inefficiency of British firms and tariff reform was not a prelude to internal reform so much as a corrective to 'unfair' competition. Protection would allow firms to use their capacity to the full, so that costs would fall; competition at home would then result in lower prices.[27]

Free trade was also deeply divided in a way that rendered it unstable at the point of victory. Although the Labour party opposed protectionism as strongly as the Liberals, a shared enemy is not the same as shared beliefs. Free trade was redefined by Labour and 'new' Liberals who argued for regulation of the economy and redistribution of income and wealth. When Labour debated its reaction to imperial preference in 1904, it agreed at once to condemn Chamberlain—and then went on to question the benefits of free trade to workers. As Keir Hardie remarked in 1903, 'production is far outstripping effective demand. The wages paid to the worker do not enable him to purchase what the labour of his hands has produced.' Free trade no longer offered an unproblematic balance between production and consumption. And did trade mean peace? 'Commerce', remarked Ramsay MacDonald, 'has become the herald of War', as in South Africa.[28] Cobden had criticized aristocrats and venal hangers-on of the state for their militarism, and wished to purge the state of their corrupting influence. In Hobson's view, the problem had re-emerged in the form of financiers who were the agents of militarism.

Might it be that free trade was leading to a degenerate society rather than to civilization? Could the development of capitalism imply bureaucracy, standardization, division of labour, and the emergence of a new mass society? Hobson brought Cobden into a new alliance with Ruskin: the demoralizing pursuit of wealth merely generated 'illth' for workers as the slaves of machinery. Production should be organized in small workshops where artisans found fulfilment and served discriminating consumers, breaking the link between standardized production and standardized consumption. Free trade was now to be connected with the development of an organic community, with a stress on moral well-being rather than a blind pursuit of comparative advantage. Comparative advantage should be subordinated to the greater good of a balanced, harmonious social order. Although such views could lead to 'insular capitalism' or national self-sufficiency, Hobson did not feel that the answer was to adopt protectionism or imperial preference; it was to transfer socially created wealth to the workers who created it. The mere pursuit of free trade was not necessarily an agent of civilization: it might lead to sweated labour at home and abroad.[29] The emphasis shifted from free trade as the guardian of consumption to concern for the circumstances of production and the conditions shaping purchasing power. An individual should not have the freedom to buy in the cheapest market if it meant poverty for others; and the distribution of income should be rectified to ensure that workers received their fair reward. Opposition to imperial preference and support for free trade could therefore move from an attack on 'food taxes' to positive action against the social problems of unfettered exchange and in support of balance in society.

Although the hegemony of free trade was not lost in 1914, there were signs that it would soon face increasing challenge. The dominance of free trade and its subsequent demise cannot be understood only in terms of political culture and electoral calculation within Britain; we need to analyse the emergence of a global world economy and the tensions it created. Why did the world economy become so globalized in the second half of the nineteenth century, and why did the process go into reverse between the wars? After all, globalization might be created by other factors than the reduction in trade barriers on which politicians spent so much emotional energy. Collapse might be the result of political tensions created by the lack of symmetry between gains and losses within an increasingly integrated world economy, so leading to difficulties for governments in making a credible commitment to a liberal trade system.

Trade and the Pattern of Settlement, 1850–1914

One indication of the emergence of a global economy is a reduction in price differentials. In 1870, the price of grain in Liverpool exceeded the price in Chicago by 57.6 per cent; by 1913, the divergence was down to 15.6 per cent. Similarly, the spread of cotton prices between Liverpool and Bombay fell from 57 per cent in 1873 to 20 per cent in 1913.[30] Liberal politicians stressed the reduction in trade barriers in creating a more integrated world economy and permitting a rise in volumes of trade. The adoption of free trade was a major political event; did it also mark an *economic* turning point, producing a rapid growth in the world economy and above all in the export sector in Britain? In the period 1841–5, net customs revenue still amounted to 32.2 per cent of the net value of imports, and free traders easily assumed that the subsequent fall to 6.1 per cent in 1876–80 lay at the basis of Britain's prosperity after 1850.[31] Cobden, so it appeared, had been vindicated. Liberals were confident that

Britain's abolition of tariffs led to a growth in the demand for imports, so increasing income abroad and creating a demand for British exports.

Their case that international trade was connected with growth seems plausible. Foreign trade rose from about 10 per cent of national income in the 1830s to 30 per cent in the 1870s, before falling back slightly to 27 per cent between 1900 and 1913. Economic growth in the mid-century might seem to be export led; and slower economic growth in the later nineteenth century might also be linked with the pattern of exports. The continuation of export growth at the same rate as between 1854 and 1872 might have raised the overall growth rate of the economy to 4.1 per cent rather than 1.75 per cent.[32] This contentious 'counterfactual' is taken to imply that free trade and the growth of exports explained the buoyancy of the British economy. The figures also suggest that the subsequent slowing down of economic growth was caused by a slackening of export growth. Might it have been sensible at this point to shift to protection in order to encourage the domestic economy? By no means all historians would agree, arguing that protection had little impact upon rates of growth in other countries.

The argument has been taken a stage further by Deirdre McCloskey who suggests that trade policy and the growth of international trade were not crucial to growth. She develops a counterfactual calculation of what would happen if the net import of commodities as a proportion of national income had stayed at the level of the 1830s (12 per cent) and had not risen to the actual figure of 1913 (26 per cent). According to her counterfactual estimates, agriculture's share of total domestic production would have been 22 per cent rather than 16 per cent in 1913, and the share of manufactures would have fallen from 38 per cent to 31 per cent. These relatively small changes led McCloskey to suggest that British industry was *not* highly dependent upon exports. She then develops the counterfactual a step further by asking what would have happened if Britain's share of world trade in manufactures had not fallen in the late nineteenth century. This calculation suggests that the output of industrial goods in Britain would have been 43 per cent higher. The figure seems very large, but McCloskey argues that the release of resources from the export trade might have found some alternative employment. In any case, British demand for foreign goods might simply have increased the price of imports compared to exports, with no gain to the welfare of Britain. If these calculations are to be believed, neither the adoption of free trade nor the later slowing down of export growth were of great significance for the development of the British economy.[33]

Counterfactual calculations do have their virtues in producing some rough estimate of the implications of the policy actually adopted against the alternative proposed at the time and pursued in other countries. The estimates provide some sense of the opportunity costs of the policy. But how realistic are McCloskey's estimates and the conclusion she draws? The answer depends on whether the

TABLE 6.2. *Terms of trade, UK, 1840–73 (1880=100)*

	Export prices	Import prices	Terms of trade
1840	128.5	122.3	105.1
1857	111.7	128.3	87.1
1873	135.2	115.4	117.2
1880	100.0	100.0	100.0
1900	91.7	76.4	120.0

Note: High number = favourable to UK.
Source: Imlah, *Economic Elements*, 94–8.

composition of the national income matters as well as the rate of growth and the level of output. A counterfactual estimate that the agricultural sector might have been a fifth larger in 1913 if protectionism had continued does suggest that landowners and farmers had a point in opposing repeal of the corn laws. The belief was about the type of society and economy, not just the overall level of the national income. Essentially, Britain would have been more like the economies of continental Europe. Further, belief that British demand for imports led to a deterioration in the terms of trade and a drop in welfare is highly questionable. The supply curve for agricultural commodities is inelastic in the short term, so higher demand results in a marked increase in prices and in the profits of producers. As a result, producers have an incentive to increase production. The expansion of cultivation is likely to outstrip demand, so that prices tumble. It is difficult to see how Britain's adoption of free trade produced a long-term deterioration in the terms of trade (see Table 6.2). Although the terms of trade did move against Britain up to 1857, the trend was reversed until 1873, followed by a slight downturn and a recovery around the turn of the century. Despite the problems experienced by farmers and landowners, the majority of people gained from the opening up of trade. The real loss of welfare might be experienced by indigenous peoples whose land was expropriated, and who suffered from famine as they were incorporated into the world economy.

A more telling criticism of the free traders is that changes in tariff levels were not the most important variable in the expansion of world trade and the emergence of a global economy. In reality, the marked drop in transport costs was much more important than changes in tariffs. British freight rates dropped by 70 per cent in real terms from 1840 to 1910. As Douglass North has remarked, 'The declining cost of ocean transportation was a process of widening the resource base of the western world.'[34] The fall in freight rates was irregular, interrupted by periodic peaks, yet with a clear downward trend (see Table 6.3).

The most obvious reason for the fall in freight rates was the replacement of sail by steam. However, steam cannot explain the drop in the first half of the

TABLE 6.3. *American export freight rates, 1815–1904 (1830=100)*

1815	363
1835	87
1840	135
1842	82
1847	117
1850	57
1854	101
1857	67
1873	117
1877	80
1880	97
1887	50
1890	64
1894	42
1900	63
1904	31

Source: North, 'Ocean freight rates and economic development', 549.

nineteenth century, and sail was still dominant in the long-haul trades where the reduction was greatest. At this stage, competition from steam placed pressure on sailing ships to become more efficient. Steamships could not compete with sail in the bulk, long-haul trades and were, accordingly, confined to trades with high-value, low-volume commodities, especially non-immigrant passengers and mail. A number of other influences contributed to the fall in freight rates up to the 1880s: technical improvements; better knowledge of winds and currents; investment in docks; telegraphs; and the greater volume of trade. From the 1880s, steam was the decisive influence on freight rates. The development of the compound steam engine from 1854 reduced fuel consumption, and as better boilers allowed pressure to be increased, so fuel consumption fell. More cargo space was available, and the labour costs of stokers fell. In 1872, the best cargo steamers used 2.1 pounds of coal per horsepower per hour; by 1891, consumption had been reduced to 1.52 pounds.[35] The design of ships also changed. Bulk cargoes were carried in tramp ships, going wherever cargoes were to be found. Designs were developed to create large holds which could be easily loaded and emptied. The profitability of tramp ships was also helped by the growth of the coal export trade. In contrast to tramp ships, liners carried more valuable cargoes and passengers, and operated to a fixed timetable. Here, the concern was speed, with considerably higher fuel

TABLE 6.4. *Wheat price spreads of Britain, Bavaria, and France with the USA, 1870 and 1913(%)*

	1870	1913
Britain	54.1	−0.8
Bavaria	44.0	37.1
France	43.8	29.3

Source: O'Rourke and Williamson, *Globalization and History*, 104.

consumption—and the development of a lucrative trade in migrants helped to reduce fares.

The increase in tariffs at the end of the century was, at least in part, a reaction to the reduction of transport costs and the social, political, and economic impact of price convergence between Europe and the New World. The cost of shipping a bushel of wheat from New York to Liverpool fell from 21 cents in 1873 to 3 cents in 1901, and improvements in internal transport meant that more land was available for cultivation. On the whole, farmers in the New World prospered. In these countries, the greatest concern was the impact of migration on wage rates. The question facing politicians in Europe was how to react to the flood of cheap grain from the New World. In Britain, tariffs were not imposed to protect agriculture when prices dropped sharply after 1870. Consequently, land prices and rents fell. In Germany and France, farmers secured tariffs from 1879 and 1892 so that prices did not converge with the USA to anything like the same extent as in Britain (see Table 6.4). Unlike in Britain, land prices and rents in France and Germany remained stable. Trade policy was not the major cause of globalization and convergence in prices; rather, the real importance of policy was how to respond to international price convergence caused by freight rates. The reaction depended in part on the size of the agricultural sector which shaped the electoral calculation of politicians. In 1871, only 23 per cent of the British workforce was engaged in agriculture compared with 51 per cent in France. This variation also shaped the impact of food imports on welfare. In Britain, the loss to agriculture from low prices and rents was outweighed by the gains to urban consumers; in France, the loss to agriculture from low prices would, in the absence of a tariff, have produced an overall fall in real wages.[36]

The general outcome was convergence within the Atlantic economy: imports of wheat and meat reduced food prices in Europe and above all in Britain; and migration from Europe resulted in higher wages. But globalization could also lead to divergence. In Asia and Africa, integration into the global economy was much more destructive, making them more susceptible to famine and disease. In India, the production of local grains was displaced by cotton, wheat, jute, and indigo for export to Britain. The expansion of cash crops forced farmers onto drier soils, and they also lost their entitlements to forests and pastures. Investment in new irrigation systems benefited the export sector, but communal systems of irrigation were disrupted and co-operative systems of management were replaced by individual occupation in return for paying revenue to the state. At the same time, traditional systems of relief were disrupted by the colonial state. Village grain reserves no longer held surpluses. Regulation of prices, tax relief in times of hardship, and welfare provision by the landed elite were all undermined. The policy pursued by the British rulers of India was similar to the approach adopted at home in the eighteenth century—to abandon price controls and to encourage a free market in grain as the best means of stimulating a secure supply of foodstuffs. However, in eighteenth-century Britain, the shift to a free market was linked with measures to stabilize prices in order to prevent both hardship for domestic consumers at times of high prices and bankruptcy for farmers at times of low prices. In Britain, these policies were only abandoned in 1846, long after a highly commercialized and stable market was in place. In India, the British rulers moved straight to a free market without mitigating its impact on domestic producers and consumers. The result was disaster when drought and famine struck in 1876–9 and 1896–1902. Nevertheless, India continued to export food: in 1877, 1,409,000 quarters of wheat were exported to the United Kingdom, double the level of 1876 and more than four times the level of 1875.[37] British consumers benefited from falling food prices while their Indian subjects were starving.

At the time of the famine of 1876–9, the viceroy of India was committed to the virtues of the free market, insisting that high prices were the 'natural saviours' of the situation. The gloomy doctrines of Malthus held sway and it followed that relief would only make a bad situation worse. Lord Salisbury, the Secretary of State for India and future Conservative Prime Minister, denounced as a 'species of International Communism' any idea that British trade should be penalized for the sake of India.[38] Both the India Office in London and the viceroy in India agreed that the famine and poverty must not lead to the creation of a poor law in India, which they feared would have the same disastrous consequences as the old poor law in England. Although a fund was created for famine relief, the terms were extremely stringent and linked with draconian measures to control the movement of population.

The government hoped that the famines of the 1870s would not be repeated, and that the expansion of a free market would resolve the problem. In fact, the famine was repeated in 1896/7 and 1899–1902. The problem was not an absolute shortage, for surpluses in Bengal and Burma could cover the shortfalls in western and central India. The real difficulty was a lack of purchasing power; railways were of no use in transporting grain which could not be bought and the surplus was instead exported to Europe. Neither did the famine fund provide much assistance. The government of India was concerned that the cost of relief would threaten the finances of India. It was anxious about the costs of the 'home charges' to Britain, which were increasing in real terms as a result of the deterioration of the rupee against the pound in the last quarter of the nineteenth century, as well as wishing to send funds to pay for war in Afghanistan and South Africa. As we will see, Lancashire was not willing to accept import duties on cotton goods as an alternative source of revenue. Consequently, internal taxation was maintained even in the areas hit by famine, on the grounds that relief would 'demoralize' the population. The famines contributed to peasant indebtedness, the sale of land, and the growth of servile labour. Looked at from India, China, or Africa, Palmerstonian and even Cobdenite free trade were far from peaceable and harmonious. At home in Manchester, the result might be celebrated as the spread of comparative advantage and harmonious exchange between the peoples of the world. An Indian peasant farmer or nationalist politician might, with some justice, see the process as an unequal imposition of a new order, involving forced disruption and a huge loss of welfare.[39]

Britain secured a remarkable share of world trade in manufactures in the emerging global economy of the mid-nineteenth century. In 1913, its share was much smaller and the emergence of competition both in domestic markets and overseas prompted concern about the loss of national efficiency. However, the alarm of both contemporaries and modern historians should be kept in perspective. The total volume of goods entering world trade was rising, and Britain only experienced a fall in its share of a larger total, rather than an absolute loss of trade. Although the rate of growth of exports did fall between 1883 and 1901, the figure returned to its earlier peak in the Edwardian period and Britain remained the world's largest exporter of manufactures (see Tables 6.5 and 6.6). Similarly, a widening gap between exports and imports was reversed in the early twentieth century: the trade deficit widened from about 30 per cent of exports in the 1870s and 1880s to 50.2 per cent between 1896 and 1900, before narrowing to 23.5 per cent between 1911 and 1913. The balance of payments remained around 4 per cent of GDP up to the First World War, which marked a serious deterioration (see Table 6.7).

TABLE 6.5. *Share of world trade in manufactures of UK, USA, and Germany, 1880–1913 (%)*

	1880	1890	1913
United Kingdom	41.4	40.7	29.9
United States	2.8	4.6	12.6
Germany	19.3	20.1	26.5

Source: Saul, 'Export economy', 12.

TABLE 6.6. *Annual growth rate of*
UK exports, 1856–1913 (volume)

1856–65	2.4
1865–74	4.5
1874–83	3.3
1883–90	2.1
1890–1901	1.3
1901–7	4.8
1907–13	3.8

Source: Pollard, *Britain's Prime and Britain's Decline*, 4.

TABLE 6.7. *Ratio of balance of payments on current account*
to GDP, Britain, 1855–1951 (average of annual percentages)

1855–73	4.5	1921–9	2.2
1874–90	5.0	1930–8	−0.9
1891–1913	5.0	1948–51	0.0

Source: Matthews, Feinstein, and Odling-Smee, *British Economic Growth*, table 14.7, 442.

The shortcomings of Britain's export trade were to become apparent after the First World War when exports of a number of commodities collapsed in absolute terms, and led to mass unemployment and depression. Generally, British manufacturing exports were narrowly based on semi-finished goods and capital goods. Consumer goods were not a large element in exports which were, indeed, increasingly imported. Manufactured goods' share of imports rose from 5.5 per cent by value in 1860 to 17.3 per cent in 1880 and 25 per cent in 1900. The appearance of increased quantities of foreign metals, chemicals, synthetic dyestuffs, scientific instruments, and motor cars suggested that Britain was falling behind its major competitors. Indeed, the most rapidly growing export was not a manufactured good but coal.[40] The exploitation of the south Wales coalfield was impressive; it entailed a massive investment in railways and docks, and the creation of new communities of miners. Coal provided export cargoes, improving the efficiency of the British merchant marine and supplying coaling stations around the world as well as fuel for European railways. But critics were concerned that Britain was exporting its mineral wealth.

Hindsight suggests that the structure of trade in the late nineteenth and early twentieth centuries laid the basis for problems after the war. In 1899, only 17.7 per cent of British exports of manufactures were in sectors whose share of world trade was rising and 18.6 per cent in sectors whose share was stable; trades with a declining share of world trade accounted for 62.9 per cent of British exports of manufactures. Above all, British manufacturing exports were heavily dependent on textiles. In 1854, textiles (cotton and wool) comprised 44.6 per cent. In 1870, their share had increased to a combined total of 49.2 per cent. In 1910, textiles accounted for a total of 31.9 per cent. Before the First World War, any weakness in the commodity structure of trade was compensated by the geographical direction of trade, with an increasing reliance on the empire and primary producers. Primary producers were expanding their share of world trade up to 1914. The empire's share of exports of cotton goods rose from 34.7 per cent in 1870 to 51.7 per cent in 1913, and of iron goods from 21.7 to 48.2 per cent. The strategy of exporting a narrow range of goods continued to be relatively successful up to the First World War; only 1.4 of the 11.5 percentage point decline in Britain's share in world trade in manufactures between 1899 and 1913 may be explained by the commodity and geographical composition of trade.[41]

The real problem was not the structure of trade so much as a loss of competitiveness. British export prices fell by only 14.5 per cent between 1872 and 1913, in comparison with 47 per cent in German export prices. If relative prices had remained at the level of the early 1870s, British exports would have been 10 per cent above their actual level in 1911–13. Even more crucial was the fact that the elasticity of demand for British goods was low: for a 10 per cent increase in world income, the demand for British exports would grow at about 8 per cent.[42] The problem was already becoming apparent in a number of sectors before the First World War. South Wales was a high-cost producer of coal, facing increasing competition from Germany and from oil from the Middle East. The strikes of 1910 reflected the concern of coal-owners that higher wages and improved working conditions imposed by the government would price them out of European markets. Similarly, the cotton industry of Lancashire had no monopoly on the supplies of raw cotton or the most efficient machinery. Generally, the response was to sell the same commodities at uncompetitive prices, by moving into imperial or primary producing markets, and specializing in particular 'niche' markets where Britain's flexible industrial technology could meet specific needs. But the problems should not be exaggerated for the strategy was successful up to 1914.

As transport costs fell and the world economy became more integrated, so the pattern of settlements changed. Until the 1860s, settlement patterns were based upon a number of discrete patterns each focused upon Britain. Each trading pattern arose out of particular circumstances, and influences only passed from one to the other via Britain. By the 1870s, a new pattern was emerging based upon the industrialization of Europe, Japan, and America. Self-contained trading patterns gave way to a single world economy with multilateral settlements revolving around Britain and its large, open market. Britain penetrated Indian markets for cotton goods in the second

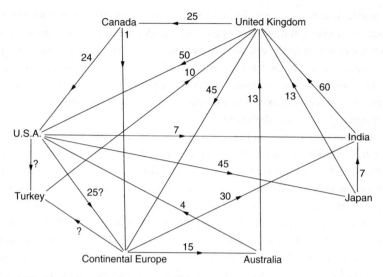

FIG. 6.1. World pattern of settlements, 1910 (£m)
Note: The arrows point in the direction of the country having a surplus.
Source: Saul, *Studies,* 58.

quarter of the nineteenth century, and was now a major exporter to India. Britain's share of Indian exports fell, and markets for Indian raw cotton, jute, rice, wheat, and hides expanded elsewhere in the world. As a result, India ran a deficit with Britain which was covered by its surplus with industrial Europe, China, Japan, the United States, and South America. The overall Indian surplus went to pay the 'home charges' to Britain, interest and invisibles, and returned profits. Indian nationalists claimed that there was a 'drain', a removal of the benefits of the export surplus from India which contributed to the poverty of the subcontinent. Whatever the truth of the nationalist case, India was essential to the British pattern of settlements.[43] By running surpluses with areas of the world with which Britain was in deficit, India allowed Britain to avoid tariffs or a lack of competitiveness in other countries. India exported more raw cotton or jute to Europe or the United States where Britain was not able to surmount tariff barriers or compete on prices; so long as Britain was able to continue exporting its goods—especially cotton textiles—to India, all was well. The trade between Britain and the east was now part of a single worldwide network of multilateral payments, with Britain and India the twin pillars.

Europe and North America increased their imports from primary producing countries, and ran up heavy balance of payments deficits. Britain was the exception: it had a balance of payments surplus with primary producers. These industrializing nations were able to cover their deficits with the primary producers because Britain's import of manufactures resulted in a balance of payments deficit with Europe and North America. In 1910, Britain's balance of payments deficit with the USA amounted to £50 m and with Europe to £45 m, allowing these economies to cover their trade deficits with the primary producers. The circle was completed by Britain's exporting goods to the primary producers and receiving large sums from interest payments and invisible earnings. Britain was the centre of a complex pattern of multilateral settlements, with India producing the bulk of the surplus to cover the deficit with other parts of the world.[44]

The relationship between Britain and India was problematical. Lancashire cotton interests obviously wished to have open access to its largest market, and feared the growth of an Indian cotton industry behind tariff walls. The government in India, on the other hand, was concerned about raising revenue. A tariff on imports was politically more attractive than increased internal taxes which would fall on the peasantry. The government of India introduced a tariff in 1859 in response to the financial crisis after the Mutiny, but the Lancashire lobby secured its reduction on cotton yarn and cloth in 1862, and its abolition in 1882. Tension was already developing between the demands of Lancashire and the imperatives of British rule in India. War or famine would lead to pressure on revenue, and the depreciation of the rupee in the late nineteenth century increased the burden of the 'home charges'. The deteriorating financial position of India led to a return of import duties in 1894, at a time when a fall in the value of the rupee was making British goods in India more expensive as well as improving the competitiveness of Indian producers in Asian markets. The government of India was concerned about the practicalities of raising taxes in India; the British government was concerned about the electoral implications of alienating opinion in Lancashire. The British government insisted that the import duty on cotton goods should be offset by an excise duty on Indian-produced cotton goods. In 1896, pressure from Lancashire meant that the import and excise duties on cloth were reduced and cotton yarn was exempted. There was a complicated political interplay between the demands of Lancashire and the British government for free trade, and of Bombay and the government in India for protection and financial stability. Whether the British government would placate Lancashire or India depended upon circumstances. In 1919, India was granted fiscal autonomy so that the government in India had the right to decide upon taxes without being overruled by the Cabinet at home. The British government was anxious for India to contribute to the reduction of the national debt and the need to conciliate Indian opinion was imperative. The outcome was that tariffs were increased.[45]

The marketing system for British goods rested on a division between manufacturers, commission agents, and financiers. Manufacturers retreated from direct sales in mid-century and the larger merchant houses such as Barings moved from dealing with goods to 'accepting' bills of exchange. The actual selling of British goods was in the hands of commission agents, usually with a partner or agent in Britain. There was a lengthy interval between the shipment of the goods by the manufacturer, their sale, and the receipt of payment from the consumer, which led to reliance on bills of exchange, a promise to pay for the goods in the future. In order to obtain money more quickly, these bills were taken by 'acceptance' houses. Such specialization reduced the need of manufacturers to provide large amounts of trade credit, and it encouraged the development of a large army of commission agents and merchants. The system offered a wide geographic coverage and flexibility, with a number of potential drawbacks. The marketing system established barriers between production and selling, between the manufacturer and the consumer. There were signs that this pattern was starting to change in the later nineteenth and early twentieth centuries, with the development of travelling salesmen in sectors such as clothing, and the appointment of agents as direct representatives of manufacturers. Despite these trends, the marketing system was not transformed and some historians complain that it entrenched a small-scale, fragmented system of production.[46] This criticism of the finance and marketing of British industry often rests on an inappropriate comparison with Germany and America, where the involvement of banks in the provision of long-term capital is taken as a model of good practice. As we have seen, the assumption may be misplaced: the financial institutions in Britain were providing trade credit to industry which was not seeking long-term capital, and the City had a flexible response to changes in the world economy.

Certainly, the City of London was crucial to the strength of Britain's balance of payments prior to the First World War. Britain was the world's major exporter of manufactures, and also the major importer of food, raw materials, and increasingly of industrial commodities. As a result, the balance of merchandise trade was in deficit every year after 1822. This deficit was covered by two other items—interest and dividends from overseas investments and 'invisible' earnings from shipping, insurance, and banking services which meant that the overall balance of payments on current account was in surplus (see Table 6.8). In the opinion of some commentators, the success of the City of London was at the expense of industry. In the words of Sir Hugh Bell, City men were 'the mere hangers-on of industry . . . [they] might be likened . . . to the maggots in the cheese'.[47] Such complaints form the basis of the concept of 'gentlemanly capitalism', the fusion of land and finance in opposition to industrial capitalism in the north and midlands. As we noted in Chapter 4, the division is overdrawn, for the City and industry were by no means distinct: merchant bankers funded trade, and insurance companies provided protection against the risks of an urban, industrial society.

Earnings from overseas investment were crucial to the surplus in the balance of payments. Critics point to the dangers that followed. Might it be that the earnings on overseas investments provided a 'cushion' which made the exporters of manufactures more conservative and less dynamic in the competition for foreign markets?[48] The

TABLE 6.8. *Balance of payments on current account. UK, 1850–1910 (£m)*

	Merchandise trade	Overseas investment earnings	Invisibles	Bullion and specie	Balance on current account
1850	−19.6	+9.4	+21.8	−1.0	+10.6
1870	−57.5	+35.3	+76.8	−10.5	+44.1
1890	−86.3	+94.0	+99.6	−8.8	+98.5
1910	−142.7	+170.0	+146.7	−6.7	+167.3

Source: Mitchell and Deane, *Abstract of British Historical Statistics*, 333–5.

argument is flawed, for it confuses macroeconomic structures with microeconomic responses. Although the balance of payments was in surplus at the level of the economy as a whole, an individual industrialist in search of profit still had every reason to search for markets. Against such criticisms, defenders of capital exports argued that investment income allowed Britain to import more goods, so that the level of consumption of the British population was higher. The export of capital also connects with the gold standard: by recycling Britain's large surpluses, international monetary liquidity was maintained. If Britain simply retained its surpluses on current account, the liquidity of the world economy would be threatened The export of capital cannot be separated from the entire structure of multilateral settlements and the functioning of the world economy.

In addition to earnings from investments, Britain received a large income as the carrier, insurer, and merchant for a large part of world trade. Although America and Germany had caught and overtaken British industrial productivity, the country still had a considerable advantage in the provision of services. London was the hub of finance and insurance; the British merchant marine was still the most efficient and largest in the world. The success of these services did not only reflect the power of rentiers and financiers or gentlemanly capitalists. As we have seen, the City included major insurance firms, offering cover for the risk of old age or ill health, responding to the risk of life in an urban industrial economy, and then investing their funds throughout the world for the best return. Invisible earnings reflected much more than the City of London. The most important contributor to the surplus in the balance of payments was shipping, which accounted for two-thirds of the invisible earnings. Of course, London was a major shipowning centre, but so were Liverpool, Hull, and Cardiff. The demand for shipping depended largely upon bulk commodities rather than more valuable manufactured commodities. In 1840, the largest single category of world merchandise carried by sea was timber (20.5 per cent); the next was grain (9.5 per cent). By 1887 the volume of trade had grown sevenfold, and the most striking changes were the increases in the share of coal and in grain.[49] There was also a trend towards long-haul journeys, with a higher proportion of grain coming from America. The ports and their shipowners and merchants were closely linked with the industrial economy. Grain, tobacco, and sugar were imported and stored or processed at the docks, before being sent on to urban consumers. All of these trades generated income from insurance, freight, and financial services, which should not be seen as the product of a distinct gentlemanly capitalism located in the City of London. Of course, London was itself a major port and processing centre handling commodities from around the world, and was the largest single market for imported foodstuffs and raw materials. The financial services of the City of London cannot be separated from the needs of the industrial economy: the members of Lloyd's insured ships carrying goods produced and consumed by the industrial economy; the Baltic Exchange created a market for freights and for grain; the textile warehouses of Fore Street handled vast quantities of cotton, wool, lace, and hosiery from the factories of the north and midlands; the dealers of Mincing Lane dealt in tea and coffee for the grocery stores of the nation.

The increasing levels of world trade, and its changing structure, meant that the demand for shipping rose. In the short term, the demand was inelastic. High freight rates generated a construction boom in the shipyards of the north-east of England and the Clyde, resulting in an oversupply of tonnage and a period of low freight rates. The shipping industry was therefore prone to fluctuations in freight rates and in construction. A major problem facing the industry was how to stabilize demand by cutting prices in the downturn of the freight cycle and offering favourable credit terms. The difficulty was particularly acute for tramp ships rather than regular liners with a much more certain market for high-value passengers and cargo. Tramp ships were much cheaper, and voyage costs were the largest item in total costs. A number of points follow. The barriers to entry in the liner trade were high, and relatively few, highly capitalized joint-stock companies emerged. In the mid-1870s, these firms started to create 'conferences' or agreements to fix freight rates and minimize competition to protect their investment. In the case of tramps, barriers to entry were low and there were a large number of small owners. Entry was easy—and so was departure. It was a world of cut-throat competition. British tramps competed with foreign owners with lower wage costs which helps to explain the anti-unionism of British owners. The tramp ship owners could not collude in fixing freight rates which would be impossible in an internationally competitive industry. Instead, they created the Shipping Federation to oppose unionization. Above all, British tramps were more modern so that the repair bill and fuel costs were held down. Until 1914, British owners were generally successful in keeping one step ahead of foreign tramp owners, buying the most efficient ships on easy terms from British builders. The dominance of British shipping rested in part upon the success of British shipbuilding in the age of steam—a clear connection between the earnings on invisibles and the industrial economy of the north and Scotland.[50]

London dominated the insurance market in shipping, and goods carried in British ships were insured and financed in Britain. Wool grown by squatters in Australasia, for example, was financed and marketed by London-based merchants. A large part of the price difference between the sheep-station in the outback and the factory in Bradford went to the British shipowners, insurers, merchants, warehouses, and brokers. The colonists were aware and resentful of this situation. By the end of the century, Australasian banks and finance houses moved into the business, and sales were organized in Australian cities in an attempt to cut out the London middlemen. Even so, the Australian concerns were often in effect run from London, and relied heavily upon British capital and credit.[51]

Britain's position at the centre of world trade and finance attracted foreign merchants to London and, to a lesser extent, Liverpool. One example was the grain trade. The major new area of supply after the repeal of the corn laws was the Black Sea. The trade was in the hands of Greek merchants. They started to move to London early in the nineteenth century, for British citizenship allowed them to have a base in Constantinople which was the vital centre of trade. The massacre of the Greeks on the island of Chios in 1822 led to the dispersal of merchants' families, who settled in London, Manchester, Odessa, and Marseilles. By 1852, there were about 200 Greek merchants in London. Their trading position rested upon the connection between wheat and cotton textiles. They imported wheat into Britain from the Black Sea and exported British cotton goods to the Middle East. The operation of this trade system was helped by interlocking family partnerships in the major trade centres. In some ways, the Greeks exploited older ways of doing business, relying on patriarchal ties, using cash or barter. But many other merchants and financial houses also relied on family or religious ties. A number of Jewish and other German families from Hamburg, Frankfurt, and Leipzig moved to Britain, forming an interlocking network of family and partnerships with European connections, drawing upon experience of trade and exchanges within a mosaic of small states with complex currencies and customs. They needed direct representation in Britain, for Germany was a major market for British textiles in the early nineteenth century. The best example is the Rothschilds, who initially moved to Britain to trade in textiles but soon moved into government loan contracting in the Napoleonic wars.[52]

The transformation of merchant houses was associated with changes in the institutional framework of the City of London. In the eighteenth and early nineteenth centuries, commerce in London was based at the Royal Exchange and in the coffee houses where merchants swapped information and read the press from various areas of the world. Some of these coffee houses were transformed into formalized exchanges, such as the Baltic which became the centre for the grain trade and freights, or Lloyd's which became the main market for ships' insurance. One feature of all of these markets and exchanges was that they were self-regulating. For the most part, they were highly specialized and competitive so that their commissions and charges were low, and they could win business on a world market. Firms were obliged to specialize by the rules of the exchanges: the Stock Exchange did not allow members to have 'outside' interests; the Baltic Exchange would only permit six members of the Stock Exchange to join. Leading features of the London markets included freedom from regulation; a highly competitive structure without minimum commissions; and the ability to tap abundant and cheap sources of finance on the money market which was increasingly supplied by the joint-stock banks. British or British-based merchants and financiers were able to compete with the financial centres of Amsterdam, New York, and Frankfurt and keep their competitive position even when the dominance of British industry was under threat.[53]

At the outbreak of the First World War, free trade was in the ascendant and the balance of payments was extremely strong. Despite the emergence of the United States and Germany as major industrial economies, and the threat of increased competition in export markets, the balance of visible trade was no worse than in the later nineteenth century. The impressive flow of income from foreign investments and invisibles meant that Britain was the world's largest creditor. Despite the increasing financial might of Wall Street, the City of London was still the world's greatest financial centre. The First World War marked a fundamental change. As Table 6.9 indicates, the First World War was the culmination of growth in trade relative to GDP. By the 1920s, free trade was under serious threat, Britain was facing the prospect of a deficit on its balance of payments, and the world's multilateral payments system was under serious strain.

TABLE 6.9. *Import duties as a percentage of total imports and total trade as a percentage of GNP, in France, Germany, UK, and USA, 1913*

	Import duties as % of total imports	Total trade as % of GNP
France	8.7	39
Germany	7.9	40
UK	5.6	48
USA	21.4	11

Source: Estevadeordal, 'Measuring', 91.

TABLE 6.10. *Merchandise exports as a percentage of GDP at 1990 prices, France, Germany, UK, and USA, 1870–1950*

	1870	1913	1950
France	4.9	7.8	7.6
Germany	9.5	16.1	6.2
UK	12.2	17.5	11.3
USA	2.5	3.7	3.0

Source: Maddison, *World Economy*, 363.

Deglobalization and the Decline of Free Trade

The First World War had serious repercussions for Britain's balance of payments. Obviously, the needs of the armed forces were paramount and industrial production concentrated on the war effort at the expense of exports. The threat to British shipping, and the need to conserve financial resources, led to shortages of raw materials. During the war, British firms lost many of their export markets and at the end of the war they faced profound problems in regaining their position. British coal producers, for example, faced profound difficulties, with a continued shift to oil. But the basic problem was not a drop in coal consumption; it was that British coal was expensive. The difficulty appeared before the war, above all in south Wales. It became even worse at the end of the war, with a marked increase in labour costs in 1919. In many cases, Britain's export position was affected by the reaction at the end of the war as much as by the war itself. During the short-lived speculative boom in 1919–20, wages rose and priced many British goods out of export markets.

The boom also meant that many industrial concerns incurred serious debts. At the end of the war, the immediate need to replace depleted stocks led to high demand and prices for various commodities. In the cotton industry, for example, many firms took the opportunity to float as public companies, selling their assets at inflated prices and borrowing money from banks. When the boom broke, the industry was in serious difficulties. The problem was not confined to manufacturing industry, for shipping faced similar difficulties. At the end of the war, demand for shipping was also high to restore stockpiles of goods around the world. Having poured their reserves into securing ships at grossly inflated prices, owners were then hit as freight rates dropped. As a result, they lost much of the pre-war advantage. Further, the sale of foreign investments and the rise of New York as a major financial centre meant that other invisible earnings were lower than before the war. The result was a reduction in the balance of payments surplus and the onset of deficit in the 1930s. The relationship between the surplus on invisibles and the deficit on visible trade was upset (see Tables 6.7 and 6.11).

TABLE 6.11. *Balance of payments in the UK, 1913–37 (£m)*

	Merchandise trade	Overseas investment earnings	Other invisibles	Bullion and specie	Balance on current account
1913	−146	+210	+129	−12	+181
1922	−183	+175	+150	+13	+155
1931	−407	+170	+134	+33	−70
1937	−431	+210	+176	−99	−144

Source: Mitchell and Deane, *Abstract of British Historical Statistics*, 333–5.

Even at their peak in 1929, British exports were still about 20 per cent below the volume of 1913, compared with an increase in world trade in manufacturers by 37.5 per cent between 1913 and 1929. Britain did not benefit from the recovery of world trade, and its share of world trade in manufactures slumped from 30.2 per cent in 1913 to 20.4 per cent in 1929 (at 1913 prices).[54] There are three possible explanations: that Britain was exporting the 'wrong' sort of goods; that it depended on the 'wrong' area of the world; or that its goods were uncompetitive. The geographical spread was not a matter of concern up to 1929, for British exports went to more rapidly growing areas of world trade. Britain was more dependent on exports to semi-industrial countries (55.9 per cent of manufactured exports in 1913) than on exports to industrial countries (19.2 per cent of exports); trade to these two groups grew by 83 and 74 per cent respectively up to 1929. Geographical coverage was more of a problem after 1929, when markets in semi-industrial countries were hit by import substitution. More serious than the geographical coverage was Britain's heavy dependence on sectors with a declining share of world trade. In 1913, 67 per cent of British manufacturing exports were in sectors with a declining share, and only 14 per cent in sectors with an expanding share. Even so, the sectoral coverage was not the main problem.[55] The major reason was lack of competitiveness.

The structure of multilateral settlements also changed after the war, creating serious difficulties for Britain's international position. Before the First World War, Britain's surplus with India covered deficits with the USA and Europe; after the war, the surplus with India declined and problems emerged. Britain's trade surplus with the tropics allowed it to secure dollars and so cover the deficit with the United States—so long as the USA imported raw materials and tropical foods, and lent overseas. After 1928, this was no longer the case. Primary producers were not able to earn or borrow dollars, and Britain was not able to cover its deficit with the USA. One response was to turn to other parts of the empire as some compensation for the weakening of Britain's trading position with India. There was a conscious attempt to increase imperial trade through better trade facilities and colonial development.

In 1913, the empire took 37.2 per cent of British exports, rising to 41.5 per cent in 1929, before falling back to 38.8 per cent in 1931.[56] Meanwhile, the empire was becoming less dependent on the British market for sales of its goods. Even if the system of imperial preference advocated by Joseph Chamberlain were adopted, it would face serious problems, for Canada was more likely to look to the United States than to Britain for its markets and might well wish to develop its own infant industries rather than to provide a secure market for British goods.

Britain finally abandoned free trade in the early 1930s and adopted at least a form of imperial preference. Multilateralism gave way to discrimination and bilateral deals, as in so many other parts of the world. The first glimmer of change appeared during the First World War when controls were needed to save on both shipping space and scarce foreign exchange. In 1915, the Liberal free trade Chancellor of the Exchequer, Reginald McKenna, introduced import duties on a range of goods, including movies and cars. The question was how to react at the end of the war. During the war, advocates of protection saw their chance and industrialists argued that the government should adopt a much more positive commitment to trade. In their view, the German state backed firms such as AEG and Siemens in the Middle East and the British government should adopt the same policies if it were not to lose the trade war. A government committee recommended the creation of an industrial trading bank, and the British Trade Corporation was created in 1917. Although the government supported the BTC in the war, it soon pulled out and the venture failed in 1926.[57] The McKenna duties did survive the war. The Safeguarding of Industries Act 1921 gave protection for five years to key industries. Free trade seemed to be in retreat. Many Conservatives were protectionists; opinion in the City and industry was shifting in favour of duties; and a committee was established to show the pragmatic need for protection to defend the balance of trade. The change in sentiment encouraged the Conservatives to fight the election of 1923 on a platform of protection, only to be defeated. The first minority Labour government abolished the McKenna duties, and the Chancellor, Philip Snowden, celebrated his proposals of 1924 as 'the greatest step ever made towards the realization of the cherished Radical ideal of a free breakfast table'.[58] When the Conservatives returned to office later in 1924, a number of influential free traders in the Cabinet hoped to hold the line. Nevertheless, the McKenna duties were restored and support for liberal internationalism was in retreat.

The war marked a shift in attitudes towards trade policy and business organization. Before the war, industrial support for tariffs was largely based on reciprocity or retaliation to force other countries to reduce their duties. Problems were seen as arising from 'unfair' competition rather than any need for internal reform of the structure of industry. This approach changed in the 1920s, when tariffs were designed to 'modernize' or rationalize British industry, encouraging a shift to larger and more efficient units. The state should provide tariffs and then leave industry to resolve its own problems; industrialists were not interested in direct state involvement in their affairs or in corporatism. State and economy should remain separate—at least until the 1930s. Such a diagnosis was shared by erstwhile free traders such as Alfred Mond, who created Imperial Chemical Industries in 1926. As the name implied, he soon adopted imperial preference. At this time, industrialists were still divided. Most motor manufacturers, for example, favoured protection, while the Cotton Spinners' and Manufacturers' Association remained free traders. The FBI was therefore reluctant to state an opinion. The balance moved in favour of protection with the slowness of recovery in the 1920s. In 1925, the National Union of Manufacturers launched a campaign to extend safeguarding, and the Empire Industries Association argued the case for imperial preference. A significant symbolic event was the decision of the Manchester Chamber of Commerce to support protection in 1930. Later that year, twenty-three leading bankers signed a resolution in favour of protection and the FBI opted for protection with the support of 96 per cent of the trade groups who voted. The steady erosion of free trade sentiment and the growth of protectionism prepared the ground for a swift change of policy in response to the slump in the early 1930s.[59]

The shift was not only a matter of material advantage and interest group politics, for the wider political culture of free trade was collapsing. Before the war, free trade could be presented as an ideology of consumption. After the First World War, the rhetoric of consumption and the consumer was increasingly separated from free trade. When Mond argued for 'safeguarding' or protection of industries against 'unfair' competition in 1921, he suggested that there was no reason why 'the British manufacturer or the British workman [should] be compelled, in the interests of some so-called consumer, *in vacuo*, to see the destruction of our industries'.[60] An open market for the benefit of the consumer was no longer desirable when policies were needed to protect employment and to prevent 'dumping'. The interest of the consumer could be better secured by regulation. The co-operative movement, for example, demanded a ban on sweated imports and the adoption of controls over resources to balance the needs of producing and consuming countries. Cheap food was no longer an unmitigated blessing if it meant a collapse in export markets and unemployment in the export industries of Lancashire or south Wales, where the co-operative movement was so strong. The emphasis shifted from free trade as a guarantee of the rights of the consumer to an interest in organized consumer councils and the socialization of food trades to weaken the hold of traders and profiteers.[61] Free trade was no longer the obvious means of protecting the consumer interest; organization and regulation were much more important. As we have seen, the process of separation between consumers and free trade started before the war, with the Labour party stressing the need for a just distribution of resources as a prerequisite for free trade. After the war, Hobson's vision of a society of small-scale producers and enlightened consumers was rejected by the Labour party's conference in 1928. Instead, Labour adopted the approach of Sidney Webb and the Fabians who actively supported large-scale production as efficient and a step towards socialized industry.[62] Although the Labour party continued to support free trade, it was linked with a redistributionist agenda, an attack on socially created wealth and Rent. The needs of the consumer were to be guaranteed not by free trade but by high wages and welfare benefits, secured by redistributive taxation and nationalization.

The pursuit of Cobdenite internationalism shifted from free trade and the blessings of comparative advantage to what Hobson called 'organised economic internationalism'.[63] A new internationalism of collective agreements was needed to deal with antagonisms. Although protectionism remained a sign of hostility and conflict over the scarce resources of the world, the mere imposition of free trade was not enough. A world of peace and prosperity could only be achieved through positive action, by regulation and international co-operation.[64] At the same time, expert opinion moved towards protection. In October 1930, the majority of the Committee of Economists of the Economic Advisory Committee decided in favour of protection. They argued that wages were 'sticky' and could only be reduced at considerable social cost, so that it was difficult to correct the balance of trade by cutting money costs. Keynes argued that tariffs would increase prices and so reduce the *real* wage more easily than by cutting money wages; the result would be higher profits.[65] Lionel Robbins and a group of economists at the LSE were sceptical, and questioned whether a reduction in real wages would help exporters who were more concerned with the level of money wages and costs.[66] The issue remained open and the Labour government tried to avoid action. But pressure for change was mounting on the minority Labour government, from its allies as well as opponents. The TUC joined with the FBI to send a memorandum to the Prime Minister on the need for inter-Commonwealth trade. Although they stopped short of an explicit demand for imperial preference, the balance of opinion was clearly shifting. Meanwhile, the Conservative Research Department drafted a tariff which allowed the National government to introduce protection very rapidly after its election victory in 1931. At least initially, the motivation was not to preserve jobs so much as to support the exchange rate from the threat of a massive depreciation in sterling after Britain left the gold standard. Protection was one way of controlling the level of sterling and prices.

Adoption of protection was the result of a gradual erosion of free trade from the turn of the century. Many industrialists had started to move towards reciprocity; they rejected Joseph Chamberlain's much more wide-ranging and dogmatic policy of imperial preference, without necessarily supporting free trade in the equally dogmatic form of the Liberal party. Meanwhile, Labour's support for free trade entailed a shift towards redistribution and a rejection of other elements of nineteenth-century liberal political economy. Although free trade seemed to have triumphed in the elections of 1906 and 1910, it was already undergoing metamorphosis from within. The impact of the First World War, the loss of export markets, and the development of Labour thinking on domestic welfare continued to erode free trade in the 1920s, preparing the way for the introduction of high tariffs after the economic crisis of 1931.

In 1931, a 10 per cent tariff was imposed on finished and semi-manufactured imports; raw materials were still allowed into the country free of duty; and a new body—the Import Duties Advisory Committee—was established to take decisions over higher duties on specific commodities out of politics. In 1932, a conference was held at Ottawa to convert this emergency tariff into imperial preference. The Import Duties Act of 1932 exempted imperial goods from the duties, and allowed bargaining with other countries so that trade blocs would be created. By 1934, the empire took 44.0 per cent of British exports. Imperial preference was linked with the abandonment of the gold standard, the adoption of low interest rates, and controls over competition within Britain. The government's priority shifted towards preserving domestic employment and industry. Plans to restore multilateralism at the World Economic Conference in 1933 foundered, for the British and other governments were reluctant to sacrifice their manufacturing industries. The United States adopted a policy of economic nationalism, introducing much higher duties in 1930. For its part, the British government concentrated on negotiating bilateral agreements with primary producers in Argentina, Denmark, and the Baltic, who were very dependent on British markets.

The scope for action was very limited. Primary producers might wish to secure access to British markets, but were reluctant to drop their tariffs on British goods. The low prices of primary commodities and the severity of the depression meant they wished to maintain industrial employment. The British government was reluctant to push for access to imperial markets too strongly, for countries such as Australia and Canada wished to protect their own industries from collapse and imperial unity might be threatened. In any case, the British government surrendered some of its bargaining power by offering non-imperial countries privileged access to its markets. British manufacturers already had a high share of imperial markets in manufactures, and a solution to their difficulties was more likely to be found by increasing exports to non-empire countries, where they were discriminated against.

British agriculture had little protection, for the agreement at Ottawa gave imperial food free access to the domestic market. The outcome is not surprising for, despite the protests of the Ministry of Agriculture, the government was much more concerned about the domestic consumer of food. Although the collapse of primary prices hit British farmers, agriculture employed only 6.4 per cent of the workforce in 1931 and a rise in food prices would have a serious impact on domestic consumption and the standard of living. In negotiating 'most favoured nation' agreements' with other countries, the Ministry of Agriculture argued for quota restrictions to limit the volume of imports. However, quotas threatened British recovery and the government preferred 'levy-subsidies'—a charge on imports to subsidize British farmers. The proposal soon collapsed, for foreign countries resented subsidizing British farmers and the levies would increase prices to British consumers. In 1937, the competing demands for cheap prices, assistance to farmers, and access to export markets were resolved by paying subsidies to farmers. As a result, food prices were kept low and the gap between world prices and British costs was met by the taxpayer. The government was then able to use its leverage to increase exports to countries with whom it signed most favoured nation agreements. Meanwhile, various scheme were devised to regulate the output and price of primary products such as rubber and copper, to prevent low profits and demand from threatening the survival of firms and the stability of colonial economies. Of course, these schemes would also raise the price of imports for British industry and their customers—a serious political issue for the British government which had to balance these competing pressures.[67]

The various bilateral agreements and trading schemes proved disappointing and the USA started to press for reductions in trade barriers. Cordell Hull, the US Secretary of State from 1933 to 1944, adopted a Cobdenite stance, arguing that 'unhampered trade dovetailed with peace; high tariffs, trade barriers and unfair economic competition with war'.[68] The Reciprocal Trade Agreements Act of 1934 marked the start of a reduction in American tariffs, for many industrialists now saw the need for larger foreign markets. In 1938, a deal was negotiated between the USA, Britain, and Canada in an attempt to reduce trade barriers and discrimination, but the British government did not accept that bilateralism had failed and gave little away. Despite statements in favour of multilateral trade, little was done to achieve liberalization of trade and to dismantle the Ottawa system. As we shall see in Chapter 9, the war and Britain's financial plight increased American leverage, without as much of an impact as might be thought.

How much difference did protection make to the British economy? As noted in Chapter 5, the combination of devaluation and protection meant that the import penetration of the early 1920s was now reversed and domestic producers took a larger share of the market. Between 1920 and 1929, imports of manufactures rose by 65.7 per cent; between 1929 and 1937, they fell by 17.6 per cent.[69] But historians are not agreed on the importance of protection in stimulating recovery. Forrest Capie points out that the vital point is not the nominal rate of tariffs; it is the effective level of protection, defined as the extent to which value added with protection exceeds value added without protection. Estimates of the effective level of duty by Capie show that the tariff did not reflect the needs of large, powerful industries so much as smaller industries and the regions. As a result, the tariff did not achieve the ambition of the IDAC of protecting the most vulnerable industries. Even Neville Chamberlain was sceptical about the impact of imperial preference. By 1940, he was arguing that multilateral trade was preferable and that Britain must end the 'vicious policy of economic nationalism'.[70] His change of policy was no doubt influenced by need for American support, but even without the desire to conciliate Cordell Hull, it was by no means clear that protection assisted recovery.

The removal of international competition in the 1930s was complemented by the erosion of competition within Britain, with a move to regulated markets and price controls. The approach adopted in the 1930s may be termed 'productivism': the invisible hand of the market was no longer sufficient for efficiency and rational business structures were needed. The trend was confirmed by wartime rationing and controls, and by the policies of Labour after the war. The re-creation of competition at home and abroad only started from the late 1950s, and was slow and partial until the 1970s. In a later chapter, we will assess the consequences of these limits on competition for the performance of the British economy. Did they lead to a 'low-effort equilibrium', an absence of commitment by capital and labour to raise productivity and increase competitiveness? The immediate concern in the next chapter is another element of the global economy: the export of capital. The era of free trade before the First World War was linked with massive and unprecedented levels of capital exports; by the 1930s, capital exports had more or less ceased and were only to recover at the end of the twentieth century. The rise and fall of capital mobility was one of the most striking features of the history of globalization between 1851 and 1951.

NOTES

1. Keynes, *Economic Consequences of the Peace, Collected Writings* (hereafter *CW*), ii. 6–7.
2. Keynes, 'National self-sufficiency', *CW* xxi. 236; *General Theory*, *CW* vii. 382.
3. Gambles, 'Rethinking the politics of protection', 936, 940.
4. Howe, *Free Trade and Liberal England*, 92, 93, 96.
5. Ibid. 95, 98.
6. Ibid. 160.
7. Ibid. 94.
8. Marsh, *Bargaining on Europe*.
9. Howe, *Free Trade and Liberal England*, 192.
10. This is the sort of approach found in Marrison, *British Business and Protection*.
11. *Parliamentary Debates*, NS 23, col. 658 (19 Mar. 1830).
12. Howe, *Free Trade and Liberal England*, 230.
13. Trentmann, 'Political culture and political economy', 229.
14. Trentmann, 'Civil society, commerce, and the "citizen-consumer" ', 319–20.
15. McKibbin, *Ideologies of Class*, 31.
16. Quoted in Cain and Harrison (eds.), *Imperialism*, 82.

17. Drage, *The Imperial Organization of Trade*, 299, 301.

18. Hobson, 'The general election of 1910', 112–13.

19. Robertson, *Trade and Tariffs*.

20. On Hobson, see Cain, *Hobson and Imperialism*, and Matthew, 'Hobson, Ruskin and Cobden'; Hobson, *The Crisis of Liberalism*, 73.

21. See Burgess, 'Lord Rosebery and the Imperial Federation League'.

22. On Chamberlain, see Marsh, *Joseph Chamberlain*, 522, 582, ch. 18; Green, *The Crisis of Conservatism*, 21, 39, 194, 223, 239, 245, 246.

23. Trentmann, 'Transformation of fiscal reform', 1012–13, 1018–20; Caillard, *Imperial Fiscal Reform*.

24. Pollard, *Britain's Prime and Britain's Decline'*, 239, 244.

25. Memorandum from H. A. Gwynne to J. Chamberlain reprinted in Mock, *Imperiale Herrschaft und Nationales Interesse*, 1024–8, 1037–40; entries in *Oxford Dictionary of National Biography*.

26. Clarke, 'End of laissez faire', 494.

27. Trentmann, 'Transformation of fiscal reform', 1025–9.

28. Trentmann, 'Wealth versus welfare', 74–5, 76.

29. Hobson, *Evolution of Modern Capitalism*, cited in Trentmann, 'Civil society, commerce, and the "citizen-consumer" ', 315; Matthew, 'Hobson, Ruskin and Cobden', 19, 21–2, 26; Trentmann, 'Wealth versus welfare', 77.

30. O'Rourke and Williamson, *Globalization and History*, 43, 53.

31. Nye, 'Myth of free trade Britain', 26.

32. Meyer, 'Input-output approach'.

33. McCloskey, *Enterprise and Trade*, chs. 7 and 8; Hatton, 'Demand', 576.

34. North, 'Ocean freight rates and economic development', 537, 541–2.

35. Craig, *The Ship: Steam Tramps and Cargo Liners*, 14.

36. O'Rourke and Williamson, *Globalization and History* 100, 113.

37. See Daunton, *Progress and Poverty*, ch. 20; Davis, *Late Victorian Holocausts*, 27.

38. Steele, *Lord Salisbury*, 102 and Roberts, *Salisbury*, 143.

39. Davis, *Late Victorian Holocaust*; Washbrook, 'Commercialization' and 'Economic development'.

40. Saul, *Studies*, 11, 37.

41. Tyszynski, 'World trade', 292.

42. Hatton, 'The demand for British exports', 582, 586.

43. Saul, *Studies*, 205.

44. Ibid. 233–6.

45. Harnetty, 'Imperialism'; Klein, 'English free traders'; Dewey, 'End of the imperialism of free trade'.

46. Nicholas, 'Overseas marketing', 489–90.

47. *City Press*, 19 Mar. 1910. Cited in Daunton, 'The City and industry', 187.

48. Pollard, *Britain's Prime and Britain's Decline*, 52–3, 83–4, 113.

49. Craig, *The Ship*

50. Sturmey, *British Shipping*, 12–13.

51. Barnard, *Australian Wool Market*, 139–46, 177–8.
52. Chapman, *Rise of Merchant Banking*, 4, 17–18.
53. Daunton, ' "Gentlemanly capitalism" ', 185–7; Michie, *London Stock Exchange*, 20–36.
54. Tyszynski, 'World trade'.
55. Ibid., 289.
56. Drummond, *British Economic Policy*, 18–28; Broadberry, *Productivity Race*, 96.
57. Davenport-Hines, *Dudley Docker*, 58.
58. Hansard, 5th series, 172, col. 1610, 29 Apr. 1924.
59. Trentmann, 'Transformation of fiscal reform', 1042–4; Trentmann, 'The strange death of free trade', 246–7; Capie, *Depression and Protectionism*, 55, 71–4.
60. Trentmann, 'The strange death of free trade', 248.
61. Trentmann, 'Civil society, commerce, and the "citizen-consumer" ', 321–2; Trentmann, 'Bread, milk'.
62. Thompson, 'Hobson and the Fabians'; Trentmann, 'Wealth versus welfare', 93–6.
63. Trentmann, 'Civil Society', Harvard University Center for European Studies, Working Paper 66 (1997), 28.
64. Ibid. 28–9.
65. Skidelsky, *John Maynard Keynes*, 370–2, 374–6.
66. In Beveridge (ed.), *Tariffs: The Case*, ch. 14.
67. See Ch. 2; on regulation of primary products, see McFadyean, *Rubber Regulation*.
68. Quoted Rooth, *British Protectionism and the International Economy*, 284.
69. Solomou, *Themes*, 145.
70. Capie, *Depression and Protection*, ch. 8; Abel, *British Tariffs*, 134.

FURTHER READING

Abel, D. R. E., *A History of British Tariffs, 1923–1942* (1945)

Ashley, W. J., *The Tariff Problem* (3rd edn., 1911)

Baker, C., *An Indian Rural Economy, 1880–1955: The Tamilnad Countryside* (Oxford, 1984)

Barnard, A., *The Australian Wool Market, 1840–1900* (Carlton, Victoria,1958)

Beveridge, W. (ed.), *Tariffs: The Case Examined* (1931)

Burgess, M. D., 'Lord Rosebery and the Imperial Federation League, 1884–93', *New Zealand Journal of History*, 13 (1979)

Caillard, V., *Imperial Fiscal Reform* (1903)

Cain, P., 'Political economy in Edwardian England: the tariff reform controversy', in A. O'Day (ed.), *The Edwardian Age: Conflict and Stability, 1900–14* (1979)

—— *Hobson and Imperialism: Radicalism, New Liberalism, and Finance, 1887–1938* (Oxford, 2002)

—— and Harrison, M. (eds.), *Imperialism: Critical Concepts in Historical Studies* (2001)

Caldwell, J., 'Malthus and the less developed world: the pivotal role of India', *Population and Development Review*, 24 (1998)

Capie, F., 'Tariff protection and economic performance in the nineteenth century', in J. Black and L. A. Winters (eds.), *Policy and Performance in International Trade* (1983)

—— 'The pressure for tariff protection in Britain, 1917–31', *Journal of European Economic History*, 9 (1980)

Capie, F., *Depression and Protectionism: Britain between the Wars* (1983)

Chapman, S. D., *The Rise of Merchant Banking* (1984)

Chauduri, K. N., 'India's international economy in the nineteenth century: an historical survey', *Modern Asian Studies*, 2 (1968)

—— *The Economic Development of India under the East India Company, 1814–58* (1971)

Clarke, P. F., 'The end of laissez faire and the politics of cotton', *Historical Journal*, 15 (1972)

Craig, R., *The Ship: Steam Tramps and Cargo Liners, 1850–1950* (1980).

Crouzet, F., 'Trade and empire: the British experience from the establishment of free trade until the First World War', in B. M. Ratcliffe (ed.), *Great Britain and her World, 1750–1914* (1975)

Daunton, M. J., 'The City and industry: the nature of British capitalism, 1750–1914', in G. Alderman and C. Holmes (eds.), *Outsiders and Outcasts: Essays in Honour of W. J. Fishman* (1993)

—— *Progress and Poverty: An Economic and Social History of Britain, 1700–1850* (Oxford, 1995)

Davenport-Hines, R. P. T., *Dudley Docker: The Life and Times of a Trade Warrior* (Cambridge, 1984)

Davis, M., *Late Victorian Holocausts: El Niño Famines and the Making of the Third World* (2001)

Dewey, C., 'The end of the imperialism of free trade: the eclipse of the Lancashire lobby and the concession of fiscal autonomy in India', in C. J. Dewey and A. G. Hopkins (eds.), *The Imperial Impact: Studies in the Economic History of Africa and India* (1978)

Drage, G., *The Imperial Organization of Trade* (1911)

Eichengreen, B. J., *Sterling and the Tariff, 1929–32* (Princeton, 1981)

Estevadeordal, A., 'Measuring protection in the early twentieth century', *European Review of Economic History*, 1 (1997)

Ferguson, N., *The World's Banker: The History of the House of Rothschild* (1998)

Gadgil, M., and Guha, R., 'State forestry and social conflict in British India', in D. Hardiman (ed.), *Peasant Resistance in India, 1858–1914* (Oxford, 1992)

Gambles, A., *Protection and Policy: Conservative Economic Discourse, 1815–1852* (Woodbridge, 1999)

—— 'Rethinking the politics of protection: Conservatism and the corn laws, 1830–52', *English Historical Review*, 113 (1998)

Ganguli, B. N., *Dadabhai Naoroji and the Drain Theory* (1965)

Green, E. H. H., 'Radical Conservatism and the genesis of tariff reform', *Historical Journal*, 28 (1985)

—— *Crisis of Conservatism: The Politics, Economics and Ideology of the British Conservative Party, 1880–1914* (1995), 236.

Greenberg, M., *British Trade and the Opening of China, 1800–42* (1951)

Gregg, E. S., 'Vicissitudes in the shipping trade, 1870–1920', *Quarterly Journal of Economics*, 35 (1921)

Harnetty, P., *Imperialism and Free Trade: Lancashire and India in the Mid Nineteenth Century* (1972)

—— 'The Indian cotton duties controversy, 1894–6', *English Historical Review*, 77 (1962)

—— 'The imperialism of free trade: Lancashire and the Indian cotton duties controversy, 1859–62', *Journal of British Studies*, 6 (1966)

Hatton, T. J., 'The demand for British exports, 1870–1914', *Economic History Review*, 2nd ser. 43i (1990)

Hobson, J. A., 'The general election of 1910', *Sociological Review*, 3 (1910)

—— *The Crisis of Liberalism* (1909)

—— *Evolution of Modern Capitalism: A study of Machine Production* (1906)

Howe, A., *Free Trade and Liberal England, 1846–1946* (Oxford, 1997)

Hyde, F. E., *Far Eastern Trade, 1860–1914* (1973)

Imlah, A. H., *Economic Elements in the Pax Britannica: Studies in British Foreign Trade in the Nineteenth Century* (Cambridge, 1958)

Kaiwar, V., 'The colonial state, capital and the peasantry in Bombay Presidency', *Modern Asian Studies*, 28 (1994)

—— 'Nature, property and polity in colonial Bombay', *Journal of Peasant Studies*, 27 (2000)

Keynes, J. M., *The Collected Writings of John Maynard Keynes*, ii: *The Economic Consequences of the Peace* (1971)

—— *The Collected Writings of John Keynes*, xxi: *Activities 1931–39: World Crises and Policies in Britian and America*, ed. D. Moggridge (1982)

Kitson, M., Solomou, S., and Weale, M., 'Effective protection and economic recovery in the United Kingdom in the 1930s', *Economic History Review*, 44 (1991)

Klein, I., 'English free traders and Indian tariffs, 1874–96', *Modern Asian Studies*, 5 (1973)

McCloskey, D., *Enterprise and Trade in Victorian Britain: Essays in Historical Economics* (1981)

McFadyean, A., *The History of Rubber Regulation, 1934–43* (1944)

McKibbin, R. I., *The Ideologies of Class: Social Relations in Britain, 1880–1950* (Oxford, 1990)

Maddison, A., *The World Economy: A Millennial Perspective* (Paris 2001)

Maizels, A., *Industrial Growth and World Trade* (Cambridge, 1963)

Marrison, A. J., 'Businessmen, industries and tariff reform in Great Britain, 1903–30', *Business History*, 25 (1983)

—— *British Business and Protection, 1903–1932* (Oxford, 1996)

Marsh, P. T., *Bargaining on Europe: Britain and the First Common Market, 1860–92* (New Haven, 1999)

—— *Joseph Chamberlain: Entrepreneur in Politics* (New Haven, 1994)

Matthew, H. G. C., 'Hobson, Ruskin and Cobden', in M. Freeden (ed.), *Reappraising J. A. Hobson: Humanism and Welfare* (1990)

Meyer, A. J., 'An input-output approach to evaluating British industrial production in the late nineteenth century', *Explorations in Entrepreneurial History*, 8 (1955)

Michie, R. C., *The London Stock Exchange: A History* (1999)

Mitchell, B. R., with P. Deane, *Abstract of British Historical Statistics* (Cambridge, 1982)

Mock, W., *Imperiale Herrschaft und Nationales Interesse: 'Constructive Imperialism' oder Freihandel in Grossbrittanien vor dem Ersten Weltkrieg* (Stuttgart, 1982)

Mukerjee, T., 'The theory of economic drain: the impact of British rule on the Indian economy, 1840–1900', in K. E. Boulding and T. Mukerjee (eds.), *Economic Imperialism* (1972)

Nicholas, S., 'The overseas marketing performance of British industry, 1870–1914', *Economic History Review*, 2nd ser. 37 (1984)

North, D. C., 'Ocean freight rates and economic development, 1750–1913', *Journal of Economic History*, 18 (1958)

Nye, J. N., 'The myth of free-trade Britain and fortress France: tariffs and trade in the nineteenth century', *Journal of Economic History*, 51 (1991)

O'Brien, P. K., and Pigman, G. A., 'Free trade, British hegemony and the international economic order in the nineteenth century', *Review of International Studies*, 18 (1992)

O'Rourke, K. H., and Williamson, J. G., *Globalization and History: The Evolution of a Nineteenth-Century Atlantic Economy* (1999)

Platt, D. C. M., *Latin America and British Trade, 1806–1914* (1972)

Pollard, S., *Britain's Prime and Britain's Decline: The British Economy, 1870–1914* (1989)

Raghavan, T., 'Malguzars and peasants: The Narmada Valley, 1860–1920', in D. Ludden (ed.), *Agricultural Production and Indian History* (Delhi, 1994)

Rea, R., *Free Trade in Being* (1908)

Roberts, A., *Salisbury: Victorian Titan* (1999)

Robertson, J. M., *Trade and Tariffs* (1908)

Rooth, T., *British Protectionism and the International Economy: Overseas Commercial Policy in the 1930s* (1993)

Satya, L., *Cotton and Famine in Berar, 1850–1900* (Delhi, 1997)

Saul, S. B., *Studies in British Overseas Trade, 1870–1914* (Liverpool, 1960)

Skidelsky, R., *John Maynard Keynes: The Economist as Saviour, 1920–1937* (1992)

Solomou, S., *Themes in Macroeconomic History: The UK Economy, 1919–1939* (Cambridge, 1996)

Steele, D., *Lord Salisbury: A Political Biography* (1999)

Sturmey, S. G., *British Shipping and World Competition* (1962)

Sykes, A., *Tariff Reform and British Politics, 1903–13* (1979)

Thompson, N., 'Hobson and the Fabians: two roads to socialism in the 1920s', *History of Political Economy*, 26 (1994)

Tomlinson, B. R., 'The political economy of the raj: the decline of colonialism', *Journal of Economic History*, 42 (1982)

—— *The Economy of Modern India, 1860–1970* (Cambridge, 1993)

Trentmann, F., 'Civil society, commerce, and the "citizen-consumer": popular meanings of free trade in late nineteenth- and early twentieth-century Britain', in F. Trentmann (ed.), *Paradoxes of Civil Society: New Perspectives on Modern German and British History* (New York, 2000); longer version in Center for European Studies, Harvard, Working Paper 66

—— 'The transformation of fiscal reform: reciprocity, modernization, and the fiscal debate within the business community in early twentieth-century Britain', *Historical Journal*, 39 (1996)

—— 'The strange death of free trade: the erosion of "liberal consensus" in Great Britain, c.1903–1932', in E. F. Biagini (ed.), *Citizenship and Community: Liberals, Radicals and Collective Identities in the British Isles, 1865–1931* (Cambridge, 1996)

—— 'Wealth versus welfare: the British left between free trade and national political economy before the First World War', *Historical Research*, 70 (1997)

—— 'Political culture and political economy: interest, ideology and free trade', *Review of International Political Economy*, 5 (1998)

—— 'Bread, milk and democracy: consumption and citizenship in twentieth-century Britain', in M. Daunton and M. Hilton (eds.), *The Politics of Consumption: Material Culture and Citizenship in Europe and America* (Oxford, 2000)

Tyszynski, H., 'World trade in manufactured commodities, 1899–1950', *Manchester School*, 19 (1951)

Washbrook, D., 'The commercialization of agriculture in colonial India: production, subsistence and reproduction in the "Dry South," *c.*1870–1930', *Modem Asian Studies*, 28 (1994)

—— 'Economic development and social stratification in rural Madras: the "dry Region" 1878–1929', in C. J. Dewey and A. J. Hopkins (eds.), *The Imperial Impact* (1978)

Watts, S., *Epidemics and History: Disease, Power and Imperialism* (New Haven, 1997)

Whitcombe, E., *Agrarian Conditions in Northern India, i: The United Provinces under British Rule, 1860–1900* (Berkeley, 1972)

....

CHAPTER 7

Capital Exports

IN 1930, Keynes was in little doubt that international capital flows were harmful to British welfare:

I believe that *laissez faire* in foreign lending is utterly incompatible with our existing wages policy. For if individuals are entirely free to lend their savings without discrimination in whatever quarter of the world they obtain the greatest reward . . . the proportion of the joint product which we award to labour as compared with the proportion which we award to capital cannot be greater here than it is in other parts of the world . . . relatively to its efficiency . . . . Either we shall be in a state of chronic disequilibrium . . . or we shall have to force down wages in England until capital gets the same proportion of the product as in Germany.

We have now reached this point, that our wages policy is definitely set to a more liberal remuneration of the worker relatively to his efficiency than prevails in a good many other countries . . . this . . . is definitely incompatible with the policy of *laissez faire* towards foreign investment.[1]

Here was a clear statement of the priority of domestic welfare over the international economy. Wages should not be forced to adjust to the outflow of capital; rather, capital movements and exchange rates should adjust to high British wages. In a trade-off between domestic welfare, capital mobility, and fixed exchanges, Keynes willingly gave priority to the first. Prior to the First World War, the trade-off between domestic welfare, capital exports, and exchange rates was much less certain. The outflow of capital could plausibly be seen as producing export markets and providing cheap imports of food. Further, fixed exchange rates seemed to imply low prices and monetary stability. Between 1851 and 1913, the global economy combined fixed exchange rates with capital mobility and an active domestic monetary policy was not possible. A reduction in interest rates to stimulate the domestic economy at a time of recession would put the exchange rate under pressure and provoke an export of capital. Hence the domestic economy would not be stimulated and interest rates would rise to protect the exchange rate. This policy mix of fixed exchanges and capital mobility could not be maintained between the wars or restored after the Second World War. In the 1920s, the government's attempt to return to fixed exchange rates was increasingly at odds with capital mobility which threatened domestic prosperity, and in the 1930s both were abandoned. In the attempt to reconstruct the world economy after 1945, capital mobility was sacrificed to a desire to restore fixed exchange rates and domestic welfare. The aim in this chapter is to analyse the rise and fall of capital mobility. In the next chapter, we turn to the rise and fall of fixed exchange rates.

The Age of Global Capital

A desire to maintain domestic welfare through high wages and restrictions on capital exports was not welcomed by those who received high returns from abroad. There was a flood of investment overseas in the half-century before 1914, which was (according to its critics) undertaken by a large rentier class living on their 'unearned' income who were passive portfolio investors rather than making direct active investment in foreign ventures: they had no control over the concerns in which the money was placed, but were merely 'coupon clippers' who received interest by wielding a pair of scissors to cut out and return the coupons on the bonds. Many commentators at the time and since have criticized such investment behaviour, which they believe harmed Britain's welfare. Equally, many British investors eagerly exploited the opportunities of the global economy and combined their own economic advantage with a comforting thought that they were making productive use of world resources and spreading peace, prosperity, and civilization. Certainly, the change in the structure of British national wealth is striking, with a marked decline in the proportion of wealth in land, and a rise in overseas assets from just under 7 per cent in 1850 to over a third by the First World War (see Table 7.1).

The level of overseas investment has been estimated by three methods. One is an indirect calculation based on the balance of payments: capital exports are the residual after all other current transactions have been taken into account.[2] Although

TABLE 7.1. *Net national wealth, UK, 1850–1913 (%)*

	Net domestic	Land	Overseas assets	Net national wealth
1850	39.9	53.3	6.8	100.0
1870	45.3	40.3	14.4	100.0
1890	45.9	28.0	26.1	100.0
1913	46.1	18.6	35.2	100.0

Source: Feinstein and Pollard (eds.), *Studies in Capital Formation*, 469.

such a procedure produces an annual aggregate of capital exports, it cannot be used to establish the composition of investment by sector and area. A second method provides more detail, through an analysis of publicly quoted issues floated in Britain for overseas destinations which excludes direct investment by firms. A third measure is based on estimates from tax records, which can be grossed up to produce a rough estimate of the level of investment.[3] Each of these measures has its shortcomings. D. C. M. Platt has claimed that errors in the data have led to a considerable exaggeration. The figure usually placed on the accumulated stock of British capital overseas in 1913 is £3.7 billion for portfolio investment in quoted securities, or about £4 billion when an allowance is made for direct investment by firms. Platt suggested that the figure of portfolio investment should be reduced by about 30 per cent, so that total investment is cut to about £3 billion.[4] Such a reduction would affect any assessment of its impact upon the British economy. Most historians accept that the higher figure is the more plausible, and that the level of overseas investment in 1913 was in the order of £4 billion, a conclusion supported by the congruence between the estimates from all methods of calculation.[5]

The data on publicly quoted securities provide some sense of the timing and direction of investment. There were three upswings: from a trough in 1867 to a peak in 1872; from a trough in 1877 to a peak in 1889; and from a trough in 1893 to a peak in 1913. Overseas investment formed a relatively low proportion of total investment in the 1890s, standing at 37 per cent of gross domestic fixed capital formation; in the boom of the late 1880s, it was 62 per cent; and in the unprecedented outflow from 1905 to 1914 it reached 76 per cent. The scale of investment abroad was extraordinarily high on any relative measure, amounting to about a third of all British capital in 1913.[6] International capital movements only regained the levels of the late nineteenth and early twentieth century around 1990, when no single country was as dominant as Britain. Most of the outflow of capital went to a few recipients, with the United States, Canada, Argentina, Australia, and India accounting for over half Above all, two sectors took the bulk of the capital: government bonds and railways accounted for two-thirds of British overseas investment. Generally, British investment went into social overhead capital, which accounted for about 69 per cent, compared with a much smaller share for extractive and manufacturing industries (12 and 4 per cent respectively). The relative importance of these sectors varied between regions, with railways dominating in North America and Argentina, and government bonds in Australia, India, South Africa, and Brazil. Railways alone accounted for 31.7 per cent of investment—and despite the importance of government bonds, investment in private concerns was more significant than public investment. In all, 36.3 per cent of investment was in government securities. However, the crucial difference was not between private and public outlets, for most investors were looking for fixed-interest securities in both sectors. Most of the investment was outside the empire, which accounted for 40 per cent compared with 59 per cent for independent foreign countries and 1 per cent for foreign dependencies. The division between empire and foreign countries was considerably less significant than the contrast between temperate areas of recent white settlement and the tropics which were much less attractive to investors. These general patterns varied over time. In the upswings, the private sector increased relative to the public. In periods of retraction, investment concentrated on government bonds and retreated to the empire. Each upswing had its own character. In the first, railways were less important and most investment was in government bonds, above all to Russia, France, and Germany. In the next, investment was more broadly based through the medium of finance, land, and investment companies, and into mining and manufacturing. The major destinations were the United States, Australia, Argentina,

TABLE 7.2. *Distribution of British overseas capital calls, 1865–1914 (%)*
(a) **By area and country**

	Percentage	Rank order
North America	34.3	
USA	20.5	1
Canada	10.1	2
South America	16.8	
Argentina	8.6	3
Brazil	4.2	7
Asia	14.0	
India	7.8	5
Japan	1.9	11
China	1.8	12
Europe	12.0	
France	1.4	15
Italy	1.0	18
Austria-Hungary	1.0	19
Australasia	10.8	
Australia	8.3	4
New Zealand	2.1	9
Africa	10.6	
South Africa	6.4	6
Egypt	1.6	13
Rhodesia	1.1	16
Multi-continent	0.9	
Oceania	0.7	
Total	100.0	

Source: Stone, *Global Export of Capital,* tables 59 and 61.

(b) Sectoral composition of capital calls, 1865–1914, total and selected areas (%)

	All	USA	Argentina	India	Australia
Government	36.3	5.8	22.4	45.8	65.8
Railways	31.7	61.6	57.5	40.5	0.0
Public utilities	6.3	9.5	8.9	3.1	3.5
Financial	7.3	6.3	5.4	1.5	11.6
Raw materials	10.0	10.1	1.0	9.1	26.3
Industrial and misc.	7.2	16.5	6.1	2.7	4.1
Shipping	1.3	0.5	0.8	1.1	1.2
Total private	63.7	94.2	77.6	54.2	34.2

Source: Stone, *Global Export of Capital,* tables 60 and 62.

(c) Distribution of capital calls for 15 major recipients, 1865–1914 (%)

Debentures	68.2
Government	35.2
Railway	22.0
Others	11.0
Ordinary shares	22.6
Preference shares	6.4
Notes	2.8
Total	100.0

Source: Stone, *Global Export of Capital,* table 63.

and India. The final, massive, upswing from 1893 to 1913 accounted for over half of all investment overseas, and was dominated by government loans and railways.[7]

Critics of overseas investment claim that the City of London acted as the conduit and that the financial institutions and their clients spurned domestic investments in the search for security and high returns abroad. The role of the City and the nature of overseas investment formed the basis of a debate which started to call into question the view that Britain's involvement in the international economy was broadly beneficial to society as a whole.

Although Liberals remained loyal to free trade up to 1914, some began to express doubts about capital exports. Did they produce prosperity for Britain and the world economy, or did they lead to impoverishment at home and conflict abroad? Perhaps the pursuit of self-interest was no longer producing general prosperity, and the state was dominated by a class of rich financiers making profits at the expense of society. Such was the fear of J. A. Hobson. Income and wealth were unevenly distributed, and in the words of Leo Chiozza Money, there was 'a great multitude of poor people, veneered with a thin layer of the comfortable and the rich'. The large number of poor led to 'under-consumption' at home; the rich with more money than they could possibly consume were 'over-saving'. There was no point in investing savings at home, since the market was so weak; and because investment at home was depressed, wages remained low. The interpretation had clear implications for social reform, for it suggested a policy of redistributive taxation. In the opinion of Hobson and Chiozza Money, the export of capital offered the solution to the dilemma of the rich who were looking for an outlet for their surplus savings. 'While capital has gone oversea [*sic*] in a never-ending stream', wrote Chiozza Money, 'the people whose united activities produced the commodities embodied in that capital have remained poor for lack of the proper investment of capital at home . . . .' An uneven distribution of income and wealth, according to these critics, produced a maldistribution of occupations. The small class of the rich demanded personal services and luxuries, whereas a more even distribution of income would lead to mass production of consumer goods and investment at home. 'Too many of our population', wrote Chiozza Money, 'are engaged either in the direct production of luxuries or in the production of useful articles to be exchanged for foreign luxuries.' There was a further danger, that the flow of capital abroad would lead to imperialism and international conflict as financiers demanded protection for their investments.[8]

Such was the assessment of overseas investment by some 'new Liberals'. They were not rejecting Cobdenite principles outright, for they were not hostile in all circumstances to capital exports or to a liberal world economy based on free trade and international specialization. Their criticism was confined to overseas investment and free trade arising from a maldistribution of income at home, creating a distortion of the economy and politics through the power of rich rentiers and financiers. Their aim was to tackle the inequalities. Hobson did not believe that imperialism and conflict were inevitable, intrinsic features of capitalism—a view held by Lenin and later Marxist historians. Hobson held that the capitalist economy could be purged of pathological features. He rejected Cobden's view that the pursuit of individual self-interest was in the general interest. Instead, he argued that the operation of the economy might generate inequalities, leading to a deviant form of overseas investment. It was necessary for the state to intervene to ensure that the economy *did* operate in a harmonious and just manner. This gave a more active role to the state than did Cobden, without totally rejecting Cobdenite principles. Indeed, shortly before the First World War Hobson was willing to argue strongly in favour of capital exports on the Cobdenite ground that they produced prosperity and international co-operation. His opposition was to aberrant forms of capital exports which distorted the international economic and political system, and led to a misallocation of resources in the domestic economy. His fear was that capital exports might, in certain circumstances, produce poverty for some and riches for others. and he wished to have capital exports, like free trade, based upon a wide and egalitarian home market.[9]

'Old' Liberals were less critical and less willing to admit that a free trade economy could produce international tension and a misallocation of resources. Consequently, they were disinclined to see the need for redistributive taxation. Such was the view taken by Robert Giffen, who argued that overseas investment was based on an efficient allocation of resources which created domestic prosperity and welfare. Hobson and Chiozza Money were propounding a heresy which was anathema to orthodox Liberals. Underconsumption contradicted Say's law, that supply created its own demand. On this view, the production of goods produced an equivalent in purchasing power, which was translated into effective demand in the form of consumption or of savings in productive investment. Say's law assumed that full employment was normal, and that over-saving or underconsumption was impossible. Giffen was therefore willing to defend overseas investment. 'A rich class at home living on its foreign income', claimed Giffen in 1905, 'is, on the whole, a desirable class for a country to possess.' He denied the existence of any maldistribution of income and wealth. Overseas investment, so he argued, produced prosperity in a number of ways. First, investment in the infrastructure of new countries produced cheap food, which meant a higher standard of living for British workers, and so led to a demand for new consumer goods. Secondly, investment overseas was just as beneficial as investment at home, for it created a demand for British goods abroad. He claimed that British investment in Argentina would generate economic activity, increase incomes, and lead to a higher demand for British consumer goods. The use of British capital in the construction of new railways would also entail the purchase of capital equipment. A third argument deployed by Giffen was that, far from being a diversion from profitable investment at home, 'the existence of a field for investment abroad is to be welcomed as a relief for a plethora that would be dangerous'. The retention of funds at home would, he claimed, drive down the yield on government bonds. On such grounds, Giffen rejected Hobson's attack on capital exports.[10] David Lloyd George accepted Giffen's optimism for most of his tenure as Chancellor of the Exchequer. He expected that overseas investment would lead to an increase in food production in the world economy, so reducing food prices and ending the erosion of the standard of living of workers. Overseas investment would, he hoped, stimulate domestic recovery.[11] There was, according to such a view, a coincidence between the private profits of overseas investors and the welfare of society as a whole.

The debate has continued among historians, just as fiercely and in much the same terms. At the heart of the debate was the assumption that the investors were passive rentiers, holding shares in their portfolios without control over the concerns—a body of 'gentlemanly capitalists' spurning the needs of industrial capitalism in the north and midlands. The argument of Cain and Hopkins has been supported by Lance Davis and his collaborators.[12] Is there anything to be said on the other side? The re-emergence of the global economy and capital mobility at the end of the twentieth century has given new life to the debate between those who see capital exports and globalization as progressive and beneficial, and those who view them as a baneful exploitation of the poor.

One problem with data on foreign investment is the difficulty in capturing direct investment compared with passive portfolio investment. New issues of publicly quoted overseas securities may be aggregated from advertisements and listings, but it is not easy to measure investments made within firms. Detailed work on trading companies suggests that the rough correction of 10 per cent for direct investment may be too low. An increase in the relative weight of direct investment compared with passive portfolio investment would affect the interpretation of the causes and consequences of overseas investment. Arguably, the level of direct investment has been understated because historians have been misled by the later experience of America where direct investment by firms entailed transnational corporations erecting plants in foreign countries. The model is the Ford Motor Co. or Singer Sewing Machine Co., transferring new technologies created for their own domestic market to other countries. Although there were some British transnationals of this type before 1914, they were few in number. Generally, British firms with foreign ventures were not in high-technology industry so much as in the service sector and in consumer products with backward integration of British firms to obtain assured supplies of raw materials such as the palm oil plantations of Lever Brothers in West Africa. British overseas industrial presence was largely in textiles.[13]

Above all, the search for American-style transnationals has the unfortunate effect of ignoring other, specifically British, organizational patterns. These took the form of the investment group and the free-standing company. Investment groups with overseas assets are not always readily identifiable, for the parent firm might be a partnership or private company whose activities abroad were carried on under separate names. These investment groups emerged from merchant houses or trading companies, following a different path from the better-known shift from merchanting to finance exemplified by the Barings or Rothschilds. The result has been to skew our understanding of the operation of the City of London and the global or imperial reach of British capitalism. Proponents of gentlemanly capitalism stress a shift from trade into finance. However, an alternative trajectory was possible: merchants might become multinational trading companies or investment groups. They might handle one particular commodity in many areas of the world; they might diversify from one commodity in one area of the world into a wide range of goods within that location; they might develop ancillary interests in services and transport; and they might take on production in plantations, mines, and factories.

One of the best-known examples is Matheson and Co. The firm originated in Scotland and developed as a major merchant house in the east. By 1914 its head offices were in London, and other parts of the group consisted of shipping (the China Coast Steam Navigation and Indo-China Steam Navigation), railway construction (the Shangai–Woosung Railway and the China Railway Co.), financial services (the Canton Insurance Office and the Ewo Bank of Shanghai), and mining (the Transvaal Exploration Co. and the Caucasus Copper Co.). There were further interests through Jardine, Matheson, and Co. in Hong Kong. By 1913, the capital of Jardine Matheson was about £2.5 m. More specialist was Harrison and Crosfield, with a capital of £1.226 m in 1913. This firm initially traded in tea, moving into the ownership of plantations and the establishment of branches to handle distribution, and hence to a wider range of trade, as well as agencies for insurance and shipping companies, and a large investment in rubber plantations. By the First World War it had interests in Malaya, the Dutch East Indies, and India, and secondary interests in Ceylon, the USA, Canada, Australia, and New Zealand. These firms emerged not only from the City of London and a 'gentlemanly' nexus of land and finance, but also from Liverpool and Glasgow, with close connections to the domestic economy and its demands for tea and cocoa, copper and rubber.

With few exceptions, the investment groups were amorphous and loose, so that they are less easily identified than the merchant banks. They were also unlike American transnationals which are often taken as the measure of rational, modern economic behaviour. In reality, the British trading companies were equally efficient and flexible. The American concerns were usually transferring a distinctive technology which reflected the particular circumstances of the home economy, and could most easily be adopted within a plant owned and managed by the parent firm. In the case of British trading companies, the problems and opportunities were different. In most cases, their fixed assets were not large, and they operated with other people's technologies, processes, and brands. Their advantage rested on 'soft' skills—knowledge, information, and human relationships. They acted as intermediaries between different regions of the world, with different cultures and methods of transacting business; they judged risk and reputation, and they created trust. In the process, they reduced the costs of transactions, information gathering, and risk assessment. The companies developed by recruiting and retaining staff which might involve socializing them into the culture of the concern. The ownership structure was often complicated. Indeed, some—such as the Swire group and Jardines—remain major concerns in China and the Pacific rim, using their experiences in the first global age of the late nineteenth century to exploit new opportunities in the second global age of the late twentieth century.[14]

Unlike the investment group or trading company, the free-standing company raised capital through publicly quoted issues, so that their activities are captured by estimates of portfolio investment. However, it is misleading to treat them as rentier investment, for they often took a more risky, active role. Most analyses of British overseas investment adopt a strict definition of direct investment, which is required to meet two criteria: control by the British investor; and investment through subsidiaries and branches rather than the Stock Exchange. Arguably, the relevant criterion is control, which might be possible by holding a sizeable bloc of shares purchased on the Stock Exchange. The definition of direct investment adopted more recently is a stake of more than 20 per cent, which would shift a sizeable part of overseas investment from portfolio to direct.[15] Certainly, free-standing companies were direct rather than passive portfolio investment. These companies were registered in Britain to conduct business overseas. They did not grow out of the domestic operations of existing companies, and they usually had only a small office in London to monitor overseas operations and to raise funds on the London capital market. They might be associated with a company promoter, or with mining engineers such as the future American President Herbert Hoover. City solicitors formed another link. Others were associated with trading houses such as Matheson and Co. The free-standing company did not itself offer a complete package of management, marketing, and production, for it relied on various functional specialists. Free-standing companies in relatively advanced countries found it difficult to compete with domestic concerns and they often disappeared after raising finance on the London market. In areas where indigenous management was weak, free-standing companies might have a continuing role and possibly make a transition to fully-fledged companies. Such a transformation was made by Burmah Oil. These companies were making a distinctive form of direct investment, quite unlike American multinationals.[16]

Furthermore, the new issues of publicly quoted securities were not entirely at the expense of investment in Britain. The purchasers of stock might include foreigners attracted to the London capital market; and British investors could be using short-term foreign money coming to London to finance trade. Merchant banks could use short-term money to purchase long-term securities, relying on the continuing flow of new short-term money and the knowledge that securities could, if necessary, be sold on the active secondary market in London. Consequently, the flow of interest on this seemingly 'British' overseas investment was a net gain to the national income, produced by the efficiency of the London money market in converting short-term deposits into long-term securities.[17] Of course, the passive 'coupon clippers' who incurred the wrath of Hobson and Keynes did exist. But were they so clearly demarcated from industrial capitalism? Essentially, the debate is over two visions of society: between those who believed that global or cosmopolitan capitalism was the way to prosperity; and those who argued for national capitalism, paying more attention to the social costs and welfare implications of a liberal economy. Linked with this division was another: the moral interpretation of profit. In the early twentieth century, a growing number of new Liberal and Labour politicians and commentators argued that income from passive investments was 'unearned' and should be taxed at a higher rate than earned income. These divides over the nature of capitalism and the morality of investment income were—and are—intensely politicized and ideological, and it is not possible to provide a clear objective answer to the question of whether foreign investment 'paid'.

Rather than attacking rentiers as parasitic, they might be viewed as prudent investors. Advisers on investments in the later nineteenth century produced advice on the structure of portfolios, showing how a diversified scheme led to a better return in income and capital appreciation than purely British investments.[18] Of course, the ownership of foreign investments reflected the highly skewed distribution of income which Chiozza Money and others felt to be unjustifiable. In 1870, perhaps 250,000 investors held paper assets, rising to a million in 1913. Data from estates left at death in 1913/14 suggest that 54.5 per cent of all stocks, funds, and shares were held by individuals leaving over £50,000 at death, who accounted for 40.2 per cent of all assets liable to death duties.[19] As Davis and Huttenback suggest, residents in London held 58.5 per cent of shares in imperial firms and 50.9 per cent in foreign firms, compared with only 20.8 per cent in domestic firms. Meanwhile, residents of non-metropolitan England held 59.1 per cent of domestic shares, 25.8 per cent of foreign, and 21.2 per cent of imperial.[20] In their opinion, England had two capital markets, which tends to support Hobson's interpretation. But too much should not be read into these figures.

Portfolio investment in foreign securities might arise from the industrial economy as part of the life cycle of businessmen. An industrialist or trader might start his career in debt. When the debt had been cleared, he would initially invest additional funds in the firm. A large part of investment in industry came from retained profits within family firms and partnerships; and much of the external capital remained personalized rather than institutional. The formal financial institutions of the City of London concentrated on a different set of needs at the next stage of the life cycle, when businessmen wished to supplement investment within the firm by safer investments outside the business. The final stage was to retire and become a rentier.[21] Until family firms and partnerships were granted limited liability in 1907, security for old age and dependants necessitated taking money out of the business into land, urban house property, or debentures, stocks and shares, and life insurance policies. The assets of retired men or their widows and dependants in the industrial and commercial cities of Britain offered a ready source of funds. Concerns such as the Australian Mercantile Land and Finance Co. tapped these sources by selling debentures to finance mortgages and loans to 'squatters' in Australia.[22]

In any case, a family business or partnership might not be able to absorb surpluses beyond a certain point. The excess funds might be placed in property, or in securities traded on the Stock Exchange. Rather than overseas investment starving domestic industry of capital, a proportion of overseas investment came from the surplus funds of industry. One example of the process is Dundee, where the economy was based on jute and hemp—a trade with strong imperial links with Bengal for the supply of raw materials, as well as ownership of mills. The families in these firms received fixed interest on the money they left in the partnership, as well as a share of the gross profits. They were inclined to leave profits to accumulate in order to obtain a steady 5 per cent, so that the problem was less a shortage of funds for expansion than what to do with the available money. One response was to convert the partnership into an investment trust administering a range of investments unconnected with textiles. One such firm—Cox Brothers—started to invest in American railroads in the 1870s, American land in the 1880s, Japanese and Australian government bonds, as well as a variety of English companies. By 1907 these investments amounted to £147,000.[23]

In 1870, most wealthy investors held their assets overwhelmingly in government bonds and railway shares or debentures. The narrow range widened in the later nineteenth century.[24] The emergence of a market in depersonalized investments is an important cultural and economic phenomenon. The willingness to purchase bonds or stock rested on trust in the company directors, mining engineers, or auditors who valued the assets, and the financial intermediaries. Trust might be misplaced, and there were notorious scams. The frauds in insurance in the 1830s and 1840s were satirized by Charles Dickens in *Martin Chuzzlewit* (1844) and the theme ran through to Anthony Trollope's *The Way We Live Now* (1875). Fiction was no more fantastical than reality. Stocks were watered and prospectuses deceived. False impressions and deceit were a common theme in mid-Victorian culture. But satire and fraud should not obscure a more general point, that a larger number of British investors were willing to trust impersonal, paper investment more or less anywhere in the world.

In addition to the London Stock Exchange, there were twenty-two provincial exchanges in Britain in 1914, supplemented by solicitors, brokers, issuing houses, and promoters. These exchanges were extremely efficient in listing securities, but were they providing reliable information? Members of the Stock Exchange were more concerned to regulate their dealings with each other than with the unwary outsider, and there was a persistent danger that dealers colluded to raise the value of stocks, allowing those in the know to sell their holdings before prices collapsed. Insider trading was endemic and unregulated. Membership of the Exchange was easy, and the numbers rose from 2,573 in 1884 to 5,463 in 1905.[25] The buyer and the seller of stocks lacked the same knowledge, and the problem of asymmetric information increased with distance. There was a real risk of what economists call 'moral hazard' or, more bluntly, deception and fraud. What was needed was an institutional system to provide some indication of reputation, and to distinguish between risk and uncertainty. An investor might accept risk, but uncertainty was a different matter, preventing a rational calculation of the merits of the investment. The answer was to rely on someone whose reputation could be trusted—a newspaper, a promoter, a mining engineer. Risk and uncertainty were reduced and distinguished by institutional innovation. The methods might involve bundling investments into a single portfolio and the participation of a respected bank or broker in an underwriting syndicate. Resolving the problems of asymmetries, and reducing transaction costs, were major achievements of the later nineteenth century.[26]

The solutions were not perfect: agents had their own interests which are more likely to be aligned with their principals than with the investors. Australian banks and finance houses, for example, misled British investors by presenting uncertainty of their prospects as risk which would provide a high return. A good case is the Australian Freehold Banking Corporation, which was renamed the Standard Bank of Australia when an office was opened in London. The change of name removed any hint that the bank was engaged in land speculation; savers were misled into thinking they were putting money into a commercial bank and not a mortgage bank. It failed in 1893.[27] Clearly, great care was needed in assessing the reputation of these agents and intermediaries. Many of the major concerns had an interest in their longer-term reputation; and many colonial issues were backed by officials—the High Commissioners and Agent Generals, or the Crown Agents acting through private brokers in the City. The dominions had relationships with major banks in London: the London and Westminster, for example, acted for New South Wales and the Transvaal. Merchant banks acted for foreign governments. British merchant banks, American investment banks, Canadian bond houses, and formal securities markets with some concern for the status of listed securities provided a degree of security. The market—and the savers—were sophisticated, understanding that 'symbolic capital' (depersonalized, mobile, and easily transferable claims on real assets) was both safe and profitable.

One way of diversification and minimization of risk and uncertainty was through finance companies or investment trusts. Finance companies were established in the 1860s in imitation of the Crédit Mobilier in France, where they were used to purchase securities in a range of ventures and mobilize capital for major projects. The initial concerns floated in London were reasonably well funded, linked with established firms with knowledge of finance, trade, and investment needs. But a flurry of speculation followed in the mid-1860s, promising impossibly high returns for lending money and financing trade rather than investing in long-term projects.

The speculative bubble burst in 1866.[28] The investment trust proved to be more stable and conservative. The first was established in 1868 to purchase a range of stocks and shares which were held in a common 'pot' for the investors in the fund. Another pioneer was Robert Fleming, who started his career as a bookkeeper in Dundee before creating an investment trust to cater for the needs of wealthy businessmen and transferring to London. These trusts allowed individuals to diversify their portfolio, offering a reasonably safe way of moving from government bonds to private securities. Their clientele was drawn from the wealthiest members of society, and increasingly from institutional investors. In 1914, about 90 per cent of their investments were held in overseas securities.[29] Institutional investments were also available to more modest incomes. For most members of the middle class, life insurance was a more sensible option than purchasing securities or placing funds in an investment trust. In 1853, Gladstone gave tax breaks to life insurance policies as an encouragement to the 'industrious' middle class to provide for their old age and for dependants after their death. The business was highly competitive, and the concerns were anxious to improve their returns in the face of declining yields in British mortgages, British government and local authority bonds, and domestic railways. Between 1870 and 1913, the proportion of the total portfolio of insurance companies invested in mortgages fell from just under a half to less than a quarter; and the proportion of British government and local authority bonds from 17 to 7 per cent. The companies looked abroad, so that these insurance companies selling policies to modestly prosperous members of the middle class were themselves large investors in foreign assets. At the Royal Exchange, for example, the share of overseas government bonds and railways rose from 10 per cent in 1890 to 23 per cent in 1909; as other overseas investments were added, the share rose to 45 per cent in 1913.[30] Not surprisingly, the insurance companies were important players in the securities market, starting to underwrite new issues. Looked at from one perspective, the choice could be seen as risk averting and conservative, damaging to British industry. But looked at from another perspective, the decision of the insurance companies could be seen as dynamic and adventurous—a decision to invest in the process of globalization of the later nineteenth century in the interests of their policy holders at home. Certainly, these insurance companies were highly successful, responding to the needs of the domestic middle class in dealing with social risk and security. Overseas investment and the City of London were not so rigidly divided from the domestic economy of industrial towns as the proponents of 'gentlemanly capitalism' would claim.

The crucial questions were: why were funds not placed in domestic securities or reinvested in industry; and how far did overseas investment crowd out domestic investment? One possible answer is that the investors were risk averse, a criticism that might apply to Cox Brothers as much as to southern rentiers. Arguably, they should have placed their surplus funds in the development of new ventures. Giffen rejected such a criticism on the grounds that their response was rational: there was a 'plethora' of funds at home, and overseas investment was a sensible outlet.[31] Many recent historians have followed, claiming that overseas investment was a 'sink for unemployed capital' and that the choice was between investment abroad or not at all. On such an interpretation, the export of capital was a net gain, for its retention at home would drive down the marginal rate of return without fundamentally increasing the rate of growth. One advocate of the rationality of overseas investment has pointed to the absurdity of keeping capital at home by wondering whether Britain needed two Forth Bridges or Bakerloo lines. Contemporaries made precisely the same point.[32] Both contemporaries and historians have therefore defended capital exports as an optimal use of resources. They point out that overseas investment was largely self-financing from the later 1870s. The outflow of capital produced an inflow of dividends and interest which exceeded the new capital raised. Net foreign lending between 1870 and 1874 was £392 m, and the net property income from abroad £227 m; between 1875 and 1879, the figures were respectively £152 m and £281 m. The net inflow of funds was reversed only in the peak periods of foreign investment in the late 1880s and before the First World War, and even then only modestly. This net inflow reduced the strain of overseas investment, for the sums received were recycled into further capital exports. Britain's rentier position might therefore have its origins in the foreign lending of the mid-Victorian period, without imposing a burden on the domestic economy.[33]

How plausible is this defence? The case in favour of capital exports rests in part upon the challengeable assumptions of neo-classical economics. One assumption is full employment, so that the investment of more capital at home would not lead to an increase in labour utilization—a somewhat unlikely proposition. Critics of high levels of overseas investment pointed out that one result was the employment of large numbers of people in domestic and personal services who could have been reallocated to more productive work. Neither is it clear that resources were allocated in an optimal manner according to marginal rates of return. Neo-classical economists assume that investors followed the dictates of the market, allocating capital to obtain the highest rate of return and to achieve the maximum level of growth. On this argument, capital went overseas because the rate of return was higher abroad. Some historians remain sceptical, suggesting that investors were conservative risk-averters, opting for safety abroad rather than seeking higher returns in more risky domestic ventures. The issue turns on the relative rates of return on home and overseas investment. In his survey, Sidney Pollard concluded that yields were not definitely and consistently higher abroad, and 'the general impression tends in the direction of "too much", rather than the "correct", quantity of foreign investment'. On this view, the retention of capital at home and a higher level of domestic investment would reduce the price of capital relative to labour, producing a higher ratio of capital to labour, and encouraging a large increase in consumption per head. The adoption of an investment rate similar to that of Germany might, so Crafts argues, have produced a 25 per cent increase in investment per head in 1911, with a significant increase in growth rates. Although existing industry might not have suffered unduly from shortages of capital, and most of the investment abroad was self-financing, it could nevertheless be argued that the retention of capital at home would have stimulated new industries by changing relative factor costs and raising incomes.[34]

A 'plethora' of funds at home might have been no bad thing, whether to raise the capital intensity of industry or to provide finance for social overhead capital and government expenditure on social policy. By 1914, Lloyd George realized that capital exports were not necessarily beneficial in securing economic recovery and supplying cheap food; he was aware of the contradiction between capital exports and domestic social reform. The expected reduction in food prices was not appearing, and there was social unrest as real wages stagnated. Rather than solving the problem, the high level of capital exports was making it difficult for the government to borrow money in order to finance its social welfare policies. Here was a clear case of 'crowding out'. As interest rates rose, local authorities were less able to invest in public health or schools, and their spending fell.[35] The identity between private profit and social gain stressed by Giffen in 1905 and initially accepted by Lloyd George was less apparent by 1914 as food prices continued to rise and the government's room for financial manoeuvre became more limited. Perhaps cities *did* require more investment in their infrastructure. There were many other possible outlets for capital than a second Forth bridge or Bakerloo line. The identity between private profit and social gain from overseas investment was always fortuitous, and was becoming strained by the time of the great boom in overseas investment between 1905 and 1914. Although capital exports in the late 1880s might well have led to 'crowding in' as low returns at home sent capital abroad, there is a distinct possibility of 'crowding out' during the great wave of foreign investment prior to the First World War

British exports of capital were justified by Giffen as a way of ensuring high sales of British goods, but as time passed the link became less clear. By the early twentieth century, it was less likely that the export of British capital to build a South American railway would lead to the purchase of British locomotives or steel. Britain supplied about three-quarters of the capital for Argentinian railways, yet the Germans had as many orders for equipment. Only in India did a direct and strong tie survive between the export of capital and capital goods.[36] The significance of indirect links is more difficult to establish, and here India was again important because of its centrality in the pattern of settlements in the world economy. The recipients of British capital might not increase their purchases of goods from Britain; they might increase their imports from India and so lead to higher sales of Lancashire cotton goods to the

Indian market. Even if capital exports *did* stimulate demand for British industrial goods in this indirect and tenuous way, it is not clear that the results were beneficial, for it tied British industry to traditional staples, so bolstering the profitability of the existing industrial structure.

The flow of income from overseas investments covered the deficit on the balance of trade, so that Britain could purchase more food than it could otherwise afford. Looked at positively, capital exports 'purchased' a higher standard of living for the British population. Income from foreign investments rose from 2.8 per cent of GDP in 1855–73, reaching as much as 9.2 per cent in the years immediately before the war.[37] As we have seen, the contribution to the balance of payments was considerable. Not all commentators were convinced. Hobson and Chiozza Money were sceptical that the flow of dividends improved the welfare of Britain, claiming that foreign earnings *created* the trade deficit by producing a stream of frivolous imported luxuries to cater for the whims of Edwardian plutocrats. This was a useful piece of propaganda rather than a sustainable point, for the deficit had a longer history than the export of capital, and trade figures do not bear out the contention that Britain's trade deficit was created by imports of luxury goods. More seriously, the large surplus on the balance of payments created by the inflow of interest payments was a potential source of danger for the world economy: it might start to threaten liquidity. Debt service would place pressure on debtor countries unless Britain sent even more funds abroad, which would lead to a further increase in inward payments. The problems posed to the world economy by a powerful creditor were apparent at the end of the Second World War, when the United States had a large trade surplus as well as loan repayments. How could other countries secure the dollars to meet their obligations? The problem was less serious before 1914, for Britain had a trade deficit and the system of multilateral payments reduced pressure. A debtor country did not need to find sterling to meet its gross payment to Britain, for it paid any outstanding balance left after taking account of its other commitments. Between the wars, the collapse of multilateral payments and a serious drop in the price of export commodities increased the strains in the system of payments. Indebtedness could, in the end, create instability in the borrowing countries, so stimulating economic nationalism. They might adopt policies of import substitution to improve their balance of payments, and attempt to export more goods which could force prices down and so create a further deterioration in their external position. Signs of these difficulties were scarcely apparent before 1914; they were obvious between the wars and were one of the major issues in the debates over reconstruction after the Second World War.

Pollard has also argued that Britain, the creditor nation, suffered as well as the debtors. In his view, the flow of income from abroad removed the incentive to strengthen the balance of trade. Pollard argued that 'the pressure for massive, long-term, future-directed changes in economic structure and emphasis was fatally weakened'.[38] This is not convincing, for Pollard confuses the macroeconomic impact of the balance of payments with the microeconomic behaviour of individual firms. Why should industrialists conclude that they had no need to seek new export markets because Britain as a whole had a balance of payments surplus? Even if they did realize that Britain had a surplus, they were more concerned with their own individual profitability and with the growing fear of competition in export markets. What can be accepted is that the decline in 'invisible' income from overseas investment and services between the wars exacerbated the deficit in trade, so placing serious strain on Britain's external position, and threatening the gold standard and free trade. In a sense, the invisible income from loans underwrote free trade before the First World War.

The potential difficulties of international liquidity were not pressing before 1914. Rather than threatening stability, supporters of overseas investment claimed that it stabilized the world economy on which Britain was so dependent, and contributed to the smooth operation of the gold standard and international settlements. This contention has some plausibility, for British capital exports were counter-cyclical: when the British economy was depressed, capital was exported, and vice versa. The result was beneficial for the world economy and hence for Britain. When the British economy was booming, a market existed for goods produced by other countries, which kept the world economy buoyant. Although the demand for imports slackened when Britain was depressed, the availability of British capital exports gave an impetus to the world economy. British capital exports returned funds to the world economy, rather than accumulating money in Britain and threatening the liquidity of the world economy. The openness of British markets meant that those countries borrowing money could sell commodities and maintain payments.[39] This pattern of free trade and capital exports therefore helped to check the spread of depression—a positive outcome compared with the American response between the wars. In the 1920s, the American domestic economy boomed and capital was exported up to 1928; capital exports then fell, so intensifying the slump in world trade and making repayments more difficult. According to this interpretation, the Americans were reducing liquidity in the world economy, and tariff barriers were erected which closed the American market to the goods produced as a result of overseas investment of the 1920s. America's creditors defaulted or curtailed imports in order to improve the balance of payments to pay their debts. By contrast, Britain helped to stabilize the world economy before the First World War, providing a counterbalance through its capital exports which prevented depression from spreading. This was not an act of altruism, for the British economy—far beyond the City of London—was heavily dependent upon the world economy and capital exports were an important element in maintaining the global economy and in assisting British prosperity.

This argument became weaker as time passed. Although British capital exports were higher than ever between 1905 and 1914, they had to offset the much greater weight of the American economy. The ability of Britain to stabilize the world economy was reduced, and a gap was starting to open between the costs and benefits of capital exports. In any case, more attention was being paid to the domestic implications of overseas investment. Would it be possible to allow a high level of capital exports to continue, given that it reflected a maldistribution of income and wealth, and harmed domestic welfare? The politics of capital exports had started to change, in parallel with debates over free trade. Like free trade, capital exports were meant to ensure cheap food, and there was clearly something to be said for this claim. The sectoral and geographic distribution of publicly quoted securities shows that British capital exports were not 'wasted' in providing funds for profligate governments in Turkey or Russia which failed to produce any real benefits for the domestic economy. The data provide some support for the view that the British economy benefited from investment in railways and infrastructure in developing economies, so leading to increased production of food and raw materials, and raising the standard of living of the working class. Critics might counter that the benefits of opening new areas of the world were not only obtained by Britain, for other countries received cheaper food and raw materials without incurring the loss of domestic investment. For that matter, just how important was British capital in securing the lower prices of food and raw materials? It would be difficult to argue that the American west required British capital, and the price of American wheat depended upon internal considerations rather than the flow of funds across the Atlantic. It might be that British capital allowed the borrowing countries to construct the basic infrastructure and to release their own capital for more remunerative investments, while increasing the price of funds within Britain. The possibility started to become more worryingly apparent just before the First World War when the price of food failed to drop and the cost of local authority loans rose. Welfare might instead be secured by redistributive taxation to stop overseas investment, and by reform of the labour market to secure adequate nutrition. Free trade and capital exports were not enough to secure welfare—and industrialists might similarly conclude that they were not enough to secure export markets.

Although the historical debate on the impact of capital exports has become increasingly sophisticated, the issues still have not been settled. The argument in the end comes down to the question of what sort of society was preferable. Should Britain be a productive state, or would it become a 'nation of bankers and commission agents, supporting armies of unemployed loafers'?[40] Should Britain pursue a path of economic nationalism or global cosmopolitanism? The contested definition of British identity and culture informed much of the debate.

The Demise of Capital Mobility

The outbreak of the First World War abruptly ended the boom in capital exports. Up to 1914, there were virtually no controls on the export of capital beyond rules on the securities which could be held by trustees. The situation changed with the war, for all available resources were needed to buy food and raw materials. Further, the British government needed to borrow huge sums of money, and could not allow foreign loans to compete. At the turn of 1914 and 1915, the government imposed regulations on new issues, and created a Capital Issues Committee to vet both domestic and foreign issues. The committee allowed some imperial loans, but took a very strict line on foreign issues, which were explicitly banned in 1917. At the same time, existing foreign investments, especially in the United States, were sold in order to obtain dollars. Britain's long-term investments were therefore lower at the end of the war, and the flow of income from dividends and interest dropped from £210 m in 1913 to £200 m in 1920.[41] Before 1914, overseas interest covered the trade deficit; between the wars, it met half or less of the deficit. The question to be faced was whether capital exports should be encouraged as a route to growth in the international economy, or whether they were a threat to British welfare.

The regulations were not abolished at the end of the war, but the Treasury did allow the CIC to adopt a more flexible approach. As the Treasury explained, controls were continued 'to protect the foreign exchanges and to conserve capital for development within the United Kingdom'.[42] A concern for domestic recovery and stability was now moving to the ascendant. Above all, the government was anxious about competition with its own borrowing. The government needed to convert a large short-term or 'floating' debt into long-term securities, and could not allow capital exports to drive up the cost. The regulation was repealed later in 1919 after a large loan was successfully floated. Even so, a free capital market was not fully restored: the Bank of England attempted to regulate issues, relying on its moral authority rather than compulsion, and depending on the guidance of the Treasury which, in theory, had no power over foreign issues. The Bank and Treasury worked together, relatively harmoniously and without any formal authority. The obvious, cynical, conclusion would be that the Bank and Treasury colluded in the international interests of the City against domestic considerations. Reality was more complicated. In 1920, they gave priority to local authority loans for council houses, followed by the needs of the empire and only then foreigners. Domestic political considerations were important, as in the complementary debate over taxation and debt redemption (see Chapter 14). Although restrictions on empire borrowers were reduced in the early 1920s, foreign fixed-interest issues were still limited in order to prevent competition with the government's own borrowing needs. In 1924, the embargo was lifted before controls were reimposed as part of the preparations for restoring the gold standard. As the head of the Treasury remarked in 1924, 'there is a real risk that the success of the policy we recommend may be jeopardized by excessive foreign lending'.[43]

The government was in a quandary, for in an ideal world it wished to have both capital exports and fixed exchange rates. This was not entirely a pro-City policy, for the Federation of British Industries was opposed to a ban on capital exports. The authorities shared the view, for a Treasury memorandum pointed out in 1925 that overseas investment offered the 'substantial advantages' of an income from abroad, commissions for the City, and orders for British industry—with the caveat 'if we can afford to acquire them'.[44] The condition expressed a crucial change since 1913: overseas investment was contingent, assessed in terms of the national interest, with a much more important domestic element than before the First World War.

In the late nineteenth century, capital mobility was linked with fixed exchange rates under the gold standard, and an active domestic monetary policy was not possible. When the British government returned to gold in 1925, fixed exchanges were in conflict with capital mobility as a result of the growing concern for domestic welfare. In order to raise the value of the pound and to maintain it after the return to gold, the Bank wished to restrict the supply of sterling and to increase the exchange rate. The government could increase the bank rate to protect the pound; or it could limit capital exports. Little debate was needed to reach the conclusion that the former was politically more difficult than the latter so that the government opted to reintroduce fixed exchange rates, but to limit capital mobility. In preparation for the return to gold, foreign loans were restricted at the end of 1924, and in 1925 the embargo was extended to the empire. The Colonial Office was alarmed and a secret Overseas Loans Committee was set up by the Cabinet to consider 'the capacity of this country to meet the demands for capital at home and abroad, with particular regard to the requirements of Empire development and to the maintenance of our export trade'. The Committee feared that removing the embargo would place strain on the resources of Britain—yet it also realized that British investors were evading it by purchasing securities in New York. The choice was to impose explicit regulation of financial markets or to abandon the embargo, as was in fact done later in 1925. Freedom was restored until 1929.

The Treasury continued to justify capital exports in much the same way as Giffen. As a leading official remarked in 1928, 'what we invest in foreign loans must, sooner or later, be exported; and insofar as it is sunk in development schemes for the Empire, it is probably exported almost at once in the form of capital goods'. The Treasury clung to the belief that the export of capital was necessary to stimulate the export of commodities: the British people were consuming more and saving less than before the war, so that less money was available to invest abroad, and exports of goods accordingly did not return to pre-war levels. Here, they argued, was the danger of the Liberal plan of 1928 and 1929 for domestic investment in public works and industry at the expense of capital exports. By diverting money from foreign investment, the Treasury feared that exports would fall or imports would rise, with harmful effects on industry. But the theoretical hostility to domestic investment was moderated by pragmatism. The Treasury was cautious when the Conservatives responded to the Liberal plans by suggesting imperial investment. A desire to constrain all spending schemes led the Treasury to minimize the impact of imperial investment on the domestic economy: over half of any investment would be spent on colonial land and labour; only the sum actually spent on British goods would help the domestic economy to a very modest extent. The Treasury's position now shifted to argue that overseas investment had no long-run effect on employment: if invested abroad, it might lead to employment in producing exports; if invested at home, it would lead to direct employment. An embargo on capital exports was reintroduced in 1929 in response to pressure on the pound and the deterioration in Britain's external position. Domestic politics dictated the choice of measures to defend the pound: the option of raising interest rates was now constrained by concern for employment at home, and capital exports were more likely to be sacrificed—an approach confirmed after the war when fixed exchange rates were restored, but linked with controls on capital exports and active domestic policies to secure full employment.[45]

Even in money terms, the level of new overseas issues fell below the pre-war level. In 1914, new overseas issues were £158.9 m; the highest level after the war was £148.4 m in 1927, falling to £46.0 m in 1931. The relationship with the balance of payments changed. Before the First World War, capital exports returned Britain's large surpluses on current account to the world economy; now, there was little surplus, for the net balance fell from £252 m in 1920 to a deficit of £26 m in 1926; it rose to a surplus of £117 m in 1930 before falling back into deficit from 1931 to 1936.[46] Capital exports changed character, relying on converting short-term deposits in London into long-term loans which was now much more risky and speculative. Before the First World War, most short-term money in London was linked with trade and therefore relatively stable; after the war, short-term money was more prone to sudden movement in response to insecurity. The increased volatility of so-called 'hot money' caused problems if short loans were recalled and long-term securities could not be realized—as happened in the crisis of 1931. Capital movements came to be seen as disruptive of the world economy and exchanges rather than a counter-cyclical, stabilizing influence. In the 1930s, capital exports virtually ceased, and Britain became a net *importer* of capital, in part because foreign companies constructed British plants to circumvent tariff barriers.[47] According to a United Nations report on international capital movements, the United Kingdom's net capital exports between 1922 and 1928 amounted to an average of $407 m a year;

TABLE 7.3. *Accumulated net assets abroad, 1856–1950, UK (£m)*

1856	260	1920	4,410
1900	2,560	1930	5,450
1913	4,180	1938	5,160
		1950	580

Source: Feinstein, *Statistical Tables*, T110.

between 1931 and 1935, the United Kingdom was a net importer of $74 m a year.[48] Estimates of accumulated net investment abroad at current prices, based on balance of payments data, show a massive rise before the First World War, with only a modest increase to 1930, followed by a slight decline to the Second World War and collapse as resources were realized to pay for the war (see Table 7.3).

The decline in the importance of capital exports had serious consequences for the City of London which played such an important role in the globalization of the world economy before 1914. Before the war, Schroders was one of the two dominant merchant banks in the City: its capital in 1913 was £3.65 m compared with £4.56 m for the largest concern (Kleinworts), and £1.22 m for the third (Antony Gibbs). Schroders had been a major issuing house for foreign loans since 1853; in 1931, it made its last issue, a sum of £3 m for the Compania de Salitre de Chile. The circumstances point to the problems of international lending. The Chilean nitrate industry was suffering from low prices and competition from artificial fertilizers, and the government took control of the industry to impose 'rationalization'. The loan was therefore needed to manage contraction and not to fuel growth. The public was reluctant to take up the bonds, and their caution was confirmed when payments were suspended in 1932 and the Chilean government abandoned the plan. The Chilean bond issue was one of the last new capital issues in the City for another forty or so years. Not surprisingly, Schroders turned to domestic issues. In 1924, the firm handled a debenture issue of £550,000 on behalf of a mining, brick-making, and chemicals concern in Derbyshire and the West Riding, and Schroders moved from mining concerns to new and expanding firms in need of large sums of money. In 1926, Schroders and Barings combined to issue £4 m of debentures to finance a shipbuilding programme for the British Tanker Corporation; and in the next few years, a syndicate of Schroders, Barings, and Rothschilds issued loans of £13.2 m for extensions to the London underground. In 1926, Schroders went still further, taking an active role in introducing a new technique of cold steel pressing of car bodies in a joint venture with an American firm and Morris Motors. The new firm, Pressed Steel, constructed a plant at Oxford to supply Morris—and a similar venture was started in Germany. In 1935, it set up Leadenhall Securities to provide venture capital to medium-sized concerns, in order to bring them to a stock market flotation within five years. Critics of the City might suggest that such initiatives were too little, too late. The answer might be that technology had changed, with a greater need for external finance to invest in 'lumpy' plant. Further, Britain no longer had the financial and economic reach to compete with Wall Street. The City was not to return to anything like its former role in the world until the 1960s.[49]

Conclusion: The Political Economy of Global Capital

Capital mobility is possible under two sets of conditions. The first set was under the gold standard, when domestic monetary policy and active economic management were subordinated to fixed exchange rates and capital mobility. The second set of assumptions, at the end of the twentieth century, was to sacrifice exchange rate stability in order to pursue an active domestic monetary policy and permit capital mobility. In the 1930s, capital mobility and exchange rate stability were abandoned in a desperate attempt to pursue domestic policies of economic nationalism; and when the world economy was reconstructed at the end of the Second World War, capital movements were sacrificed in order to impose exchange rate stability in conjunction with active domestic economic policies. The rise and fall of capital mobility and the ability to pursue a domestic monetary policy are indicated by interest rate differentials between the United States and United Kingdom which were small under the gold standard and much wider in the 1930s (see Table 7.4).

The political economy of capital exports underwent a considerable change in Britain, with a growing awareness of the dangers for domestic welfare and the need for the state to pursue active domestic policies. Much of the historical debate has been too introverted. British investment could be seen by the recipients as the provision of a scarce resource on reasonable terms—or as exploitative and imperialistic, a threat to the autonomy of independent countries and a drain on the colonies and dominions. The political situation varied, according to the institutional systems and social structures of the debtors, and changed over time. In Australia before the First

TABLE 7.4. *Nominal interest rate parity, US–UK domestic interest rates, 1890–1939*

	Per cent p.a., standard deviation
1890–1913	0.39
1919–24	2.06
1925–30	0.95
1931–9	2.05

Source: Obstfeld and Taylor, 'Great depression', table 11.2, 362.

World War, for example, government loans were in the hands of representative bodies and most non-governmental loans went to Australian-owned and operated concerns. Consequently, capital imports were unproblematic. By contrast, criticism of British capital was much more vociferous in Argentina, where most of the loans were to companies registered in Britain, with British directors. There was direct conflict between British and Argentinian concerns in banking, and British-dominated railways or meat packers were attacked for their insensitivity.[50] The backlash against global capital flows become more intense after the First World War, when the price of primary products fell sharply, placing strains on the balance of payments and on domestic prosperity. The outcome in Argentina was an extreme form of nationalism; in Australia, a growing resentment at the economic costs of loans. Economic nationalism grew as the process of globalization went into reverse.

Globalization had its losers as well as its winners; it was about power and force as well as an efficient use of the world's resources. Globalization led to convergence between the countries of Europe and the New World as resources moved back and forth. As capital and labour left Europe, so wages and the cost of borrowing rose there and fell in the Americas. The political response varied. American workers were suspicious of the impact of mass migration on their wage rates; in time, many representatives of British workers came to suspect that export of capital was at the expense of their welfare. The return flow of food hit European landowners and farmers, who had a greater or lesser voice depending on their numbers and the constitutional system. In Britain, landowners had little voice compared with urban consumers so that the outcome differed from France and Germany. In Africa and Asia, incorporation into the world economy usually entailed a loss of independence and a divergence from the wealth of the developed world. Historians have written the history of globalization prior to the First World War as a story of convergence–a comforting story of economic progress lost in the 1920s and 1930s when domestic forces blocked the commitment to internationalism.[51] But this is only part of the story. In the white settler economies of the Americas, Australasia, and South Africa, and Asia and the rest of Africa, British capital was used to exploit land and to bring it within a commercialized world economy, in many cases removing it from indigenous peoples without compensation or on highly disadvantageous terms. In India, the investment in railways and irrigation incorporated Indian food into the world economy, but at the expense of famine at home. The Maori of New Zealand might have some modest recognition of their rights—but they lacked the reputation to borrow from London banks. The indigenous peoples of Australia had no rights: the continent was defined as *terra nullius*, and the original inhabitants seen as barely human. In some cases, land rights were confirmed in order to create stable local systems of governance and to permit taxation. Even so, confirming native title or property rights could have the same effect as in eighteenth-century Britain: land was removed from the web of custom and made more marketable, so that society was destabilized. Many of the arguments within British history about the domestic impact of capital exports seem parochial—can there really be much dispute that they made the resources of the world available to British and western consumers, with a growing gap between the world's rich and poor?

NOTES

1. Keynes, 'Evidence before the Macmillian Committee on Finance and Industry', 6 Mar. 1930, *Collected Works*, xx. 147–8.
2. Imlah, *Economic Elements*, ch. 3.
3. Simon, 'Pattern of new British portfolio foreign investment' and the more recent and extended use of his data by Stone, *Global Export of Capital*; Pollard, 'Capital exports', 492.
4. Platt, *Britain's Investment Overseas*, 57–60.
5. Feinstein, 'Britain's overseas investment'.
6. For the scale of investment, Pollard, *Britain's Prime and Britain's Decline*, 61; for dating of cycles of investment, Stone, *Global Export of Capital*, 7.
7. Stone, *Global Export of Capital*, 13, 21, 23; Simon, 'Pattern of new British portfolio foreign investment', 40–1.
8. Chiozza Money, *Riches and Poverty*, 43, 147–8; Hobson, *Imperialism*, 134, 378–80.
9. Lenin, *Imperialism*. For the difference between Lenin and Hobson, see Clarke, *Liberals and Social Democrats*, 96–7. Hobson's changing views are in Cain, *Hobson and Imperialism*.
10. Giffen, 'Notes', 493.
11. Offer, 'Empire and social reform', 126–7.
12. Cain and Hopkins, *British Imperialism: Innovation and Expansion* and *British Imperialism: Crisis and Deconstruction;* Davis and Huttenback, *Mammon and the Pursuit of Empire*, 274–6 Davis and Gallman, *Evolving Financial Markets*, 208.
13. Nicholas, 'British multinational investment', 613–14; Wilkins, 'European and North American multinationals', 15; Fieldhouse, *Unilever Overseas*, 494.
14. Jones, *Merchants to Multinationals*, ch. 7; Chapman, 'British-based investment groups'; Marriner and Hyde, *The Senior*.
15. Svedberg, 'The portfolio-direct composition of private foreign investment', 764–5; Stone, 'British direct and portfolio investment', 696; Daunton 'Gentlemanly capitalism', 136.
16. Jones, *International Business in the Nineteenth Century*, 172–3; Wilkins, 'Free-standing company', 260–1; Chapman, 'British-based investment groups', 232.
17. Michie, *London and New York Stock Exchanges*, ch. 5.
18. Rutterford, 'World was their oyster'.
19. Davis and Gallman, *Evolving Financial Markets*, 153, 197.
20. Davis and Huttenback, *Mammon and the Pursuit of Empire*, 209.
21. Morris, 'The middle classes and the property cycle', 92.
22. Daunton, 'Firm and family', 171–2.
23. Lenman and Donaldson, 'Partners' incomes', 3, 12–13.
24. Davis and Gallman, *Evolving Financial Markets*, 153.

25. Michie, *The London Stock Exchange*, 77, 86.
26. Davis and Gallman, *Evolving Financial Markets*, 753–68.
27. Ibid. 816–17.
28. Landes, *Bankers and Pashas*, 52–61.
29. Davis and Gallman, *Evolving Financial Markets*, 150–3; Cassis, 'The emergence of a new financial institution', 140–1, 150–1, 145.
30. Davis and Gallman, *Evolving Financial Markets*, 145–50; Supple, *Royal Exchange Assurance*, 330–48; Trebilcock, *Phoenix Assurance*, ii. 63–91.
31. Giffen, 'Notes', 485, 491–2.
32. McCloskey, 'No it did not', 539; Pollard, *Britain's Prime* 73.
33. Pollard, *Britain's Prime*, 69.
34. Pollard, 'Capital exports', 513; Kennedy, 'Foreign investment', 416–17, 436–7; Kennedy, 'Economic growth and structural change', 112, 114; Crafts, 'Victorian Britain did fail', 537.
35. Offer, 'Empire and social reform' 133, 137–8.
36. Davis and Gallman, *Evolving Financial Markets*, 720–2.
37. Pollard, *Britain's Prime*, 61–2.
38. Ibid. 109–10.
39. Saul, *Studies*, 110–15, 128–30; Kindleberger, *World in Depression*, 39–41, 292.
40. George Wyndham, quoted in Green, *Crisis of Conservatism*, 236.
41. Mitchell and Deane, *Abstract*, 335.
42. Quoted in Atkin, 'Official regulation', 325.
43. Clarke, 'Treasury's analytical model', 182; Atkin, 'Official regulation'.
44. Atkin, 'Official regulation', 334.
45. Ibid. 326.
46. Ibid., 335. Mitchell and Deane, *Abstract*, 335.
47. Scott and Rooth, 'Protection and the growth of overseas multinational enterprise'.
48. Roberts, *Schroders*, 249, 268.
49. Ibid 151, chs. 7, 9; Kynaston, *The City of London: Illusions of Gold, 1914–45*.
50. Davis and Gallman, *Evolving Financial Markets*, 817–19, 822–5.
51. For example, O'Rourke and Williamson, *Globalization and History*; James, *End of Globalization*.

FURTHER READING

Atkin, J., 'Official regulation of British overseas investment, 1914–1931', *Economic History Review*, 23 (1970)

Cain, P. J., 'J. A. Hobson, Cobdenism, and the radical theory of economic imperialism, 1898–1914', *Economic History Review*, 2nd ser. 31 (1978)

—— *Hobson and Imperialism: Radicalism, New Liberalism, and Finance 1887–1938* (Oxford, 2002)

—— and Hopkins, A. G., *British Imperialism: Innovation and Expansion, 1688–1914* (Harlow, 1993)

—— —— *British Imperialism: Crisis and Deconstruction, 1914–1990* (Harlow, 1993)

Cairncross, A. K., *Home and Foreign Investment, 1870–1913: Studies in Capital Accumulation* (Cambridge, 1953)

Cassis, Y., 'The emergence of a new financial institution: investment trusts in Britain, 1870–1939', in J. J. van Helten and Y. Cassis (eds.), *Capitalism in a Mature Economy: Financial Institutions, Capital Exports and British Industry, 1870–1939* (Aldershot, 1990)

Chapman, S. D., 'British-based investment groups before 1914', *Economic History Review*, 38 (1985)

Chiozza Money, L. G., *Riches and Poverty* (1905)

Clarke, P. F., 'Hobson, free trade, and imperialism', *Economic History Review*, 2nd ser. 34 (1981)

—— *Liberals and Social Democrats* (Cambridge, 1978)

—— 'The Treasury's analytical model of the British economy between the wars', in M. O. Furner and B. Supple (eds.), *The State and Economic Knowledge: The American and British Experience* (Cambridge, 1990)

Crafts, N. R. F., 'Victorian Britain did fail', *Economic History Review*, 32 (1979)

Daunton, M. J., ' "Gentlemanly capitalism" and British industry, 1820–1914', *Past and Present*, 122 (1989)

—— 'Firm and family in the City of London in the nineteenth century: the case of F. G. Dalgety', *Historical Research*, 62 (1988)

Davis, L., and Gallman, R., *Evolving Financial Markets and International Capital Flows: Britain, the Americas and Australia, 1865–1914* (Cambridge, 2001)

—— and Huttenback, R., *Mammon and the Pursuit of Empire: The Political Economy of British Imperialism, 1860–1912* (Cambridge, 1986)

Denoon, D., *Settler Capitalism: The Dynamics of Dependent Development in the Southern Hemisphere* (Oxford, 1983)

Edelstein, M., *Overseas Investment in the Age of High Imperialism: The United Kingdom, 1850–1914* (1982)

—— 'Foreign investment and the empire, 1860–1914', in R. C. Floud and D. N. McCloskey (eds.), *The Economic History of Britain since 1700*, ii (Cambridge, 1981)

Feinstein, C., 'Britain's overseas investment in 1913', *Economic History Review*, 43 (1990)

—— and Pollard, S. (eds.), *Studies in Capital Formation in the United Kingdom, 1750–1920* (Oxford, 1988)

—— *Statistical Tables of National Income, Expenditure and Output of the U. K., 1855–1965* (Cambridge, 1972)

Fieldhouse, D., *Unilever Overseas: The Anatomy of a Multinational, 1895–1965* (1978)

Ford, A. G., 'Overseas lending and internal fluctuations, 1870–1914', *Yorkshire Bulletin of Economic and Social Research*, 17 (1965)

Freeden, M. (ed.), *Reappraising J. A. Hobson: Humanism and Welfare* (1990)

Giffen, R., 'Notes on imports versus home production, and home versus foreign investment', *Economic Journal*, 15 (1905)

Green, E. H. H. *Crisis of Conservatism: The Politics, Economics and Ideology of the British Conservative Party, 1880–1914* (1995)

Hobson, J. A., 'The general election of 1910', *Sociological Review*, 3 (1910)

—— *Imperialism: A Study* (1902)

Imlah, A. H., *Economic Elements in the Pax Britannica: Studies in British Foreign Trade in the Nineteenth Century* (Cambridge, 1958)

Jones, C., *International Business in the Nineteenth Century: The Rise and Fall of a Cosmopolitan Bourgeoisie* (Brighton, 1987)

Jones, G., *Merchants to Multinationals: British Trading Companies in the Nineteenth and Twentieth Centuries* (Oxford, 2000)

Jones, H., *The End of Globalization: Lessons from the Great Depression* (Cambridge, Mass., 2001)

Kennedy, W. P., 'Economic growth and structural change in the U.K., 1870–1914', *Journal of Economic History*, 42 (1982)

—— 'Foreign investment, trade, and growth in the United Kingdom, 1870–1913', *Explorations in Economic History*, 11 (1974)

Keynes, J. M., *The Collected Writings of John Maynard Keynes*, xx: *Activities, 1924–31: Rethinking Employment and Unemployment Policies*, ed. D. Moggridge (1981)

Kindleberger, C., *The World in Depression, 1929–1939* (2nd edn., Harmondsworth, 1987)

Kynaston, D., *The City of London: Golden Years, 1890–1914* (1996)

—— *The City of London: Illusions of Gold, 1914–45* (1999)

Landes, D., *Bankers and Pashas: International Finance and Economic Imperialism in Egypt* (1958)

Lenin, V. I., *Imperialism: The Highest Stage of Capitalism*, in *Collected Works of Lenin*, ed. G. Hanna, xxii (Moscow, 1964)

Lenman, B., and Donaldson, K., 'Partners' incomes, investment and diversification in the Scottish linen area, 1850–1921', *Business History*, 13 (1971)

McCloskey, D., 'Did Victorian Britain fail?', *Economic History Review*, 23 (1970)

—— 'No it did not: a reply to Crafts', *Economic History Review*, 32 (1979)

Marriner, S., and Hyde, F. E., *The Senior: John Samuel Swire 1825–1898: Management in Far Eastern Shipping Trades* (Liverpool, 1967)

Michie, R. C., 'Crisis and opportunity: the formation and operation of the British Assets Trust, 1897–1914', *Business History*, 25 (1983)

—— *The London and New York Stock Exchanges, 1850–1914* (1987)

—— *The London Stock Exchange: A History* (Oxford, 2001)

Mitchell, B. R., with P. Deane, *Abstract of British Historical Statistics* (Cambridge, 1962).

Morris, R. J., 'The middle classes and the property cycle during the industrial revolution', in T. C. Smout (ed.), *The Search for Wealth and Stability: Essays in Economic and Social History Presented to M. W. Flinn* (1979)

Nicholas, S. J., 'British multinational investment before 1939', *Journal of European Economic History*, 11 (1982)

Obstfeld, M., and Taylor, A. M., 'The great depression as a watershed: international capital mobility over the long run', in M. D. Bordo, C. Goldin, and E. N. White (eds.), *The Defining Moment: The American Economy in the Twentieth Century* (Chicago, 1998)

Offer, A., 'Empire and social reform: British overseas investment and domestic politics, 1908–14', *Historical Journal*, 26 (1983)

O'Rourke, K. H., and Williamson, J. G., *Globalization and History: The Evolution of a Nineteenth-Century Atlantic Economy* (Cambridge, Mass., 1999)

Platt, D. C. M., *Britain's Investment Overseas on the Eve of the First World War: The Use and Abuse of Numbers* (Basingstoke, 1986)

Pollard, S., *Britain's Prime and Britain's Decline: The British Economy 1870–1914* (1989)

—— 'Capital exports, 1870–1914: harmful or beneficial?', *Economic History Review*, 2nd ser. 38 (1985)

Pomeranz, K., *The Great Divergence: China, Europe and the Making of the Modern World Economy* (Oxford, 2000)

Roberts, R., *Schroders: Merchants and Bankers, 1870–1914* (1992)

Rutterford, J., 'The world was their oyster: international diversification pre-World War I', in Rutterford, J., Upton, M., and Kodwani, D. (eds.), *Financial Strategy: Adding Stakeholder Value* (2nd ed., Chichester, 2006)

Saul, S. B., *Studies in Overseas Trade* (Liverpool, 1960)

Scott, P., and Rooth, T., 'Protectionism and the growth of overseas multinational enterprise in interior Britain', *Journal of Industrial History*, 3 (2000)

Sigsworth, E. M., *Black Dyke Mills: A History* (Liverpool, 1958)

Simon, M., 'The pattern of new British portfolio foreign investment, 1865–1914', in J. H. Adler (ed.), *Capital Movements and Economic Development* (1967)

Skidelsky, R., *John Maynard Keynes: The Economist as Saviour, 1920–37* (1992)

Stone, L., 'British direct and portfolio investment in Latin America before 1914', *Journal of Economic History*, 37 (1977)

—— *The Global Export of Capital from Great Britain, 1865–1914: A Statistical Survey* (Basingstoke, 1999)

Supple, B., *Royal Exchange Assurance: A History of British Insurance* (Cambridge, 1970)

Svedberg, P., 'The portfolio-direct composition of private foreign investment in 1914 revisited', *Economic Journal*, 88 (1978)

Trebilcock, C., *Phoenix Assurance and the Development of British Insurance*, ii: *The Era of the Insurance Giants, 1870–1984* (Cambridge, 1998)

Wilkins, M., 'The free-standing company, 1870–1914: an important type of British foreign direct investment', *Economic History Review*, 41 (1988)

—— 'European and North American multinationals, 1870–1914: comparisons and contrasts', *Business History*, 30 (1988)

....

CHAPTER 8

The Rise and Demise of the Gold Standard

In 1865, R. H. Patterson, a leading financial journalist, saw gold as a sign of civilization and international peace, complementing free trade in a vision of Cobdenite peace and prosperity.[1] The convertibility of bank notes into gold imposed morality and discipline on businessmen and on the government. The discipline prevented militaristic ministers from printing notes to wage war; and it limited speculation by businessmen by preventing over-expansion of credit. Gold was a measure of intrinsic value which helped resolve difficulties in measuring value in a highly commercialized capitalist economy. Gold *was* a measure of intrinsic value. It was easily assumed that only prosperous countries with a highly developed cash economy could afford to use it; and equally that less advanced and civilized countries were condemned to the lesser metal of silver. Indeed, a gold pound coin was 'Sovereign'. To question gold was tantamount to an attack on the queen whose head appeared on the newly designed gold sovereigns and half-sovereigns of 1893. Exchange controls were inconceivable.[2] The gold standard and gold sovereign were not technical issues, but were embedded in political culture.

In the late nineteenth century, Patterson's vision of gold was linked with an unprecedented level of globalization, and Britain was at the centre of the world's financial markets and trading systems. It was one element in an 'inconsistent trinity' of capital mobility, fixed exchange rates, and an active domestic monetary policy. Any state can have two of these policies, but not all three. In the late nineteenth and early twentieth centuries, the British state opted for capital mobility and fixed exchanges which precluded an active domestic monetary policy. Any action to support the international exchange rate at its fixed level would lead to a flow of capital in or out of the country. Hence low interest rates to prevent an appreciation of a currency would stimulate an outflow of capital so offsetting any benefit of cheap money for the domestic economy. Such a policy choice has been explained as the result of the power of the City and the marginalization of industry and labour, but such a view is far too simple. Many workers and industrialists saw the gold standard as a guarantee of stability and prosperity.

After the disruptions of the Great War, a return to the gold standard seemed to offer the obvious way of restoring stability and growth—and in 1925 Churchill announced the resumption of the gold standard at the pre-war parity of £1 to $4.86. Not everyone was convinced. To Keynes it was a sign of barbarity, a relic of another age. The problem with the gold standard, in his opinion, was that it forced costs to adjust 'automatically' to the fixed exchange rate at the expense of unemployment and misery. Critics no longer saw the gold standard as a guarantee of morality; it was, in the opinion of G. D. H. Cole in 1924, nothing but superstitious idol worship.[3] In the 1920s, officials, politicians, bankers, and most industrialists accepted the return to gold—but the experiment failed in 1931 with Britain's abandonment of gold, the onset of a deep, persistent depression, and the collapse of globalization. The demise of the gold standard was now seen as liberation from the restrictions of international exchanges. In 1931, the British government chose only one element of the 'inconsistent trinity'—an active domestic monetary policy. In retrospect, the cost seemed too high: the world economy faced serious crisis, and the pursuit of national prosperity by individual countries led to international depression. During the war, attention turned to a new system of stable exchanges which could be subordinated to domestic considerations. In Keynes's view, international monetary policy should be guided by the need for domestic full employment, an approach he attempted to turn into reality at Bretton Woods in 1944. The result was to combine fixed exchanges with active domestic monetary policies, and to sacrifice capital mobility. Britain could now adopt its own interest rates independently of other countries.[4]

The Golden Age of Gold, 1850–1914

The battle over the British gold standard was fought and won in the early nineteenth century, with the restoration of convertibility in 1821 and the triumph of the 'currency school' in the Bank Charter Act of 1844 which fixed the circulation of bank notes by the gold reserves of the issuing banks. In theory, the operation of the gold standard was automatic. It rested on the convertibility of domestic money into gold at a fixed price, so that a bank note for £10 could be changed into ten gold sovereigns. Similarly, a $10 bank note could be converted into ten gold dollars. The amount of gold in the country's reserve should remain a fixed proportion of the amount of money in circulation. The domestic convertibility of bank notes into gold was linked to free import and export of gold, which led to fixed exchange rates. The physical amount of gold in a sovereign was 486 per cent of the amount of gold in a dollar, so the exchange rate was $4.86 to £1. In theory, the international monetary system was self-regulating, and any balance of payments problems would be rectified by the 'price-specie-flow' mechanism. This mechanism was at the heart of contemporary understandings of the workings of the gold standard. The result was that country A with a balance of trade deficit would send gold to its creditors in country B, so reducing its money supply and causing prices to fall. Conversely, country B increased its money supply and prices would rise. The readjustment of relative prices would automatically correct the balance of trade, for goods produced in country A became more, and in country B less, competitive. Subsequently, economists have looked for different adjustment mechanisms which gave less weight to the flow of gold. The mechanism is different but the result is the same: automatic adjustment of the balance of payments with little possibility of a domestic monetary policy to protect employment and wages. International exchanges were rigid, and the domestic economy needed to adjust. At most, the exchange rate varied between the so-called 'gold points' at which it became profitable to import or export gold after taking account of the costs of freight and insurance in moving gold. This, it seemed to commentators looking back in nostalgia from the turmoil of the 1920s, was the 'golden age' of the gold standard when the world economy would not experience severe disruption. It was easy to assume that the mechanism could be restored. But as the experience of the 1920s was to show, matters were not so straightforward for the success of the gold standard before the Great War was contingent on economic, social, political, and cultural preconditions. Restoring the gold standard proved to be no guarantee of renewed prosperity.

Although most contemporaries and many later economists portrayed the gold standard as automatic, it was in no sense 'natural'. Although Britain adopted the full form of the gold standard in 1821, there were few other adherents until the 1870s. At the time of the International Monetary Conference at Paris in 1867, the only European countries on gold were Britain and Portugal.[5] In the 1920s, the restoration of gold was linked with a conscious search for stability in a disrupted world and it was easy to read the same motivation into the past, explaining the adoption of the gold standard in the 1870s as a decision to create stable exchange rates. Such an interpretation says more about the assumption of the 1920s than about the initial emergence of the gold standard. Why should stability emerge in the 1870s on the basis of gold rather than a silver-based or bimetallic system found elsewhere in Europe? The monetary system in the mid-nineteenth century was not inherently unstable, for the stocks of the bimetallic countries—above all France—kept the exchange rates between gold and silver within reasonable limits. In 1865, the Latin Monetary Union between France, Italy, Belgium, and Switzerland—and later Greece—attempted to create monetary unification on the basis of bimetallism under French leadership. Rather than seeing the emergence of the gold standard as a natural way of establishing harmony in the world economy, it is to be understood in terms of the collapse of the LMU's bimetallic standard in 1873, and the need to *restore* stability on a new basis.[6]

One possible way of explaining the shift to gold is that the balance between the supply of silver and gold altered. If the volume of silver production rose more than gold extraction, silver coinage would depreciate and countries had a reason to shift to gold to stabilize currencies. The explanation is appealing, but it does not fit the timing of the adoption of gold by the major economies before the onset of depreciation in silver. In any case, the logic could be reversed: the price of silver might fall as a result of a drop in *demand*.[7] Another possible explanation of a shift to gold rests on the domestic politics of debtors and creditors. The argument depends on an economic calculation that debtors have an interest in rising prices to reduce the real burden of their payments, and would therefore favour silver; creditors have an interest in falling prices to increase the real worth of their income and would therefore favour gold. Again, this explanation does not work. The division makes sense in the 1880s and 1890s when prices were falling sharply and many debtors and exporters of agricultural commodities (often the same people) were hit by a mounting burden of servicing their loans. Hence many American farmers campaigned for the monetization of silver in order to increase prices and reduce the real value of their debts. At the same time, creditors favoured stable or falling prices which increased the real value of their loans and receipts of interest. It is tempting to read these considerations back into the 1850s and 1860s, and to argue that the shift from silver to gold was the result of a change in the political balance in European countries between agrarian interests (who supported inflation and silver) and urban capitalists (who supported stable prices and gold). Again, there were problems with timing. In the mid-nineteenth century, gold was associated with *inflation* after the massive discoveries in California and Australia; the link between easy money and bimetallism did not appear until 1876.[8]

Both interpretations adopt a narrow, deterministic approach to the shaping of economic policy, as a reaction to price signals or market conditions, mediated by interest groups defined in material terms. Debates over policy should be seen in a more complex way in terms of political cultures and normative assumptions about the functioning of society. Arguably, the major change in the 1850s and 1860s was the emergence of a general sentiment in favour of a liberal political economy. The growth of trade, the reduction of trade barriers, and the creation of international bodies provided the context for monetary integration and convergence. The emergence of Britain as the dominant economic power meant that Peel's policies of free trade, sound money, and fiscal balance were the model to emulate or to rival. Gold was a political or cultural choice, a central element in a liberal, bourgeois order of constitutional monarchy and national liberty. Once it reached a critical mass, joining was also economically rational for economies with a large share of trade with other countries on the gold standard, offering access to the world's major markets.

Above all, the German states were moving towards unification and wished to standardize their currencies on the basis of gold. Their problem was how to get enough gold to make this feasible, and how to dispose of silver as it was demonetized. The defeat of France in 1870–1 and the imposition of an indemnity of 5 billion francs, or a third of the French GNP, provided the answer. Germany now had the means to secure gold and could dispose of its silver through the French bimetallic system. In 1871, the Reichstag switched to gold, and suspended the minting of silver. In response, the French resisted the German schemes and stopped coining silver in 1873 in order to prevent the inflow of German bullion and to stop pressure on the bimetallic ratio between silver and gold. The result was merely to reinforce the flight from silver to gold, so that bimetallism was virtually defunct. The gold standard moved to dominance within Europe—and once it became the basis of a large amount of trade, other countries with significant trading links with the gold bloc opted to join. Some countries adopted a fully-fledged gold standard, with automatic convertibility into gold; others adopted a gold exchange standard with conversion at the discretion of the authorities. Increasingly, the silver standard was associated with poor countries and with states with weak banking systems or financially irresponsible governments. The move to gold resulted in a 'tighter' monetary policy after 1873 and contributed to falling prices for the next quarter of a century. At this point, the politics of money changed, with pressure from debtors and agrarian exporters to re-monetize silver and adopt bimetallism. Above all, gold became the symbol of stability and prosperity, conveniently ignoring that it emerged in the first place from an earlier instalment of Franco-German conflict. The collapse of France's bimetallic project of fixed silver–gold exchange rates was central to the emergence of the gold standard, not as the result of a search for stability and mutual co-operation but in response to political conflict and warfare.[9]

Once the gold standard was widely accepted, why did it function with remarkably little friction? Adherence to the gold standard made good sense in terms of economic self-interest. The gold standard was a 'commitment mechanism' which allowed politicians and officials to bind their and their successors' freedom of action to change policy. A country's commitment to the gold standard usually rested on an explicit and transparent rule, so that any abandonment of convertibility was a sign of desperation in times of war or national emergency. Crucially, this commitment put the gold standard beyond political contention. Maintenance of gold and convertibility became a 'constitutional' rule. It was a sign of financial prudence and reputation, a proof of rectitude, removing the risk of currency depreciation and so allowing access to capital imports from Britain and other countries on better terms. Acceptance of the binding rules of the gold standard reduced the costs of borrowing; it also limited the scope for domestic monetary policy. Gold was portrayed as 'natural' or at least apolitical, an automatic mechanism removing the need to respond to different economic and social interests. Like free trade, the gold standard purged the state of corrupting influences.[10]

Of course, many argue that the gold standard was an element in 'gentlemanly capitalism' designed to benefit the City against industry, to favour creditors versus debtors. In the opinion of Barry Eichengreen, the gold standard was only possible in the late nineteenth century because workers lacked political 'voice' to criticize the impact of international monetary policies on the domestic economy. The gold standard would collapse, according to this interpretation, when workers secured 'voice' and understood the impact of monetary policies on their economic condition.[11] However, the gold standard was more than the self-interest of the City masquerading as the national interest, and more than a failure of democracy. The absence of an active domestic monetary policy might be positively welcomed as a way of excluding political or financial manipulations of monetary policy, purging the state of interest. Like free trade, gold was also a policy to help consumers, for the fall in prices after 1873 led to the largest and most sustained rise in the standard of living in the nineteenth century. Certainly, unions and Labour did start to protest against the domestic implications of gold in the 1920s, and we have noted that Keynes pointed to the need to reverse priorities, to make international monetary policy adjust to domestic stability. But this is not to say that workers were without voice in the heyday of gold, for the gold standard could easily be seen as beneficial in the later nineteenth century. Falling prices allowed consumers to buy more within a liberal world economy; and it was easy to link gold with free trade in a dynamic, expanding global economy. When free trade and capital exports were debated, the operation of the gold standard was barely mentioned. Perceptions changed in the inter-war period, when domestic stability and prosperity seemed incompatible with the gold standard which was now contributing to the depression of export industries, and leading to pressure on wage rates and employment. The change in attitude was not a response to workers' securing a voice; economic circumstances and political calculations changed.[12]

The only possible exception to the widespread commitment to gold in Britain before 1914 was the bimetallist campaign of the 1880s and 1890s to monetize silver in addition to gold. The bimetallist movement arose from the fall of silver prices relative to gold from the 1870s. The London price of an ounce of silver was around 61*d*. from the 1850s, and after reaching a peak of 69*d*. in 1873 fell to 25.8*d*. in 1900–4. This had serious consequences for India. Although exporters stood to gain from the low value of the rupee, the growth of the export sector might distort the economy and also meant very high prices for British imports and an increased cost of the 'home charges' paid to Britain in sterling. The depreciation of the rupee was creating difficulties, leading to higher taxes to cover the home charges. Potentially, the depreciation of silver also affected interests within Britain. The Lancashire cotton industry was heavily dependent upon the Indian market. 'It is impossible', commented the special committee of the Liverpool Chamber of Commerce in 1879, 'that India can continue to purchase from England at the rate expected when her money is discredited 20 per cent.' Lancashire might lose its market in India, and the Indian textile industry might develop, protected from imports by the high price of British goods and able to take over markets in other silver-based countries such as China and Japan. There were also fluctuations in the exchanges between gold and silver currencies which made it difficult to be certain about profits. More generally, the gold standard resulted in price deflation which benefited creditors at the expense of debtors, and led to a squeeze in the profits of industrialists, farmers, and aristocratic landowners. Such concerns led to the campaign for bimetallism. According to the bimetallists, the gold standard was supported by the City or moneyed interest, threatening to create a nation of 'mortgagors and rentiers' against producers, who were suffering from overvaluation and falling prices. H. H. Gibbs complained that the banking interest 'has chosen to put itself shoulder to shoulder with the men who live on their interest and toil not, neither do they spin'.[13]

Did this campaign mark a fundamental divide between finance and production? The concerns of Lancashire did not amount to a serious threat to the gold standard. More immediately, the Lancashire cotton masters and merchants wished to prevent India from imposing tariffs. After all, the problem of the rupee could be resolved by extending the gold exchange standard to India, not by converting Britain's currency to bimetallism. In 1893, the Indian government expressed a willingness to exchange gold for rupees at a rate of fifteen to the pound, and at the same time Indian mints were closed to the free coinage of silver on private accounts. Above all, most organized workers supported gold for they benefited from falling prices; far from being merely a pro-City policy, gold was part of the social contract between the state and workers. Indeed, Gibbs indicates the dangers of any interpretation based on a City/industry divide, for he was himself a City merchant banker. His business dealt with silver-based countries in Latin America, so his campaign for bimetallism had a justification. More than that, it reflected Gibbs's wider concern for a society based on Anglicanism and hierarchy, unlike the Cobdenite world of free trade. The forces against gold were modest, contained both by a widespread acceptance that gold and free trade meant prosperity for British consumers, and by the rhetoric of natural order.[14]

The world economy was expansive and remarkably stable in the later nineteenth century, when London was the centre of the international monetary system. It was easy for contemporaries to make a connection: the gold standard was the source of stability and prosperity; and it worked because of the power of Britain. Of course, the fact that two things coexist is no proof that one caused the other. The world economy was booming for other reasons, and the seemingly smooth operation of the gold standard and Britain's apparent ability to manage the system were the consequences rather than the cause of prosperity.

It is difficult to see how the 'price-specie-flow' mechanism of the gold standard could operate to create stability in the way predicted by theory, for the process of adjustment was faster than could be expected from shipping gold from one country to another and waiting for it to affect prices. The price-specie-flow mechanism was a cultural interpretation of the natural and untroubled operation of the gold standard. Shipments were small; relative prices did not move very far; and banks did not necessarily allow gold to affect the amount of money in circulation. An alternative interpretation suggests that adjustments came about through the action of the Bank of England to pre-empt flows of gold and to protect the reserves so that the key was not the automatic operation of the gold standard but British power. 'During the latter half of the nineteenth century', remarked Keynes, 'the influence of London on credit conditions throughout the world was so predominant that the Bank of England could almost have claimed to be the conductor of the international orchestra.'[15] This is to argue that the success of the gold standard before 1914 depended on a hegemonic economic power—and that the absence of such a power after 1918 explains the failure of the gold standard. How far can the existence of a hegemonic power explain stability before the Great War and instability between the world wars?[16]

At the end of the First World War, the government's committee of inquiry chaired by Lord Cunliffe emphasized the power of the Bank of England in stabilizing the world economy and the gold standard through its management of interest or discount rates. Higher interest rates would postpone new ventures, reduce demand for capital goods, cut employment, and hit consumption. Lower demand at home would discourage imports and encourage exports, and the balance of trade would be adjusted. The Committee praised this mechanism as 'an automatic machinery by which the volume of purchasing power in this country was continuously adjusted to world prices of commodities in general'.[17] But was the Committee's stress on the power of the Bank of England any less wishful thinking than the 'price-specie-flow' mechanism?

Whether the Bank could have such an impact may be doubted. The supposedly automatic operation of the interest rate mechanism rested on a complex institutional structure, and the task of making the Bank rate effective took about twenty years. The process started in 1871, and for a long time there were two rates in London—the market rate and the Bank rate. Although the Bank had some influence on the wider market as one of the largest purchasers of bills, its relative power diminished as the scale of the market increased. Only after 1890 did the Bank move towards a more effective policy, by competing more aggressively in the market for bills and by the use of 'open market operations'. By varying the supply of bills on the market, the

Bank might have been able to bring the market rate into line with the Bank rate. By the turn of the century, it had a degree of influence on the market, allowing the Bank rate to play the role assigned to it by the Cunliffe Committee. Even so, the system was not as automatic as the Committee assumed, for the Bank had considerable discretion over how and when to react. The directors were unlikely to have been the conductors of the international gold standard from the late 1890s, for they did not have enough power. Even if the Bank sold all of its securities in 1913 in order to buy gold, it would only increase the world's reserves by 0.5 per cent. The more modest actual adjustments made by the Bank's directors are highly unlikely to have influenced the course of the international economy. The Bank of England, in the words of McCloskey, 'was no more than the second violinist, not to say the triangle player, in the world's orchestra', and the stability of the international monetary system before 1914 did not depend on the hegemonic power of London.[18]

Such considerations have led other historians to argue that the explanation of the stability of the gold standard was not the presence of a hegemonic power but rather the existence of 'a decentralized, multipolar system' which depended on credibility and co-operation. According to Eichengreen, Britain, France, and Germany were committed to economic policies designed to maintain equilibrium in the balance of payments, to defend reserves, and ensure convertibility. Confidence in their commitment to gold meant that capital moved in large volumes and with great speed, so stabilizing exchange rates. Eichengreen emphasizes that central banks co-operated in dealing with financial crises before 1914, unlike in the 1920s and 1930s—a claim that is questionable, for the evidence suggests that 'central bank co-operation was probably not decisive in the operation of the gold standard'. The banks only helped each other if it was in their own interest and their approach may better be understood as a mixture of 'hatred, neglect and indifference'.[19] Such a view is compatible with the initial creation of the gold standard from conflict, and the distinct lack of co-operation between the Banks of Prussia, France, and Britain in the early 1870s. Not surprisingly, the conflicts of the 1870s reappeared in the run-up to the First World War. Eichengreen's arguments should be restated. There was, as he argues, a credible commitment to gold, but it was based on the consent of most people rather than ignorance or subordination. Inter-bank co-operation was less significant than the fact that politicians in each country pursued independent policies to maintain gold and to secure the advantage of belonging to the major trade bloc of the world. Tensions might be resolved not by co-operation between central banks but by a process more in line with the realities of the world before 1914: the power of European nations over their colonies. The core gold bloc countries could draw on specie from the periphery by the use of coercion or influence; in particular, London could utilize the reserves of India. The credibility of the commitment to gold was vital, as Eichengreen argues, but it could rest on power and individual national interest rather than co-operation.[20]

The gold standard was underpinned by the structure of the world economy as well as by the credible commitment to gold. In the second half of the nineteenth century, the world economy was moving towards unified markets as a result of 'arbitrage', the process of buying and selling goods to take advantage of minor variations in prices between, say, London and New York. Consequently, prices converged between parts of the world economy. This applied equally to the movement of goods with the drop in transport costs and to financial markets. 'Arbitrage operations among the great security markets of the world', it was noted by the *New York Tribune* in 1914, 'tend to annihilate space and time.' This could not have been said in 1850, when there was no integrated security market and a price differential of about 14 per cent was needed between Britain and America before it became worthwhile to buy in one market and sell in another. Change in international dealings started in 1851 when the first telegraph cable from Dover to Calais linked the exchanges in London and Paris. In 1866, the first cable was provided to New York, when the cost of transmitting a single word was £20, falling to 2s. by 1906. The creation of instantaneous communication allowed an international market to emerge. In 1860, the price of American railroad securities on the London and New York Stock Exchanges overlapped only 8.5 per cent of the time, with an average divergence of 4.8 per cent of the average price. In 1870, the price of American government bonds overlapped 73.6 per cent of the time, with an average divergence of 0.52 per cent of the average price. London was at the centre of a new international market which emerged between 1850 and 1914: the turnover of the London Stock Exchange in 1914 was ten times that of New York, and it was also the most international, reflecting the importance of British investors and the efficiency of the market. Specialist arbitrage firms emerged—there were 262 in 1909—which were subject to minimal controls. Membership of the Stock Exchange was cheap and easy, and the London market was much more liberal and flexible than Paris and New York. Once London established a reputation as the market with the widest range of securities at the most competitive prices, its attractiveness became self-perpetuating. The fact that London was the key to the system of arbitrage in securities and in commodities meant that the role of the Bank of England might be more significant than its limited sources would suggest, for the Stock Exchange and the commodity markets were intimately linked with the London money market.[21]

The fact that the Bank of England held a comparatively small gold reserve did not matter as long as confidence in sterling was high, and London could attract gold by raising the Bank rate and encouraging an inward flow of short-term capital. The general buoyancy of trade helped, for lines of credit from banks were taken up when trade was expanding, so forcing up interest rates and pulling in short-term funds which reduced the strain on the exchanges. Further, the combination of current and capital account adjustments was particularly important in maintaining stability and liquidity in the world economy. Britain was a long-term investor in the deficit countries, which kept the system in balance. Even so, debtor and creditor nations were not in untroubled harmony. The amount of gold in the world was very unevenly distributed, for most capital importers were on silver or the gold exchange standard without an internal supply of gold coinage. The gold standard might place strains on silver-based countries which had to pay interest in depreciated silver currency. There might well be resentment at the power of foreign capital. At the same time, depreciation of silver currencies gave their exports an advantage; the issue was whether this benefited native producers or the British-controlled export sector and the British consumer who received cheap food and raw materials. Before 1914, strains over capital exports were kept within narrow limits by the general liquidity of the world economy and Britain's reinvestment of its surplus. The tensions were to become much more serious after the First World War when debtor nations had serious difficulties in covering their deficits as prices fell.

The pre-war gold standard was based on a conjuncture of circumstances which could easily be upset. There would be serious problems if the flow of long-term capital changed so that surpluses were not recycled—and critics of capital exports were already complaining that domestic interests were being sacrificed. External tension arose from the emergence of other financial centres, and particularly New York. The United States moved into surplus on its balance of payments by the First World War, so attracting gold from the rest of the world which was in effect removed from circulation. American banks placed their seasonal surpluses on the London money market which was now susceptible to crises in the notoriously unstable American financial system. At the same time, internal changes within the London money market created difficulties. In the later nineteenth century, joint-stock banks became an increasingly important source of funds for discount houses and merchant banks, and the Bank of England became less important in the creation of liquidity. In the 1890s, there was an uneasy balance. The situation became more precarious as the power of the joint-stock banks increased after the mergers of the 1890s. There would also be problems if changes in the structure of trade disrupted the pattern of multilateral settlements, if Britain's ability to adjust the pattern of settlements through flows of capital was reduced, or the role of British credit in financing much of world trade was eroded. None of these conditions could be taken for granted; all were changing up to 1914.[22] Above all, the credibility of national commitments to gold could not be assumed after the First World War. The change did not come about simply because workers secured 'voice'; it was much more because the gold standard now genuinely did threaten deflation and a loss of jobs.

On and off Gold, 1914–1944

The war forced Britain to suspend the gold standard, and the attempt to restore and retain it in the 1920s collided with a much greater need to consider the domestic repercussions of monetary policy. Before the First World War, the pound was not overvalued against the dollar and the greater problem was the appreciation of gold-based currencies against silver. Consideration of this issue was largely technical, involving deliberations to bring the silver-based rupee into line with the gold-based pound. Despite the ambitions of the bimetallic campaign, monetary policy was not central to British politics before the First World War. After the war, the problem was much more serious, for British wages and prices rose sharply. The desire to return to gold at the pre-war parity of £1 to $4.86 therefore implied a reduction in British prices and wages, which would not be easy. The gold standard was no longer a guarantee of low prices and high levels of consumption; it was a threat to jobs and incomes. At the end of the war, the Labour party and trade unions were arguing that workers paid an undue share of the costs of the war. Why should they now also suffer a reduction in wages and a loss of jobs in order to bring costs into line with America?

Prior to 1914, few people considered the domestic repercussions of monetary policy. In the 1920s, the return to the gold standard meant deflationary policies. As Keynes pointed out, this amounted to a clash between two theories of economic society:

The one theory maintains that wages should be fixed by reference to what is 'fair' and 'reasonable' as between classes. The other theory [is] . . . that our vast machine should crash along, with regard only to its equilibrium as a whole, and without attention to the chance consequences of the journey to individual groups.

Under this second theory, 'the object of credit restriction . . . is to withdraw from employers the financial means to employ labour at the existing level of prices and wages. The policy can only attain its end by intensifying unemployment without limit, until the workers are ready to accept the necessary reduction of money wages.' But why should they accept these 'hard facts'? 'The gold standard', argued Keynes,

is an essential emblem and idol of those who sit in the top tier of the machine. I think that they are immensely rash in their regardlessness, in their vague optimism and comfortable belief that nothing really serious ever happens. Nine times out of ten, nothing really serious does happen—merely a little distress to individuals or to groups. But we run a risk of the tenth time (and are stupid into the bargain), if we continue to apply the principles of an economics which was worked out on the hypotheses of *laissez-faire* and free competition to a society which is rapidly abandoning these hypotheses.[23]

Keynes's answer was simple: 'in modern conditions wages in this country are, for various reasons, so rigid over short periods, that it is impracticable to adjust them to the ebb and flow of international gold-credit.'[24] What was involved was a fundamental reordering of economic priorities. Instead of preserving a fixed exchange rate by adjusting costs, wages, and prices on the principles of a *laissez-faire* society based on free competition, the exchange rate should be varied. In 1925, Keynes's proposition was heresy. By 1929, the Minister of Labour was able to utter such doubts in Cabinet.[25] After 1931, Keynes's proposition rapidly became orthodoxy.

The subsequent abandonment of gold in 1931 and the recovery of the British economy with low interest rates meant that the decision to return to gold in 1925 came to be seen as a mistake. Is this to say that the adoption of a strict monetary policy and return to gold was designed to benefit the City of London? The desire to return to the gold standard should be understood on its own terms. The wider political culture of the gold standard did not suddenly dissolve after the war and even many trade unionists and Labour politicians continued to support it.

At the end of the war, monetary policy was lax. The government was more concerned by the threat of unemployment and social unrest, and the need for low interest rates to finance social reform (especially building council houses), than by the concerns of the Treasury for sound money. The balance of opinion was soon transformed. Cheap money contributed to a short-lived boom from April 1919. Demand was high as merchants and shops restocked after the war; banks lent money to businesses; and powerful, militant trade unions secured higher wages. Inflation became a serious concern. The Treasury attempted to reassert control, arguing that a stricter monetary policy was needed to check inflation. Treasury officials feared that a continuation of speculation might result in a smash, and that the economy should be deflated.

In February 1920, the Bank of England urged the adoption of higher interest rates as unavoidable, despite the harmful impact of deflation on some classes of the community. At this point Keynes agreed, pointing out that 'A continuance of inflationism and high prices will not only depress the exchanges but by their effect on prices will strike at the whole basis of contract, of security, and of the capitalist system generally.'[26] Higher interest rates were intended to restore stability as a short-term measure, but when the boom ended in April 1920 interest rates were *increased* to 7 per cent to deal with the problem of short-term debt. A major concern was the legitimacy of government finances, a fear of loss of confidence if short-term debt were not converted to long-term loans, or the threat of inflation if the short-term debt was repaid. High interest rates were also needed to prepare for the return to gold. The post-war boom was coming to an end, so that monetary policy intensified rather than caused the slump. Despite the severity of the downturn, Treasury officials were reluctant to reduce interest rates, arguing that monetary stringency was a corrective to post-war speculation, and that high interest rates were needed to return to the gold standard. Lower interest rates would not lead to long-term recovery. In the opinion of the Treasury, economic growth rested on the international economy and not on a shift to home demand. The real problem was high costs, and any attempt to restore competitiveness and regain overseas markets would be threatened by easy credit. Of course, British industry could not be competitive at the pre-war parity unless wages and prices were sharply reduced. Although the pain was not in doubt, the decision to return to gold and to maintain high interest rates was not entirely a sacrifice of industry to the interests of the City. The Treasury was concerned with the legitimacy of government finances, with export competitiveness, and long-term recovery. Whether the policy would succeed was a different matter.[27]

In 1925, the initial period of suspension of convertibility expired and the gold standard would be restored unless the Chancellor made a conscious decision to renew suspension. He would need convincing arguments, for the return to gold had been in preparation since 1920. In retrospect, the decision to return to gold at the pre-war parity of $4.86 seemed misguided. As Keynes warned:

We are depending for the reduction of wages on the pressure of unemployment and of strikes and lock-outs . . .

The Bank of England is *compelled* to curtail credit by all the rules of the gold standard game. It is acting conscientiously and 'soundly' in doing so. But this does not alter the fact that to keep a tight hold on credit . . . necessarily involves intensifying unemployment. . . . What we need to restore prosperity today is an easy credit policy. We want to encourage business men to enter on new enterprises . . . Deflation does not reduce wages 'automatically'. It reduces them by causing unemployment. The proper object of dear money is to check an incipient boom.[28]

He was not alone in his concern. In 1925, Alfred Mond warned that 'we are to be harnessed to the money rate of New York, our trade is to be further depressed whenever there is a flurry on Wall Street, because some people seem to think that we must be hanged on a cross of gold'.[29] Concern about the impact of a deflationary monetary policy was also expressed by the Federation of British Industries, by Reginald McKenna (the former Chancellor and chairman of the Midland Bank), and by *The Economist*.[30]

Churchill was well aware of these concerns and was alarmed that 'The whole question of a return to the Gold Standard must not be dealt with only upon its financial and currency aspects.' He feared that high interest rates to preserve the gold standard would harm trade and employment, and expose the government to the complaint that it 'favoured the special interests of finance'.[31] He was wary of Montagu Norman's (the Governor of the Bank of England) contemptuous dismissal of merchants, manufacturers, and workmen. In Norman's opinion,

The cry of 'cheap money' is the Industrialists' big stick and should be treated accordingly. The restoration of Free Gold will require a high Bank Rate: the Government cannot avoid a decision for or against Restoration: the Chancellor will surely be charged with a sin of omission or of commission. In the former case (Gold) he will be abused by the ignorant, the gamblers and the antiquated Industrialists; in the latter case (not Gold) he will be abused by the instructed and by posterity.

Plain and solid advantages can be shown to exist which justify—and seem to require—this sacrifice.[32]

Churchill was not easily convinced. He remarked with some acerbity that Norman was 'perfectly happy in the spectacle of Britain possessing the finest credit in the world simultaneously with a million and a quarter unemployed'. He even posed the heretical question whether France, with its financial recklessness, was worse off than Britain with sound finance and high unemployment. Churchill challenged the Treasury to justify its financial policy of unemployment and dearth: 'I would rather see Finance less proud and Industry more content. . . . the fact that this island with its enormous resources is unable to maintain its population is surely a cause for the deepest heart searching.'[33] The decision to return to gold was by no means made lightly; it was made with more discussion than any other economic decision in the inter-war period.

The Treasury, and above all Otto Niemeyer, responded to Churchill's challenge. Niemeyer denied that financial policy was the main cause of unemployment and rejected inflation as an option, arguing that it offered only a temporary increase in spending power until the credit of the country was destroyed. 'I assume it to be admitted', he warned Churchill, 'that with Germany and Russia before us we do not think plenty can be found on this path.' It followed that 'economic employment can only be given to the extent to which commodities can be produced at a price which existing uninflated wealth can pay for them'. He was clear on the best means of increasing demand for British goods:

what we have to do . . . is (1) to stabilize our currency in relation to the main trading currencies of the world, (2) to reconstruct the broken parts of Europe and (3) to encourage thrift and the accumulation of capital for industry. . . .

. . . the root idea I am convinced is right, and the only way to enable this small island bound to buy and sell largely abroad . . . ultimately to support its population.

In Niemeyer's view, gold would lead to a more effective recovery: The issue, he pointed out, was not a fundamental divide between industry and finance; it was that bankers took a longer view than manufacturers.[34] The return to gold was therefore justified as an employment policy which assumed that recovery rested on the international rather than domestic economy.

Return to gold was as much a moral as an economic policy. In the words of Cecil Lubbock, 'a contract is, and always has been, sacred'. Not to return, or to return at a lower rate, carried the implication of fraud or default, a blow to prestige and to integrity. A major advantage of gold was that it was 'knave proof'. Politicians could delegate monetary policy to the automatism of the gold standard and the expert, technical operations of the Bank, removing the temptation to exploit monetary policy for political ends, as well as insulating politicians from criticism. When Churchill opted to return to gold, the costs seemed bearable. On some estimates, the pound was virtually back at $4.86; if it were not, the automatic adjustment of the specie-price-flow mechanism was confidently expected to correct relative prices. The pain of adjustment had already been felt in preparing for the return; even most of the opponents of deflation accepted that any further pain would be transitory. As McKenna remarked, it would be hell—but there was no alternative.[35]

In fact, the pound continued to be overvalued because British wages and costs did not fall, and American wages and costs did not rise (see Chapter 5). As a result, British exports were hampered, and interest rates were kept at higher levels to sustain the value of the pound. Returning at an overvalued rate soon led to industrial unrest and to depression in the export industries. The government could not contend that monetary policy was depoliticized and that the consequences were none of its concern. Domestic political considerations started to intrude in a much more serious way than before the First World War because the gold standard was imposing strains on workers' economic conditions. Wages and work were highly political, and it became more difficult for the authorities to decide on monetary policy according to international considerations without considering the domestic impact. Although it was theoretically bound by rules, the response of the Bank of England to movements in the gold reserve shows that it was sensitive to domestic considerations.

Concern for the domestic impact of the gold standard threatened the credibility of the commitment to fixed exchanges. Eichengreen argues that the result was to destroy central bank co-operation and hence to undermine the pre-war basis of the gold standard. As we have noted, co-operation was probably not the main prop of stable exchanges before 1914; he is right to suggest that tension between domestic and international monetary policy existed in all countries to a greater extent than before the wars. In many European countries, the independence of central bankers was compromised. The difficulty over monetary policy was linked with the conflict over taxation, for a failure to reach agreement over the level and incidence of taxes resulted in budget deficits and forced central banks to print money. The result was hyperinflation in Germany and serious inflation in France. Returning to the gold standard had the great virtue of closing debates over monetary policy. Paradoxically, the attempt to remove money from the realm of politics and to increase credibility reduced the ability of central bankers to use discretion in dealing with the strains of the international monetary system. By limiting the creation of credit and constraining international co-operation, the collapse of the international monetary system became more likely.[36] In the United States, inflation was largely avoided after the war and a different issue appeared. The Federal Reserve was made up of a number of regional boards comprising local bankers, industrialists, and politicians with little experience or interest in international monetary policy. Officials in New York saw the importance of international monetary policy; the board of governors in Washington was more concerned about domestic issues.[37] When the Bank of International Settlements was created in 1930 to resolve the difficulties of reparations and post-war debts, the Federal Reserve was not allowed to join and in any case the BIS had no remit for wider international monetary issues.[38]

The problem was less the failure of a hegemonic power to impose stability than the difficulties of maintaining a credible commitment to fixed exchanges. As yet, no supranational body could impose rules. At the same time, changes in the world economy meant that the system was inherently less stable. The disputes over war debts and post-war reparations introduced serious tensions in the world economy. There were significant changes in patterns of trade, especially with the emergence of the United States as a major exporter with a large trade surplus. As a result, the United States drew bullion and foreign exchange from the rest of the world, creating a potential problem of a lack of liquidity. The danger was avoided so long as the United States returned its surplus to the world economy by lending overseas. But in 1928, the Federal Reserve adopted a more stringent monetary policy, capital exports were reduced, strain was placed on the reserves of other countries, and central banks had to restrict credit. The imbalance in the pattern of settlements meant that any change in American policy had a major impact elsewhere, and the Federal Reserve was unwilling to reduce interest rates to deal with international strains.

Changes in the operation of the gold standard made it much more fragile. The demand for gold reserves exceeded the supply, and central banks competed through higher interest rates. One response to the shortage of gold was to adopt a gold exchange standard with a greater reliance on foreign currencies, which meant that a financial crisis in one country threatened to destabilize other countries. The United States and, to a lesser extent, France were exceptions, for they acquired large gold reserves and then in effect 'sterilized' gold by withdrawing it from circulation to prevent price rises. Their reaction was the mirror image of Britain's. In Britain, Keynes stressed the 'stickiness' of wages, costs, and prices which did not fall in line with the overvaluation of the pound. Differences emerged between Britain and the United States, where Keynes's view was widely seen as defeatist.[39] American commentators felt that Britain's avoidance of wage cuts was the source of its problems. The automatic adjustment of the specie-price-flow mechanism did not operate in the way expected, and the overvaluation of sterling persisted. For their part, British commentators complained that countries with surpluses were passing the burdens of adjustment to countries with a deficit by refusing to allow inflows of gold to affect their price level. The problem became more serious after 1928 when the United States' restrictive monetary policy led to a cut in foreign lending. Many countries with deficits on their balance of payments relied on imports of American capital, and the reduction in lending forced them to raise their interest rates and restrict credit. Producers of primary goods tried to increase their exports to obtain more foreign currency, with the result that commodity prices dropped still more and they were less able to buy manufactured imports, hitting British industrialists who were heavily dependent on these markets. The situation became still more alarming after 1929, for the American authorities responded to the crash on Wall Street with a strict monetary policy to 'purge' the economy of speculation. The structure of the gold standard in the 1920s meant that deflation was spread through the world economy; the United States did not restore liquidity to the global economy by means of capital exports, and it did not keep an open market for goods from the deficit countries.

The gold standard intensified financial crisis rather than solving problems. When central bankers in countries with the experience of inflation were faced with a domestic crisis, they could not respond with an easier money policy which would undermine the credibility of their commitment to gold and provoke a flight of money. The situation deteriorated with defaults by some debtor nations which made international lending all the riskier. Britain was spared some of the problems, for it had avoided inflation in the 1920s and its domestic banking system was stable. Nevertheless, there were serious external difficulties. Earnings on invisibles declined in 1930–1, and short-term capital left as a result of a lack of confidence in the stability of sterling and the deficit on the unemployment insurance fund. The Bank was in a dilemma. An increase in the Bank rate to defend the pound would not be popular with labour, and might only suggest that sterling was under pressure. The Bank and international bankers wished to see a return to sound finance, and some commentators saw a conspiracy to destroy the Labour government. In reality, the Bank was seeking action rather than the collapse of the government, and the Labour Chancellor welcomed external pressure to strengthen his hand.[40] The basic issue was that in any conflict between international and domestic considerations, it was becoming clear that domestic influences would have priority. The gold standard was abandoned.

The abandonment of gold reduced some of the constraints on monetary policy. The incompatible goals of domestic welfare and international credibility were already apparent in the British reaction to the crash in the United States in 1929. Interest rates were cut and the Treasury realized that cheaper money had considerable advantages, both in converting the national debt to a lower rate and stimulating economic recovery.[41] As a result of conflicting international and domestic demands, monetary policy was ineffective; commitment to gold was not credible; and the pursuit of a domestic monetary policy was constrained by concern for the international situation. After 1931, the abandonment of the gold standard opened the way for a more explicit pursuit of domestic policies. Countries with serious inflation in the 1920s tried to stay on gold and retained stringent monetary policies even after its abandonment. In their view, economic problems were created by easy credit, speculation, and financial crisis; economic recovery started with the restoration of monetary stability. The British response was different. Agreement on taxation and spending was reached, and disputes were negotiated within widely based political parties. Conflict over spending and taxation did not fundamentally disrupt social relations, and the dangers of an unbalanced budget, lax monetary policy, and inflation were avoided. As a result, continued commitment to the gold standard did not have the same force as in France or Germany where inflation and monetary instability in the 1920s made gold important as a guarantee of stability. The lack of serious inflation meant that once gold was abandoned, there was ready acceptance that political and social tensions would not follow. The difference was clear at the international economic conference of 1933. The French feared inflation and low interest rates, and clung to the gold standard; the British rejected high interest rates and were committed to low interest rates as the route to recovery. In Britain, the gold standard came to be seen as the *cause* of economic problems rather than a cure.[42]

The British government seized on the opportunity to develop a creative policy of domestic recovery. Initially, abandonment of the gold standard offered the Treasury a way of reducing the cost of servicing the national debt. The debt could only be converted to a lower interest rate if there was an expectation that interest would remain low. In 1932, almost £2,000 m of war debt was converted from 5 per cent to 3.5 per cent. The Treasury also realized that abandoning gold allowed more adventurous policies. The pound could now be modestly undervalued, so helping exporters by making their goods cheaper in foreign markets and offering protection to domestic producers by increasing the price of imports. However, depreciation posed problems as well as opportunities. Internationally, it reduced the value of overseas assets and raised the cost of repaying loans to the United States; at home, it increased the price of imports, so provoking demands for wage increases. The question was whether the pound should be allowed to drop to $3.90 or still further to $3.40. The Treasury favoured the lower rate in order to help exports, raise prices, and reduce the burden of debt. The main problem, they argued, was the discrepancy between costs and wages, which were considerably higher than before the war, and prices, which were about the same. Any attempt to bring wages and prices into line by reducing wages was undesirable, as the general strike had shown. The solution was to increase prices without a rise in costs or wages. A Treasury official explained that the policy was designed

To restore the conditions under which industry and commerce could expand. . . . If we can hold out to industry a prospect of stable or rising prices, a reasonable stability in the exchanges, cheap capital and easy money, a check to the rise in taxation and possibly some reduction, and a guarantee against revolutionary and dislocating new departures in public enterprise, confidence will revive, enterprise will quicken and employment will expand.

This policy was an alternative to Keynes's proposals for budget deficits and public works. The Treasury feared that the first would undermine confidence in national finances, without which cheap money was impossible; and the second would simply divert money from normal trade into 'hothouse schemes'.[43]

The value of the pound initially dropped to about \$3.30, and was then stabilized around \$3.40 by the Exchange Equalization Account established in 1932 with a fund to buy and sell sterling. As a result, exports had a competitive advantage. The approach to exchange rates was similar to the trade policy adopted at Ottawa: to create a sterling area including those countries most dependent on British markets. In these countries, the parities of the gold standard still applied. The sterling area was part of the policy of creating a trade bloc and a means of retaining some control over international finance. As we have seen, abandonment of gold was complemented by the introduction of a general tariff, reinforcing the shift from the open, global economy of the years before the war.

The experience of the 1930s led to considerable debate about what had gone wrong, not least amongst economists associated with the League of Nations. In their opinion, the crux of the matter was the pursuit of independent, nationalist policies without an appreciation of how depression could be spread throughout the world. Their solution was to create a new set of international institutions to prevent any one country from pursuing self-defeating, selfish policies. The outbreak of the Second World War seemed to mark the culmination of the collapse of the world economy into self-contained trade blocs and mutual suspicion—and the beginning of discussion of how to create a new post-war global economy based on mutual agreement.

NOTES

1. Patterson, *The Economy of Capital*, 42.
2. Alborn, 'Coin and country', x.

3. Keynes, 'National self-sufficiency' (1933), *Collected Writings* (hereafter *CW*), xxi. 240; Cole quoted in Brown, *England and the New Gold Standard*, 253.

4. Keynes, *A Treatise on Money*, *CW* vi. 219, 299, 354–6; Obstfeld and Taylor, 'The great depression as a watershed', 354–5.

5. See the maps in Einaudi, *Money and Politics*, 206–7.

6. Einaudi, *Money and Politics*; Flandreau, *Glitter of Gold*; Flandreau, 'French crime'.

7. Daunton, 'Britain and globalization, I', 14–21; Flandreau, *Glitter*.

8. De Cecco, *Money and Empire*, 53, 58–60; hypothesis tested by Meissner, 'New world order'.

9. Einaudi, *Money and Politics*; Flandreau, 'French crime'; Meissner, 'New world order'; Lopez-Cordova and Meissner, 'Exchange rate regimes'.

10. Bordo and Rockoff, 'Gold standard as a "good housekeeping seal of approval"'; Bordo and Kydland, 'Gold standard as a commitment mechanism'.

11. Eichengreen, *Golden Fetters, passim* but especially 6, 30–1.

12. Daunton, 'Britain and globalization, I'.

13. Green, 'Rentiers versus producers?', 597, 591–2, 598–600, 608–11; Gibbs, *A Colloquy on Currency*, 180. On the perception of a conflict between the City and industry see Green, 'The bimetallic controversy', and the doubts of Howe, 'Bimetallism' and Daunton, ' "Gentlemanly capitalism" and British industry', 151.

14. De Cecco, *Money and Empire*, 67; Howe, 'Bimetallism', 389–90.

15. Keynes, *Treatise*, *CW* vi. 274.

16. This is the view above all of Kindleberger, *The World in Depression*.

17. Committee on Currency and Foreign Exchanges after the War (Cunliffe Committee), *First Interim Report*, 1918, paras. 4–6.

18. McCloskey and Zecher, 'How the gold standard worked', 185–6.

19. Flandreau, 'Central bank co-operation', 735, 737.

20. Kaminsky, ' "Lombard Street" and India', 302–27; De Cecco, *Money and Empire*, 62–75.

21. Michie, *London and New York Stock Exchanges*, 34, 43–8, 53, 74 189.

22. De Cecco, *Money and Empire*, ch. 6.

23. Keynes, *Economic Consequences of Mr Churchill*, *CW*, 218, 224, 233–4.

24. Quoted in Skidelsky, *John Maynard Keynes*, 205.

25. Quoted in Clarke, *Keynesian Revolution*, 57.

26. Quoted in Howson, *Domestic Monetary Management*, 19–20.

27. Clarke, 'Treasury's analytical model', xx.

28. Keynes, *Economic Consequences of Mr Churchill*, 220.

29. Mond in Hansard, 5th ser. 182, cols. 786–7, 26 Mar. 1925.

30. Hume, 'The gold standard and deflation', 233–5.

31. Moggridge, *British Monetary Policy*, 65.

32. Quoted ibid. 70.

33. Ibid. 76.

34. Ibid. 77, 69; Clarke, *Keynesian Revolution*, 38.

35. Moggridge, *Domestic Monetary Policy*, 229; Hume, 'The gold standard and deflation'.

36. Eichengreen, *Golden Fetters*, 9–12.

37. Moggridge, *British Monetary Policy*, 59.
38. Eichengreen, *Golden Fetters*, 11, 259.
39. Skidelsky, *John Maynard Keynes*, 133–4.
40. Williamson, 'A "bankers' ramp"?'
41. Howson, *Domestic Monetary Management*, 68.
42. Solomou, *Themes*, xx.
43. Ibid. 68, 91, 92.

FURTHER READING

Alborn, T., 'Coin and country: visions of civilization in the British recoinage debate, 1867–91', *Journal of Victorian Culture*, 3 (1998)

Bloomfield, A. l., *Monetary Policy under the International Gold Standard, 1880–1914* (New York, 1959)

Bordo, M. D., *The Gold Standard and Related Regimes: Collected Essays* (Cambridge, 1999)

—— and Kydland, F. E., 'The gold standard as a rule', *Explorations in Economic History*, 32 (1995)

—— —— 'The gold standard as a commitment mechanism', in T. Bayoumi, B. Eichengreen, and M. P. Taylor (eds.), *Modern Perspectives on the Gold Standard* (Cambridge, 1996)

—— and Rockoff, H., 'The gold standard as a "good housekeeping seal of approval"', *Journal of Economic History*, 56 (1996)

—— and Schwartz, A. J., 'The operation of the specie standard: evidence for core and peripheral countries, 1880–1990', in J. B. de Macedo, B. Eichengreen, and J. Reis (eds.), *Currency Convertibility: The Gold Standard and Beyond* (1996)

—— —— (eds.), *A Retrospective on the Classical Gold Standard* (Chicago, 1984)

Brown, W. A., *England and the New Gold Standard, 1919–26* (New Haven, 1926)

Clarke, P. F., *The Keynesian Revolution in the Making, 1724–1936* (Oxford, 1988)

—— 'The Treasury's analytical model of the British economy between the wars', in M. O. Furner and B. Supple (eds.), *The State and Economic Knowledge: The American and British Experience* (Cambridge, 1990)

Daunton, M. J., '"Gentlemanly capitalism" and British industry, 1820–1914', *Past and Present* (1989)

—— 'Britain and globalization since 1850, I: creating a global order, 1850–1914', *Transactions of the Royal Historical Society*, 6th s.16 (2006)

De Cecco, M., *Money and Empire: The International Gold Standard, 1890–1914* (Oxford, 1974)

Drummond, I. M., *The Gold Standard and the International Monetary System, 1900–39* (Basingstoke, 1987)

Eichengreen, B. (ed.), *The Gold Standard in Theory and History* (1985)

—— *Golden Fetters: The Gold Standard and the Great Depression, 1919–39* (Oxford, 1992)

—— *Elusive Stability: Essays in the History of International Finance, 1919–1939* (Cambridge, 1990)

—— *Globalizing Capital: A History of the International Monetary System* (Princeton, 1996)

—— and Flandreau, M., 'The geography of the gold standard', in J. B. de Macedo, B. Eichengreen, and J. Reis (eds.), *Currency Convertibility* (1996)

Einaudi, L., *Money and Politics: European Monetary Unification and the International Gold Standard, 1865–1873* (Oxford, 2001).

Flandreau, M., 'The French crime of 1873: an essay on the emergence of the international gold standard, 1870–1880', *Journal of Economic History*, 56 (1996)

—— 'Central bank co-operation in historical perspective: a sceptical view', *Economic History Review*, 50 (1997)

—— *The Glitter of Gold: France, Bimetallism, and the Emergence of the International Gold Standard, 1848–73* (Oxford, 2004)

Ford, A. G., 'Bank rate, the British balance of payments and the burden of adjustment, 1870–1914', *Oxford Economic Papers*, 16 (1964)

—— *The Gold Standard, 1890–1914: Britain and Argentina* (Oxford, 1962)

Frieden, J., 'The dynamics of international monetary systems: international and domestic factors in the rise, reign and demise of the international gold standard', in B. Eichengreen (ed.),*The Gold Standard in Theory and History* (1985)

Gallarotti, G. M., 'The scramble for gold: monetary regime transformation in the 1870s', in M. D. Bordo and F. Capie (eds.), *Monetary Regimes in Transition* (Cambridge, 1993)

—— *The Anatomy of an International Monetary Regime: The International Gold Standard* (Oxford, 1995)

Gibbs, H. C., *A Bimetallic Primer* (3rd edn., 1896)

Gibbs, H. H., *A Colloquy on Currency* (3rd edn., 1894)

—— and Grenfell, H. R., *The Bimetallic Controversy* (1886)

Green, E. H. H., 'Rentiers versus producers? The political economy of the bimetallic controversy', *English Historical Review*, 103 (1988)

—— 'The bimetallic controversy: empiricism belimed or the case for the issues', *English Historical Review*, 105 (1990)

Howe, A. C., 'Bimetallism, c.1880–1898: a controversy reopened?', *English Historical Review*, 105 (1990)

Howson, S., *Domestic Monetary Management in Britain, 1919–38* (Cambridge, 1975)

Hume, L. J., 'The gold standard and deflation: issues and attitudes in the 1920s', *Economica*, 30 (1963)

Kaminsky, A. P., ' "Lombard Street" and India: currency problems in the late nineteenth century', *Indian Economic and Social History Review*, 17 (1980)

Keynes, J. M., *Collected Writings of John Maynard Keynes*, i: *Indian Currency and Finance* (1971)

—— *Collected Writings of John Maynard Keynes*, xxi: *Activities, 1931–39: World Crises and Policies in Britain and America*, ed. D. Moggridge (1982)

Kindleberger, C., *The World in Depression, 1929–1939* (2nd edn., Harmondsworth, 1987)

Lopez Córdova, J. E., and Meissner, C., 'Exchange rate regimes and international trade: evidence from the classical gold standard era, 1870–1913', *American Economic Review*, 93 (2003)

McCloskey, D. N., and Zecher, J. R., 'How the gold standard worked, 1880–1913', in D. N. McCloskey, *Enterprise and Trade in Victorian Britain* (1981)

Meissner, C., 'A new world order: explaining the emergence of the classical gold standard', *Journal of International Economics*, 66 (2005)

Michie, R. C., *The London and New York Stock Exchanges, 1850–1914* (1987)

Milward, A. S., 'The origins of the gold standard', in J. B. de Macedo, B. Eichengreen, and J. Reis (eds.), *Currency Convertibility: The Gold Standard and Beyond* (1996)

Moggridge, D. E., *British Monetary Policy, 1924–1931: The Norman Conquest of $4.86* (Cambridge, 1972)

Nevin, E., *The Mechanism of Cheap Money: A Study of British Monetary Policy, 1931–39* (Cardiff, 1955)

Obstfeld, M., and Taylor, A. M., 'The great depression as a watershed: international capital mobility over the long run', in M. D. Bordo, C. Goldin, and E. N. White (eds.), *The Defining Moment: The Great Depression and the American Economy in the Twentieth Century* (Chicago, 1998)

Patterson, R. H., *The Economy of Capital: or Gold and Trade* (Edinburgh, 1865)

Sayers, R. S., *The Bank of England, 1891–1914*, vol. i (Cambridge, 1976)

—— 'The return to gold, 1925', in L. S. Presnell (ed.), *Studies in the Industrial Revolution* (1960)

Skidelsky, R., *John Maynard Keynes: The Economist as Saviour, 1920–1937* (1992)

Solomou, S., *Themes in Macroeconomic History: The UK Economy, 1919–39* (Cambridge, 1996)

Williamson, P., 'A "bankers' ramp"? Financiers and the British political crisis of August 1931', *English Historical Review*, 99 (1984)

....

CHAPTER 9

Rebuilding the International Economic Order?

> All of us have seen the great economic tragedy of our time. We saw the worldwide depression of the 1930s. We saw currency disorders develop and spread...In their wake, we saw unemployment and wretchedness...We saw their victims fall prey, in places, to demagogues and dictators. We saw bewilderment and bitterness become the breeders of fascism, and, finally, of war.[1]
>
> (Henry Morgenthau, United States Secretary of the Treasury, 1944)

*T*hese reflections on the collapse of the international economy opened the Bretton Woods conference, where representatives of forty-four countries came together to rebuild the world's monetary system. The guiding ambition was to prevent a recurrence of 'beggar my neighbour' devaluations and a retreat into trade blocs. The Americans wished to reinstate monetary stability and multilateral trade—and their immense economic power at the end of the war allowed them to set the agenda. Many commentators assumed that the result of America's overwhelming economic power was to recreate the conditions for a liberal international economy.[2] The historical record seemed to support the argument. After all, Britain was the hegemonic economic power in the mid-nineteenth century, and the demise of the liberal world economy between the wars could be explained by the lack of a hegemonic economic power with the ability to impose binding agreements, so that the world economy collapsed into 'insular capitalism'. At the end of the Second World War, the United States appeared to have achieved an even greater measure of hegemony, with the obvious inference that a liberal world economy could be recreated.

The argument has a seductive simplicity but is far from a complete explanation of the reshaping of the world economy. Although the economic power of the United States was of considerable importance, both the chronology and form of the new liberal order were much more complex and contested than implied by a story of the rise and fall of economic hegemons. Another important influence was the changed priority of national economic policies, with a greater need to mitigate the impact of international and market forces on the domestic society and economy. The point was well put by Ragnar Nurske:

There was a growing tendency during the inter-war period to make international monetary policy conform to domestic social and economic policy . . . Yet the world was still economically interdependent; and an international currency mechanism for the multilateral exchange of goods and services . . . was still a fundamental necessity for the great majority of countries. The problem was to find a system of international currency relations compatible with the requirements of domestic stability.[3]

As Karl Polanyi argued, the reaction against the market, from both left and right, ruled out any attempt to restore an international economic order on the basis of free trade and the gold standard. In his view, the social basis of 'capitalist internationalism' had disappeared with the emergence of an active domestic state, and the international economy would need to be consciously managed by collaboration between governments.[4] Despite the economic hegemony of the United States, and its desire to return to free trade and a form of gold standard, domestic social and economic policies in Britain and the rest of western Europe could not be subordinated to international considerations to anything like the same extent as before the First World War. The international economic order constructed after 1945 differed from the old order: a compromise was struck between the liberal global order of the later nineteenth century and the national capitalism of the 1930s, so that international liberalization and domestic economic stability were mutually supportive.[5]

Bretton Woods marked a crucial step in the creation of formal institutions for international economic management. The form of these institutions reflected more than the emergence of America as a hegemon. The balance between domestic stability and international liberalization was contested in the United States and in Britain, and the outcome can only be understood through a complex interplay of ideas, institutions, and interests. The outcome was not preordained. Between the wars, negotiations collapsed into antipathy so that economic nationalism triumphed; the process might well be repeated. Alternatively, the US administration might use its undoubted economic power to insist on a return to a liberal economic order so creating a deep sense of animosity. The major issue was whether both of these potentially disastrous outcomes could be avoided.

The shape of the post-war global economy depended on the relative weight given to the different elements of an open world economy. Was free trade more important than capital flows; and were fixed exchange rates the crucial variable from which everything else would follow? The global economy involves a choice between four variables: free trade, exchange rate stability, free capital movements, and an active domestic economic policy. Essentially, it was impossible to have all four of this 'inconsistent quartet'. As we have seen, globalization in the late nineteenth century rested on the pursuit of free trade; stability in exchange rates; and lack of controls on the flow of capital. The active pursuit of domestic economic stability was not feasible: if the exchange rate is fixed and capital is allowed to move freely, any action designed to maintain the exchange rate will offset the domestic impact of the policy. If we suppose that the currency was appreciating, the interest rate could be reduced to make the pound less attractive. Low interest rates might stimulate the domestic economy—but a lack of capital control would mean that funds could go abroad. An increase in interest rates designed to prevent depreciation of the pound would encourage capital to stay at home, so offsetting the domestic impact of higher interest rates. In either case, monetary policy was driven by international considerations and an active pursuit of domestic economic stability was impossible.[6] The dominant assumption in the later nineteenth century was that prosperity flowed from the open, liberal world economy, which offered low prices for consumers and export markets for industrialists. Between the wars, the balance shifted with a greater stress on domestic considerations which made the return to gold more difficult. Eventually, fixed exchange rates, capital movements, and free trade were abandoned in favour of 'insular capitalism'. After the Second World War, domestic prosperity and stable exchanges were given priority—and trade liberalization was initially concerned with re-establishing multilateralism rather than lowering trade barriers. Capital flows were often seen as counter-productive, hindering the re-emergence of stable exchanges and multilateral trade. Both the American and British delegates at Bretton Woods accepted that capital controls were necessary to prevent domestic policies from being undermined by capital flight. If capital markets are controlled, a country may both adopt fixed exchange rates and pursue its own domestic monetary policy (see Table 9.1).

The precise mix of policies is to be explained by the increased power of domestic welfare in shaping economic policy—and a sense that the global economy between the wars foundered on the rocks of speculative capital movements. Many economists and politicians drew an obvious economic lesson from the experience of the inter-war period: an outflow of capital undermined stable exchange rates, so creating difficulties with the balance of trade and leading to protective duties. Most economists readily endorsed the proposition that the movement of *goods* 'is a prerequisite of prosperity and economic growth'.[7] As Keynes pointed out, capital flows might strangle trade rather than playing 'their proper auxiliary role of facilitating trade'. He argued that the free movement of capital was incompatible with an active domestic monetary policy. Cheap money—that is, low interest rates—remained a central element of Britain's domestic economic policy from the 1930s to 1951, and rested on strict limits

TABLE 9.I. *Policy trade-offs between domestic economic policies, capital mobility, and fixed exchanges, c.1870–1990*

Era	Countries chose to sacrifice		
	Activist policies	Capital mobility	Fixed exchange rate
Gold standard	most	few	few
Inter-war (off gold)	few	several	most
Bretton Woods	few	most	few
Float	few	few	many

Source: Obstfeld and Taylor, *Global Capital Markets*, 40.

on the flow of capital. Such considerations meant that the Bretton Woods agreement sacrificed capital mobility. Although international bankers on Wall Street and in the City of London were not entirely convinced, they were generally subordinated to a coalition of labour, industry, and leading officials and politicians. The financiers of Wall Street did achieve a greater say in American economic policy between 1945 and 1947, but the experience of financial liberalization in 1947 merely reinforced the need for tight controls on capital movements for the next two decades. During the period of fixed exchange rates, capital controls were sanctioned in order to prevent currency crises; the incompatibility between capital movements and fixed exchanges was again apparent in the strains leading to the demise of fixed exchanges after 1971.[8]

The lesson to be drawn from the economic history of the inter-war period was much less obvious in the case of trade policy, for economists and politicians disagreed over the causes of the depression of the 1930s. Although there were differences of emphasis within Britain and the United States, there was also a divergence of opinion between the two countries. In the story favoured by many American politicians and economists, Britain was the villain who led the world into depression by a selfish failure to adhere to the gold standard, by its pursuit of trade discrimination at Ottawa, and by the creation of a sterling bloc. The British government stood accused of adopting the easy option of devaluation and a retreat into imperial markets, so bringing the world economy into disarray. In the opinion of Cordell Hull, the US Secretary of State, the Ottawa agreement was 'the greatest injury . . . that has been inflicted on this country since I have been in public life'.[9] F. W. Hirst, a defender of the verities of free trade, remarked that Hull was 'a Jeffersonian Liberal Free Trader, simple and direct'. As this implies, Hull represented one strand in American thinking, rejecting the alternative approach of Alexander Hamilton who emphasized the need for national economic development behind tariff walls. In the

United States, protectionism dominated for most of the later nineteenth and early twentieth centuries, at a time when Britain was wedded to free trade. The situation was now reversed.

In 1941, negotiations over the Lend-Lease agreement to supply Britain with war materials gave Hull an opportunity to press for the reinstatement of free trade. The initial draft of clause VII of the agreement proposed that Britain should pledge itself not to discriminate against America. Keynes was scornful of proposals which he saw as a matter of almost religious conviction rather than pragmatic politics.[10] Harry Hawkins, an official in the Division of Commercial Treaties and Agreements, felt that Keynes missed the point:

What Mr. Keynes has completely failed to see . . . is that the idea of non-discrimination . . . is not a philosophical concept but rather a matter involving considerations of practical politics and economics. The imposition of high, though non-discriminatory, trade barriers for the protection by a country of its own producers does and has aroused resentment, but this resentment is mitigated by the fact that a certain degree of preference by a government for its nationals is understandable and tolerable. But discrimination in favour of other foreigners is not so regarded.[11]

Hull and Hawkins aimed to end discrimination and to replace bilateral exchanges with multilateral trade between all countries—an outcome that could be reconciled with high levels of duties. The question facing British officials and politicians was: should clause VII be accepted and imperial preference abandoned?

On the British side, the collapse of the world economy was more usually blamed on the Americans for failing to maintain liquidity. By imposing high tariffs after 1929, the Americans prevented other countries from selling their goods in one of the world's largest markets. On this account, a major problem facing the world economy was the creditor position of the United States: how were other countries to cover their trade deficits and service their loans if the United States was building up gold reserves and so starving the rest of the world of money? At the end of the war, Britain would be among the debtor nations. How was this situation to be faced?

Opinions were deeply divided between proponents of free trade and economic nationalism. While the Americans (and especially Hull) provided the driving force for free trade, the alternative form of economic nationalism was most strongly associated with the German banker and Minister of Economics, Hjalmar Schacht. His new economic order rested on a system of bilateral barter for foreign trade, with import licensing and exchange controls to limit a country's purchases.

A number of British economists—including significant figures in the Economic Section of the War Cabinet—welcomed American pressure. They accepted Hull's argument that tariffs undermined the growth of the world economy, though they saw the need for global government and an escape route if things became difficult. In 1943, James Meade renounced Britain's trade policy of the 1930s:

A protectionist world of bilateral bargaining is one in which there are no rules of the economic game. . . . But such a system could not work harmoniously for long. When every country is making bilateral agreements with every other country . . . economic relationships will become a perpetual source of diplomatic friction.[12]

Similarly, Lionel Robbins looked back with regret to the nineteenth-century liberal world order which created peace and prosperity.[13] Roy Harrod, a leading proponent of free trade, pointed out that the Americans had not agreed to support Britain in order to establish 'a system of a Schachtian kind run from London instead of Berlin'. In Harrod's opinion, Schachtianism 'rivets trade to politics and turns every new commercial development into an act of economic warfare'.[14]

On the other side were opponents of liberalization who held that multilateralism and a free economic system were doomed to failure. Their scepticism might be pragmatic. The Bank of England felt that non-discrimination was impracticable, and that the only realistic way to proceed was by controls on exchanges and trade. In the opinion of the Bank:

It can surely be foreseen that we and others will refuse to limit our internal monetary policy by reference to any external standard; that we can never again tolerate conditions in which mass movements of capital are free to overwhelm the international exchanges; that we shall maintain exchange and import controls for an indefinite period; that we shall aim at maintaining the concept and structure of a sterling area; and that we shall retain the liberty to use bilateral negotiations as an instrument for promoting international trade.[15]

Others went further, such as Leo Amery who inherited the mantle of Joseph Chamberlain and strongly supported imperial preference.

Economic nationalism was not simply an atavistic pursuit of imperial glory: it could rest on a particular reading of economic history and its projection into the future. One of the strongest advocates was Hubert Henderson. In a Treasury memorandum of 1943 he rejected any attempt

to reconstruct a war-shattered world on the basis of a freely working economic system, international credits, the reduction of trade barriers, and the out-lawry of quantitative regulation. To attempt this . . . would be to repeat the mistakes made last time . . . . It would be to invite the same failure, and the same disillusionment; the same economic chaos and the same shock to social and political stability; the same discredit for the international idea.

In his opinion, economic nationalism was not the cause of economic problems between the wars. Rather, the central problem was 'deeply rooted maladjustments in the balance of international payments'. The marked trend towards an increasing degree of collective organization and State intervention in internal economic affairs must necessarily exert a far-reaching influence on external economic policies. The idea of greater economic security is fundamentally incompatible with that of an unregulated external economy. If a country's economic life is to be rendered reasonably stable, it may be essential to safeguard it against extreme disturbance from the vicissitudes of foreign markets. No country which makes the maintenance of full employment one of its major aims can abdicate its authority to check an abnormal flood of imports which threatens to disorganize employment.

Henderson therefore advocated 'quantitative methods of regulation' in order to 'provide a reliable safeguard against violent change and a considerate means of effecting gradual change .... The old international order of the nineteenth century was based on laisser-faire and has broken down for good.'[16] As he said in 1941, controls on exchanges and trade were 'an advance in the direction of a more ordered life', and therefore incompatible with clause VII.[17] Henderson wrote to Keynes that he did not understand his opposition to the Ottawa agreement. Since it was not likely that the USA would voluntarily give up its creditor position, Britain should continue to plan its trade, and rely on imperial preference and agreements with foreign countries. His position was pessimistic: Britain's economy was weak, and there was little to be done about it beyond exploiting its favoured position in the empire.[18]

Despite Henderson's support for regulations and controls, he continued to favour a capitalist economic system and private ownership. Economic nationalism could also take a socialist form. Such a view was adopted only by a minority within the Labour party; much more common was a general suspicion of the free market as an allocative device and a widespread preference for supply-side intervention in the economy. Most economists and politicians avoided the extremes of American free trade, of the German new economic order, and of Stalinist planning, and responded to circumstances.

Above all, Keynes attempted to reach some compromise between Schachtian economic nationalism and Hull's commitment to the reconstruction of a liberal world economy. Although Keynes started life as a free trader, he moved to economic nationalism in the 1930s, largely from a desire to maintain domestic employment. In the war, he initially aimed to improve Schachtianism rather than to adopt multilateralism, assuming that the unbalanced creditor position of the United States would necessitate bilateral trade during a period of post-war adjustment. At the end of the war, Britain would have a weak balance of payments, and anyone who advocated giving up bilateral agreements 'would be as great a traitor to his country as if he were to sign away the British navy'.[19]

Keynes was later willing to move in the direction of multilateralism in trade, always provided that Britain had some safeguard during the post-war transition, and that the international monetary system was reformed, by ensuring that some of the burden of adjustment fell on the *creditor* nation. Although Keynes's priority remained domestic employment and stability, he would abandon protectionism and bilateralism in favour of reforming international monetary institutions in order to allow adjustments between creditor and debtor nations. Much depended on the political circumstances. When Harrod urged him to abandon economic nationalism and support the Americans, Keynes's reaction was that both approaches should be pursued. Keynes's collaborator, R. F. Kahn, remarked in 1941 that 'the only fundamental issue is what degree of American co-operation would be necessary to justify a return to what might be called a liberal economic system and whether there is sufficient hope of persuading the Americans . . . to make the necessary concessions'.[20] Keynes responded that the Americans would have to adjust their pursuit of *laissez-faire* policies to conditions, and that the economic system after the war would differ from free trade. Schachtianism was abandoned—on condition that a new mechanism was created to combine domestic prosperity and multilateralism.

The Treasury realized that the Americans had considerable economic power, and that outright opposition to clause VII was unrealistic. Accordingly, the Treasury adopted a pragmatic response in 1941, opting not to make a case for controls on trade but not pressing for immediate free trade. On this basis, the British and American administrations reached a compromise over clause VII of the Lend-Lease agreement. Rather than the sudden and destructive shift to non-discrimination initially proposed by the Americans, the final version required a move in the direction of non-discrimination, with the proviso that it would be 'in the light of governing economic conditions'. Further, non-discrimination was balanced by 'the expansion . . . of production, employment, and the exchange and consumption of goods'.[21] In other words, British commitment to the eventual adoption of non-discrimination depended on an American commitment to promote economic expansion, as well as a reduction of its own tariffs. Domestic stability and international liberalization were linked. But how to ensure that multilateral payments could be restored?

The problem at the end of the war was that the Americans could export vast quantities of goods, and the countries wishing to buy these goods had little ability to pay. Consequently, attention turned from the highly politicized and deeply contentious issue of trade policy to a more precise and technical issue of monetary policy. This was justified by the realization that resolving the problem of payment would allow trade liberalization to follow; trade liberalization alone would soon collapse unless means were found to allow payment for the goods entering trade. At the heart of these technical debates was the nature of the exchange rate system. One proposition was easily accepted: the competitive devaluations of the inter-war period should end, and steps should be taken to ease international settlements. But should the exchange rates be rigidly fixed as under the gold standard or should there be room for variation? And should the scheme for international settlements impose the need for readjustment on countries in surplus as well as deficit? Once more, the interpretation of the economic history of the inter-war period shaped perceptions. Generally, American officials believed that the gold standard resulted in prosperity in the 1920s, and that its abandonment led to depression. As a result, they favoured fixed exchange rates. By contrast, British officials blamed the gold standard for the economic problems of the 1920s, and assumed that its abandonment led to recovery in the 1930s. Further, the economic position of the two countries would be very different at the end of the war. America would be a creditor nation; Britain would be in debt with a massive deficit on its balance of payments. How could Britain pay for its imports and pay off its debts? The debate was over *how* the position of debtor and creditor countries should be adjusted. Should the burden fall mainly on the debtor country, with the possibility of deflation as after the First World War, or should the creditor nation also take action to reduce its surplus? At the very least, a period of transition was needed. The perceptions were strongly divergent, and it remained to be seen what balance could be struck.

In 1941, two solutions emerged: Keynes's British clearing union scheme and Harry Dexter White's American stabilization fund. These schemes formed the basis of the debate culminating in the Bretton Woods agreement in 1944. Both schemes accepted the existence of a liquidity problem and a problem of adjustment between deficit and surplus countries. There was also widespread agreement that the system of 'floating' exchange rates posed dangers. In the 1930s, competitive devaluations and speculative flows of money led to chaos and disruption. The two schemes reflected a common understanding of the economic problems of the inter-war period. They started from the aim of government co-operation to ease balance of payments adjustments at the end of the war, and to reconcile stability in the international monetary system with domestic prosperity. However, they soon diverged.

Keynes's clearing union was designed to avoid a repeat of the economic difficulties after the First World War. Keynes believed that the creditor nation should have some obligation to adjust its position; if it did not, the world economy might collapse, leading to deflation, default, protective duties, and bilateral agreements as well as political disorder. All transactions giving rise to surpluses or deficits should be settled through an International Clearing Bank, with only the net balance changing hands. If a country still remained in deficit after all balances had been settled, it could draw on an overdraft at the bank set by the value of trade before the war, so removing any immediate need for corrective action. Further, the bank would issue international currency ('bancor') which would be accepted by the creditor nation, so that some of the burden of adjustment was passed from the debtor to the creditor. Keynes also argued for a degree of flexibility in exchange rates: he wanted monetary stability without complete rigidity of fixed exchange rates. Exchange rates would be agreed between the union and its members, with provision for changes in the transitional period and the right to maintain exchange controls. The clearing union marked a step away from Keynes's earlier Schactianism. Unlike Henderson or Amery, his attitude to economic nationalism was pragmatic. He preferred an international response—on condition that the Americans could be made to behave as Britain was assumed to have acted in the nineteenth century, in maintaining liquidity and allowing settlements to be made between debtors and creditors. He believed that deficit countries should not be forced to deflate in order to meet their international obligations; and that national governments should be free to set their domestic interest rate in pursuit of full employment. He was sufficiently a realist to admit that the clearing union was utopian, and at Bretton Woods, Keynes surrendered Schachtianism without securing his scheme. The solution adopted was closer to the stabilization fund of White. Whereas the clearing union would increase the amount of funds available by means of 'bancor', the stabilization fund relied on the currencies of its members and made loans from capital contributed by them, so that it had a smaller sum for lending. The fund relied on adjustment by debtors with no obligation on the part of creditors, with more emphasis on the virtues of fixed exchange rates and the desirability of abolishing exchange controls.

The two plans offered very different routes to post-war reconstruction. The Americans thought that Keynes's scheme was inflationary and were puzzled by his idea of overdrafts and an international currency. The British thought that White's plan would lead to financial rigidity and deflation. The two views were fought out in 1944, first in a joint statement of principles and then in the Bretton Woods agreement. Perhaps 'agreement' is not the right word, for the positions were very different and the American view largely prevailed. Britain abandoned the clearing union, overdrafts, and 'bancor'; the Americans ceded a degree of flexibility in exchange rates. In addition, Britain could only negotiate for delays during an undefined transitional period. Nevertheless, the Bretton Woods system differed from the world economy of the late nineteenth and early twentieth centuries, for domestic stability had at least parity with international considerations.

The first article of the International Monetary Fund (IMF) committed it to 'the promotion and maintenance of high levels of employment and real income, and to the development of the productive resources of all members as primary objectives of economic policy'. The IMF would prevent competitive devaluations and financial crises, allowing members to draw on loans according to their contribution to the Fund's capital in order to meet a short-term deficit on their balance of payments. The Fund was obliged to accept a change of 10 per cent in exchange rates, but a larger devaluation of any currency was only permitted if the balance of payments was in 'fundamental disequilibrium'. Further, the Fund was not to object to devaluation on the grounds of its opposition to 'domestic social or political policies'. Britain secured the insertion of a transitional period: members only needed to consult the

Fund if they wished to continue restrictions beyond five years. The shortcomings of the gold standard were avoided by ensuring that countries could pursue domestic policies without being subordinated to the external balance. The dangers of floating exchanges in the 1930s were prevented by containing speculation and competitive devaluation. International monetary arrangements would be stabilized without sacrificing domestic welfare policies and economic management, and adjustments to balance of payments deficits would be gradual and incremental.[22]

The agreement was not a mere reflection of American hegemonic power; there was also intellectual convergence between British and American economists and officials over the need for workable monetary arrangements, designed to prevent the stalemate and mutual suspicion which undermined attempts to resolve economic difficulties between the wars. On both sides, the emergence of common norms and technical assumptions underpinned the belief that the post-war order should be managed and multilateral. A number of economists associated with the League of Nations turned attention away from issues of trade policy to a concern for the nature of recessions and their transmission. Rather than taking the existence of institutions for granted, they were now interested in the framework for international economic life and how it could be regulated. They did not assume that an increase in economic interdependence would reduce conflict; they realized that interdependence meant that nationalistic responses to recession could easily spread depression. Economists attached to the League hoped to instil more rational behaviour amongst governments, encouraging a shift from narrowly nationalistic responses to economic difficulties by showing how self-seeking behaviour could harm everyone, and limiting their narrow chauvinism by institutions designed to generate mutual trust in a complex, interdependent world. The attempt to create trust through joint action underpinned the United Nations and its Economic and Social Council. As Ikenberry remarks,

a transatlantic group of economists and policy specialists . . . led their governments toward agreement by identifying a set of common Anglo-American interests that were not clearly discernible to others. . . . at critical turning points, such as the end of a major war, uncertainties about power structures and unhappiness with past or current definitions of interests provide openings for rethinking. Moreover . . . elites are interested in building institutions that have a measure of legitimacy, and this reinforces the value of authoritative policy ideas.[23]

But would the agreement at Bretton Woods on the issues of monetary policy survive the political difficulties of post-war reconstruction; and could the agreement be extended to the more politicized issue of trade policy?

At the end of the war, Hull's commitment to free trade was by no means universal. In 1947, Jacob Viner remarked that 'There are few free traders in the present-day world . . . no person in authority anywhere advocates free trade.'[24] His provocative assertion could be rephrased: few economists or politicians believed that multilateralism and non-discrimination could be achieved without formal, international agreements to reimpose rules in the world economy. The point was realized by James Meade in 1942, when he argued that Keynes's clearing union would not be enough to restore prosperity to the world and to solve Britain's post-war economic problem. If Britain were to increase its exports after the war, the answer was 'the general removal of restrictions to international commerce' by increasing purchasing power in world markets, reducing trade barriers, and ending discrimination and bilateral deals. Nevertheless, he realized that balance of payments difficulties might oblige Britain to restrict payments to other countries. How to reduce trade barriers, without returning to destructive protectionism at the first sign of trouble? His solution was to complement the clearing union designed to deal with difficulties of payments with a commercial union to reduce restrictions on international commerce. Members of the commercial union would agree not to grant a preference to one member without offering it to all; and would reduce protective duties against other members. However, countries would be allowed to adopt protective measures if they were also members of the clearing union and their deficit reached a certain level. The agreement would be overseen by an International Commerce Commission.[25] Meade realized that free trade and multilateralism would not simply follow from the agreement on international monetary policy or from the ideological commitment of the American government: a formal agreement with internationally recognized and enforced rules was essential.

In 1945, the creation of an international trade organization on the lines of Meade's proposal formed the basis of the Anglo-American agreement on commercial policy and the United Nations' World Conference on Trade and Employment held at Havana in 1947 and 1948 which proposed an International Trade Organization. Meade welcomed the scheme. In his view, the ITO and IMF would re-create equilibrium in the world. Countries would still be able to use protection and controls in order to deal with balance of payments problems within an agreed system of rules and without returning to bilateralism. Deficit countries would have some freedom to restrict imports; countries with a surplus would not be allowed to restrict their purchases. Further, countries should stimulate domestic employment and external purchasing power in order to maintain worldwide demand.[26]

Meade's hopes were not realized, for the charter of the ITO was not ratified by the US Congress. The negotiation of the charter at Havana proved extremely tense, with a lack of consensus over the proposed rules. The developing countries formed a majority, and argued that they should be allowed to impose quantitative import restrictions to encourage new industries, allowing 'unequal treatment for unequally developed countries'.[27] In addition to this bold claim for preferential treatment, the developing countries refused to guarantee the security of foreign capital investments. The American delegation had to decide whether to meet the demands of the developing countries or of the industrial economies and above all Britain. The Americans opted to compromise with the developing countries. For their part, the British delegates insisted on the continuation of imperial preference and the right to use discrimination so long as balance of payments problems continued. They refused to capitulate to American threats that assistance would be denied, largely because the Americans wanted Britain to take part in a European recovery programme. The British government was able to exploit the conflict in American ambitions. The British were able to retain much of the system of imperial preference which was supported by many Labour politicians as well as by tariff reformers such as Amery. Despite the anti-imperial sentiments of the left, the empire and the sterling area appealed as an economic bloc to counterbalance American power, providing a non-dollar trading area which was crucial to Britain's balance of payments.[28] All that survived was the preliminary agreement of 1947—the General Agreement on Tariffs and Trade.

Unlike the ITO, the GATT did not have clear and formalized rules. Progress towards reducing tariffs and extending multilateralism was slow. The British government refused to end imperial preference unless the Americans agreed to reduce their own tariffs and increase access to the most prosperous market in the world. The GATT exempted all *existing* preferences and about 70 per cent of British preferences survived. American pressure for multilateralism was moderated by concern for the political stability of western Europe. What was the point in liberalizing world trade, only to disrupt the economies of Europe and encourage communism? In the liberal world economy prior to 1914, free traders assumed that their policies would benefit the domestic economy. The depression of the inter-war period destroyed such assumptions, and the attempt to return to a more liberal global economy meant that domestic stability was at least on a par with the restoration of multilateralism and free trade. Consequently, the GATT banned quantitative restrictions on trade while permitting their use in response to balance of payments difficulties—including deficits created by the pursuit of full employment.

The abortive negotiations over the ITO coincided with problems for the monetary arrangements at Bretton Woods. Keynes realized that the conditions laid down in 1944 were far too rigid. Indeed, Alan Milward argues that the Bretton Woods system collided with economic and political reality in 1947, when it was found 'to have solved nothing and to have practically no value or use as the basis of post-war reconstruction'. In the aftermath of the crisis, Milward locates 'a less comprehensive and a more painstaking and accurate construction of a system of international economic interdependence'.[29] Although Milward goes too far in marginalizing the importance of the agreement at Bretton Woods, he does have a point in claiming that grand institutional schemes were complemented by more flexible, piecemeal responses to the post-war difficulties of Britain and the rest of western Europe. Above all, the period of transition proved long and arduous. Although official par values for currencies were declared in December 1946, full convertibility of the major currencies was only achieved in 1958. During this period, American policy was forced to adapt to the political exigencies of Europe and was far from achieving hegemony.

At the end of the war, the US administration wished to recreate an open, multilateral global economy, without a continuing strategic commitment to Europe. The ambition failed, for European governments pressed for American military and economic assistance, and at the same time forced the US administration to accept a measure of support for welfare states, full employment, and economic stability, and to defend a social and economic system defined by the Europeans. The explanation was, in part, the desire of the State Department to secure hegemony by consent, seeking to legitimize American power and to strengthen its non-communist allies in Europe.

The British government faced an immediate, pressing problem: it had a serious trade deficit and, in common with the rest of western Europe, had a massive shortage of dollars. The bulk of British exports went to countries which could not pay in convertible currency, whereas imports came from countries demanding payment in gold or in convertible currencies. In the past, the deficit with the dollar economies was covered by the surplus earned by other members of the sterling area. After the war, the deficit in trade and the shortage of dollars posed very serious problems for the British government, which realized that it needed to increase exports by between 50 and 75 per cent. In the short term, more money was needed to deal with the shortfall, and the Cabinet accordingly approached the USA for a grant in 1945 and dispatched Keynes to Washington to negotiate. Keynes hoped that the Americans would accept the moral claims of Britain for reconsideration of the costs of the war to take account of its heroic efforts in standing alone against Hitler. He argued for a fair allocation of the costs of the war, which would allow Britain to recover and take part in the open world economy. Otherwise, the outcome might be bilateralism, or what he termed 'Starvation Corner'. Keynes also rejected a third option—the 'Temptation' of a loan to allow convertibility and multilateralism at once. In the event, Keynes's plea for justice was not accepted. Instead, he returned from Washington with a smaller loan than he felt was needed. The US administration insisted that the loan should require convertibility and non-discrimination. The respite offered by the American loan was short, for the result was a run on the pound in 1947 and the suspension of convertibility after a mere five weeks. By imposing an unrealistic condition, the Americans merely delayed its eventual adoption until 1958. After 1947, American policy towards Europe shifted from its earlier commitment to multilateralism and economic liberalism.

At the time, many senior American officials and politicians feared a collapse of the economies of western Europe. European capitalism seemed to be on its last legs. In 1947, the excess of dollar payments in the world amounted to $12,282 m, an imbalance which provoked serious concern. If the dollar shortage was temporary, it would be cured as recovery took its course and the immediate shortfall could be met by a reduction in spending and perhaps a grant or loan from the United States. On the other hand, if the shortage was chronic and permanent, European governments might develop their industries behind tariff walls or impose quota restrictions. The result would be a serious threat to the American ambition of creating an open world economy. Many commentators and politicians feared that the dollar deficit was long term and structural. In fact, it was temporary: by 1950, the dollar deficit was down to $2,453 m and was virtually removed in the early 1950s. But in 1947, optimism seemed misplaced. Above all, General George Marshall urged America to offer aid to Europe. The outcome was the European Recovery Programme or Marshall aid, administered by the Committee of European Economic Co-operation.[30] Whether the injection of dollars into the economies of western Europe really did rescue them may be doubted, for output and foreign trade were already growing, and the fear of imminent collapse was greatly exaggerated. What the ERP did entail was a shift in American policy to allow governments in western Europe, including Britain, to continue with policies to encourage domestic growth. Domestic stability within Europe was essential for American strategic ambitions in countering the threat of communism. In 1947, the Bretton Woods system collided with domestic programmes of growth and full employment, with the result that European governments continued to pursue growth even at the expense of economic liberalism and internationalism.

The American administration came to the belief that recovery could be achieved by creating a single economic area or customs union in western Europe. Hence European reconstruction rested on the encouragement of trade between European countries and protection or discrimination against America and the dollar zone. The exact structure of the European trading system or customs union was a matter of considerable dispute between France and Britain, and with the United States. The French wished to create a customs union, as a step towards a strong political force in western Europe. The British government was more dubious, fearing that the customs union would undermine 'economic sovereignty', offer a limited, protectionist market, and threaten the sterling area and the policy of discrimination in favour of the empire. Accordingly, the British government wished to reduce trade barriers through a European Trade Liberalization Programme without discriminating against the rest of the world through a customs union, and at the same time to retain links with America and the Commonwealth. These disputes over the European Recovery Programme meant that growth was less the result of joint action and co-operation than 'separate, often conflicting, national reconstruction policies'.[31] Only when recovery started did co-operation between the European economies become possible, above all through the European Payments Union of 1950. The members of the EPU agreed to clear their debits and balances at the end of each month, so reducing Europe's need for dollars and removing some of the constraints of the Bretton Woods system. The creation of the EPU reflected the realization that co-operation would not contradict the pursuit of domestic economic policies. Further, the US government abandoned its ambition of moving from monetary to political union within Erope. The Americans were initially hostile to the sterling area and wished Britain to become part of an integrated European economy, but came to realize that Britain would neither abandon the sterling area nor subsume itself into Europe. The Americans therefore opted to encourage interdependence between the sterling area, the dollar zone, and Europe. At the same time, the French took the lead within Europe, abandoning the wider customs union for a narrower common market. The outcome was a far cry from the American ambitions at Bretton Woods and Havana.

The British government retained imperial preference and high levels of tariffs (see Table 9.2). Further, the government turned to quantitative import controls. The scale of the activity was impressive, with the Import Licensing Department of the Board of Trade issuing 250,000 licences in 1948 alone. Import restrictions offered a high level of protection: according to Milward and Brennan, 6.7 per cent of British manufacturing output in 1954 would be lost if controls were not in place against imports from the United States, and 16.5 per cent if all controls were removed.[32] The government relied on quotas in addition to tariffs, for they could be introduced by direct executive action, without the approval of parliament or the need for debate with important interest groups. The emergence of detailed statistics and administrative mechanisms during the war meant that quotas could be used much more effectively than in the past, with many civil servants confident of their ability to control the economy. Despite the sympathy of many officials for multilateralism, concern about the post-war trading position meant that they

TABLE 9.2. *Tariff rates in the UK: ratio of duties to total imports, 1979–80*

1929	9.7	1950	31.2
1935	24.5	1970	34.3
1938	24.1	1980	12.7
1945	38.2		

Source: Broadberry, *Productivity Race*, 140.

were reluctant to dismantle import controls. As far as many Labour politicians were concerned, import controls complemented their general support for planning and direct controls over the economy. This is not to say that the government had a coherent plan: its approach was piecemeal, reflecting general assumptions rather than carefully considered control over the economy. Import controls might protect the home market as a secure basis for exports; they could assist infant and high-technology industries; and they could support old, uncompetitive industries in the depressed regions. Above all, import quotas were central to attempts to reduce the dollar deficit after 1947, when attention shifted from the post-war programme of encouraging exports to reductions in the demand for imports through austerity and direct controls.

The balance of payments problem arose in large part from the level of government spending abroad, and investments in the empire. Attlee was anxious to reduce overseas spending, but was limited by strategic considerations and the need to retain American support through a commitment to fight communism. And investment in the empire was necessary to maintain the sterling area which was vital to trade.[33] In addition to tariffs and import controls, the balance of trade deficit was adjusted by a major devaluation of the pound in 1949 by 30.5 per cent to $2.80. At the end of the war, economists were divided on the need for devaluation. Although Keynes argued that the dollar was overvalued in terms of purchasing power parity, many economists felt that devaluation was less important than a change in the pattern of trade away from sterling to dollar markets. In any case, direct controls might be more effective than devaluation in holding imports down. By 1949, financial markets were expressing growing scepticism. First, there was a wide gap between the official and black market rates of sterling. Secondly, financiers assumed that the exchange rate was sustained by import and exchange controls; if the rate were allowed to fall, controls could be removed and the balance of payments problem solved.

The balance of payments on current account returned to deficit in 1949 and officials started to accept the case for devaluation. Robert Hall of the Cabinet Office's Economic Section argued that the government's decision to rule out deflation meant that devaluation became the obvious solution. Further, the Americans believed that Marshall aid could be reduced by adjusting European exchange rates and making exports more competitive. American pressure led to an IMF inquiry, which virtually called on Britain to devalue and so led to speculation against the pound. The Chancellor of the Exchequer (Stafford Cripps) considered four possible responses: to raise interest rates; to improve competitiveness through higher productivity; to impose severe deflation on the British economy; or to devalue. The first was rejected, for the government remained committed to 'cheap money' as a means of limiting the burden of debt and encouraging wage restraint. Deflation was politically difficult; and devaluation was ruled out unless it was part of a wider solution to the dollar shortage. Consequently, he continued with the policy of improving competitiveness, supplemented by a tougher stance on wages and limits on government spending. The balance of opinion swung in favour of devaluation when Cripps was absent and his successor, Hugh Gaitskell, was convinced of the need to devalue.[34]

Once devaluation was accepted, the government needed to decide on what measures should accompany it. Cripps feared that his advisers were more sympathetic to the American 'free economy' than to the ambitions of the government, and Attlee was adamant that there should be no return to 'nineteenth century economics' by which external constraints determined domestic policies. Officials were suspicious that the government was adopting an easy option of devaluation instead of deflation and cuts in government expenditure. By the end of 1949, the gold and dollar deficit had virtually ceased. Britain's trade deficit with the dollar area rose from £301 m in 1946 to £510 m in 1947, and then fell to £88 m in 1950. By 1951, the debate over devaluation gave way to discussion of possible revaluation of the pound and the possible return to convertibility. The balance of payments seemed healthy (see Table 9.3).[35]

American ambitions for restoring a liberal world economy were still unrealized in 1951. Indeed, the outcome was closer to the prognosis of Henderson than the ambitions of Keynes. Britain had high tariffs, extensive import controls, and imperial preference; the pound was still not convertible. The period of transition had yet to end. External controls on competition were complemented by internal regulations, through rationing, price controls, nationalization, and licensing of buildings and investment. The post-war Labour government did not, as some historians have suggested, readily adopt an American approach to liberalization of trade.[36] Instead, it faced a paradox: a commitment to international economic planning (and a partial loss of national sovereignty) was in tension with national planning of the British economy. Was it possible to abandon economic nationalism and plan the national

TABLE 9.3. *Balance of payments on current account, UK, 1946–51 (£m)*

	Exports and re-exports	Imports	Visible balance	Invisible balance	Current account balance
1946	960	1,063	−103	−127	−230
1948	1,639	1,790	−151	+177	+26
1951	2,735	3,424	−689	+320	−369

Source: Mitchell and Jones, *Second Abstract of British Historical Statistics*, 142.

economy in all its aspects? As Richard Toye points out, Labour suffered from a 'planning paradox' which it did not resolve. It tried to steer a middle way between free trade and protectionism, on the lines explained by Dalton: 'Free Trade, in the old sense, is a denial of planning; tariffs in the old sense, are a caricature of planning.' He developed the point in 1941, remarking that the days of both individualist free trade and individualist tariffs had passed; what was needed was agreements between countries. A Labour party memorandum in 1942 spelled out the planning paradox created by such a policy: the state must maintain its own national control of production and prices; and at the same time 'must yield some of its attributes of economic sovereignty to an international authority which must have the power to plan and control production and distribution'. Not surprisingly, a leading Treasury official commented that Labour's attempt to combine trade liberalization abroad with planning at home led into a 'theological maze'. Usually, planning won out over liberalization. Although Labour's policy statement on *Full Employment and Financial Policy* of 1944 argued for a reduction of tariffs, this commitment to a liberal commercial policy

emphatically does not mean that there should be any return to *laissez-faire* or 'free trade' in the capitalist sense. Socialists believe in the planning of imports and exports and the present apparatus of control...should remain in existence. War time arrangements for bulk purchases...of food stuffs and raw materials, should continue. State trading...brings great benefit to the peoples. We must not let this Socialist advance be halted or turned back.

By contrast with Labour's emphasis on planning at both the national and international level, the American approach to multilateralism rested on free enterprise and the rule of the market. As Attlee remarked, 'In certain specific points...we find the United States in agreement with us, but, generally, they hold a capitalist philosophy which we do not accept.' Any failure of the Attlee government to plan the domestic economy cannot be explained by its surrender to American international objectives of a liberal international economic order; on the contrary, the government managed to avoid implementing the promises it had given to the Americans in return for assistance. The failure of planning is to be explained by domestic considerations of ideological confusion and political pragmatism rather than external constraints (see Chapter 17).[37]

The eventual restoration of freedom to markets only really started from the late 1950s with the introduction of convertibility and the start of trade liberalization. Nevertheless, the arguments at Bretton Woods and Havana were more than pious hopes. The direction of change was established and the normative assumptions of the international economic order were very different from the 1930s.

NOTES

1. Quoted in van Dormael, *Bretton Woods*, 1.
2. The classic statements on 'hegemonic stability' are Kindleberger, *World in Depression*; Gilpin, *War and Change in World Politics*.
3. League of Nations, *International Currency Experience*, 230.
4. Polanyi, *Origins of our Time*, ch. 2, 19–21.
5. Ruggie, 'International regimes', 393.
6. Obstfeld and Taylor, 'The great depression as a watershed'; Obstfeld and Taylor, 'Globalisation and capital markets'; Obstfeld and Taylor, and *Global Capital Markets*, 29.
7. Helleiner, *States and the Re-emergence of Global Finance*, 37; Dormael, *Birth*, 10.
8. Helleiner, *States and the Re-emergence of Global Finance*, ch. 2 Obstfeld and Taylor, 'Globalization and capital markets'.
9. Quoted in van Dormael, *Bretton Woods*, 25.
10. Quoted in Skidelsky, *Fighting for Britain*, 179.
11. Quoted in van Dormael, *Bretton Woods*, 24.
12. 'The post-war international settlement and the United Kingdom balance of payments', Dec. 1943, in *The Collected Papers of James Made*, ed. Howson, iii. 52.
13. Robbins, *Economic Planning*, 232–7; *Economic Consequences of the War*, 80–5, 88–94, 99.
14. Quoted in Skidelsky, *Fighting for Britain*, 213, 220.
15. Quoted ibid. 210.
16. Henderson, 'International economic history of the interwar period', 290, 291, 294.
17. Quoted in Skidelsky, *Fighting for Britain*, 200.
18. Quoted ibid. 210.
19. Keynes, 'Proposals for an International Currency Union', *CW* xxv. 21–2, 27.
20. Quoted in Skidelsky, *Fighting for Britain*, 202.
21. Gardner, *Sterling–Dollar Diplomacy*, 59.
22. James, *International Monetary Co-operation since Bretton Woods*, 50–1. For the debates leading to Bretton Woods, see Skidelsky, *Fighting for Britain*, Part II.
23. Ikenberry, 'A world economy restored', 293–4.
24. Quoted in Ruggie, 'International regimes', 396.
25. 'A proposal for an International Commercial Union', 25 July 1942, in *The Collected Papers of James Meade*, ed. Howson, iii. 52.
26. 'Bretton Woods, Havana and the United Kingdom balance of payments', ibid. 81–94.
27. Quoted in Toye, 'Developing multilateralism', 291.
28. Toye, ibid. and 'The Attlee government, the imperial preference system, and the creation of GATT'; Tomlinson, *Democratic Socialism and Economic Policy*, 28, 32.
29. Milward, *Reconstruction, 1945–51*, 464.
30. Cairncross, *Years of Recovery*, 70; Milward, *Reconstruction*, chs. 1–2.
31. Milward, *Reconstruction*, 470; Tomlinson, *Democratic Socialism and Economic Policy*, 32–4.
32. Milward and Brennan, *Britain's Place in the World*, 1, 6.
33. Tomlinson, *Democratic Socialism and Economic Policy*, 64–7.
34. Cairncross, *Years of Recovery*, 176, 196.
35. Ibid. 189, 201.

36. For example, as argued by Booth, 'How long are light years in British politics?', 24.
37. Toye, *The Labour Party and the Planned Economy*, 161, 162, 170–1, 177–84.

FURTHER READING

Booth, A., 'How long are light years in British politics? The Labour Party's economic ideas in the 1930s', *Twentieth Century British History*, 7 (1996)

Bordo, M. D., 'The Bretton Woods international monetary system: a historical overview', in M. D. Bordo and B. Eichengreen (eds.), *A Retrospective on the Bretton Woods System: Lessons for International Monetary Reform* (Chicago, 1993)

Broadberry, S. N., *The Productivity Race: British Manufacturing in International Perspective, 1850–1990* (Cambridge, 1990)

Cairncross, A., *Years of Recovery: British Economic Policy 1945–51* (1985)

—— and Eichengreen, B., *Sterling in Decline: The Devaluations of 1931, 1949 and 1967* (Oxford, 1983)

De Marchi, N., 'League of Nations economists and the ideal of peaceful change in the decade of the 1930s', in C. D. Goodwin (ed.), *Economics and National Security: A History of their Interaction*, Annual Supplement to Volume 23, *History of Political Economy* (Durham, NC, 1991)

Eichengreen, B., 'Keynes and protection', *Journal of Economic History*, 44 (1984)

Gardner, R. N., *Sterling–Dollar Diplomacy: Anglo-American Collaboration in the Reconstruction of Multilateral Trade* (Oxford, 1956)

Gilpin, R., *War and Change in World Politics* (Cambridge, 1981)

Helleiner, E., *States and the Re-emergence of Global Finance: From Bretton Woods to the 1990s* (Ithaca, NY, 1994)

Henderson, H. D., 'International economic history of the interwar period', in H. D. Henderson, *The Interwar Years and Other Papers: A Selection from the Writings of Hubert Douglas Henderson* (Oxford, 1955)

Horsefield, J. K., *The International Monetary Fund, 1945–1965*, i: *Chronicle* (Washington, 1969)

Howe, A., *Free Trade and Liberal England, 1846–1946* (Oxford, 1997)

Ikenberry, G. J., 'Rethinking the origins of American hegemony', *Political Science Quarterly*, 104 (1989)

—— 'A world economy restored: expert consensus and the Anglo-American postwar settlement', *International Organisation*, 46 (1992)

—— 'The political origins of Bretton Woods', in M. D. Bordo and B. Eichengreen (eds.), *A Retrospective on the Bretton Woods System* (Chicago, 1993)

James, H., *International Monetary Co-operation since Bretton Woods* (Washington, 1996)

Keynes, J. M., *The Collected Writings of John Maynad Keynes*, xxv: *Activities 1940–44: Shaping the Post-war World: The Clearing Union*, ed. D. Moggridge (1980)

Kindleberger, C. P., *World in Depression, 1929–1939* (2nd edn., Harmondsworth, 1987)

League of Nations, *International Currency Experience: Lessons of the Inter-War Period* (Geneva, 1944)

Meade, J., *The Collected Papers of James Meade*, iii: *International Economics*, ed. S. Howson (London, 1988)

Milward, A. S., *The Reconstruction of Western Europe, 1945–51* (1984)

—— and Brennan, G., *Britain's Place in the World: A Historical Enquiry into Import Controls* (1996)

Obstfeld, M., and Taylor, A. M., 'The great depression as a watershed: international capital mobility over the long run', in M. D. Bordo, C. Goldin, and E. N. White (eds.), *The Defining Moment: The American Economy in the Twentieth Century* (Chicago, 1997)

—— —— 'Globalization and capital markets', in M. D. Bordo, A. M. Taylor, and J. G. Williamson (eds.), *Globalization in Historical Perspective* (Chicago, 2003)

—— —— *Global Capital Markets: Integration, Crisis and Growth* (Cambridge, 2004)

Polanyi, K., *The Origins of our Time: The Great Transformation* (1945)

Robbins, L., *Economic Consequences of the War* (1939)

—— *Economic Planning and the International Order* (1937)

Ruggie, J. G., 'International regimes, transactions, and change: embedded liberalism in the postwar economic order', *International Organization*, 36 (1982)

Skidelsky, R., *John Maynard Keynes: Fighting for Britain, 1937–1946* (2000)

Tomlinson, J., *Democratic Socialism and Economic Policy: The Attlee Years, 1945–1951* (Cambridge, 1997)

Toye, R., 'Developing multilateralism: the Havana charter and the fight for the International Trade Organization, 1947–48', *International History Review*, 25 (2003)

—— 'The Attlee government, the imperial preference system, and the creation of GATT', *English Historical Review*, 118 (2003)

—— *The Labour Party and the Planned Economy, 1931–1951* (Woodbridge, 2003)

Van Dormael, A., *Bretton Woods: Birth of a Monetary System* (1978)

PART III

POVERTY, PROSPERITY, AND POPULATION

....

CHAPTER 10

Births and Marriages

When Malthus published his *Essay on Population* in 1797, fears of over-population and demographic disaster were causing alarm. By the 1830s, concern had receded: the people had not slumped into complete misery, and agriculture could sustain a much larger population without famine. Nevertheless, trade unionists still saw a solution to low wages in the encouragement of emigration, helping to reduce competition for jobs and increase their bargaining position.[1] The Malthusian League, created in 1877, offered another approach: the encouragement of birth control. These neo-Malthusians insisted that no other solution to poverty was possible or desirable.[2] Nevertheless, by the 1870s, fears of overpopulation seemed exaggerated—an increase in the population might be a blessing rather than a curse, a means of increasing demand and production.

Population Fears and Declining Birth Rates

At the end of the period, the problem seemed very different from Malthus' dire warnings. In the 1930s, demographers feared that a stationary or even declining population would reduce welfare. In 1895, few took notice of Edwin Cannan's warning that the continuation of demographic trends would lead to a decline in the growth of the population of England and Wales, until it became 'trifling' by 1941–51 and ceased entirely by 1995 when the population was expected to reach a peak of 37.4 million. A greater cause of concern was the differential drop of the birth rate between classes and the possible 'degeneration' of the population as the children of the poor came to dominate the racial stock. Between the wars, Cannan's prophecy seemed close to realization. When he returned to the issue in 1931, he pointed out that a stationary population would lead to a shift in production and consumption away from basic necessities and 'heavy industries' to 'lighter' industries. Although Cannan hesitated to say whether the stationary population was desirable, most commentators expressed deep concern. As the birth rate fell, so more books were published with alarmist titles warning of race suicide and the twilight of parenthood.[3]

When Keynes reflected on the slowing down in the growth of Britain's population, he suggested that a rising population had been an important element in the growth of Britain's economy in the nineteenth century. A declining population had the opposite effect, for demand was lower than expected and any oversupply was less easily corrected. Keynes feared that 'we have another devil at our elbow at least as fierce as the Malthusian—namely the devil of unemployment escaping through the breakdown of effective demand'. Keynes's economic policies of deficit finance were, therefore, based on the assumption that a strategy was needed to mop up surplus capacity. The alternative was to stimulate population growth. Such thinking offered support for family allowances and for post-war welfare reforms. The Labour party's programme of 1945, *Let Us Face the Future*, was pro-natalist and this concern informed the government's policies on housing and new towns.[4]

In reality, the fears of population decline were misplaced for the predictions rested on a faulty statistical analysis, and the post-war 'baby boom' took the population of England and Wales well above 37 million.[5] The population scare of the 1930s was greatly exaggerated, but it does highlight a very striking change since the Great Exhibition. The birth rate continued to rise until 1876, when a decline started on both sides of the border. By the Second World War, the birth rate per 1,000 women aged 15–44 had fallen to 40 per cent of the level of 1876 in England and Wales, and to 48 per cent in Scotland (see Table 10.1). A more accurate measure is the total fertility rate, that is the number of children a woman might expect to have on passing through the reproductive years 20–49. This reached a peak of 7.67 in

TABLE 10.1. *Birth rates per 1,000 population and women aged 15–44, England and Wales and Scotland, 1851–1938*

	England and Wales		Scotland	
	Women 15–44	Population	Women 15–44	Population
1851	34.3	145.0	—	—
1861	34.6	147.4	34.9	145.2
1871	35.0	152.1	34.5	148.6
1876	36.3	156.7	35.6	153.9
1881	33.9	147.6	33.7	146.4
1891	31.4	132.6	31.2	134.4
1901	28.5	114.5	29.5	122.1
1911	24.3	98.0	25.6	106.6
1921	22.4	89.7	25.2	103.7
1931	15.8	64.4	19.0	79.8
1938	15.1	62.4	17.7	74.0

Source: Mitchell and Deane, *Abstract*, ch. 1, table 10.

TABLE 10.2. *Age-specific fertility rates for England and Wales and total marital fertility rate for 20–49, 1800–1933*

Maternal age group	1800–24	1851	1871	1891	1911	1922	1933
20–4	0.425	0.426	0.428	0.418	0.402	0.365	0.275
25–9	0.381	0.367	0.367	0.345	0.294	0.247	0.178
30–4	0.311	0.306	0.308	0.271	0.206	0.163	0.108
35–9	0.255	0.249	0.249	0.208	0.135	0.098	0.059
40–4	0.142	0.120	0.120	0.096	0.053	0.033	0.020
45–9	0.019	0.018	0.018	0.012	0.006	0.004	0.002
Total marital fertility rate	7.67	7.43	7.45	6.75	5.48	4.55	3.21

Source: Woods, *Demography*, table 4.2, 130. The table shows the number of children born per annum to women in each age group, and the total born over the entire period age 20 to 49.

England and Wales in the early nineteenth century, then plummeted from the 1870s (see Table 10.2). Family sizes of women marrying in the 1870s were widely dispersed with no size containing more than 10 per cent of the population: 17.7 per cent of women had ten or more children, 12.5 per cent one or two, and 8.3 per cent none. The figures for women marrying in 1925 were respectively 0.6 per cent, 50.6 per cent and 16.1 per cent.[6]

Nuptuality

In Malthus' model, the key to population growth was the age and rate of marriage which influenced the number of births. The mean age of first marriage for women fell slightly, from 25.8 years in England and Wales in 1851 to 25.2 in 1871, and from 26.0 in Scotland in 1851 to 25.6 in 1881. Subsequently, the mean age of marriage for single women rose to 26.3 in England and Wales in 1911 and 26.6 in Scotland. Similarly, the proportion of females aged 20 to 24 who were currently married rose from 30.8 per cent in England and Wales in 1851 to 34.3 per cent in 1871, before falling back to 24.2 per cent in 1911.[7] These relatively modest changes could not explain the bulk of the drop in birth rates; the explanation must be found within marriage.

Although nuptuality was no longer the major determinant of fertility, marriage patterns still had a significant impact on society, and they were very different from experience at the end of the period. After the Second World War, marriages were tightly bunched around an expected age and experience was homogeneous: 80 per cent of marriages of women took place in a period of eight years between the ages of 17 and 25. Before the First World War, marriages were more dispersed.

TABLE 10.3. *Source of livelihood of spinsters, Britain, 1851 (%)*

	25–34	65–74
Active	64	27
Active including trade relatives	77	34
Living off property	1	17
State or charity	3	34
Retired	0	5
Other	17	11

Source: Anderson, 'Social position of spinsters', 380.

In 1851, 80 per cent of marriages of women were spread over about twenty years, and in 1911 over seventeen years. Indeed, many women never married: in 1911, 15.8 per cent of women aged 45–54 in England and Wales and 20.8 per cent in Scotland were single.[8] In the second half of the nineteenth century, much concern was expressed about the plight of spinsters. In 1851, there were 1.04 million unmarried women in Britain aged 25 and above, and a further 750,000 widows—in all, 8.9 per cent of the population. Most younger spinsters worked, or lived in craft, farming, or trading households where they made a contribution to the business. Many others lacked a recorded occupation and lived at home, which might involve a life of leisure or good works in prosperous families, though even here many unmarried daughters kept house for a father or nursed ailing parents. Most widows and spinsters under 55 supported themselves, and faced problems as they aged. A fortunate minority were supported by trusts or annuities provided by their fathers or husbands; the rest were forced to rely on the poor law and charity (see Table 10.3).[9]

Marriage varied by region, class, and occupation. Female nuptuality was low in south-west Wales, the northern Pennines, and in many towns in southern England. It was high in the coalfields, parts of East Anglia, and the east midlands. Generally, more urbanized places had higher, and low-density rural areas lower, rates of marriage. The pattern was affected by migration which disrupted the balance between single men and women: young men moved to urban-industrial centres such as the south Wales coalfield, and women to urban service sectors such as the suburbs of London. A high proportion of women in domestic service reduced the rate of marriage—but so did a high proportion of women employed in *any* wage labour, most obviously in the textile towns with their opportunities for retaining independence. In agriculture, 'service in husbandry' in the west and north led to delayed marriage compared with areas based on day labour (see Atcham and Mitford respectively in Table 10.4). Similar variations were found in industrial occupations. Nuptuality

TABLE 10.4. *Percentage of men and women ever married by age 30, selected districts, 1861*

	Males	Females
Sheffield with Eccleshall-Bierlow	83	85
Mitford	75	81
Bakewell	65	72
Pateley Bridge	62	72
Keighley	75	69
Atcham	54	65

Source: Woods and Hinde, 'Nuptuality and age at marriage', 125.

was high in areas based on mining and heavy industry such as Sheffield, where there were few jobs for women and men achieved relatively well-paid jobs in their early twenties. Nuptuality was low in textile districts where women had paid work and the men waited longer to receive a full adult wage rate (Pateley Bridge and Keighley). The differences between occupations are clear in a survey of 1884/5 which indicated that the mean age of first marriage of the wives of miners was 22.5 years, and of textile workers 23.4 years. The age of marriage was considerably higher in the professional middle class, with the social expectation that the husband should be well established before contemplating marriage, and that the newly married couple should set up home at the same standard as their parents. The mean age of first marriage in the professional middle class in 1884/5 was 31.2 years for men and 26.4 years for their wives; for clerks, the mean age was 26.3 for men and 24.4 for their wives (Table 10.5). A shift from service in husbandry to wage labour involving 20 per cent of the agricultural workforce in 1861 would increase the potential marital fertility in agricultural areas by 6 per cent and by 4.5 per cent in England and Wales. Similarly, a shift of 4 per cent of adult women out of domestic service would increase potential marital fertility by over 7 per cent. Until fertility was more easily regulated within marriage, nuptuality remained under strict social control and an older demographic system based upon nuptuality continued to coexist alongside a newer system based upon control of marital fertility, at least to 1914 and possibly into the inter-war period.[10]

Marriages were most often terminated by death and many women and men were left to bring up children as 'single parents'. Childbirth was hazardous, so that men often found themselves left with young children. At least they had the possibility of earning a decent wage; widows with families were often reduced to penury. By contrast, divorce was rare. Until 1857, it required a private Act of parliament, and was largely confined to notorious cases. Although the terms for divorce were relaxed

TABLE 10.5. *Mean age at first marriage for selected occupations, England and Wales, 1884–5*

Husband's occupation	Bachelors	Spinsters
Miner	24.06	22.46
Textile hand	24.36	23.43
Shoemaker, tailor	24.92	24.31
Artisan	25.35	23.70
Labourer	25.56	23.66
Commercial clerk	26.25	24.43
Shopkeeper, shopman	26.67	24.22
Farmer or farmer's son	29.23	28.91
Professional or independent class	31.22	26.40

Ogle, 'On marriage-rate and marriage-age, cited in Woods, *Demography*, 86.

in 1937, divorce remained costly, unusual, and shameful. In 1911, there were 859 petitions for divorce in England or 0.2 per cent of marriages. By 1937, the number had risen to 5,750 and in 1950 to 29,096 or 7.1 per cent of marriages. The divorce rate in Britain was one of the lowest in Europe, but legal separation was one of the highest. From the 1840s, the principle of private separation contracts was accepted in the civil courts, allowing financial terms to be enforced. Furthermore, the Divorce Act of 1857 allowed wives to obtain a magistrate's order to protect their property. These rights laid the basis for the Matrimonial Causes Act 1878, which allowed magistrates to grant women a separation order for cruelty, with housing and child custody. The rights of women were extended again in 1886, when magistrates could order maintenance to deserted wives, and in 1895 they could grant separation, maintenance, or custody if the husband was guilty of assault, wrongful desertion, or if his cruelty and neglect led his wife to leave. Private separation contracts, out of court settlements, and these various orders meant that failed marriages could be dealt with short of divorce.[11]

The age of marriage and ability to escape a miserable marriage were both important personal and cultural factors, but they were not the major determinants of the birth rate in this period. Age at marriage can only explain part of the divergence even between the number of children born to the wives of cotton textile workers and coal hewers. In 1911, the average number of births for wives aged under 45 was 2.32 in cotton and 3.68 in coal; when the fertility rate is standardized at the same age of marriage, the wives of cotton textile workers still had only 2.42 children compared with 3.56 for the wives of hewers.[12] Clearly, marital fertility varied independently of the age of marriage, and something was happening *within* marriage.

Explaining the Fertility Decline: Birth Control versus Sexual Abstinence

What exactly changed within marriage? There are two possibilities: *stopping* after the desired number of births so that conceptions ceased well before the onset of menopause; and *spacing* births over the entire period from marriage to menopause. Unless couples opted for celibacy, stopping probably involved the use of artificial methods of birth control. Spacing was less likely to require such methods, and more likely to involve traditional methods. At times of economic hardship, couples appear to have used coitus interruptus or simply reduced the frequency of sexual inter-course—both methods relying on male self-control.[13] Spacing suggests continuities with these past techniques in the different circumstances of rising prosperity in the last quarter of the nineteenth century. The high age of marriage in England created a culture of sexual abstinence *before* marriage that could be extended into marriage. Stopping would suggest much greater discontinuity, with the emergence of a different pattern of behaviour from 'natural' fertility in earlier generations where births were spread over the entire period from marriage to menopause. Which method, or what combination of methods, explains the fall in the birth rate in Britain?

Many historians have assumed that the key to the drop in the birth rate was better information on contraception and the adoption of stopping. On this view, the desire to control births was self-evident and only needed better information to become effective. Knowledge of birth control thus becomes the prime mover. Accordingly, historians have charted the growth of publications on birth control, starting with Francis Place's *Illustrations and Proofs of the Principle of Population* of 1822. But the key event for these historians was the notorious trial of Charles Bradlaugh and Annie Besant in 1877 for publishing Charles Knowlton's *Fruits of Philosophy*. Knowlton's pamphlet was first published in New York in 1832 and sold about 42,000 copies in Britain by 1876. When a Bristol publisher was sentenced to hard labour for reissuing it, Bradlaugh and Besant decided to raise a test case by informing the police of their intention to print the pamphlet. They were arrested, taken to court, and cleared. Sales surged. The Malthusian League was one outcome, with its highly conservative approach to birth control as a solution to economic problems. Other publications followed including Besant's own *The Law of Population* of 1879 which advised on coitus interruptus, the douche, condom, and, above all, the vaginal sponge; it sold 175,000 copies in twelve years.[14]

More information was available, but it is quite another matter to suggest that it was followed or that it caused the decline in fertility. Couples might read the pamphlets as a result of a pre-existing wish to reduce births, and much of the information was unhelpful. At most, the pamphlets expressed a willingness to consider the possibility of reducing births. However, there is little direct evidence that couples used 'artificial' techniques. When the Royal Commission on Population of 1944–9 asked women about their use of birth control, it found that only 2 per cent of the marriage cohort of 1900–9 employed appliance methods at *any* time; 13 per cent used non-appliance methods; 85 per cent claimed not to use contraception at all; and 30 per cent to be ignorant. The low level of use of appliance methods is entirely plausible, for condoms were expensive. Furthermore, they needed to be soaked or heated to be used. Similarly, the douche and vaginal sponge assumed facilities unavailable in crowded houses. More surprising is the finding that only 15 per cent of women in 1900–9 acknowledged *any* birth control which is scarcely plausible in view of the drop in the birth rate.[15] Some historians claim that abortion was common, but it cannot account for more than a small proportion of the 'missing' births. Abortion was both illegal and dangerous and even the highest contemporary estimate of abortions—16–20 per cent of current births—could only account for 10–15 per cent of the overall decline in live births.[16] The 'missing' births are more easily explained by the fact that 'attempted abstinence' was not considered as birth control, although it could lead to considerable spacing of births. Indeed, wives might well be unaware that their husbands were restricting their sexual advances below what they felt desirable, so that birth control meant masculine self-control and denial rather than the use of appliances. This suspicion is confirmed by evidence in a survey of middle-class women in 1914: 52 per cent of those claiming to control births did mention abstinence.[17]

The case for 'stopping' comes from the age of women at the birth of their last child. In the eighteenth century and the first half of the nineteenth century, the median age of women at the birth of their last child was 39. The age started to drop in the later nineteenth century. Women born in 1861 had their last child at a median age of 36; and women born in 1891 at a median age of 32.[18] This drop might be produced by a conscious decision to 'cluster' births in the early years of marriage, stopping as soon as the desired family size was reached by using reasonably effective methods of contraception. However, it is doubtful that such a strategy was feasible in the later nineteenth century. In the absence of reliable contraception, any decision to reach the desired family size within the first few years of marriage was extremely risky, for the chances of further conceptions up to the end of the wife's fertile years were high. Couples were also more likely to concentrate births in a few years if they were confident of the survival of children to adulthood, which was still not the case. In the absence of reliable methods of birth control and high levels of infant mortality until the early twentieth century, spacing over the entire fertile period of marriage might be more achievable. Hence the initial fall in the median age of mothers at the birth of their last child might be a secular phenomenon, reflecting a decline in the likelihood of conceiving at older ages with a fall in the level of sexual activity. In other words, 'stopping' could be a side-effect of spacing.[19]

One test of spacing is provided by data in the 1911 census of fertility for couples in the first five or ten years of their marriage. If couples relied on stopping once they achieved their preferred family size, there would be little difference in the fertility of occupations with high and low completed family sizes during this initial period of marriage. The gap would appear in the next period, when those couples opting for a small family 'stopped' and other couples continued to have children. In fact, couples in occupations with a low completed family size showed a wide divergence from other trades in the first 5–10 years of marriage, and must therefore have spaced births from early in their marriage. Furthermore, occupations where later marriage was the norm were characterized by careful regulation of fertility *after* marriage. Such a pattern indicates there was no clear divide between an earlier period (when nuptuality was the key variable) and a later period (when contraception within marriage took pride of place). The protracted process of decline in fertility involved both factors, which were adopted by the same occupational group and rested on similar cultural assumptions. A delay in marriage meant sexual abstinence: sexual self-denial was a cultural norm. The close relationship between delayed marriage and spacing suggests that 'attempted abstinence' may have been the principal means of limiting fertility. In 1914, Major Greenwood, professor of epidemiology and vital statistics at the London School of Hygiene and Tropical Medicine, remarked that the statistics on birth rate and control reflected an 'abnormal sexual life'. Simon Szreter concurs: the decline in the birth rate was achieved by 'a syndrome of self-imposed male frigidity or even impotence'.[20]

Spacing was certainly an important element in the fertility decline of the later nineteenth century, and there is little doubt that fertility was controlled by coitus interruptus and abstinence. These methods were unreliable, and the high risks of an unwanted pregnancy meant they were more likely to entail spacing over the wife's fertile years. However, the contrast between spacing and stopping should not be overdrawn, for couples were likely to be attempting *both*. The two processes are difficult to untangle, for spacing was likely to lead to stopping as a secondary phenomenon. A reduction in sexual intercourse meant a fall in the age of the wife at the birth of the last child, for the ability of a woman to conceive declines over time. When small families became established as the social norm, stopping could be pursued as a conscious strategy in order to secure the benefits of a smaller family. Above all, the children of smaller families produced by spacing came to see small families as normal and consciously attempted to achieve the pattern in their own marriages. The emergence of cheaper, more comfortable condoms assisted. With effective contraception, having children in rapid succession became more feasible, for couples had less fear of contraceptive lapses and unwanted pregnancies. Certainly, a new phenomenon emerged in the 1920s and 1930s when couples opted to postpone the birth of their first child for some time after marriage. Not only did they seek to stop families at younger ages; they also delayed starting their families until they were better established.

Explaining Fertility Decline

The choice of stopping or spacing was achieving smaller families. Why exactly did more people desire this outcome? Not all families attempted to space pregnancies, for the decision to restrict the number of children was confined to a particular group of families. In the later nineteenth century, family sizes were widely dispersed around the mean. For couples married in the 1870s, each size category of family from childless to ten children accounted for at least 5 per cent of families, and none reached 10 per cent. For couples married between 1900 and 1909, family sizes were much less dispersed: 15 per cent had a completed family size of one child, 19 per cent had two, and 16 per cent had three.[21] Clearly, a sizeable minority of couples marrying at the beginning of the period decided to restrict births, with many continuing to have large numbers of children until the inter-war period. There were general processes at work, and also variations between social groupings which might provide an insight into the reasons for falling fertility. Historians differ in the weight they give to the general versus the particular: should we stress multiple fertility declines and concentrate on variations; or should we see variations as relatively unimportant? The answer should be both, for understanding the variations between occupations or locations helps to pinpoint the precise nature of the general processes.

A number of influences can be ruled out. The mere development of an urban-industrial society cannot explain reductions in fertility, for some rural areas had low and some urban areas high fertility. Neither was the small family size diffused from the middle classes to the working classes through observation; it is much more likely that changes occurred autonomously in different groups for distinct reasons. Knowledge of appliance methods was not the key, for the fall in fertility was to a considerable extent produced by existing methods of 'spacing'. What *was* new was a change in attitudes towards family limitation, the adoption of 'a calculus of conscious choice'.[22]

A number of general processes led to a culture of choice. Family planning propaganda might be more important in creating a sense of choice than in offering practical advice. More generally, Robert Woods argues that attitudes changed with mass education. Literacy might well raise the expectations of women and give them more sense of power in the home. After all, women bore the burden of frequent conceptions: miscarriages and illnesses could lead to enforced abstinence, but not all husbands were self-controlled, and many women suffered appalling problems from frequent pregnancies. The evidence presented by women in the letters in *Maternity* offered grim stories which were reason enough to control fertility. From the Edwardian period, women were given more authority to deny the 'rights' of their husbands by doctors and health visitors who impressed on them the dangers of frequent pregnancies. However, the 'medicalization' of childbirth came *after* the start of the fertility decline, so that it can only explain part of the fall and not its onset which must depend on the ability of women in some places and social groups to impose their wishes. [23]

A rise in real wages from the 1870s encouraged a consumer-oriented culture in which a family of two or three children was respectable and more than five was not. A large family meant forgoing the pleasures of the later nineteenth century—a holiday, or a well-furnished parlour. Again, the general process was moderated by local variations between areas with a surviving culture of masculine pleasures of the pub and of a new culture of domesticity. Further, the secular decline in early childhood mortality from the 1860s and then infant mortality from the late 1890s confirmed the downward trend in fertility.

Many demographic historians explain the fall in fertility through the economics of the household, linking a number of general trends with divergences according to the circumstances of particular occupations and locations. Rowntree's survey of poverty in York developed the notion of the poverty cycle. The birth of a child would initially force a working-class family into poverty before the child entered the labour market and contributed to the family income. As a result, the family experienced a period of relative affluence before the child left home to get married. In the later nineteenth century, the cost of a child was affected by a longer period of 'drain' on the family income, and by a reduction in the period of contribution to the budget. Child labour was restricted by the Workshop Regulation Act of 1867 and the Factory and Workshop Act of 1878. At the same time, compulsory education was introduced and strictly enforced, with all except the poorest parents obliged to pay school fees until 1893.[24]

How did these shifts in the allocation of costs and benefits of children over the life cycle affect fertility? Wally Seccombe's interpretation rests on a highly instrumental approach by husbands. He argues that couples could afford one or two children without too much hardship, and until the 1870s the earnings from the first child contributed to the cost of the third or fourth child. The 'subsidy' from older children ceased in the 1870s, for the delay in the receipt of income from the first child meant that the costs of the fourth or fifth child became too great a burden, and couples opted to stop. In his view, the decision was largely the husband's, for the reduction in marital fertility depended upon his willingness to practise coitus interruptus, to abstain, or to use condoms. According to Seccombe, husbands controlled their sexual behaviour out of self-interest, coming to share their wives' aversion to pregnancy when the costs of an additional child threatened their ability to spend money on their own pleasures.[25]

The changing cost of children doubtless did influence decisions, but Seccombe's formulation is far too instrumental. Is it likely that husbands would alter their sexual behaviour with such precision in response to the changing economics of the third or fourth child? It is much more plausible that couples reduced their target family size in response to the mounting real costs of children; and that the interests of husbands and wives became more symmetrical for other less materialistic reasons. At least in some places, the interests of husbands and wives could coalesce as working-class culture became more domesticated and home based. The quality and cost of housing increased, accounting for a large part of the additional spending power of working-class families. At the same time, employers challenged workshop culture. Spending on alcohol started to decline with a shift to more commercialized recreation in the music hall and seaside resort. Of course, the pub and football match, or hobbies, continued to be male dominated, but much consumption was now home and family based. Marriage became more companionate and co-operative.

The increase in real wages in the late nineteenth century meant that children were less likely to be seen as a source of income or security in old age, and were more often seen as items of expenditure. Indeed, the extent to which they were ever a source of income should not be exaggerated, for many children did not contribute to the household budget. In 1851, about 27 per cent of boys in Britain had left home by the age of 16, rising to about 75 per cent at the age of 25. Many of these were in an intermediate category, leaving their family of origin without forming a household of their own.[26] The retreat from the family of origin towards the formation of a new household was gradual, involving a number of intermediary stages. In the late nineteenth and early twentieth centuries, more working children stayed at home and they were more likely to retain some of their earnings, with parents either asking for a contribution for board and lodgings or handing over an allowance from their earnings. Clearly, the precise bargain could create tension, and some children paid less and some more than the full cost of their keep according to family need and assumptions. A working child would probably pay more to a widowed mother or unemployed father than in a household with a male head of household in employment. Gender was also important, for a daughter was expected to stay at home, whereas a son would be expected to leave home to marry. Many of these assumptions were incorporated into social policy, which rested on unpaid care by women for the sick and elderly, and on the obligation of all wage earners to contribute to the household budget. Over time, the balance moved towards the children as a reduction in family size allowed them to be indulged to a much greater extent.

The general increase in the relative cost of children was important, but why did it have differential impact on different social groups? The household economics approach can be extended by taking account of variations in the loss of earnings of the wife in different occupations. Marital fertility was low in the cotton textile districts where women were more likely to work. By contrast, marital fertility remained high in mining and heavy industrial towns, and in districts dominated by casual labour such as the East End of London. The reasons for high fertility in these locations were somewhat different. In the heavy industrial districts and coalfields, male wages were high (and achieved in early adulthood) so there was less need for men to control fertility especially given the limited aspirations of their 'culturally autarkic' communities. The frame of reference for families in the coalfields tended to be their own past and their less well-paid neighbours rather than possibilities in other communities, and they were less likely to be affected by the culture of consumption. [27] In the East End garment industry, both wives and children could find work, and the income of adolescent children provided some protection in periods of underemployment so that the birth of additional children remained worthwhile.[28]

Household economics may also be applied to middle-class families where the decline in marital fertility started earliest and went furthest. In the later eighteenth century, the propertied classes were characterized by late marriage and a high chance of remaining unmarried. For the bourgeoisie, postponing marriage was the only respectable way of defraying the costs of running the marital home. Middle-class children were not an economic asset; on the contrary, they imposed considerable costs of education and, in the case of daughters, of marriage set-tlements or support as single women. The need to control fertility in the later nineteenth century arose from pressure on middle-class incomes as a result of the profit squeeze in industry, the fall in interest rates and rents, and 'overpro-duction' of professionals with the growth of public schools. At the same time, the costs of maintaining a middle-class lifestyle rose. Wives were expected to be 'perfect ladies', no longer helping with the business or running of the home. The wages of servants rose, as did the fees for public schools, and there was an expectation that the better-off should have a carriage and the paraphernalia of gentility.[29]

These arguments from household economics may be too deterministic, resting as they do on a calculation of the costs of a child compared with the loss of the wife's earnings. There were also wide cultural variations between towns. Many married women in textile towns did not work, but their experience as single mill lasses and their later age of marriage gave them a greater sense of independence. In the male-dominated society of the coalfield, women had less scope to achieve independence, and there was a different power balance between husband and wife These arguments start to shift the discussion away from household economics to a cultural understanding of gender relations and roles, which fits with the importance of cultural meanings of masculinity. In the opinion of Szreter, families from all classes and occupations in a particular location adopted new norms of manhood and self-control; and the fall in fertility was more complex than the assumption of contemporary surveys that the decline originated in the professional middle class and filtered down. This interpretation is, he suggests, based on the ideology of civil servants who compiled the statistical returns.[30]

The first major national survey of fertility was carried out by the government in the census of 1911. In order to carry out this survey, the General Register Office devised a social classification of Britain. All male heads of household were placed in one of five occupational categories: I professional, II intermediate, III skilled manual, IV intermediate, and V unskilled manual. The model combined two assumptions: non-manual occupations were graded by the extent to which they were professional; for manual occupations, skill levels were assumed to be synonymous with status. Businessmen did not appear as a separate category. The GRO then used the classification to consider the eugenicist assumption that the fall in the birth rate amongst the most able people in Britain—the professionals—was a threat. In fact, the GRO rejected this and favoured an environmentalist view that the decline in fertility of the higher classes was the result of *knowledge* of contraception, and would be diffused to other groups so that the threat to the racial stock would recede. The difference of interpretation had important policy implications, for it implied a programme of education rather than eugenic policies of sterilization of the unfit. Nevertheless, both approaches started from the proposition that family limitation commenced amongst the educated elite as a result of their innately superior intelligence and access to information.

In fact, the picture was more complicated than a diffusion of family limitation from the educated elite to the rest of society, as is shown by an analysis of the fertility of the 206 occupations underlying the five classes. Of the twenty occupations comprising the 5 per cent of the married population with the lowest fertility, more were in class II than in class I; and there were no class V occupations among the 5 per cent of the population with the highest fertility. The groups with the lowest fertility were somewhat miscellaneous, comprising the professions, both old (law, Church, and army) and new (civil engineers and accountants); people who retired in their late forties or early fifties or had private means; and indoor domestic servants, lodging house keepers, tobacconists, and wholesale dealers. Textile workers generally had low fertility, as did workers in the jewellery and precious metals trades in London and Birmingham. In some cases, these groups had an early age of marriage such as army officers and lodging house keepers; others married late, such as doctors, solicitors, indoor servants, and the large and growing body of clerks. The groups with the highest fertility were almost entirely coal hewers; and some well-paid workers had higher fertility than the lower paid. The level of skill was less important than the nature of the occupation and the community. Groups with the highest fertility were united by heavy physical labour alongside other men, creating a macho culture.

Data from the fertility census of 1911 suggest to some demographic historians that there were two relatively discrete locales or environments with low fertility, cutting across skill and employment status. Szreter and his colleagues claim that the same social class had different fertility levels in different types of environment or 'communication communities' which consisted of similarly socialized families linked to the dominant local labour market. The first locale was the south, dominated by non-manual occupations of wealth and privilege, and those who served them as servants and professionals. Szreter argues that the norms established by the middle class extended to other social groups. White-collar communities had low fertility for *all* occupations, for the middle class set the tone of 'acceptable' behaviour and influenced nuptiality through their demand for domestic labour. From the last quarter of the nineteenth century, more people were looking for a comfortable middle-class suburban life, with a rise in white-collar, lower middle-class occupations in London, the home counties, and larger provincial towns. In the larger second group of communities, low fertility showed highly localized and sectoral variations, largely reflecting the sexual segregation of their labour markets rather than neat variations by class or skill. The group was dominated by the textile regions. Above all, Szreter stresses the distinction between 'insular' and 'open' communities. In most working-class communities, respectability meant living within one's means, leading to cultural conservatism in self-sufficient 'communication communities', and refusing to engage with the aspirational culture of the middle class. The middle class was more competitive and aspirational, eager to distance itself from the workers through a life of gentility, based on foresight and self-control. In Szreter's opinion, the decline in fertility rested on shifting roles, norms, and social identities in these 'communication communities' with clear parameters of accepted behaviour. An example makes the point: in some 'communication communities', a man would be derided by his peers if he helped with housework or child care; in others, he would be criticized for spending time with his mates in the pub. Such differences were mediated by the culture of different environments. Professional and white-collar workers in predominantly working-class areas were slower, and working-class groups in middle-class districts quicker, to adopt new norms. At the beginning of the period, the gap between middle class and working class was wide, and society tended to be polarized. By the early twentieth century, the gap was closing. Szreter therefore argues that environment is superior to class in explaining variations in fertility. 'The overall picture to emerge is one of multiple falling fertilities in Britain: an essentially fractured and fissured set of relatively independent processes, occurring in different ways over a period of nearly a century in different locations and communities.'[31]

Szreter's emphasis on the primacy of localities or communication communities over class and occupation, and the suggestion that the decline in fertility was fractured and multiple, are useful warnings against class determinism and overgeneralization.

But is Szreter's claim strained and is it more realistic to emphasize general processes which were modified by local circumstances? Furthermore, his interpretation is not radically different from the long-standing analysis of different labour markets and household economies. Does the notion of 'communication communities' do more than simply indicate that the culture of the dominant occupation might affect other people within the locality, an unexceptionable and readily accepted point?

Sexuality

Restriction of births by spacing had different implications for sexuality from the use of appliances. If couples used artificial methods of control, they could continue the same level of sexual intercourse, with few unwanted pregnancies, and sexual activity might even *increase* with the removal of the fear of pregnancy. The adoption of artificial birth control meant, so it seems to some historians, that Victorian anti-sensualism was swept away in a wave of sexual liberation.[32] However, 'spacing' means that sexual behaviour must have become *more* rather than less controlled to reduce the birth rate, with the implication that early Victorians were more sexually active and more willing to talk about sex than their children and grandchildren.

The norm of abstinence was established in the mid- to late nineteenth century, with a repudiation of physical sexual desire by many women and men. In part, the shift reflected hostility to sexual activity as animal-like and dishonouring, reflected in the dread of gonorrhea and syphilis, and expressed in the campaign for stricter censorship and raising of the age of sexual consent. It might reflect a reduction in the opportunities of women for economic independence which made women more dependent on male wages and more vulnerable to desertion. However, the culture of anti-sexuality was much more positive than a rejection of sex as debasing or a fear of abandonment. It rested on 'a widely and warmly embraced creed' of 'aspirational anti-sensualism' rather than mere prudery.[33] Sexual activity and enjoyment were not rejected as repulsive and animalistic; almost the contrary, married love was virtually sacramental. Sex within marriage was to be pleasurable, and not to be rushed into. Although Charles Kingsley and his wife had a physically close courtship, they delayed consummating their marriage for a month for, as Kingsley explained, full intercourse was akin to their future marriage in heaven.[34] Evangelicals were adamant that the senses should not be titillated by erotic language, revealing dress, or play-going, yet they were far from hostile to sexual activity. Indeed, their wives' enjoyment mattered to many husbands, for medical opinion held (incorrectly) that ovulation was caused by orgasm which was therefore necessary for conception. Women might shun sexual pleasure from a desire to avoid another pregnancy, yet married sex was not a matter of joyless inhibition.[35] The widespread concern about masturbation (and nocturnal emissions) was not merely a sign of sexual repression;

it was linked with the fear of impotence and premature ejaculation which would prevent satisfactory intercourse and heterosexual desire.[36]

Anti-sensualism was not only religiously inspired; it was also urged by radicals, progressives, and feminists. William Lovett, the Chartist leader, summarized an important strand in radical, progressive thought when he remarked that 'man . . . has within him the capacities of the philosopher and the propensities of the savage; and whether he shall be one or the other will depend on the . . . means taken to develop the good and control the evil'.[37] Similarly, feminists developed a code of anti-sensualism, starting from Mary Wollstonecraft's *Vindication of the Rights of Women* which warned that 'when even two virtuous young people marry, it would perhaps be happy if some circumstances checked their passion'. In his important study of Victorian sexuality, Michael Mason argues that most progressive thinkers believed that the development of the intellect and non-sensual behaviour offered the way to social and political advance; the key was not Evangelical prudery so much as 'progressive anti-sensualism'.[38]

Victorian anti-sensualism was broadly based, resting on sincerely held values which commanded wide assent.[39] The question was how long this culture could be sustained. Abstinence within marriage led to frustration, and could only survive through self-control or, in Hera Cook's formulation, 'internalized sexual repression'. The low fertility of the 1930s was therefore a cause of considerable anxiety. Men were expected to have self-control—but advice literature stressed that husband and wife had mutual needs for sexual satisfaction. The trauma of the First World War led, so Susan Kent argues, to an acceptance of mutual and pleasurable sexual behaviour in marriage to reduce sexual repression which created violence. Psychiatrists and sexologists stressed sexual pleasure as normal, and feminist critiques of sexuality were marginalized. Domestic life was becoming more central to many couples and attitudes to the body changed with the emergence of looser and lighter clothing, and physical exercise. The result was that male anxieties about self-control collided with another anxiety, about the need for 'healthy' sex leading to mutual orgasm. The conflict was not easily resolved, for mechanical or barrier forms of birth control diminished sexual pleasure. Only with the development of thinner, lubricated condoms and the contraceptive pill from the 1960s were the tensions resolved—at least to the satisfaction of men, for another way of viewing the emergence of effective and convenient birth control is as a process of eroticizing married women for the benefits of their husbands.[40]

Domesticity and Family Life

Acceptance of this anti-sensualist code was connected with a decline in the importance of fatherhood as a source of identity and pride. Men's emotional involvement with child rearing declined as their role in transmitting skills was taken over by formal education and professional qualifications. The father's role was increasingly to earn a living to support a family. As far as the father was concerned, children could now be seen as economically burdensome and emotionally problematic rather than a means of expressing identity.[41] Advice books gave a smaller role to fathers, leading some virtually to abdicate from child rearing: many withheld intimacy from a fear of undermining their manhood and that of their son; others responded by asserting their status through repressive behaviour. Many men found the shifting definition of masculinity to be difficult. As middle-class families ceased to be economic units, domesticity became central to masculinity, with the assumption that a man's deepest needs were met in the home. Instead, the family became sentimental and emotional, a pattern noted by foreign visitors such as Hippolyte Taine. He was struck that 'Every Englishman . . . imagines a "home", with the woman of his choice, the pair of them alone with their children. That is his own little universe, closed to the world.' Equally, British visitors to Paris or Vienna were struck by the difference from London, noting how cafés and restaurants allowed life to continue outside the home.[42]

Increasingly, men went out to work—and hence the home and suburb could be seen as a refuge from the tribulation of a heartless commercial ethic, a place where a man could express his authentic self. The home was also central to social status. A non-working wife, a complement of servants, and a tastefully decorated and elegant home were signs of the husband's social standing. For most suburban residents engaged in salaried employment, the family was a source of identity, set apart from the workplace. This theme runs from the mid-nineteenth century to the 1930s, when the residents of the suburbs were almost paranoid in their concern for social standing. Many were recent recruits to white-collar work, leaving working-class relatives in the old inner-city districts. Deep anxiety to establish their standing as members of the new middle class led to a high degree of formality in social interaction and a stress on the self-contained family unit. For professionals and businessmen, the family and home were not only a domestic refuge: they were places for socializing, showing respectability to business colleagues and the local elite.

The impact of domesticity on the man's position was ambivalent. His masculine status depended on entering the workplace to support the family which increased his patriarchal status. At the same time, he lost authority in the home to his wife, leading to a polarization between the breadwinner and the home-maker with very different interests and education. For many middle-class men, the thought of sharing interests with women was difficult to comprehend. As Mandell Creighton, the future bishop of London, remarked to an undergraduate friend: 'Of course, at a certain age . . . you get a wife . . . and find her a very comfortable institution; but I doubt greatly whether there were ever many men who had thoughts worth recounting, who told those thoughts to their wives.' Many husbands seem to have confused the role of wife and mother. Arthur Stanley, in his mid-forties, informed his fiancée that 'I shall often flag and be dispirited; but you, now, as my dear mother formerly, must urge me, and bid me not despair when the world seems too heavy a burden to be struggled against'.[43]

Middle-class women in the suburbs might find their lives confining and limited. One response was to participate in voluntary organizations or create societies to give some shape to their lives; in the 1930s, they might escape to a matinée at the cinema or play golf at their husband's club.[44] Equally, men might feel that the elevation of the home and the wife above other social ties was undermining their own associational life, threatening to emasculate them and their sons. One response was to dispatch boys to the all-male environment of a public school. The growth of these schools is often portrayed as a sign of the 'gentrification' of the middle class, an attempt to fuse with an established agrarian or gentry elite and to reject urban, industrial society. Much more significantly, the schools resolved some of the contradictions produced by femininity and domesticity: the boy would live without the comforts of home, and would develop manly qualities of energy and resolution. Similarly, many adult men created their own all-male spheres, where they could meet and talk over commercial issues and indulge in risqué or ribald conversation. Gentlemen's clubs, Masonic lodges, golf clubs, the garden or allotment, and hobbies from pigeon racing to model railways gave men of different interests and social status some means of negotiating the limits of the home.[45]

Sexuality, Fertility, and Social Policy

Virginia Woolf's claim that sex was not talked about prior to 1910 was far from the mark.[46] The language of sexual gratification was eroded, but sex and sexuality were constantly talked about in social debate, linked with notions of health and disease, morality and immorality, surveillance and regulation. Concerns over incest, prostitution, pornography, sexually transmitted diseases, masturbation, and homosexuality were matters of great concern.

At the beginning of the period, issues of sexual morality were linked with poverty and the environmental shortcomings of great cities. As Edwin Chadwick remarked, the habits of the poor were 'of a piece' with their dwellings. The evidence collected by the Report into the Sanitary Condition of the Labouring Population suggested the connections:

I have met with upwards of forty persons sleeping in the same room, married and single . . . I found in one room a prostitute . . . she stated that she had lodged with a married sister, and slept in the same bed with her and her husband; that hence improper intercourse took place, and from that she became more and more depraved.[47]

Similarly, the campaigns for factory reform portrayed working women as sources of corruption. In 1842, one witness to the commission on the employment of children in mines had 'no doubt that debauchery is carried on . . . I think it scarcely possible for girls to remain modest who are in pits, regularly mixing with such company, and hearing such language as they do.'[48] Poverty, disease, and sexual depravity were linked in what may be termed 'moral environmentalism'. Chadwick's reports and the novels of Dickens presented images of pollution, filth, secretions, blockages in which physical degradation mirrored moral and sexual decay. Sanitation and physical improvement were essential for moral advance as explained by John Simon at the Local Government Board:

where grievous excess of physical suffering is bred, large parts of the same soil yield, side by side with it, evils of another kind . . . in some of the regions of insanitary influence, civilization and morals suffer almost equally with health . . . education . . . is little likely to penetrate, unless with amended sanitary law, nor human life to be morally raised while physically it is so degraded and squandered.[49]

Slums were plague spots, to be excised, and once drained of their pollution, society would return to health.[50] Equally, prostitutes were reservoirs of pollution, and threatening the nation's health, above all the vigour of the army and navy. As *The Lancet* pointed out, doctors should intervene in the case of a diseased woman in the same way as with typhus or smallpox, to prevent the spread of disease. In the early and mid-Victorian period, doctors were securing more control over citizens, such as in the imposition of compulsory vaccination of all children against smallpox. A similar sanitary approach to prostitution was implemented in the Contagious Diseases Acts of 1864, 1866, and 1869. Prostitutes in naval and garrison towns could be regulated and inspected by medical men and the police who had power to examine any woman suspected of being a prostitute, and to detain her in a 'lock hospital'.

These Acts provoked outcry and eventual repeal, with a significant impact on the power of state medicine. Such powerful women as Harriet Martineau and Florence Nightingale formed the Ladies' National Association, criticizing the Acts as a threat to the civil liberties of women and as a means of permitting male vice. The campaign brought together the languages of radical dissenting religion and anti-statist concern for personal rights in a challenge to medical power. Regulation of sexuality by interventionism gave way to an emphasis on *moral* reform.

The result was a shift from state medicine to a campaign for purity, launched by the National Vigilance Association in the mid-1880s. The aim was to reform male sexuality through a greater use of criminal law to regulate obscenity, indecency, incest, homosexuality, and the age of consent. The new stress on purity drew on popular scientific concepts of evolution, with its emphasis on the movement from lower to higher impulses. It was sustained by sensationalist notions of danger and violation in the popular press. W. T. Stead's infamous series of articles on 'white slavery' or child prostitution in 1885, and the reporting of the murders of Jack the Ripper in 1888, drew on melodrama, pornography, and religious outrage to present the city as a dangerous place for women. Women as well as men spoke in the debates over sexuality, attacking the double standards of men. In their opinion, the law should play a major role in protecting women and children, and preserving the moral values of the nation. In the words of Ellice Hopkins, 'whoever touches the higher life and well-being of the family still more vitally affects the wider family of the State, and threatens its disintegration'.[51] Of course, the attempt to use the state to impose morality was controversial and intensely disliked by many people. In London the progressives on the London County Council regulated music hall acts, provoking a backlash from voters who wished to preserve their opportunities for enjoyment.[52] Many civil servants and national politicians were concerned by this encroachment of purity into politics, and tried to define it as outside their remit. Consequently, most of the extension of criminal law to sexual demeanour and behaviour between 1885 and 1912 came as the result of external pressure.

Medical regulation went into partial eclipse with the repeal of the Contagious Diseases Acts. In the last quarter of the nineteenth century, the confident elite of generalist arts-educated civil servants was suspicious of doctors' claims to expertise. Then, in the Edwardian period medical discourse returned with a different emphasis. The body and slums were no longer viewed as a reservoir of corruption and vice. Rather, the slow acceptance of germ theory led to a realization that the body could mount its own defences through antibodies. What was needed was training in motherhood and education in sex 'hygiene'. The environment was now viewed in a different way, stressing the role of the individual as well as the external, physical environment. This approach marked a reassertion of the role of medicine without a 'hereditarian' emphasis on 'breeding'. The medical profession exploited alarms over the physical condition of the British population after the Boer War to urge attention to the health of schoolchildren, the care of pregnant mothers and newborn children, in order to reduce infant mortality and improve the standards of the race. Certainly, they shared the assumptions of eugenicists about the innate superiority of white and, above all, Anglo-Saxon peoples. However, the majority of the medical profession differed from eugenicists who rejected environmentalism and wished to regulate breeding. Environmentalism remained dominant, at most appealing to racial rhetoric in order to create support for greater investment in a programme of public health directed at individuals and their immediate environment. Preventive medicine moved beyond the negative and criminal approach of the purity campaign to a concern for education and training of the sexual instinct and of maternity. The People's League of Health of 1917 was one expression of the approach, with its motto that 'A Nation's Health is a Nation's Wealth'. The formation of the Ministry of Health in 1919 reflected this new emphasis on the individual's responsibility for their own health in an improved environment. Healthy and responsible parenthood, and self-controlled sexual activity through education and not criminal law, were seen as crucial for the evolution of humanity.[53]

NOTES

1. Clements, 'Trade unions and emigration', 175–8.
2. See McLaren, *Birth Control*, ch. 6.
3. Cannan, 'Probability of a cessation of the growth of population', 513; Cannan, 'Changed outlook in regard to population', 525–6; Robbins, 'Notes on some probable consequences of the advent of a stationary population', 71; Mc Cleary, *Race Suicide?*; Charles, *Twilight of Parenthood*; Hankins, 'Has the reproductive power of western peoples declined?', 188; Harrod, 'Modern population trends'.
4. Keynes, 'Some economic consequences of a declining population', 16, 17; Toye, *Keynes on Population*; Reddaway, 'Special obstacles to full employment', 304; Reddaway, 'Family endowment'; Reddaway, *Economics of Declining Population*, 127–35; Matless, *Landscape*, 243.
5. For an account of the panic and the statistical confusions, see Flinn, 'British population scare of the 1930s'.
6. Anderson, 'Life cycle', 80.
7. Ibid. 82; data from census.
8. Anderson, 'Social implications', 67–9; Mitchell and Deane, *Abstract*, 16, 18.
9. Anderson, 'Social position of spinsters', 381–2.
10. Woods, *Demography*, 72, 93–5; Hinde, 'Household structure, marriage and the institution of service', 47; Woods and Hinde, 'Nuptiality and age at marriage', 125; Anderson, 'Marriage patterns in Victorian Britain', 382–5; Haines, 'Fertility, nuptiality and occupation', 258–9; Griffiths, *Lancashire Working Classes*.
11. McGregor, *Divorce*, 11, 18, 23–4, 29, 38; Anderson, 'State, civil society and separation'.
12. Haines, 'Fertility, nuptiality and occupation', 248.
13. Wrigley, 'Family limitation', 92–5, 97–8, 104–5.
14. For the debate on birth control, and its connections with neo-Malthusianism and other ideologies, see McLaren, *Birth Control*; Soloway, *Birth Control*, 53–5, 67, 326. On evidence of withdrawal and the availability of new advice in the 1820s and 1830s, see Cook, *Long Sexual Revolution*, ch. 2.
15. Gittins, *Fair Sex*, 162–80; McLaren, *Birth Control*, 51–7; Szreter, *Fertility, Class and Gender*, 402–7.
16. Szreter, *Fertility, Class and Gender*, 431; Gittins, *Fair Sex*, 164; Knight, 'Women and abortion', 57–69; McLaren, 'Women's work and regulation of family size', 72, 78.
17. Szreter, *Fertility, Class and Gender*, 394–5, 398, 402, 405, 409.
18. Anderson, 'Life cycle', 74; Andeson, 'Social implications', fig. 3, 52.
19. Szreter, *Fertility, Class and Gender*, 432–4; Anderson, 'Highly restricted fertility', 5, 9, 13, 15.
20. Szreter, *Fertility, Class and Gender*, 393, 410.
21. Anderson, 'Life cycle', 40, fig. 7.

22. Woods, *Demography*, 169.

23. Ibid. 148–9, 164, 305–6; on the difficulties of childbirth, see Llewelyn Davies, *Maternity*.

24. Seccombe, 'Starting to stop', 170–2, 184–6.

25. Seccombe, 'Starting to stop', 171, 176–8, 186–7.

26. Anderson, 'Life cycle', 69, fig. 9, 84.

27. Szreter, *Fertility, Class and Gender*, 526; Griffiths, *Lancashire Working Classes*, ch. 7.

28. On rise in marital fertility in many East End districts 1861–1891, see Woods, 'Social class variations', 35–7.

29. Banks, *Prosperity and Parenthood*, 5, 82, 85, 89–90, 130–4, 196–201.

30. Szreter, *Fertility, Class and Gender*, part II.

31. Ibid 364, 530, 533.

32. Mason, *Victorian Sexuality* 57–61 64, 218 assumed that there had to be birth control to account for sexual liberation.

33. Mason, *Victorian Sexual Attitudes*, 49; Cook, *Long Sexual Revolution*, 62, 65, 67, 89, 90, 92; Hall, *Hidden Anxieties*, 3–4.

34. Quoted in Mason, *Victorian Sexual Attitudes*, 19.

35. Ibid 176, 200–1, 203.

36. Ibid 210–15.

37. Ibid 117–19, 121, 125.

38. Mason, *Victorian Sexuality*, 5, 215, 218–19, 220, 222, 223, 225.

39. Ibid 44–5.

40. Cook, *Long Sexual Revolution*, 121, 123, 161–2, 182; Hall, *Hidden Anxieties*, 75, 82, 88, 93, 138; Kent, *Making Peace*, 140.

41. Szreter, *Fertility, Class and Gender*, 462.

42. Davidoff and Hall, *Family Fortunes*, ch. 7; Tosh, *Man's Place*, 5–8, 28; Olsen, *City as a Work of Art*, 217–18, 242–4.

43. Tosh, *Man's Place*, 68, 110.

44. McKibbin, *Cultures and Class*, 421

45. Tosh, *Man's Place*, 117–19, 168–9, 177.

46. Quoted in Mort, *Dangerous Sexualities*, p. xi.

47. Ibid. 31.

48. Ibid. 37.

49. Quoted ibid. 53; Trotter, *Circulation*, 103–12.

50. See Yelling, *Slums and Slum Clearance*, 10.

51. Mort, *Dangerous Sexualities*, 96.

52. Pennybacker, *Vision for London*, 219, 228–9.

53. Mort, *Dangerous Sexualities*, 133, 139.

FURTHER READING

Anderson, M., 'The modern life cycle', *Social History*, 10 (1985).

—— 'Marriage patterns in Victorian Britain: an analysis based on Registration District data for England and Wales, 1861', *Journal of Family History*, 1 (1976)

Anderson, M., 'The social position of spinsters in mid-Victorian Britain', *Journal of Family History*, 9 (1984)

—— 'Highly restricted fertility: very small families in the British fertility decline', *Population Studies*, 52 (1998)

—— 'The social implications of demographic change', in F. M. L. Thompson (ed.), *The Cambridge Social History of Britain, 1750–1950*, ii: *People and their Environment* (Cambridge, 1990)

Anderson, O., 'State, civil society and separation in Victorian marriage', *Past and Present*, 163 (1999)

Banks, J. A., *Prosperity and Parenthood: A Study of Family Planning among the Victorian Middle Class* (1954)

—— and Banks, O., *Feminism and Family Planning in Victorian England* (1964)

Cannan, E., 'The probability of a cessation of the growth of population in England and Wales during the next century', *Economic Journal*, 5 (1895)

—— 'The changed outlook in regard to population, 1831–1931', *Economic Journal*, 41 (1931)

Charles, E., *The Twilight of Parenthood* (London, 1934)

Clements, R. V., 'Trade unions and emigration, 1840–80', *Population Studies*, 9 (1955)

Cook, H., *The Long Sexual Revolution: English Women, Sex and Contraception, 1800–1975* (Oxford, 2004)

Davidoff, L., and Hall, C., *Family Fortunes: Men and Women of the English Middle Class, 1780–1850* (1987)

Davin, A., 'Imperialism and motherhood', *History Workshop*, 5 (1978)

Dupree, M. W., *Family Structure in the Staffordshire Potteries, 1840–80* (Oxford, 1995)

Flinn, M. W., 'The British population scare of the 1930s', in J. Schneider (ed.), *Wirtschaftskräfte und Wirtschaftswege V* (Stuttgart, 1981)

Garrett, E., Reid, A., Schurer, K., and Szreter, S., *Changing Family Size in England and Wales: Place, Class and Demography, 1891–1911* (Cambridge, 2001)

Gittins, D., *Fair Sex: Family Size and Structure, 1900–39* (1982)

Griffiths, T., *The Lancashire Working Classes, c.1880–1930* (Oxford, 2001)

Haines, M. R., 'Fertility, nuptuality and occupation: a study of coal mining populations and regions in England and Wales in the mid-nineteenth century', *Journal of Interdisciplinary History*, 8 (1977)

Hall, L., *Hidden Anxieties: Male Sexuality 1900–1950* (Cambridge, 1991)

—— *Sex, Gender and Social Change in Britain since 1880* (Basingstoke, 2000)

Hankins, F. H., 'Has the reproductive power of western peoples declined?', in G. H .L. F. Pitt-Rivers (ed.), *Problems of Population: Being the Report of the Proceedings of the General Assembly of the International Union for the Investigation of Population Problems* (New York, 1971)

Harrod, R. F., 'Modern population trends', *Manchester School*, 10 (1939)

Hinde, P. R. A., 'Household structure, marriage and the institution of service in nineteenth-century rural England', *Local Population Studies*, 35 (1985)

Kent, S. K., *Making Peace: The Reconstruction of Gender in Interwar Britain* (Princeton, 1993)

Keynes, J.M., 'Some economic consequences of a declining population', *Eugenics Review*, 29 (1937)

Knight, P., 'Women and abortion in Victorian and Edwardian England', *History Workshop Journal* (1977)

Llewelyn Davies, M., *Maternity: Letters from Working Women Collected by the Women's Co-operative Guild* (1915; Virago edin., 1978)

Mckibbin, R., *Classes and Cultures: England, 1918-51* (Oxford, 1998)

McLaren, A. A., *Birth Control in Nineteenth-Century England* (1978)

—— 'Women's work and regulation of family size: the question of abortion in the nineteenth century', *History Workshop*, 4 (1977)

Mc Cleary, G. F., *Race Suicide?* (1945)

McGregor, O., *Divorce in England: A Centenary Study* (1957)

Mason, M., *The Making of Victorian Sexuality* (Oxford, 1994)

—— *The Making of Victorian Sexual Attitudes* (Oxford, 1994)

Matless, D., *Landscape and Englishness* (1998)

Mitchell, B. R., with P. Deare, *Abstract of British Historical Statishics* (Cambridge, 1962)

Mort, F., *Dangerous Sexualities: Medico-moral Politics in England since 1830* (2nd edn, 2000)

Ogle, W., 'On marriage-rates and marriages-ages, with special reference to the growth of population', *Journal of the Royal Statistical Society, 53 (1890)*

Olsen, D. J., *The City as a Work of Art: London, Paris, Vienna* (1986)

Pennybacker, S. D., *A Vision for London, 1889–1914: Labour, Everyday Life and the LCC Experiment* (1995)

Reddaway, W. B., 'Special obstacles to full employment in a wealthy community', *Economic Journal*, 47 (1937)

—— 'Family endowment reconsidered', *Review of Economic Studies*, 5 (1938)

—— *The Economics of Declining Population* (1939)

Robbins, L., 'Notes on some probable consequences of the advent of a stationary population in Great Britain', *Economica*, 9 (1929)

Roper, M., and Josh, J. (eds.), *Manful Assertions: Masculinities in Birtain since 1800* (1991)

Seccombe, W., 'Starting to stop: working-class fertility in Britain', *Past and Present*, 126 (1990)

Soloway, R.A., *Birth Control and the Population Question in England, 1877–1930* (1982)

Stone, L., *Broken Lives: Separation and Divorce in England, 1660–1857* (Oxford, 1993)

Szreter, S., *Fertility, Class and Gender in Britain, 1860–1940* (Cambridge, 1996)

—— 'Victorian Britain, 1937–1963: towards a social history of sexuality', *Journal of Victorian Culture*, 1 (1996)

Teitelbaum, M. S.,' The British fertility decline: demographic transition', in *The Crucible of the Industrial Revolution* (Princeton, 1984)

Thompson, F. M. L., 'Changing perceptions of land tenures in Britain, 1750–1914', in D. Winch and P. K. O'Brien (eds.), *The Political Economy of British Historical Experience 1688–1914* (Oxford, 2002)

Tosh, J., *A Man's Place: Masculinity and the Middle-Class Home in Victorian England* (New Haven, 1999)

Toye, J., *Keynes on Population* (Oxford, 2000)

Trotter, D., *Circulation: Defoe, Dickens, and the Economies of the Novel* (Basingstoke, 1988)

Walkowitz, J. R., *City of Dreadful Delight: Narratives of Sexual Danger in Late-Victorian London* (Chicago, 1992)

Woods, R., *The Demography of Victorian England and Wales* (Cambridge, 2000)

—— 'Social class variations in the decline of marital fertility in late nineteenth century London', *Geografiska Annaler*, 66B (1984)

—— and Hinde, P. R. A., 'Nuptuality and age at marriage in nineteenth-century England', *Journal of Family History*, 10 (1985)

—— and Smith, C. W., 'The decline of marital fertility in the late nineteenth century: the case of England and Wales', *Population Studies*, 37 (1983)

Wrigley, E. A., 'Family limitation in pre-industrial England', *Economic History Review*, 19 (1966)

Yelling, J.A., *Slums and Slum Clearance in Victorian London* (1986)

....

CHAPTER II

Death and Disease

In 1861, Prince Albert died at the age of 42—popularly thought to be a victim of typhoid. Not even the most influential members of British society were immune from an early death caused by pollution and infectious disease. His widow, Queen Victoria, continued to mourn until her own demise in 1901, and death and its rituals were central to Victorian culture. Novels, poems, biographies, and pictures featured countless death scenes, watched over by family members. An elaborate ritual ensued: a vigil and last visit; the draping of windows; the wearing of mourning clothes and jewellery; the use of black-bordered writing paper; a funeral procession, followed by interment and frequent visits to the grave. Only the monarch could go to the elaborate extremes of the Albert memorial, but many of her subjects did their best with stained glass windows and memorial plaques. Even the poorest took out life insurance policies to avoid the ignominy of a pauper burial denying the family its rituals of loss and commemoration. For the poor, as for better-off members of society, rituals were critical to negotiating the identity of the dead and the relationship with the bereaved.[1]

Death was central to Victorian culture—but its presence and visibility did not imply that it was untroubling. By her bedside, Victoria kept a copy of Tennyson's *In Memoriam*, a poem on the death of his friend Arthur Henry Hallam at the age of 22. The poem was one of the major statements on death in a culture permeated by eschatology: the meaning of death, judgement, heaven, and hell was debated in poetry, hymnody, novels, and paintings. Tennyson's poem expressed the grief which afflicted so many in Victorian Britain. The question facing Tennyson was how to bear grief and loss. Was the grave the end of existence or rebirth? 'Thou madest man, he knows not why, | He thinks he was not made to die; | And thou hast made him: thou are just.' If God was just, death could not be an end. But belief was hedged round by doubt and hesitation. If the grave was not the end, what lay 'behind the veil'? Tennyson rejected the idea of hell, of 'the gulfs beneath, | The howlings from forgotten fields'. Nevertheless, individuality might cease. Tennyson hoped it would survive: 'Eternal form shall still divide | The eternal soul from all beside; | And I shall know him when we meet: | And we shall sit at endless feast, | Enjoying each the other's good.'[2]

Tennyson's poem is often seen as an expression of religious doubt in the face of science which culminated in the publication of Darwin's *The Origin of Species* in 1859. More accurately, it captures shifting understandings of death. The epitaphs on gravestones established the identity of the deceased and the relationship with those who mourned, often expressing the hope that the departed was not dead but sleeping, waiting to be reunited with those who survived. But where had the departed gone, and in what form did they continue to exist? Death might be the gate to heaven which appeared, in Michael Wheeler's phrase, as 'more like a middle-class suburb in the sky than the city of God'. Equally, heaven might appear as a timeless, placeless state of praise and spiritual union. Perhaps death led to judgement and transformation. The common belief of eternal damnation and punishment seemed too harsh to many Anglicans and moderate Protestants. Perhaps the wicked would be completely annihilated, either after a period of retribution or at the point of death. Or perhaps everyone would survive after a period of purification, a comforting universalism which offered all the chance of paradise. Gladstone was troubled: what would happen to morality if terror were removed? Certainly, the idea of hell and eternal punishment was not lost. In 1872, Archbishop Tait rejected the literalist notion of hell and asserted it was a spiritual condition rather than a place, marking separation from God who was love. The idea of a retributive God had weakened by the late nineteenth century—a shift with large consequences for economic and social policy as well as for understandings of personal salvation.[3]

Cultural and emotional responses to death and the afterlife shifted towards a less gloomy eschatology. Yet as religious doubt developed so did interest in psychic research and spiritualism. In 1917, Max Weber assumed that the modern world would be associated with secularization and 'disenchantment'. However, the notion of 'disenchantment' is misleading.[4] The quest for a spiritual element might involve a search for the transcendental in nature or the occult and mystical religion, an interest readily compatible with new ideas of multiple and shifting consciousness and personalities. The inner world was not fixed, but fragmented and complex—a view expressed by Freud and by novelists, but also by the Theosophical Society. The theosophists took Christianity as a metaphor for pagan mysteries and the occult, in which all creation was part of a cosmic soul. More orthodox was the Society of Psychical Research, established in 1882 to investigate the evidence for a spiritual life. Henry Sidgwick, who became president of the Society, believed that a sense of immortality was vital for ethics. Unfortunately, his attempt to contact the dead gave him more insight into human credulity than the proof he so desired. Although Keynes mocked Sidgwick's attempts to establish the immortality of the soul, he joined the committee of the University of Cambridge section of the Society in 1911.[5]

Spiritualism attracted many, not least in response to the First World War which led to a surge of interest in spiritualism in order to deal with loss. The cataclysm of the war posed an immense problem of how to accept so many deaths, and how to commemorate their sacrifice. Although the war is often associated with the dissolution of traditional forms of literary expression, the more immediate response was to cope though traditional sentiments and forms rather than anger, a sense of debt rather than of waste.[6]

Responses to death and the afterlife are central to the history of all societies, and it would be possible to write at length on the intellectual, emotional, and cultural history of death in Britain between 1851 and 1951. The concern here might appear more mundane: how was disease controlled and life expectation raised? By 1951, the expectations of life and health were very different from 1851, and not surprisingly death retreated from the central position it held in the intellectual and emotional life of Victorian Britain. It became a silence rather than an ever-present commentary.

Life Expectancy and the Retreat of Mortality

Many children born in England and Wales in 1851 could not look forward to a contented old age, for life expectancy at birth was 41. The chances of a long life were somewhat better for children born in the countryside and considerably worse in towns with more than 100,000 residents (Table 11.1).

Low life expectancy at birth reflected the very high chances of succumbing to disease in the first year of life, for 15.3 per cent of all babies born in England and Wales in 1851 were dead before their first birthday (see Table 11.2). The fall in infant mortality only started from 1900, falling to barely a third of its earlier peak by the outbreak of the Second World War. Once the dangers of infancy were passed, childhood posed many threats from infectious diseases. The initial and most substantial reduction in mortality came in childhood and adolescence between the ages of 1 and 15, starting from the mid-nineteenth century. By what means was the death rate for this age

TABLE 11.1. *Life expectancy at birth, England and Wales, 1851 and 1911*

	1851	1911
London	35	52
Over 100,000	34	51
10,000–100,000	38	53
Rural	45	55

Source: Woods, 'Effects of population redistribution', 650.

TABLE 11.2. *Crude death rate per 1,000 and infant deaths under 1 per 1,000 live births, England and Wales and Scotland, 1851–1951*

	England and Wales		Scotland	
	Death rate	Infant mortality	Death rate	Infant mortality
1851	22.0	153		
1861	21.6	153	20.3	111
1871	22.6	158	22.2	130
1881	18.9	130	19.3	113
1891	20.2	149	20.7	128
1901	16.9	151	17.9	129
1913	13.8	108	15.5	110
1921	12.1	83	13.6	90
1931	12.3	66	13.3	82
1938	11.6	53	12.6	70
1945	12.6	46	13.2	56
1951	12.5	30	12.9	37

Source: Mitchell and Deane, *Abstract*, 36–7; Mitchell and Jones, *Second Abstract*, 24.

group curtailed? In the last quarter of the nineteenth century, mortality also fell for young adults. Gains for older adults were delayed until after the Second World War, when medical treatment started to limit the toll of degenerative diseases. Overall, the results are striking: by 1911, life expectancy at birth in England and Wales had risen to 53 and the discrepancy between town and country was much smaller.[7]

Why did the death rate start to fall in the second half of the nineteenth century, with differential declines in infant, child, and adult mortality? An assessment of the causes depends on a careful analysis of the causes of death, for different diseases are transmitted in different ways and are therefore susceptible to control by different methods. They also affect different age groups. A fall in mortality from smallpox might indicate that medical intervention was a major influence, through the use of vaccination or by isolating infectious people and tracing their contacts. The significance of medical treatment versus public health may be tested by comparing the impact of different policies at different times and places. If the major fall in mortality was in airborne or pulmonary diseases, the crucial variable was less likely to be investment in the urban infrastructure than general improvement of diet, or better housing and working conditions; at some point, public action to control pollution by noxious fumes and smoke might have an impact. A fall in deaths from water-borne diseases would suggest that the crucial variable was investment in the urban infrastructure to supply clean water and effective sewerage, which depended on political will.

The timing of mortality decline by age groups provides further guidance to the most important variables. The initial drop in the death rate was concentrated on children rather than infants or adults, so directing attention to diseases that were less likely to be influenced by investment in water and drainage. The delay in the fall in infant morality would suggest that some causes of death were less tractable than others. Infant mortality was more likely to be influenced by improved cleansing of streets, and by standards of hygiene within the home and patterns of infant care. Clearly, a marked improvement in the mortality rate in large cities would direct attention to the policies pursued by local authorities rather than general, national processes, and might support the case for the significance of collective investment in the infrastructure.

To some commentators, the heroes of the story were the doctors. Others are sceptical about the claims of the medical profession, particularly Thomas McKeown, a heterodox doctor who doubted the ability of his more technocratic colleagues and their therapies. In his view, the medical profession was of scant importance compared with economic growth. His argument rested on analysing the various causes of death, seeing which diseases were in retreat, and then eliminating or minimizing various factors on the grounds that they could not explain the most significant falls in deaths from particular diseases. The first factor to be rejected was autonomous declines in micro-organisms, which could explain deaths from scarlet fever and some of the decline in tuberculosis. Scarlet fever accounted for 20.3 per cent of the decline in mortality in England and Wales between 1851–60 and 1891–1900. Secondly, he rejected improvements in the environment, whether as a result of immunization or public health measures to improve sanitation. The only disease affected by immunization was smallpox, which accounted for a mere 6.1 per cent of the decline in mortality. Similarly, sanitary reform mainly affected water-borne diseases, which fell into two groups. The first was typhus, enteric fever, and simple continued fever. Nineteenth-century doctors confused enteric fever or typhus (spread by lice) with typhoid (spread by infected water), so that not all of the decline in deaths in this group—22.9 per cent—can be explained by investment in water and sanitation. The second group of water-borne diseases—cholera, dysentery, and diarrhoea—were spread by polluted water, and accounted for 8.9 per cent of the decline in mortality. Although the decline in water-borne diseases was significant, McKeown suggests that the decline in mortality from tuberculosis was of prime importance, accounting for 47.2 per cent of the fall in deaths. Since medical therapies for treatment of tuberculosis and other diseases were not effective, McKeown concluded that the standard of living and especially improvements in diet explain the decline in mortality from tuberculosis and, to a lesser extent, typhus.[8] McKeown therefore asserted the primacy of air- over water-borne diseases, and hence the secondary role of public health measures.

His argument is not convincing because of flaws in the data and methodology. The importance of diet emerges only by default: other possible factors are dismissed, leaving diet as the only possible explanation without subjecting this variable to the same critical examination. The attention devoted to diet in the 1930s by nutritionists such as John Orr showed that the important variable was not how much money people had but how they spent it. The standard of living could rise without leading to the intake of vitamins or minerals for health. Is it so evident that only general resistance to disease caused by an improved standard of living and, above all, diet could reduce airborne diseases? A higher standard of living might be important in explaining a decline in deaths from tuberclosis, but mediated through housing rather than diet. Equally, preventive medicine might play a major role. In any case, were airborne diseases as important as McKeown believed? The data are not as clear-cut as he claims, for mortality from other pulmonary diseases rose.

These considerations led Simon Szreter to stress the primacy of water-borne diseases which probably accounted for a third of the reduction in the nineteenth century, with the decline in tuberculosis as a secondary response to the reduction of other debilitating diseases (see Table 11.3). This leads him to emphasize the role of preventive medicine and public investment in the infrastructure of cities. His account restores the medical profession to a central role through its ability to work

TABLE 11.3. *Contribution to the fall in death rate, 1848/54–1901 (percentage of decline)*

Airborne micro-organisms		
Respiratory tuberculosis	30.0	
Bronchitis, pneumonia, influenza	+10.0	} 20.0
Scarlet fever, diphtheria	13.3	
Smallpox	5.0	
Other	3.3	
Water-and food-borne micro-organisms		
Cholera, diarrhoea	11.7	
Typhoid, typhus[a]	16.7	
Other	3.3	
Other micro-organisms		
Principally convulsions	15.0	
Other conditions		
Not micro-organisms	8.3	
Total	100.0	

[a] Misallocated; should be other micro-organisms.

Source: Recalculated from Szreter, 'The importance of social intervention', 8.

with the state. So, how did it become possible to invest so much more in the health of cities in the last quarter of the nineteenth century?

Investing in the Urban Infrastructure

One explanation for the fall in the level of mortality in the later nineteenth century was that urban areas caught up with the countryside. In rural areas, the infant mortality rate was often less than 100 per 1,000 live births in 1861; in some towns, it was still 150 in 1911.[9] As a result, some demographic historians argue that geography was more important than social class or occupation for mortality.[10] On this view, the largest differential in infant and child mortality was determined by physical environment rather than by the income and occupation of the father. Towns were less healthy than the countryside, the inner city was less salubrious than the suburbs, and industrial areas were particularly deadly. A member of the middle class living in a smoky, polluted town would experience a higher level of infant or child mortality than someone in the same occupation in Oxford or Cheltenham. Place mattered.

In Szreter's view, the improvement in mortality in the later nineteenth century followed a period of serious deterioration in urban conditions as a result of a failure of investment in the infrastructure, with a fall in life expectancy at birth in large towns of 100,000 and above from 35 in the 1820s to 30 in the 1840s. It followed that the improvement in mortality in the final quarter of the century arose from a higher level of investment.[11] Not all demographic historians have accepted the case for a rise in mortality in the second quarter of the nineteenth century. Robert Woods questions whether so much emphasis should be placed on a relatively small part of the population in the largest towns. He also objects that, in the absence of adequate data, Szreter takes material from Glasgow as representative—a proposition he feels rests on insecure foundations. In any case, Woods suggests that decline might arise from the particular circumstances of the 1830s and 1840s with the visitation of cholera and migration from Ireland rather than from a systemic breakdown in governance.[12] Nevertheless, Szreter's contention does seem plausible, for other evidence from smaller towns in various parts of the country supports a general decline in urban life expectancy and a deterioration in infant mortality.[13] Investment in cities and industrializing towns was low in the second quarter of the nineteenth century. Problems of collective action were not resolved; investment by private utility companies was still modest; and housing was tightly packed. In Liverpool in 1841, about a quarter of the population lived in courts, with houses packed around a small open space containing a common privy and ashpit. In Bristol, the Royal Commission on the Health of Towns of 1843/5 found that only 5,000 people out of 130,000 had piped water.[14]

In the early nineteenth century, the structure of urban government in England and Wales was unable to cope with the environmental problems of rapid population growth. In Scotland, the burghs had a greater sense of continuity and effectiveness: the Merchants' House and Traders' House—forms of corporate guilds—were represented on town councils which often had assets allowing them to take action. In England the corporations were usually self-electing oligarchies. A closed corporation of Tory-Anglicans was easily criticized for using resources for partisan ends, and the finances of the corporation consequently lacked transparency and accountability. As a result, ratepayers were reluctant to pay their taxes, and the financing of urban improvements relied on borrowing and debt. Further, many rapidly growing towns fell outside the existing corporations. The corporations were complemented by various ad hoc bodies—improvement, police, lighting, or paving commissioners—supported by the better-off residents. Although these commissioners did invest in the expanding cities there were serious problems. The commissioners were criticized for their limited representation. Paving and lighting a few streets in the better-off districts did little to protect their residents from cholera which required investment in the sanitation of the town as a whole. Indeed, an improvement in one direction could lead to difficulty in another. The expansion of the market for water by the commercial companies in London resulted in more water closets connected to sewers which were designed for surface water only, so polluting the Thames and the drinking water supply.

Action was needed to create a new sense of legitimacy in urban governance. In London, the Metropolitan Board of Works was created in 1855 and constructed a new system of sewers costing £4.1m—a massive sum which resolved some of the problems of sanitation in the metropolis.[15] Elsewhere, the corporations were reformed by the Municipal Corporations Act of 1835. The Act ended the closed oligarchies by laying down a standard franchise and regular elections, but the franchise was more limited and more open to manipulation than might at first appear. The proportion of adult males with a municipal vote varied: in 1865, only 13.3 per cent of adult men in Liverpool had a vote; by contrast, as many as 63 per cent of adult men in Bradford did. Generally, spending was lowest where the franchise allowed domination by small ratepayers who took a myopic view of investment. Recovery started with the extension of the franchise. The Municipal Franchise Act 1869 reduced the qualifying period; small occupiers of houses who paid rates via their landlords also secured the vote; and multiple occupiers of the same property were given the vote in 1878. By 1884, 47.1 per cent of adult men in Liverpool had a municipal vote and 77.4 per cent in Bradford. Extension of the franchise led to higher levels of social spending: the small property owners were now contained by an alliance between large property owners or professionals with an interest in investment in the urban infrastructure and working men. The classic example of such an alliance was Birmingham, where members of the business elite moved into the council, most strikingly Joseph Chamberlain in the 1870s. The general rise in the proportion of men with the vote and the variation between towns allow a statistical test of the relationship between the franchise and spending. This shows a U-shape: a limited franchise dominated by larger ratepayers led to higher investment; a somewhat wider franchise led to dominance by small ratepayers and lower spending; and a much wider franchise led to higher spending.[16]

These political changes were complemented by developments in the capital market. Loans from central government to local authorities under the Public Works Loans Act 1853 were on strict terms and the Treasury was reluctant to accede to the pressure of the Local Government Board for more generous terms. Smaller authorities continued to borrow from the government, but from the 1870s larger authorities turned to the London capital market. As interest rates fell, large capital schemes became possible until the rise in interest rates after 1905 choked off investment in the urban infrastructure.[17]

Although the extension of the franchise allowed local politicians to build a coalition of support, problems did not end. The nature of any scheme, and the precise allocation of costs and benefits, were open to dispute. For example, the water company in Wakefield drew its supply from the river which was polluted and unsuitable for domestic use but a good source for the local textile industry which needed soft water. The company proposed to draw pure water from wells, which was desirable for domestic use but too hard for the textile industry. Local industrialists blocked the scheme and the company was purchased by the town council which was slow to invest in a new supply of pure, soft water suitable for both domestic and industrial use.[18] Similarly, water consumers disputed the structure of tariffs and questioned whether authorities with spare capacity should sell to neighbours at marginal cost. Problems also arose over the disposal of waste: one town's solution was another's problem. In Leeds, local landowners complained about the pollution of the river Aire caused by the discharge of raw sewage. The appeal court found in their favour, and the corporation was required to ensure that its sewage was purified and deodorized. The politics of water and waste involved complex and contested issues of assessing costs and benefits, of defining where the liberty of one person to cause harm should be constrained.[19] Hence the willingness of local authorities to invest in pure water supplies and main drainage, and the use of water closets in place of middens and privies, varied.

Not only did cities such as Glasgow and Birmingham have costly waterworks and sewers, trams and gasworks, they also invested in art galleries, libraries, and universities. Urban residents were certainly healthier and more long-lived as well as better educated: by the 1850s, the life expectancy at birth in towns of 100,000 was back to 34, and then passed the previous level to reach 38 in the 1870s, 40 in the

1880s, and 42 in the 1890s.[20] In Szreter's opinion, the decline in mortality was mainly due to the success of the public health movement.[21] He does have a powerful point about the low level of investment in cities in the second quarter of the nineteenth century, and the huge spurt in investment in the urban infrastructure in the last quarter of the nineteenth century. But was it quite as influential as he assumes? Collective action was not only a matter of capital projects; as Szreter is well aware, it also involved regulating the urban environment, isolating people with infectious diseases, cleaning the streets, and disposing of rubbish. Further, the influence of economic growth and the standard of living was more than a matter of diet and resistance to disease. Higher levels of income allowed more women to retreat from paid work and devote their time to housework and child care, and, above all, led to better-quality housing.

Further, the role of place over class should be treated with caution. Place did matter, but class and occupation were still important. Even in the most unhealthy industrial towns, members of the wealthy middle class could escape to the suburbs, whereas manual workers were tied to the polluted inner city. The flight of the middle class is often linked with an aversion to industry and a retreat into rural nostalgia; a more compelling reason was the very real danger in polluted cities. The middle class also had political clout to improve their own environment. The environment was more important for infants and young children; for adult men, life chances were affected by a combination of occupation and social class. Data for England and Wales in 1860–1 and 1871 show a relatively high life expectancy at age 20 of 41.71 years for barristers and solicitors and 42.21 for carpenters. However, the life expectancy was low for both middle-class doctors (39.34), and for workers in pottery and earthenware trades (32.65), and file-makers in the towns of the Black Country (31.87), as a result of respiratory complaints. Income levels did not necessarily make much difference to the death rate of adults.[22]

Domesticity, Cleanliness, and Behaviour

A more realistic interpretation of the decline in mortality avoids large claims for any one variable and stresses interaction between causes. Above all, any understanding of the decline of mortality in childhood indicates the range of factors involved. Childhood diseases depended for their transmission on close personal contact, and prevention was difficult in the absence of immunization. At best, local authorities could stop parents from sending children with symptoms to school and encourage them to keep infected pupils in the home. The Infectious Diseases Notification Act 1889 and the Public Health (London) Act 1891 gave medical officers of health the power to isolate individuals, and so to check the spread of disease. The task was difficult. In Islington in 1896 the medical officer found 1,252 children with an infectious disease in school.[23] In this case, investment in the urban infrastructure was less significant than monitoring urban living.

Similarly, the decline in childhood mortality from whooping cough from 1870 reflected improved nursing care, better housing, and diet. Deaths from whooping cough were also affected by the incidence of rickets. In turn, rickets arose from a deficiency of vitamin D, and seems to have declined in the late nineteenth century with improvements in nutrition and child care. In this case, diet had some role and preventive medicine very little. Again, mortality from measles was affected by respiratory complications to which preventive medicine made no contribution. Rather, the key variables were the incidence of rickets, overcrowding, and care of the sick child. Diet also had an impact, for the level of fat consumption makes a difference between fatal and mild infection. At first sight, diphtheria seems to reflect the success of medical therapy with the regular use of a new serum treatment from 1895, but the fall in the death rate started before it was available. Although some historians argue that the virulence of the disease declined, there is no direct evidence. The most likely causes for a decline in its impact were improved living conditions and controls of infected children. Scarlet fever arises from streptococci present in most people's throats and nasal passages; many children develop an infection, but its frequency and seriousness are affected by their general health. The spread of infection by respiratory droplets is more likely in crowded living conditions. Recovery was linked with care, warmth, bed rest, a good diet, and a reduction in the pressure of large families.[24] In all these childhood diseases, the role of investment in water and sewers was modest; preventive medicine played some part; and the major reason was improved living conditions and patterns of child care.

The next group of diseases with declining mortality mainly affected young adults. The only disease in which medical intervention might have had an impact was smallpox, where compulsory vaccination was carried out. However, the effectiveness of vaccination was limited and other forms of preventive medicine were more significant. Port sanitary authorities were created in 1872 and helped to prevent the entry of diseases into Britain, and at the local level contacts were traced, houses cleaned, and infected people isolated. By 1907, compulsory vaccination was abandoned.[25]

Cholera, dysentery, enteric fever, diarrhoea, and typhoid were spread by infected drinking water, and the reduction in mortality certainly depended on investment in better drains and water supplies, as well as improved domestic hygiene and plumbing. These diseases were also spread by the huge number of flies attracted by horses used for transport, and cows which were housed in the metropolis to provide milk; large numbers of animals were also driven into Smithfield to provide meat. Vegetable waste and ashes from fireplaces mixed with the contents of privies created stench and attracted flies. The threat to health was lessened by the use of more easily cleaned granite setts or asphalt, by controls on animal waste, and by the introduction of efficient waste collections.[26]

Typhus was carried by lice and its incidence was linked with social dislocation and serious overcrowding, and above all with mass migration from Ireland. Lower mortality depended on cleanliness, which was easier with improved housing conditions from the 1870s. Local authorities had power to cleanse, whitewash, or demolish infected property, and from 1897 could spend money on cleaning infected people.

One of the most significant drops in mortality was in tuberculosis. Again, many historians argue that the virulence of the disease declined. In fact, a strong case can be made for the role of living conditions and prevention. Mass screening in the Second World War showed that a very large number of people had been exposed to the disease without developing tuberculosis. The problem arose where the infection was reactivated or the person was re-infected. For many people, a small level of exposure created resistance and the germs remained inactive. Much depended on the level of exposure, for infection usually requires fairly intimate and close contact with a person in the active phase of infection. A fall in mortality was helped by slum clearance, constant water supplies, controls on overcrowding, ventilation and cleaning, better health, and a reduction in employment in trades with a high incidence of infection. The medical profession did little or nothing to cure tuberculosis until the Second World War, but the public health system might well have checked its spread.

The National Association for the Prevention of Tuberculosis was launched in 1898. In 1911, the new insurance scheme gave free institutional treatment to the insured; it was extended to everyone in 1913 when the illness also became a notifiable disease. By 1918, a state-financed and controlled system for prevention and treatment was in existence, relying on institutional treatment. There was no cure but the sanatoria did isolate patients in the highly infectious, active stages. Although patients remained infectious on their release, the chance of passing on the disease was much reduced; and steps were taken to prevent them from working in food trades. Public education campaigns against spitting helped to check the spread of the disease, and controls were imposed on milk supplies which were another vector. The Second World War marked a major change in treatment and the possibility of a cure. The introduction of mass radiography from 1943 meant that the disease could be tackled in its early stages. The same year, the first effective anti-tuberculosis drug—streptomycin—was discovered. By 1949, milk was categorized, with a programme of pasteurization and testing for tuberculin, and in 1953 vaccination started in schools.[27]

The role of the state in public health initiatives was therefore important, not simply as a result of large-scale investments in clean water and sewers but also in raising standards of cleanliness and disseminating awareness of how diseases were spread. Local authorities provided refuse collection and effective street cleaning; sanitary inspectors and medical officers visited houses, controlled anti-social habits, and isolated infectious disease. The way children were nursed changed, as did patterns of visiting the sick or of dealing with corpses. The change was not only the result of intervention by public officials, for people had more money and better accommodation to keep themselves and their houses clean. There was a cultural change in responses to diseases and dirt. The rise in the standard of living meant the ability to buy cleaning materials which were amongst the first mass-produced, branded goods, as well as the availability of more easily washed floor coverings. The initial phase of urbanization meant a flow of people from low-mortality rural areas to high-mortality towns. In the second half of the nineteenth century, the pattern was reversed with a flow to the suburbs.[28] Above all, housing conditions improved from the 1870s. Stricter public regulation after the Public Health Act of 1875, and controls over courts, insanitary common privies, and cesspits, prevented the recurrence of health problems, and local authorities cleared some of the worst slums. The Housing of the Working Classes Act 1890 marked the modest beginnings of public housing—a programme which expanded after the First World War. The Housing Act of 1930 marked a new phase of slum clearance, imposing a duty on local authorities to clear property and construct council houses for the displaced residents. But the main explanation for higher-quality accommodation was the rising standard of living and the ability to spend more on rent. In the 1930s, the boom in owner-occupation transformed British cities.[29]

Prosperous members of the middle class in all cities could afford more spacious housing than less well-paid manual workers. However, housing conditions varied between cities independently of income and social class. Some of the poorest housing was found in Scotland. In Glasgow, 55.7 per cent of the population lived in overcrowded conditions of more than two people per room in 1911. In England, the worst housing conditions were in the north-east. In Gateshead, 33.7 per cent of the population was overcrowded in 1911, with rent levels at 66 per cent of the level of London in 1905. By contrast, only 1.1 per cent of the population of Leicester was overcrowded with rents at 48 per cent of London.[30] Whilst housing conditions improved everywhere and contributed to a fall in the death rate, they also varied markedly and contributed to the variation in mortality.

What was more difficult to control was air pollution. The notorious 'smog' of London and other great cities killed many into the 1950s, and highly polluted industrial processes affected residents as well as workers. Controls were hard to achieve. The Smoke Abatement Act of 1853 only applied to steam engines, and required them to use the 'best practicable means' of limiting pollution; in 1875 all authorities were given power to adopt anti-smoke measures, with little effect for domestic fuel was excluded until 1956. Local residents or landowners could take legal action against polluters, but the legal process was costly and uncertain. Even when legislation was introduced in the Alkali Acts of 1863, 1874, and 1881, the most serious pollution from copper was excluded and the wording of 1853 was repeated to require the best practicable means of controlling emissions. The definition of this term assumed that what was practicable or reasonable depended on what was economically feasible.[31] Not surprisingly, deaths from polluted air continued to be high. Economic growth did not only reduce mortality through better housing conditions and investment in the urban infrastructure. It could increase it through the consumption of more domestic coal, the production of more industrial fumes—and the purchase of mass-produced cigarettes. Tobacco smoke was an inescapable pall in cinemas, public houses, and transport, a presence in most homes in the country.[32]

Infant and Maternal Mortality

The decline in infant mortality from 1900 was particularly significant, for infants accounted for a large proportion of all deaths and the improvement in their chances of survival was the main reason for the rise in life expectancy at birth above 50.[33] Why did the fall in infant mortality start thirty or so years after the fall in childhood mortality, and why was it then so marked?

Neonatal mortality in the first month of life and post-neonatal mortality between one month and a year have different explanations. Neonatal mortality largely depends on the health of the mother and obstetric practice. Obstetric practice did not improve until the 1930s, and reduction in neonatal mortality was probably a response to the improved health of mothers as a result of better diet and the longer interval between births. In the case of post-neonatal mortality, the major influence was the poor level of sanitation which led to diarrhoea and dysentery, particularly when the weather was hot. Outbreaks of diarrhoea could have a sudden and devastating impact: the infant death rate per 1,000 live births in England and Wales rose from 105 in 1910 to 130 in 1911, before falling to 95 in 1912.[34] When the impact of seasonal outbreaks of diarrhoea is discounted, the underlying level of infant mortality possibly started to decline from about 1891. It is difficult to point to any striking change to explain it. Although large-scale investment in sewers and clean water played a role, probably of greater significance were improved standards of street cleaning and rubbish disposal, and cleanliness within the home.[35]

Some medical men seized on a simple explanation of the high level of infant mortality—working women neglected their duties as mothers. However, this conclusion is not convincing. Mortality was also high in some areas where women did *not* work, and it might be lower where women did work. After all, working mothers could improve the chances of life by supplementing low family incomes. As Eilidh Garrett remarks, 'industrial squalor seems to have been the most likely source of peril for young lives, not the employment of married females'.[36]

The criticism of working mothers easily became a much more general attack on their ignorance. In Edwardian Britain, motherhood was given a new dignity in protecting and nurturing an imperial race, so that it was all the more important that women should be trained in the skills of mothercraft. Bodies such as the Women's League of Service for Motherhood and the St Pancras School for Mothers, and classes in elementary schools, attempted to educate women. Although much of the advice was patronizing, knowledge of hygiene and child care did make a difference. Jewish families in the poorest districts of the East End had much lower rates of infant mortality than their gentile neighbours, showing that care of infants within the home could compensate for the poor physical environment.[37]

The improvement in the care of babies and young children was not only the result of the initiatives of public health officials and philanthropists. Women had more time as a result of a decline in the birth rate, and improvements in female education after 1870 gave them greater access to written information. Furthermore, the allocation of time within the household changed. During the eighteenth century, women shifted from unpaid activities within the household to participation in the market, selling their labour and increasing the cash income of the family. The reallocation of household time was probably beneficial to the welfare of families. In the later nineteenth and early twentieth centuries, more women retreated from the labour market as their husbands' wages rose, and devoted more time to housework and child care, securing a greater gain to welfare than their own (modest) earnings could produce. The shift in the allocation of household time reinforced the improvement in housing conditions and the availability of cheap, mass-marketed soaps and detergents.

Infant feeding practices have considerable impact on mortality and changes led to a sharp drop in infant deaths. Between 1900 and 1920, the feeding of infants and their mothers improved as a result of state intervention. The incidence of breast-feeding and its duration were crucial to the chances of survival. Medical officers of health realized that artificial feeding led to higher infant mortality and so encouraged breast-feeding. Their data indicated that breast-feeding in the first month was high but variable, reaching 97.4 per cent in Middlesbrough (1908/9, 1914/15, 1918), though only 70.7 per cent in Cambridge (1906–15, 1917–19). An improvement in the diet of mothers resulted in more breast milk and some local authorities therefore provided mothers with dietary supplements. The safety of artificial feeding was also improved by switching from bottles with long, unhygienic tubes to short-teat bottles. The quality of infant food improved, both through advice to mothers about inappropriate food such as condensed milk and the development of safer foods such as dried cow's milk. In some towns, pure milk was supplied through 'milk depots'. The Milk (Mothers and Children) Order of 1918 allowed local authorities to supply food and milk to expectant and nursing mothers and to children up to the age of 5, free in cases of need. Such relatively simple changes could have a dramatic effect. In Norwich, the decline in the use of long-tube bottles and the provision of sterile dried cow's milk led to a fall in infant mortality from 174 per 1,000 live births in 1905 to 86 in 1919.[38]

A number of local authorities pioneered home visits to pregnant women, bringing them within the reach of medical specialists, and these schemes were taken up by the Local Government Board in 1914 (see Chapter 16). The Midwives Act of 1936 created a system to deal with childbirth, operated by local authorities under the supervision of the Ministry of Health and the Central Midwives Board, and run by domiciliary midwives rather than obstetric consultants. The system was locally planned and offered continuity of care. But it was not entirely free at point of delivery, and the effectiveness of the programme varied according to local political decisions on spending. In some local authorities means tests were lenient and more mothers were paid grants, with a co-ordinated service throughout the neonatal period. In other cases, the system was much less well organized and mothers were expected to pay more. In London, variations in spending affected maternal mortality. In Stepney, a poor district with casual labour and high levels of overcrowding, maternal mortality was low, largely because of the care of teaching hospitals located there. In Hampstead, a more prosperous district, mothers who used a GP or midwife were more likely to die as a result of childbirth. Nevertheless, the level of spending on maternal and infant services did make some difference, for the drop in infant mortality was more rapid in areas with an active policy of provision.[39] Generally, midwives, antenatal care, and postnatal health visitors served to reinforce an existing trend rather than to initiate the decline in infant mortality.

The confident condemnations of working-class mothers by predominantly male, middle-class commentators failed to appreciate the material needs of poor women. It was easy to blame high infant mortality on the failings of the poor rather than the conditions in which they lived.[40] One explanation for the improvement in infant mortality rate was the decline in fertility from the 1870s which increased the interval between births so that mothers were healthier, and had more time and resources to cope with fewer children. Feminists had a point in suggesting that one very practical way of helping poor women was to pay them a family allowance for looking after children. In fact, family allowances were not paid until 1948, not least because of the opposition of male trade unionists.[41]

War and Depression

The processes described so far were long term and gradual. A possible exception was the impact of the First World War. Mechanized warfare had appalling consequences for those who survived so that many returning soldiers needed rehabilitation and care. The personal and emotional costs were high—as were the financial costs. War might also lead to gains in civilian health. Jay Winter argues that the health of the young, men above the age of military service, and women improved: diets were maintained or improved as a result of the levelling up of the low wages of unskilled workers and a shift from low-paid to better-paid jobs. Despite an increase in mortality from respiratory diseases, overall mortality of the civilian population fell. His calculation of the impact of the war on male deaths suggests that the mortality rate increased for men of military age, but fell for those above the age of 45. He also argues that female mortality declined, and that infant mortality fell more rapidly during the war than at any time from 1900 to 1930, with the greatest decline in the areas with highest mortality. Similarly, Richard Wall uses evidence collected by the London County Council on children to suggest that their health improved during the war.[42]

Wage differentials certainly did narrow during the war, and London did not suffer anything like the crisis of food supplies and health found in Berlin. But was there really such a marked improvement in health? The improvement in mortality for men above military age was modest even on Winter's showing.[43] It is doubtful that the death rate of women or of infants fell any faster during the war, or more rapidly in the areas of highest mortality. Generally, food supplies were restricted during the war: could the dietary gains of the poorest compensate for the losses experienced by others; and does nutrition have such a direct impact on mortality?[44] Winter's more recent work is cautious, suggesting that London's mortality remained stable during the war, with influences leading to higher mortality balancing gains from improvements in nutrition for others. Indeed, he found that the war meant a loss of 'some of the momentum of pre-war mortality decline', a more realistic conclusion than a major, positive impact on civilian health.[45] The most plausible conclusion is that the demographic impact of the war was not as favourable as Winter initially argued, and that long-term trends were more significant.

What about the depression of the 1930s? In this case, Winter suggests that 'it would be wrong to perpetuate the view that among the costs of the Depression of the early 1930s in Britain was a deterioration in the health of women in childbirth and of their infants'. In his view, infant and maternal mortality improved, and the class differential did not widen. Winter argues that the depression had less impact on public health than often supposed because social protection policies were effective and secured wide acceptance.[46] The optimistic view of inter-war health was presented at the time by statistics from the Ministry of Health. By 1932, Newman was able to report that no borough in England or Wales had an infant mortality rate above 100: his work, it would seem, had been virtually completed with its reduction to an 'irreducible minimum'. Infectious diseases were under control, and malnutrition had been reduced to a mere 1 per cent.[47] But there were dissentient voices. The medical officer at Stockton-on-Tees found many children suffering from malnutrition, and claimed that mortality was higher in the new council estates. In the early 1930s, left-wing critics publicized the poor conditions of health in the depressed areas. The Ministry of Health and Board of Education responded with surveys which reaffirmed the positive conclusion that the condition of the most depressed areas was little worse than the average and was improving. In 1939, Newman denied that bad housing had any role; the problem was personal behaviour. Politicians were reassured, and in 1933 the Minister of Health informed the Commons that 'there is no available medical evidence of any general increase in physical impairment . . . as a result of . . . unemployment'.[48]

Such optimism seems implausible. The evidence used by public health officials concentrated on national averages for England and Wales. Little was said about Scotland, where infant mortality came seventeenth in the League of Nations ranking of infant mortality. Even the national figures raise doubts about the 1930s: the rate of decline in infant mortality slowed down, and England and Wales fell behind other western countries. Regional variations remained: in Manchester, infant mortality ranged from 44 to 143 between wards. In 1943, Richard Titmuss used the scant data released by the Ministry to argue that class differentials in infant mortality were widening. The statistics are not consistent: in some cases, the differential widened, and even where it narrowed, the movement was modest. Data on feeding of children was suspect: even the Ministry was surprised that no child in the severely depressed towns of Ebbw Vale and Aberdare was classed as suffering from 'bad nutrition'. Under-recording was admitted, and the data ignored developments in the science of nutrition. More sophisticated tests found serious deficiencies of iron, and in 1936, John Orr concluded that 50 per cent of the population was undernourished. Not surprisingly, the Ministry of Health was sceptical, for such figures cast doubt on the triumphs of public health. But attitudes were starting to change.[49]

Mass unemployment and depression were serious threats, and the shift to full employment after the war, as well as the development of a national system of welfare, led to considerable advances. But should we go so far as Webster in arguing that before the Second World War 'the total machinery of welfare was inadequate . . . Welfare services were too thinly spread and too erratic to serve more than a residual function . . .'?[50] This is to take correction of the optimism of Newman too far. Could any welfare system cope with a depression on the scale of the 1930s, given the expectations of the time? The evidence presented in this chapter shows how medical bureaucrats did reduce death from infectious diseases and managed the threats of the urban environment. Where they were unrealistic was in believing that they could also overcome the effects of poverty and economic hardship.

The Changing Life Cycle

Low life expectancy at birth reflects the perils of infancy and childhood. Anyone who survived those years had a reasonable chance of reaching old age. Whether the survivors would enjoy a contented retirement was another matter. Until the introduction of a modest state pension in 1908, a fixed age of retirement was unusual and was largely confined to salaried workers. Self-employed professionals and traders usually took out insurance policies providing an annuity for their old age and for their dependants on their death. For most workers, there was little choice except to work as long as possible, supplemented by family support and possibly small sums of sick pay from a friendly society, with the grim prospect of admission to the workhouse as a last resort. As life expectancy rose, the elderly imposed greater burdens on families, friendly societies, and the poor law, and led to pressure for reform. The introduction of pensions offered a small supplement to other sources of income, and created a definite age of retirement to ease the elderly out of the labour market.

Disease and death also meant a break-up of families. Single-parent families were a major source of poverty and usually the result of the death of a spouse. The experience of married couples in England and Wales in 1826 indicates the problem: after ten years, 18 per cent of marriages were broken by death, rising to 36 per cent after twenty years.[51] By 1950, lower death rates for adults and improvement in maternal mortality meant that fewer marriages were broken by the early demise of one partner, and at the same time more grandparents survived to assist with the care of children. Indeed, the 'traditional' three-generation working-class family celebrated in the sociological studies of the 1950s and early 1960s was a relatively recent phenomenon.

Changes in birth and death rates should be combined to understand the changing life cycle of families. At the beginning of the period, women were relatively old at the birth of their last child and life expectancy was low. A woman born in 1831 would, on average, marry in 1854; she did not long survive the marriage of her youngest child, on average in 1891; she would die in 1897 and not survive to see the birth of her last grandchild in 1909. Few women had living parents to assist with the rearing of young children. The pattern changed for women born in 1861, who were likely to survive five years beyond the birth of their last grandchild. More women had children at a younger age and life expectancy increased, so that over 60 per cent of women born in the 1900s had both parents alive in the 1930s when they were raising their own children. The figures may be turned around from the perspective

TABLE 11.4. *Life course of women born in 1831 and 1861 in England and Wales whose families experienced events at median ages*

	Women born in	
	1831	1861
Median age of marriage	22	23
Birth of first child	23	24
Birth of last child	38	35
Marriage of first child	45	48
Marriage of last child	60	60
Last grandchild aged 5	78	73
Death of husband	62	66
Own death	66	73

Source: estimated from Anderson, 'Life cycle', fig. 3.

of the elderly: how likely were they to have surviving children to support them in old age? A woman born in the 1850s who lived to 75 was likely to have a large number of grandchildren: more than half had more than five living grandchildren. The situation was different for women born in the 1900s: fewer than 14 per cent had more than five living grandchildren at the age of 75, and over half had no grandchildren at all. Indeed, 43 per cent of these women had no children to care for them in old age. Clearly, these changes had major consequences for social policy and for social life.[52]

Environment versus Eugenics

Public intervention had important consequences for the relationship between the individual and the state. Many of the strategies implied intervention in the privacy of the home. This was the price to pay for a relative lack of intervention in other freedoms, and was a mark of a relatively harmonious relationship between citizens and the state. The alternative was rigid quarantine of goods and travellers, compulsory vaccination, and regulation of prostitutes. In the case of cholera, the British government rejected quarantine and opted for investment in sanitation and the inspection of houses. Such drastic and effective intervention was less possible in continental Europe, where suspicion of the state was more marked. Rather than entering the private sphere of the family and investing in the infrastructure, the French concentrated on policing the borders. In the case of smallpox, the British government initially adopted compulsory vaccination, but abandoned it in favour of notification, isolation, and disinfection. In other European countries, a one-off process of vaccinating children seemed less problematic than the attempt to secure continuing compliance with the state. Similarly, the repeal of the Contagious Disease Acts led to treatment of infected men and women in clinics provided by local authorities. The emphasis was on education and voluntary treatment. In Britain, sanitary investment was better than quarantine in dealing with cholera; surveillance and voluntary vaccination were more effective than compulsion in handling smallpox; and medical care and education were preferable in dealing with sexually transmitted diseases.[53]

The success of the public health movement limited the impact of eugenics in Britain. F. W. Galton and Karl Pearson argued that social welfare threatened the fitness of the race by allowing the survival of the unfit, and they turned to policies of selective breeding by sterilizing the mentally incapable. Such policies reached their appalling conclusion in Nazi Germany, but even liberal democratic countries in Europe and North America introduced eugenicist legislation. Although eugenics originated in Britain, and very powerful claims were made for the importance of heredity after 1900, the practical influence on policy was slight. One explanation was that public health officials, firmly entrenched in the machinery of government, were doubtful of the eugenic approach. Far from succumbing to eugenicists, their claims made the environmentalists more assertive in their explanation of poverty. Public health officials were able to turn the debate over the future of the race to their own advantage, pressing their claim to expertise at the expense of generalist civil servants, and drawing on germ theory and bacteriology to widen the definition of the environment. Individuals were not treated as isolated social atoms, but as part of the wider social relations of health and illness. A narrow concern for sewers and cleaning streets gave way to a growing realization that diet, housing, hygienic practices, and social behaviour were significant elements. Indeed, they could appropriate Social Darwinian rhetoric in order to argue that collectivist co-operation was the highest form of evolution.

In the debate over physical deterioration after the Boer War, the environmentalist interpretation prevailed. Far from coming together with eugenics in a new alliance, the environmentalist public health movement fought back. Eugenicists attacked the public health professionals as fatal to biological progress; they retorted that the eugenicists were Malthusian cranks. Men such as Alfred Eicholz of the medical staff of the Board of Education denied that people's occupations and social position reflected their inherited intellectual ability. Rather, a person's place in the labour market explained physical defects in schoolchildren, and divergences in living conditions led to differences in behaviour and culture. In Eicholz's view, the physical deterioration of the poor was almost entirely due to their current environment. The work of physical anthropologists led to the same conclusion: individuals varied without clear differences between classes. The Interdepartmental Committee on Physical Deterioration, appointed to consider the fitness of the British race after the crisis of the Boer War, accepted the line against the eugenicists. The challenge of the hereditarians mainly served to push the environmentalists to a much greater appreciation of impersonal social and economic forces which created a self-reinforcing circle of impoverishment and disadvantage. Rather than forming an alliance with eugenicists, they joined forces with town planners and housing reformers to tackle the relationship between urbanism and health. They utilized the language of degenerationism to create support for social planning, and stressed the need for education in motherhood rather than heredity.[54]

NOTES

1. Strange, 'Only a pauper whom nobody owns', 150.
2. Tennyson, *In Memoriam*, lines 6.5–8, Prelude 10–12, 1.3–4, 55.17–20, 45.16, 56.28, 41.15–16, 47.4, 47.6–10.
3. Wheeler, *Heaven, Hell and the Victorians*, especially 28–31, 73–76, 120–2, 178–9; and see also Rowell, *Hell and the Victorians*; Curl, *Victorian Celebration of Death*, 7–19, for example.
4. Weber, 'Science as a vocation'; Chadwick, *Secularization of the European Mind in the Nineteenth Century*, 239, 258.
5. Skidelsky, *Keynes*, i. 37, 264; Oppenheim, *The Other World*; Gould, *Founders of Psychical Research*.
6. Winter, *Sites of Memory*, 5, 76.
7. Woods, 'Effects of population redistribution', 650.
8. McKeown and Record, 'Reasons for the decline of mortality'; McKeown, *Modern Rise of Population*.
9. Woods, 'Causes of rapid infant mortality decline', I, 353.
10. Woods, *Demography*, 28; Williams, 'Death in its season'.
11. Szreter and Mooney, 'Urbanization, mortality', 104.
12. Wood, *Demography*, 370–1.
13. Szreter and Mooney, 'Urbanization, mortality', 99–101; Armstrong, 'Trend', 102–6; Huck, 'Infant mortality', table 1, 534.
14. Daunton, 'Introduction', 3.
15. Halliday, *Great Stink*; Daunton, 'Taxation and representation', 33.
16. Aidt, Daunton, and Dutta, 'Retrenchment hypothesis'; Szreter, 'Economic growth', 704–6; on Birmingham, see Hennock, *Fit and Proper Persons*.
17. Millward and Sheard, 'Urban fiscal problem', 503–5; Offer, 'Empire and social reform', 130, 133.
18. Hamlin, 'Muddling in Bumbledom', 70–1.
19. Daunton, 'Taxation and representation', 29–30; Hamlin, 'Muddling in Bumbledom', 61–9.
20. Szreter and Mooney, 'Urbanization, mortality', 104.
21. Szreter, 'The importance of social intervention'.
22. Woods, Demography, ch. 6.
23. Hardy, *Epidemic Streets*, 268–72.
24. Ibid. 56–8, 82–3, 103.
25. Hardy, 'Smallpox in London'; Fraser, 'Leicester and smallpox'.

26. Winter, *London's Teeming Streets*; Turvey, 'Street mud, dust and noise'; Thompson, 'Nineteenth-century horse sense'; Morgan, 'Infant mortality', 115.

27. Bryder, *Below the Magic Mountain*.

28. Woods, *Demography*, 379.

29. Daunton, *House and Home*; Daunton, *Property Owning Democracy?*

30. Daunton, *House and Home*, 55, 67, 81.

31. Brimblecombe, *Big Smoke*; Newell, 'Atmospheric pollution'; Brenner, 'Nuisance law'; McClaren, 'Nuisance law'; Simpson, 'Victorian judges'; Daunton, 'Taxation and representation'.

32. See Hilton, *Smoking*, 2.

33. Williams and Mooney, 'Infant mortality', 185.

34. Mitchell and Deane, *Abstract*, 37.

35. This comes from Woods, *Demography*, 305–6: but also in Woods, Watterson, and Woodward, 'Causes of rapid infant mortality decline, I'.

36. Garrett, 'Was women's work bad?', 312; also Graham, 'Female employment' and Garrett and Reid, 'Satanic mills, pleasant lands?'

37. Marks, *Model Mothers*, 1–3, 99.

38. Fildes, 'Infant feeding practices', 255, 265, 275–6, table 3, 262.

39. Marks, *Metropolitan Maternity*; Peretz, 'Maternity service for England and Wales'; Peretz, 'Regional variations in maternal and child welfare'; Peretz, 'Costs of modern motherhood'.

40. Garrett and Reid, 'Satanic mills, pleasant lands'.

41. Davin, 'Imperialism and motherhood'; Pedersen, *Family, Dependence*, 32–59.

42. Winter, *Great War*, 124, 141, 142, 147–8; Winter, 'Surviving the war', 522; Winter, 'Some paradoxes', 15; Wall, 'English and German families', 44–53.

43. Winter, 'Some paradoxes', 15.

44. Harris, 'Demographic impact', 351, 353, 358, 364; for another critique, see Bryder, 'The First World War: healthy or hungry?'

45. Winter, 'Surviving the war', 522–3.

46. Winter, 'Infant mortality', 440, 460.

47. Quoted in Webster, 'Healthy or hungry thirties?', 112.

48. Quoted ibid. 115, 122.

49. Ibid. 116, 118–23, 124, 125.

50. Webster, 'Health, welfare and unemployment', 229.

51. Anderson, 'Life cycle', fig. 5, 79.

52. Ibid. 74–5.

53. Baldwin, *Contagion*, 532, 534.

54. Szreter, *Fertility, Class and Gender*, 121, 215, 228, 234; Jones, *Social Hygiene*, 1; Porter, 'Enemies of the race'.

FURTHER READING

Aidt, T., Daunton, M., and Dutta, J., 'The retrenchment hypothesis: an example from the extension of the franchise in England and Wales', at http://www.econ.cam. uk/faculty/aidt/papers/web/Retrenchment/pdf

Anderson, M., 'The emergence of the modern life cycle', *Social History*, 10 (1985)

Armstrong, W. A., 'The trend of mortality in Carlisle between the 1780s and 1840s: a demographic contribution to the standard of living debate', *Economic History Review*, 34 (1981)

Baldwin, P., *Contagion and the State in Europe, 1830–1930* (Cambridge, 1999)

Benjamin, B., 'The urban background to public health changes in England and Wales, 1900–50', *Population Studies*, 17 (1964)

Brenner, J. F., 'Nuisance law and the industrial revolution', *Journal of Legal Studies*, 3 (1974)

Brimblecombe, P., *Big Smoke: A History of Air Pollution in London since Medieval Times* (1987)

Bryder, L., 'The First World War: healthy or hungry?', *History Workshop Journal*, 24 (1987)

Bryder, L., *Below the Magic Mountain: A Social History of Tuberculosis in Twentieth-Century Britain* (Oxford, 1988)

Chadwick, O., *The Secularization of the European Mind in the Nineteenth Century* (Cambridge, 1975)

Curl, J. S., *The Victorian Celebration of Death* (Newton Abbot, 1972)

Daunton, M., *House and Home in the Victorian City: Working-Class Housing, 1850–1914* (1983)

—— *Property Owning Democracy? Housing in Britain* (1987)

—— 'Introduction', in M. Daunton (ed.), *Cambridge Urban History of Britain*, iii: *1840–1950* (Cambridge, 2000)

—— 'Taxation and representation in the Victorian city', in R. Colls and R. Rodger (eds.), *Cities of Ideas: Civil Society and Urban Governance in Britain, 1800–2000* (Aldershot, 2004)

Davin, A., 'Imperialism and motherhood', *History Workshop*, 5 (1978)

Dwork, D., *War is Good for Babies and Other Young Children: A History of the Infant and Child Welfare Movement in England, 1898–1918* (1987)

Dyehouse, C., 'Working class mothers and infant mortality in England, 1895–1914', *Journal of Social History*, 12 (1978–9)

Fildes, V., 'Breast feeding practices during industrialisation, 1800–1919', in F. Faulkner (ed.), *Infant and Child Nutrition Worldwide* (Boca Raton, Fla., 1991)

—— 'Infant feeding practices and infant mortality in England, 1900–1919', *Continuity and Change*, 13 (1998)

Fraser, S., 'Leicester and smallpox', *Medical History*, 24 (1980)

Fraser, W. Hamish, and Maver, I. (eds.), *Glasgow*, ii: *1830–1912* (Manchester, 1996)

Garrett, E. M., 'Was women's work bad for babies? A view from the 1911 census of England and Wales', *Continuity and Change*, 13 (1998)

—— and Reid, A., 'Satanic mills, pleasant lands: spatial variation in women's work, fertility and infant mortality as viewed from the 1911 census', *Historical Research*, 67 (1994)

Gould, A., *The Founders of Psychical Research* (1968)

Graham, D., 'Female employment and infant mortality: some evidence from British towns, 1911, 1931 and 1951', *Continuity and Change*, 9 (1994)

Halliday, S., *The Great Stink of London* (Stroud, 1999)

Hamlin, C., 'Muddling in Bumbledom: on the enormity of large sanitary improvements in four British towns, 1855–1885', *Victorian Studies*, 32 (1988–9)

Hardy, A., *The Epidemic Streets: Infectious Disease and the Rise of Preventive Medicine, 1856–1900* (Oxford, 1993)

—— 'Smallpox in London: factors in the decline of the disease in the nineteenth century', *Medical History*, 27 (1983)

Harris, H., 'The demographic impact of the First World War: an anthropometric perspective', *Social History of Medicine* (1993)

Hennock, E. P., 'Finance and politics in urban local government in England, 1835–1900', *Historical Journal*, 6 (1963)

—— *Fit and Proper Persons: Ideal and Reality in Nineteenth-Century Urban Government* (1973)

Hilton, M., *Smoking in British Popular Culture, 1800–2000* (Manchester, 2000)

Huck, P., 'Infant mortality and living standards of English workers during the industrial revolution', *Journal of Economic History*, 55 (1995)

Jones, G., *Social Hygiene in Twentieth-Century Britain* (1986)

Law, C. M., 'The growth of urban population in England and Wales, 1801–1911', *Transactions of the Institute of British Geographers*, 41 (1967)

McClaren, J. P. S., 'Nuisance law and the industrial revolution: some lessons from social history', *Oxford Journal of Legal Studies*, 3 (1983)

McKeown, T., *The Modern Rise of Population* (1976)

—— and Record, R. G., 'Reasons for the decline of mortality in England and Wales during the nineteenth century', *Population Studies*, 16 (1962)

Marks, L., *Model Mothers: Jewish Mothers and Maternity Provision in East London, 1870–1939* (Oxford, 1994)

—— *Metropolitan Maternity: Maternal and Welfare Services in Early Twentieth-Century London* (Amsterdam, 1996)

Maver, I., 'Glasgow's city government', in W. H. Fraser and I. Maver (eds.), *Glasgow, i: 1830–1912* (Manchester, 1996)

Millward, R., and Bell, F. N., 'Economic factors in the decline of mortality in late nineteenth-century Britain', *European Review of Economic History*, 2 (1998)

—— and Sheard, S., 'The urban fiscal problem, 1870–1914: government expenditure and finance in England and Wales', *Economic History Review*, 48 (1995)

Mooney, G., 'Did London pass the "sanitary test"? Seasonal infant mortality in London, 1870–1914', *Journal of Historical Geography*, 20 (1994)

Morgan, N., 'Infant mortality, flies and horses in later nineteenth-century towns: a case study of Preston', *Continuity and Change*, 17 (2002)

Newell, E., 'Atmospheric pollution and the British copper industry, 1690–1920', *Technology and Culture*, 38 (1997)

Offer, A., 'Empire and social reform: British overseas investment and domestic politics, 1908–1914'. *Historical Journal*, 26 (1985)

Oppenheim, J., *The Other World: Spiritualism and Psychical Research in England, 1850–1914* (1985)

Owen, A., *The Place of Enchantment: British Occultism and the Culture of the Modern* (Chicago, 2004)

Pedersen, S., *Family, Dependence, and the Origins of the Welfare State: Britain and France, 1914–45* (Cambridge, 1993)

Peretz, E. P., 'A maternity service for England and Wales: local authority maternity care in the interwar period in Oxfordshire and Tottenham', in J. Garcia, R. Kilpatrick, and M. Richards (eds.), *The Politics of Maternity Care* (Oxford, 1990)

Peretz, E. P., 'Regional variations in maternal and child welfare between the wars: Merthyr Tydfil, Oxfordshire and Tottenham', in D. Foster and P. Swan (eds.), *Essays in Regional Local History* (Hull, 1992)

—— 'The costs of modern motherhood to low income families in interwar Britain', in V. Fildes, L. Marks, and H. Marland (eds.), *Women and Children First: International Maternal and Infant Welfare, 1800–1950* (1992)

Porter, D., ' "Enemies of the race": biologism, environmentalism and public health in Edwardian England', *Victorian Studies*, 34 (1991)

Rowell, G., *Hell and the Victorians* (1974)

Saville, J., *Rural Depopulation in England and Wales, 1851–1951* (1957)

Simpson, A. W. B., 'Victorian judges and the problem of social cost: Tipping v St Helen's Smelting Co. (1865)', in A. W. B. Simpson, *Leading Cases in the Common Law* (Oxford, 1995)

Skidelsky, R., *John Maynard Keynes: Hopes Betrayed, 1883–1920* (1983)

Smith, F. B., *The Retreat of Tuberculosis, 1850–1950* (1988)

Strange, J.-M., 'Only a pauper whom nobody owns: reassessing the pauper grave, *c.*1880–1914', *Past and Present*, 178 (2003)

Szreter, S., 'The importance of social intervention in Britain's mortality decline *c.*1850–1914: a reinterpretation of the role of public health', *Social History of Medicine*, 1 (1988)

—— 'Economic growth, disruption, deprivation, disease and death: on the importance of the politics of public health for development', *Population and Development Review*, 23 (1997)

—— *Fertility, Class and Gender in Britain, 1860–1940* (Cambridge, 1996)

—— and Mooney, G., 'Urbanization, mortality, and the standard of living debate: new estimates of the expectation of life at birth in nineteenth-century British cities', *Economic History Review*, 51 (1998)

Tennyson, Alfred Lord, *In Memoriam: Authoritative Text Criticism: A Norton Critical Edition*, ed. E. Gray (New York, 2004)

Thompson, F. M. L., 'Nineteenth-century horse sense', *Economic History Review*, 29 (1976)

Turvey, R., 'Street mud, dust and noise', *London Journal*, 21 (1996)

Wall, R., 'English and German families and the First World War, 1914–1918', in R. Wall and J. Winter (eds.), *The Upheaval of War: Family, Work and Welfare in Europe* (Cambridge, 1988)

Weber, M., 'Science as a vocation', in *Max Weber: Essays in Sociology*, ed. H. H. Gerth and C. Wright Mills (Oxford, 1958)

Webster, C., 'Healthy or hungry thirties?', *History Workshop Journal*, 13 (1982)

—— 'Health, welfare and unemployment during the depression', *Past and Present*, 109 (1985)

Wheeler, M., *Heaven, Hell and the Victorians* (Cambridge, 1994)

Williams, N., 'Death in its season: class, environment and the mortality of infants in nineteenth-century Sheffield', *Social History of Medicine*, 5 (1992)

—— and Mooney, G., 'Infant mortality in an "age of great cities": London and the English provincial cities compared, *c.*1840–1910', *Continuity and Change*, 9 (1994)

Winter, J., *London's Teeming Streets, 1830–1914* (1993)

—— 'Infant mortality, maternal mortality and public health in Britain in the 1930s', *Journal of European Economic History*, 8 (1979)

—— *The Great War and the British People* (Basingstoke, 1986)

—— 'Some paradoxes of the First World War', in R. Wall and J. Winter (eds.), *The Upheaval of War: Family, Work and Welfare in Europe, 1914–1918* (Cambridge, 1988)

—— *Sites of Memory, Sites of Mourning: The Great War in European Cultural History* (Cambridge, 1995)

—— 'Surviving the war: life expectation, illness and mortality rates in Paris, London and Berlin, 1914–1919', in J. Winter and J.-L. Robert, *Capital Cities at War: London, Paris, Berlin, 1914–1919* (Cambridge, 1997)

—— 'The decline of mortality in Britain, 1870–1950', in T. C. Barker and M. Drake (eds.), *Population and Society in Britain, 1850–1980* (1982)

—— and Robert, J.-L., *Capital Cities at War: London, Paris, Berlin, 1914–1919* (Cambridge, 1997)

Woods, R. I., 'The effects of population redistribution on the level of mortality in nineteenth-century England and Wales', *Journal of Economic History*, 45 (1985)

—— 'The structure of mortality in mid-nineteenth century England and Wales', *Journal of Historical Geography*, 8 (1982)

—— *The Demography of Victorian England and Wales* (Cambridge, 2000)

—— Watterson, P. A., and Woodward, J. H., 'The causes of rapid infant mortality decline in England and Wales, 1861–1921', Parts I and II, *Population Studies*, 42 (1988) and 43 (1989)

CHAPTER 12

Rich and Poor

In their preface to the 1851 census, George Graham and Horace Mann were confident that Britain could escape from the 'stationary state'. The world of Malthus, Mill, and Engels was giving way to new possibilities, not only because the 'hare' of population became much slower but also because the 'tortoise' of resources put on a spurt of growth. Much higher levels of GNP per capita now became possible, breaking through the limits of the late eighteenth and early nineteenth centuries.

Charles Feinstein has calculated that real weekly earnings in Britain between 1778–82 and 1853–7 rose by less than 30 per cent. Indeed, real incomes were largely static up to the early 1830s, and gains in the mid-1830s were lost in the depression of 1838–42 with recovery only starting in the mid-1840s. The situation was even less impressive when a number of other factors are taken into account. The number of dependants supported by each wage earner rose and reduced the standard of living of the average family by about 10 per cent. Part of the improvement in real wages was a recompense for poor conditions and early death in towns; poor relief also fell. These two factors probably reduced the gains by a further 5–10 per cent, so that the overall gain in the standard of living of the average working-class family was only 10–15 per cent between 1778–82 and 1853–57. In the words of Feinstein, 'the historical reality was that [the working class] had to endure almost a century of hard toil . . . before they really began to share in any of the benefits of the economic transformation they had helped to create'.[1] Most of the advance came after 1873 as prices fell, the number of dependants started to decline, and the worst problems of urban sanitation were resolved.

The problems of poverty were not solved, for the distribution of income and wealth was highly unequal and remained so up to 1914 and beyond. Indeed, inequality was considered by many to be a prerequisite for economic growth by offering incentives to enterprising businessmen. In his budget of 1853, Gladstone rejected redistributive taxation: the best way of stimulating welfare was to allow the rich to retain their money for saving and investment. Poverty and hardship would be reduced as the benefits of growth filtered down; and at the same time, the state should encourage workers to take responsibility for social risks through savings banks and friendly societies. 'New Liberals' and neo-classical economists took a somewhat different view, arguing that the distribution of wealth might *contribute* to misery. Might rich families spend their money on luxuries or send their savings overseas, so distorting the home market and domestic investment to the detriment of welfare? Such thoughts led to policies designed to redistribute income and wealth.

The distribution of GNP was also affected by the nature of the labour market and the structure of the economy. The nature of the work process influenced the distribution of wages, with wide discrepancies between skilled or supervisory and unskilled or subordinate labour. During the First World War, labour shortages gave unskilled workers a better bargaining position and differentials narrowed within the working class; there was a shift from capital towards labour. At the same time, the emergence of white-collar or lower middle-class occupations meant that there were more occupations with salaries at least on the same level as skilled manual workers, and with greater security. As the structure of employment changed, so did the nature of social mobility. How far could unskilled workers move into skilled jobs, and how easily could manual workers join the white-collar workforce?

The position of women connects with these issues. Women's wages were only half the male rate even when their work was similar, and many of the new white-collar jobs were given to women as a deliberate strategy to reduce labour costs. Women were usually obliged to resign on marriage and lacked the career prospects of their male counterparts. These assumptions were generally shared by women as well as by their employers and husbands: a non-working wife was a symbol of status, a working wife of pressing need. Indeed, the decision to stay at home might lead to greater gains for welfare than entering the labour market by improving domestic cleanliness, child care, and diet. Only with the widespread diffusion of labour-saving machinery and changes in retailing could women contemplate combining work and family responsibilities except in necessity. The general increase in the GNP per capita was therefore complicated by changes in its distribution within the working class, between capital and labour, and between men and women.

Measuring the Standard of Living

The standard of living made some modest improvements in the 1840s: the index of average full-employment real earnings (1778–82=100) rose from 115.9 in 1840 to 133.4 in 1843, falling back to 116.4 in 1847 and returning to 133.4 in 1849. In the 1850s, the gains were modest and hesitant. In the 1860s, the higher level was sustained, reaching 149.4 in 1869. In the early 1870s, average real earnings moved to much higher levels, from 160.4 in 1873 to 179.2 in 1882.[2] The welfare of the British people was reaching new levels. The onset of more rapid advance from the 1850s and especially after 1873 makes sense of other changes. The pressure of dependants on wages was reduced with a fall in the birth rates, and rising living standards changed attitudes to children on whom more money was spent. The consumption of food became more varied, and more money could be allocated to housing, consumer durables, and leisure. The hours of work also started to fall.

The quarter-century from 1873 has often been termed the 'great depression', and a Royal Commission was established in 1883 to inquire into the Depression of Trade and Industry. Whatever the 'great depression' might have been, it was not a period of depression in the standard of living of the working class (see Table 12.1). At the beginning of the twentieth century, improvement slackened or was even reversed. The wage index compiled by A. L. Bowley indicated a fall in the rate of growth of money wages and a reduction in real wages between 1899 and 1913. However, the break in trend was probably less marked than Bowley thought, for he excluded distribution, domestic service, road and rail transport, and central and local government. Some of the missing occupations had a more rapid growth of money wages than others he included—the building trade, for example, was experiencing a slump. Neither did Bowley utilize data on the period shortly before the First World War and he therefore missed the spurt in money wages at the end of the period. Feinstein's wage index for the period 1880–1913 covered a wider range of occupations and utilized additional data on the sectors included by Bowley. Feinstein indicates that real wages grew at an annual rate of 1.58 per cent between 1882 and 1899, and fell to a growth rate of 0.29 per cent between 1899 and 1913. The break in trend survived without an actual fall in the standard of living.[3]

A reduction in the rate of growth of real income to a third of its former level poses a number of problems. Why were money wages maintained during the period of falling prices after 1873; how is the break in trend after 1899 to be explained;

TABLE 12.1. *Nominal and real wages in the UK, 1856–1913 (annual percentage growth rates)*

	Bowley			Feinstein		
	Money wages	Cost of living	Real wages	Money wages	Cost of living	Real wages
1856–73	2.03	0.40	1.62			
1873–82	-0.98	-2.01	1.03			
1882–99	1.01	-1.01	2.03	0.92	-0.66	1.58
1899–1913	0.76	1.23	-0.46	1.26	0.97	0.29

Source: Feinstein, 'What really happened?', 330, 344.

and what were the economic and social consequences? This issue connects with the gold standard which meant that the exchange rate could not be allowed to 'float' downwards in order to maintain competitiveness in export markets and to price foreign goods out of the domestic market. One explanation often proposed for the success of the gold standard before 1914, and for difficulties after its restoration in 1925, is that wages were flexible before the war and rigid in the inter-war period. In fact, money wage rates did not fall in most trades before 1914 with the exception of the coal industry and iron and steel trades where wages were, in some cases, regulated by a 'sliding scale' which determined wage rates by the selling price of output. But in general, money wages were maintained during the period of falling prices and employers opted to reduce the wage cost by increasing the workload and imposing tighter discipline.

In every industry, a 'frontier of control' defined the balance between the demands of the employer and the desire of the workforce for discretion and some autonomy. Falling prices gave employers an incentive to push the frontier of control to their advantage. The outcome was that unit wage costs in industry fell so that wage costs were reduced without an attack on money wage rates.[4] The ability of employers to intensify the pace of work depended on a number of circumstances. One was the nature of the final product. For example, compositors in Fleet Street retained greater control over the work process than engineers. Newspapers were not open to foreign competition and a loss of one day's production could never be restored. Compositors could therefore resist attempts to increase their pace of work. In engineering, the market was increasingly competitive and it was possible to regain lost production after a stoppage. Hence engineering employers were more inclined to take a firm line with workers.[5] The competitive structure of any industry was a further influence. A high level of competition made it more difficult to overturn traditional patterns of work. Boards of conciliation in the cotton industry embedded the existing pattern of work: they allowed employers to increase the pace of work by co-operating with the upper grades of workers, without breaking free of the institutional pattern which limited the adoption of new technology.[6] A change in the frontier of control was easier where oligopoly gave a few employers more power, or where employers had a desire to submerge their differences. In the building industry, contractors wanted some certainty that wage rates would not escalate or that workers would not down tools so that the terms of the contract were not met. Consequently, employers agreed to a formalized system of bargaining with the unions.[7] Although some historians interpret these agreements as a sacrifice of control over the workplace by the union leaders in return for recognition, the outcome was usually to secure tighter control within an existing institutional pattern rather than a serious attempt to break the power of workers as in the United States. Hence money wage rates were relatively stable, and employers preferred to increase the work effort within the existing pattern of control, without moving to strict internal managerial control or using higher wages to increase the 'effort bargain'.

What happened around 1899? Bowley's data suggest that prices rose and the rate of growth of money wages between 1899 and 1913 was 20 per cent lower than in 1882–99. However, Feinstein's corrected figures show that the annual rate of increase of money wages was actually 37 per cent *higher*. The index of money wages is weighted to allow for changes in the structure of employment, and accordingly combines two influences. The first is a structural shift towards higher wage occupations. Textiles, with a net output per head of £73 in 1907, lost 295,000 workers between 1881 and 1907 in the UK, whereas metals with a net output per head of £100 gained 370,000 workers. Shifts from occupations with low to high output affected the level of money wages in the economy. The other influence was improvement in wages by people who stayed in the same occupation which reflected wage bargaining. The role of structural change through a shift to more highly paid sectors of the economy remained constant at 0.3 per cent per annum in the two periods, whereas the contribution of changes in money wages within sectors rose from 0.61 per cent per annum between 1882 and 1899 to 0.95 per cent per annum between 1899 and 1913.[8] Of course, the increase in money wages was at the expense of considerable labour unrest shortly before the war.

Another possible reason for the change in the pattern of real income growth was that the rate of productivity growth fell so that there was less scope to increase money wages until employers were forced to make concessions. Measures of real GDP per worker are contradictory. Measures based on output data indicate that the rate of growth of GDP per worker slowed in the 1870s. On the other hand, measures based on income data show a fall in the rate of growth of real GDP per worker from 1.43 per cent between 1882 and 1899 to 0.31 per cent between 1899 and 1913 which could explain the deceleration in real employment income per worker.[9] If the income data are indeed accurate, the fall in the rate of growth of real wages is explained.

Another possible explanation of the trend in real wages is a shift in the terms of trade or, more generally, in the price of consumers' goods compared with other prices. The improvement in real wages was largely the result of a fall in food prices. Could it be that Britain in the later nineteenth century benefited from a favourable movement in the terms of trade? The explanation for changes in the growth of real wages might, in other words, be located in the world economy (see Table 6.2). However, the movement was not large. What about the movement of prices for consumers against other prices? If the cost of living index fell more than the general price index, individual consumers would gain; they would lose if the cost of living index rose more than the general price index. Consumers did benefit to some extent from changes in relative prices between 1882 and 1899, but the overall impact on trends in real income was modest.[10]

The explanation of the break of trend in real wages therefore remains open. What about outcomes? Marshall pointed to one possible outcome of the movement in real wages: a depression in profits and interest in the latter part of the nineteenth century led to an increase in the share of wages and salaries in GNP. The rapid fall in agricultural rents and agricultural prices contributed to a shift in the distribution of income within rural society in favour of the labourer, and the share of farm property income fell sharply up to 1913. There was a similar trend in industry: the share of profits in industrial income fell by 10 per cent between 1870–4 and 1890–4, before a modest recovery up to the First World War. Nevertheless, labour's share of GNP remained fairly stable (see Table 12.2). Although agricultural rents fell, the rent of housing rose in the later nineteenth century. House prices and rents fell sharply after the building boom at the turn of the century but at the same time property income from abroad increased. Overall, labour's share of national income fluctuated within narrow limits up to the First World War which marked a major redistribution from property to labour by 10 per cent. The gains were held up to the Second World War which marked a further shift of about 5 per cent towards labour (see Table 12.2).

How is the wartime shift in the distribution between capital and labour to be explained? Initially, prices rose rapidly and the standard of living was under pressure. In the second half of the war and in the post-war boom, money wages rose faster than prices and contributed to inflationary pressure. As a result, profits were squeezed

TABLE 12.2. *Factor shares as a percentage of GNP at current prices, Britain, 1856–1951*

	1856	1873	1913	1924	1937	1951
Wages	43.5	41.4	36.6	40.6	38.6	41.9
Salaries	6.9	6.3	11.9	17.3	18.1	20.0
Employers' contributions	0.0	0.0	1.0	2.1	2.5	3.8
Self-employment	7.4	6.7	6.5	6.6	5.9	5.2
Total labour income	57.8	54.4	56.0	66.6	65.1	70.9
Income from abroad	2.2	4.4	8.5	5.0	4.2	2.7
Rent	4.8	5.2	6.4	5.3	6.4	3.4
Farm property income	10.1	7.2	2.4	1.8	1.1	1.9
Profits	25.1	28.8	26.7	21.3	23.2	21.1
Total property income	42.2	45.6	44.0	33.4	34.9	29.1

Source: Matthews, Feinstein, and Odling-Smee, *British Economic Growth*, table 6.1, 164.

and were further eroded by inflation and taxation of excess profits, and by the impact of depression in the staple industries. Although profits recovered somewhat between the wars, they remained below the level of 1913. During the Second World War, excess profits were taxed at a still higher rate, and the post-war Labour government was suspicious of the profit motive. The share of profits in GNP fell back to the level of 1924. The decline accounts for just over 5 per cent of the gain of labour between 1913 and 1924 or 1951. At the same time, employers' contributions through social insurance increased in both world wars. The second major element of redistribution was property income from abroad. This was remarkably high in 1913 but it fell sharply over the First World War, and again slightly between the wars with a further marked fall over the Second World War. The third variable was rent—a category which includes housing, agricultural land, and commercial property. During the First World War, the share of rent fell slightly, which benefited working-class tenants; the fall was more marked over the Second World War.

The gains of workers over the First World War created serious difficulties for the plan to return to the gold standard at the pre-war parity. British costs were too high to make an exchange rate of £1 to $4.86 sustainable, and money wages would need to fall faster than prices. Reductions in real wages were only modest up to 1924, when they again started to rise. Real wages improved markedly up to the Second World War—and the number of dependants also fell, so that more money was available for spending on consumer goods.

Keynes, Beveridge, and other social scientists were puzzled by the 'stickiness' of wages in the inter-war period. The level of unemployment was higher than before 1914 so that employers had a strong bargaining position. In 1922, Keynes complained that average wage levels were 80 per cent above pre-war levels and pointed out that when account was taken of the reduction in hours, wages were probably double pre-war levels. He saw the danger of a loss of trade, but realized the political dangers of attempting to reduce wages. He rejected the theory of the 'economic juggernaut' with its assumption that workers should adjust to the economic machine—and realized that the government, for all its call for adjustments, lacked the political will to carry through the implications of its own policies. The experience of the general strike exposed the limits of the government's policy of wage reductions. Keynes's explanation was in part a political calculation of the dangers of cutting wages, and a sense of social injustice that workers should be forced to adjust to the dictates of a fixed exchange rate in order for others to benefit.

But he remained puzzled by the 'stickiness' of wages and uncertain of the reasons. On some occasions, he suggested that wages were set by 'social and historical forces', and that at no point in history had wages ever been flexible in a downward direction without social unrest and protests. On other occasions, he suggested that welfare benefits allowed workers to refuse wage cuts despite the fall in prices and unemployment, a view endorsed by Beveridge in the 1920s and more recently by Benjamin and Kochin who claimed that welfare benefits prevented labour markets from clearing. Beveridge changed his view in the 1930s when he was actively engaged in administering the benefits, as did Keynes in his evidence to the Macmillan Committee in 1931 when he firmly rejected the suggestion that welfare prevented the operation of 'economic laws'.[11] The implication was that economists should not assume that downward flexibility was 'correct' or 'normal'; it was a choice, and economists could only measure the consequences.

Industrialists were more concerned with labour costs per unit of output than with money wages. In the later nineteenth century, money wages rose at a time of falling prices, and industrialists responded by increasing work intensity and reducing unit labour costs. Similarly, in the inter-war period productivity rose and industrialists did not need to launch an attack on money wages if unit labour costs were falling and their profits recovering. Certainly, welfare benefits were not a major factor. A more plausible explanation for the maintenance of money wages at a time of high unemployment is the distinction between 'insiders' and 'outsiders' in the labour market. Insiders were offered decent wages to encourage hard work and to reduce turnover; employers would not use 'outsiders' to undercut wages, for they lacked work discipline and skills. The exclusion of 'outsiders' entailed a decline in the employment of older men. Before the First World War, between 60 and 70 per cent of men aged 65 and above were still at work; the proportion declined in the 1920s and 1930s so that the figure was down to 47.5 per cent in 1931. Data collected by the *New Survey of London Life and Labour* suggest that older workers could no longer sustain the work effort to retain a full male wage; employers were less inclined to allow short-term work or a lower work effort than in the past.[12] Crafts found that long-term unemployment in the depressed regions and among the elderly did not constrain the wages of insiders with jobs. Hence a reduction in benefits for the long-term employed would reduce their welfare without creating jobs.[13]

The inter-war period was therefore a period of gains in welfare for families in work. Real wages rose and a continued fall in the number of dependants freed money to be spent on consumer goods, better housing, and leisure. On the other hand, unemployed families suffered hardship, despondency, and ill health. The Second World War brought the 'outsiders' back into the labour market. Inflation was kept under control so that real wages rose over the war and the immediate post-war period. From 1947 to 1951, 'austerity' and the export drive meant that real wages in 1951 were below the level of the 1930s (see Table 12.3). Of course, these figures are complicated by the high levels of taxation and the payment of welfare benefits, so that the impact on welfare is more difficult to measure.

TABLE 12.3. *Wages and the cost of living in the UK, 1914–51 (average of 1906–10 = 100)*

	Wage rates	Cost of living	Real wage rates
1914	106	106	100
1916	122–7	155	79–82
1918	185–91	216	86–8
1920	276–314	266	104–18
1921	307	241	127
1924	211	212	100
1929	206	173	119
1933	196	148	132
1938	218	166	131
1942	288	231	125
1945	327	245	133
1947	365	266	137
1951	434	333	130

Source: Routh, *Occupation*, table 3.1.

Wage Differentials and Cycles

The aggregate indices of money and real wages capture the broad trends in the standard of living yet neglect significant social trends. Unemployment among Teesside shipbuilders, for example, was as high as 40.5 per cent in 1908 and 30.1 per cent in 1909. Shipbuilding, like other capital goods industries, experienced marked cycles: high freight rates led to a spurt in construction followed by overcapacity and low prices until the volume of trade caught up with available shipping space.[14] The reality for such workers was different from the improvement in earnings shown in statistics calculated on the basis of full-time employment, and they responded by creating trade union unemployment funds to 'smooth' earnings. The statistics collected by these unions allow a correction for the level of unemployment, but capture only part of the impact of the trade cycle through short-time working or overtime. The variation for workers in casual sectors was even greater, with seasonal employment and variations over the week. These workers could not afford to join a union welfare scheme, and they developed other stratagems.

The length of the normal working day or week changed over the period in a few sharp breaks. In many trades, working hours fell from 60 to 54 hours a week in the early 1870s, with the next cut in 1919/20. Usually, unions demand higher wages rather than shorter hours because employers are more likely to accept an increase in the wage rate than a change in hours. Furthermore, workers with a preference for leisure are unlikely to resist an increase in wages, whereas workers with a preference for income are more likely to oppose a loss of wages in return for leisure. Consequently, the reduction in hours came at periods of unusual prosperity and bargaining power when an increase in wages could be combined with an increase in leisure, so removing the clash of preferences.[15]

The wage indices provide a single national figure and neglect regional and occupational variations. Regional wage variations remained wide up to 1914 when national bargaining and economic change led to a narrowing. Coal miners provide a good example. In 1914, hewers in south Yorkshire had a daily wage of 10s. 3d.; in Leicestershire the daily wage was 7s. The high level of internal migration merely prevented regional differentials from becoming wider. In 1850, the high-wage areas were London, the north, and parts of the midlands; by 1914, the lowlands of Scotland and south Wales were added. Since the high-wage areas were not necessarily those with high prices, the standard of living diverged. The high-wage areas were also, with the exception of London, areas of high unionization; it followed that collective bargaining maintained differentials before the First World War.[16] The pattern changed after the war when national bargaining started to erode differentials and the previous high-wage areas experienced persistent depression between the wars. Consequently, the pattern of regional differentials was overturned and the high-wage areas were now London and the midlands.

Occupations differed in the pace of change. Taking all sectors, annual earnings rose by 27.5 per cent between 1881 and 1913, but the increase varied from 86.8 per cent in coal mining to 7.7 per cent in footwear and nil in female clothing. Modest wage increases can be explained in part by mechanization (in footwear, clothing) or the ease of entry into trades with a lack of organization (road haulage, clothing). Trades with large wage increases lacked major technical change. Hewers in coal mines were able to demand higher wages for their strenuous hand labour, helped by the low elasticity of demand for coal and the secular increase in its price. Between the wars, the range of variation was considerably less, reflecting the decline of casual labour, the completion of mechanization, and the arrival of national bargaining.[17]

Wage indices not only mask wide regional and occupational variations; they also hide the spread of wages within any occupation. Up to 1914, the range was very wide, particularly where wages were determined by piece rates. On Teesside, the earnings of steel workers in 1913-14 in any week varied from 18s. to 37s.[18] There were also wide discrepancies between grades. A large part of British industry was characterized by internal subcontracts with skilled workers dividing the payment and available work in order to protect their own position. In engineering in 1880, the time rate for an unskilled worker was about 60 per cent the time rate for a skilled worker; the gap was still greater in the case of earnings. The gap closed during the First World War and post-war boom, when labour shortages meant that unskilled workers had a stronger bargaining position, and the government encouraged decasualization. The

TABLE 12.4. *Time rate of unskilled as a percentage of the time rate of skilled workers, in building, shipbuilding, engineering, and railways, 1885–1950*

	Building	Shipbuilding	Engineering	Railways
1885	63.6	54.0	60.0	50.5
1914	66.5	55.2	58.6	54.3
1920	81.0	77.2	78.9	81.2
1925	75.6	68.8	70.9	69.4
1933	75.2	68.3	71.2	61.6
1937	75.0	71.2	74.1	61.0
1950	84.1	81.7	84.7	77.4

Source: Knowles and Robertson, 'Differences', 111.

wage differential between skilled and unskilled workers did not return to pre-war levels and it narrowed again during the Second World War: flat-rate changes in wages were awarded as 'temporary' wartime bonuses designed to meet rising costs of living, and were then incorporated into the basic rate (see Table 12.4).[19]

By contrast, the differential between men's and women's wages remained remarkably stable (Table 12.5). Women made some gains in the lower professional grades but differentials in manual grades widened so that the overall weighted position was worse in 1950 than in 1913/14. The differential did not reflect any difference in the value of women's work for it was a social and cultural phenomenon. Male trade unionists developed the notion of a family or 'breadwinner's' wage as a sign of respectability and pride. Such an argument appealed to many middle-class commentators who stressed the need for women to stay at home; many women shared their belief. Housework and child care were strenuous and demanding activities in their own right, and paid work outside the home was an additional burden. Shifting these cultural assumptions took time: in 1946 the Labour government accepted the recommendation of the Royal Commission on Equal Pay that women should not have the same wage as men.[20]

Of course, the largest single female occupation for much of the period was in domestic service. In the late nineteenth century, indoor domestic service employed 36 per cent of working women in England and Wales; in 1951, only 11 per cent were employed in the sector. By the twentieth century, more young women were moving into retailing and offices. More married women entered the labour market during and after the Second World War (see Table 12.6), but their prospects for promotion and advancement remained poor. Married women might contribute to the family income by taking in lodgers or washing, or by part-time cleaning or child minding. It was difficult for women in some areas to find paid employment, particularly in heavy industrial districts and coalfields, compared with textile districts where many

TABLE 12.5. *Women's wages as a percentage of men's averages, Great Britain,*
1913–1956

	1913/14	1922/4	1935/6	1955/6
Lower professional	57	67	69	72
Managers/admin.	(40)	33	38	54
Clerks	42	46	46	57
Foremen	46	57	57	61
Skilled manual	72	78	75	57
Semi-skilled manual	72	78	75	57
Unskilled manual	44	57	57	52
All (1911 weights)	53	58	56	52

Source: Routh, *Occupation*, 123.

TABLE 12.6. *Female employment by marital status, England and Wales and*
Scotland, 1911–51 (%)

	England and Wales			Scotland		
	Married	Single	Widowed/divorced	Married	Single	Widowed/divorced
1911	14	77	9	5	87	7
1921	14	78	8	6	87	7
1931	16	77	7	9	86	6
1951	40	52	8	23	69	7

Source: McIvor, *History of Work*, 38.

married women worked. In 1911, only 6.9 per cent of married and widowed women
in Barrow were in full-time employment compared with 35 per cent in Preston (see
Table 12.7).[21]

As the women in Preston realized, working women had great difficulties in
combining two onerous tasks of factory work and domestic chores, and many
turned to child minders and spent more money on laundry and convenience foods.
Work outside the home did not offer liberation and freedom: it was a huge burden,
added to the unremitting domestic tasks of washing clothes, cleaning, shopping, and
cooking. Indeed, women's labour in the home might produce a greater gain in the
family's welfare through increased cleanliness, nutrition, and health. Washing clothes
took a full day of heavy physical labour, involving heating water, pounding clothes by
hand, and passing them through a wringer. Heating and in many cases cooking was
done on an open fire or range, with the need to carry coal, clean the grate, and battle

TABLE 12.7. *Women employed by region, England and Wales, 1931*

	Percentage of total employed
Lancashire and Cheshire	41.9
Greater London	39.9
Durham and Northumberland	23.1
South Wales	19.5
England and Wales	34.2

Source: McIvor, *History of Work*, 39.

TABLE 12.8. *Occupation distribution of women, England and Wales, 1881–1951 (%)*

	1881	1901	1931	1951
Personal service	—	42.0	34.7	23.4
Indoor domestic	36.0	33.0	23.8	11.5
Other		9.0	10.9	11.9
Clerks, typists, etc.	—	1.3	10.2	20.4
Commerce and finance	—	6.8	10.8	12.1
Professional and technical	5.5	7.5	7.0	8.3
Textile goods / dress	17.7	16.1	9.0	7.0
Textile workers	17.0	14.0	10.4	6.0

Source: James, 'Women and work in 20th century Britain', 291.

against dust and grime. Water for washing was heated on the fire, so that bathing was an effort—particularly onerous for the wives of miners who returned home in their pit clothes. Floors had to be scrubbed, and privies kept clean. Of course, infants and children needed to be nurtured, from washing nappies to caring for them in sickness. These daily and unremitting tasks constrained the life of women who had to manage limited budgets. These tasks became easier with the emergence of improved sanitation, cleaning materials, and floor coverings, and the appearance of gas cookers, electric light, and even vacuum cleaners. However, for most women housework and child care remained a heavy burden up to 1950. Washing machines and refrigerators were still rare in working-class households, and shopping remained labour intensive. Indeed, the purchase of time-using goods such as radios and gramophones was much more rapid than time-saving goods such as washing machines.

Women's tasks were not confined to domestic chores. Men dealt with their employers in the workplace; women dealt with landlords and shopkeepers, playing a crucial role in the management of the budget; and they faced agents of the state who inspected and monitored their care of the home and children. The skill of the wife was critical to the welfare of the family. Very often, success depended on drawing on assistance from kin and neighbourhood in mutual support. It was hard work but it was also a source of pride, which delivered considerable gains in welfare to the family. As Joanna Bourke points out, when household earnings reached a reasonable level, 'the value of a woman investing all her time in unwaged domestic production outstripped the value of her wage'. Rising wages therefore led to women's labour within the home, and the increased welfare of working-class families was created not only by higher wages at work but also by improved housewifery. Men developed their own form of masculine housework in decorating and gardening, using their increased leisure time and spare cash.[22]

The structure of the family economy was of crucial importance for the standard of living, a point realized by B. S. Rowntree in his pioneering study of poverty in York. He found that 9.9 per cent of the total population lived in 'primary poverty' in 1899, that is below the level of income needed to maintain mere physical efficiency. These poor families were not a fixed group, for a much larger part of the population moved into and out of poverty at some stage. An individual, argued Rowntree, was likely to experience three periods of relative comfort and three of hardship. The first child would be born into relative comfort. By the time the first child reached the age of 5, the family was probably pushed into poverty as further children were added to the family and the mother was less able to provide a supplementary income. This phase of poverty would last until the first child reached the age of about 14 and started to earn. When children left home in order to marry, they entered a new phase of poverty around the age of 30 as they had a family of their own, until their own children started to earn. Middle age was therefore a period of relative prosperity. When their children left home and the strength of the male breadwinner started to fail, income fell and old age was eked out in poverty. The figure of 9.9 per cent of the total population in primary poverty was therefore a 'snapshot' of those who were in one of the poverty phases.[23]

Rowntree's concept of the 'poverty cycle' is useful, yet he did not attach it to any particular occupation. Different occupations had different patterns of income over a career which can be captured by a distinction between 'family time' and 'industrial time'.[24] 'Family time' is Rowntree's poverty cycle: the timing of marriage, the birth of children, the departure of a young adult from home. The precise timing varied over time and between occupations, and interacted with 'industrial time' which had two dimensions. The first was the pattern of trade cycles. In one family the transition to a period of strain in the life cycle might coincide with depression, whereas in another it might coincide with an upturn in the economy. The second consideration was the particular organization of work in any occupation with different timing of promotion to a full adult wage. Wage rates might be more or less identical in two trades but with very different patterns of lifetime earnings which had major consequences for the standard of living. Did an occupation offer the prospect for advancement from poorly paid to well-paid grades? Was the highest income reached in young adulthood or was it delayed? And how did adult male wages connect with family earnings? An increased income for the male head of household might allow a reduction in the contribution of children and wives, so that family earnings grew less rapidly.

The coal and cotton industries in Lancashire illustrate the point. A comparison of average adult male wages suggests that hewers were better paid than spinners. However, the timing and certainty of attaining the adult wage differed in the two trades. In coal, promotion from the juvenile grade of hauling to the adult grade of face work was virtually certain. This was achieved before marriage, with promotion to hewer coming around the age of 27 so that children were born at a time of peak earnings. The hewer experienced a gradual fall in earnings as his strength failed, with the likelihood of demotion to work on the surface at a much lower rate. In the case of cotton, promotion from the juvenile or subordinate grades to the adult grade of spinner was less certain and often delayed until the late twenties, after marriage. The precise age and likelihood of promotion depended upon the rate of expansion of the industry, and the problem intensified as the cotton industry entered a decline after the First World War. Promotion might coincide with the point at which the family started to move out of poverty as children went to work, and affluence was likely to continue for a longer period than in the coal industry for the minder could work into old age. Hardship in young adulthood was consequently offset by relative affluence in late middle age. There were therefore significant differences in the relationship between 'family time' and 'industrial time' in two major industries in one area.[25]

Wage scales might be used to secure long-term loyalty and discipline within a bureaucratic form of employment. For example, the Post Office created a wage scale for letter-carriers which rose over an individual's career. The letter-carriers were divided into various classes with an incremental wage scale within each class; in addition, up to six 'good conduct stripes' (with an extra weekly payment) could be earned at intervals of five years. The concern of the Post Office was to secure obedience by creating a long-term commitment. A similar pattern was found in other bureaucratic organizations, and white-collar occupations such as clerks in insurance companies. The flow of income over the life cycle was manipulated by promotion hierarchies and company pension schemes.[26]

The distribution of wages relates to the debate over the so-called 'labour aristocracy'. Many commentators in the 1840s thought that Britain faced social unrest and the prospect of revolution. In the 1960s and 1970s, Marxist historians followed Lenin in explaining the shift from unrest to stability in the middle of the nineteenth century: the employers divided the proletariat by creating a 'labour aristocracy' in regular, well-paid jobs who became the allies of capital against the subordinate grades.[27] How plausible is this? Few historians now accept the existence of a revolutionary potential or the existence of a class-conscious proletariat, so that there is little to explain. Neither was the emergence of a group of well-paid industrial workers a particular feature of the 1850s. The social processes for securing a high income varied, and it makes little sense to lump together coal hewers, cotton minders, platers in shipbuilding, and postmen into a single category of 'labour aristocrats'. Their privileged position arose from different processes with different social implications, at varying stages of the life cycle.

Whether well-paid workers joined friendly or co-operative societies depended on personal decisions, and often reflected family income rather than the male wage. These new institutions of the better-paid or respectable workers formed part of a process of consolidation and not the disintegration of a previously united working class. Unlike the craft exclusivity of artisans in earlier periods, such societies were open to anyone with the ability to pay. The ethic of respectability and self-help had a specifically working-class character. Members of the middle class defined these concepts in terms of independence from others and reliance upon the assets of an individual family. Skilled or more affluent workers interpreted the concepts in terms of freedom from dependence upon the middle class through their own institutions of collective self-help. Indeed, in the later nineteenth century and into the twentieth century, the lines between skilled and unskilled workers became more blurred as they formed a cohesive culture around their own institutions. As a result, culture up to 1950 was highly cohesive within both the working and middle classes without being integrated between the classes.[28]

Poverty

After the riots in London in 1886, Charles Booth decided to measure the level of poverty in the metropolis. He started by considering east London, in the belief that he would find there 'the most destitute population in England'. He went on to find that poverty was just as bad in south London, a conclusion which reinforced his belief that the metropolis had unique problems.[29] Hence Rowntree's claim in *Poverty* (1901) that a similar level of poverty was typical of the provinces was startling. The subtitle of his book gave one answer: it was *A Problem of Town Life*. In York he found that 27.84 per cent of the total population or 43.4 per cent of the working class lived in 'primary' and 'secondary' poverty. Primary poverty accounted for 9.91 per cent of the total or 15.46 per cent of the working-class population. In the case of secondary poverty, the income was in excess of the bare minimum yet it was spent in such a way that the family fell below the poverty line. Such a level of hardship was, Rowntree contended, a general phenomenon.

Rowntree found that the most common cause of poverty was low wages for men in regular employment, which accounted for 51.96 per cent of cases, followed by large families (22.16 per cent) and death of the chief wage earner (15.63 per cent). York would be typical of the level of poverty in provincial towns (as Rowntree contended) if the proportion of low-paid, unskilled labourers was the same as elsewhere. But Rowntree himself admitted that York lacked any highly paid industry. The existence of his own firm in the city hints at its distinctiveness: the manufacture of confectionery required a large, cheap workforce to package goods and to work in fairly simple processes of production. Booth himself was sceptical of its typicality, and his secretary remarked in 1908 that 'Mr Booth has never attempted to apply these propositions to the country generally where the conditions of life are in so many respects different from those prevailing in London'. Further comparative studies justified Booth's caution.[30] A survey of five provincial towns undertaken in 1912–14 by Bowley found that the level of primary poverty varied. In York, 12.7 per cent of working-class households were in primary poverty. The level was higher in Reading (23.3 per cent), a town with some similarities to York, and in Warrington (13.4 per cent), a town based on chemicals. There was less poverty in the shoemaking town of Northampton (8.9 per cent), the coal-mining community of Stanley (6.0 per cent), and the cotton-spinning town of Bolton (7.6 per cent).[31]

The major cause of primary poverty was low wages or irregular earnings which together accounted for 54.8 per cent of families in primary poverty in York. The towns with the highest level of primary poverty were those where unskilled labour and casual underemployment were endemic. The Charity Organization Society report of 1908 gave three definitions of casual labour: (1) engagement by the hour or day (this pattern applied, for example, to dock labourers); (2) a succession of jobs which might last from a few days to a few months, with 'leakage' or discontinuity between them as in building; (3) seasonal work with uncertainty about the beginning and end of a season, and fluctuating demand. This would apply, for example, to stokers in gas works.[32]

Every town had some casual labour in each category. The problem was particularly acute in towns with a large waterfront labour market and domestic industry or 'outwork'. In Liverpool, dockers were taken on at seventeen leading 'stands' and they had little idea of how many jobs were available. A docker would concentrate on a few stands where he was known to the foremen responsible for hiring, and it was in the interests of the foremen to spread work among a pool of men so that there were always enough applicants to meet the peak demand. The core of 'professional' dockers was supplemented by men who turned up when there was no other work; and the demand varied according to the season. In her analysis of the Liverpool waterfront labour market, Eleanor Rathbone pointed out that the problem was exacerbated by the organization of the labour market. Each stand had a certain number of men tied to it, who were in aggregate more than the docks ever needed. Rathbone and other reformers wished to create a single labour market with more regular employment.[33]

The existing system had advantages for employers who could tap the casual labour market at low rates of pay. The casual dockers themselves were sceptical about the desirability of decasualization. Habits adjusted to casual work so that a cultural transformation would be needed in the event of the introduction of regular work. 'There can be no doubt', remarked Rathbone, 'that the sense of being "their own masters" enjoyed by the men . . . [is] some compensation for the irregularity of their earnings.' The hardship was felt less by the dockers than their wives and children, for husbands usually handed over a fixed amount. The result was that 'the standard of family life is fixed by the amount earned in the slack months', creating a cycle of deprivation.[34] Pressure for change was more likely to come from union leaders who saw regular employment as essential to the achievement of recognition and a strong bargaining position. Some employers saw an advantage in a more organized labour market but many saw a threat to their profits.

The other major area of casual employment was domestic production or outwork. The scale declined between 1850 and 1914, but social problems intensified in surviving trades. Where did outwork disappear and where did it survive? The Charity Organization Society noted:

where expensive machinery is used, there is a strong incentive to reduce cost by continuous running. . . . Even though demand may be fluctuating, goods will be made for stock during slack periods until the fear of over-production and the rent for warehouses overbalances the gain from continuous working.[35]

The ability to stockpile depended upon the commodity: it was easier to make cotton cloth ahead of demand than garments which were affected by fashion and seasonality. The attractions of mechanization also depended on a sufficiently high demand. The rising standard of living in the last quarter of the nineteenth century encouraged the production of ready-made clothing in factories.

Even when the market did change, outwork continued, above all in tailoring. R. H. Tawney pointed out:

At one end of [the industry] are the large factories, equipped with every variety of power-driven machinery, relying mainly on female labour, and employing workers whose labour is so minutely graded that one woman may spend her whole time making the thirtieth part of a garment. At the other end is the living-room of the isolated outworker, who takes out materials either direct from the factory or from a middleman, and works upon them at home. Intermediate between these two extremes are the workshops, employing from five to forty workers.

The cheap, hand-driven sewing machine could be used in small workshops or at home. Low overheads and the ability to lay off workers allowed competition with factory production. 'The special characteristic of these short contracts', commented the COS, 'consists in transferring to the employee the responsibility of finding sufficient work . . . The employer gains from avoiding the necessity to pay wages for more labour than he needs.' Factory-based tailoring in Leeds and outwork in London were complementary as well as competing, undertaking different parts of the trade and covering seasonal variations.[36]

The distribution of factories and workshops in tailoring was, Tawney found, 'dependent mainly on the alternative employments for women and the level of men's earnings in different parts of the country'. The survival of outwork and sweatshops was 'a development into which employers deviate in those districts whose peculiar economic conditions make large numbers of married women anxious to supplement their husbands' earnings':

in the north of England women work in the tailoring trade when they are young. . . . In London . . . they have to work when they are older partly because they have not been able to obtain a competence when they are young . . . . For it is, of course, very largely from the wives and daughters of the worst paid and most irregularly employed male workers that the ranks of the home-workers in the tailoring trade are recruited. . . . The . . . low wages of one industry spreads like an infection to industries which are apparently quite unconnected with it.

'Sweated' female labour was the other side of the coin of male casual employment.[37]

Casual underemployment and seasonality had a major impact on family survival strategies. Where mechanization transformed the urban economy, greater regularity of employment resulted: industrialists attempted to keep their capital in production with periodic disruptions during downturns. As we have noted, the manufacture of capital goods was particularly liable to fluctuation. The average level of unemployment in shipbuilding on the Wear between 1902 and 1913 was 15.8 per cent, with a peak of 46.9 per cent in 1908 and a low of 2.8 per cent in 1913. By contrast to these heavy engineering districts dependent on the export market, in London and district unemployment in engineering varied between 6.8 per cent in 1908 and 2.1 per cent in 1911. The industry here was more diversified. Indeed, the emphasis on casual underemployment in London obscures the fact that employment in many trades was more regular than in northern industrial districts. The problem of cyclical unemployment was also less acute in cotton textiles and other semi-finished and consumer goods.[38]

The structure of the labour market and the inadequacy of wages were not the only reasons for poverty. Death, illness, and old age together accounted for 20.74 per cent of primary poverty in York. Another reason was the size of families which accounted for 22.16 per cent of primary poverty. Illness, old age, and death were less susceptible to control than family size.[39] All had the incentive, if not the means, to devise institutions to mitigate the impact on the family economy. Strategies for coping with the hazards of life ran from acts of desperation to careful, long-term management of resources which started to merge with the behaviour of the middle class.

Before the First World War, the state took action to deal with the problems of casual and sweated labour. Trade boards were established in the 'sweated' industries in order to raise wages and to stop employers from passing costs of ill health and deprivation on to the rest of society. The aim was not to subvert the market but to ensure that employers paid the real cost of labour. Similarly, labour exchanges were established: by centralizing hiring and giving regular dockers preference, the worst problems of casual labour could be resolved. The approach was pioneered in Liverpool but progress was slow as use of the labour exchanges was voluntary. The rank-and-file workers feared a loss of autonomy or their exclusion from the list of preference dockers, and went on strike against the scheme. Success depended on an alliance between state officials and union leaders who saw the advantages of organization. Above all, progress required compulsion, but the state was reluctant to impose change, and neither employers nor the union welcomed state intervention. The war provided the opportunity for the power of the union leadership increased. They proposed registration of dockers through the union, with a promise to work regularly in return for the payment of 75 per cent of their wage for every day on which they presented themselves for work, whether or not they were engaged. The scheme was less about decasualization than creating a closed shop and financial security. The issue became less urgent as the market for casual labour declined and welfare benefits became more generous. The most serious social problem facing the government between the wars was no longer casual employment but long-term unemployment in the depressed areas. Eventually, the dockers secured compulsory registration in 1940 which was incorporated into the Dock Labour Scheme of 1947—a closed shop which gave the union control over the waterfront.[40]

Consequently, the nature of poverty changed. Rowntree returned to his analysis of poverty in York in 1936 and 1950. In 1936, he found that 31.1 per cent of the working class and 17.7 per cent of the total population lived in poverty. The explanation was predominantly unemployment (28.6 per cent of cases) and low wages (32.8 per cent). The level of poverty had fallen from 27.8 per cent of the total population in 1899. By 1950, the figure had fallen dramatically to 1.66 per cent of the total population and 2.77 per cent of the working class. In 1950, unemployment did not account for any poverty, and low wages for only 1 per cent. Poverty was now overwhelmingly a matter of sickness and old age. As Rowntree and Laver realized in 1950, the explanation was partly the result of changes in the labour market, but the welfare state also had a role. If welfare benefits had remained at the same level as in 1936, they calculated that between 31.1 and 22.2 per cent of working-class households would be in poverty in 1950.[41]

Social Risk and Survival Strategies

The standard of living increased more rapidly in the later nineteenth century, and many working-class families had an unprecedented degree of affluence and comfort. At the same time, poverty remained a major concern. In the course of the debate, the meaning of poverty was redefined. Despite the improvement in the standard of living, the risk of poverty and hardship remained ever present as a result of old age or sickness or trade depression. Poverty was not confined to those with low wages: everyone faced social risks. The need to adjust the family budget to cope with child care, illness, old age, and death, and with the vagaries of the trade cycle and economic change, meant that working-class families developed strategies which allowed them to survive. However, families on the lowest income could not afford many of these strategies. *In extremis*, they could turn to the hated poor law or to charity from the middle class, yet most self-respecting working families preferred to make the best use of resources under their own control. These survival strategies were crucial and helped lay the foundations for the development of state welfare reforms.

Such stratagems appeared fruitless to many middle-class observers; to working-class families they were rational. One device was the pawnshop. Goods bought in prosperous months could be 'hocked' in less prosperous times. There was little sense in tying up assets in the form of an overcoat during the summer when there was an immediate need for cash. Middle-class observers were appalled by the high rate of interest charged by pawnbrokers. Yet the number of pawnbrokers' licences in Britain rose from 3,390 in 1870 to a maximum of 5,087 in 1914, and then fell to 2,672 in 1939—a clear sign of the rise in working-class living standards, and of the growth of other forms of debt.[42]

Another stratagem was credit, usually from local shopkeepers who allowed 'tick' during the winter. The costs were again high, for goods were bought in small quantities which increased the unit price, and the shopkeeper increased margins to cover defaulters. Credit might be used to buy clothing, furniture, and other consumer goods. 'Tallymen' visited housewives in working-class districts, selling goods which were paid for in instalments. Clothing clubs were established by workers or by shopkeepers, and small sums were subscribed, usually on the basis of twenty-one payments of 1s. for goods to the value of £1. Another scheme was 'check trading': a voucher was obtained from a company and paid for in instalments, but could at once be redeemed for goods at a participating store. Credit was not necessarily a strategy of desperation, for it could be used by well-paid workers to purchase more expensive goods. Hire purchase schemes emerged by the 1860s, for pianos, sewing machines, and furniture. Another major expenditure was rent, and one solution to financial difficulties was to 'flit'. However, landlords might permit arrears to be repaid in better times, particularly in the case of respectable workers. Frequently, tenants adjusted the rent to their budget by taking in lodgers.[43]

The flow of income and outgoings could be adjusted by various means, ranging from hand-to-mouth existence to the planned purchase of expensive consumer goods. Even better-paid workers were not immune to fluctuating incomes, and they developed their own distinctive strategies. In principle, co-operative stores attempted to win working-class families away from credit by requiring payment in cash, with members receiving a 'dividend' at the end of the year according to the amount they had spent. In practice, the ban on credit trading was modified in the face of realities: 75.5 per cent of English co-operative societies in 1905 admitted to giving credit. Many societies adopted a policy of high dividends, with 58.9 per cent of members in 1900 belonging to societies paying over 2s. 6d. in the pound. The stores were being used as a form of 'forced' savings by more affluent working-class families: they built up a fund upon which they could draw for a holiday or a larger purchase. Such a system of contractual saving through a mark-up in prices was more rational than voluntary savings through a savings bank, and it had the benefit of establishing a claim to credit during a period of hardship.[44]

Working-class families attempted to insure themselves against various eventualities. The most common was insurance against death in order to pay for a decent funeral. A group of people formed a burial club and paid a levy on the death of a member or a weekly subscription. The larger local societies used collectors who went from door to door to receive premiums in return for a commission. 'Collecting' societies developed from this practice. These were essentially commercial ventures: there were no shareholders, and they were operated by the collectors and officials of the society who received commissions and salaries. The Royal Liver had 1,957,139 members by 1905. Management costs accounted for 40 per cent of the premiums, with 27.5 per cent of this sum going to the collectors in commissions and fees. The business soon attracted more conventional insurance companies. Costs were comparable to the collecting societies, amounting to 41.5 per cent of premiums in the Prudential in 1887. The industrial assurance companies came to dominate the market, with 21.2 m paid-up policies in 1901; by 1936, this had risen to 62.9 m. Critics complained that the policies were bad value, and that using scarce resources for an elaborate funeral was inappropriate. They missed the point, for burial by the parish was considered the ultimate indignity. The weekly visit of the collector was a visible sign of status as well as increasing the chances of maintaining payment.[45]

Most working-class families aspired to insure against sickness. The most important agencies were the 'affiliated' friendly societies, national organizations with central reserves and branches around the country which provided both medical treatment and sick pay. Total membership amounted to 2.8 m by 1910 and a peak of 3.1 m in 1922–6. The largest was the Independent Order of Oddfellows. Subscriptions often lapsed when the family budget was under pressure, so that payments into the fund were lost to the advantage of more prosperous workers who maintained their eligibility. The subscription ranged from 4*d*. to 8*d*. a week, giving members the right to medical attendance from a doctor, and sick pay of about 10*s*. a week. The local branches met weekly or fortnightly to transact business, and the members ran the societies themselves, assessing the claims of fellow members. Display, status, and sociability were crucial. Many of the 'ordinary' societies with single branches offered similar benefits and rituals: they provided sick pay and medical treatment to 1.6 million members in 1910.

The emphasis in the affiliated friendly societies was on achieving status within the working-class community and securing protection from hardship, rather than acquiring the means of social mobility. The societies were based upon respectability and self-help. Working-class families were unlikely to accumulate enough assets to face a prolonged period of sickness, and it made more sense to share risks by creating a common fund. 'Contingency insurance' was a more rational response than savings; social display was more realistic than social mobility. However, some societies concentrated on sick pay rather than medical treatment. Centralized societies offered national coverage, transacting business by post without contact between members. The Hearts of Oak had 64,421 members in 1875, and expanded to 428,000 by 1933. Centralized societies appealed to a higher stratum of the working class, and new forms of leisure reduced the appeal of branch meetings and rituals. The deposit societies, with 0.4 m members in 1910, were a halfway house between a centralized society and a savings bank. The largest, the National Deposit Friendly Society, was formed in 1872 and it was run from a central office in London. It had 45,000 members by 1900, and 1.2 m in 1933. Members paid as much as they wished each week, partly into the benefit fund and partly to the member's personal account. During a period of illness, the sick pay was partly paid from the benefit fund; the remainder came from the member's account. The member could draw on the account for other purposes so that it was in part a savings fund. The centralized and deposit societies marked a point of transition to a more individualistic response to insecurity, appealing to clerical workers to whom fellowship with manual workers was a threat to status.[46]

Other institutions provided medical treatment without sick pay. The coverage is difficult to establish, for many did not register with the government. Clubs were formed to provide medical treatment in return for a payment of 1*d*. a week, usually supplying their members with a doctor who was paid a capitation fee for consultations and drugs. Much more impressive were the medical services in the coalfields, especially in south Wales where coverage extended from working miners to their families, and often to sick and unemployed miners, the old, and widows. These medical services emerged from clubs at individual pits, initially run by employers who deducted 2*d*. or 3*d*. in the pound which was handed to the doctor. In the later nineteenth century, the miners won control of the clubs, and they paid the doctors a fixed salary. The balance was used to provide midwives, nursing services, dentistry, and cottage hospitals. Many doctors were resentful of such lay control and were concerned by the financial limits and poor terms of the friendly societies. Accordingly, doctors in working-class communities seized on the state scheme of health insurance in 1911 as an opportunity for winning professional independence and a better financial deal.[47]

Only a minority of the working class could afford insurance against unemployment. In 1908, about 10 per cent of the male workforce had unemployment benefit, predominantly in metals, engineering, and shipbuilding (293,666), mining and quarrying (392,542), textiles (310,499), and transport (118,277). Some craft unions offered welfare benefits to cover sickness, funerals, or a payment to widows. Most unions did not accumulate funds or earmark them for specific purposes, which led to problems when a strike used up the money. The provision of welfare benefits was something of a mixed blessing. On the one hand, it increased the attraction of membership. On the other, the subscription could price membership out of the reach of workers, and the need to protect welfare benefits might limit their willingness to strike.[48]

In some cases, welfare benefits were organized in occupational schemes separate from the union. By 1881, seven funds covered the major coalfields, all providing cover against loss of earnings from accidents and sometimes adding medical treatment and pensions. The Northumberland and Durham Miners' Permanent Relief Society provided accident benefit after a colliery disaster in 1862; it developed into the largest private occupational scheme in the country. By 1914, 90 per cent of the miners in the north-east of England were members, paying 6*d*. a week for a weekly pension of 8*s*. With these exceptions, the provision of pensions was one of the major gaps in the system of working-class self-help, for few workers could afford to set aside enough money. To some extent, the societies paid disguised old age pensions by giving reduced sick pay to members who were too feeble to work. Union provision of pensions was similarly minimal.[49]

Working-class notions of self-help differed from those of the middle class. The middle class interpreted thrift in a more individualistic way through accumulation of assets. The government attempted to extend such an approach to the working class through the Post Office Savings Bank which was intended to supplement the trustee savings banks set up by middle-class philanthropists to receive small sums from the workers. Very few workers had sufficient resources to accumulate enough to cover even minor crises; the savings banks were used for short-term, specific purposes such as a seaside holiday. Workers needed certainty, so that contingency insurance was attractive. The key was the level of income; by the later nineteenth century at least a sizeable proportion of the British workforce could afford to join friendly societies offering contingency insurance. What they could not afford was accumulation of assets on a sufficient scale to provide protection against hardship.[50] Paul Johnson argues that the members were using collective means towards competitive goals, which leads him to downplay the cultural and ideological component of the co-operative and friendly societies. The motivation could be both mutual and competitive, with a widely shared belief in the values of the societies extending beyond a purely rational or instrumental approach. Of course, working people on limited means wished to achieve security, but they might also have a vision of the sort of society in which they wished to live. Competition for status was not necessarily at odds with a cohesive culture of working-class communities.[51]

The gaps left by self-help were covered, however inadequately, in a number of ways. One was the poor law; another was informal assistance within the working-class family and community. A third means was employer paternalism or welfare capitalism. The paternalism of factory communities was a feature of isolated villages under the control of employers who took a close interest in their workers. At Saltaire near Bradford, Titus Salt provided houses, schools, library, church, almshouse, and hospital which catered for his workers from cradle to grave. Such initiatives covered only a tiny proportion of the workforce, and most employers in large industrial towns preferred to provide facilities through voluntary organizations.[52] What did develop from about 1870 was a different form of welfare provision by employers—occupational pensions.

In 1859, a non-contributory pension scheme was introduced for the civil service. It covered not only elite administrators but also the employees of the Post Office, the largest single employer in the country. Private employers followed, both for salaried staff and manual workers. The larger joint-stock banks and insurance companies moved to formal pension schemes in the 1870s, and most railway companies had schemes for managerial and clerical staff by the 1880s. Self-help could elide with paternalism. The Great Western Railway, for example, obliged its workers to join the GWR Enginemen and Firemen's Mutual Assurance, Sick and Superannuation Society. Such pension schemes were a response to particular problems of control, for employers did not have the option of using internal subcontracting, and they needed to secure the loyalty and reliability of staff handling money or the lives of passengers away from immediate supervision. Indeed, company welfare might form part of an anti-union strategy. Dismissal meant not only the loss of a job but also of accumulated pension rights. Occupational pension funds entailed a shift from the discretionary award of a charitable gift to the certainty of provision according to formal bureaucratic rules. More generally, company pension schemes were often part of a wider change in labour policies to create an 'internal labour market' of incremental wage scales, formal promotion procedures, and rules to cover hiring and firing. However, most British manufacturers relied on state provision of welfare.[53]

Philanthropy was much more important and many employers preferred to operate through the voluntary organizations of the town. Between 1850 and 1914, philanthropy moved beyond individual knowledge of the local poor to a more impersonal and institutional character. New bodies proliferated, each appealing for funds to aid particular classes of need. This was not welcome to the Charity Organization Society which saw a potential threat to social order from competing philanthropy. In its view, the breakdown of personal ties between donor and recipient removed the need for recipients to be deserving and for the gift to lead to desirable social behaviour. The answer was a more orderly, bureaucratic approach based on referral to a committee to enquire into applicants' moral qualities. The deserving poor would be helped to independence; the undeserving would be left to the poor law. Social problems were seen as the outcome of personal rather than structural problems, and society was perceived as a collection of separate, individual wills. From about 1900 the debate between these perceptions was at the heart of British politics.[54]

The COS did not convert many charitable and voluntary organizations to its cause. 'Conspicuous compassion' allowed the middle class to achieve status in the community through honorific vice-presidencies and membership of committees. Charity offered purpose to middle-class women. A further motivation was what Beatrice Webb called a collective consciousness of sin by guilt-stricken members of the middle class. At settlement houses such as Toynbee Hall in the East End of London, university students lived amongst the poor, seeking to recreate face-to-face contacts and social relationships, and understand social problems. They included R. H. Tawney, William Beveridge, and Clement Attlee.[55]

Most charities and voluntary organizations had a different perception of society from the COS's reliance on case-work. To many philanthropists, the problem was a religious one. Temperance and sabbatarian organizations sought to rescue men and women from the perils of drink and vice. Temperance coffee houses, boys' clubs, and the Young Men's and Women's Christian Associations offered safety from the snares of the city. Pressure groups aimed to influence government policy. Churches and chapels were eager to maintain existing membership and win new adherents. Most denominations spawned an institutional structure which allowed congregations to spend their leisure within the church. Sectarian competition was, in the eyes of the COS, inefficient and wasteful—rather missing the point. Even members of the COS started to accept a different approach to the relationship between charity and the state, turning to Guilds of Social Help to co-operate with local welfare services, providing the human face to relief.[56]

The COS did have a point that voluntary organizations overlapped in some ways and left major gaps in other areas, not least in the provision of medical services. Perhaps half of the doctors in the country were under contract to friendly societies or medical aid clubs, and general practitioners were supplemented by semi-philanthropic provident dispensaries, and by out-treatment at hospitals. The hospitals were themselves divided into two broad categories: the poor law infirmary; and the voluntary hospitals which were funded in a number of ways. They appealed to individuals who were given 'tickets' to distribute to the poor. They created 'hospital Sundays' to raise collections at church services; and 'hospital Saturdays' for collections from workers. In London, the Prince of Wales created a fund in 1897 as part of the celebration of Queen Victoria's diamond jubilee. These interests came into conflict for a voice in the management of the hospitals, clashing with the medical profession which was acutely sensitive about its own autonomy. These tensions were to shape the intervention of the state into health care, in the introduction of health insurance in 1911 and the National Health Service in 1948.[57]

Social Mobility

When Mill reflected in *The Principles of Political Economy* on the structure of British society, he felt that social distinctions were so entrenched that they were 'almost equivalent to an hereditary distinction of caste'. Yet in a later edition of his *Principles*, Mill believed that economic growth was undermining social hierarchies so that 'human beings are no longer born to their place in life'. The classic statement was Samuel Smiles's *Self Help*, with its confidence that 'what some men are, all without difficulty might be'. More nuanced was Walter Bagehot's view that Victorian Britain lay somewhere between the egalitarianism of the United States and the 'irremovable inequalities' of castes in India.[58] Bagehot's point was that most people would not expect to rise from rags to riches, but they might hope that they or their children might rise from unskilled to skilled manual work, or from artisan to clerk.

Many recent cultural historians assume that Britain between 1851 and 1951 was characterized by two very powerful and coherent working- and middle-class cultures. In Ross McKibbin's influential interpretation, workers and the middle class created their own associations and leisure activities which were self-contained. In his view, Britain was divided into two class cultures which were much more important than other identities. These cultures were individually very powerful and cohesive, but in his view there was little in the way of a common culture. Perhaps boys' comics, Hollywood films, some popular music and radio programmes, and women's romances reached across class lines—but only partially and not sufficiently to constitute a common culture. If there was a 'democratic culture', it was found in the suburban world of the new middle class. Each culture gave identity to its members, without connecting. Trade unions rested on adversarial bargaining and the assumption that interests were divergent and mutually exclusive. However, the introverted and cohesive nature of working-class culture meant that fundamental inequalities were not challenged, for the basic institutions of society—the courts, parliament, and monarchy—were seen as fair. Resentment, argues McKibbin, was 'depoliticized'. If he is right, did such marked class cultures act as barriers to social mobility? If men or women were socially mobile at work or in marriage, did these barriers lead to a crisis of cultural identity? Was social mobility largely confined within each class culture? Or were these class cultures themselves a response to the dissolving power of mobility?[59]

Andy Miles and David Vincent provide some support for McKibbin's account. They point to two processes. On the one hand, barriers between manual workers and the middle class became more rigid; on the other, divides within the working class become less marked. Hence the working class was becoming more homogeneous.[60] These trends are apparent in data on income differentials which show that the gap between skilled and unskilled workers narrowed. However, the gap between working-class and middle-class occupations remained wide. Table 12.9 shows that the differences between skilled male manual workers, and male lower professional workers and managers, were wider in inter-war Britain than in 1913/14. By 1955/6, the gap had disappeared in the case of male lower professional workers, who now earned less than skilled manual workers.

The same pattern of homogeneity within classes and barriers between classes is confirmed by an analysis of marriage. When women and men married, they gave the occupations of their fathers in the register so that it is possible to see how many improved on the occupational status of their parents, and how many marriages crossed class boundaries. The data are available only up to 1914 and only capture the difference between the status of parent and child at the point of marriage. The data indicate that mobility increased up to 1914: in the marriage cohort of 1839–54, about a third of sons experienced some mobility; the figure rose to just under a half in the marriage cohort of 1899–1914. However, mobility was mainly within a class. At the beginning of the period, over three-quarters of the sons of unskilled workers remained in that category at marriage; by the First World War, over half were in higher categories than their fathers. Unskilled jobs were declining in importance, with the proportion of men recording themselves as unskilled falling from 29.8 per cent in 1839–59 to 17.5 per cent in 1899–1914. In 1839/54, skilled and unskilled workers were distinct: the fathers of over two-thirds of skilled grooms were themselves skilled, and the fathers of over three-quarters of unskilled grooms were unskilled. By 1899–1914, a majority of the sons of unskilled workers were in semi-skilled or skilled jobs at the time of marriage; and about a third of the sons of skilled workers were downwardly mobile. The working class was therefore becoming more homogeneous. Crossing the divide into the middle class was still rare. Fewer than 10 per cent of men with working-class fathers had middle-class occupations by the time they married, and those who succeeded usually joined the

TABLE 12.9. *Occupational class averages as a percentage of the mean of all occupational groups, men and women, Britain, 1913–56*

	1913–14	1922–4	1935–6	1955–6
Men				
1. Professional				
(a) Higher	405	372	392	290
(b) Lower	191	204	190	115
2. Managers etc.	247	307	272	279
3. Clerks	122	116	119	98
4. Foremen	152	171	169	148
5. Skilled manual	131	115	121	117
6. Semi-skilled manual	85	80	83	88
7. Unskilled manual	78	82	80	82
Men's average	116	114	115	119
Women				
1. Professional				
(a) Higher	—	—	—	(218)
(b) Lower	110	137	130	82
2. Managers etc.	99	102	104	151
3. Clerks	56	68	64	60
4. Foremen	70	98	96	90
5. Skilled manual	54	56	53	60
6. Semi-skilled manual	62	63	62	51
7. Unskilled manual	35	47	43	40
Women's average	62	66	64	60

Source: Routh, *Occupation*, 124, from Savage and Miles, *Remaking*, 26–7.

lower middle class where wages were little better than for skilled manual workers (see Table 12.9). Even those who became clerks were usually in sectors without prospects of future social mobility; bank clerks with the opportunity of career progression to bank manager were largely recruited from white-collar families. Although barriers within the working class remained, the increased flexibility within the working class contrasts with limited movement across the boundary with the middle class. The result was 'the demographic "making" of the English working class'. The notion of distinct, cohesive working- and middle-class cultures does make sense in 1914.[61]

The rigidity of class barriers may also be measured by the frequency with which children of skilled workers married the children of unskilled workers, or children of working-class fathers married the children of middle-class fathers. Marriage across class lines might reinforce occupational mobility and allow newcomers to be assimilated into their new class. Equally, men who experienced occupational

TABLE 12.10. *Social class of grooms compared with social class of fathers, Britain, 1839–1914 (%)*

Father's class	Year of marriage	Son's class				
		I	II	III	IV	V
I	1839–54	36.7	43.3	15.0	5.0	0.0
	1859–74	53.5	30.2	7.0	4.7	4.7
	1879–94	46.6	25.9	20.7	5.2	1.7
	1899–1914	36.2	31.9	19.1	2.1	10.6
II	1839–54	2.9	45.1	29.8	10.9	11.3
	1859–74	3.7	52.9	23.2	10.5	9.8
	1879–94	1.9	51.7	25.4	14.0	7.0
	1899–1914	2.5	51.4	24.7	13.6	7.9
III	1839–54	0.1	4.9	80.7	5.2	9.1
	1859–74	0.4	6.4	75.3	8.1	9.8
	1879–94	0.2	7.5	72.0	11.0	9.3
	1899–1914	0.5	8.2	63.6	16.5	11.1
IV	1839–54	0.4	6.4	30.5	47.8	14.9
	1859–74	0.4	5.1	33.1	46.7	14.7
	1879–94	0.7	8.6	33.9	45.4	11.4
	1899–1914	0.3	8.5	34.6	43.7	12.9
V	1839–54	0.0	2.4	18.0	8.4	71.2
	1859–74	0.0	2.6	19.9	12.1	65.4
	1879–94	0.0	3.0	21.5	17.7	57.9
	1899–1914	0.2	3.6	28.9	23.0	44.4

Notes: I = Independent and professional.
    II = Business, farming, and white collar.
    III = Skilled craft, outwork, factory, mining, transport, and services.
    IV = Semi-skilled industrial, agricultural, transport, and services.
    V = [unskilled?].
Source: Miles, 'How open', table 2.1.

mobility might marry women from their initial social background, so isolating themselves from their new occupational status. In other cases, men who retained the same occupational status married women from a different social background. These different patterns each introduced an element of heterogeneity into the class system. Just how frequent were these cross-class marriages?[62]

Men had few chances of meeting women from other classes at work. For women, the pattern was different, especially with a fall in the proportion of women employed as domestic servants. Female servants would meet the male head of household and sons in a menial capacity, and any closer relationship would transgress sexual propriety. As the proportion of women working in clerical and secretarial jobs for male employers rose, so did the prospect of friendly relations and courtship. By 1931, women accounted for 42 per cent of clerical workers, and over half were young. The opportunities for social mobility for young women were therefore greater than for their brothers. Though their chances of career progression were much lower, girls (and their mothers) saw office work as an opportunity for fashionable clothes and spending money, courtship, and possibly a good marriage. Consequently women had a greater likelihood of marrying men from a higher social background, and women were somewhat more likely to change their social class through marriage than men were to change their social class through occupational mobility. Almost half of women married a man whose class position was different from their fathers', compared with 37 per cent of men. Women were also more likely to be downwardly mobile. The relationship between class and gender was therefore complicated.[63]

Of course, these trends cannot capture the social meanings of marriage across occupational and class lines. Did women marrying into a higher social class lose contact with their family of origin, and were they accepted into their family of marriage? Did brothers and sisters or cousins experience contradictory patterns of upward and downward mobility by marriage or by career, and how were divergences within families handled? Cohesive class cultures made these boundaries difficult to negotiate.

What happened to social mobility after the First World War? Marriage data are no longer available, and we must rely on social surveys. In his 1924 study, Bowley found that only 18.1 per cent of the children of unskilled workers remained in that class; 53.7 per cent moved into the skilled working class.[64] Many sociologists assume that social mobility did not increase between 1918 and 1951. The first thorough sociological investigation of social mobility was published in 1954 by David Glass and his collaborators. They collected evidence from men, starting with a group born before 1890, and then by decade up to 1920-9. In the cohort born before 1890, 33.4 per cent of men had the same status as their fathers; in the cohort born 1920–9, the figure was 37.0 per cent. The proportion with a higher status than their father only rose from 31.8 per cent to 33.7 per cent. Glass stressed the close relationship between the status of father and son, and in turn the importance of parental status on the type of education. Although Glass expected greater social mobility as a result of the 1944 Education Act, the later study of John Goldthorpe did not find this.[65]

How plausible are these claims that social mobility was stable? Occupational change was not only a matter of the growth of middle-class jobs; it also meant a change in the pattern of recruitment. Improved literacy and education meant that more men and women could compete for the new types of middle-class employment. Urbanization increased opportunities to identify jobs, with a wider range of social contacts and less reliance on parents or kin. Above all, barriers of entry into better-paid positions weakened. The nature of skill shifted from traditional crafts and apprenticeships to more bureaucratic or 'credentialist' patterns of employment.[66] Vincent has used oral history interviews, and Miles has analysed autobiographies to show the changing balance between different career paths. They produce similar career typologies. Vincent suggests four types. The first was formal vertical bureaucracy, with entry dependent on credentials and promotion based on selection or examination. The second was a career based on knowledge, comprising artisans and teachers, lawyers and doctors. The third rested on the construction of a business. The fourth career was dynastic, with transmission of property between generations. Individuals might then adopt one of four trajectories. In 'gold watch' careers, a worker remained with a single employer where it was possible to move up an incremental scale and secure a pension. In 'migrating' careers, individuals took a sequence of jobs. The third option was to 'meander' from one unrelated job to another. Finally, an individual might have a 'fractured' career, leaving one type of work and moving in a new direction.[67]

In Vincent's sample, 51 per cent of men had 'gold watch' careers, 26 per cent migrated, 9 per cent meandered, and 14 per cent experienced a fractured career. The pattern was very different for women: only 7 per cent followed 'gold watch' careers, 18 per cent migrated, 30 per cent meandered, 34 per cent experienced fracture, and 11 per cent had no career. Most women ended their careers at marriage, and re-entry usually meant casual work. Although the First World War and slump had serious consequences for the careers of many workers, the sample covered by the oral history evidence comprised the 'golden age of the gold watch career', between a more casual pattern in the nineteenth century and the more recent emergence of 'labour market flexibility'. In the period covered by Vincent's sample, large numbers of men (and some women) had security from economic disruption or war. They did not experience significant social mobility but they did have stability and a measure of affluence.[68] The pattern is very similar in Miles's data. Miles's typology has three main career types. The first was informal, through entrepreneurship. The second was a formal career through bureaucratic progression or promotion within a single company. The third was the non-career, based on a single switch of direction, more frequent switching between a number of occupations before settling on one, or a continued meandering between largely unrelated jobs. The longer timescale of his evidence shows the shift from 'switching' and 'meandering' to a more formal and bureaucratic model (see Table 12.11). The change is apparent in the means used to find a job: only 10 per cent of autobiographers born between 1816 and 1864 mentioned applying for a job, compared with 46 per cent of those born between 1865 and 1914; similarly, the proportion mentioning an advertisement rose from 5 to 32 per cent, an interview from 8 to 25 per cent, and examination from 5 to 21 per cent.[69]

TABLE 12.11. *Career typologies, for men born 1723–1815, 1816–64, and 1865–1914, Britain (%)*

Career type	Writers' date of birth		
	1723–1815	1816–64	1865–1914
1. Informal	36.2	32.2	30.4
Entrepreneurial	(19.2)	(17.8)	(11.3)
Professional	(17.3)	(14.4)	(19.1)
Union-political	nil	(13.9)	(7.1)
2. Formal	nil	4.8	16.0
Bureaucratic	(nil)	(2.4)	(8.9)
Company	(nil)	(2.4)	(8.9)
3. Non-careers	63.5	49.0	46.4
Single switch	(20.2)	(23.6)	(25.0)
Switching	(26.0)	(19.7)	(16.7)
Meander	(17.0)	(5.3)	(4.8)
Number	104	208	168

Source: Miles, 'How open?', table 2.7.

Bureaucratic and credentialist recruitment weakened family influence over their sons' careers: patronage or purchase of a place became less important. But families could gain an advantage in the new credentialist world through investment in education.[70] Credentialism in the upper levels of the civil service excluded everyone except young men with a knowledge of the classics. Even at lower levels of public employment, credentials could be used as a social filter. Promotion opportunities probably declined with an increase in scale of organizations, and hence more lower- or middle-level positions; and the more formal, bureaucratic system was biased against women. In Lloyds Bank the initial bureaucratization of work created prospects of career mobility which then declined in the inter-war period; and the promotion prospects of men were maintained at the expense of women.[71]

Not all historians accept the existence of a cohesive class culture, on the grounds that it rests on somewhat romanticized autobiographies by writers such as Richard Roberts and Richard Hoggart, or on post-Second World War social surveys by Michael Young and the Institute of Community Studies. Baines and Johnson used data from the *New Survey of London Life and Labour* for 1929-32 to argue that under 10 per cent of young men entering the labour market closely followed their fathers' trades, and mobility across the lines of skilled, semi-skilled, and unskilled was normal. But do these data really overturn the notion of a cohesive class culture? This interpretation does not require sons to follow exactly the same occupation as their father, and mobility within the working class confirms its homogeneity. If the argument of McKibbin is to be challenged, it must be on the basis of the cultural identity of the class, and whether it really was so cohesive.[72]

The increasing homogeneity of the working class was not without strains, for skilled men mounted a defensive reaction against the threat to their autonomy and status. Skilled men relied on internal subcontracting to maintain some authority. They controlled entry into the workplace, passing many of the burdens of adjustment to lower grades while covering themselves against hardship through their own mutual societies. Such sectionalism was challenged by employers in the engineering lockout of 1898 and in the 'dilution' of skilled labour in the First World War. But the change was not easily imposed by employers, many of whom were wary of conflict with powerful unions. The change was partly the result of employers winning the loyalty of supervisors, removing them from the shop floor to join the ranks of management. It was also the result of a growing involvement of the state through labour exchanges, national insurance, and schools. Unions needed more voice in these new institutions, so moving their concerns away from immediate shop-floor issues to national politics. The TUC started to press for redistributive transfer payments in the 1890s rather than exclusive mutual associations for the better-off workers, and this trend continued into the inter-war period. Issues of unemployment pay and means testing brought skilled and unskilled workers together in a new form of industrial politics.[73]

Conclusion: Towards Equality?

The Labour government was committed to a more equal society, whose classic statement was Tawney's *Equality*. Hugh Dalton, Labour's post-war Chancellor, pursued a more equal distribution of income and wealth throughout his career. Douglas Jay summed up the case: 'economic inequality is . . . bad because it propagates a false scale of values: a false servility on the one hand, and a false compliance on the other. . . . But besides all this inequality is evil because it is unjust.' Equality might be secured through access to health care and education, through control over private capital, and by shifts in the distribution of income and wealth. The different criteria did not necessarily move in the same direction: nationalization could remove the economic power of capitalists without affecting wealth or income distribution. Free health care would not affect income distribution but did affect the quality of life.[74]

The impact of higher levels of taxation, as well as full employment, might be expected to lead to greater equality of income. But who paid the taxes and who took the benefits? Any answer is fraught with difficulties, for many members of the middle class were successful in using the new universal welfare schemes, and at least part of the cost fell on working-class consumers of alcohol and tobacco. Contemporaries were divided in their estimates. Probably, gains were made by incomes below

TABLE 12.12. *Changes in the distribution of wealth, Britain, 1911–54*

	Percentage of total wealth owned by top		
	1 per cent	5 per cent	10 per cent
1911–13	69	87	92
1924–30	62	84	91
1936–8	56	79	88
1954	43	71	79

Source: Atkinson, *Unequal Shares*, 21.

the threshold for income tax of £500 p.a. in 1948/9, and losses above that figure. A. M. Cartter produced three calculations, and his middle estimate suggested that public expenditure raised the income of those on £135 p.a. or less by 56.7 per cent, on £135–250 by 28.6 per cent, and on £250–500 by 13.4 per cent. The income of those earning £500–750 fell by 4.8 per cent and £750–1,000 by 12.4 per cent. Most of the gains for workers were in collective rather than personal consumption—and they were available to all members of society as universal benefits.[75]

What happened to wealth? At first sight, there was considerable progress towards equality (see Table 12.12). But the shift was less striking than the figures suggest. Higher and progressive levels of death duties did not only lead to a reduction in great fortunes but to a shift in the distribution of assets. Gifts before death meant that wealth shifted from the very rich to the merely rich. Such a strategy helps to explain why the top 1 per cent of wealth holders lost and the next 4 per cent gained. The use of trusts and settlements meant that redistribution was limited, and inherited wealth was preserved within families. Despite Labour's ambition, action was difficult given the ease of avoidance of death duties.[76]

In 1951, the British people had higher incomes, longer lives, fewer dependants, and more opportunities for leisure than could be imagined by even the most optimistic visitors to the Great Exhibition. The structure of occupations changed, so that more people had regular work with a degree of security. The middle class expanded and casual employment declined. How did these changes affect patterns of consumption?

NOTES

1. Feinstein, 'Pessimism perpetuated', 649–52.
2. Figures from ibid., appendix table 1.
3. Feinstein, 'What really happened?', table 4, 344.
4. Phelps Brown, *Century of Pay*, 126–32; Hobsbawm, 'Custom, wages and work load'.
5. Zeitlin, 'Engineers and compositors'.

6. Lazonick, 'Industrial relations and technical change'.

7. Price, *Masters, Unions and Men*.

8. Feinstein, 'What really happened?', 344–5; Feinstein, 'New estimates', 607, 612; Ashworth, 'Changes', 64.

9. Feinstein, 'What really happened?', 336–8, 344.

10. Ibid. 340, 348–9.

11. Skidelsky, *Economist as Saviour*, 133–4, 203–6, 242, 347–9; Harris, *William Beveridge*, 353–4, 359–60; Ch. 5.

12. Baines and Johnson, 'Did they jump or were they pushed?', 949, 953, 969–70.

13. Crafts, 'Long-term unemployment and the wage equation', 247–8, 253.

14. Hall, 'Wages, earnings and real earnings', 208.

15. Bienefeld, *Working Hours in British Industry*, 177–8, 222–6.

16. Hunt, *Wage Variations*, 57, 72, 104–5, 285, 354.

17. Feinstein, 'Variety and volatility'.

18. Hall, 'Wages, earnings and real earnings', 210.

19. Knowles and Robertson, 'Difference'; also Routh, *Occupations*, table 2.27; Penn, *Skilled Workers*, 100.

20. Pederson, *Family*, 36–9, 48–51; Lewis, *Women in England*, 164.

21. Lewis, *Women in England*, 156; McIvor, *History of Work*, ch. 7; Roberts, *A Woman's Place*, 39–40, 81, 101; Roberts, 'Working class standards of living in Barrow and Lancaster'.

22. Ross, *Love and Toil*; Ross, 'Survival networks'; Bourke, *Working-Class Cultures in Britain*, ch. 3 and *Husbandry to Housewifery*; Chinn, *They Worked All their Lives*, ch. 2; Davin, *Growing up Poor*; Hardyment, *From Mangle to Microwave*.

23. Rowntree, *Poverty*, 111, 136–8.

24. Haraven, *Family Time and Industrial Time*.

25. Griffiths, *Lancashire Working Classes*, ch. 2.

26. Daunton, *Royal Mail* Part III; Hannah, *Inventing Retirement*, chs. 1 and 2.

27. Hobsbawm, 'Labour aristocracy'; Foster, *Class Struggle and the Industrial Revolution*; Gray, *Labour Aristocracy*.

28. McKibbin, *Ideologies of Class*, xx–xx; Crossick, *Artisan Elite*, xx–xx.

29. Booth, *Life and Labour*.

30. Rowntree, *Poverty*, 120, 298, 300–1; Hennock, 'Measurement of poverty', 213–6.

31. Hennock, 'Measurement', 225.

32. Rowntree, *Poverty*, 120; Charity Organization Society, *Special Committee on Unskilled Labour*, 2.

33. Rathbone, 'Conditions of dock labour' 28–9; also Beveridge, *Unemployment*.

34. Rathbone, 'Conditions of dock labours', 54.

35. COS, *Special Committee on Unskilled Labour*, 5.

36. Tawney, *Tailoring Industry*, 10; COS, *Special Committee on Unskilled Labour*, 3.

37. Tawney, *Tailoring Industry*, 115; Stedman Jones, *Outcast London*, Part I.

38. Southall, 'Origins of the depressed areas'; Southall, 'Regional unemployment patterns'.

39. Rowntree, *Poverty*, 120.

40. Phillips and Whiteside, *Casual Labour*.

41. Rowntree, *Poverty and Progress*; Rowntree and Lavers, *Poverty and the Welfare State*, 30–1, chs. 3 and 4.

42. Johnson, *Saving and Spending*, 165–88.

43. Ibid. 144–65.

44. Ibid. ch. 5.

45. Ibid. ch. 2; Gosden, *Self Help*, 119–42.

46. Johnson, *Saving and Spending*, 48–74; Gosden, *Self Help*, ch. 4.

47. Johnson, *Saving and Spending*, 70–2; Earwicker, 'Miners' medical services'.

48. Thane, 'Working class and state "welfare" ', 884–5; Johnson, *Saving and Spending*, 74–80.

49. Hannah, *Inventing Retirement*, 6; Johnson, *Saving and Spending*, 80–3.

50. Johnson, *Saving and Spending*, ch. 4.

51. Ibid. 231–2; Gurney, *Co-operative Culture*, 8–11; Alborn, 'Senses of belonging', 562.

52. Reynolds, *Paternalist*; Joyce, *Work, Society and Politics*.

53. Hannah, *Inventing Retirement*, chs. 1 and 2.

54. Stedman Jones, *Outcast London*, Part III.

55. Stedman Jones, *Outcast London*, 258–61, 285; Webb, *My Apprenticeship*, 179–80.

56. Yeo, *Religion and Voluntary Organisation*; Cahill and Jowett, 'New Philanthropy'.

57. Waddington, *Charity and the London Hospitals*; Prochaska, *King's Fund*.

58. Miles, 'How open?', 20; Mitch, 'Inequalities which every one may remove', 158–9.

59. McKibbin, *Ideologies*, 166; McKibbin, *Classes and Cultures*, 527–8.

60. What follows is from Savage and Miles, *Remaking*, ch. 2.

61. Ibid. 30–40; Miles, *Social Mobility*, 22–3, 24, 27, 34, 48–9, 178–9; Miles, 'How open?', 23–4.

62. Mitch, 'Inequalities which every one may remove', 144, 156–8.

63. Savage and Miles, *Remaking*, 25, 39–40; Miles, *Social Mobility*, 152–62; Todd, 'Poverty and aspiration', 122–3, 125–6, 139, 140.

64. Calculated by Ginsberg, 'Interchange', 565.

65. Glass, *Social Mobility*, 187–8, 216–17, 329, 337; Goldthorpe, *Social Mobility and Class Structure*, 251–2; Goldthorpe, 'On economic development', 563.

66. Miles, *Social Mobility*, 29, 34, 48–9, 61, 64–5, 95–6, 178–9; Kaelble, *Social Mobility in the 19th and 20th Centuries*, 128.

67. Vincent, 'Mobility, bureaucracy and careers' 224–5; Miles, 'How open?', 18–39.

68. Vincent, 'Mobility, bureaucracy and careers', table 11.2.

69. Miles, 'How open?', 30–3.

70. Vincent, 'Mobility, bureaucracy and careers', 218; Miles, 'How open?', 35; Miles, *Social Mobility*, 115, 114.

71. Daunton, *Royal Mail*, ch. 7; Miles, *Social Mobility*, 113, 184–5; Savage, 'Career mobility and class formation'.

72. Baines and Johnson, 'In search of the "traditional" working class'.

73. Melling, 'Non-commissioned officers'; Savage and Miles, *Remaking*, 56.

74. Ellison, *Egalitarian Thought*; Tomlinson, *Democratic Socialism*, 263–5.

75. Tomlinson, *Democratic Socialism*, 278-80; Weaver, 'Taxation', 207–13; Cartter, *Redistribution*, 63.

76. Atkinson, *Unequal Shares*, 21–4; Tomlinson, *Democratic Socialism*, 281–2.

FURTHER READING

Abel Smith, B., *The Hospitals, 1800–1948* (1964)

Alborn, T., 'Senses of belonging: the politics of working-class insurance in Britain, 1880–1914', *Journal of Modern History*, 73 (2001)

Alexander, S., Davin, A., and Hostettler, E., 'Labouring women: a reply to Eric Hobsbawm', *History Workshop Journal*, 8 (1979)

Ashworth, W., 'Changes in the industrial structure, 1870–1914', *Yorkshire Bulletin of Economic and Social Research*, 17 (1965)

Atkinson, A. B., *Unequal Shares: Wealth in Britain* (1972)

Baines, D., and Johnson, P., 'Did they jump or were they pushed? The exit of older men from the London labour market, 1929–31', *Journal of Economic History*, 59 (1999)

—— 'In search of the "traditional" working class: social mobility and occupational continuity in interwar Britain', *Economic History Review*, 52 (1999)

Barnsby, G. J., 'The standard of living in the Black Country during the nineteenth century', *Economic History Review*, 24 (1971)

Benson, J., 'English coal-miners' trade union accident funds, 1850–1900' *Economic History Review*, 28 (1975)

—— 'The thrift of English coal-miners, 1860–95', *Economic History Review*, 31 (1978)

Beveridge, W., *Unemployment: A Problem of Industry* (1909)

Bienefeld, M. A., *Working Hours in British Industry: An Economic History* (1972)

Booth, C., *Life and Labour of the People in London*, 9 vols. (1892–7)

Bourke, J., *Working-Class Cultures in Britain 1890–1960* (1994)

—— *Husbandry to Housewifery: Women, Economic Change, and Housework in Ireland, 1890–1914* (Oxford, 1993)

Bowley, A. L., and Burnett-Hurst, A. R., *Livelihood and Poverty* (1915)

Brabrook, E. W., *Provident Societies and Industrial Welfare* (1896)

Bythell, D., *The Sweated Trades: Outwork in Nineteenth-Century Britain* (1978)

Cahill, M., and Jowitt, T., 'The new philanthropy: the emergence of the Bradford City Guild of Help', *Journal of Social Policy*, 9 (1980)

Cartter, A. M., *The Redistribution of Income in Postwar Britain* (New Haven, 1955)

Chapman, S., 'Some policies of the cotton spinners' trade unions', *Economic Journal*, 10 (1900)

Charity Organization Society, *Special Committee on Unskilled Labour, Report and Minutes of Evidence* (1908)

Childs, M. J., 'Boy labour in late Victorian and Edwardian England and the remaking of the working class', *Journal of Social History*, 23 (1987)

Chinn, C., *They Worked All their Lives: Women of the Urban Poor in England, 1880–1939* (Manchester, 1988)

Crafts, N. R. F., 'Long-term unemployment and the wage equation in Britain, 1925–39', *Economica*, 56 (1989)

Crossick, G. J., *An Artisan Elite in Victorian Society: Kentish London, 1840–80* (1978)

Daunton, M. J., *House and Home in the Victorian City: Working-Class Housing, 1850–1914* (1983)

—— 'Down the pit: work in the Great Northern and south Wales coalfields, 1870–1914', *Economic History Review*, 34 (1981)

—— *Royal Mail: The Post Office since 1840* (1985)

Davidson, C., *A Woman's Work is Never Done* (1982)

Davin, A., *Growing up Poor: Home, School and Street in London, 1870–1914* (1996)

Davies, A., *Leisure, Gender and Poverty: Working-Class Culture in Salford and Manchester, 1900–39* (Buckingham, 1992)

Earwicker, R., 'Miners' medical services before the First World War: the south Wales coalfield', *Llafur*, 3 (1981)

Ellison, N., *Egalitarian Thoughts and Labour Politics: Retreating Visions* (1994)

Englander, D., *Landlord and Tenant in Urban Britain, 1838–1918* (Oxford, 1983)

Erickson, C., *British Industrialists, Steel and Hosiery, 1850–1950* (Cambridge, 1959)

Feinstein, C. H., 'Changes in the distribution of the national income in the United Kingdom since 1860', in J. Marchal and B. Ducros (eds.), *Distribution of the National Income* (1968)

—— 'What really happened to real wages? Trends in wages, prices, and productivity in the United Kingdom, 1880–1913', *Economic History Review*, 43 (1990)

—— 'New estimates of average earnings in the United Kingdom, 1880–1913', *Economic History Review*, 43 (1990)

—— 'Pessimism perpetuated: real wages and the standard of living in Britain during and after the industrial revolution', *Journal of Economic History*, 58 (1998)

—— 'Variety and volatility: some aspects of the labour market in Britain, 1880–1913', in C. Holmes and A. Booth (eds.), *Economy and Society: European Industrialisation and its Social Consequences* (Leicester, 1991)

Foreman-Peck, J., 'Seedcorn or chaff? New firm formation and the performance of the interwar economy', *Economic History Review*, 38 (1985)

Foster, J., *Class Struggle and the Industrial Revolution: Early Industrial Capitalism in Three English Towns* (1974)

Gazeley, I., 'The cost of living for urban workers in late Victorian and Edwardian Britain', *Economic History Review*, 42 (1989)

Gilbert, B. B., 'The decay of nineteenth-century provident institutions and the coming of old age pensions in Great Britain', *Economic History Review*, 17 (1965)

Ginsberg, M., 'Interchange between social classes', *Economic Journal*, 39 (1929)

Glass, D. V. (ed.), *Social Mobility in Britain* (1954)

Godley, A., 'Enterprise and culture: Jewish immigrants in London and New York, 1880–1914', *Journal of Economic History*, 54 (1994)

Goldthorpe, J. H., 'On economic development and social mobility,' *British Journal of Sociology*, 36 (1985)

Goldthorpe. J. H., et al., *Social Mobility and Class Structure in Modern Britain* (Oxford, 1980, 1987)

Gosden, P. H. J. H., *Self Help: Voluntary Associations in Nineteenth-Century Britain* (1973)

Gourvish, T. R., 'The standard of living, 1890–1914', in A. O'Day (ed.), *The Edwardian Age: Conflict and Stability, 1900–1914* (1979)

Gray, R., *The Labour Aristocracy in Victorian Edinburgh* (Oxford, 1976)

Griffiths, T., *The Lancashire Working Classes c.1880–1930* (Oxford, 2001)

Gurney, P., *Co-operative Culture and the Politics of Consumption in England, c.1870–1930* (Manchester, 1996)

Hakim, C., 'A century of change in occupational segregation, 1891–1991', *Journal of Historical Sociology*, 7 (1994)

Hall, A. A., 'Wages, earnings and real earnings in Teesside: a reassessment of the ameliorist interpretation of living standards in Britain, 1870–1914', *International Review of Social History*, 26 (1981)

Hannah, L., *Inventing Retirement: The Development of Occupational Pensions in Britain* (1986)

Haraven, T. R., *Family Time and Industrial Time: The Relationship between the Family and Work in a New England Industrial Community* (1982)

Hardyment, C., *From Mangle to Microwave: The Mechanisation of Homework* (Cambridge, 1988)

Harris, J., *William Beveridge: A Biography* (Oxford, 1977)

Harrison, B., 'Philanthropy and the Victorians', *Victorian Studies*, 9 (1965–6)

Hennock, E. P., 'The measurement of poverty: from the metropolis to the nation, 1880–1920', *Economic History Review*, 40 (1987)

Hobsbawm, E. J., 'The Labour aristocracy in nineteenth-century Britain', in J. Saville (ed.), *Democracy and the Labour Movement: Essays in Honor of Dona Torr* (1954)

—— 'Custom, wages and workload in nineteenth-century industry', in A. Briggs and J. Saville (eds.), *Essays in Labour History* (1967)

—— *Labouring Men. Studies in the History of Labour* (1964)

Hobson, J. A., 'The social philosophy of Charity Organisation', *Contemporary Review*, 70 (1896)

Howarth, E. G., and Wilson, E., *West Ham: A Study in Social and Industrial Problems* (1907)

Hunt, E. H., *Regional Wage Variations in Britain, 1850–1914* (1973)

James, E., 'Women and work in twentieth century Britain', *Manchester School*, 30 (1962).

Joyce, P., *Work, Society and Politics: The Culture of the Factory in Later Victorian England* (Brighton, 1980)

John, A. V., *By the Sweat of their Brow: Women Workers at Victorian Coal Mines* (1984)

Johnson, P., *Saving and Spending: The Working-Class Economy in Britain, 1870–1939* (Oxford, 1985)

Kaelble, H., *Social Mobility in the Nineteenth and Twentieth Centuries: Europe and America in Comparative Perspective* (Leamington Spa, 1985)

Knowles, K. G. C., and Robertson, D., 'Differences between the wages of skilled and unskilled workers, 1880–1950', *Bulletin of the Oxford University Institute of Statistics*, 13 (1951)

Lazonick, W., 'Production relations, labor productivity, and choice of technique: British and US cotton spinning', *Journal of Economic History*, 41 (1981)

—— 'Industrial relations and technical change: the case of the self-acting mule', *Cambridge Journal of Economics*, 3 (1979)

Le Grand, J., *The Strategy of Equality* (1982)

Lewis, J., *Women in England, 1870–1950* (1984)

McLelland, K., 'Time to work, time to live: some aspects of work and the reformation of class in Britain, 1850–80', in P. Joyce (ed.), *The Historical Meanings of Work* (Cambridge, 1987)

Mark-Lawson, J., and Witz, A., 'From "family labour" to "family wage"? The case of women's labour in nineteenth-century coalmining', *Social History*, 13 (1988)

—— Savage, M., and Warde, A., 'Gender and local politics: struggles over welfare 1918–39', in L. Murgatroyd et al. (eds.), *Localities, Class and Gender* (1985)

Matthews, R. C. O., Feinstein, C. H., and Odling-Smee, J. C., *British Economic Growth, 1856-1973* (Oxford, 1982)

McIvor, A. J., *A History of Work in Britain, 1880–1950* (Basingstoke, 2001)

McKibbin, R., *The Ideologies of Class: Social Relations in Britain, 1880–1950* (Oxford, 1990)

—— *Classes and Cultures: England, 1918–1951* (Oxford, 1998)

Melling, J., ' "Non-commissioned officers": British employers and their supervisory workers, 1880–1920', *Social History*, 5(1980)

Miles, A., 'How open was nineteenth-century British society? Social mobility and equality of opportunity, 1839–1914', in A. Miles and D. Vincent (eds.), *Building European Society: Occupational Change and Social Mobility in Europe 1840–1940* (Manchester, 1992)

—— *Social Mobility in Nineteenth and Early Twentieth Century England* (Basingstoke, 1999)

—— and Vincent, D., 'A land of "boundless opportunity"? Mobility and stability in nineteenth-century England', in S. Dex (ed.), *Life and Work History Analyses: Qualitative and Quantitative Developments*, Sociological Review Monograph 37 (1991)

Mill, J. S., *Principles of Political Economy* in *The Collected Works of John Stuart Mill*, iii. ed. J. M. Robson (Toronto, 1965)

Mitch, D., ' "Inequalities which every one may remove": occupational recruitment, endogamy, and the homogeneity of social origins in Victorian England', in A. Miles and D. Vincent (eds.), *Building European Society* (Manchester, 1992)

More, C., *Skill and the English Working Class, 1870–1914* (1980)

O'Connell, S., and Reid, C., 'Working-class consumer credit in the UK, 1925-60: the role of the check trades', *Economic History Review*, 58 (2005)

Oddy, D., 'Working-class diets in late nineteenth-century Britain', *Economic History Review*, (1970)

Offer, A., *Property and Politics, 1870–1914: Landownership, Law, Ideology and Urban Development in England* (Cambridge, 1981)

Pederson, S., *Family, Dependence and the Origins of the Welfare State: Britain and France, 1914–1945* (Cambridge, 1993)

Penn, R., 'The course of wage differentials between skilled and non-skilled manual workers in Britain between 1856 and 1964', *British Journal of Industrial Relations*, 21 (1983)

—— *Skilled Workers in the Class Structure* (Cambridge, 1985)

—— and Dawkins, D. C., 'Structural transformations in the British class structure: a log linear analysis of marital endogamy in Rochdale, 1856–1964', *Sociology*, 17 (1983)

Phelps Brown, E. H., *Egalitarianism and the Generation of Inequality* (Oxford, 1988)

—— with Browne, M. H., *A Century of Pay: The Course of Pay and Production in France, Germany, Sweden, the United Kingdom and the United States of America, 1860–1960* (1968)

Phillips, G., and Whiteside, N., *Casual Labour: The Unemployment Question in the Port Transport Industry 1880–1970* (Oxford, 1985)

Pollard, S., 'Real earnings in Sheffield, 1851–1914', *Yorkshire Bulletin of Economic and Social Research*, 9 (1957)

—— 'Wages and earnings in the Sheffield trades, 1851–1914', *Yorkshire Bulletin of Economic and Social Research*, 6 (1954)

Price, R., *Masters, Unions and Men: Work Control in Building and the Rise of Labour, 1830–1914* (Cambridge, 1980)

Prochaska, F., *Philanthropy and the Hospitals of London: The King's Fund, 1897–1990* (Oxford, 1992)

Rathbone, E., 'Report of an inquiry into the conditions of dock labour at the port of Liverpool', *Transactions of the Liverpool Economic and Statistical Society* (1903–4)

Reid, A., 'Politics and the division of labour 1880–1920', in H. J. Mommsen and H.-G. Husung (eds.), *The Development of Trade Unionism in Britain and Germany* (1985)

Reynolds, J., *The Great Paternalist: Titus Salt and the Growth of Nineteenth-Century Bradford* (1983)

Roberts, E., 'Working-class standards of living in Barrow and Lancaster, 1890–1914', *Economic History Review*, 30 (1977)

—— 'Working-class standards of living in three Lancashire towns, 1890–1914', *International Review of Social History*, 27i (1982)

—— *A Woman's Place: An Oral History of Working-Class Women 1890–1940* (Oxford, 1984)

Ross, E., 'Survival networks: women's neighbourhood sharing before World War I', *History Workshop Journal*, 15 (1983)

—— *Love and Toil: Motherhood in Outcast London, 1870-1918* (Oxford, 1993)

Routh, G., *Occupation and Pay in Great Britain, 1906–1979* (2nd ed., 1980)

Rowntree, B. S., *Poverty: A Study of Town Life* (1901, 4th ed., 1902)

—— *Poverty and Progress: A Second Social Survey of York* (1941)

—— and Lavers, G., *Poverty and the Welfare State* (1951)

Saul, S. B., 'House-building in England, 1890–1914', *Economic History Review*, 15 (1962–3)

Savage, M., 'Career mobility and class formation: British banking workers and the lower middle classes', in A, Miles and D. Vincent (eds.), *Building European Society: Occupational Change and Social Mobility in Europe, 1840–1940* (Manchester, 1992)

—— 'Women and work in the Lancashire cotton industry, 1890–1939', in J. A. Jowitt and A. J. McIvor (eds.), *Employers and Labour in the English Textile Industries* (1988)

—— and Miles, A., *The Remaking of the British Working Class, 1840–1940* (1994)

Skidelsky, R., *John Maynard Keynes: The Economist as Saviour, 1920–1937* (1992)

Slaven, A., 'Earnings and productivity in the Scottish coal-mining industry during the nineteenth century', in P. L. Payne (ed.), *Studies in Scottish Business History* (1967)

Southall, H. R., 'Regional unemployment patterns among skilled engineers in Britain, 1851–1914', *Journal of Historical Geography*, 12 (1986)

—— 'The origins of the depressed areas: unemployment, growth and regional economic structure in Britain before 1914', *Economic History Review*, 41 (1988)

Stedman Jones, G., *Outcast London* (Oxford, 1971)

Summerfield, P., *Reconstructing Women's Wartime Lives* (1998)

Tawney, R. H., *The Establishment of Minimum Rates in the Tailoring Industry* (1915)

Thane, P., 'The working class and state "welfare" in Britain, 1880–1914', *Historical Journal*, 27 (1984)

Todd, S., 'Poverty and aspiration: young women's entry to employment in interwar England', *Twentieth Century British History*, 15 (2004)

Tomlinson, J., *Democratic Socialism and Economic Policy: The Attlee Years, 1945–51* (Cambridge, 1997)

Vincent, D., 'Mobility, bureaucracy and careers in early twentieth-century Britain', in A. Miles and D. Vincent (eds.), *Building European Society: Occupational Change and Social Mobility in Europe, 1840–1940* (Manchester, 1992)

Waddington, K., *Charity and the London Hospitals, 1850–98* (Woodbridge, 2001)

Weaver, F., 'Taxation and redistribution in the UK', *Review of Economics and Statistics*, 32 (1950)

Webb, B., *My Apprenticeship* (1926)

Webb, S., and Webb, B., *Industrial Democracy* (1902)

Yeo, S., *Religion and Voluntary Organisations in Crisis* (1976)

Zeitlin, J., 'From labour history to the history of industrial relations', *Economic History Review*, 40 (1987)

—— 'Industrial structure, employer strategy and the diffusion of job control in Britain, 1850–1920', in H. J. Mommsen and H.-G. Husung (eds.), *The Development of Trade Unionism in Britain and Germany* (1985)

—— 'Engineers and compositors: a comparison', in R. Harrison and J. Zeitlin (eds.), *Division of Labour: Skilled Workers and Technological Change in Nineteenth-Century Britain* (Brighton, 1985)

....

CHAPTER 13

Cultures of Consumption

In 1851, consumption was a matter of survival for many—of finding enough to eat, and clothes, shelter, and heat to remain healthy. The poorest members of society had their pleasures too, from family and friends, the consolations of religion, or the sociability of the public house. But as the economy grew, more people were able to escape from the narrow constraints of mere survival (see Table 3.1). They could spend money on leisure, and might even take a holiday. The Great Exhibition and the Festival of Britain were themselves part of the economy of enjoyment—and the needs of a more affluent Britain were supplied by department and chain stores, music halls and cinemas, radio and gramophone, seaside resorts, sport, and leisure pursuits. Every town developed its spaces for leisure, which became highly commercialized and commodified. Some towns were devoted to enjoyment, from working-class Blackpool to middle-class Eastbourne, and the countryside was redefined for cultural consumption. The growth of manufacturing was intimately connected, for many consumer goods offered entertainment. And as real wages rose, more was spent on better-quality housing and its domestic comforts.

Decisions over how to spend the growing margin of income above subsistence were by no means straightforward. How much should be spent on immediate visceral enjoyment and pleasure—a trip to the music hall or a week at the seaside—and how much on long-term, prudential delayed gratification by saving for old age or investing in education? The choice was cultural and social, and much debated by moral critics. Gladstone wished to increase prudence through the Post Office Savings Bank, and the Charity Organization Society complained about the lack of moral discipline of the poor. These concerns were shared by reactionary and progressive critics who complained about the power of advertising, the manipulation of desire for debased ends. John Ruskin and William Morris despised the flow of cheap goods and meretricious taste, calling for a revival of craftsmanship and discrimination; their sentiments fed into the thinking of many members of the Labour party who remained suspicious of commercialization and competition. One way of rebalancing the pursuit of immediate gratification against long-term prudence was to shift

TABLE 13.1. *Consumers' expenditure in the UK, 1900–55*

	1900–4	1915–19	1925–9	1935–8	1939–45	1946–50	1951–5
Percentage of total expenditure at current prices							
Food	33.1	37.7	33.1	29.2	29.7	29.2	33.5
Alcohol	10.9	8.0	8.0	6.8	10.7	9.5	7.4
Tobacco	1.7	2.4	3.1	3.9	7.8	8.9	7.6
Rents, rates, water	11.3	8.1	9.3	11.0	10.2	7.4	6.9
Fuel and light	4.4	4.0	4.0	4.2	4.7	3.9	4.1
Clothing	9.2	10.7	10.8	9.7	9.6	10.8	10.4
Durable household goods	3.5	4.1	5.3	6.2	3.7	5.9	7.0
Transport/comm.	5.5	5.2	7.3	7.7	5.8	6.9	8.0
Other goods	4.8	6.2	5.9	6.6	6.6	6.9	6.7
Other services	15.6	13.5	13.2	14.7	11.4	10.5	8.3
Expenditure per head at constant 1938 prices (1938 = 100)							
Food	78.2	76.1	89.8	99.5	95.9	108.5	115.1
Alcohol	229.4	144.9	114.1	98.1	104.8	96.0	93.5
Tobacco	46.8	62.7	73.5	93.5	120.3	113.5	110.3
Rents, rates, water	68.0	77.8	84.3	97.3	108.9	104.8	105.7
Fuel and light	80.4	81.1	85.9	97.2	110.6	114.1	126.1
Clothing	87.7	72.6	92.8	100.0	75.9	93.6	96.2
Durable household goods	53.0	49.9	86.5	110.5	46.7	78.6	100.5
Transport/comm.	35.4	43.9	73.6	95.4	79.0	108.7	128.7
Other goods	48.2	62.3	73.9	95.0	84.7	96.8	105.5
Other services	96.9	89.4	81.6	98.0	76.8	77.9	67.8
Total	82.7	77.1	86.5	98.7	89.8	99.2	103.7

Source: Stone and Rowe, *Measurement of Consumers' Expenditure*, ii, tables 55, 57.

spending from personal choice to collective decision. Undesirable desire could be regulated or banned as advocates of temperance desired; or consumption could be shaped by taxation. Consumption was politicized, with moral and cultural definition of what was a basic necessity, what a luxury, and what morally suspect or wasteful.

The ability to purchase more expensive goods rested on the use of credit, which posed the question of legal rights which troubled the courts and legislators. Did consumers need to be protected against retailers; or did shopkeepers need to be protected against customers? The very act of buying implied moral choice: was a commodity produced by 'sweated' labour; were foreign goods 'dumped' to the detriment of British workers, or were they a sign of the benefits of comparative advantage? Would commercial radio and television undermine British culture? The composition of consumption was also gendered. The house was a place of work for women and of relaxation for their families. Should priority be given to buying time-saving devices to ease women's housework; or should it be spent on family entertainment?

Just how much did consumer spending grow, and where did most of the additional spending go? (see Table 3.1)[1] Food remained more or less steady at around a third of consumers' expenditure. If we compare 1900–4 with the last period of peace in 1935-8, we see that real expenditure per capita rose, not surprisingly given the poor quality and tedium of the diet of many people at the beginning of the period. More and better-quality food contributed to improved health. Up to 1935-8, the composition of food consumption did not change radically (see Table 13.2). Wartime and post-war rationing led to a decline in per capita consumption of meat and bacon, oils and fats, and sugar, preserves, and confectionery; by contrast, per capita consumption

TABLE 13.2. *Consumers' expenditure on food in the UK, 1900–55*

	1900–4	1915–19	1925–9	1935–8	1939–45	1946–50	1951–5
Percentage of expenditure on food at current prices							
Bread and cereals	16.0	16.7	14.4	15.0	17.9	17.5	15.2
Meat and bacon	31.3	31.0	31.3	28.9	23.6	17.7	22.7
Fish	3.5	4.1	4.1	4.0	4.8	4.9	3.6
Dairy products/eggs	12.9	11.6	13.1	14.8	15.9	16.0	15.5
Oils and fats	8.6	8.1	7.9	7.4	4.1	3.8	5.2
Vegetables	7.5	7.7	7.1	8.2	10.9	12.9	11.0
Fruit and nuts	4.1	4.5	6.9	6.5	4.3	8.6	7.8
Sugar, preserves, cfry.	9.5	10.5	9.4	8.2	7.9	7.8	9.5
Beverages	5.9	5.2	5.3	5.5	4.9	4.8	4.9
Other food	0.7	0.7	0.7	1.6	5.5	5.5	4.7
Expenditure on food per head at constant 1938 prices 1938 = 100							
Bread and cereals	81.1	90.0	85.8	97.8	—	109.2	103.0
Meat and bacon	95.0	89.2	99.6	100.3	—	75.3	85.1
Fish	86.1	75.9	96.3	100.9	—	156.5	114.8
Dairy products/eggs	69.7	61.4	85.1	99.1	—	132.0	135.3
Oils and fats	65.4	64.9	81.0	101.0	—	73.2	79.5
Vegetables	58.8	54.3	84.6	97.7	—	146.2	145.7
Fruit and nuts	63.9	63.9	103.0	106.6	—	138.0	161.4
Sugar, preserves, cfry.	88.7	88.7	83.8	99.1	—	86.9	123.0
Beverages	67.5	73.5	90.7	99.3	—	102.0	107.9
Other food	16.3	14.3	26.5	81.6	—	326.5	369.4
Total	78.2	76.1	89.7	99.5	—	108.5	115.1

Source: Stone and Rowe, *Measurement of Consumers' Expenditure*, ii, tables 59 and 61.

of fish, dairy products and eggs, vegetables, fruit, and 'other foods' rose. Bread and cereal consumption remained more or less constant, with a modest fall between the wars reversed during the Second World War. The share of dairy products and eggs rose at the expense of oils and fats; and a larger proportion was spent on fruit and vegetables. The increase in 'other foods' reflects the rise of convenience foods. These changes seem to have continued into the early 1950s, except for a fall in fish consumption and a continued rise in the consumption of fruit and sugar/confectionery.[2]

The share of consumers' expenditure on housing, rates, and water charges fell between the wars as a result of rent control, before rising to its earlier level in the 1930s and then falling back with the return of rent controls. The cost of fuel and light remained reasonably stable. Real per capita spending on rents, rates, and water charges did increase by about one and half times between 1900–4 and 1946–50, reflecting the greater standards of domestic comfort. What the figures cannot capture are the shifts in architectural form and layout; and the emergence of widespread owner-occupation. In the case of clothing, the proportion of total expenditure and real per capita spending were both reasonably stable. Much more significant than any change in spending on clothing was the rise in the importance of consumer durables. Although they were a small proportion of total spending, the share rose up to the Second World War and real per capita expenditure slightly more than doubled between 1900/4 and 1935/8. Spending fell during the Second World War, and by the early 1950s had only returned to the level of the early 1930s. The share of consumer spending on transport increased. It included both public and private transport, not least spending on bicycles and motor cars. Real per capita expenditure rose by more than two and a half times between 1900–4 and 1935–8, and threefold by 1946–50. In the case of both consumer durables and motor cars, increased spending entailed the purchase of expensive items for which credit was needed. This posed significant cultural and legal problems.

The proportion of spending on alcohol fell from 1900–4, with a reversal during the Second World War. The change in real per capita consumption is striking, falling by about 60 per cent over the first half of the twentieth century. The reduction in spending on alcohol reflected, in part, political intervention. Nonconformist Liberals and the United Kingdom Alliance demanded abolition. Although their success was limited to closing public houses in Wales on Sundays, licensing laws were tightened and duties increased. The price of alcohol rose more than other goods at the same time that new and cheaper goods became available, so encouraging a switch in consumption.[3] As we shall see, leisure was separated from the consumption of alcohol and became a commercial venture in its own right. The tightening of licensing laws as well as the reduction in spending resulted in a change in the structure of the brewing industry as firms competed to purchase 'tied' public houses.

Consumption of tobacco increased, despite the fact that its relative price also increased. Between 1900–4 and 1945–51, its share of total consumer expenditure rose by 7.2 per cent, the largest single shift over the period. Up to the middle of the nineteenth century, annual tobacco consumption was about 2 pounds per adult over the age of 15; by the middle of the twentieth century it was 7 pounds. About 80 per cent of men and 40 per cent of women were smokers in 1948, though most women were light smokers. For women, smoking lacked respectability until the inter-war period when it was encouraged by advertisers as a sign of liberation and popularized in many Hollywood movies. The anti-tobacco movement was less successful than the campaign against drink: it was a marginal fringe element in the temperance movement, making the same point about enslavement to a habit and threat to health. Such claims were derided by the pro-smoking lobby, and the only success of the anti-tobacco movement was the prohibition of its sale to children under the age of 16 in 1908. After that, the campaign against tobacco stopped, and was replaced by a more modest claim by the National Society of Non-Smokers for some smoke-free areas on trains or buses. Smoking was, as A. J. P. Taylor remarked, 'the essential social habit of the age'.[4]

The data on consumers' expenditure indicate that the wars and not the slump of the early 1930s were the major periods of reduction. In 1913, consumers' expenditure at 1938 prices was £3,544m, falling to £3,045m in 1918 or a drop of 14.1 per cent. In 1938, consumers' expenditure was £4,392m, falling to £3,751m in 1943 or a drop of 14.5 per cent. Rationing and price controls were major political concerns in the two world wars. By contrast, the slump of the early 1930s had little impact. Consumers' expenditure in 1929 stood at £3,765m in constant 1938 prices; at the trough of the slump in 1933 it stood at £3,937m and continued to grow to the Second World War.[5] The problem of lack of demand and overcapacity between the wars came largely from outside Britain: the domestic market was buoyant, and the period marked a continued development of new attitudes to consumption. As the number of dependants fell, so families had more cash and time for a variety of pursuits and pastimes. The inter-war period was not only marred by the hardship of the coal mines of south Wales or the shipyards of the Tyne and Clyde. There were also modern factories producing vacuum cleaners, cinemas portraying the glamour of Hollywood, and mock-Tudor semi-detached houses by the thousand in the new suburbs.

Housing and Domesticity

The largest component of expenditure after food was rent. Although the price of most goods and service fell in the second half of the nineteenth century, rents were a major exception and the rent index rose from 82.6 in 1874 to 90.5 in 1880, 100.0 in 1900, and 102.4 in 1913.[6] The explanation was partly the technical conservatism of the building industry, but also a marked improvement in housing quality. The Public Health Act of 1875 permitted any sanitary authority to impose regulations on standards of construction, street widths, and the density of development. Such regulations expressed a concern to check the spread of disease by improving the circulation of air and reducing density. But the quality of housing was rising in any case. Better-quality housing and a shift to a culture of domesticity were among the more striking features of the second half of the nineteenth century. Houses became larger and were more likely to be self-contained, with piped water and gas typical features of working-class accommodation. The market for cheap furniture, linoleum, fabrics, and wallpapers expanded, and new consumer goods emerged.

There were, however, many variations. Glasgow was dominated by tenement flats, with 85.2 per cent of dwellings in 1911 having three rooms or less. In Newcastle-upon-Tyne, 58.3 per cent of dwellings had three rooms or less. By contrast, in Leicester only 6.1 per cent of houses had three rooms or less. Such variations affected the death rate and incidence of disease. Rents also varied markedly, and not necessarily in line with wages. The Board of Trade survey of rents and wages in 1905 showed that, if London is taken as 100, the rent index in Leicester was 48 and the index for the wage of a skilled building worker stood at 94. By contrast, rents in Glasgow and Newcastle were higher than in Leicester (76 in both cities) and wages lower (91 and 90 respectively).[7]

The variation in housing styles over the country and the change over time affected the nature of domestic life. At the beginning of the period, cities were still constricted by the limits of transport, and growth often meant an increase in density in courts and alleyways, where families shared privies or a standpipe or pump. The by-laws were designed to reduce the density of development and to create more 'open' layout. Public and private spaces were delineated, with water and sanitation confined to a single property and the responsibility of a single household. As the houses became more distinct, so the streets became more public. Municipal by-laws sought to control their use. In Birmingham, playing of musical instruments or shouting on any street within 50 yards of a dwelling or 100 yards of a hospital was regulated; as was playing cricket and football on land adjoining a street in such a way as to cause danger. Jostling pedestrians or obstructing the free use of the street became offences. The aim of such rules was to control street hawkers and musicians, and the use of public spaces for recreation and trading. Of course, children continued to kick balls on the streets, though even they ran the risk of punishment. Certainly, the use of market squares or main roads for bull-baiting, mass football matches, and fairs was much more rigidly controlled. The elite withdrew its consent to the popular use of public space, and recreation and leisure was more strictly confined to parks, or to football and cricket pitches with controlled entry.[8] The task of defining the private from the public spaces was more difficult in Scottish cities where high-rise tenements dominated and internal staircases and communal areas continued to cause concern for cleanliness and good order.

As we have seen, the level of overcrowding varied so that in some cases allocation to special purposes was difficult. In some regions, sub-letting was common—37.4 per cent in Cardiff and 44.4 per cent in Tottenham—in response to the high average size of property and, in the London suburbs, to the high level of rents. Sub-letting might entail a single lodger, or two families sharing space designed for one. It might also be a way of coping with the poverty cycle, allowing a family to earn some extra money when their income was under strain with the arrival of children; the wife might offer cooking and washing as well as a room to a lodger. In other towns, with a smaller house size and low rents, sub-letting was infrequent: in Oldham and Leicester in 1911, only 1.6 and 1.8 per cent of the population respectively lived in accommodation with sub-letting. In the inter-war period, local authorities tried to control sub-letting by their tenants.

Aspiring and respectable working-class families tried to use the housing in a particular way. The 'parlour'—the room at the front of the house—was set aside for special occasions. Visitors would be received in this formal space; it was the room for courtship and for laying out a body before burial, and perhaps for Sunday lunch or tea. Mrs Loane, a keen observer of working-class life, complained that this room was taboo—a place where expensive objects were kept locked away, behind drawn curtains, rather than used. But that was the point: it was a sign of respectability. Until non-coal space heating became more common, it was difficult to heat a room for a short period, and the cost of pianos and furniture was too high to allow frequent use.

By contrast, the kitchen was used for everyday life, with cooking and washing relegated to a scullery in many of the new houses. Gas entered working-class households with the introduction of prepayment slot meters in the 1890s. Many customers installed gas cookers: by 1914, 73 per cent of all consumers in the South Metropolitan area had slot-meters, and 82.8 per cent of consumers had gas cookers. Gas cooking reduced the labour of women and the additional cost seemed well worth paying. Gas was much slower in spreading to water heating and was much more expensive than coal by something over three times. In 1942, only 26 per cent of households with an income of less than £300 had a piped hot water supply for baths and 9 per cent for washing clothes. Lack of facilities at home meant that many families used public bath houses and wash houses supplied by local authorities, or sent out their washing to be done by other women. In 1942, 27 per cent of these families did not wash their clothes at home, and 28 per cent regularly used public wash houses. Gas was also used for lighting, replacing paraffin lamps. Water became more common in working-class houses. In the 1840s, only one in twelve of the population of Newcastle-upon-Tyne had access to piped water; by 1914, piped water was virtually universal, though not yet baths. Water-borne sanitation became much more common, replacing privies or pails. In Newcastle the proportion of houses with water closets rose from 65.2 per cent in 1883–5 to 88.6 per cent in 1913, and in Manchester from 26.4 per cent in 1899 to 97.8 per cent in 1913. Architects of local authority housing tended to agree with Mrs Loane and tried to remove the parlour as a wasteful use of space in favour of a single large living room. The use of space was different in middle-class homes. There, the sitting room was the setting for everyday life and was not kept for special occasions. The middle class usually had a distinct dining room and used the kitchen simply for food preparation, and often as a space for servants. In many new middle-class suburban houses in the 1930s, the kitchen was a small space with a hatch to serve the dining room. In more prosperous middle-class homes, bedrooms were also used during the day as private sitting areas—something not possible in working-class or modest middle-class housing given the cost and labour of heating by coal fires. In larger middle-class houses men had their own spaces in a library or study; in modest middle-class or working-class houses they found refuge in their garden sheds or allotments.

Towns differed in the speed of change and many old slum properties survived even into the 1930s. Some local authorities started to sweep away the worst property under local Acts, such as in Glasgow in 1866, but the Artisans and Labourers Dwellings Improvement Act of 1875 gave any local authority the power to clear slum areas. The problem with the Act was that the owners of existing property received generous compensation so that the cleared sites were expensive. Many of the poor families who had been displaced moved to the adjacent area where crowding increased. In London, many of the sites were taken by the Peabody Trust which built blocks of flats on cleared sites and insisted that the tenants pay their rent regularly. In 1882, the obligation to rehouse the population was dropped in provincial towns, and reduced to half in London. In some cases, the initiative for rebuilding passed to local authorities. Initially, they were permitted to build replacement houses on condition that they sold within ten years, but from 1890 they could retain property and also build additional rather than replacement housing, on a very modest scale. The process of slum clearance became much more intensive in the 1930s, for the Housing Act of 1930 required every local authority to survey and clear slum areas; the owners were now given much less compensation, and the local authority received a subsidy from the central government for every person cleared.

Before the First World War, about 90 per cent of housing was rented. Scotland and England diverged in their legal systems which affected the social relations between tenant and landlord. Until 1911, most Scottish tenants were required to take a property for an entire year, with only about 20 per cent of working-class tenants on shorter monthly lets. The tenancies expired at the same time which created a discrepancy between the housing market and the labour market with its short-term contracts. Landlords sent a 'missive' to their tenants several months before the expiry of the tenancy, asking if they wished to stay for the next year—so committing the tenant to a property despite a possible change of work or family circumstances. The Scottish system also created tensions in the family budget, for there was a discrepancy between weekly wages and the payment of rent at longer intervals. Furthermore, tenants were required to pay rates directly to the council in a lump sum. In England, tenancies were usually for a week in working-class property, so that there was no discrepancy between the housing and labour markets. Rents usually included rates and were paid weekly in line with the receipt of wages. The landlords 'compounded' the rates, handing over payment to the local council in return for a generous commission. Long lets in Scotland were associated with the law of hypothec which gave landlords the right to seize goods up to the value of rent for the entire year. The level of litigation between landlord and tenant was high in Scotland, almost entirely in the monthly let property. Landlords complained that their powers over recalcitrant tenants in the monthly let property were too weak. An application for eviction was made at the end of a month, when notice was given for a third of the period; if the tenant did not move, the landlord applied for a warrant of eviction, but the tenant could lodge an objection for a small fee which usually gave ten or eleven days. The landlords were concerned at the loss of income at the hands of tenants who knew how to play the system. In 1911, the complaints of the long-let tenants about the missive system came together with the complaints of the landlords against the monthly tenants. Shorter lets were introduced to end the problem of missives in long-let property. At the same time, the rates were incorporated into the rent and paid to the council by the landlord in return for a commission of 2.5 per cent. The landlords suffered as a result of a higher turnover of tenants, and complained that the commission was too low. But they were compensated by much more draconian powers of eviction against short-let tenants. Tenants of the better flats were gaining flexibility at the expense of their poorer neighbours.

English landlords relied on the common law power of 'distress' or seizure of goods for outstanding rent. This power was limited in the later nineteenth century, for county court judges were often sympathetic to hard-pressed tenants and unimpressed by the character of the bailiffs. Landlords did have the right of summary eviction under the Small Tenants Recovery Act of 1838: if the tenant of a house with a rent of under £20 was in arrears, the landlord could give a week's notice, followed by a warrant for ejectment ordering the tenant to leave in twenty-one days. Hence the tenant could secure up to four weeks rent free before leaving. Not surprisingly, the landlords pressed for greater powers which came to nothing. In practice, the level of litigation was low. Dishonest tenants were more likely to 'flit', leaving the house without paying; and landlords were often willing to allow arrears to respectable tenants to help them over a period of financial difficulty.

The improvement of housing standards was not without its problems, for the bottom of the housing market was depleted by demolitions. Conditions might in consequence deteriorate in the inner city. When replacement housing was supplied, it was usually too expensive for the poorest families. The housing problem would, it was hoped, be resolved as property was vacated by families moving to new suburban houses. Whether or not the strategy succeeded depended on the building cycle. In boom periods overbuilding led to falling rents, and a high level of vacancies, so that poorer families could move into better accommodation. Equally, there were periods when the market was very tight and rents rose before a renewed period of frantic building. The boom at the turn of the century led to a high level of vacancies, falling rents, and a serious decline in capital values, exacerbated by higher interest and rates which landlords could not pass to their tenants. At the same time, interest rates were higher and rates were rising. Landlords faced difficulties in passing on these costs at a time of stagnant real wages and slack in the housing market. At the same time, local authorities in England were eager to reduce the compounding allowance in order to increase their yield. In the opinion of Avner Offer, the outcome was that a cyclical downturn in the housing market had been converted into a permanent structural change.[9]

Certainly, there were difficulties before the First World War, but the argument for permanent change may be exaggerated. In some towns, housing building for rent was still at a high level before the First World War. Small investors might well have returned to the market when the yield recovered compared with other outlets. But the outbreak of war made the issue irrelevant. Tenants were not impressed by what they saw as profiteering by landlords who increased rents. Rent strikes and mass demonstrations, especially in Glasgow, led to the Rent and Mortgage Interest (Restrictions) Act of 1915 and mortgage interest was also fixed. The result was that both landlords and mortgagors faced a serious fall in their profits during the war.

Rent controls were due to expire after the war, but their demise would result in a large increase in rents in response to inflation and the shortage of property—and the government feared the consequences for public order. In 1919, the government allowed rents to be increased by 10 per cent and in 1920 by 40 per cent above pre-war levels; and in 1923, decontrol started when tenants vacated a property. It was still not possible to end controls completely and to allow the private market to operate. In 1931, controlled houses still accounted for 69.1 per cent of all houses in the private rental market and 78.1 per cent in the working-class market. Although controls were liberalized in 1933, they continued on some houses right up to the Second World War when rents were fixed at 1939 levels. New houses were not covered by the controls, but few landlords and builders were willing to enter the rental market after the First World War. Much more important were the local authorities. Their building programme was modest before 1914, but now moved to a new level. If they could build houses and remove the shortages, decontrol could be undertaken. In fact, the shortage was not removed: a total of 500,000 houses were planned, but the programme proved to be too costly, and there were difficulties in securing land and finance. Costs rose from an estimated £600 a house in 1918 to £1,200 in 1920. The local authorities were only liable for any losses up to the revenue from a rate of 1*d*., so much of the burden fell on central government at a time when it faced other serious financial difficulties. In 1923 the Conservative government introduced less generous subsidies for both council and private housing, and passed most of the cost on to local authorities; in 1924, Labour introduced higher subsidies, predominantly for public building. After 1930, the emphasis shifted from additional housing to replacement for slums. The result of the local authority initiative was a major change in the housing market, with a fall in the proportion of private rental and a rise in public housing (see Table 13.3).

Almost a third of new housing in inter-war England and Wales was public, and even more was built after the Second World War. Between 1944 and 1949, 423,300 local authority houses were built in England and Wales, and only 128,000 private houses; in Scotland the figures were 62,100 and 4,800. The social consequences were considerable.[10] Most of the new public housing was built on large suburban estates, usually without local employment. Men had to travel to work at additional cost; women were often not able to find part-time employment and were removed from the markets of the inner city and from family members who could assist with child care. Children seeking work had to travel, and on marriage left the estate until they secured a place on the local authority housing list. Furthermore, most estates were poorly provided with social facilities. The suburban estates were often in another local authority area which led to political tensions and a lack of investment in the social infrastructure. A comparison between Birmingham's estate at Kingstanding and the town of Shrewsbury was used to point the difference. Both had a population

TABLE 13.3. *Housing tenure in England and Wales, 1938*

| | Houses built | | |
	Pre-war	Inter-war	All
Owner-occupied	27.1	49.1	34.9
Public rental	negligible	31.5	11.2
Private rental:			
Controlled	41.3 ⎫ 72.9	nil ⎫ 19.4	26.6 ⎫ 53.9
Non-controlled	31.6 ⎰	19.4 ⎰	27.3 ⎰
Total	100.0	100.0	100.0

Source: Ministry of Health, *Departmental Committee on Valuation for Rates*, 7.

of 30,000. In Shrewsbury, there were thirty churches, twenty halls, and two libraries; at Kingstanding, there was one church and one hall. One response was to shift to inner-city flats, a strategy pursued in London. Another adopted after 1945 was to build new towns to link work and housing, to provide a full range of social and commercial services, and to bring classes together.

Managing the new council property posed difficulties. Local authorities had to select tenants, and then make sure that they looked after the property and that they did not sub-let or fail to pay the rent. Initially, priority was given to ex-servicemen but this gave way to various measures of housing need, moderated by a concern that the new tenants should be able to pay. Fixing the rent was not easy. Slum clearance tenants were less able to pay rents, and any losses fell on the local ratepayer. Moving into a new council property could impose strain on family budgets, and the medical officer for Stockton found an increase in the death rate as a result of a decline in diet caused by higher rents. The basis for determining the rent of individual houses did not relate to the ability to pay so much as the cost of construction and the level of subsidy, so that better-paid men might have larger houses and cheaper rents than poor slum clearance tenants. One response was to introduce differential rents according to need, by increasing rents for some in order to reduce rents for slum clearance tenants. Such policies were unpopular, and in Birmingham in 1939 tenants staged a rent strike.[11]

The decline of the private rental market also led to owner-occupation, largely for middle-class families. Investment in dwellings rose from 13 per cent of total investment in 1900-9 to 21 per cent in 1920-9 and 32 per cent in 1930-8. The number of private houses built without subsidy rose from 133,000 in 1931 to a peak of 292,000 in 1934. One explanation was the lower cost of borrowing. Building societies had more funds and changed their liquidity ratios; interest rates fell, they cut the initial deposit, and extended loan periods. The societies were better organized and managed, and their mortgage lending increased significantly. Between 1928 and 1934, the weekly cost of borrowing £500 fell by about a third. As the housing market became saturated, builders and building societies colluded in the dubious practice of the 'builders' pool' in order to expand sales. Loans for as much as 100 per cent of the value were advanced on houses which were overvalued and possibly of poor construction. If the purchasers failed to keep up payment, the builders bought the houses back to guarantee the loan. Owners were tempted into taking loans which were too large, on property which was not worth what they paid—a state of affairs which led to complaints and a legal decision against the practice in 1939. Lower costs of borrowing probably accounted for about half of the initial increase in housing investment, and demand also increased as a result of a change in the structure of the population: the rate of growth of the population was low, but the number of families increased. Furthermore, large houses became impracticable with the decline in domestic servants and the rise in electrical appliances. The cost of housing fell markedly, with a reduction in building costs and land prices.[12]

How important was house building to recovery in the 1930s? Some historians have argued that house building itself had limited linkages with the rest of the economy. But new housing does lead to a demand for new furnishings, consumer durables, and even motor cars for transport from the suburbs. The boom meant a rise in the proportion of houses wired for electricity. In the 1930s, the proportion of houses wired for electricity rose from 31.8 per cent of houses in 1932 to 65.4 per cent in 1938.[13]

Houses were sites for the consumption of consumer durables which brought entertainment into the home, and used spare time as did the music hall and cinema. Other consumer goods saved time, such as vacuum cleaners and washing machines. As Gary Becker argues, commodities compete with work in the allocation of 'discretionary' time: would a household spend money on goods which used up discretionary time, or on goods which increased the amount of discretionary time? The answer was that most preferred to buy goods which used discretionary time. Table 13.4 indicates that radios moved from 1 to 20 per cent of all households in three years, whereas washing machines took twenty-three years.

The explanation is in part technical, for it proved easier to produce goods that made leisure more attractive than it did to reduce housework. Visiting the 'live' music hall or theatre was an occasional pleasure; listening to the radio or gramophone or going to the cinema could be done every night. Knowledge of the latest programme or popular 'hit' was an important part of social life and failure to participate was to suffer from a sense of social exclusion. Such commodities were symbols of status and appealed to all members of the household. Indeed, listening to the radio was a common feature of domestic life. To reduce the amount of housework was much more difficult. Household appliances are not status goods: they are kept out of sight or stored in utility rooms. Furthermore, they had little impact on the actual amount

TABLE 13.4. *Diffusion rate of household appliances: percentage of households*

Appliance	Household penetration begins (1%)	Additional years to penetration		
		20%	50%	75%
Radio (UK)	1923	3	10	20
TV (E&W)	1949	5	9	12
Electric iron (E&W)	1909		24	30
Vacuum cleaner (E&W)	1915	18	40	47
Clothes washer (E&W)	1934	23	30	

Note: E & W = England & Wales.
Source: Bowden and Offer, 'Household appliances and the use of time', 729.

of time spent in housework for they encouraged certain tasks to be undertaken more often. They might shift some work such as washing bed linen back to the household; or, in middle-class households, substitute for domestic servants. The time spent by women on housework actually increased between 1937 and 1961, most strikingly for middle-class women. In any case, the benefit of labour-saving (or perhaps -creating) domestic appliances was largely felt by housewives, whereas decisions on the purchase of a costly consumer durable were likely to be made by the husband.[14]

Credit

Consumption entails a legal and social relationship between the person selling and buying the commodity. Purchases were not made by purely rational economic individuals, but were permeated with social and cultural assumptions. Personal character and personal credit were connected—and both were fluid. At the beginning of the period, men's bodies could still be seized as collateral for their debts; by the end of the period, imprisonment for consumer debt was marginalized. Assessment of character was crucial in deciding whether to extend credit. Creditors tried to divine personal worth and character from their debtors' clothing, marital relations, patterns of spending, and perceived social status, and customers tried to create a persona of creditworthiness. The notion of an individual economic actor was complicated, for the male head of household was legally liable for the actions of his servants, wife, and children, who might purchase goods without his knowledge but could not be imprisoned for debt incurred in his name. How did the shopkeeper stand if the head of household denied responsibility? Consuming was a contested issue, involving cultural practices, social relationships, and legal principles.

Many poor people had recourse to 'tick', buying basic necessities on credit and paying later. The local shopkeeper was part of the community and had to make a judgement about the reliability of the customer; 'tick' was more likely to be offered if the person was known to be reliable but experiencing difficulties. A stranger, or someone known to be unreliable, was more likely to be denied credit. In order to deal with the problems of greater anonymity in large towns, shopkeepers formed trade protection societies to exchange information on potentially risky customers, formalizing debt collection, offering legal services, and establishing credit enquiry departments. However, credit was not only a recourse for straitened members of the working class. Holding an account with a wine merchant or tailor was a sign of status for the middle classes. The shopkeeper might be in a position of social subservience, and conscious of the need to retain prestigious clients, needing to judge when to move from more or less subtle hints that payment would be appreciated to use of the courts. Consumer markets were sustained by 'informal' retail credit, and traders awarded differential credit according to the perceived differences in personal character and social standing. Consumers presented themselves to retailers, shaping their identity as respectable and trustworthy; the shopkeeper had to assess whether the customer was what he or she seemed. Particular difficulties arose in dealing with sons and wives who were pledging the credit of the male head of household. Would a father pay bills run up by his feckless son at his Cambridge tailor and wine merchant? At what point could the shopkeeper refuse further purchases without alienating a potentially valuable customer and his friends? Would a husband honour the bills run up by his wife at her dressmakers? And if the aggrieved parent or spouse refused to pay, would the courts side with them or with the shopkeeper?

In the eighteenth century, the largest category of prisoner was debtors, and debtors' prisons were sanctuaries rather than sites for punishment. Members of the middle class could seek refuge there until their debts were discharged. The prisons were largely run by their inmates who could rent rooms, purchase food, leave to work, and receive alms—and while in prison, they were immune from the claims of their creditors. Residents were seen as victims of misfortune as much as authors of their own downfall. In the mid-nineteenth century, the nature of the prisons changed, as higher-status debtors were removed and confinement became more a matter of enforcing the contractual duties of working-class debtors. The debtors' prisons were incorporated into the criminal system and converted into places of punishment. The process started with local small claims courts or courts of request, which created summary justice for small debts with imprisonment in the house of correction. A series of Acts between 1838 and 1846 went a stage further. Jurisdiction over claims of less than £20 (increased to £50 from 1850, and to £100 from 1902) passed from local 'courts of request' to the county courts, where judges had the power to send debtors to prison for up to six weeks, and to send them back if they failed to pay their debts as agreed by the court. Their supposedly irresponsible consumption was punished, and contracts enforced. By contrast, in the 1860s imprisonment was abolished for more substantial debts. In 1861, the law of bankruptcy, which previously only applied to traders, was extended to non-traders if they paid a fee of £10. By this means, personal debtors secured protection of their goods and bodies, and they could be discharged of their debt by partial repayment of 10s. in the pound, or less if agreed by the creditors. The fee effectively excluded working-class debtors. In 1869, superior courts lost the power of imprisonment for debt, but county courts retained it for debts of less than £50. In 1897, there were 7,282 bankruptcies, compared with over 1.1m plaints to recover small debts, whose average amount up to the First World War was £3. Between the wars, imprisonment for debt declined. County court imprisonment peaked at 11,986 in 1906, fell to 293 in 1918, then rose to an inter-war peak of 4,041 in 1932 when it was more likely to be used for failure to pay maintenance or bastardy orders and local rates.[15]

These legislative changes could be interpreted as the creation of 'class law': larger, propertied, or middle-class debtors avoided prison and full payment of their debts; the poor faced summary eviction for non-payment of rent or imprisonment for failing to pay their debts, with repeated imprisonment until they paid in full. In Paul Johnson's opinion, the law 'both embodied and justified middle-class views about the latent fecklessness and immorality of manual workers and about the latent industry and honesty of the property-owning classes'. He suggests that 'class-based legal prejudice was combined with the supposedly value-free operation of untrammelled market competition'. Johnson argues that the free market was constrained by suspicion about the moral laxity of the working class. Hence institutions for thrift were biased: the POSB gave a low return to working-class savers and used their deposits to reduce the national debt. Life insurance on infants was restricted as a result of fear that working-class parents were killing their children. Above all, he argues that attitudes to debt were deeply affected by a divergence between the moral worth of the middle class and the moral degradation of the working class. In his view, the new county courts paid little attention to custom or to discretion. They were not imposing the norms of the free market and contract; rather they made the free market and contract 'subservient to moral prejudice'. In Johnson's view, parliament, the law, and the courts were systematically biased against the working class, and these assumptions were accepted by the population as a whole. The biases were, he argues, sustained by evolutionary theories which stressed a movement from instinct and gratification (found amongst savages and working men who spent their wages on instant pleasure) to reason and prudence (found amongst middle-class families who could defer their desires).[16]

Bias certainly existed in the treatment of debt but was it really as intense as Johnson argues? The fear of gratification overcoming prudence was not only a criticism of workers; it also applied to middle-class women and sons who could subvert the supposedly rational and prudential control of family assets. Biases in the legal system were challenged as well as entrenched. Above all, judges used their moral assumptions to protect workers from their creditors: the free market and contract were not subverted only by treating workers as incapable of acting prudently, but also by viewing traders as unscrupulous. County court judges were instructed to consider the contractual and social circumstances of the debt, and they had some discretion in ordering payment or imprisonment. The Act of 1846 therefore did not mark a complete break with equity and the creation of the county courts was more than an imposition of contractual obligations on workers. But did this mean that the judges had more scope to introduce class bias? Johnson sees class bias against workers; Finn sees judges using their discretion to protect workers and their wives. Many county court judges were drawn from families involved with the Church, army, civil service, and law rather than commerce and industry, and they were themselves critical of individualism and the materialism of capitalism, wishing to moralize the market and limit the reach of purely contractual behaviour. They were not necessarily sympathetic to the traders who came before them. Of course, county court judges often interpreted the debts through the lens of political economy, and welcomed their ability to punish debtors and to insist on repayment. But they saw that thrift was not enough to deal with poverty, and that credit was not a sign of dissipation. Judges might be hostile to creditors who wished to enforce their contractual rights without consideration of the need to act equitably. Might imprisonment for small debts merely encourage traders to behave more unscrupulously? Judges could fulminate against the wiles of drapers who led women into purchases for which their husband would be responsible, and in such cases they often refused the creditor's claim. Judges were more than the agents of a class system of law, and they were ambivalent towards the market. The point was realized by Ellen Wilkinson, the MP for the depressed Tyneside constituency of Jarrow, who pointed out that 'the county court judge has over and over again stood as the friend of the poor and unfortunate litigants'.[17]

Credit relations were permeated with moral and cultural assumptions, and were considerably more complicated than the imposition of class bias. Gender was equally important, and the nature of the individual and his or her goods were assessed and measured. Was this commodity a necessity or a luxury for that person? Was the trader unscrupulous in seducing consumers into inappropriate action, and so undermining patriarchal authority in the home? Or was he the innocent victim of deceitful and imprudent consumers? Women shopped, acting as the agents of their husbands who generally paid for and owned the goods, so creating a fear in the minds of alarmed cultural conservatives that women's desires, and their manipulation by retailers, would corrupt the home and weaken the husband. Samuel Smiles feared women's passions would subvert society, for their 'rage for dress and finery . . . rivalled the corrupt and debauched age of Louis XV of France' and would ruin both their husband and trader. The legal right of a wife to pledge her husband's credit was uncertain. What would happen if women were seduced into buying goods, pledging their husbands' credit? Female desires could destroy their husbands if they were obliged to honour the debt, or harm traders if the husbands refused to pay. Both parties turned to the law for protection, and judges had to decide between the two claims. Generally, they favoured husbands. A husband could deny responsibility for debts incurred by his wife if he could show that the goods were not necessary and that he had forbidden her to buy them. In a crucial legal case of 1864, Mr Jolly, a draper, claimed that he sold goods to Mrs Rees with the presumption she could pledge her husband's credit. Mr Rees argued he had explicitly forbidden his wife to act as his agent and that he was not liable. The court agreed with Mr Rees. Although a man living with his wife might be assumed to have given her authority to pledge his credit, he had the right to revoke it without any public notice. Not surprisingly, retailers were alarmed: How were they to know whether a woman had the authority to buy goods on her husband's credit?. Even if the husband had not explicitly forbidden his wife to purchase goods, the courts might still absolve him from his wife's debts on the grounds that the purchase was not necessary. Mr Sharpe, the Keeper of Records at the Guildhall in London, refused to pay for a sealskin coat purchased by his wife from Whitley's for £12; he argued it was extravagant and he should not be liable. The judge found for Sharpe against Whitley. The jacket, he opined, 'may be perfectly "suitable" ... but it cannot be called necessary, and, if the husband is not generous enough or rich enough to indulge his wife in the luxury, she must go without'. Male heads of households were not autonomous economic individuals; they appeared before the courts as social individuals whose economic choices were made by members of their families, in ways that were ambiguous and disputed.[18] In 1935, their status was simplified by the Married Women and Tortfeasors Act which made wives personally responsible for their debts.

The cultural definition of what was 'necessary' and what was a luxury was at the heart of the dispute between Sharpe, his wife, and Whitley's store. Under the law of necessaries, the credit of the head of household was shared by dependent family members. The point applied to sons as well as to wives. What, for example, was a 'suitable and agreeable' purchase by an undergraduate for his father's station in life? The issue vexed the Cambridge county court in 1883. The defendant's son contracted a debt of £2 7s. for sherry, brandy, and maraschino for a party in his college rooms; after careful deliberation of the boundary between need and luxury, the judge ruled that maraschino and brandy were not necessary, but was uncertain about the sherry. Closer enquiry established that the student was the eldest of ten children of a clergyman who did not drink beer, wine, and spirits for reasons of economy. The judge therefore ruled that the sherry was also a luxury, so that the wine merchant could not enforce a contract made by a minor on his father's presumed credit. As Finn comments, 'commodities participated in the unstable meanings, strategies, structures and practices of social life . . .. Necessaries in one context and luxuries in the next, these goods assumed social meanings that reflected the station in life of their purchasers rather than their use value or their exchange value alone.'[19]

As well as 'informal' credit, a number of more formal systems of borrowing emerged. By the later nineteenth century, credit was needed even by the most affluent members of the working class—and indeed by many members of the middle class—to buy more expensive consumer goods. A piano, living room furniture, or a motor car could not be purchased from the weekly wage or monthly salary, and would often involve payment in instalments to spread the cost over a period of months or even years. Hence the emergence of hire purchase in the second half of the nineteenth century, starting with Singer's sewing machines in the 1860s and pianos and bicycles in the 1880s, and growing particularly rapidly between the wars. Rough estimates suggest that there were around a million current agreements in 1891, rising to 24 million in 1936. In 1924, consumers entered into around 2 million new agreements, and in 1936 as many as 7 million. Such agreements were crucial to the expanding market for consumer durables: more than 70 per cent of sales of motor cars, bicycles, electrical appliances, and working-class furniture relied on hire purchase.[20]

Hire purchase was both economically necessary and socially ambivalent. Ownership of a piano, new furniture, electrical goods, or a motor car was a marker of social status. Between the wars, magazines such as *Woman's Own* idealized the 'professional' housewife who provided nourishing meals, domestic harmony, and emotional and physical health, all of which demanded the purchase of labour-saving consumer durables, comfortable furnishings, and home entertainment.[21] Attaining the standards of the 'ideal home' was a sign of status; purchasing the goods through hire purchase was a sign that they could not be afforded. Consequently, recourse to hire purchase was a guilty secret in suburbia or the parlours of respectable working-class families. Not surprisingly, advertising for HP offered assurances such as 'we guarantee delivery in plain vans'.[22]

The lack of openness created an imbalance between traders and consumers who had difficulties in obtaining information on the reputation of different companies, and who were reluctant to publicize their experiences at the hands of shady dealers. Consequently, many traders were able to charge excessive prices at extremely high interest rates. Many traders did not even provide a copy of the contract. The hire purchase agreement often limited customers' rights, denying any implied warranty under the Sales of Gods Act 1893. As one judge remarked, the clause should read: 'we will sell you rubbish and you shall have no redress.' The commodity remained the property of the trader during the agreement, and the customer was paying a rental charge for its use so that failure to make even the last payment allowed repossession. Hard-nosed traders could take repossession on the slightest pretext—a practice known as 'snatch back'. They might tempt customers into taking out a new contract for another item which was added to an existing agreement—and failure to meet payments on the new contract meant that the item covered by the previous contract was also repossessed. Not surprisingly, these abuses were criticized. Although retailers were within their legal rights, many judges sympathized with customers and were willing to use adverse publicity against unscrupulous traders. Such concerns were shared by respectable traders who preferred to use hire purchase to increase their turnover rather than to make high profits from individual sales on dubious terms. When legislation was introduced to remove some of the worst abuses in a private member's bill in 1938, it was sponsored by social workers with the support of the Hire Traders' Protection Society.[23]

How far did the problems prevent the diffusion of consumer durables between the wars? The example of the motor car industry is instructive. British motor manufacturers in the inter-war period assumed that the upper- and middle-class market had not yet been saturated; they therefore concentrated on this segment of the market rather than creating a new market. Car ownership in England rose from 5 per cent of households in 1924 to 20 per cent in 1938. By contrast, a mass market was created in the USA, through hire purchase (General Motors) or price cuts (Ford). In 1919, Continental Guaranty of America created United Dominions Trust to provide credit for motor cars in Britain, and there were seven concerns by 1937. By 1928, 60 per cent of cars in the UK were sold on instalments, and the terms were among the best in Europe, and in some respects better than in the USA. The main reason for a slower diffusion of mass car ownership was the difference in the price of cars. In Britain, Ford's strategy of cutting prices did not work and its increase in sales barely covered the fall in profits per vehicle. Ford's experience showed that price reductions did not increase market share or profits, and other companies preferred to continue with the existing strategy of retaining higher prices and concentrating on the middle-class market. The key factor was the decision of producers on pricing and the nature of the market rather than credit terms.[24]

Leisure and Enjoyment

In 1850, many leisure activities were associated with alcohol consumption. Publicans encouraged customers to spend more and to stay longer by providing entertainment, and music halls allowed the sale and consumption of alcohol in the auditorium. Sporting activities tended to be informal—a matter of meeting on a patch of waste or common ground, without a clearly defined pitch or time, and without a clear structure of competition. Animal baiting and fights between dogs, cocks, and bulls continued, though by 1850 usually without the sanction of the civic elite. The result, in the eyes of many moral reformers, could be disorder. As we have noted, many local authorities wished to remove disruptive activities from public spaces. At the same time, the growth of income and leisure time meant that entrepreneurs had new opportunities to supply leisure in more expensive facilities, which meant that they also wished to ensure that activities were respectable to attract more affluent members of the working class or even the middle class. Indeed, the commercialization of leisure could give opportunities to moral reformers, for venues often needed licences to operate. The result might be tension over the content of recreational activities.

Moral reformers were anxious that recreation should raise standards, and their assumptions collided with the norms of the rest of society. The United Kingdom Alliance campaigned to close down the drink trade, and temperance did have its successes. Sabbatarians wished to ensure that Sunday was observed as a day of peace and reflection—and they managed to close most shops and places of entertainment. The Royal Society for the Prevention of Cruelty to Animals campaigned for better treatment of cab horses as well as against dog and cock fighting. The Young Men's (and later Women's) Christian Association provided havens of safety, and social purity crusades tried to control prostitution, vice, and debauchery. The motivation was partly Evangelical disapproval of moral transgression. It was also a matter of disciplining the workforce and establishing new standards of urban order, to create a purer and more public-spirited society. Moral integrity was a badge of citizenship: the rich had to show that they were stewards of their wealth just as much as the poor were to act honestly. Of course, the boundaries were vague and the definition of the limits of acceptable behaviour continued to be debated throughout the period. However, the power of these various bodies declined from the 1880s, as single-issue movements lost their purchase in wider party structures and moral reform was displaced by a greater concern for structural reform. [25]

An important part of rational recreation was the codification of sports. If hearty games could civilize the boys of Rugby School, they might equally transform the life of East End boys and channel youthful exuberance. Sport was also a way of winning religious adherents though was not always sustained. In Bolton, the Christ Church Football Club was started by an Anglican clergyman but within four years the team walked out to form Bolton Wanderers.[26] Football was soon experiencing a change towards a professional, commercialized activity. When the Football Association was formed in 1863, it was a middle-class body. In the 1870s, it started to lose its middle-class and amateur identity, a process encouraged by the creation of the FA Cup in 1871 which attracted northern working-class teams to compete with southern gentlemen, with a clear culmination to the season. The FA Cup final of 1883 was a symbolic moment, when Blackburn Olympics defeated Old Etonians. In 1884, the FA banned professional players. In response, the northern working-class clubs seceded and formed their own association, which led the FA to accept professionalism in 1885; Scotland followed in 1893. In 1888, a national football league was created in England, with its headquarters in Preston in tension with the FA in London. By 1914, there were about 158 professional teams in England and Wales, and another 30 in Scotland. Average attendance in the first division in England rose from 4,600 in 1888/89 to 23,100 in 1913/14. Most clubs were limited liability companies, run by boards drawn from local traders, publicans, and small businessmen who were attracted by local prestige, with both political and commercial importance in addition to their own interest in the game. Dividends were limited to 5 per cent, and most profits were returned to the game. Of course, many young men continued to play the game: there were about 12,000 clubs and 750,000 registered players in England in 1914, and it became part of the Board of Education's Physical Training Syllabus in 1909. In 1914, the king attended his first cup final, which became an established part of royal duty. But grammar and public schools avoided the game. Professionalism, mass spectatorship, and commercialization meant that the middle class largely withdrew. As F. E. Smith pointed out in 1911, football assisted the policemen and social workers, keeping workers happy; without it, there would be 'nothing but misery, depression, sloth, indiscipline and disorder'. Some historians suggest that this was the purpose of football, which is a very different matter. In reality, was a means of enjoyment and identity, not a conscious policy of manipulation to produce a culture of consolation.[27]

Cricket and rugby union football escaped the curse of professionalism. In the case of cricket, professional 'players' were allowed into county teams alongside 'gentlemen' amateurs who retained control over the game and ensured that paid working men were kept in their place. It remained the summer sport of public schools, as well as a popular professional club game in Lancashire and Yorkshire, managing to combine the classes within a single code. In the case of rugby, the clash between middle-class amateurism and working-class professionalism split the game into union and league. The Rugby Football Union was formed in 1871, when the game was still largely middle class; by the 1880s, many working men were playing in northern towns, where they introduced knock-out competitions and leagues. The RFU was wary about organized leagues and hostile to professionalism. In 1895, twenty-two northern clubs formed the Northern Union or, from 1922, the Rugby League.[28] Hence sport was generally segregated on class lines.

New forms of rational entertainment emerged from within the working class, so that the process was not entirely one of imposition by the morally concerned middle class. Men might organize excursions, fishing, or a game of cricket or football. Men and women might form a choral society. In some cases, societies might cross class lines. In Leeds, the Philharmonic Choir was founded in 1870, attracting leading conductors and commissioning new work. In the south Wales mining valleys, a similar choral tradition emerged, usually based on male voices rather than mixed choirs. These choirs competed in eisteddfods which were such a feature of Welsh identity in the later nineteenth century. Choirs also competed in national competitions at the Crystal Palace. Such recreation also crossed the lines of religious identity: Anglicans and nonconformists, total abstainers and modest drinkers could come together for choral competitions. Brass bands were formed in many industrial districts, often with links with military music; they bought their instruments with loans from the makers or with support from their employers. One of the most famous was the Black Dyke band which was formed around 1855 with the backing of John Foster and Sons, the owner of the woollen mill. By the early twentieth century there were perhaps 40,000 bands in the United Kingdom; as with the choral societies, they competed in regional and national competitions, an endemic feature of popular culture with its pride in success and local patriotism.

Such musical activities grew out of the active associational life of the industrial districts and cut across denominations and class. They generated commercial activity, for bands were supplied with instruments and sheet music; and choirs and bands recorded for the new gramophone industry. The line between popular and serious music was blurred. Sir Arthur Sullivan's father was sergeant bandmaster at the Royal Military College and subsequently teacher of clarinet at the new Royal Military School of Music. Arthur sang in the Chapel Royal, winning a scholarship to the Royal Academy of Music and to Leipzig. He wrote extensively for the chorally based music festivals. Symphonic music did not offer a living as it might in Germany; in the highly commercial and urban society of Britain, writing popular ballads did. *The Lost Chord* was his greatest success, selling 200,000 copies of sheet music; and his setting of the stirringly Evangelical hymn 'Onward Christian Soldiers' earned him a royalty at every reprinting. Of course, his greatest success was in works for the musical theatre, and most famously with W. S. Gilbert, where the wit of Gilbert's words was matched by the clever parodies of opera, madrigals, and popular songs. The impresario Richard D'Oyly Carte turned Gilbert and Sullivan into big business and a national institution. Sullivan himself conducted the orchestra of the Philharmonic Society as well as for musical festivals such as Leeds. He moved in the social world of the monarchy and aristocracy, and appealed to the lower middle class.[29]

Musical entertainment took many forms, from the oratorios performed at music festivals, to cathedral choirs and nonconformist hymns, to music hall songs and ballads. The producers of sheet music were impresarios who shaped musical taste, creating the careers of singers and composers. Alongside them were the owners of chains of music halls. These emerged from singing saloons provided by enterprising publicans. By the 1850s, some publicans were charging for admission rather than making their profits from sales of drink and attracting audiences more by the quality of the acts and the comfort of the venue. The smaller halls started to decline, particularly after the tightening of licensing and safety controls in the 1880s. In 1851, Charles Morton opened the Canterbury Hall in Lambeth on the site of his pub's skittle alley, and in 1861 he extended his operations to the West End. The Oxford music hall on Oxford Street was the first purpose-built music hall of a new breed. But the largest was the Alhambra on Leicester Square with a capacity of 3,500. The Alhambra was operated by a joint-stock company, and by 1866 a boom of construction and flotations created thirty-three large halls in London, with an average capacity of 1,500. There was a further spate of construction in the 1880s.

Music halls, with town halls and other public buildings, and the new department stores, were part of the reconstruction of the town centres. The provinces followed, and a number of entrepreneurs created chains in the north and midlands. Care had to be taken that large-scale investments were not threatened by regulations and the revoking of licences, for to many moral reformers the music halls remained a demotic challenge to civilized behaviour. The reformers turned to the renewal of licences as a way of enforcing their views, and town councils came under pressure either to refuse licences or to impose censorship. They were concerned for safety and imposed fire regulations, which could also be used as a way of securing control over acts. The LCC employed a team of inspectors to visit the halls, noting down risqué lyrics and observing the behaviour of the audience. In 1894, the LCC refused any new licence for a music hall selling alcohol, and closed the Empire on Leicester Square because of the conduct of women soliciting members of the audience. The owners responded by ensuring that their acts were beyond reproach but the halls could never be entirely freed from moral danger—the popularity of singers such as Marie Lloyd or George Formby relied on transgression of the limits of respectability. Morton started a system of turns whereby performers might appear in four or five venues a night, with the greatest stars under exclusive contract to one chain. The performer was removed from the audience to the stage, with a shift from sitting around tables with friends, drinking and talking. But even when fixed seating became the norm, there could still be lively exchange between stage and customers. The audience was largely drawn from the working class but with some clerks and shop-workers, and perhaps a more louche set of young middle-class men. By the end of the century, as they became more variety halls, members of the middle class might attend. The halls became ever more elaborate, with singers, dancers, acrobats, or tableaux of historical events, and short films by the early twentieth century.

Critics of the music hall have seen it as undermining a radical working-class culture by offering what Stedman Jones calls a culture of consolation. But why should the music hall be politically radical and was it merely a way of consoling under the control of commercial interests? Entrepreneurs had to be aware of the public controls, but they also knew their audiences; and many of the acts mocked and ridiculed, in a tame way, figures of authority.[30]

By the 1880s, the technique of recording sound was discovered. At this stage, recordings were made acoustically, placing performers near a large horn which transferred the sounds into vibrations scored into a soft surface. Initially, the majority of recordings sold in Britain were made and sold by the American firm Columbia; in 1897, the Gramophone Company was established in London, by an American entrepreneur who drew on American technology and recordings as well as starting to record British artists from 1898. In 1901 an agreement was made with the American Victor Co. to share markets: Victor took the Americas and Far East, and the Gramophone Co. the rest of the world. The Columbia and Gramophone Co. competed for a growing market using advertising and branding, and creating budget labels. By 1914, total annual sales of records in Britain were nearly 4 million and during the war sales of popular and patriotic songs increased. The piano was in retreat before a wave of records.

Between the wars, recording technology changed with the introduction of electrical recordings, followed more slowly by electrical reproduction. In 1931, Elgar opened a new recording studio at Abbey Road, conducting the London Symphony Orchestra in one of his own works. But above all, the recording firms moved into jazz, big bands, and dance music rather than music hall stars and classical composers, and above all from America. In the early 1930s, sales of players declined which could indicate that the market was saturated. More surprisingly, the total number of records sold felt sharply from a peak of 59.2m in 1930 to 20.0m in 1935. The explanation was not the impact of depression but the emergence of radio broadcasting as receivers fell in price and improved in quality. In 1926, when the BBC was chartered, 25 per cent of households had a radio; by 1939, the figure was over 80 per cent. The BBC did not permit advertising or 'plugs', which meant that the record companies sponsored programmes on foreign stations which broadcast into Britain. For example, HMV broadcast on Sunday afternoon from Radio Paris from the end of 1931. In response to the declining market, the Gramophone Co. and Columbia merged in 1931 to form Electrical and Musical Industries (EMI), and by the Second World War the only other company was Decca. As well as competing at home, the two firms co-operated in marketing each other's labels in different parts of the world. The Gramophone Co. also manufactured electrical goods at its large factory, including radio receivers—and started to research into the development of television which formed the basis of the first broadcast by the BBC in 1936.[31]

Between the wars, the most popular recordings were no longer British music hall stars, and there was a much greater emphasis on dance music. The first *palais de danse* opened in 1919 and was soon copied around the country. Although the popularity of dancing declined in the 1920s with the growth of cinemas and radio, it emerged as a mass recreation in the 1930s in the hands of chains such as Mecca which commercialized dancing and appealed to a lower middle- and working-class clientele. The halls were important as sites of social interaction and courtship, and of physical expression for women and young people.[32]

Commercialism transformed recreation, and at the same time the idiom changed to be much more democratic and American in inspiration. How does this leave McKibbin's notion of two distinctive and cohesive class cultures? In his view, British society had a high level of social cohesion but not social integration: classes maintained clear boundaries, knowing that their own rights would not be infringed.[33] But rigid class lines were less obvious in the dance music of the 1920s and 1930s, and commercial firms wished to exploit markets with more standardized music without regard for cultural boundaries. The working and lower middle classes were the largest share of the market. As James Nott comments, 'the voice of popular culture within the nation's culture as a whole was increasingly prominent'. It entailed a culture of domestic enjoyment, sentimentality, and romance. Music and pleasure became much more widely available, and at a higher standard—a point not always welcomed by cultural conservatives who decried the destruction of an 'authentic' popular culture and a contamination of society by meretricious and superficial escapist entertainment. 'Hits' came and went more quickly, but this was not necessarily a sign of decline. There was more music, often at a higher standard of execution and sophistication, and available to most members of society. The cultural balance of power was shifting towards entrepreneurs, undermining notions of what was respectable and of value. This criticism was often linked with a suspicion of 'Americanization'. British 'folk' music was losing out, so it seemed, to Jewish and black idioms from America. The trend could be checked by quotas on American films and by the monopoly of the BBC in broadcasting. Some historians stress that culture was being controlled and regulated, but this is to interpret the process in too negative a way. The trend of democratizing and nationalizing popular culture could not be halted. James Nott stresses the emergence of a common national culture and the dictates of commerce sanitized popular culture. He prefers to argue that the new forms of music and entertainment 'significantly increased the social and expressive possibilities of working-class life'.[34]

This was true of the cinema, which provided excitement and romance, an escape from routine, and an opportunity for courtship. By 1914, Manchester had as many as eleven cinemas with a further seventeen in Salford. In 1924, the Conference on Christian Politics, Economics, and Citizenship commented with approval on cinema going: it was cheap enough for the poorest members of society, opening up a new world of interest and recreation for people living in poor conditions. Moral concern was much less than in the music hall. However, the licensing of music halls by town councils posed a threat if it were applied to cinema; it was one thing to modify acts to the needs of a particular town, but films could not be re-edited. The industry successfully argued for self-regulation through the British Board of Film Censors which was created in 1912 to ensure that nothing was shown to undermine the morals of the audience. The result, in the opinion of Jeffrey Richards, was to control the content of films to prevent treatment of religious and political issues, or the mocking of authority. The government was delighted to leave the task to the BBFC as an unofficial body which was concerned, as its president pointed out in 1919, not to extenuate crime or undermine marriage and morality. In 1917, the president set out forty-three rules—including bans on the depiction of prostitution, premarital and extramarital sex, nudity, orgies, sweating, abortion, and sexual perversion. The Board was wary of horror films for pandering to the love of the morbid; and hospital films for showing intimate details. Its concerns could sometimes become political: the Board banned *Battleship Potemkin*, fearing that it would lead to a breach of the peace. Hollywood films were also banned, such as *The Bitter Tea of General Yen* (1933) for dealing with miscegenation or *Night Must Fall* for its sexual content. On the other hand, the Cambridge University Socialist Society picketed a Cambridge cinema showing *Lives of a Bengal Lancer* as propaganda for military dictatorship in India. In the later 1930s, some films did have a political edge: *The Stars Look Down* argued for nationalization of the mines, and *The Citadel* for a national health service.

Cinema was accessible to women, unlike most spectator sports and the public house, and to children and adolescents. Admission figures are first available for 1934 when 903m visits were made in Britain, rising to 1,027m in 1940. By 1938, there were 4,967 cinemas. Larger companies emerged to handle production and distribution: Gaumont and Associated British Picture Corporation owned cinemas and made films; a third concern, the Odeon, made an exclusive deal with United Artists. These three circuits had 1,011 cinemas by the war, two-fifths of the total. A social survey of Merseyside found that 40 per cent of the population went to the cinema in any one week, and 25 per cent of the population went twice, with the manual working class going more often. Above all, sons and daughters and young married couples went; middle-aged and elderly men preferred the pub, darts, and pigeons. If age was important so was class: 35 per cent of those in lower-income groups went once a week or more, but only 25 per cent of the middle-income groups and 19 per cent of upper-income groups. Of those who went at least once a week, 69 per cent were women. Middle-class women attended in suburban cinemas, taking tea with friends after shopping. Most films were historical or romantic comedies or musicals, and above all from Hollywood, offering an image of a glamorous and less hierarchical society which alarmed social conservatives.

In 1923, only 10 per cent of films shown were made in Britain, in 1926 only 5 per cent. In 1927, the Cinematograph Films Act imposed a quota of British films, rising to 20 per cent in 1933. Most British films were low-quality 'quota quickies', though United Artists did support Korda in making high-quality films. Before the First World War, European films took as much as 60 per cent of the American market; in the 1920s, they had a tiny share, and also lost a large part of their domestic market. The most plausible explanation is that the First World War came at a critical time when production was shifting to more expensive 'feature' films. Just at the point where the cost of making films rose, the war prevented European producers from investing—and the Americans secured a lead which was difficult to erode. Most feature films made little or no profit, and the studios relied on a few successful movies which were difficult to predict—hence the need for a large output which European makers could not afford. Hollywood had the technical expertise with external economies from sharing resources, as well as a suitable climate. By 1924, few British films were being made and entry by new producers was difficult. They did not have the output to survive an unpopular movie; and producers might be tempted to appeal to the market by producing an expensive film with high risks. Success was almost as bad, for the director and actors might be tempted to Hollywood. The British film industry was well aware of its difficulties. As a memorandum of 1930 pointed out, westerns were scarcely possible, and crook and underworld dramas were hampered by the lack of gang warfare and machine gun battles in British cities. Britain was too civilized and law-abiding; and British court rooms far less dramatic, with less corruption and too many wigs.[35]

Gambling was a common pastime, a key part of working-class culture. A 'flutter' on a horse, greyhound, or pigeon was an enjoyable way of adding some excitement to the day. Until the First World War, most betting was on horses, and most of it was illegal, carried on at street corners or back alleys, with look-outs posted against police or informers. Under the Street Betting Act of 1906, betting was legal on the course or on credit through licensed bookmakers. Here was a clear example of legal bias: what was permitted for middle- and upper-class men with access to credit was not allowed for workers. However, illegal betting flourished, and the police often turned a blind eye. If they did arrest the look-out his fine would be paid by the bookmaker, so satisfying the police's need to show action without disrupting the trade. The financial penalties were modest; in some cases, bribes to the police were larger. Betting offered excitement and stimulation, through calculation and knowledge of form and handicaps; it meant intellectual initiative in making decisions. The business was run by workers for workers; it was illegal but honest. What was legal, and popular among men and women, was betting on football results. By the Second World War, about 10 million people were on the books of the 'pools' promoters, and as much as a third of the population participated. Most men and women only wagered a small amount, carefully observing the limits of what they could afford. Betting offered a way of exercising judgement and, as Ross McKibbin argues, for many poor families it was as rational as saving small sums which could not transform their lives or provide against insecurity. A 'win' might allow a 'treat'; the loss of a few pennies would not cause hardship. Opposition came from nonconformists, from 'official classes' who feared it would lead to ruin—and from the labour movement.[36]

Hobbies were popular. Allotments were used to grow vegetables but they were also a club where men could meet, talk, and compete, represented by the leek competitions of the north-east with their rules on the proportion of white to green, diameter to length, and so on. Men took immense pride in their achievements. Competition was rife—in pigeon racing or fishing, brass bands or choirs, or dog breeding. They offered a form of intellectual activity, of discipline and skill apart from officially sanctioned achievements.[37]

Every large town had its own entertainment district; seaside resorts were dedicated to pleasure. In Lancashire the survival of the traditional 'wakes week' meant that a town's mills closed down for a period in the summer. The workers were not paid but many saved small sums to stay in a boarding house in Blackpool, and to enjoy the funfair and variety shows. In mining areas or in shipbuilding, regular annual closures were not normal, and periods off work were related to the cycle of production, or to the payment of wages when there would be a day off. In south Wales, the miners in 1888 had a holiday on the first Monday in every month with the result that leisure was based on day excursions rather than a week away from home. Between the wars, paid holidays were becoming the norm, considered to be 'essential to a reasonable standard of living'. By 1937, about 4m of 18.5m working people had a paid holiday, and a higher proportion took a holiday away from home. The prospect of legislation led to a spurt to pre-empt legislative action, which came with the Holiday with Pay Act 1938. By the war, over 11 million workers had paid holidays. Seaside resorts continued to expand, and the first holiday camps offered a rival attraction to the seaside boarding house.[38]

Representing the Consumer

Consumption and the consumer were defined in moral, cultural, and social terms. They also acquired political resonance. We have seen that utilities posed important questions: how were customers to be protected from rapacious companies? The state intervened to impose regulation in various ways, reflecting the political balance of advantage between different stakeholders. The definition of consumption and the consumer also affected trade policy and taxation. Were the interests of the consumer assured by free trade or did free trade imply exploitation of 'sweated' labour abroad, and the destruction of jobs at home? Should indirect taxes shape consumption by taxing undesirable commodities and removing duties from necessities? If so, who was to define what was a necessity and what was undesirable, on what terms?

Free trade was linked with the rights of the consumer. It involved more than the dominance of a free market and *laissez-faire*, for it offered the consumer the right to free exchange of goods without fear of exploitation. Free trade allowed goods to be purchased in the cheapest market without the danger of protective duties to increase the profits of favoured interests; and the state should take steps to ensure that monopolistic utilities did not take advantage of their power to boost their profits at the expense of the rest of society. The politics of bread in the tariff reform controversy could easily expand into a wider concern for what the worker was earning in terms of what he or she could buy—a shift in progressive thought confirmed by the introduction of minimum wage legislation, the concept of the poverty line, and the concern for the distribution of income and wealth.

The widening definition of the consumer interest was encouraged by the First World War. During the war, consumer protests and strikes against shortages and unfair allocation of goods created difficulties. The War Emergency Workers National Committee, for example, called for government control of the food supply and the introduction of maximum prices for necessities. In November 1917, the government introduced compulsory rationing and bread was subsidized. Food Control Committees were created to oversee the local administration of distribution and rationing. The membership was drawn from a wide spectrum of society: in January 1919, 25 per cent of members were working class, 17.8 per cent women, and 11 per cent from the co-operative movement. In January 1918, a Consumers' Council was established to advise the Ministry of Food. Membership included six representatives of the co-operative movement, three from the parliamentary committee of the TUC, three from the WEWNC, and three from industrial women's organizations. J. R. Clynes, the chairman of the Council, defined its role as to 'see with an eye on the consumer whether the interests and rights of consumers were being properly watched or not'. The ploy of containing criticism proved an illusion, for the Council developed a socialist politics of consumption, arguing for subsidized milk for nursing mothers and children under 5, the state purchase of wholesalers, and state intervention in the supply of commodities. But the Council was divided. Some members opposed decontrol at the end of the war; others argued for decontrol and saw the real threat as state trading. After the war, the Council was largely ignored and it resigned in 1920/1. However, it had created a precedent for the formal recognition of a consumers' interest.[39]

After the First World War, the politics of consumption shifted to more active state protection of the consumer against profiteers and combines, and as a means of raising standards of health and nutrition. Before the war, Lloyd George used the large loaf as a symbol of the benefits of free trade compared with the small German loaf; after the war, the rhetoric of the large loaf disappeared. The health of the British people, and above all children, seemed to depend on the purity of milk. In other words, consumer politics moved towards a more active involvement of the state in consumption.[40]

The Labour movement was divided. The co-operative movement created its own party which was affiliated with Labour, arguing that the politics of the factory should be replaced, or at least complemented, by the politics of the shop. The co-operative movement stressed the duties of the 'citizen consumer', with obligations and duties to create a more just society through the act of consumption. Nothing came of the ideas of the co-operative movement, and the ILP was also marginalized. The ILP's programme of a living wage was devised by John Hobson and was linked with his interest in Ruskin who remained, with William Morris, an important influence. The ILP argued for discriminating consumption of distinctive goods: individuals could express their identity as consumers and at the same time encourage small workshops which would give self-expression to workers. This emphasis was defeated in the

Labour party in favour of nationalization and asceticism, and the efficiency of mass production.[41]

How should consumers fit into a planned economy? Political and Economic Planning argued that 'the State must be consumer-minded rather than producer-minded', suggesting that a much more conscious policy was needed than in the days of free trade. The consumer interest should be represented and the consumer educated as a way of improving the efficient allocation of resources. Consequently, a Consumer Research Council should set standards and encourage higher-quality manufacture, offering a central source of consumer information, and in the process improving the efficiency of firms and raising the quality of goods. Such an approach was expressed in *What Consumers Need* (1934). Informed consumers would discipline the economy from the side of demand. This approach to consumption was based on the 'customer consumer', an ally of large retailers who was concerned with value for money and efficiency rather than the ethical nature of the production of goods.[42]

More pragmatically, the trade unions and Labour mounted campaigns on the cost of living, and Stanley Baldwin used food prices as a populist issue. He established a Royal Commission on Food Prices in 1924-5. The Commission argued that prices were biased in favour of the producer, and as a consequence a Food Council was set up to analyse chains of production and retailing. Its activities peaked in 1929-31 over the London milk combine of United Dairies, but the Council lacked powers and had no real success. Labour introduced Consumer Council Bills in 1930 and 1931 to create more powerful bodies to investigate raw material and farm prices. Again, the proposals came to nothing, and they were based on a negative consumerism designed to fix prices, control profiteers and combines, and protect the consumer of necessities. The Councils were a first stage to nationalization, and wages and work were more significant to Labour than price and consumption. As a result of Labour pressure, the National government did make the Food Council part of the agricultural marketing schemes but was no more than a façade, a way of deflecting criticism from the producers. Not surprisingly, the consumer bodies within the various marketing boards were ignored, and the voice of the farmers was dominant.[43]

In the Second World War, rationing was immediately introduced. Women were mobilized to implement and advise on rationing and austerity through the Women's Voluntary Service and the Women's Institute. However, there was no representative body on the lines of the Consumer Council. Instead, the Consumer Needs Section was established in 1941 to collect data on the impact of the schemes. On the whole, workers were satisfied with the morality of utility schemes and purchase tax which taxed luxuries at high rates and exempted the standard, government-approved items. Although a recent account of wartime and post-war rationing suggests that black markets were extensive and the culture of 'fair shares' contested, the reality was somewhat more complicated. The black market was probably limited in scope, and individuals interpreted their compliance or resistance according to their notions of what was reasonable.[44]

After the war, Labour's approach rested on shaping the consumer through public control of the economy, using rationing, subsidies, and price controls to offer fair shares to all consumers. The concern was less with representation of the consumer than supply-side initiatives. Nationalized industries subsumed the consumer in public control. Consumer councils were set up in the nationalized industries, but they were weak, for the interests of the consumer were seen as synonymous with public control, and competing claims of workers and consumers could be resolved by productivity gains. The Parliamentary Secretary to the Ministry of Fuel and Power summed up the approach in 1946 when he asked: 'How can an organisation which is running an industry for the public interest exploit anyone?' Emanuel Shinwell, the Minister of Fuel and Power who was responsible for nationalizing the coal industry, felt that consumers had no need for protection since there was 'no inducement on the part of those administering the industry to take advantage of the consumer'. The post-war Labour government replicated what it criticized between the wars in agricultural marketing: weak consumer representation.[45]

Labour thinking after the war was more concerned with the politics of necessity than with affluence. Its post-war policies gave priority to productive, rational purchases of utility goods over the pursuit of novelty and fashion or luxury and extravagance. The rhetoric made sense in terms of the need to hold down domestic consumption in favour of the export drive, but it had deeper roots in a concern about the pursuit of luxury at the expense of the common good. The electoral dangers were becoming clear by 1950. Michael Young inserted various consumer issues into Labour's manifesto in 1950, proposing consumer protection and information in the market-place, through an independent consumer advice service and legislation on hire purchase and false description. The theme was picked up by Harold Wilson in the aftermath of the narrow election victory of 1950:

It is pretty clear that at the last election a good number of those who voted against us . . . were voting as consumers, and were expressing their . . . view about the cost of living, and the . . . nationalised industries. Apart from housing, the Conservative Party will presumably base their main appeal . . . on questions affecting the consumer, and . . . once again many electors will vote against us because they regard their gains as producers . . . as being not due to the Labour Government . . . while the responsibility for their *consumer* troubles they are ready to lay at the Government's door.

Wilson argued that Labour needed to present itself as the party of the consumer through a Consumers' Charter. Although Attlee saw this approach as 'the shape of things to come', it was dropped in 1951. Christopher Mayhew pointed to the problem: 'The party has been built up as a party of producers, but the last election showed that the electorate was tending to vote more as consumers.'[46]

NOTES

1. The analysis here rests on Stone and Rowe, *Measurement of Consumers' Expenditure and Behaviour*, ii. Data for 1900-19 were compiled by Prest, *Consumers' Expenditure*. Data are consolidated in Feinstein, *National Income, Expenditure and Output*, which provides detailed annual estimates of consumers' expenditure from 1900 to 1965 in tables 24 and 25, and aggregate estimates in table 5.

2. Stone and Rowe, *Measurement of Consumers' Expenditure*, ii. 128–32.

3. Dingle, 'Drink and working class living standards'; Stone and Rowe, *Measurement of Consumers' Expenditure*, table 58.

4. Stone and Rowe, *Measurement of Consumers' Expenditure*, table 58; Hilton, *Smoking*, 2, and chs. 3, 5, and 6 on evils of smoking; Taylor, *English History*, 392.

5. Feinstein, *National Income, Expenditure and Output*, table 5.

6. Singer, 'Index'.

7. The discussion of housing here relies on Daunton, *House and Home* and Englander, *Landlords and Tenants*.

8. Reid, 'Decline of Saint Monday'; Griffin, *England's Revelry*; Bailey, *Leisure and Class*.

9. Offer, *Property and Politics*, 271–2.

10. Mitchell and Jones, *Abstract*, 117–8.

11. For council housing and rent controls, see Daunton, 'Introduction' and Ryder, 'Council house building in County Durham', Finnigan, 'Council housing in Leeds', and Dresser, 'Housing policy in Bristol'; on Dagenham, Olechnowicz, *Working-Class Housing*; Marriner, 'Cash and concrete'; Wilding, 'Housing and Town Planning Act, 1919'; Swenarton, *Homes Fit for Heroes*; Schifferes, 'Council tenants and housing policy'.

12. Feinstein, *Domestic Capital Formation*, 36; Richardson and Aldcroft, *Building in the British Economy*, 42–3, 56, 74–5; McIntosh, 'A note on cheap money', 168; Broadberry, 'Cheap money'; Humphries, 'Interwar house building'; Scott, 'Selling owner-occupation'; Richardson and Aldcroft, *Building in the British Economy*; Craig, 'The house that jerry built?'

13. Bowden, 'Consumer durables revolution', 44, 45.

14. Bowden and Offer, 'Household appliances and the use of time'.

15. Finn, *Character of Credit*, 326; Johnson, 'Class law', 157–63.

16. Johnson, 'Class law', 147–50, 157, 162–3, 164, 166–7.

17. Finn, *Character of Credit*; Finn, 'Working class women', 126, 127, 142–8; Wilkinson quoted in Scott, 'Twilight world,' 221.

18. Rappaport, 'Halls of temptation'; Rappaport, 'Husband and his wife's dresses', 53, 66–7; and Rappaport, *Shopping for Pleasure.*; Finn, *Character of Credit*.

19. Finn, *Character of Credit*, 274–7.

20. Scott, 'Twilight world', 197–8; Bowden, 'New consumerism', 242–62.

21. See for example Greenfield and Reid, 'Women's magazines', 162–4.

22. Scott, 'Twilight world', 206, 213, 215

23. Ibid.

24. Bowden and Turner, 'Demand for consumer durables'.

25. See Roberts, *Making English Morals*.

26. Bailey, *Leisure and Class*, 139.

27. Ibid. 138–44; Mason, *Association Football*; Vamplew, *Pay Up*.

28. Bailey, *Leisure and Class*, 144–5; Vamplew, *Pay Up*, 64-6; Smith and Williams, *Fields of Praise*.

29. Entries in *ODNB*; information on choirs and bands from their websites.

30. On music halls, Bailey, *Leisure and Class*, ch. 7; Pennybacker, *Vision for London*; Bailey (ed.), *Music Hall*; Russell, *Popular Music*; Stedman Jones, 'Working-class culture'.

31. Nott, *Music for the People*, appendix and tables 1, 2, 3; Martland, *Since Records Began*.

32. Nott, *Music for the People*, chs. 5, 6, 7; Fowler, *First Teenagers*, chs. 4 and 5.

33. McKibbin, *Ideologies*, 166.

34. Nott, *Music for the People*, 226–35.

35. Davies, *Leisure*, 74; Richards, *Age of Dream Palace*, part 1; Bakker, 'Decline and fall of the European film industry', 342–3.

36. Davies, *Leisure*, ch. 6; McKibbin, *Ideologies*, ch. x.

37. McKibbin, *Ideologies*, ch. x.

38. Walton, 'Demand for working-class seaside holidays'; Walton, *English Seaside Resort*; Pimlott, *Englishman's Holiday*, ch. 13; Ward and Hardy, *Goodnight Campers*.

39. Hilton, *Consumerism*, 66–74.

40. Trentmann, 'Bread, milk'.

41. Thompson, 'Hobson and the Fabians'.

42. Beauchamp, '*Getting Your Money's Worth*', 131, 133; Hilton, *Consumerism*, 99–107.

43. Hilton, *Consumerism*, chs. 2, 3, and 4.

44. Zweiniger-Bargielowska, *Austerity in Britain*.

45. Beauchamp, '*Getting Your Money's Worth*', 136; Hilton, *Consumerism*, 146.

46. Beauchamp, '*Getting Your Money's Worth*', 137–8; Hilton, *Consumerism*, 155.

FURTHER READING

Allan, C. M., 'The genesis of British urban redevelopment with special reference to Glasgow', *Economic History Review*, 18 (1965)

Bailey, P., *Leisure and Class in Victorian England* (1978)

—— (ed.), *Music Hall: The Business of Pleasure* (Milton Keynes, 1986)

Bakker, G., 'The decline and fall of the European film industry: sunk costs, market size and market structure, 1890-1927', *Economic History Review*, 58 (2005)

Beauchamp, C., "*Getting Your Money's Worth*: American models for the remaking of the consumer interest in Britain, 1930s–1960s', in M. Bevir and F. Trentmann (eds.), *Critiques of Capital in Modern Britain and America: Transatlantic Exchanges 1800 to the Present Day* (Basingstoke, 2002)

Bowden, S., 'The new consumerism', in P. Johnson (ed.), *Twentieth Century Britain: Economic, Social and Cultural Change* (1994)

Bowden, S., 'The consumer durables revolution in England, 1932-38: a regional analysis', *Explorations in Economic History*, 25 (1988)

—— and Offer, A., 'Household appliances and the use of time: the United States and Britain since the 1920s', *Economic History Review*, 47 (1994)

—— and Turner, P., 'The demand for consumer durables in the United Kingdom in the interwar period', *Journal of Economic History*, 53 (1993)

Briggs, A., *The History of Broadcasting in the United Kingdom*, ii: *The Golden Age of Wireless* (1965)

Broadbery, S. N., 'Cheap money and the housing boom in interwar Britain: an econometric appraisal', *Manchester School*, 87 (1987)

Craig, P., 'The house that jerry built? Building societies, the state and the politics of owner-occupation', *Housing Studies*, 1 (1986)

Cross, G. S., *Time and Money: The Making of Consumer Culture* (New York, 1993)

Daunton, M, 'Introduction', in M. Daunton (ed.), *Councillors and Tenants: Local Authority Housing in English Cities, 1919-39* (Leicester, 1984)

—— *House and Home in the Victorian City: Working-Class Housing 1850-1914* (1985)

—— *A Property Owning Democracy? Housing in Britain* (1987)

Davies, A., *Leisure, Gender and Poverty: Working-Class Culture in Salford and Manchester, 1900-1939* (Milton Keynes, 1992)

Dingle, A. E., 'Drink and working class living standards in Britain, 1870-1914', *Economic History Review*, 25 (1972)

Dresser, M., 'Housing policy in Bristol, 1919-30', in M. Daunton (ed.), *Councillors and Tenants* (Leicester, 1984)

Englander, D., *Landlord and Tenant in Urban Britain, 1838-1918* (Oxford, 1983)

Feinstein, C., *Domestic Capital Formation in the United Kingdom, 1920–38* (Cambridge, 1965)

—— *National Income, Expenditure and Output of the United Kingdom, 1855–1965* (Cambridge, 1972)

Finn, M. C., 'Working class women and the contest for consumer control in Victorian county courts', *Past and Present*, 161 (1998)

—— 'Women, consumption and coverture in England, c.1760–1860', *Historical Journal*, 39 (1996)

—— *The Character of Credit: Personal Debt in English Culture, 1740-1914* (Cambridge, 2003)

Finnigan, R., 'Council housing in Leeds, 1919–39', in M. Daunotn (ed.), *Councillors and Tenants* (Leicester, 1984)

Fishwick, N., *English Football and Society, 1910-1950* (Manchester, 1989)

Fowler, D., *The First Teenagers! The Lifestyle of the Young Wage-Earners in Inter-war Britain* (1995)

Greenfield, J., and Reid, C., 'Women's magazines and the commercial orchestration of femininity in the 1930s: evidence from *Woman's Own*', *Media History*, 4 (1998)

Griffin, E., *England's Revelry: A History of Popular Sports and Pastimes 1660–1850* (Oxford, 2005)

Hilton, M., *Smoking in British Popular Culture 1800–2000* (Manchester, 2000)

—— 'The fable of the sheep, or private virtues, public vices: the consumer revolution of the twentieth century', *Past and Present*, 176 (2002)

—— *Consumerism in Twentieth-Century Britain* (Cambridge, 2003)

Holt, R., *Sport and the British: A Modern History* (Oxford, 1989)

Humphries, J., 'Interwar house building, cheap money and building societies: the housing boom revisted', *Business History*, 29 (1987)

Johnson, P., 'Class law in Victorian England', *Past and Present*, 141 (1993)

Jones, S. G., *Workers at Play: A Social and Economic History of Leisure, 1918–1939* (1986)

McIntosh, R. M., 'A note on cheap money and the British building boom, 1932–37', *Economic Journal*, 61 (1951)

McKibbin, R., *The Ideologies of Class: Social Relations in Britain, 1880–1950* (Oxford, 1990)

Maiwald, K., 'An index of building costs in the United Kingdom, 1865–1938', *Economic History Review*, 7 (1954)

Marriner, S., 'Cash and concrete: liquidity problems in the mass production of "homes for heroes"', *Business History*, 18 (1976)

Martland, P., *Since Records Began: EMI, the First Hundred Years* (1997)

Mason, T, *Association Football and English Society, 1863-1915* (Brighton, 1980)

Muthesius, S., *The English Terraced House* (1982)

Mitchell, B. R., and Jone, H. G., *Second Abstract of British Historical Statistics* (Cambridge, 1971)

Nott, J. J., *Music for the People: Popular Music and Dance in Interwar Britain* (Oxford, 2002)

Offer, A., *Property and Politics, 1870–1914: Landownership, Law, Ideology and Urban Development in England* (Cambridge, 1981)

Olechnowicz, A., *Working-Class Housing Between the Wars: The Becontree Estate* (Oxford, 1997)

Pennybacker, S., *A Vision for London, 1889–1914: Labour, Everyday Life and the LCC Experiment* (1995)

Pimlott, J. A. R., *The Englishman's Holiday: A Social History* (1947)

Prest, A. R., *Consumers' Expenditure in the United Kingdom, 1900-1919* (Cambridge, 1954)

Rappaport, E. D., ' "A husband and his wife's dresses": consumer credit and the debtor family in England, 1864–1914', in V de Grazia with E. Furlough (eds), *The Sex of Things: Gender and Consumption in Historical Perspective* (Berkeley, 1996)

—— ' "The halls of temptation": gender, politics, and the construction of the department store in late Victorian London', *Journal of British Studies*, 35 (1996)

—— *Shopping for Pleasure: Women in the Making of London's West End* (Princeton, 2000)

Reid, D., 'The decline of Saint Monday', *Past and Present*, 71 (1976)

Richards, J., *The Age of the Dream Palace: Cinema and Society in Britain 1930–39* (1984)

Richardson, H. W., and Aldcroft, D. H., *Building in the British Economy between the Wars* (1968)

Roberts, M. J. D., *Making English Morals: Voluntary Association and Moral Reform in England, 1787–1886* (Cambridge, 2004)

Russell, D., *Popular Music in England, 1840–1914: A Social History* (Manchester, 1987)

Ryder, R., 'Council house building in County Durham, 1900–39: the local implementation of national policy', in M. Daunton (ed.), *Councillors and Tenants* (Leicester, 1984)

Saul, S. B., 'House building in England, 1890–1914', *Economic History Review*, 15 (1962–3)

Schifferes, S., 'Council tenants and housing policy in the 1930s', in Political Economy of Housing Workshop, *Housing and Class* (1976)

Scott, P., 'The twilight world of interwar British hire purchase', *Past and Present*, 177 (2002)

—— 'Selling owner-occupation to the working classes in 1930s Britain', University of Reading Economics and Management Discussion Papers 23 (2004).

Singer, H. W., 'An index of urban land rents and house rents in England and Wales, 1845–1913', *Econometrica*, 9 (1941)

Smith, D., and Williams, G., *Fields of Praise: Official History of the Welsh Rugby Union, 1881–1981* (Cardiff, 1980)

Stedman Jones, G., *Outcast London: A Study in the Relationship between Classes in Victorian Society* (Oxford, 1971)

—— 'Working-class culture and working-class politics in London, 1870-1914', *Journal of Social History* (1974)

Stone, R., and Rowe, D. A., *The Measurement of Consumers' Expenditure and Behaviour in the United Kingdom, 1920–38*, II (Cambridge, 1966)

Swenarton, M., *Homes Fit for Heroes: The Politics and Architecture of Early State Housing in Britain* (1981)

—— and Taylor, S., 'The scale and nature of the growth of owner-occupation in Britain between the wars', *Economic History Review*, 38 (1985)

Tarn, J. N., *Five Per Cent Philanthropy: An Account of Housing in Urban Areas between 1840 and 1914* (Cambridge, 1973)

Taylor, A. J. P., *English History,' 1914–45* (Oxford, 1966)

Thompson, N., 'Hobson and the Fabians: Two roads to socialism in the 1920s', *History of Political Economy*, 26 (1994)

Trentmann, F., 'Bread, milk and democracy: consumption and citizenship in twentieth-century Britain', in M. Daunton and M. Hilton (eds.), *The Politics of Consumption: Material Culture and Citizenship in Europe and America* (Oxford, 2001)

Vamplew, W., *Pay Up and Play the Game: Professional Sport in Britain, 1875-1914* (Cambridge, 1988)

Walton, J. K., *The English Seaside Resort: A Social History, 1750-1914* (Leicester, 1983)

—— *The Blackpool Landlady: A Social History* (Manchester, 1978)

—— 'The demand for working-class seaside holidays in Victorian England', *Economic History Review*, 3 (1981)

Ward, C., and Hardy, D., *Goodnight Campers! The History of the British Holiday Camp* (1986)

Wilding, P., 'The Housing and Town Planning Act, 1919: a study in the making of social policy', *Journal of Social Policy*, 2 (1973)

Wohl, A. S., *The Eternal Slum: Housing and Social Policy in Victorian London* (1974)

Yelling, J. A., *Slums and Slum Clearance in Victorian England* (1986)

Zweiniger-Bargielowska, I., *Austerity in Britain: Rationing, Control and Consumption, 1939–1955* (Oxford, 2000)

PUBLIC POLICY AND THE STATE

PART IV

PREJUDICE, LAW, AND THE STATE

....

CHAPTER 14

Taxing and Spending

'There is something repulsive to human nature', wrote Gladstone's biographer John Morley, 'in the simple reproduction of defunct budgets.' Gladstone might have been surprised by Morley's remark, for budgets were central to his political success and to the forging of the mid-Victorian consensus which removed taxation from the centre of political contention. Cobden was nearer the mark when he suggested that 'When a government deals unjustly by the people with respect to taxation, that constitutes the whole matter of account between them.'[1] As Gladstone and Cobden realized, taxation was crucial to the relationship between the citizen and the state.

Consent to taxation was important for the form of the state in Britain. The balance of central and local spending shifted over the period. The local tax system became much less responsive from about 1900, whereas the central state was more flexible; welfare spending accordingly moved from the localities to the centre. Similarly, the ability to finance welfare from redistributive central government taxation meant that contributory insurance schemes became less important. The structure of welfare affected the response to the depression of the 1930s, for transfer payments contributed to the stability of consumption in Britain. The ability of the state to secure finance determined its ability to wage war as well as to pay for welfare. This was not simply a matter of collecting taxes, but also of securing loans. Individuals would only subscribe to loans if they had confidence in the stability of national finances and the credibility of the state's commitment to honour its debts. The cost of the First World War placed immense strain on government finances, and in some countries, difficulties in negotiating taxes meant that the burden of the debt was reduced through hyperinflation. By contrast, Britain managed to place post-war government finances on a secure basis which contributed to the financial stability of the inter-war period. Of course, the tax system also expressed normative assumptions about the nature of the economy and human motivation. Was growth created by offering incentives to the rich; or would the result merely be envy and waste? Was growth the outcome of equality and a sense of inclusiveness, or would this reduce motivation to work and invest? Would high levels of taxation blunt growth or create social justice?

Between the middle of the nineteenth century and the middle of the twentieth century, the level of government expenditure rose in two 'steps'. In 1850, total government expenditure stood at 11 per cent of GNP, a marked reduction from the peak of the 'fiscal-military state' of the Napoleonic wars, when the figure reached 23 per cent. The Boer War marked a temporary increase to 14 per cent of GNP or 13.3 per cent of GDP in 1900. Spending was then displaced by the First World War—and did not fall back as after the Napoleonic wars. Total government expenditure was 20.5 per cent of GDP in 1920 and 26.0 per cent in 1937. The Second World War resulted in another displacement to 37.5 per cent in 1951: much of the additional spending went on welfare. In 1900, public spending on social services accounted for 2.3 per cent of GDP, rising to 10.5 per cent in 1937 and 14.1 per cent in 1951. By contrast, spending on defence was 6.0 per cent of GDP in 1900 and 7.6 per cent in 1951.[2] Why did the public sector, and especially spending on welfare, become so large, and with what impact on the economy? The impact was affected not only by how much was spent, but how it was raised. Did the level and incidence of taxation create economic problems whether by harming incentives or by burdening the poor?

The Gladstonian Fiscal Constitution

The fiscal basis of the Victorian state was negotiated by Sir Robert Peel and William Gladstone in their budgets of 1842 and 1853, complementing the repeal of the corn laws in 1846 and the passing of the Bank Charter Act in 1844. The Bank Charter Act was designed to ensure monetary stability. The repeal of the corn laws and the gradual reduction in duties on other imports marked an attempt to create political balance and social harmony. The ambition of Peel, as expressed in 1830, was to bring as many people as possible within the realm of consumption, allowing them to enjoy tea, coffee, and sugar without paying excessive taxes. At the same time, adjusting the balance of the tax system would remove the complaint of radicals and many industrial interests that taxation was falling on the poor and producers to the benefit of rentiers and aristocratic hangers-on. Peel realized that stability rested on fiscal justice between classes, a sentiment that lay behind his decision to reintroduce the income tax in 1842 which provided revenue to cover the tariff revisions of 1842 and 1845.

The Tories feared that the income tax implied an end to protection. Many radicals and free traders were alarmed that it would give the state more money for warfare, and they pressed for retrenchment as an alternative. Others admitted the need but wished to differentiate the tax between income from 'spontaneous' and 'industrious' earnings. 'Spontaneous' income from land or bonds continued regardless of the energy or health of the individual. By contrast, 'industrious' income from trade or the professions depended on the maintenance of life and good health, and ceased entirely at death. Consequently, a proportion of industrious incomes needed to be saved and the advocates of differentiation argued that it should be exempted from taxation. The principle of differentiation was taken up by Disraeli in an attempt to secure the allegiance of urban trade and industry to the Conservative party. By 1852, Disraeli was anxious to redefine the Conservatives as a party appealing to commercial and industrial interests as well as to landed society. He was convinced that free trade was politically necessary, and in introducing his budget he faced a difficult task. On his own benches, he had to conciliate landowners and commercial interests who claimed that they were damaged by free trade. He offered landowners a reduction in the duties on malt; yet he could not conciliate them too much for fear of alienating urban and industrial interests. To the urban and industrial interests, he offered differentiation of the income tax. But his attempt to convert the Tories from a narrow party of the landed interest into a national party failed. The distinction between earned and unearned income was criticized by many as a breach of faith with holders of government bonds who now faced the prospect of paying a higher rate of tax on their interest payments than other groups. Most significantly, Disraeli had to find the money to pay for concessions to landowners and 'earned incomes' and his proposals alienated other groups. It seemed to be a piece of class legislation which took away from the urban middle class with one hand what it appeared to give with the other, leaving farmers and landowners as net gainers. The failure marked the end of the campaign for differentiation for fifty years.

The incoming Chancellor, Gladstone, feared that differentiation would set one interest group against another—landowners and rentiers versus industrialists and professionals. A visit to Naples made him aware of the dangers of a decadent aristocracy battening upon a repressed middle class; Gladstone felt that the answer was balance and justice. The fiscal policy of the state should not be a source of disruption but should integrate society. He wished to encourage commerce and trade within the framework of pre-industrial social relationships based on the rule of an enlightened aristocracy. Indeed, he hoped that a satisfactory fiscal policy might remove the need for further political reform. He rejected differentiation in 1853, on the grounds that the tax system could be balanced even in its absence. After all, assets left at death paid inheritance duties and land was liable to the local property rate. His one concession to 'industrious' incomes was tax relief on life insurance policies—a concession in favour of prudence and self-reliance which was to have serious consequences for the pattern of saving. The case for differentiation was rejected, until it reappeared in different political circumstances after 1900. The budget of 1853 also marked a shift in attitudes of free traders towards the income tax. Gladstone offered a further round of reductions in import duties, and Cobden now accepted that the income tax not only provided revenue to extend free trade, but could act as a restraint on militarism. Gladstone's aim was to create an identity between the payment of income tax and the franchise, so that voters would be mindful of the impact of government expenditure, and would support retrenchment. The payment of income tax was therefore a means to constrain government expenditure, and in return for self-control by the electors Gladstone offered its abolition by 1860—an ambition that was never achieved.

Whatever the disagreement over differentiation, in the second half of the nineteenth century there was widespread acceptance that the guiding principle of proportionality did not imply graduation of the tax system. The principle of proportionate taxation according to 'ability' implied that everyone should pay as nearly as possible the same share of their income in tax by whatever means the revenue was collected. Indirect taxes fell proportionately more heavily on the poor; and the need for a large revenue and ease of collection meant that articles of general consumption were taxed. Direct taxes should therefore offset the heavier burden of indirect taxes on the poor, but without redistributing income. The rate of income tax should not be increased or progressive on higher incomes. John Stuart Mill opposed graduation: a minimum income 'needful for life, health and immunity from bodily pain' should be left untaxed, but all income above this threshold should pay the same flat rate. He argued that larger incomes were a sign of energy, providing the savings necessary for a prosperous economy. Placing a higher tax on large incomes would be socially harmful.[3] In Gladstone's famous remark, money should be allowed to fructify in the pockets of the people—that is, the income of the rich would be used more effectively by them than by the state. Rich people would be more likely to save and invest and create work for poorer members of society. Hence savings were prudent for the individual and for society as a whole, leading to personal security and generating economic growth. These propositions were called into question by John Maynard Keynes in the 1930s, who pointed out that savings did not necessarily convert into investment; savings could reduce consumption and individual prudence could become, in aggregate, undesirable for the economy. What Mill and Gladstone did accept was that inheritances should be taxed, for inherited wealth gave some (possibly undeserving) people a start in the race for prosperity. Higher taxation of assets left at death could be justified on grounds of equality of opportunity. In 1853, Gladstone introduced a new succession duty—a tax on assets left at death.

Gladstone's budget was designed to shackle the state, encouraging voters to support retrenchment in order to remove the income tax. For the next forty or fifty years, the level of spending by the central government increased less rapidly than the growth of GNP. Between 1850 and 1890, total government expenditure grew at a slower rate than GNP, by 0.76 per cent for every 1 per cent increase in GNP. Most of the items of spending which grew faster than GNP were the responsibility of the local state. Between 1850 and 1890, the annual average real rate of growth of central government spending was 1.5 per cent; local government spending grew almost twice as fast, at 2.9 per cent.[4] Why was central government taxation held down? One answer is that nineteenth-century states needed less money for warfare. The cost of servicing the national debt (an item reflecting the costs of past wars) grew by only 0.38 per cent p.a. between 1850 and 1890, and defence spending by 0.92 per cent.[5] But this is not the entire explanation, for in the twentieth century any slack in defence spending or debt charges was taken up by civilian spending on welfare.

Gladstone hoped that the connection between taxation and voting would contain spending ambitions. In the 1860s, he was willing to extend the vote beyond the ranks of income tax payers to the better-off working men. In 1866 he proposed to extend the vote to men paying an annual rent of £7, which entailed 'an income very generally obtainable by the artisans and skilled labourers'.[6] Gladstone saw a close connection between the franchise and paying taxes, arguing that since the working class paid about a third of the taxes, they might be offered a majority of the electorate in about a third of the borough seats. In fact, Disraeli broke the link in the Reform Act of 1867, and the franchise was further extended in 1884. Here was a new danger: might an electorate dominated by voters below the median income seek to transfer resources from the rich? On the whole, the answer up to the end of the nineteenth century was 'no'. The attitude of most working-class electors was shaped by their suspicion of state spending as wasteful and inefficient. Most artisans and skilled workers felt that their claim to respectability rested on self-reliance. Their ambition was to create autonomous institutions whose stability was guaranteed by state regulation and legal recognition—above all, by trade unions and friendly societies.

The slow growth of spending by the central state reflected administrative or accounting procedures. Many of these devices were introduced prior to 1850, but in the second half of the nineteenth century they became a fairly rigid and uncompromising set of principles. The aim was to make the state and its citizens prudent and responsible. Taxes should not be hypothecated—that is assigned to a particular purpose which would mean that the revenue would always be spent: they should be paid into a single consolidated budget, and allocated to particular budget headings. This rule was linked with annual votes of parliament and the refusal to allow spending plans to run from year to year, which would tie the hands of subsequent governments. Further, funds could not be 'vired', that is reallocated from one budget head to another. A surplus on one head could only be used for one purpose—to pay off the national debt. Unless by mischance or unexpectedly low yields of taxation, the budget could not be in deficit. The national debt was now viewed as a protection for British liberties in times of national danger, rather than a massive burden. But debt should only be incurred in times of danger, for as H. H. Asquith remarked in 1906 'the Government is competing for and locking up funds

TABLE 14.1. *Government expenditure per capita at constant prices and as a percentage of GNP, UK, 1810–1900*

	Per capita (constant prices) (1790 = 100)	% of GNP
1810	191	23
1830	164	17
1850	179	11
1870	191	9
1890	272	8
1900	519	14

Source: Middleton, *Government versus the Market*, 90.

that might otherwise be available for commercial and industrial purposes'.[7] By these means, the spending of the central government was constrained. At the same time, it was legitimized: the central state was seen as efficient and transparent, able to respond to new needs for welfare after 1900.

The rising demand for revenue eventually imposed strains on the Gladstonian fiscal constitution. Although Peel and Gladstone promised that the income tax was temporary, in reality it became a permanent element. In the second half of the nineteenth century, the most striking change was a fall in the proportion of the central government's revenue from indirect taxes with the reduction in import duties in accord with the principles of free trade, and the limitation of excise duties to a few commodities. As Table 14.2 shows, the move from indirect taxes started with the repeal of the corn laws and other reductions in duties in the 1840s, and continued for the rest of the century. At first, protective or unremunerative duties were abolished or reduced. In the 1870s, the policy shifted. Robert Lowe, the Chancellor, claimed that his problem was 'to know how to get rid of all the money which persisted in pouring in upon him'. In his budget of 1873, he abolished many indirect taxes and duties.[8] The remaining indirect taxes were, so free trade Liberals claimed, voluntary: no one needed to consume tobacco or drink beer. But the increase in military spending during the Boer War was to impose strains on the existing fiscal structure. Should the additional revenue be secured from widening the range of indirect taxes; or should the revenue come from reform of the income tax?

Local Taxation

Taxation was not only a matter for the central government; as noted earlier, local government spending grew more rapidly than GNP in the nineteenth century. Relief

TABLE 14.2. *Contribution to UK Exchequer revenue of direct and indirect taxes, 1846–1930 (%)*

	Indirect	Direct
1846–50	69.8	30.2
1860–5	64.9	35.1
1871–5	65.4	34.6
1891–5	56.0	44.0
1901–5	48.8	51.2
1919–20	42.5	57.5
1929–30	35.9	64.2

Source: Matthew, 'Disraeli, Gladstone and the politics of mid-Victorian budgets', 638; Daunton, *Just Taxes*, 46.

of poverty was the responsibility of the Boards of Guardians; education fell upon the school boards; borough councils raised rates to pay for the provision of sewers, parks, police, and the other services. All relied on a property-based tax or rate, which was uneven in its incidence and increasingly inflexible. By the end of the nineteenth century, local taxation was in crisis and it proved easier to shift some of the costs from the rates to central taxation or insurance contributions. The relationship between the cost of urban government and the rate base reached a turning point in the 1870s. Between 1873/4 and 1878/9, the rateable value in England and Wales rose by 16.6 per cent, and the income from the rates by 15.3 per cent, so that the rate in the pound did not increase. The pattern then changed: between 1878/9 and 1883/4, the rateable value increased by 9.3 per cent and the income from the rates by 14.4 per cent, and continued to increase inexorably.[9]

The lack of buoyancy in rateable value may be easily explained. The most rapid period of urbanization was over by 1880, and continued urban growth was often outside the limits of the existing municipal boundaries. Suburbs with a low rate in the pound would, of course, jealously guard their independence from towns eager to incorporate them. At the same time, the costs of urban government mounted. This was in part the result of central government directives imposing minimum standards on schools or police. It was also a response to the fact that much local expenditure was now 'lumpy', requiring the issue of bonds which had to be paid regardless of the changing political complexion of the council and the financial burden. By 1914 local authority debt amounted to £656.2 m, not far short of the national debt which stood at £706 m.[10] Expenditure was more capital intensive, and once the decision to build a new reservoir or tramway had been taken and the bonds issued, the payment of interest was inevitable.

The nature of the urban political process was changing. In the mid-Victorian period, it was possible to reverse an upward trend. Expenditure was not dominated to the same extent by capital projects and the servicing of debt, so that retrenchment was more feasible. Indeed, a characteristic feature of the towns of mid-Victorian Britain was a ratepayers' backlash as a party of 'economists' took over the council from the instigators of schemes leading to higher rates. This alternation of periods of expenditure and retrenchment followed a local pattern. In the case of Birmingham, the 'economists' came to the fore in the mid–1850s, and were only finally overturned in the early 1870s, most obviously during the mayoralty of Joseph Chamberlain. The chronology in Leeds was different. There the 'economists' started to emerge in the 1870s. They gained control in the 1880s and persisted until the 1890s. The election of Archie Scarr, a market trader, as mayor in 1887 marked the apotheosis of the petty trader, contrasting with the national political status which Chamberlain had attained by this time.[11] By the end of the century, however, the cycle of periods of expenditure succeeded by long periods of retrenchment was much reduced.

Quite apart from changing financial circumstances, the ratepayers' interest of small tradesmen and house-owners was no longer so powerful by the late nineteenth century. Although most towns had a ratepayers' organization, it was usually somewhat peripheral in its emphasis on individualism and myopic decisions on investment. At least among professionals and larger businessmen, as well as officials, there was a greater willingness to use the municipality to invest in the urban infrastructure. The campaigns of the ratepayers' association might appear to be a diversionary tactic, for to many Liberals the real reason for high rates was landowners' avoidance of their fair contribution to local taxation. Other interests counteracted the claims of the ratepayers. A more bureaucratic and professional form of local government emerged by the early twentieth century, as councillors handed over executive functions to professional staff. The local Trades Council might have a greater political clout than the ratepayers' association so that the council might be forced to pay union wages to its own staff and award contracts only to employers agreeing to union terms.

The ratepayers' associations had a valid point, for the costs of urban government were mounting. As a result, owners of rented houses were facing a serious crisis. In England, rates were in theory paid by the occupier and not by the owner; in practice, the owners of most working-class housing in England 'compounded', paying the rates in return for a commission and hoping to cover themselves by adjusting their tenants' weekly payment. Difficulties arose in the early twentieth century as rates mounted, and the glut of housing after the building boom around 1900 meant it was difficult to pass the increased burden of rates on to the tenants. Landlords consequently faced an erosion of their profit margins, and also of the capital value of their houses. In Scotland, the problem was different. Until 1911, it was very rare for landlords to pay rates on behalf of the tenants and both parties paid directly to the council so that the pressure on the landlord's profit margin was accordingly less. In 1911, the English system of compounding was introduced with a considerably lower allowance, so that landlords faced a serious erosion of their profit margin. The structure of local taxation was therefore creating serious problems for investors in the towns and cities of Britain.[12]

A major political issue from the late nineteenth century was how to solve the problem of the increasing cost of local government and a narrow, inequitable tax base that affected not only borough councils but also the Boards of Guardians and school boards. There were a number of possibilities. One was to increase the income from municipal trading. Another was to widen the tax base. Property owners complained, for example, that merchants in Liverpool with valuable ships or cargoes in the harbour or on the seas might make no contribution to local taxation beyond the rates on their office. Was this fair when their cargoes passed through the municipally maintained streets, were protected by the police, and the burdens of supporting casual dockside labour fell on the poor rates? Such considerations led some to argue for a local income tax. Similarly, the building of a park or the improvement of the drains benefited local property owners who should be asked to pay. It was also argued that education and poor relief were national concerns for which all should pay out of national taxation. Above all, Conservatives and Liberals were divided over the position of the owners of property. Were landowners escaping their fair share of taxation?

In his *Principles of Political Economy*, Mill looked back to Ricardo's claim that landowners would secure most of the benefits of increased production and population as land prices and rents were driven up. In Mill's opinion, the income of landowners increased without 'exertion or sacrifice'. It followed that 'it would be no violation of the principles on which private property is grounded, if the state should appropriate this increase of wealth, or part of it . . . This would . . . merely be applying an accession of wealth, created by circumstances, to the benefit of society.'[13] This was not a point with which Gladstone could agree, for it threatened to use the tax system as an instrument of class conflict. Such attacks re-emerged at the end of the nineteenth century.

Radicals had long been hostile to aristocratic landowners and their leasehold estates, with a demand that leases should be 'enfranchised' or given the right to buy the freehold. In the 1880s, the issue was broadened with the publication of Henry George's *Progress and Poverty*. He argued that land received an 'unearned increment', for high levels of rent arose less from any effort of the owner than from the endeavours of the rest of society. The community created the increment in value, and was therefore justified in expropriating it by a tax on land values, which would offer two benefits. One was a reduction in land prices, since the owners would now have no incentive to hold out for high prices. The other was a shift in the incidence of taxation away from the building and towards the land upon which it was erected.[14]

The attack upon landowners offered a solution to the problems of local government finance, or at least an electorally attractive proposal for the Edwardian Liberal party. The attempt to reduce land prices was also seen as a solution to the problem of urban housing, and the use of cheap land on the suburban fringe was part of the policy proposed by the garden city movement. Low fares on municipal trams could decant the poor of the inner city to cheap suburban land, whose price was reduced by taxation designed to force it onto the market. The land campaign connected with the emergence of lower-density housing development which was being proposed before the First World War, and which was encouraged by the Housing and Town Planning Act of 1909. Although the aesthetic of the garden city movement did triumph, it was implemented after the war through very different means of the council estate. Otherwise, the strategy proposed by Henry George and seized on by Lloyd George in his land taxes in the budget of 1909 came to nothing. It was simply not practicable to define land as a reprehensible form of property apart from the house erected upon it. In the majority of cases the owner of the house also owned the freehold of the land. Land was in any case a small—and decreasing—proportion of the total national income. The opening of new agricultural areas in the Americas and Australasia in fact led to falling land prices and a reduction in the share of rent in the national income.[15] Nevertheless, interest in appropriating land values did not disappear and was implemented by the Labour government in 1947.

The attack upon landowners did have a political appeal in holding together an alliance within the Liberal party. Most of the remaining Whig landowners departed in the mid–1880s over the issue of Irish home rule, which made an attack upon the land politically more attractive. Here was a way of appealing to working-class electors without alienating middle-class voters. The blame for high house rents could be laid at the door of rapacious landowners. Industrial problems could be blamed upon high mineral royalties and land prices. A link could be forged with rural interests in Wales and Scotland where there was hostility towards Anglican landowners and the demands of the Church. Although the land question was unrealistic as a solution to the problems of local taxation, it did have a massive symbolic role.

The implementation of a policy on local taxation in the late nineteenth century was largely a matter for the Conservatives. At first, central government income was used in an ad hoc way to relieve the rates but in 1888 the Chancellor tried to reach a permanent solution by assigning the revenue from certain licence duties to the localities. The result was to make the structure of central government assistance more inflexible. Although the revenues increased the grant in the short term, in the longer term the limited nature of the assigned duties created a lack of buoyancy and flexibility. In the 1890s, the Conservative governments failed to provide further assistance to the towns and concentrated upon aid to the country and Church. The problem of local taxation was becoming serious, and coincided with a mounting financial burden in imperial taxation created by the Boer War.[16] Here was one explanation for the Conservative interest in tariffs. The difficulties of local government finance had other ramifications. The mounting problems of the voluntary schools resulted in an extension of rate support to Anglican and Catholic voluntary schools in the Education Act of 1902. The cost of the poor law was a further cause for concern. In the early years of the twentieth century, the Conservative government was grappling, none too successfully, with a crisis in local and imperial finance which was challenging the Victorian consensus of trade and fiscal policy, and threatening to reopen the nature of educational and social policies.

Reform of local government finance came to nothing. The Liberal solution of taxation of land values was abandoned after the First World War, and produced little revenue. As a result, local government did not have access to any buoyant or responsive tax, and increasingly came to rely on subventions from the central government. The attempt to limit the demands of local government in 1888 soon failed, and new grants-in-aid were offered. Pressures on the central government budget and a threat to its balance meant that the Treasury was anxious to control local authority spending. Concern was particularly intense in the case of the poor law, where Labour-controlled Guardians offered more generous payments to the unemployed. There were two responses. One was to move power away from 'irresponsible' local authorities to more dependable bodies. The second was to replace percentage grants with fixed 'block' grants. The new system was introduced in 1929, along with a partial derating of industry which was designed to remove the burden of heavy local taxation on the staple industries in depressed areas.[17] Although local spending accounted for a large part of welfare between the wars, the initiative was clearly shifting to the central state—a trend largely supported by Labour which realized that revenue from the central state was more redistributive between classes and regions.

Remaking the Fiscal Constitution

At the turn of the nineteenth and twentieth centuries, pressures mounted for higher levels of spending both on defence and welfare. The fiscal military state was reborn in a new form. The Boer War placed immediate pressure on the fiscal constitution, which continued with the naval race in the Edwardian period. The nature of military technology changed and a new alliance was forged between the state and science which turned away from a free trade rhetoric of peace to a successful claim for more funding in pursuit of power and security. The great new battleships demanded highly sophisticated systems of 'fire control'; and the state was heavily involved in the development of aircraft. Indeed, Britain was developing a 'warfare state' as well as a 'welfare state'.[18] The beginnings of a shift may be seen in the 1890s, when the expansion of unskilled trade unions led the Trades Union Congress to greater sympathy towards tax-funded welfare. The change was carried through in the policies of the Labour party which argued for tax-funded welfare and redistribution. Support for state-funded welfare did not come only from workers: many of the reforms were actively backed by employers anxious to improve efficiency and by state officials. The important point was the capacity of different bodies to supply welfare—a reasonably efficient and acceptable central tax system was more able to respond to demands for increased spending on welfare than other institutions (whether employers, charity, or self-help bodies) and the local state whose source of funding was limited to the rates.

The challenge of Conservatives to free trade meant that Liberals had to respond with an alternative fiscal policy. One way was to extend Mill's attack upon unearned incomes. The political symbolism of land, which had an appeal to many Liberals, was used by Lloyd George in the 'people's budget' of 1909 and in his land campaign of 1912–14 in order to rally support. In practice, it was a distraction from a solution to the problems of local government finance. Of greater practical significance was a shift of various social services from the poor law: old age pensions (1908) were funded from general national taxation; health and unemployment insurance (1911) from insurance contributions paid by workers and their employers. Costs were transferred from local to central government, and at the same time the pattern of central taxation started to change with a rejection of proportionality and an acceptance of graduation.

Gladstone believed that higher levels of taxation placed a burden on the prudent and benefited the indigent; he assumed that the incomes of the well-to-do led to savings and hence to investment and progress. Social problems were a matter of moral regeneration of the individual rather than changes in the distribution of income. Such views were challenged in the later nineteenth century, in part from the marginal revolution in economics. Alfred Marshall's *Principles of Economics* stressed the marginal cost of producing another unit of output and the marginal satisfaction to be derived from consuming it. The satisfaction to be derived from an additional £1 of income was less for someone earning £1,000 than for someone earning £200, so that a higher tax rate on the larger income caused less loss of satisfaction. Proportionate taxation according to ability could therefore be redefined as an equal marginal sacrifice.[19] This did not mean a pursuit of equality to the exclusion of other considerations. F. Y. Edgeworth feared that redistribution might simply encourage the poor to take more leisure and have more children. Furthermore, it might reduce savings and investment by the rich and so constrain economic growth, offset by the improved efficiency of workers who now had more income and welfare. Economists such as Edgeworth went beyond Mill in accepting the case for progressive, graduated taxation, but tempered the principle of equality with 'prudential considerations'.[20] A similar approach was developed by A. C. Pigou, who applied Marshall's marginal economics to welfare: he argued that a transfer of resources from rich to poor would scarcely affect the efficiency of the rich, but would raise the efficiency of the poor.[21] Marginal economics complemented the case for spending on public health and social welfare, defining progression as the norm. Although the marginal revolution in economics did not initiate the change in policy, it did alter the context for refutation, transferring intellectual authority from opposition to support of progressive taxation.

At the same time, officials at the Treasury and Inland Revenue came to accept the need for progression. In part, the shift arose from a change in personnel, but there was also a pragmatic realization that progression might be needed to raise more revenue with a minimum of friction. Prior to the Liberal government of 1906, the leading officials devised various administrative stratagems to argue that progression was impossible; after the Liberals came to power, the new generation stressed the need for more flexibility in the fiscal system. Data collected during the debate over Irish home rule showed that the poor were taxed heavily in relation to their income; and studies on the distribution of income by Chiozza Money showed just how much of the nation's income went to the rich.[22] A higher rate of tax on the rich was accepted by officials, who also accepted that savings and investment need not suffer if more modest middle-class incomes were relieved of the heavy burden of taxation.

Of course, some commentators were eager to push the case for redistribution further. Much of the change in perception came from writers outside the mainstream of economics, especially Sidney Webb and J. A. Hobson. The Webbs and the Fabian Society took Rent in a collectivist direction. They stressed the notion of 'parasitic trades', which took two related forms. The first was the partial maintenance of workers in trades with low levels of wages by other trades and the taxpayer who picked up the costs of ill health or irregular employment. The second, and wider, definition of parasitism assumed that the continued efficiency of industry relied upon the health and strength of the workforce. A trade which did not pay a wage sufficient for adequate food, clothing, and housing undermined health and efficiency, and left to itself, the market would lead to degeneration rather than progress. The answer was for the state to intervene and prescribe a 'National Minimum'.[23] Such arguments led the Webbs to advocate state direction of the labour market, extension of public ownership of industry, and large-scale production with limited choice.

This approach was anathema to most 'new Liberals' who wished to remove the constraints preventing men and women from taking charge of their own lives, rather than to make them dependent upon the state. The new Liberals aimed to make liberal capitalism work more efficiently rather than to replace it. Hobson proposed removing Rent by taxation, leaving individuals to make their own choice in the market, and encouraging discriminating consumption from small producers. Any income above the necessary cost of production was the surplus: it could be productive or unproductive. The unproductive surplus led to luxury trades and irregular work, producing excessive saving and underconsumption, and hence leading to unemployment and imperialism. The answer, argued Hobson, was the transfer of the unproductive surplus or 'economic rent' from private owners to the public, which would increase total consumption and put an end to unemployment. Once the state had captured rent, it could allow competition and individualism to play their part.[24] Here was an expression of the new Liberal notion of 'organicism', the belief that individual self-interest might be at the cost of other members of society, and that socially created value did not 'belong' to an individual and was therefore a legitimate source of taxation, repaying what was due to society. Once society, as a rational organism, had corrected the incidence of costs and benefits, the individual should be left to cope, rather than being reduced to dependency upon the state.[25] Hence the notion of rent and the 'unearned increment' was extended from land by arguing that all large incomes must contain a considerable 'social' element unearned by the individual which should be appropriated by the state. This approach would radically change fiscal policy.

The emphasis on social value and fiscal policy implied a changing definition of social problems. To Gladstone, social problems arose from individual failings and the solution was the moral regeneration of the individual. By contrast, the new Liberals stressed systematic failings, so that some people were not receiving sufficient income to take charge of their own lives. It was therefore impracticable to reform the individual's character without first removing the barriers to independence and success. 'Social value' could be called upon to increase wages or to finance social reforms, which would allow for greater success and prudence. The ambition of the new Liberals was the same as Gladstone's; it was the means which differed. Individual responsibility would be better developed by removing burdens 'too great for average human nature to bear'.[26]

Such was the background to the adoption of differentiation between earned and unearned income in 1907. It was part of the Liberal government's strategy of countering Chamberlain's demand for tariff reform with its promise of revenue and full employment by devising an alternative fiscal policy based on free trade. Asquith's budget of 1907 accepted that 'the problem of Free Trade finance' was to show that 'the burden can be placed where it ought to rest—on the vast surplus wealth of the community' through differential taxation of earned and unearned incomes.[27] Lloyd George's budget of 1909 applied the notion of social value through the taxation of land—a symbolic act which did not produce much revenue. More significantly, Lloyd George adopted graduation of the income tax. Winston Churchill's defence of the budget provides a clear expression of 'the new attitude of the State towards wealth':

Formerly the only question of the tax-gatherer was, 'How much have you got?'... But now a new question has arisen.... 'How did you get it?'... This refusal to treat all forms of wealth with equal deference, no matter what may have been the process by which it was acquired, is a strenuous assertion in a practical form, that there ought to be a constant relation between acquired wealth and useful service previously rendered.[28]

Here, it seemed, was a fundamental breach in the consensus of the 1850s.

The approach of the new Liberals was not welcomed by all Liberals, let alone Conservatives, and was at the heart of the constitutional crisis of 1909. The change was decried by A. V. Dicey, one of the most vigorous critics of Liberal policies. Until the budgets of Asquith and Lloyd George, 'a taxing Act was generally held open to censure if it imposed a special burden upon one class of the community; it was still more generally agreed that taxation should be imposed mainly, one might almost say exclusively, to meet the financial wants of the State'. He believed that the budget of 1909 departed from these principles by attacking the rich and landowners, and used taxes for political and social ends.[29] Yet despite Dicey's concerns, it would be wrong to see Lloyd George as fully embracing a Hobsonian view of the budget and jettisoning Gladstone. He was, in fact, more conservative than some of his critics allowed.

He hesitated about following Hobson's argument about 'underconsumption' and 'over-saving'. It was one thing to attack landowners, to raise the wages of 'sweated' labour through the trade boards, or to decasualize the labour market through labour exchanges. It was quite another to mount a major policy of income redistribution—not least for fear of alienating middle-class voters to the Conservatives, but also because it was still commonly assumed that prosperity followed from the savings of the rich. The extent to which the finance of the Liberal welfare reforms was redistributive should certainly not be exaggerated. The insurance schemes were largely contributory so that costs fell upon wage earners rather than the rich. Since the contributions were flat rate, they imposed a higher burden upon unskilled than skilled workers. Although taxation was less regressive, it had not yet become noticeably progressive, and the Labour party argued for a further shift away from flat-rate insurance contributions to a more progressive system of finance of welfare. Indeed, one of the strategies adopted by Lloyd George was to reduce taxation of middle-class family men. In 1909, he introduced tax breaks for children under the age of 16, which meant that many modest middle-class incomes paid less tax. Neither did Lloyd George follow Hobson's critique of foreign investment as a product of over-saving. Rather, he followed the line that investment abroad would lead to cheaper food and raw materials, and to a demand for British exports. It was only from 1912, as the costs of government mounted and recovery was not apparent, that Lloyd George extended his 'land campaign' and in 1914 moved to a fully graduated income tax.[30]

Since the Liberals came to power, the maximum rate of direct taxation on earned incomes had risen from 9d. to 2s. 8d. in the pound (3.75 to 13.3 per cent), and death duties from 8 to 20 per cent. The Liberal governments of 1906–14 therefore placed more emphasis upon fiscal policy in response to the Conservative demand for tariffs, and to overcome the problem of local taxation and social reform. Rather than directly facing up to the problems of local taxation, the Liberal response was to shift the burden from the poor rates to the central government. The reform of the tax system also gave Britain a considerable advantage over other countries. Britain entered the war with a highly effective system of income tax, which could be shifted in a more progressive direction without too many problems. Furthermore, the British government was able to secure loans on easier terms than its counterparts in the rest of Europe. At the outbreak of the war, the national debt was 27.6 per cent of the net national product in Britain, compared with 44.4 per cent in France and 86.5 per cent in Germany, and the yield on French bonds was 0.6 per cent higher and in Germany 0.7 per cent higher than in Britain.[31] The British financial system was more responsive to the demands of warfare.

Financing the First World War and its Aftermath

The share of government spending dropped as a proportion of GNP from the close of the Napoleonic wars, and the increase at the start of the twentieth century did not regain earlier levels (see Table 14.3). The outbreak of the First World War led to a displacement of government spending back to the level of the Napoleonic wars—with a fundamental difference that the level of spending remained high at the end of the war. A second divergence from the Napoleonic wars was the greater reliance on loans than on taxation, a choice with major consequences for post-war reconstruction. Later commentators were surprised that the British government did not rely more heavily on taxes, for their contribution to total revenue was considerably below the Napoleonic wars, Crimean War, and Boer War—let alone the Second World War. The Treasury was well aware of the discrepancy, pointing out that 47.1 per cent of the cost of wars between 1793 and 1815 and 52.6 per cent of the cost of the Crimean War came from taxes.[32] A higher level of taxation would have removed excess spending, as Keynes argued. It would also have reduced the costs of debt service after the war, which caused such political difficulties. But the view of most Treasury officials and the Chancellor was that taxes had gone as high as possible, with an increase in progression and a fall in the threshold for

TABLE 14.3. *Total public expenditure as a percentage of GDP at current prices and by function, UK, 1900–51*

	Total	Debt interest	Defence	Social services
1900	13.3	1.6	6.0	2.3
1907	10.9	1.8	2.7	3.1
1913	11.9	1.7	3.1	3.7
1920	20.5	5.7	6.1	4.9
1924	23.6	7.9	2.9	8.0
1929	5.4	5.4	2.6	9.2
1937	26.0	5.4	4.9	10.5
1948	37.0	5.1	6.3	17.6
1951	37.5	4.7	7.6	14.1

Source: Middleton, *Government versus the Market*, 91.

payment of income tax, as well as the imposition of an excess profits tax. The Chancellor argued that the country had reached the limit of taxation that was possible without encroaching on the standard of life necessary for efficiency. In a sense, he was right—unless the government opted to ration and control goods. During the First World War, the government was slow to move away from the market towards rationing and controls, preferring to pursue a policy of 'business as usual'. The government was also somewhat constrained, for the Liberals were firmly opposed to indirect taxes and the Conservatives were wary of still higher levels of direct taxation. It seemed that the most the government could realistically achieve was to raise taxes to cover the so-called 'normal year', ensuring that the revenue from permanent taxes (that is, apart from wartime impositions such as the excess profits duty) covered interest on loans plus ordinary peacetime expenditure at pre-war levels. This policy led to serious problems after the war, for the cost of debt service was high and there was little chance of restoring pre-war levels of spending. The crucial issue was how the costs of servicing the debt would be handled—and here the strength of the British fiscal and political systems came into play. At the outbreak of the war, debt service amounted to 9.7 per cent of the gross income of the government; in 1919/20, it was 24.8 per cent, and in 1930/1 34.2 per cent.[33] At the end of the Napoleonic wars, the payment of interest to a rentier class led to considerable political tension, and similar dangers were apparent at the end of the Great War. Opposition to the high costs of servicing the debt came from different directions, each with its own mutually incompatible solution.

The first solution came from Labour, building on the pre-war concept of Rent and socially created wealth to demand the conscription of wealth or a 'capital levy'.

Conscription for the armed forces was introduced in 1916, and the Labour movement argued that wealth should similarly be called on to contribute to the costs of the war. Men gave their lives and health; property and wealth were protected, making high profits during the war and receiving significant interest payments after the war, extracted from productive enterprise. The attack on passive, socially created wealth took on a more radical edge, and Labour argued for a one-off levy of all capital assets to redeem the national debt. Initially, some economists supported the proposal. But the political dangers soon became clear: might the money raised be spent on welfare rather than reducing taxes; might assets be retained by the government as a step towards a socialized economy; and might the levy be repeated? The Labour leadership started to have doubts; the result might be to disrupt capital markets for little net benefit, and to alienate electors who feared an attack on property.[34]

At the same time, many industrialists were alarmed that debt service and high taxes on income and profits would penalize them in post-war competition. At the end of the war, the excess profits duty was retained, and British industrialists complained that their profits were being eroded so that industry lacked capital for recovery. Recent estimates of real return on equity capital after tax suggests that their fears were justified: it fell from 10.0 per cent in 1910–14 to 8.7 per cent in 1915–20 and 3.1 per cent in 1921–4. Industrialists complained that they were heavily burdened in comparison with other countries where agreement on taxes proved difficult and the national debt was reduced by the expedient of inflation.[35] Of course, inflation posed its own serious problems of disrupting social relations and destabilizing the currency, and creating suspicion about the actions of the state. The Treasury feared that rising prices after the war were like a drug, which would stimulate only with increased doses until the economic health of the nation collapsed. The Federation of British Industries argued for a reduction in taxes made possible by cuts in spending or even budget deficits, or a shift to indirect taxes. Similar complaints came from the lower middle-class campaign against 'waste'. Many salaried workers and recipients of fixed incomes complained that they lost from the redistribution of income during the war. On the one hand, they attacked profiteers; on the other, they attacked 'selfish' trade unionists able to secure higher wages and so outstrip inflation. The post-war coalition government was therefore caught between Labour and 'anti-waste': how could it please one without alienating the other? 'Waste' could be cut by abandoning a 'land fit for heroes', which would strengthen the claims of Labour that the 'heroes' were being sacrificed to idle rentiers who had not 'earned' their interest payments.[36]

Meanwhile, the City and the government were extremely concerned about the level of the short-term floating debt. In the final stages of the war, the government issued short-term loans, and there was a serious danger that these would have to be repaid with a risk of inflation. The Treasury was deeply alarmed and believed that the short-term debt should be paid off by keeping taxes high, or by converting it into long-term loans which would seemingly increase the cost of debt service. Churchill feared that the policy could be interpreted as favouring the City and finance over industry, but the issue was more complex than an alliance of the Treasury and City. On the whole, the City wished to pay off the floating debt by an increase in the income tax and supertax for three years—a strategy which would play into the hands of both Labour and the campaigners against waste. The government had a clearer sense of the complex political requirements, as well as a shrewd realization that it needed to secure financial stability for its own purposes and not simply for the City. If the short-term bills could not be renewed, the government would be forced to borrow from the Bank of England, so that credit would expand, and prices would rise in an inflationary spiral. The dangers were apparent in Germany, where lack of demand for the floating debt led to its monetization and hyperinflation.

The government was more successful than its counterparts in the rest of Europe in negotiating between these conflicting interests. The anti-waste campaign was contained by the 'Geddes axe'. A committee on national expenditure, chaired by Sir Eric Geddes, met in 1921/2 and recommended reductions in spending. The savings were less swingeing than many wished but contained the campaign against 'waste'. The government was aware that it could not reduce the debt by increasing the income tax as the City demanded; neither could it shift to indirect taxes or a sales tax which would alienate Labour and play into the hands of the advocates of a capital levy. In the opinion of the Treasury, the only sector which had the capacity to pay more taxes was industry and the excess profits duty was renewed and a new tax on corporate profits was introduced. The Treasury was adamant that it could not reduce taxes through a budget deficit or by delaying the redemption of the debt, for paying off the debt was essential to prosperity. Holders of government bonds would be repaid; and they would then use the funds to invest in industry. In other words, maintaining taxation and redeeming the debt were a form of 'compulsory thrift'. Above all, the Treasury argued that economic disruption was caused by the inability of foreign governments to service their debt so that confidence in their finance collapsed.[37]

By 1924, the taxes on profits could be abandoned, and the worst of the difficulties were over. In 1925, the Chancellor, Winston Churchill, was able to extend the pre-war strategy by reducing income tax on modest middle-class incomes for married men with children, making a bid for the support of a crucial section of the electorate. The result was a 'dip' in the level of taxation for these families compared with those who were poorer and richer, as well as childless couples and single people. The difficulties of the tax system were negotiated, without a collapse of consent. In Britain, the level of taxation remained at a much higher level after the war; and there was a further shift in the direction of direct taxes as a result of the decision to avoid a major new indirect tax (see Table 14.2). The principles of class neutrality and balance laid down by Peel and Gladstone survived. The Treasury ethos or view was immensely strong, imposing restraints on the actions of politicians. The concern was for political and financial stability—and it largely succeeded.

The successful negotiation of these fiscal concerns at the end of the war might be criticized for cutting expenditure or for imposing a policy of deflation which harmed industry. But there is another and more positive way of considering the government's policy: it contained more damaging and destructive policies. By converting the short-term debt, government finances were put on a stable basis. Consent to taxation meant that transfer payments remained relatively generous, and consumers' expenditure held up in the depression. In many ways, the pain of the early 1920s paid off in the 1930s, when Britain experienced less social, economic, and political disruption than the rest of Europe. Above all, leading Conservatives were anxious to present themselves as representatives of families and of producers, turning Labour's attack on passive rentiers away from the demand for a capital levy and nationalization to a defence of capitalism and private property. Taxes on active wealth creation should be reduced and passive inherited wealth should be taxed; property should be distributed as widely as possible. As Stanley Baldwin put it, capital was made up of the savings of the rich and poor. Baldwin's vision of society opposed Labour's policy of seizing socially created wealth from a small group of exploiters. His argument was more nuanced than the attack on 'waste', for he was also anxious to maintain social expenditure in order to create a sense of fairness and to create social harmony and political stability on the basis of incentives and a wide distribution of property throughout society.[38]

Of course, Labour politicians were wary of Baldwin and Churchill. Although the Labour leadership retreated from the capital levy on grounds of electoral expediency, the party was still committed to nationalization and to equality, arguing that economic growth was not created by individual incentives so much as by superseding the market. Hugh Dalton, one of the leading financial experts within the Labour party and Chancellor after the Second World War, moved away from the capital levy to argue for the appropriation of socially created wealth by higher levels of death duties and an additional surtax. Most Labour politicians were also suspicious of an active capital market which took decisions in pursuit of private gain. Philip Snowden, the Chancellor in the minority Labour administrations between the wars, argued that 'a nation can save as well as an individual . . . . When the nation spends revenue or loan capital on useful works there is the assurance that it is saved.'[39] Here was an argument for nationalization, or at least for investment by the technocratic managers of responsible corporations. Such ideas were implemented by Dalton after the war.

In the 1920s, an alternative approach was proposed by the Independent Labour party which adopted Hobson's policy prescriptions. His approach to taxation assumed that income and wealth should be redistributed in order to create more affluent and discriminating consumers, who could then purchase goods from small producers. Hobson was eager to reduce the element of socially created wealth taken by individuals, but he gave much less weight to nationalization and a greater role to competition and to individuality in consumption. He believed that acquisitiveness and the market were helpful in creating a dynamic economy, expressing social needs and allocating resources. Such an approach was rejected by the Labour party conference in 1928 which turned instead to the Fabians and Sidney Webb. To them, the market implied waste and irrational consumer choice; the emergence of large-scale units was welcomed as a step towards nationalization. The decision was crucial to the future of Labour's economic policy and attitudes to competition and affluence, with an emphasis on bureaucratic management, suspicion of private profit, consumption, and the market.[40]

In the aftermath of the financial crisis of 1931 and the collapse of the Labour government, the party pondered the future direction of economic policy. To some, the depression of the 1930s confirmed that capitalism was deeply flawed and unstable, and that nationalization was needed. Others were less sure. A group of younger democratic socialists, including Hugh Gaitskell and Douglas Jay, started to develop an alternative approach. In their opinion, nationalization could be combined with private ownership and control of private investment. It was not enough to adopt Keynes's policy of deficit finance and borrowing in a recession, for there was a danger of strengthening the rentier class. They argued for a redistribution of income and wealth, taking unearned income to fund generous social services and so removing the dangers of underconsumption. Meanwhile, credit and investment should be controlled by nationalizing the Bank of England and replacing Stock Exchange speculators by a National Investment Board. Growth did not rest on personal incentives and profits which merely led to socially created, unearned income.[41]

Financing the Second World War and its Aftermath

The finance of the Second World War brought these debates to the fore. Even before the formal declaration of war in September 1939, politicians and civil servants realized that taxation was preferable to loans in order to avoid the difficulties of inflation during the First World War and the strains of the post-war debt. The Treasury was aware of the dangers of increasing taxes for rearmament too soon before the outbreak of war. As a result, the Treasury condoned borrowing from 1935 in order to spread the cost, moving away from 'sound' finance. In 1937, Neville Chamberlain started to raise taxes. During the war, taxes moved to a new level. Rates of income tax were increased and a much larger number of people were brought within its reach; an excess profits tax was introduced at a rate of 100 per cent; and a new indirect or purchase tax was imposed. Government spending rose and remained higher than before the war: in 1938, total public expenditure amounted to 25.2 per cent of national income, rising to 44.7 per cent in 1944 and remaining at 44 per cent in 1948/9.[42] Loans were much less significant than during the First World War, and interest rates were also lower so that debt service after the war was not such a serious issue. Although there was some discussion of a capital levy, the debate was much more muted. But the question remained of how the tax system should relate to direct controls over the economy. Keynes felt that taxation could do most of the work of managing the economy during the war. He argued that the government could work out the 'inflationary gap' between incomes and goods available for consumption; this 'gap' of excess spending could then be removed by a combination of taxes and 'deferred pay' which would be returned at the end of the war. As a result, the debt would be widely spread and repayment could be timed to offset any post-war depression. In order to secure working-class support, and to deal with the problems of the low birth rate, he also suggested the payment of family allowances. By these means, inflation would be controlled and individuals could make their own choice of how to spend their money in a free market. However, the package was not implemented in full. Male trade unionists feared that family allowances and deferred pay were means of reducing their wages. Many civil servants shared the hostility to the scheme, arguing that the state would be taking control over the individual's decision of when to save and when to spend. This missed the point that individuals would be left to their own devices in spending what remained after paying taxes and deferred pay. The alternative was a detailed control over all consumer choices which is what actually happened: goods were rationed, and subsidies paid to some necessities. Many items were produced to specified 'utility' standards. Further, the purchase tax rates ranged from exemption for utility goods to 100 per cent on luxuries. As a result, consumer choices were distorted. The problem was to become more apparent after the war.[43]

Labour thinking continued to stress the attack on unearned income and wealth. Certainly, domestic consumption needed to be held down in order to release goods for export markets and to prevent inflationary pressures. At the heart of Labour's policy was an attack on 'socially functionless' wealth and a desire to create greater equality. Transfers to rentiers were held down by low interest rates; and Dalton increased the surtax on large incomes and death duties, as well as removing low-paid workers from the income tax. The Labour government also embarked on a programme of nationalization: perhaps the largest was the Town and Country Planning Act 1947 which gave state control over the right to develop land with the levy of a 'development charge' of 100 per cent on the increase in site values. A significant element in post-war policy was the differential profits tax introduced in

1947. At the end of the war, the profits tax was retained and Dalton decided to vary the rate between profits distributed to shareholders and retained in the company for re-investment. Distributed profits paid a higher tax, on the grounds that they would create large fortunes from socially created wealth, and would stimulate inflation by provoking demands for wage increases. One way of holding down wage demands and cost-push inflation was therefore to limit distributed profits. Retained profits in the hands of efficient managers would encourage economic growth without creating large incomes and widening income differentials. Differential taxation of profits implied a particular view of the market and the sources of economic growth. It assumed that resources were not allocated most efficiently by an external capital market. These decisions should be left to the nationalized industries and managers of large corporations—and it followed that the National Investment Board was no longer needed, for technocratic decisions could be made without the need for complex changes in the structure of government. It implied a productionist, supply-side approach to the economy which stressed the creation of rational, large-scale ventures with economies of scale, and the generation of new technology from within. It rejected the notion that new products and innovation came from small-scale concerns with access to external capital; and it denied that high profits or income created incentives.[44]

Of course, the approach of the Labour government was open to criticism. Keynes criticized the encouragement of retentions on two grounds. It could be a tax-avoidance measure, for retentions increased the value of shares and capital appreciation was tax free. Retention might also be a conservative response by managers who secured a buffer for future inefficiency. The Federation of British Industries pointed to the danger of penalizing new firms which needed access to external capital, pointing out that 'there is too much emphasis on safety and too little on enterprise'. The concern was shared by Nicholas Kaldor who feared that the limitation of dividends and high levels of profits tax was ossifying the industrial structure. Paul Chambers, who left a senior position in the Inland Revenue for ICI, pointed out that low interest rates might reduce the cost of debt service but at the expense of distorting the capital programme. Increasingly, the Treasury and government's economic advisers argued that Labour's fiscal policies were creating inflexibilities and rigidities. Although the consequences of differential profits taxation should not be exaggerated, they do symbolize many of the features of post-war economic policy with its suspicion of the market as an allocative device. It formed part of what has been called a 'low-effort equilibrium': wages would be held down in return for a reduction in profits, which removed the incentive for either party to improve productivity. A large part of manufacturing output was covered by price agreements, and both industrialists and the unions were loath to advocate antitrust policies. Furthermore, import duties were still high and many imports were controlled, so there was little overseas competition. The fiscal system was part of this low-effort, low-productivity system. The pursuit of growth by retained profits, the sacrifice of profits to wage restraint, the weakness of an active capital market, complemented the low level of price competition.[45]

The purchase tax, food subsidies, and utility scheme also distorted choices. In 1949/50, subsidies amounted to £410m of a total public expenditure of £3,375.3m. The purchase tax and other indirect taxes were designed to shape consumption, as well as raising revenue for the government. These aims were not entirely compatible, for the best way of securing large sums was a flat-rate tax across a wide range of goods. Further, the result might be to harm the export drive. Utility goods were not appealing to foreign consumers, and the development of new, attractive goods was checked by the high level of taxation on the domestic market. As the Board of Customs and Excise pointed out, the allocation of resources was distorted. Relative prices were affected by the payment of subsidies to some goods, and the imposition of high levels of purchase tax on others. The Board claimed that incentives were reduced, for a basic, subsidized standard of living was easily achieved and any further improvement was difficult as a result of heavy taxes.[46] Many officials were therefore eager for a shift in policy, but the room for manoeuvre of the incoming Conservative government was strictly limited.

The influence of high levels of taxation and social spending on growth started to trouble some commentators by 1950. The Treasury pointed out that about 60 per cent of private taxes went in social benefits which weakened the connection between work and income. The Treasury and economic advisers argued that spending on welfare was a drain on efficiency. Robert Hall, an economic adviser at the Treasury, complained that

The social services are part of the citizen's real income; but a part that is independent of his output and service to the community. . . . The full benefits of the policy of full employment can only be secured if labour is responsive to incentives to earn more and to move freely between occupations. Our financial policy at present produces the opposite effect.

Hall's case has been repeated by more recent historians who argue that Britons rewarded themselves with generous welfare at the expense of productivity growth. Certainly, a striking feature of the post-war period was the high level of popular support for collective provision of social goods, sustained by a sense that taxation was reasonably equitable and public delivery reasonably efficient. How did social policy change from the heyday of the poor law at the start of the period to the creation of the welfare state at the end, and what visions of economic growth and social relations were embodied in the changing responses to welfare? How far did the post-war welfare state in fact harm incentives and growth?[47]

NOTES

1. Morley, *Life of William Ewart Gladstone*, I. 461; Cobden quoted in Matthew, 'Disraeli, Gladstone and the politics of mid-Victorian budgets', 616. This chapter draws on Daunton, *Trusting Leviathan* and *Just Taxes*.

2. Middleton, *Government versus the Market*, table 3.1, 90, and table 3.2, 91; Middleton, *The British Economy since 1945*, 77.

3. Daunton, *Trusting Leviathan*, 155–7; Mill, *Principles*, 804–9.

4. Middleton, *Government versus the Market*, table 3.1, 90.

5. Ibid. Mann, *Sources of Social Power*, 365–78, 381, 388–9, 504.

6. Matthew, *Gladstone*, 140.

7. Daunton, *Trusting Leviathan*, 71.

8. Buxton, *Finance and Politics*, ii. chs. 23 and 25.

9. Daunton, *House and Home*, 204.

10. Wilson, 'Finance of municipal capital expenditure', 31–5; Bellamy, *Administering Central–Local Relations*, 88–9; Millward and Sheard, 'Urban fiscal problem', 501–35.

11. Hennock, *Fit and Proper Persons*.

12. Englander, *Landlord and Tenant*, 8; Daunton, *House and Home*, ch. 6.

13. Mill, *Principles*, ii. 408.

14. George, *Progress and Poverty*; see Offer, *Property and Politics*, ch. 12.

15. See Offer, 'Ricardo's paradox', 236–52.

16. Offer, *Property and Politics*, 207–17.

17. Daunton, *Just Taxes*, 341.

18. Mann, *Sources of Social Power*, ii. 394–5; Turner, *Contesting Cultural Authority*, ch. 8 on science and the state; Edgerton, *England and the Aeroplane* and *Warfare State*. See also the discussion of education in Ch. 15 below.

19. Marshall, *Principles of Economics*, 449–50.

20. Edgeworth, *Papers Relating to Political Economy*, ii. 101–5, 130–2. See Ch. 1 above.

21. Pigou, *Wealth and Welfare*, especially ch. 9 and see above Ch. 1.

22. Daunton, *Trusting Leviathan*, ch. 11; Chiozza Money, *Riches and Poverty*.

23. For example, Webb and Webb, *Industrial Democracy*, 766–84.

24. Hobson, *The Industrial System*, pp. v. vii, 81, 138–9, 224 especially chs. 4 and 14; Hobson, *Taxation and the New State*; Hobson, *The Evolution of Modern Capitalism*; Hobson, *The Problem of the Unemployed*, 91, 100–3; Hobson, *The Economics of Distribution*.

25. Hobhouse, *Liberalism*, 202, 209.

26. Ibid. 182–3.

27. Clarke, *Liberals and Social Democrats*, 113.

28. Churchill, *Liberalism and the Social Problem*, 377–8.

29. Dicey, *Law and Public Opinion*

30. Offer, 'Empire and social reform', 119–38; Daunton, *Trusting Leviathan*, ch. 11.

31. Emy, 'Impact', 108, 119, 129; Ferguson, *The Pity of War*, 127, 131.

32. Daunton, *Just Taxes*, 38.

33. Calculated from Mitchell and Deane, *Abstract of British Historical Statistics*, 394–5, 398–9.

34. Daunton, *Just Taxes*, 68–9, 187–9.

35. Ibid. 86; Arnold, 'Profitability and capital accumulation in British industry', table 3; Gilbert, *Churchill Companion*, vol. v part I, 996–9, W. S. Churchill to O. Niemeyer, 20 May 1927.

36. Daunton, *Just Taxes*, 76.

37. Daunton, 'How to pay for the war'.

38. Williamson, *Baldwin*, 171, 180–1, 336, 338–41, 343, 353, 358; Jarvis, 'British Conservatism'.

39. Snowden, *Wealth or Commonwealth*, 15.

40. Thompson, 'Hobson and the Fabians'.

41. Tomlinson, 'Attlee's inheritance'.

42. Contemporary estimates by the Treasury, cited in Daunton, *Just Taxes*, 176.

43. Ibid. 182–4, 188–9.

44. Tomlinson, *Democratic Socialism*, 273, 275 and 'Attlee's inheritance', Daunton, *Just Taxes*, 196–212, 350–1; Whiting, *Labour Party*, 83–90.

45. Daunton, *Just Taxes*, 202–4, 222–3; Broadberry and Crafts, 'British economic policy and industrial performance', 83.

46. Daunton, *Just Taxes*, 240; Tomlinson, *Democratic Socialism*, 270–1.

47. Quoted in Daunton, *Just Taxes*, 226; Tomlinson, *Democratic Socialism*, 275–6; Barnett, *Audit of War*.

FURTHER READING

Arnold, A. J., 'Profitability and capital accumulation in British industry during the transwar period, 1913–24', *Economic History Review*, 52 (1999)

Balderston, T., 'War finance and inflation in Britain and Germany, 1914–18', *Economic History Review*, 42 (1989)

Barnett, C., *The Audit of War: The Illusion and Reality of Britain as a Nation* (1986)

Bellamy, C., *Administering Central–Local Relations, 1871–1919: The Local Government Board in its Fiscal and Cultural Context* (Manchester, 1988)

Biagini, E. F., 'Popular Liberals, Gladstonian finance and the debate on taxation, 1860–74', in E. F. Biagini and A. J. Reid (eds.), *Currents of Radicalism* (Cambridge, 1991)

—— *Liberty, Retrenchment and Reform: Popular Liberalism in the Age of Gladstone, 1860–80* (Cambridge, 1992)

Blake, R., *Disraeli* (1966)

Broadberry, S. N., and Crafts, N. R. F., 'British economic policy and industrial performance in the early post-war period', *Business History*, 38 (1996)

Bulpitt, J., *Territory and Power in the United Kingdom: An Interpretation* (Manchester, 1983)

Buxton, S., *Finance and Politics: An Historical Study, 1783–1885*, 2 vols. (1888)

Chiozza Money, L. G., *Riches and Poverty* (1905)

Churchill, W. S., *Liberalism and the Social Problem* (1909)

Clark, C., 'Public finance and changes in the value of money', *Economic Journal*, 55 (1945)

Clarke, P. F., *Liberals and Social Democrats* (Cambridge, 1978)

Cronin, J. E., *The Politics of State Expansion: War, State and Society in Twentieth-Century Britain* (1991)

Daunton, M. J., 'How to pay for the war: state, society and taxation in Britain, 1917–24', *English Historical Review*, III (1996)

—— *House and Home in the Victorian City: Working-Class Housing, 1850–1914* (1983)

—— *Trusting Leviathan: The Politics of Taxation in Britain, 1799–1914* (Cambridge, 2001)

—— *Just Taxes: The Politics of Taxation in Britain, 1914–79*, (Cambridge, 2002)

Dicey, A. V., *Law and Public Opinion in England* (2nd edn., 1914)

Edgerton, D., *England and the Aeroplane: An Essay on a Militant and Technological Nation* (Basingstoke, 1991)

—— *Warfare State: Britain, 1920–1970* (Cambridge, 2006)

Edgeworth, F. Y., *Papers Relating to Political Economy*, II (1925)

Emy, H. V., 'The impact of financial policy on English party politics before 1914', *Historical Journal*, 15 (1972)

Englander, D., *Landlord and Tenant in Urban Britain, 1838-1918* (Oxford, 1983)

Ferguson, N., 'Public finance and national security: the domestic origins of the First World War revisited', *Past and Present*, 142 (1994)

—— *The Cash Nexus: Money and Power in the Modern World, 1700–2000* (2001)

—— *The Pity of War* (1998)

George, H., *Progress and Poverty: An Enquiry into the Causes of Industrial Depressions and of Increase of Want with Increase of Wealth—the Remedy* (1879)

Gilbert, M., *Churchill Companion*, vol, v, part I, *The Exchequer Years 1992–29* (1980) 996–9, W. S. Churchill to O. Niemeyer, 20 May 1927.

Harling, P., and Mandler, P., 'From "fiscal-military" state to laissez faire state, 1760–1850', *Journal of British Studies*, 32 (1993)

Hennock, E. P., *Fit and Proper Persons: Ideal and Reality in Nineteenth-Century Urban Government* (1973)

—— 'Finance and politics in urban local government in England, 1835–1900', *Historical Journal*, 6 (1963)

Hobhouse, L. T., *Liberalism* (1911)

Hobson, J. A., *The Industrial System: An Inquiry into Earned and Unearned Income* (1909)

—— *The Problem of the Unemployed* (1896)

—— *The Evolution of Modern Capitalism* (1894)

Hobson, J. M., 'The military-extraction gap and the wary Titan: the fiscal-sociology of British defence policy, 1870–1913', *Journal of European Economic History*, 22 (1993)

Jarvis, D., 'British Conservatism and class politics in the 1920s', *English Historical Review*, III (1996)

Keynes, J. M., *A Tract on Monetary Reform* (1923), in *Collected Writings of John Maynard Keynes*, vol. iv (1971)

Kolthammer, F. W., *Some Notes on the Incidence of Taxation on the Working-Class Family* (The Ratan Tata Foundation, Memorandum on Problems of Poverty, I, 1913)

Lindert, P. H., 'The rise of social spending, 1880–1930', *Explorations in Economic History*, 31 (1994)

—— 'What limits social spending?', *Explorations in Economic History*, 33 (1996)

Macdonald, A., 'The Geddes Committee and the formulation of public expenditure policy, 1921–22', *Historical Journal*, 32 (1989)

McKibbin, R., 'Why was there no Marxism in Great Britain?', English Historical Review, 99 (1984)

Mann, M., The Sources of Social Power, ii: The Rise of Classes and Nation States, 1750–1914 (Cambridge, 1993)

Marshall, A., Principles of Economics: An Introductory Volume (1890)

Matthew, H. C. G., 'Disraeli, Gladstone and the politics of mid-Victorian budgets', Historical Journal, 22 (1979)

—— Gladstone, 1809–74 (Oxford, 1986)

Middleton, R., Government versus the Market: The Growth of the Public Sector, Economic Management and British Economic Performance, c.1890–1979 (Cheltenham, 1996)

—— The British Economy since 1945: Engaging with the Debate (Basingstoke, 2000)

Mill, J. S., Principles of Political Economy (7th edn., 1871)

Millward, R., and Sheard, S., 'The urban fiscal-problem 1870–1914: government expenditure and finances in England and Wales', Economic History Review, 48 (1995)

Mitchell, B. R., with P. Deane, Abstract of British Historical Statistics (Cambridge, 1962)

Morgan, E. V., Studies in British Financial Policy, 1914–25 (1952)

Morley, J., The Life of William Ewart Gladstone, 3 vols. (1903)

Murray, B. K., The People's Budget, 1909/10: Lloyd George and Liberal Politics (Oxford, 1980)

Nottingham, C. J., 'Recasting bourgeois Britain? The British state in the years which followed the First World War', International Review of Social History, 31 (1976)

Offer, A., Property and Politics, 1870–1914: Landownership, Law, Ideology and Urban Development in England (Cambridge, 1981)

—— 'Empire and social reform: British overseas investment and domestic politics, 1908–14', Historical Journal, 26 (1983)

—— 'Ricardo's paradox and the movement of rent in England c.1870–1910', Economic History Review, 33 (1980)

Peacock, A. T., and Wiseman, J., The Growth of Public Expenditure in the United Kingdom (1961)

Peden, G. C., British Rearmament and the Treasury, 1932–39 (Edinburgh, 1979)

Pigou, A. C., Wealth and Welfare (1912)

Smith, A., An Enquiry into the Nature and Causes of the Wealth of Nations, ed. R. H. Campbell, A. S. Skinner, and W. B. Todd 2 vols. (Oxford, 1976)

Snowden, P., Wealth or Commonwealth: Labour's Financial Policy (1929)

Thompson, N., 'Hobson and the Fabians: two roads to socialism in the 1920s', History of Political Economy, 26 (1994)

Tomlinson, J., 'Attlee's inheritance and the financial system: whatever happened to the National Investment Board?', Financial History Review, 1 (1994)

—— 'Welfare and economy: the economic impact of the welfare state, 1945–51', Twentieth Century British History, 6 (1995)

—— Democratic Socialism and Economic Policy: The Attlee Years, 1945–1951 (Cambridge, 1997)

Toye, R., 'Keynes, the Labour movement and how to pay for the war', Twentieth Century British History, 10 (1999)

Turner, F. M., Contesting Cultural Authority: Essays in Victorian Intellectual Life (Cambridge, 1993)

Webb, S., and Webb, B., Industrial Democracy (1897; 1920 ed.)

Whiting, R. C., 'The Labour party, capitalism and the national debt, 1918–24', in P. J. Waller (ed.), *Politics and Social Change in Modern Britain: Essays Presented to A. F. Thompson* (Brighton, 1987)

—— 'Taxation policy', in H. Mercer, N. Rollings, and J. Tomlinson (eds.), *Labour Governments and Private Industry: The Experience of 1945–51* (Edinburgh, 1992)

—— *The Labour Party and Taxation: Party Identity and Political Purpose in Twentieth-Century Britain* (Cambridge, 2000)

Williamson, P., *Stanley Baldwin: Conservative Leadership and National Values* (Cambridge, 1999)

Wilson, J. F., 'The finance of municipal capital expenditure in England and Wales, 1870–1914', *Financial History Review*, 4 (1997)

Zimmeck, M., 'Gladstone holds his own: the origins of income tax relief for life insurance policies', *Bulletin of the Institute of Historical Research*, 58 (1985)

CHAPTER 15

Education

'The preservation of internal peace', remarked James Kay-Shuttleworth in 1832, '. . . depends on the education of the working classes.'[1] His concern was less with the production of educated workers to benefit the economy and more with the maintenance of social order. At the time he wrote, the state provided very little in the way of financial aid to education. In England, a modest subsidy was offered from 1833 to elementary schools provided by religious societies; only in Scotland did the parishes fund a system of public education. England was a laggard during the industrial revolution in terms of student enrolment. From the 1890s, the gap closed, and by the First World War enrolment in primary schools was actually higher in England than in Scotland and Germany, which experienced declining levels of enrolment (see Table 15.1). Although England and Wales caught up with the leading countries in primary school enrolments from the 1890s, public spending continued to lag (see Table 15.2). As Peter Lindert remarks, the leaders in tax-funded schooling were not the leaders in poor relief. England and Wales led in the provision of poor relief; the pioneers in tax-funded schooling were Prussia and North America, as well as Scotland.[2]

By the 1950s the Conservative government was willing to invest in education. In 1955, David Eccles, the Minister of Education, remarked that 'problems such as forestalling inflation, preventing and settling strikes, and abandoning restrictive practices will, in the end, only be solved by better education'.[3] In the view of the Conservatives, education offered a way both of creating a skilled and productive workforce, and of providing an incentive for social mobility, personal responsibility, and responsiveness to market opportunities. The different emphases of Kay-Shuttleworth and Eccles suggest a shift in the purposes of education over a century or more.

At any time formal schooling was a mixture of two characteristics. One feature was the process of socialization and the reproduction (or reshaping) of the existing social structure; the other was the training of a workforce. These two aspects were often in tension. In the view of many historians, education in this period was more concerned

TABLE 15.1. *Student enrolment rates in primary schools per 1,000 children aged 5–14, 1830–1930*

	1830	1850	1870	1890	1910	1930
England and Wales (public and private)	274	498	609	657	748	755
Scotland (private and public)	n.a.	592	697	802	729	675
Prussia (public and private)	695	730	732	755	764	n.a.
Germany (public only)	n.a.	n.a.	n.a.	742	720	699
France (public and private)	388	515	737	832	857	803
USA (public only)	546	681	779	857	896	835
(public and private)	n.a.	n.a.	n.a.	971	975	921

Source: Lindert, *Growing Public*, i, table 5.1, 91–2.

TABLE 15.2. *Percentage of GNP devoted to tax-based social spending, c.1850*

		Relief of poor	Public education (all levels)
England and Wales	1820/1	2.66	0
	1850	1.07	0.07
France	1833	0.63	0.13
United States	1850	0.13	0.33

Source: Lindert, *Growing Public*, i, table 1.1, 8.

with socialization or morality than with productivity.[4] A common complaint is that the British educational system was anti-industrial and anti-technical, so providing one explanation for the 'decline' of the British economy.[5] The dominance of classical education in the public schools and old universities, so the argument runs, gave primacy to an aristocratic, gentlemanly culture. Similarly, elementary education for the working class is often criticized for maintaining the social hierarchy and inequalities to the neglect of technical education and social mobility. Both critiques come together in a common complaint that the British state spent too little, too late on education. But are these criticisms accurate and realistic—or should they be read as self-serving appeals to justify more money for particular types of education?

Elementary education

In 1955, Eccles argued that spending on education was the acceptable face of welfare—a position adopted in Scotland at a much earlier period. The patterns of public spending in England and Wales and in Scotland were very different at the start of the period covered by this book, and the divergence had its origins in the sixteenth and seventeenth centuries. In England, parishes provided tax-funded relief for the poor. In Scotland, the poor law was much more limited and parishes or burghs normally provided a school and paid the salary of a teacher, who was expected to have attended university. These schools were supervised by the Kirk, and the teacher was in a sense a junior minister financed in part by a local tax on landowners.[6] The basic principle of the Scottish educational system was that schools served both the middle class and the poor, unlike the dual system of England. The parish and burgh schools could send pupils to the Scottish universities which did not have any formal entrance examination until 1892, and took in students at the age of 15–16 as well as older working-class men. Here was the basis of the Scottish myth and occasional reality of the 'lad of parts'—the clever boy from a poor family. The Scottish educational system could easily idealize a golden age of social inclusiveness and mobility—but how far was it achieved?

In the 1860s, 33 per cent of students at Scottish universities came from the professional classes and 16 per cent from the commercial and industrial middle classes; as many as 23 per cent were the sons of workers, a figure not achieved in England for another century.[7] But there were limits. Poverty and the need to send children to work was one constraint; the availability of schools was another. The law required each parish to provide one school—a serious shortcoming in large parishes with a scattered population. The idealized version of the Scottish educational system only worked in some areas, most particularly in the north-east where the parish schools fed pupils to Aberdeen's two universities. Particular problems emerged as Scotland urbanized, for the burgh schools could not cope and might opt to concentrate on secondary education for the middle classes. From the 1820s, the parish and burgh schools were increasingly supplemented by 'sessional schools' provided by the Church of Scotland on the lines of the voluntary schools in England. The process was carried still further after the 'Disruption' or split in the Church which led the new Free Church to compete. The parochial schools were therefore a minority, and many of the new schools did not offer a basic classical education which might allow a 'lad of parts' to enter university. Nevertheless, Scotland's educational system did achieve higher literacy rates than in England. In 1855, 89 per cent of Scottish men and 77 per cent of Scottish women were able to sign their names in the marriage register, compared with 70 and 59 per cent in England and Wales.[8] (See Table 15.3.) By 1900, England caught up with Scotland—and the gender gap in literacy was also closed. In 1900, 98 per cent of men and 97 per cent of women in Scotland could sign their names at marriage; in England, the figure was 97 per cent for both men and women.[9]

Whether or not it reflected reality, idealization of the parish school shaped policy by justifying a more inclusive form of education than in England. In 1820,

TABLE 15.3. *Percentage of grooms and brides signing the marriage register, 1855*

	Grooms	Brides	All
Scotland			
Selkirkshire	100	100	100
Midlothian	94	90	92
England			
Westmorland	86	76	81
Nottinghamshire	70	56	63
Lancashire	67	41	54

Source: Stephens, *Education in Britain, 1750–1914*, 29–30.

the influential Presbyterian minister Thomas Chalmers praised socially inclusive education as a source of stability and mutual goodwill. In the words of the Revd John Macleod in 1878, the result was an 'absence of those sharp lines of demarcation which separate the several grades of society in other countries'.[10] By contrast, a stratified system of education was taken for granted in England. In 1868, James Fraser contrasted England with the United States with its common schools—a system he believed could only work in a young society. In England, he suggested, 'the grades of society, so marked and manifest, will always probably demand, and in fact necessitate, a corresponding graduation of schools'. Matthew Arnold agreed: 'The education of each class in society has, or ought to have, its ideal determined by the wants of that class.'[11]

At the start of the period, there was no systematic provision of elementary education in England on the lines of the Scottish parish schools. English education had developed rapidly from about 1530, and was probably ahead of both France and Scotland by 1640. It then slowed down from about 1680, and England fell behind the levels of literacy in Scotland and other European countries.[12] The explanation is possibly a reaction to the radicalism of the Civil War and a desire to reimpose social and political stability. Education and literacy could appear subversive:

Giving education to the labouring classes of the poor . . . would . . . be prejudicial to their morals and happiness; it would teach them to despair their lot in life, instead of making them good servants in agriculture, and other laborious employment to which their rank in society had destined them . . . it would enable them to read seditious pamphlets, vicious books, and publications against Christianity; it would render them insolent to their superiors.[13]

The high level of state spending during the Napoleonic wars and the desire to retrench after 1815 led to considerable suspicion about public expenditure, and not only from Tory backwoodsmen. Wider constitutional and religious issues complicated public funding for education. The expansion of schooling from the later eighteenth century was linked with an upsurge of radicalism and religious dissent, a challenge to the authority of the Anglican establishment which resulted in the provision of schools under the control of the Anglican Church and landed elite. Nonconformists also responded with their own schools. These initiatives were formalized by the Church of England's National Society (formed in 1811) and the nonconformist British and Foreign School Society (formed in 1810). But state involvement was problematical. When full membership of the political nation depended on adherence to the Church of England, any state funding would presumably need to be under the auspices of the Church. Equally, if the state offered funding to all voluntary schools, it would conflict with the constitutional principle that only Anglicans were full members of the political nation. The problem was resolved with the repeal of the Test Act in 1829 which limited public life, at least in theory, to Anglicans, and the passage of the first Reform Act in 1832.[14]

These considerations delayed central government spending until 1833 but more important still was the lack of effective local tax spending. In Prussia, France, and the United States, the initial development of tax-funded education was the result of local autonomy, allowing particular districts with a high demand for schooling to take the initiative without being blocked by the central government.[15] The same applied to Scotland where the parishes provided funding and motivation. In England and Wales, the parishes concentrated on poor relief whose costs were rising rapidly in the later eighteenth century. When the poor law was reformed in 1834 and new Boards of Guardians were instituted, they were explicitly forbidden to provide schools.[16] Initial state aid therefore came from the centre and was directed to the voluntary schools. In 1833, the state supplied some grant aid towards the cost of building and running 'voluntary' schools in England, which was extended to Scotland in 1834. The grant in England rose from £20,000 in 1833 to £775,000 in 1862, when the government introduced 'payment by results'.[17]

The constitutional changes of 1829 and 1832 prepared the ground for the introduction of grant aid, and so did alarms over political radicalism and disorder. Education might teach discipline and religion, provided it was not in the 'wrong' hands. In 1802, the owners of cotton and woollen mills were obliged to offer some education to their apprentices. The measure was promoted by Robert Peel and adopted in his family's mills. In 1833, the Factory Act required factory owners to ensure that child workers had a regular education, no longer within the factory but in a school chosen by the parents or factory inspector. Of course, some factory owners resented the loss of control over their workers and tried to evade the Act, but most complied. Indeed, the firms most active in providing education sometimes argued that it should become a state responsibility.[18] Concern for education was part of the debate over public order in the age of the Chartists. The problem was not just a lack of schools for the wrong type of schools could be as bad as no schooling. Many commentators were equally alarmed that workers were turning to cheap private schools which educated about a third of working-class pupils in England in 1851 and a quarter in Scotland. In the words of Thomas Lacquer, there was a 'bewildering but widely supported network of small schools'.[19] These schools were not susceptible to outside supervision. Unlike the voluntary schools, they were answerable to parents and teachers had to be more sympathetic to the demands of the working-class economy.

Many commentators in both England and Scotland feared that the working class was succumbing to crime and disorder. The remedy was to 'moralize' children through schools. The school, like the workhouse and the prison, would impose institutional discipline and surveillance. In 1840, Kay-Shuttleworth complained that 'the influence of the teacher of a day-school over the minds and habits of the children attending his school is too frequently counteracted by the evil example of parents and neighbours, and by the corrupting influence of companions with whom the children associate in the street and court in which they live'.[20] It was therefore all the more important that the school should be removed from the influence of the neighbourhood by making the teachers independent of parents. From 1839, the voluntary schools came under the supervision of Her Majesty's Inspectors of Schools. Teacher training colleges were expanding from the 1830s, and in 1846 the government laid down a career structure for the teaching profession, with a defined social status above the working class. In the opinion of Richard Johnson,

the early Victorian obsession with the education of the poor is best understood as a concern about authority, about power, about the assertion (or the re-assertion?) of control. This concern was expressed in an enormously ambitious attempt to determine, through the capture of educational means, the patterns of thought, sentiment and behaviour of the working class. Supervised by its trusty teacher, surrounded by its playground wall, the school was to raise a new race of working people—respectful, cheerful, hard-working, loyal, pacific and religious.[21]

The denominational schools, with their trained teachers and formalized systems of management, provided such a style of education.

The state-funded and inspected voluntary schools, like the public elementary schools after 1870, wished to supplant rather than supplement education provided through the home and locality. Education involves more than formal schooling, for many skills are learned in the home, in play, or engagement in work. By contrast, the voluntary and elementary schools adopted a mechanical approach to learning. What they learned was separated from the working-class community which the teachers and authorities mistrusted. In particular, payment by results made teaching a matter of ensuring that tests were passed. Pupils progressed from standard to standard only when they met the threshold of attainment and, as David Vincent puts it, they had an acquaintance with rather than a command of literacy.[22]

These criticisms of Victorian education and the argument that voluntary and board schools were opposed to working-class culture should not be pressed too far. The motivation for public spending might have been primarily social discipline, but investment in education still provided greater economic opportunities. Basic literacy allowed men to run trade unions, friendly societies, and co-operatives with their formalized rules and procedures. They might still learn more about gardening, domestic skills, or trades from their home and workplace—but even so, formal education gave them more freedom to extend their knowledge. Despite the criticism of Victorian board schools as places of discipline and order, a survey carried out in the 1960s of 444 people born between 1870 and 1908 suggests a much more positive picture. In all, 67.5 per cent of working-class respondents had a positive attitude to school, compared with only 14.4 per cent negative and 18 per cent mixed. Many expressed gratitude to teachers; the new board schools were seen as modern and impressive. The regret expressed by the respondents was that education came to an end too soon. After the Second World War, the sociologist Ferdynand Zweig claimed that 20 to 25 per cent of working men were self-educated. Mutual improvement societies flourished, and their ethos was carried over into the Workers' Educational Association, the co-operative movement, and Working Men's Club and Institute Union. The Royal Arsenal Co-operative Society of Woolwich, for example, spent almost £1,000 on education in 1910, rising to £18,792 in 1937. In 1874, a survey of 312 clubs in the WMCIU found that 21 per cent held classes, 33 per cent ran lectures, and nearly all had libraries. In south Wales, the coal miners established a network of libraries, and gave donations to support the new University College of Wales at Aberystwyth and the National Council of Labour Colleges. And the culture was not just one of reading: there were choral societies, brass bands, gardening clubs.[23]

In any case, control was contested for attendance was initially neither compulsory nor free. Education was entirely at the discretion of the working-class family. David Mitch estimates that state subsidies or free places accounted for only a quarter of the rise in enrolments between 1833 and 1899 with the remainder explained by the desire of parents to send their children to school. In other words, the rise of popular literacy reflected an interplay of private demand and public policy.[24] A larger part of the change in attendance came from the desire of parents to send their children to school. Criticism of the voluntary schools and, after 1870, the school boards should not romanticize the private schools as did some historians in the 1970s who celebrated them for their lack of control on dress, their easy attitudes to admissions and withdrawal, and their unstructured curriculum.[25] But it was not only the inspectors of schools and advocates of surveillance who felt that the result could be verminous children, lacking in discipline and structure. Might it not be that parents themselves preferred the voluntary or board schools, with their trained teachers and orderly approach?

Government-inspected schools were mainly attended by the children of skilled workmen and concentrated on the younger age groups. In the midlands in 1864, for example, 48.9 per cent of pupils at inspected elementary schools were 8 or younger and 72.2 per cent 10 or younger. Education was a short-term process: 38.7 per cent of pupils in the midlands attended for less than a year, and 76.2 per cent for three years or less. Education involved the payment of a fee, and the sacrifice of the child's wage, and in 1858 James Fraser believed that earnings of 1s. 6d. a week for a boy of 10 and 2s. for a boy of 11 would 'outbid the school'. The cost to a family of keeping a child mounted from the age of 10, and at the same time their potential income increased, so that the incentive to send a child to work was intense. The Royal Commission on the State of Popular Education condoned the decision. 'Independence is of more importance than education; and if the wages of the child's labour are necessary . . . it is far better that it should go to work at the earliest age . . . than it should remain at school.'[26] Unskilled working-class families were not likely to see the longer-term virtue of education when it led to present poverty. The children who experienced school therefore came from a higher social stratum than the offspring of the 'demoralized' working class whom Kay-Shuttleworth wished to reach.

State assistance to the voluntary schools resulted in an expansion in school places. In 1835, the Anglican schools in Nottingham had an attendance of 665 pupils, the nonconformists 1,082, and the Catholics 243; by 1870 the Anglicans had an attendance of 5,354 in comparison with 1,197 for the nonconformists and 462 for the Catholics.[27] But there were still gaps and the voluntary schools could not provide sufficient places within their resources. Pressure for a publicly financed school system started in Scotland, where the Free Church, struggling to provide their own schools after the Disruption, saw the advantage of a non-sectarian public school system. Between 1854 and 1869, five bills were presented to reform the Scottish educational system. In the event, the breakthrough came in England. The explanation was not only the extension of the franchise in 1867.[28] The battle lines were drawn in the late 1860s between the radical, nonconformist National Education League and the National Education Union. The League wanted a free, universal, compulsory, and non-sectarian educational system which would absorb the voluntary schools; the Union wished the denominational schools to provide the basis of elementary education. A bill introduced by W. E. Forster in 1869 pleased neither interest. Forster proposed that the educational needs of each district should be assessed; the voluntary bodies would then have a year to provide schools. At the end of this period, school boards would fill any gaps, with the right to decide whether the schools would be secular, denominational, or non-denominational. The ensuing religious squabble dominated the parliamentary debate with the result that board schools were only to teach non-denominational religion. Nevertheless, elections to the school boards continued to be fought on religious lines. The state turned away from merely assisting and supervising the religious societies to direct provision of schools; meanwhile, the voluntary schools lost their public subventions and continued alongside the growing public sector. Once a compromise had been thrashed out in England, the way was open for reform in Scotland in 1872. Britain now had a localized system of public schooling, supported by the local taxation of the school boards, plus state subventions.

When the school boards started their work, the existing provision varied across England. In Nottingham, for example, only 307 places were needed or 2.3 per cent of the total, whereas in London the deficiency was 103,863 places, or 22.8 per cent of the total required.[29] The board schools very soon moved from supplementing the voluntary schools to become the most important providers of working-class education. The British and Foreign Society, and subsequently the Wesleyans, largely opted out of the provision of schools and handed their buildings to the boards. By the end of the century only the Anglicans and the Catholics saw a continuing role for voluntary schools. In Nottingham, for example, the board schools had 28,546 pupils in 1903, the Anglicans 13,079, and the Catholics 2,473; there was no nonconformist school after 1892.[30] The Anglicans had a monopoly of schools in many rural areas which led to resentment from nonconformists who were obliged to send their children to be indoctrinated by the parson and squire. Meanwhile, the voluntary schools complained that the teaching of the 'Three Rs' was not religious, and that they should be subsidized for their 'secular efficiency'. The problems were to become even worse when school fees were abolished, and the resources of the voluntary sector came under still greater strain.

The private sector of working-class education withered away. The school boards entailed greater authority and control than was possible in state-subsidized voluntary schools and private schools. These developments have been reduced by some writers to no more than a desire to discipline and moralize the working class so as to create, in the words of R. H. Tawney, 'an orderly, civil, obedient population with sufficient education to understand a command'. Tawney was criticizing the poverty of the education offered by elementary schools. Many politicians and officials were explicit in arguing that a prime task of elementary schools was indeed to instil order and discipline. In 1875, the Board of Education's code for elementary schools laid down an obligation 'to bring up the children in habits of punctuality, of good manners and language, of cleanliness and neatness; and also to impress upon them the importance of cheerful obedience to duty'. H. G. Wells, a former teacher, commented that 'the Education Act was . . . an Act to educate the lower classes for employment in lower class lines, and with specially trained, inferior teachers'. Girls were trained for their domestic future. The board schools are therefore seen by some commentators as little more than agencies to reinforce class and gender lines.[31]

However, parents were initially under no compulsion to send their children to the board schools, and increased attendance might reflect their preference. After all, schools funded by poor parents were not likely to have good facilities or trained teachers—and the new school boards were elected on a reasonably wide franchise, with a degree of democratic control. Parents could also select board schools for their children according to their financial ability. Initial fears that board schools would bring together the children of skilled artisans with the dirty and verminous children of the poor were overcome in a hierarchy of schools to cater for different groups according to their ability to pay. In the late 1880s, the London School Board supplied 110,000 basic places at 1*d*. a week, 180,000 at 2*d*., and 100,000 at 3*d*., with 60,000 at 4*d*. and above.[32]

The question of compulsion and fees raised issues of civil rights: should parents be forced to send their children to school and pay fees? Should the state cover the full cost, or was education a part of parental responsibility? The Royal Commission of 1861 opposed payment of fees for the poor, and was willing to excuse non-attendance in order to preserve the independence of working-class families. The Education Act of 1870 left the issue of compulsory attendance to local discretion. In Scotland, the Act of 1872 introduced compulsory attendance between the ages of 5 and 13. When national compulsion came to England and Wales in 1880, full-time attendance was required only from the age of 5 to 10. In 1899, local authorities were given the right to raise the age to 14, and in 1918 the national school-leaving age was increased to that figure. Even so, exemption from full-time attendance could be secured for children who reached a certain standard and were 'beneficially at work'. In 1893, there were only 693 half-timers in London, but 93,969 in Lancashire where children entered the cotton mills. The introduction of compulsion preceded the removal of fees. In 1888, the Cross Commission argued that education was part of the responsibility of parents and that the existing balance between parental duties and public assistance should be maintained. Poor families that faced serious difficulties in finding the 'school pence' could be assisted in two ways. The school boards and voluntary organizations could remit fees, a power used sparingly. Alternatively, parents could seek help from the poor law Guardians. In all, 9 or 10 per cent of children in England and Wales had free education before the final abolition of fees for elementary education in 1891.[33]

Compulsory education was enforced by the School Attendance Officers. They scheduled all houses with a rateable value below £25, listed the children, investigated claims for the remission of fees, and cautioned and summoned parents who could be fined. Persistent absentees were sent to truant and industrial schools. These measures divided opinion. The poor resented the loss of their children's earnings, and they had the support of some doctors, clergymen, and magistrates. Older children, especially daughters, cared for their younger siblings, and being 'needed at home' was often accepted as a reason for non-attendance. On the other hand, the measures had the support of radicals and better-off members of the working class, as well as many middle-class reformers. Certainly, the level of attendance improved considerably, from 65.8 per cent in London School Board schools in 1872 to 89.0 per cent in 1905. The level of attendance of boys was higher than for girls: in 1886/7, the average attendance of boys in London was 82 per cent and of girls 76 per cent.[34]

The school boards encouraged attendance, and tensions with working-class communities lessened as standards of living improved. Equally schools were under pressure from parents to provide better education. Elementary schools were changing, in part in response to the concern for national efficiency exposed by the Boer War and competition from the industrial economies of Germany and the United States. By 1904, the elementary code marked a change from disciplining children, and placed emphasis upon the development of intelligence and clear reasoning. In the next few years, school meals and medical inspection aimed to ensure that pupils were adequately fed and fit. Indeed, the code of 1904 proposed that one function of elementary schools was to discover pupils who had ability, so that they might be passed to the secondary schools.

Secondary Schools

The emergence of secondary education took different forms in England and Wales from Scotland. In Scotland, there was less distinction between schools for the elite and middle class and for the poor: the parochial and burgh schools provided a route to the universities. Unlike England, the Scots in the early nineteenth century did not have either boarding schools for the elite or grammar schools for the middle class and poor scholars. Instead, pupils left the parochial or burgh schools at around 14 or 15 and received a form of secondary education in the junior classes of the universities. By the 1820s, middle-class reformers were arguing for change, pressing for secondary schools by repositioning the burgh schools and by creating private 'proprietary' schools. Unlike in England, these secondary schools were largely for day pupils. Burgh schools were maintained by town councils, with masters supplementing their income from fees. Head teachers were less powerful, and the schools were often run by the teachers as a group; children moved from school to school to receive tuition from individual teachers. Although this freedom gave way to a more rigid curriculum and a greater sense of corporate identity in the later nineteenth century, day schools remained the norm. The residential and collegiate tradition was weak both in schools and universities, and education was much more in the hands of the family.

In Scotland, publicly funded secondary schools came earlier than in England. In 1872, burgh schools were transferred to the school boards, and 'higher-class' schools specialized in secondary education. From 1886, the Scottish Education

Department started to inspect secondary schools, which received state grants in 1892. In addition, secondary education developed from the elementary schools in the form of 'higher-grade' schools. Although secondary education was becoming more sharply differentiated from elementary education, the Scottish system retained a distinctive feature: secondary schools shared the same curriculum and prepared their students for entry to university. By contrast, the higher-grade schools in England offered a more vocational education and did not lead on to university.

Scottish universities remained more democratic than in England but needed to reform as the educational system changed. As a result of the more systematic hierarchy of schools, with pupils transferring from one to the other by means of examinations, reformers pressed for closed entry to university by means of examinations and the removal of the junior classes. These changes led to resistance from the lower middle class and artisans who might be excluded, but also from many professors who feared a shift from a distinctive general philosophical curriculum to more specialized courses. The changes were only completed in 1892 when entrance examinations were imposed. The age of entrants rose from 14 or 15 to 17 or 18. Despite these changes, social recruitment remained much wider than in England, for Scottish secondary education was more generally available. In 1860, 16.9 per cent of the fathers of male students at the university of Glasgow were shopkeepers, clerks, and small businessmen, and 18.6 per cent manual workers; in 1910, the proportions were higher, at 19.7 per cent and 24.0 per cent.[35]

Of course, not all Scottish children went to secondary school in the late nineteenth century, and the stress on an academic curriculum meant that vocational training was neglected. After 1903, children who were not considered suitable for secondary education went to supplementary classes in the elementary sector, with a vocational bias. Criticism led to a further change after the war: in 1921, the Scottish Educational Department recommended a clear division between elementary and secondary education at the age of 12 when children would be sent to different schools, whether for a full five years of secondary education or two to three years in an 'advanced division'. Although implementation started in 1923, progress was slow until 1936 when secondary education was offered to all children.

The system of secondary education in England was different: it was stratified by class with highly distinctive curricula rather than forming a single graduated system; there was less ability to transfer to university; and the assumption that schools should provide social mobility was not widely accepted at the beginning of the period. The difference in attitude was clear in the deliberations of the Taunton Commission on endowed schools of 1864–7, largely the old grammar schools created by the benefactions of rich merchants in the fifteenth and sixteenth centuries, as well as some of the great public schools. The Commission proposed three grades of school, not seen as successive stages so much as distinct forms of education for different social groups. The first type of school should be designed for children staying at school until the age of 18, who would be prepared for university; the second would cater for pupils leaving at the age of 16; the third for those leaving at the age of 14. A small concession was given to the possibility of boys moving from one class to another by the suggestion that Latin might be taught in common. The resulting Endowed Schools Act of 1869 aimed to end the old pattern of giving scholarships through patronage, and to award them by merit. Critics saw the reform as a means of removing the rights of the poor, for 'merit' was tested through examinations requiring specialist training at preparatory schools. Opportunities were few: in the whole of England, there were perhaps 5,500 scholarships in 1900.[36] There was nothing like the parochial school tradition of Scotland: for bright children at elementary schools, and especially girls, the best opportunity for social mobility was to attend a teacher training college.

A few reformers did argue for a scholarship system designed to provide social mobility for the pupils of elementary schools. T. H. Huxley informed the London School Board in 1871 that he would like 'a great educational ladder' from the gutter to the university for children of superior ability to reach their intended place.[37] Huxley was a leading supporter of Charles Darwin; many 'Social Darwinists' came to a different conclusion. F. W. Galton and Karl Pearson, the creators of eugenics, believed that ability was tied to inheritance and to class, so that the most able children were found in the middle class—and the sharper decline in the birth rate of the middle class threatened deterioration in the racial stock. Two questions followed. First, should mental testing be used to sustain the link between inherited ability and class, and to locate the mentally unfit for sterilization in order to sustain the fitness of the race? Or should testing be used to find able children, regardless of their class and background? Secondly, should the 'great educational ladder' lead to a form of secondary schools modelled on the public schools and grammar schools, or could it be constructed from higher-grade schools and technical schools? These questions came together in the Education Act of 1902.

The Cross Commission reported in 1888, shortly after the Royal Commission on the Depression on Trade and Industry raised alarm about the competitive ability of the British economy. The Cross Commission wished to limit the role of public elementary schools, arguing that they should offer some training in science and the use of tools without becoming so attractive that the education of wealthier members of society fell upon local taxation. Neither should the board schools invade the 'proper sphere' of secondary education. The Commission was adamant that 'Nothing should be done which might discourage existing voluntary effort on the part of the manufacturers and employers of labour to promote technical instruction' or which would replace practical training at work with 'artificial' training in school. The role of the state was narrowly defined: elementary schools were not to develop into secondary or technical schools; rather, the educational system was to reflect and even reinforce the existing class structure of society.[38]

The minimalist approach of the Cross Commission was at odds with the expansion in the role of board schools. As in Scotland, the school boards started to supply higher-grade schools for pupils who wished to stay on beyond the seventh grade. The Board of Education did not award grants to the higher-grade schools; another government department—the Department of Science and Art—did. The syllabus of the higher-grade schools was very different both from their counterparts in Scotland and secondary schools in England: it was dominated by science and technical subjects, and did not provide a route to the universities. The pupils came from the lower middle class and skilled working class: in 1897, 46.6 per cent of the parents of boys at public secondary schools were lower middle class, 8.1 per cent skilled artisans, and 1.0 per cent unskilled workers; for higher-grade schools, the figures were 42.0, 32.7, and 7.3 per cent. In 1897, 91.7 per cent of the pupils of higher-grade schools came from the elementary schools compared with only 48.9 per cent in the grammar schools; the proportion from the skilled and unskilled working class was 34.1 per cent and 6.8 per cent.[39] In addition, some towns started to provide a form of vocational, technical education in the so-called central or junior technical schools. After 1889, the new county and county borough councils could raise a rate of up to 1*d.* to provide technical schools, supplemented by the grant of 'whisky money'—the proceeds of a tax on spirits—in 1890.

In many cases, middle-class boys and, to a growing extent, girls were trained for white-collar positions by attending private commercial schools. Clark's Civil Service and Commercial College, for example, provided courses to train girls and boys to type or work the new mechanical calculating machines. For many upper working-class or lower middle-class families, this was the realistic summit of their ambition. Much professional training was still provided on the job. Although doctors needed to attend a medical college, many solicitors and most accountants learned within the firm from the age of 16. A new career pattern was emerging for commercial employment, with promotion within an organization and examinations to validate skills, which gave opportunities for social mobility without the need for extended periods of formal education. Much of the literature on education concentrates on the provision of formal schooling and misses such continued training after leaving school.

In the opinion of many contemporaries, secondary education properly defined was confined to the private and charitable sector, and did not include higher-grade and technical schools. At the top of the system were the old-established public schools such as Eton and Winchester, as well as newer schools created in their image in the nineteenth century such as Shrewsbury and Marlborough. The elite of these schools formed the Headmasters' Conference. In addition, 'proprietary' schools were established as companies. These schools varied from national institutions with a high standing to local schools for the children of tradesmen. In many towns, endowed grammar schools were turned into middle-class schools by the second half of the nineteenth century. Unlike in Scotland, the schools of the elite segregated the children into single-sex environments under the control of teachers, and apart from the family.

In the mid-Victorian period, the public schools were reformed. When Thomas Arnold became headmaster of Rugby in 1828, he took steps to deal with the problems caused by boys ruling the school. He aimed to introduce 'godliness and good learning' through cultivating a code of gentlemanly self-control and honour. Headmasters were often clergymen and many had been fellows at Oxford or Cambridge: they were anxious to teach classical learning and religious principles. As the Clarendon Commission pointed out, the aim was to create 'the capacity to govern others and control themselves'.[40] Brooke Foss Westcott (1825–1901), a master at Harrow and future professor of divinity at Cambridge and bishop of Durham, explained that 'Frivolity, inactivity, and aimlessness seem equally remote from the true idea of living. I should say that we live only so far as we cultivate all our faculties . . . The means of living then will be our own endowments . . . ; the aim of living, the good of man; the motive of living, the love of God.'[41] Many historians take a less elevated approach to the public schools, seeing them as a device to incorporate the sons of the professional and financial elite into the norms of the landed gentry and aristocracy through the classics and literary culture. The influence of the public schools cannot be denied: between 1886 and 1916, over 60 per cent of Cabinet ministers attended public school, with Eton alone accounting for 34.7 per cent. Not surprisingly, the radical positivist Frederic Harrison complained that the public schools 'bred our present aristocratic conservatism in Church and State'—and the criticism echoed down the generations.[42] Even those who did not attend the public schools might be affected, for the grammar schools mimicked their curriculum.

However, the public schools had other social outcomes. They provided a male sphere to counter the feminizing influence of the home. The word 'manliness' recurred time and again: in Thomas Hughes's lectures of 1876 on *The Manliness of Christ* or the comment of Edward Thring (headmaster of Uppingham School from 1853 to 1887) that 'the whole efforts of a school ought to be directed to making boys manly, earnest and true'.[43] Childishness and effeminacy, gambling and drinking, were to be replaced by self-command, duty, and action. As David Newsome remarks, 'the pursuit of manliness had become something of a cult'. Tom Hughes explained in *Tom Brown at Oxford* that 'a man's body is given him to be trained and brought into subjection, and then used for the protection of the weak, the advancement of all righteous causes, and the subduing of the earth'.[44] Here was a particular vision of British imperialism—an almost Spartan disregard for comfort allied with fairness and honesty. At its best, it meant a lack of pomposity and a stress on straightforwardness. But it could easily become a pursuit of unthinking athleticism and amateurism. Academic achievement could give way to muscularity or even regimentation—to compulsory organized games and the officer training corps. As the century passed, games became more important and schools invested large sums in new sporting facilities. Athletes were considered to be men of integrity and steadfastness, summed up in the motto of the public schools: 'Run Straight and Play the Game'.[45] Here, according to the headmaster of Harrow, was the basis of British superiority. 'Englishmen are not superior to Frenchmen or Germans in brains or industry or the science and apparatus of war, but they are superior in the health and temper which games impart.'[46]

Indeed, the public schools were not imposing a stable and unchanging landed culture to which newcomers assimilated. The culture and ethos of the schools themselves changed both to reflect the emergence of more professional teachers and in response to the wider society. Of course, the public schools taught classics, but this cannot be taken as a rejection of a commercial and industrial society. A social analysis of the career of sons compared with their fathers indicates that the public schools produced more entrants into trade and commerce.[47] In any case, the cultural work of classics was more complicated than a rejection of industry, commerce, and science. They provided a common culture for the educated elite, fulfilling a function of social integration without necessarily leading to a denial of the virtues of economic change. Indeed, the classics could provide a vocabulary to understand and domesticate otherwise threatening developments. The modern world was understood through reference to the ancient; classics and literary culture more generally did not so much preclude debates over science as provide a common language and frame of reference, allowing scientists to legitimize themselves, to make their new ideas comprehensible, and to domesticate their startling notions as unthreatening. As Gillian Beer remarks, classics 'makes an appeal to the cohesion of those who have shared an education . . . Classical reference and quotation serve to place the current scientific text close to the ancient philosophers and poets, then still at the authoritative centre of written culture.' Of course, the language was not always inclusive, for it created a common discourse among elite men whilst excluding women and men who did not receive a classical education.[48] A classical education was not so much about a rift between arts and science; it was more about a social gulf between the educated and the non-educated. For example, the Northcote–Trevelyan reforms of the civil service imposed competitive examinations which presupposed education in the elite public schools and the universities of Oxford and Cambridge, and so excluded able young men from different backgrounds.

When the Royal Commission on Secondary Education (Bryce) of 1895 considered the subject, it complained that 'growth has not been either continuous or coherent'.

504 · *Public Policy and the State*

The Commission recommended that secondary and technical education should be reorganized under a single body for each locality, alongside the school boards which would continue to provide elementary education. The local authorities would fill any deficiencies and establish means of transferring able pupils. The Bryce Commission differed from the Cross Commission in accepting that secondary education need not be only literary. This seemed to offer the prospect of social mobility, breaking down the existing assumption that secondary education entailed a particular form of literate culture.

In fact, the secondary education system created by the Education Act of 1902 followed the recommendations of neither Commission. The Act arose from a combination of two concerns: the financial position of the voluntary schools; and the debate over the proper role of secondary education. Although the nonconformists handed over their schools to the new boards, the Anglicans continued to expand their system after 1870. The task proved difficult for the resources of the Church of England were hit by the agricultural depression of the late nineteenth century. The Catholics attempted to provide schools for the children of Irish immigrants in the great cities but faced difficulties in raising funds. The religious schools experienced problems in matching the scale and financial resources of the board schools which were in the ascendant. The voluntary system was still a major, and troubled, part of school provision and in 1896 the Conservative government introduced a bill to provide rate support. The nonconformists were outraged: why should the Church of England, and even worse the Catholics, be subsidized?

The nature of the secondary education system returned to the political agenda as a result of the crisis of the higher-grade schools created by the combined—and divergent—efforts of Sidney Webb and Robert Morant. Webb, a leading figure in London politics, was a self-made man who enrolled in evening classes at the Birkbeck Institute and City of London College in order to enter the civil service and read for the bar. Rather like Huxley, he wanted a single body for education from the elementary school to the university. Robert Morant, a civil servant at the Board of Education, held a similar view that higher-grade schools were a 'dead end'. Morant and Webb agreed that the higher-grade schools should be ruled illegal or *ultra vires* and the courts agreed in 1900. Legislation was therefore crucial in order to place secondary education on a proper footing—and this provided the Conservatives with a chance to break the deadlock of 1896 and rescue the voluntary sector. In 1902, rate funding for voluntary schools was introduced and school boards were abolished. Education was handed to local education authorities which were to pay the salaries and running costs of voluntary schools as well as the existing board schools; and they were given powers to provide secondary education. After 1870, election to the school boards was contested on grounds of religion to ensure that no one denomination would subvert the non-denominational character of the schools. Women could be elected, and working men secured seats. Further, the boards and head teachers responded to parental demands for higher-grade schools and classes in particular skills. By abolishing the school boards, the Act of 1902 reduced direct democratic control, for the local education authorities were now drawn from the wider county or borough council, elected on non-educational and increasingly programmatic party lines, and with greater professional control.

Webb ignored the religious dimension, and was willing to work with the Conservative government to create a single, coherent administrative system. Nonconformist Liberals were horrified at financial support for Catholics and the Church of England, above all in rural areas where there were few board schools. The consequent mobilization of nonconformity contributed to the Liberal victory in 1906. Not only did Webb ignore religion; his vision of secondary education differed from that of Morant. Webb wished to supplant the higher-grade schools because they did not lead to higher education: his ambition was to provide opportunity for able children. Morant wished to remove higher-grade schools in order to construct a narrow version of secondary education designed to maintain the existing social system. The debate was essentially between the views of the Cross Commission and Bryce Commission, which were replicated within the Board of Education by Morant and Michael Sadler, a civil servant at the Board from 1895 to 1903. Sadler opposed higher-grade schools but accepted the Bryce Commission's wider definition of secondary education. He complained in 1901 of the 'very insufficient provision of the highest kinds of technical, scientific and professional training, deliberately and skillfully adjusted to the most recent needs of modern life'. He believed that pupils who did not attend grammar schools should be provided with a distinctive system of education, an approach inspired by the German distinction between the classical *Gymnasium* and the *Realschule*. By contrast, Morant adhered to the conventional view that secondary education should involve the public school ethos and curriculum. Morant's view triumphed: the new county schools were to provide a literary education, less dominated by the classics than the public schools and with a greater emphasis on history and English literature. His approach seemed intensely conservative, yet his aim was to encourage social mobility within a particular channel.[49]

The new local education authorities had power to create maintained grammar schools, and in 1907 the government offered more generous grants if 25 per cent of places were free. A 'capacity catching' system was created. But the ladder of opportunity was narrow. In 1912, there were 5.5m pupils in elementary schools, and only 49,120 former elementary school pupils in maintained secondary schools. As one Labour politician commented, the 'educational ladder' often did not reach the earth and often had rungs missing.[50] The process of selection was largely in the hands of the local elite, and was open to abuse or at least bias. Many were hostile, and the *Times Educational Supplement* warned in 1910:

In an old country like England, where lines of class distinction are sharply drawn, they cannot be ignored or set aside in practice, however anxious we may be to open the best educational advantages to everyone. Most secondary school headmasters would welcome a contingent of capable working-class boys to be absorbed into the life of the school . . . but many of them are alarmed lest, if it be known or surmised that the numbers thus coming up from below are large enough to affect the tone and character of the school, the parents of paying pupils will hold aloof.[51]

The nature of secondary education in grammar schools forced scholarship children to assimilate to a particular culture and ethos, for they offered not only a formal qualification but also codes of dress, speech, and manners. The new grammar schools were unlike higher-grade schools that developed from the needs and ambitions of working-class families. Secondary education was not a means of creating a more technically sophisticated workforce; it was to be a means of recruiting more able children to the ranks of the clerical and professional workforce.

The Trades Union Congress was highly critical of the 1902 Act's approach to the move from elementary to secondary education as more concerned with social rank than educational attainment. The secondary education system had little to do with responding to demands for a more technically trained workforce; it was more to do with the maintenance of a particular culture to which successful children from lower classes would have to conform. As Ramsay MacDonald pointed out, it was 'nothing to do with the improvement of national education'.[52] Morant's approach was open to criticism on grounds of social justice and for ignoring the needs of the economy, but the complaint may be exaggerated. The grammar schools were akin to German *Gymnasium* in their stress on a literary education; and there was a growing need for professional and administrative workers with literary skills and social confidence. It is not clear that the problem was the failure of schools to produce scientifically trained workers; it was rather in their poor employment opportunities.

How were children to be selected for the secondary schools? From the 1880s, educationalists and doctors were concerned to measure the ability of children in the elementary schools, less to select the able than to discover 'mentally defective' children for special education. In 1899, permissive legislation allowed the creation of special schools and in 1914 local authorities were required to provide them. The legislation did not indicate a triumph for eugenics: defective children were seen as an educational problem rather than a medical problem. More sophisticated methods of testing were needed to identify these children, and George Newman, the chief medical officer of the Board of Education, believed that mental tests should be included in the work of the school medical service with the aim of educating children to the best of their ability by understanding the constraints on their achievement. Even when the tests were designed by hereditarians such as Cyril Burt the context was concern for the child's development, with a stress on environment rather than heredity.[53] The concept of 'mental age' implied that mental defects were not simple and absolute. According to Alfred Eicholz, the official responsible for special schools at the Board of Education, children might develop over time and could not be categorically separated from the 'normal' child.[54]

Tests were also used to classify normal children as part of the process of separating them into different types of school. After 1907, greater care was needed to select elementary pupils to take the free places in the grammar schools and intelligence testing became commonplace. Tests assumed that 'general intelligence' could be isolated and measured at an early age. As Burt explained to the Spens Committee of 1938, 'Intellectual development during childhood appears to progress as if it were governed by a single central factor . . . It appears to enter into everything which the child attempts to think, or say, or do.'[55] The Spens Committee accepted that this general intelligence or all-round cognitive ability could 'predict with some degree of accuracy the ultimate level of a child's intellectual powers'.[56]

At what age could general intelligence be tested? In 1920, a Committee of the Board of Education concluded that 11 was the best age to transfer pupils to secondary education and this became the norm. In 1926, the report of the Consultative Committee of the Board of Education, under the chairmanship of Henry Hadow, proposed that primary education should end at 11 when children should be divided into three streams of secondary education: grammar schools for those with academic, literary, and scientific abilities; modern schools for those with practical skills; and senior classes attached to the elementary schools for the rest.[57] Progress was slow: junior technical schools were given little attention, and all-age elementary schools continued to teach 43.4 per cent of pupils aged 11–16 in 1937.[58] In 1938, the Consultative Committee under the chairmanship of Will Spens suggested that differentiation at the age of 11 should be into grammar, technical high, and modern schools. However, technical schools never became a significant element in secondary education and neither did continuation schools for those who left school to enter work. The idea of continuation schools had considerable support before and during the First World War, and was proposed in the post-war Education Act before falling victim to economy cuts. At the same time, many industrial firms economized on apprenticeships which formed the traditional basis of training. In 1937, one worried commentator concluded that 'for the vast majority of young boys and girls who have left elementary schools . . . there is no technical training or vocational training of any kind available. This great mass of children, the great majority in modern industry, do not receive any training at all.'[59]

Both the Hadow and Spens reports argued that the different types of school should have 'parity of esteem'—a laudable but implausible and expensive claim. Between the wars, the major problem was the lack of finance to implement the

TABLE 15.4. *Percentage of children from different social classes attending grammar and independent schools, by social background, England and Wales*

	Children born		
	Before 1910	1910–19	1920–9
Professional/managerial	37	47	52
Other non-manual/skilled manual	7	13	16
Semi/unskilled	1	4	7

Source: Sanderson, *Educational Opportunity*, 29.

recommendations. At the end of the First World War, the Hilton–Young Committee recommended that the proportion of free places should be increased to 40 per cent, with an eventual expansion of secondary education places for 75 per cent of children aged 11–16—an ambitious target at a time when only 9.5 per cent of elementary schoolchildren went on to secondary education.[60] The Labour party wished to proceed even more rapidly: in 1922, R. H. Tawney pressed for 75 per cent as a medium-term target, and an end to all fees.[61] The proportion of free places in England and Wales did increase from 30.3 per cent in 1913/14 to 47.3 per cent in 1937/8; and the proportion of children aged 13–14 at grant-aided secondary schools rose from 9.3 per cent for boys and 8.1 per cent for girls in 1920/1 to 13.8 per cent and 12.7 per cent in 1937/8.[62] But the ambitions of the Hilton–Young report, let alone of the Labour party, were far from being realized. When a working-class child won a free place at a grammar school, the extra costs of school uniform and books led many parents to decline the chance. Not surprisingly, there were marked discrepancies in the proportion of children attending grammar school by social class (see Table 15.4). Children from middle-class families could still attend grammar schools by paying fees, regardless of ability; by contrast, many able children from lower social classes were excluded by their poverty.

The 11-plus examination became the crucial event deciding a child's future. It did not always involve the use of intelligence testing and was not welcomed by social conservatives who wished to control upward social mobility. In 1922, Martin Conway, the Conservative MP for the English universities, remarked that what was needed was a 'sieve', a means of finding merely those children of the 'finest ability'. In his opinion, 'If you succeed in getting that, you really get all that is required, because the number of really able and most highly developed and educated people that are wanted will never be very many'.[63] Others took a more progressive line, wishing to find any one who could benefit. Educational psychologists accepted that abilities differed, and that selection was necessary to assign children to the most appropriate school. Their concern was not only to fit children into the existing structure of society; they were also developing more effective methods of teaching to make the most of their differing ambitions.

The Hadow and Spens reports informed the Education Act of 1944 which introduced free secondary education for all, and divided children into different types of school according to their general intelligence. The minister, R. A. Butler, wished to introduce schools which were different in character though equal in quality. He seized on Sir Cyril Norwood's report of 1943 on *Curriculum and Examinations in Secondary Schools* which denied the importance of 'general intelligence' and instead divided children into broad mental types: those capable of understanding a complex argument, with sensitivity to language and proof, and an interest in learning for its own sake; those who could handle applied science or art, with an 'uncanny insight into the intricacies of mechanism'; and those who dealt with concrete and practical issues. In Norwood's opinion, sorting children between these schools was the work of teachers rather than of tests—an argument which gave more weight to social assumptions and cultural training. Norwood was conservative, arguing that children's minds were shaped by culture and class, and that they should have education appropriate to their social position. The Butler Act was therefore less radical in intent than later appeared, and education had another appeal: it was cheaper than welfare reform. As the Chancellor remarked, he would prefer to give money to Butler than 'throw it down the sink with Sir William Beveridge'.[64]

The 1944 Act meant that the grammar schools now catered for the most able regardless of class or income. Not everyone approved. Social conservatives feared that the result was to lose 'the boy who was not good academically, but one who had character, loyalty and other virtues'.[65] Character and background might be more important than cleverness. By contrast, some Labour politicians wished to move to 'multilateral' schools for all abilities, a proposal with some support in the late 1930s. However, most Labour politicians approved of grammar school education free of charge for those with ability. Differentiation had considerable support, provided that selection was fair and efficient. Eric James (headmaster of Manchester Grammar School) claimed in 1951 that Britain was experiencing 'an immense social change, the slow creation of an elite of merit, a transfer of power to those whose qualification for wielding it is neither birth nor wealth, but talent'.[66]

Later critics of Labour's acceptance of the 1944 Act argued that Labour was 'stolidly committed to the values and ethos of the existing order. . . . It sought to distribute the benefits of that order, not to change it'.[67] The criticism might be too strong: if grammar school places were available only on grounds of merit, and able working-class children were offered the best academic education, was that such a conservative policy? But the critics started to win the debate, and Labour's policy changed in 1951 when the party conference passed a resolution in favour of multilateral schools. Many children found the grammar schools alien and the

TABLE 15.5. *Percentage of children from different social classes entering grammar schools, 1953*

	SW Herts	Middlesbrough
Professionals, business, and managers	59	69
Clerical workers	44	37
Foremen, small shopkeepers	30	24
Skilled manual	18	14
Unskilled manual	9	9
All children	22	17

Source: Sanderson, *Educational Opportunity*, 45.

local education authorities lacked sufficient funds to ensure that access to grammar schools was equitable between areas. At one extreme, 8 per cent of children in Gateshead attended grammar schools; at the other, 60 per cent of children in Merioneth had places. There were still very marked discrepancies in the chances of attending grammar school by occupational background: in the early 1950s, only about 10 per cent of working-class children went to grammar school. The supposedly objective 11-plus contained its own cultural biases, especially in the English test—and might reflect decisions made at an earlier stage by teachers who selected pupils at the age of 7 or 8 for special teaching, as well as parents' willingness to pay for coaching. Even when working-class children secured a place in grammar school, many left before taking the school-leaving certificate: in 1949, 14.5 per cent of boys and 17.6 per cent of girls left under 16.[68] In reality, the tripartite system became a dual system of grammar schools for about 20 per cent of the most able, and secondary modern schools for about 70 per cent, with technical schools taking a mere 3 to 4 per cent. The majority of children were condemned to schools that were widely seen as catering for 'failures'.

Higher Education

Although a very small proportion of the population attended university in England, their students included the governing elite and many financiers. The result, in the opinion of many historians, was unfortunate: they contributed to the creation of a social elite with a cultural aversion to industry, technology, and science. C. P. Snow expressed this idea in an extreme form in his lectures of 1959 on the 'two cultures': the arts, he suggested, were in the ascendant and science was held in low esteem. His assertion forms part of a wider interpretation of British culture from the close of the nineteenth century, which many historians have seen as turning away from modernity to the pursuit of nostalgia.[69] These historians argue that even when the universities did undertake scientific research, their concern was with 'pure' science. On this account, Britain failed to develop a system of higher education akin to the land grant colleges in the United States, the *grandes écoles* of France, or the *Technische Hochschulen* of Germany.

It is easy to find speeches and pamphlets suggesting that the universities ignored trade, industry, and the professions; and even to find statements that this outcome was desirable. When J. S. Mill was installed as Rector of St Andrew's University in 1867, he remarked that 'There is a tolerably general agreement about what a university is not. It is not a place of professional education. . . . Their object is not to make skilful lawyers and physicians or engineers, but capable and cultivated human beings.' His view was not universally accepted. Perhaps the strongest claim for scientific and technical education came in Lyon Playfair's reflections on the lessons of the Great Exhibition:

Raise Industry to the rank of a profession, as it is in other countries—give to your Industrial universities the power of granting degrees involving high social recognition to those who attain them, and you will draw off the excess of those talented men, to whom the Church, the Bar, and Medicine offer only a slender chance of attaining eminence.[70]

His words could be read in two different ways—as an attempt to assert the value of science and industry against the dominance of the classics in the later nineteenth century; or as a successful counter-attack, an appeal for support and funding.

The question may be approached through the after-life of the Great Exhibition. At its close in 1851, the Crystal Palace was dismantled and reconstructed at Sydenham where it provided a home to spectacular concerts as well as political rallies. By the inter-war years, the Crystal Palace had declined into shabby old age and its spectacular destruction by fire fulfilled its destiny as a metaphor for British history. But the later history of the Great Exhibition was played out not only at Sydenham: the Royal Commissioners continued to manage an estate in South Kensington bought with the profits of the Great Exhibition. 'Albertopolis' became the home of a number of major artistic and scientific institutions. The development of these institutions—the Victoria and Albert, Natural History, and Science Museums, the Royal Schools of Art and of Music, and the various scientific institutions at South Kensington which came together to form Imperial College in 1907—makes Albertopolis a key site for understanding British responses to industry, empire, education, art, and identity. Imperial College, a centre of technocratic education formed through the amalgamation of a number of earlier institutions, symbolized the connection between empire and science. It inherited the buildings of the Imperial Institute which aimed to test imperial commodities, gather commercial data, and teach oriental languages. It did not display an aversion to trade and industry, for its first director was Frederick Abel, an industrial chemist who specialized in explosives at the War Office.[71] It brought together the Royal School of Mines, established to explore the mineral resources of Britain and its empire, with the Royal College of Chemistry, which aimed to link science and industry. It incorporated the Normal School of Science which was inspired by the French *École Normale* and later became the Royal College of Science. In 1902, in the aftermath of the Boer War, the eighth duke of Devonshire (whose father created the Cavendish Laboratory in Cambridge), Lord Rosebery, and A. J. Balfour proposed the formation of Imperial College in response to the great research centres of the German Reich.

The creation of Imperial College symbolized a change in perceptions of Britain's economic problems. The Great Exhibition was organized less to celebrate British economic success as the workshop of the world than to rectify its deficiencies of taste and design, particularly compared with the French. After the exhibition, the project was continued by the South Kensington Museum (later renamed the Victoria and Albert Museum), which provided a repository of good taste, and by the Government Schools of Design and National Art Training School, the precursor of the Royal College of Art. By 1902, the focus shifted from taste to science. The dominance of British industry was now threatened by Germany rather than France, by productive efficiency and science rather than style. Confidence in the superiority of private initiatives now seemed suspect. At the time of the exhibition, Henry Cole claimed that 'No public works are ever executed by any foreign government which can vie for magnificence, completeness or perfection with those that our countrymen execute for themselves.'[72] On the whole, scientists agreed. In 1851 George Biddle Airy, the Astronomer Royal, argued that 'in Science . . . our national genius inclines us to prefer voluntary associations of private persons to organizations of any kind dependent on the State'.[73] At this stage, science was enrolled in the cause of peace—a vision expressed at the Great Exhibition. By the end of the nineteenth century, scientists were more doubtful of the need for distance from the state, and they moved towards nationalism and militarism, claiming that the state should provide them with more money as a measure of national security.[74]

Far from being marginalized and ignored by an arts-educated and anti-scientific political elite, their pleas were heeded. Sir Henry Tizard, the Rector of Imperial College, embarked on a programme of expansion in 1936/7; he was also a leading figure in aeronautics and radar, who aimed to foster co-operation between science and industry. Such close links between science, the state, and militarism marked a major shift from the peaceful image of the Great Exhibition to a technocratic, warfare state.[75] The story is not one of British neglect of science, with a triumph of rural nostalgia and the emergence of mutual incomprehension between the 'two cultures'. Accounts of British cultural history should give more weight to men such as the third Lord Rayleigh—a Nobel prize-winning physicist as well as landowner. He was head of the Cavendish Laboratory in Cambridge, created with a grant from the seventh duke of Devonshire who was conscious of his relationship to Henry Cavendish (1731–1810), the discoverer of hydrogen and pioneer researcher on electricity. Devonshire, like Rayleigh, was the best mathematician of his year at Cambridge, where mathematics was as important as classics. Rayleigh campaigned for the creation of a state-funded National Physical Laboratory. When it opened in 1902, the Prince of Wales remarked that it was 'the first instance of the State taking part in scientific research . . . Does it not show in a very practical way that the nation is beginning to realise that if its commercial supremacy is to be maintained, greater facilities must be given for furthering the application of science to commerce and industry.'[76] In fact, it was a revival rather than an initiation of state support. In the eighteenth and early nineteenth centuries, the state sponsored scientific research through the Royal Observatory, Admiralty, geological survey, and other agencies but backed away from direct involvement in the second half of the nineteenth century. By 1902, a new alliance was being forged. The story of Albertopolis and its institutions is about the shift from a voluntary, hands-off approach to a new technocratic concordat between the state and science. Indeed, some radical scientists claimed—with some justice—that science had been diverted from its role in benefiting humanity to become a tool of war and power.[77]

The institutions forming Imperial College highlight two approaches to science and to the distinction between 'pure' and 'applied' science. One model is the college of science, where science was taught as beneficial in its own right as well as for its application, as in the Royal College of Chemistry. The second was the polytechnic where science was part of a systematic professional training, as in the case of the School of Mines. It is not at all clear that the model of a college of science was anti-industrial and indicated a cultural aversion to application. Many industrialists were sceptical of the polytechnic model, feeling that 'pure' science offered a foundation for practical training in the workshop or company laboratory. Was the polytechnic model applicable to Britain where training through articles and pupillage created a supply of mechanical engineers who were highly competitive in obtaining positions throughout the world? Pupillage was arguably more responsive to the needs of the great private engineering contractors and industrial concerns. Knowledge could be passed on within the firm, and through the proceedings of the professional bodies. The German system of *Technische Hochschulen* and the French *écoles* were created above all to supply the state, which was less appropriate for Britain. In France, the teaching of the *École Polytechnique* was dominated by pure mathematics, and was little concerned with the needs of industry: between 1880 and 1914, 74.1 per cent of its students went into the army and only 13 per cent into industry.[78] Even in the case of Germany, the crucial issue was how to convert academically trained graduates into industrial scientists or engineers within the firm. In the new, technically advanced industries of the later nineteenth and twentieth centuries, much research took the form of adaptation on the shop floor, and success depended on the close integration of the laboratory with production; the point was not the supply of graduates so much as the existence of successful firms providing experience at the leading edge of practice.

Both models of scientific education were applied in Britain in the later nineteenth century, with support from industrialists and scientists, and with different outcomes depending on local peculiarities of institutional politics. At Glasgow, the great physicist William Thomson, Lord Kelvin, was concerned with the development of the second law of thermodynamics and with practical engagement with the needs of industry. He was closely involved in the construction of the transatlantic telegraph cable, and in the development of compass binnacles for steamships. His understanding of the second law of thermodynamics or entropy arose from practical engineering concerns with the loss of heat from industrial machines. In Manchester, John Owens, a textile manufacturer, left money to establish a college which opened in 1851. Initially, Owens College followed an arts-based curriculum but changed its approach in 1857 with the arrival of Henry Roscoe as professor of chemistry who raised money from the local textile and engineering firms. Although the college seemed to adopt the model of a college of science, it also put on courses in applied science. Meanwhile, the Manchester Mechanics Institute was transformed into the Manchester Technical School in 1879, with the aim of supplying apprentices to local industries. It was more on the lines of a polytechnic, and received support from the city council as well as leading industrialists. In time, the Technical School also started to teach general science, so that the two institutions overlapped. They came together in much the same way as Imperial College: Owens College became the University of Manchester in 1904 with the Technical School joining as the Faculty of Technology in 1905. In Manchester and in London, the polytechnic and university came together in a single institution; in other cities, such as Birmingham, they remained distinct—not because of any hostility or aversion so much as a decision by members of the local elite who sat on both the council of the university and the town council not to use public funds to support the technical school as a rival to the university.[79]

In the twentieth century, the expanding universities and their academic staffs moved to a concern for their own professional status. Although some academics continued to assist local industry, universities tended to move away from the local economy. In Manchester, the work of Rutherford, Bohr, and Geiger on nuclear physics was of little interest to local industrialists, yet their 'pure' research had major national significance in the development of nuclear weapons and power. The emergence of research laboratories in private firms as well as in the state created

TABLE 15.6. *Average years of formal educational experience of the population aged 15–64 in 1913*

	Primary	Secondary	Higher	Total
UK	5.30	1.90	0.08	7.28
France	4.31	1.77	0.10	6.18
Germany	3.50	3.35	0.09	6.94
USA	4.90	1.83	0.20	6.93

Source: Middleton, *Government versus the Market*, 244.

a need for more graduates, trained in general principles. The aircraft industry, for example, needed advanced mathematics to understand aerodynamics. 'Pure' research had practical application in warfare and peace, and was far from a sign of cultural aversion to industry.

Conclusion

Education has many implications, for social mobility, personal fulfilment, and economic growth. To many critics, the concern of the British state was to protect the social order at the expense of investing in human capital. Yet as Table 15.6 indicates, the poverty of Britain's educational system should not be overstated: by 1913, pupils were spending more years in formal schooling than in other countries. Did the length of education really make a difference to levels of literacy and numeracy? The history of education has largely been written through the lens of policy rather than the experience of pupils and their attainments—and has missed the continued training provided at work and through leisure pursuits. The cultural and social history of education is much wider than schooling, and is still to be written.

NOTES

1. J. Kay-Shuttleworth, *The Moral and Physical Condition of the Working Class*, 18.
2. Lindert, *Growing Public*, i. 19.
3. Quoted in Lowe, *Welfare State*, 200–1.
4. Johnson, 'Educational policy', 119; Mitch, 'Under-investment in literacy?', 565–6.
5. For extreme statements, see Wiener, *English Culture*, 16–25, 132–7 and Barnett, *Audit of War*, 210–23, 287–92.
6. See Daunton, *Progress and Poverty*, 463–7.
7. Anderson, *Education and Opportunity*, 150–1.
8. Anderson, *Education and the Scottish People*, 305.
9. Ibid. 305
10. Anderson, *Education and Opportunity*, 12, 14.

11. Marsden, *Unequal Educational Provision*, 91.
12. Stone, 'Literacy and education', 136–9.
13. Davies Giddy, Future President of the Royal Society, quoted in Lindert, *Growing Public*, i. 100.
14. Colley, 'Whose nation?' for a general discussion of the issue of state nationalism.
15. Lindert, *Growing Public*, i, ch. 5.
16. Prest, *Liberty and Locality*, 15.
17. Stephens, *Education*.
18. Sanderson, 'Education and the factory'.
19. Lacquer, 'Working-class demand', 202.
20. Johnson, 'Educational policy', 111.
21. Ibid. 119.
22. Vincent, *Literacy and Popular Culture*, 93.
23. Rose, *Intellectual Life*, 78–9, 131–6, 146, 149–50, 235, 237.
24. Mitch, 'Impact of subsidies', 389–91; Mitch, *Rise of Popular Literacy*, 209–11.
25. Lacquer, 'Working-class demand', 201; also Johnson, 'Educational policy' and Colls, ' "Oh happy English children" '.
26. Wardle, *Education and Society*, 59–60; Hurt, *Elementary Schooling*, 34–50; Rubinstein, *School Attendance*, 5.
27. Wardle, *Education and Society*, 51–3.
28. Lindert, *Growing Public*, i. 114.
29. Wardle, *Education and Society*, 86; Rubinstein, *School Attendance*, 22.
30. Wardle, *Education and Society*, 87.
31. Tawney, *Education, the Socialist Policy*, cited in Simon, *Education and the Labour Movement*, 119; *Royal Commission, Elementary Education*, 301; Landes, *Unbound Prometheus*, 341; Davin, *Growing up Poor*, 153.
32. Rubinstein, *School Attendance*, 83–9; Hurt, *Elementary Schooling*, 71–4.
33. Rubinstein, *School Attendance*, 37; Hurt, *Elementary Schooling*, 101, 157–61, 188–9.
34. Davin, *Growing up Poor*, 102, 106; Rubinstein, *School Attendance*, 112.
35. Anderson, *Education and Opportunity*, 310–11.
36. Sanderson, *Educational Opportunity*, 20.
37. Quoted in Sutherland, *Ability*, 107.
38. *Royal Commission, Elementary Education*, 156.
39. Roach, *Secondary Education*, 96; Marsden, *Unequal*, 117.
40. Berghoff, 'Public schools', 148.
41. Quoted Newsome, *Godliness and Good Learning*, 91.
42. Berghoff, 'Public schools', 148, 149; Perkin, 'The recruitment of elites in British society', 231.
43. Quoted from Newsome, *Godliness and Good Learning*, 195.
44. Ibid. 214.
45. Mangan, *Athleticism*, 179.
46. Mangan, *Games Ethic*, 35.
47. Berrghoff, 'Putlic schools', xx.
48. Turner, *Contesting Cultural Authority*, 263, 272; Beer, *Open Fields*, 210.

49. *Royal Commission on Secondary Education, 1895,* 17 Allen, *Morant;* Grier, *Achievement.*

50. Sutherland, *Ability,* iii.

51. Ibid. 285, Anderson, *Education and Opportunity,* 250.

52. Simon, *Education and the Labour Movement.*

53. Contrary to Lowe, 'Eugenicists, doctors and the quest for national efficiency' and 'Eugenics and education'; critique by Sutherland, *Ability,* 86 ff.

54. Sutherland, *Ability,* 90.

55. Wooldridge, *Measuring the Mind,* 237.

56. Sutherland, *Ability,* 153.

57. Ibid. 176.

58. Sanderson, *Educational Opportunity,* 29.

59. Gollan, *Youth in British Industry,* 44, quoted in Sanderson, 'Education and economic decline', 44.

60. Sanderson, *Educational Opportunity,* 26–7.

61. Tawney, *Secondary Education for All,* 8–9.

62. Sutherland, *Ability,* appendix i, tables 1.1 and 1.2.

63. Ibid. 287–8.

64. Wooldridge, *Measuring the Mind,* 242–3; Jeffreys, 'R. A. Butler', 422, 425–6, 430–1.

65. Quoted Wooldridge, *Measuring the Mind,* 255.

66. James, *Education and Leadership,* quoted in Wooldridge, *Measuring the Mind,* 259.

67. Barker, *Education and Politics,* 158–9.

68. Sanderson, *Educational Opportunity,* 47, 52, 56, 61.

69. Snow, *Two Cultures.*

70. Quoted Sanderson, *Universities and British Industry,* 5; Argles, *From South Kensington to Robbins,* 16–17, from Bogue, *Lectures on the Results of the Great Exhibition of 1851,* vol. i.

71. Hobhouse, *Crystal Palace,* 226.

72. Ibid. 13–14.

73. Quoted in Turner, *Contesting Cultural Authority,* 203.

74. Turner, *Contesting Cultural Authority,* ch. 8.

75. Edgerton, *Warfare State* and *England and the Aeroplane.*

76. www.npl.co.uk/about/historical_events/1902.html.

77. Werskey, *Visible College* 185–99.

78. Fox and Guagini, 'Britain in perspective' 133–50.

79. Smith and Wise, *Energy and Empire;* Guagini, 'Fashioning of higher technical education'; Fox and Guagini, 'Flexible university' and *Laboratories.*

FURTHER READING

Adamson, J. W., *English Education, 1789–1902* (1930)

Allen, B. M., *Sir Robert Morant* (1934)

Anderson, R. D., 'Education and the state in nineteenth-century Scotland', *Economic History Review,* 36 (1983)

—— *Education and Opportunity in Victorian Scotland* (1983)

Anderson, R. D., 'Secondary schools and Scottish society in the nineteenth century', *Past and Present*, 109 (1985)

—— 'Education and society in modern Scotland: a comparative perspective', *History of Education Quarterly*, 25 (1985)

—— 'School attendance in nineteenth-century Scotland', *Economic History Review*, 38 (1985)

—— *Education and the Scottish People, 1750–1918* (1995)

—— 'In search of the "lad of parts": the mythical history of Scottish education', *History Workshop Journal*, 19 (1985)

Argles, M., *From South Kensington to Robbins: An Account of English Technical and Scientific Education since 1851* (1964)

Banks, O., *Parity and Prestige in English Secondary Education* (1955)

Barker, R., *Education and Politics, 1900–1951: A Study of the Labour Party* (1972)

Barnett, C., *The Audit of War: The Illusion and Reality of Britain as a Nation* (1986)

Beer, G., *Open Fields: Science in Cultural Encounter* (Oxford, 1996)

Berghoff, H., 'Public schools and the decline of the British economy, 1870–1914', *Past and Present*, 129 (1990)

Bud, R. F., and Roberts, G. K., 'Thinking about science and practice in British education: the Victorian roots of a modern dichotomy', in P. W. G. Wright (ed.), *Industry and Higher Education: Collaboration to Improve Students' Learning and Training* (1990)

Cassis, Y., 'Bankers in English society in the late nineteenth century', *Economic History Review*, 38 (1985)

Colley, L., 'Whose nation? Class and national consciousness in Britain, 1750–1830', *Past and Present*, 113 (1986)

Colls, R., ' "Oh happy English children!": coal, class and education in the north-east', *Past and Present*, 73 (1976)

Cruickshank, M., *Church and State in English Education* (1963)

Daunton, M., *Progress and Poverty: An Economic and Social History of Britain, 1700–1850* (Oxford, 1995)

Davin, A., *Growing up Poor: Home, School and Street in London, 1870–1914* (1996)

Dyehouse, C., *Girls Growing up in Late Victorian and Edwardian England* (1981)

—— *No Distinction of Sex? Women in British Universities, 1870–1939* (1995)

Edgerton, D., *Science, Technology and the British Industrial 'Decline', 1870–1970* (1996)

—— *Warfare State: Britain, 1920–1970* (Cambridge, 2006)

—— *England and the Aeroplane: An Essay on a Militant and Technological Nation* (1991)

Floud, R., 'Technical education and economic performance: Britain, 1850–1914', *Albion*, 14 (1982)

Fox, R., and Guagini, A., 'Britain in perspective: the European context of industrial training and innovation, 1880–1914', *History and Technology*, 2 (1985)

—— —— 'The flexible university', *Social Studies of Science*, 16 (1986)

—— —— *Laboratories, Workshops and Sites: Concepts and Practices of Research in Industrial Europe, 1800–1914* (1999)

Gollan, J., *Youth in British Industry: A Survey of Labour Conditions Today* (1937)

Gosden, P. H. J. H., *Education in the Second World War: A Study in Policy and Administration* (1976)

Graves, J., *Policy and Progress in Secondary Education, 1902–42* (1943)

Grier, L., *Achievement in Education: The Work of M. E. Sadler, 1885–1935* (1952)

Guagini, A., 'The fashioning of higher technical education in Britain: the case of Manchester, 1851–1914', in H. F. Gospel (ed.), *Industrial Training and Technological Innovation* (1991)

—— 'Worlds apart: academic instruction and professional qualifications in the training of mechanical engineers in England, 1850–1914', in R. Fox and A. Guagini (eds.), *Education, Technology and Industrial Performance in Europe, 1880–1939* (1993)

Guttman, W. L., *The British Political Elite* (1968)

Hennock, E. P., 'Technological education in England, 1850–1926: the uses of a German model', *History of Education*, 19 (1990)

Hobhouse, H., *The Crystal Palace and the Great Exhibition: Art, Science and Productive Industry: A History of the Royal Commission for the Exhibition of 1851* (2002)

Hurt, J. S., *Elementary Schooling and the Working Classes, 1860–1918* (1979)

Jefferys, K., 'R. A. Butler, the Boad of Education and the 1944 Education Act,' *History*, 69 (1984)

Johnson, R., 'Educational policy and social control in early Victorian England', *Past and Present*, 49 (1970)

Kay-Shuttleworth, J. P., *The Moral and Physical Condition of the Working-Class Employed in the Cottan Manufacture in Manchester in 1832 (1832*; repr. Marchester, 1969)

Lacquer, T. W., 'Working-class demand and the growth of English elementary education, 1750–1850', in L. Stone (ed.), *Schooling and Society: Studies in the History of Education* (1976)

Landes, D., *Unbound Prometheus: Technological Change and Industrial Development in Western Europe from 1750 to the Present Day* (1969)

Lindert, P. H., *Growing Public: Social Spending and Economic Growth since the Eighteenth Century* (Cambridge, 2004)

Lowe, R., *The Welfare State in Britain since 1945* (2nd edn., 1999)

Lowe, R. A. 'Eugenicists, doctors and the quest for national efficiency', *History of Education*, 8 (1979)

—— 'Eugenics and education: a note on the origins of the intelligence testing movement,' *Educational Studies*, 6 (1980)

Lowndes, G. A. N., *The Silent Social Revolution* (1937)

Mangan, J. A., *Athleticism in the Victorian and Edwardian Public School* (1981)

—— *The Games Ethic and Imperialism* (1983)

Marsden, W. E., *Unequal Educational Provision in England and Wales* (1987)

Middleton, R., *Government versus the Market: The Growth of the Public Sector, Economic Management and British Economic Performance, c1890–1979* (Cheltenham, 1996)

Mitch, D. F., 'The impact of subsidies to elementary schooling on enrolment rates in nineteenth-century England', *Economic History Rewiew*, 39 (1986)

—— 'Under-investment in literacy? The potential contribution of government involvement in elementary education to economic growth in nineteenth-century England', *Journal of Economic History*, 44 (1984)

—— *The Rise of Popular Literacy in Victorian England* (1992)

Newsome, D., *Godliness and Good Learning* (1961)

Pedersen, J. S., *The Reform of Girls' Secondary and Higher Education in Victorian England* (1987)

Perkin, H., 'The recruitment of elite in British society since 1800', *Journal of Society History*, 12 (1978–9)

Prest, J., *Liberty and Locality: Parliament, Permissive Legislation and Ratepayers' Democracies in the Nineteenth Century* (Oxford, 1990)

Purvis, J., *Hard Lessons: The Lives and Education of Working-Class Women in Nineteenth-Century England* (1989)

Roach, J., *Public Examinations in England, 1850–1900* (Cambridge, 1971)

—— *Secondary Education in England, 1870–1902* (1991)

Rose, J., *The Intellectual Life of the British Working Classes* (New Haven, 2001)

Rose, N., *The Psychological Complex: Psychology, Politics and Society in England, 1869–1939* (1985)

Royal Commission appointed to enquire into the Elementary Education Acts, 1888, Final Report

Royal Commission on Secondary Education, 1895, Report

Rubinstein, D., *School Attendance in London, 1870–1904: A Social History* (Hull, 1969)

Sanderson, M., 'Literacy and social mobility in the industrial revolution in England', *Past and Present*, 56 (1972)

—— 'Education and the factory in industrial Lancashire, 1780–1840', *Economic History Review*, 20 (1967)

—— (ed.), *The Universities and British Industry, 1850–1914* (1972)

—— *The Universities in the Nineteenth Century* (1975)

—— *Educational Opportunity and Social Change in England* (1987)

—— 'Technical education and economic decline, 1890–1980s', *Oxford Review of Economic Policy*, 4 (1988)

—— *The Missing Stratum: Technical School Education in England, 1900–1990* (1994)

Schofield, R. S., 'Dimensions of illiteracy, 1750–1850', *Explorations in Economic History*, 10 (1973)

Simon, B., *Education and the Labour Movement, 1870–1920* (1965)

—— *The Politics of Educational Reform, 1920–40* (1974)

—— and Bradley, I. (eds.), *The Victorian Public School: Studies in the Development of an Educational Institution: A Symposium* (Dublin, 1975)

Smith, C., and Wise, N., *Energy and Empire: A Biographical Study of Lord Kelvin* (Cambridge, 1989)

Snow, C. P., *The Two Cultures*, introd. S. Collini (Cambridge, 1993)

Stephens, W. B., *Education in Britain, 1750–1914* (Basingstoke, 1998)

Stone, L., 'Literacy and education in England, 1640–1900', *Past and Present*, 42 (1969)

Sutherland, G., *Policy-Making in Elementary Education, 1870–1895* (1973)

—— *Ability, Merit and Measurement: Mental Testing and English Education, 1880–1940* (Oxford, 1984)

Tawney, R. H., *Some Thoughts on the Economics of Public Education* (1934)

—— *Secondary Education for All: A Policy for Labour* (1922)

—— *Education, the Socialist Policy* (1924)

Turner, F. M., *Contesting Cultural Authority: Essays in Victorian Intellectual Life* (Cambridge, 1993)

Vincent, D., *Literacy and Popular Culture: England, 1750–1914* (1989)

Wardle, D., *Education and Society in Nineteenth-Century Nottingham* (1971)

Werskey, G., *Visible College: A Collective Biography of British Scientists and Socialists of the 1930s* (1978)

Wiener, M. J., *English Culture and the Decline of the Industrial Spirit, 1850–1980* (Cambridge, 1981)

Wooldridge, A., *Measuring the Mind: Education and Psychology in England, c.1860–c.1990* (Cambridge, 1994)

....

CHAPTER 16

From the Poor Law to the Welfare State

All societies experience social risks and attempt to resolve them in a variety of ways. Death is a universal experience. Employment varies across the seasons and trade cycle. Work itself poses risks of accident and disease. Child bearing was risky, with high levels of maternal mortality; and infancy was extremely dangerous. Husbands might become widowers with young children; wives could be widowed and left to support the family; children faced growing up in single-parent families or as orphans. Self-employed professionals or traders experienced business failure or illness which could lead to genteel poverty or worse. The risks were myriad and ever present.

The history of social policy has sometimes been written as an internal account of legislative change marching towards the creation of the welfare state.[1] Historians now have a greater sense of contingency and variation. Of course, the growth of state action is important: public expenditure rose from around 11 per cent of GNP in 1850 to 37.5 per cent of GDP in 1951 and a large share of this increased public spending was taken by social services. In 1907 expenditure on social services was 3.1 per cent of GDP. In 1951, it had risen to 14.1 per cent.[2] The rise of public welfare spending deserves attention, without falling into the trap of assuming an inexorable rise of the welfare state and without ignoring other ways of dealing with risk.

One way of considering the development of social policy is through demography. Families need to make a choice between devoting their scarce resources to children or to the elderly, and their decision was shaped by the relative proportion of these two age cohorts, and the timing of the family cycle.[3] Given the late age of marriage in England, many couples in nuclear families were raising their children at the same time that their own parents were in need of assistance, creating what has been called 'nuclear hardship'. Families often relied on the poor law to support their elderly. We have noted how a fall in the birth rate in the later nineteenth century stimulated programmes for mothers and infants; and how the changing pattern of births and deaths influenced intergenerational support. But demographic influences are not the entire story. Employers might be willing to provide some work for the elderly; in other cases, they might introduce pension schemes in order to ease them out of the labour market. The attitudes of the elderly themselves might change. Economists assume that individuals make rational choices on the basis of self-interest to maximize their utility. In their view, welfare policy would reflect the rational decisions of significant groups in response to changes in the franchise. Thus the extension of votes to unskilled workers might be expected to lead to an increase in spending on social policies; and the state might seek to introduce institutional constraints to contain their demands. Further, the choice of welfare policy would be shaped by the level of income and the stage of economic growth. If incomes were relatively modest, most people would opt for a basic, standard form of welfare provision; if income levels rose, they might prefer to purchase their own mix of welfare.

Despite the powerful insights of rational-choice economics, it neglects the role of interest groups, institutions, and ideas. In the 1960s and 1970s, many social historians were influenced by a variety of Marxist interpretations of social policy. They pointed not to the rational choice of individuals but to the power of capital. For example, welfare might be offered to skilled workers to secure their allegiance as 'labour aristocrats'; their self-help organizations might be 'captured' by the state as a mechanism of social control or pensions might be used to restructure the labour force. On this view, the state was fulfilling the needs of the capitalist class.[4] As these interpretations declined in popularity, so another approach attracted historians: the work of Michel Foucault. He stressed the emergence of confinement under the guidance of experts. Criminals had once been punished through chastising the body by whipping, branding, or execution; in the nineteenth century, they were confined in prisons under the gaze of warders and chaplains. Lunatics or the feeble minded had once been allowed to wander the streets; now they were placed in asylums and homes under medical inspection. The rise of residential institutions was linked with the growth of professional authority. Unlike the Marxist accounts, Foucault saw power as diffuse and pervasive, permeating society through the subjection of individuals to authority.[5]

Many historians are wary of such overarching generalization with its lack of precision. Institutions did expand in the nineteenth and twentieth centuries, but we should be careful to analyse the constraints of funding and to note the counter-currents. Expert medical advice might be divided and lead in directions other than confinement: eugenicists preferred to solve social problems by sterilization; many other doctors favoured an environmental solution. Further, the influence of doctors was contained by generalist civil servants. The role of ideas was also somewhat more complex than Foucault allowed: he was less interested in detailed analysis of formal ideas about the role of the state or the place of the individual in society than general 'discourses'. As we shall see, an understanding of developments in social policy in Britain between 1851 and 1951 does require an understanding of the different forms of liberal ideology, Idealism, and socialism.

Institutions played a major role in shaping policy outcomes and political scientists have studied the role of interest groups. Policies were shaped by a range of interests: industrial employers, trade unions, women's organizations, charities with knowledge of particular social problems, medical practitioners and public health officials, insurance companies and friendly societies. State agencies had their own concerns, and gave more or less power to the permanent civil service or to bodies of expert opinion. In order to understand the emergence of social policies, we need to appreciate how the structure of the state intersected with social relations, and with existing institutions of welfare provision which provided both information and administrative capacity.[6]

Any welfare system comprises a mixture of personal or familial, commercial, charitable, and state action, with a changing balance and complicated interconnections. After all, the state might allow or require a risk to be covered through commercial insurance (as for motor accidents) ; or might give tax breaks to life insurance. It might make existing working-class organizations 'approved societies' within the state system. It might give power to charitable bodies, as in the case of homes for orphans, or work alongside them in the provision of social services. Indeed, welfare provision should not only be categorized according to whether it was delivered by commercial, charitable, or state schemes. Each form of provision may also be categorized according to four variables.

First, was the risk pool inclusive or exclusive? A scheme covering the entire population reflects the average risk in society, and transfers costs from high-risk to low-risk individuals. An alternative was some form of insurance based on a limited risk pool confined to those who paid contributions and met other criteria of eligibility. The principle of contributory insurance was embodied in the legislation of 1911 and in the Beveridge Report of 1942. The initial state scheme for unemployment insurance only covered a few trades with a reasonably accurate body of data on the risk involved. Similarly, private health insurance schemes excluded high-risk individuals. Public welfare is not necessarily any more inclusive than commercial or charitable provision. Secondly, what was the nature of redistribution? It could be from low- to high-risk individuals, which might also mean a redistribution from rich to poor, though the outcome depended on the method of finance. A public scheme might be funded from progressive taxation, so that it was redistributive between rich and poor; or through insurance contributions which might fall regressively on the poor through a flat-rate payment. Schemes might be intergenerational, transferring money from those who were currently active to the elderly; or they might be intra-personal over an individual's life. Thirdly, entitlement could be solidaristic or contractual. In the former case, every member of society could claim according to need and without reference to payments. In the latter case, benefits were linked to contributions. Finally, was management central or local, public or private? Compulsion might not entail public provision of the service (the case of motor insurance), and might not entail comprehensive coverage (the case of unemployment insurance in 1911). Central provision might be less flexible and more bureaucratic than local provision by parishes or charities; but local provision removed the possibility of redistribution from rich to poor areas in the face of economic depression.[7]

This chapter focuses on the public provision of welfare within the context of these wider issues and approaches; commercial provision and self-help have been considered in earlier chapters. Attention is focused on the public sector, whose role was increasing over the period, but was always shaped by these other forms of provision.

The New Poor Law

Although the English poor law is often portrayed as harsh and repressive, the Elizabethan poor laws gave the able-bodied poor an absolute statutory right to tax-funded public relief. The New Poor Law of 1834 was designed to tighten the terms upon which relief was offered, without removing the right to public assistance. In many ways, the Elizabethan principle of a right to relief shaped the development of the modern British welfare state, for it offered a tax-funded, inclusive risk pool of the entire population. In a sense, unemployment and health insurance in 1911 marked a retreat from the poor law, for the risk pool was much narrower.

The Elizabethan poor law was reformed as a result of the deliberations of the Royal Commission on the Poor Law and the Act of 1834. The report of the Royal Commission and the Act embodied a particular view of the relationship between welfare and economic efficiency. The strongest criticism came from Malthus, who feared that grants in support of wages would undermine prudence. The poor could afford to have more children, so putting pressure on supplies of food and forcing up prices. In his view, the poor law should be abolished in order to instil prudence and protect welfare. The Royal Commission shared these fears, but was more optimistic about the ability to feed and employ a larger number of people if a free market was created. By withdrawing relief in aid of wages, and making wages dependent on entry into the workhouse where conditions would be 'less eligible' than the lower grade of independent labourer, workers would become 'more steady and diligent'. A virtuous circle of growth and prosperity would be set in motion. The 'frugal habits' of the poor would be strengthened, so that they would work harder and increase the demand for labour.[8]

Tax-financed relief of poverty as a statutory right was a feature of the English poor law, unlike in Scotland where the old poor law gave able-bodied men no legal entitlement to relief. In the event of a depression or harvest failure, relief was expected to come from charity or the collection of a 'voluntary assessment'. When reform of the Scottish poor law was considered, the exclusion of able-bodied men was defended on the grounds that it would merely offer 'a premium to indolence'. Thomas Chalmers, a leading religious minister and founder of the Free Church, preferred the traditional values of paternalism. Social problems arose from moral failings and could only be solved by personal responsibility assisted by philanthropy. Chalmers opposed the granting of a right to relief. It was an individualistic approach that insisted on personal self-help assisted by discriminating charity—and it was to inform debates in England in the middle of the century, above all through the Charity Organization Society. There was some scepticism even in Scotland. W. P. Alison, the leading critic of the Scottish poor law, argued that 'the poor would be on a more independent footing and would not be so much debased, if it were declared that they had a right to relief which they got, instead of going to ask it as a charity'. In his view, the poor should have a legal right to relief, for industry and mining had created a new social order. [9]

The Scottish Poor Law Amendment Act of 1845 did not entirely follow Chalmers's policy. The Kirk was replaced by parochial boards under a Central Board of Supervision which introduced bureaucratic, legal assessments of relief. However, the able-bodied did not gain a clearly stated, legal right to relief. Their position was at best ambiguous for a legal decision in 1849 established that an able-bodied man had no right to relief when unemployed, and even the element of discretion was removed in 1864 when the courts ruled that relief could not be given unless the applicant was both destitute *and* disabled. The Board of Supervision felt that the court's interpretation was too extreme, and urged the parochial boards to interpret the decision reasonably. In 1878, the Board permitted relief when other organizations failed and refusal to offer relief would lead to disability. The problem facing the poor law authorities was how to bend the law of 1845 in order to relieve the able-bodied poor in the conditions of an urban, industrial society. [10]

In England, the Royal Commission and the Act of 1834 concentrated on able-bodied paupers, above all in the rural south. The debate did not really consider urban, industrial districts with their own distinctive problems of cyclical unemployment. In practice, able-bodied men formed a very small proportion of those relieved in the workhouses and most relief remained 'outdoor' (see Table 16.1).

The continued reliance on outdoor relief was in part explained by cost. Work-houses were expensive and it was cheaper to maintain a pauper at home. Constructing workhouses to cope with large-scale cyclical unemployment in industrial areas was impractical. The Bradford workhouse could hold only 260 paupers, yet on 1 July 1848 the union was relieving 13,521; the able-bodied adults amounted to 1,397 and all but one were in receipt of outdoor relief. In such cases, the Poor Law Board was obliged to suspend the Outdoor Relief Prohibitory Order of 1844. In 1852, the Relief Regulation Order permitted unions to give able-bodied men outdoor relief

TABLE 16.1. *Poor relief in England and Wales, 1 January 1874*

	% of relieved
Paupers receiving indoor relief	15.5
outdoor relief	84.5
Of paupers receiving indoor relief	
adult able-bodied	13.5
adult non-able-bodied	53.5
children	31.3
vagrants	1.7
Adult able-bodied males	
indoor relief	28.6
outdoor relief	71.4

Source: Local Government Board, *Fourth Annual Report* (1875), appendix 386–7.

after performing a labour 'test'; able-bodied women could receive outdoor relief without a test. In Bradford, 39.4 per cent of cases of outdoor relief in November 1878 were relief in aid of wages. In 1881, the Local Government Board was resigned to the fact that 'the old abuse of relief in aid of wages must largely prevail in some form or other'. Assistance was also offered to low, irregular incomes such as widows and the old.[11] Widows might earn small sums as cleaners or in sweated trades, with a supplementary allowance from the poor law. Workhouses are usually portrayed as dreaded poor law Bastilles, but conditions might have been more eligible than independence based upon a pittance of outdoor relief supplemented by menial, poorly paid labour.

Although outdoor relief remained more important than indoor relief, from about 1870 the proportion of indoor relief did rise. Outdoor pauperism fell from around 45 per 1,000 population in the 1850s to 22.1 in 1908. Meanwhile, the level of indoor pauperism remained stable at around 6.5 to 6.8.[12] Part of the fall in the rate of outdoor relief is to be explained by the spread of friendly societies and union welfare schemes, and the general improvement in the standard of living which allowed families to cope with social insecurity. Working-class families were not entirely powerless, for they turned to the poor law when their own resources were inadequate, selecting who should have access to their own limited funds and who was best passed to poor law. Parents applied for remission of school fees; wives sought medicine for sick husbands; daughters looked for assistance for parents. By applying for public aid for one member of the family or wider kin, resources were freed for others. As Lynn Lees remarks, the stigma of relief was more powerful in the minds of officials than of the poor. They could challenge the claims of the Guardians that care of 'liable relatives' was a family responsibility.[13] The shift in the pattern of relief also reflected a change in the operation of the new poor law in the 1860s and 1870s. During the 1860s, the poor law faced strains which created pressure for reform. In London, severe distress in the winters of 1860/1, 1867/8, and 1868/9 led to a surge of outdoor pauperism.[14] A new, urban, equivalent of the old poor law in the rural south appeared to have emerged which led to demands for a more rigorous enforcement of the principles of 1834. A second problem facing the poor law was the Lancashire cotton famine in the early 1860s, when a combination of depression and disruption of supplies during the American Civil War threw large numbers out of work. The poor law could not cope and unemployment clearly had economic and political causes beyond the control of any workman. Hence historians have often interpreted the provision of employment in useful public works in the Public Works (Manufacturing Districts) Act of 1863 as a breach in the ideology of deterrence and the beginning of a new approach to welfare. But the Act also marked an attempt to enforce the deterrent principles of 1834. By removing respectable and deserving working men from the poor law, undeserving able-bodied men could be left to a harshly punitive and deterrent poor law.[15]

A third crisis of the 1860s related to the treatment of the sick poor and children. The report of 1834 accepted outdoor relief for the sick and suggested that those who required 'indoor' relief should receive 'appropriate treatment' in an institution apart from the workhouse. Practice fell short, for the sick were often placed in a general, mixed workhouse; and outdoor medical relief was patchy. The medical services of the poor law faced criticism in the 1850s and 1860s. Louisa Twining and the Workhouse Visiting Society of 1858 expressed concern that the workhouse should 'facilitate recovery in the case of the temporary sick, and ensure the comfort and care due to the incurable and infirm' who should be relieved with 'none of the penal elements which belong to the treatment of the idle and vicious pauper'.[16] The medical profession was seeking better conditions, both for patients and for themselves. The Medical Act of 1858 established a system of registration, creating a greater sense of professional status and contributing to pressure for independence from the control of cost-conscious Guardians. In the mid-1860s, the case for reform was reinforced by scandals in London's workhouses. Florence Nightingale pressed for the employment of trained nurses in place of paupers; the British Medical Association and *The Lancet* launched inquiries; and the Metropolitan Poor Law Medical Officers' Association was formed. In 1866, the Poor Law Board concurred.

The medical services of the new poor law became an important element in hospital provision in mid-Victorian Britain. The Metropolitan Poor Law Amendment Act of 1867 accepted that the principle of deterrence should not apply to the sick. 'There is one thing', the President of the Poor Law Board assured the Commons, 'which we must peremptorily insist on—namely, the treatment of the sick in the infirmaries being conducted on an entirely separate system'. The sick were therefore to be taken out of the workhouses in London and treated as invalids. The Poor Law Board amalgamated the medical services of the Unions in London into larger units, and created public dispensaries to provide outdoor relief. The Metropolitan Asylums Board was created to provide fever or isolation hospitals for the whole of London. Although the Act of 1867 only applied to London, the basic principles were extended to the rest of the country, and in 1893 county councils and in 1909 county borough councils were empowered to establish fever hospitals. Public dispensaries appeared in larger provincial cities, and in the late 1860s, about a third of the inmates of workhouses in the provinces and between a third and a half in London were receiving medical care. The poor law had 'developed into the State medical authority for the poor', supplemented by isolation hospitals provided by local authorities.[17]

Reform of the poor law medical services did not necessarily mean that the Webbs' claim was correct that a new principle of 'greater eligibility' replaced deterrence.[18] An important motive behind the Act of 1867 was to separate medical treatment in order to make the workhouse more deterrent for the able-bodied poor. In any case, the measures of 1867/8 were challenged. Although doctors were eager to improve services, Guardians feared a ratepayers' revolt. In the 1870s the Poor Law Board attempted to reduce outdoor medical relief, arguing that treatment in poor law infirmaries would prevent abuse and proposing that the family of the sick poor should enter the workhouse. The Board insisted that 'the stamp of pauperism is plainly marked upon all relief' by requiring that the word infirmary should not be used without the prefix 'pauper' or 'workhouse'.[19] The use of outdoor relief through dispensaries also fell. General practice did not develop through public, salaried doctors in poor law dispensaries, and the poor law concentrated on hospitals. General practitioner services were instead provided by friendly societies and the outpatient departments of voluntary hospitals, both of which had their own problems. Doctors complained that the friendly societies' fees were low and that their income from private patients was reduced both by the societies and the voluntary hospitals. The doctors' concern about the 'abuse' of voluntary hospitals' charity was shared by the COS which favoured the creation of self-supporting 'provident dispensaries' aimed 'chiefly at the formation and deepening of habits of self-reliance and forethought'.[20] The provision of medical treatment therefore remained a confusing and complex system.

The attempt to revert to a deterrent, indoor system of medical relief was doomed to fail. Most people who entered poor law infirmaries were in employment. There was no alternative to the poor law infirmary in many towns, and even where voluntary hospitals did exist, their beds were mainly intended for 'acute' illnesses. As medical care improved, hospitals ceased to be refuges for the poorest members of society. Although the Local Government Board referred to 'paupers', most Boards of Guardians spoke of patients. In 1881, a Royal Commission recommended that the concept of less eligibility should be abandoned, stressing that the problem was 'one of public safety . . . and extirpation of epidemic infectious disease'.[21] From 1883, patients in metropolitan asylums no longer lost the vote, and the provision was extended to sick paupers in general in 1885. The number of beds in the public sector in England and Wales increased from 83,000 in 1891 to 154,000 in 1911, outstripping the voluntary hospitals which rose from 29,000 to 43,000.[22] The provision of an increasingly sophisticated and 'de-pauperized' public hospital system had not been anticipated by the creators of the new poor law.

The poor law was therefore remade in the 1860s with the creation of specialist institutions for categories to whom 'less eligibility' did not apply. There was not a single trend away from the principles of 1834: rather, 'greater eligibility' or curative treatment for some was associated with deterrence for the able-bodied poor. This restructuring was possible as a result of removing a number of legal and administrative problems which were not addressed in 1834. One was the creation of a more secure financial base which allowed Guardians to build expensive institutions and so to shift from outdoor relief of the able-bodied poor. The Act of 1834 required each parish in a Union to pay the costs of its own poor, so that ratepayers in the poorest parishes paid the bulk of the costs of relief while more prosperous parishes escaped. Not surprisingly, the Guardians were obsessed with saving money. This constraint was linked to the law of settlement: applicants for relief could be threatened with return to their parishes of settlement in order to reduce the number of applicants. Such a strategy was more appealing to urban parishes than building an expensive workhouse. In 1846, the practice was threatened by Sir Robert Peel, who compensated landed interests for the repeal of the corn laws: residence for five years now led to 'immovability' so that urban parishes would be less able to pass the burden of supporting the poor to rural parishes. Immovability threatened poor urban parishes with a large increase in costs with the result that the charge of the irremovable poor was shifted to the common fund of the entire union in 1847. In the 1860s, the cotton famine and the problems of poverty in east London led to a more thorough reform. In 1861, the period for 'irremovability' was reduced to three years and in 1865 to one, and each parish now contributed to the common fund in proportion to the rateable value of property rather than its expenditure on relief. Although Guardians were still concerned about economy, there was now greater equality between rich and poor parishes, so providing more secure finance for constructing workhouses and specialist institutions. The definition of entitlement moved from the parish to the state which took more responsibility for finance: the Aliens Act of 1905, and subsequent welfare measures, questioned the limits of benefit of aliens from abroad rather than other parishes within Britain.[23]

The attempt to draw a firm line between the morally respectable and 'demoralized' poor was articulated by bodies such as the London Society for Organizing Charitable Relief and Repressing Mendacity which was formed in 1868 and soon renamed the Charity Organization Society. It was inspired by Thomas Chalmers, who divided a parish in Glasgow between deacons to assess the needs of the poor. The COS aimed to co-ordinate charity and to assess individual applicants so that only the deserving were assisted, and the undeserving were left to the deterrent poor law. It feared that the tie of deference between rich and poor had been severed in large cities; it would be restored by interviewing each applicant for charity to ensure that the gift led to a sense of obligation. The nexus between donor and recipient would be resurrected, and large towns reordered on the basis of small-scale paternalistic communities. The government was sympathetic. In 1869, the President of the Local Government Board, George Goschen, issued a circular criticizing lax policies on outdoor relief in London. As part of this strategy, poor law finance in the metropolis was reformed. The Metropolitan Poor Amendment Act of 1870 allowed poor unions in the East End to draw on the resources of rich unions in the West End for indoor relief but not outdoor relief. In 1871, the Local Government Board circular on outdoor relief insisted that Guardians rigidly apply the principles of 'less eligibility', and reiterated the moral precepts of 1834.[24]

Was the attempt to impose deterrence feasible? Application of the COS principle and the 1871 circular varied among unions. In some cases, there was close collaboration between Guardians and the COS. Generally, outdoor relief fell to a lower level between the mid-1870s and 1900. The attempt to distinguish between deserving and undeserving poor continued to inform government policy. In response to riots in London in 1886, Joseph Chamberlain issued a circular recommending that local authorities should provide public works schemes to keep the genuinely unemployed out of the reach of the poor law. The approach was revived in London in 1904 as the economy headed towards a slump. Joint distress committees were created, separating the deserving poor from the undeserving. Such an approach was extended in the Unemployed Workmen's Act of 1905.[25] The measures of 1863, 1871, 1886, and 1904/5 were not rejections of deterrence and the principles of 1834: they were designed to deal with exceptional distress amongst the deserving.

A key element in the new poor law of 1834 was to end the abuse (as the Commissioners saw it) of the old poor law. The new Boards of Guardians were brought firmly under the control of electors who paid for relief by giving large property owners and occupiers more votes and disenfranchising anyone who received support. Guardians needed to reach a high threshold of property in order to serve, and others were appointed ex officio and by nomination so that the system was highly biased against beneficiaries. The electoral system changed with the Local Government Act of 1894 which abolished ex officio and nominated Guardians; removed the property qualification for Guardians; and ended plural voting. Consequently, working men (as well as some women) were elected Guardians. The Act did not immediately lead to greater generosity of treatment, for the division of the poor into deserving and undeserving poor had a strong hold even among socialists, and the labour movement was divided on how best to respond. The Marxist Social Democratic Federation believed that the poor law could be turned against capitalism. In their view, the poor law was designed to force workers into the labour market which could be subverted by the provision of generous relief, so removing the reserve army of labour and undermining capitalism. Such a policy was adopted by George Lansbury, an SDF Guardian at Poplar and future leader of the Labour party. The Poplar union shifted towards generous outdoor relief after 1893, and 'Poplarism' became a byword for extravagance. The ILP and Labour party were more ambivalent. Their preference was to abolish a tainted system. As a result, there was tension in Poplar between Lansbury and Will Crooks of the Labour party.[26] As we have seen, pressure for change in the poor law also came from other groups, including professionals eager to increase their standing and remuneration.

Most recipients of indoor relief were the 'indigent' poor. 'The house was not a workhouse', commented the chairman of the Burnley Guardians, '. . . It was for the old and infirm and the destitute poor.' Poor law institutions on both sides of the border were predominantly specialist residential institutions, which were increasingly seen as the best means of treating social and medical problems. Institutions were no longer viewed as negatively deterrent but as curative. By the end of the nineteenth century, institutions were 'a universal panacea'.[27] The increasing institutionalization of late Victorian society had alarming financial consequences. The mean number of indoor paupers relieved in England and Wales was 123,004 in 1849/50, 143,084 in 1875/6, and 215,377 in 1899/1900; outdoor paupers meanwhile fell from 885,696 to 606,392 and 577,132.[28] Not only were there more indoor paupers: they were more expensive as a result of the creation of new institutions and rising salary costs. By the end of the nineteenth century, the costs of locally funded welfare led to demands for reform—and at the same time, the relationship between welfare policy and economic efficiency was being debated with a new intensity. Could an efficient, productive economy rest on the principles of 1834 and the creation of a moral, self-reliant workforce—or should there be more investment in maintaining the skills and health of the workforce, and removing impediments to their well-being?

In 1907, Sidney and Beatrice Webb set out what they saw as the main trends in the development of the English poor law. Their analysis was a piece of propaganda, part of their campaign to break up the new poor law which, they contended, had already been abandoned in practice. The principles of 1834 were held together by a belief in laissez-faire; by 1907, so the Webbs argued, these principles were more honoured in the breach than in the observance. National uniformity had given way to regional variation, except for vagrants. Otherwise, the central authority permitted a range of approaches to the relief of the able-bodied, children, the sick, and old. Able-bodied men were maintained at home in return for some work which was no worse than that undertaken by an independent labourer. The departure from the principles of 1834 was still more obvious in the case of the sick and children. The Webbs concluded that the English poor law had ceased to follow the principles contained in the Act of 1834 and had moved towards a new set of principles based upon 'Curative Treatment, Universal Provision and Compulsion'. Reform, argued the Webbs, was necessary and inevitable.[29]

Of course, the Webbs were not writing dispassionate history; they were reading into the historical record precisely those trends that justified the break-up of the poor law and the adoption of their own policies. Certainly, the operation of the poor law changed between 1834 and 1907; whether history was marching to the tune of the Webbs is a different matter. The fundamental principles of the new poor law were modified with the emergence of a different set of assumptions about the relationship between social spending, economic efficiency, and personal character. But the Webbs were looking for a collective and autocratic system of welfare, with the state taking control of the lives of its citizens. The reforms of the Liberal government of 1906–14 took a very different form. The Liberals did not wish to undermine character by making people dependent on state welfare; they wished to build up character and self-help. The beneficiaries of the Liberal reforms were somewhat selective, concentrating on men and on skilled workers. Meanwhile, the Labour party was developing its own programme of benefits to unskilled workers financed by general taxation. The changes in the welfare system were not just a response to demands from the poor for assistance, for welfare spending might be sought by employers as a means of raising productivity and efficiency—the question was who would pay, on what terms would relief be given, and to whom?

The Liberal Welfare Reforms

The simmering problems of local taxation and the onset of a depression led the Conservative government to appoint the Royal Commission on the Poor Laws and the Relief of Distress in 1905. Legislation on social issues during the Victorian era did not fundamentally challenge the settlement of 1834 and was more in the nature of pragmatic responses to particular concerns. At the same time, other forms of welfare provision grew up. In the private sector, insurance companies provided annuities to the more prosperous members of society; most workers took out small policies to pay for a decent funeral. Friendly societies offered sick pay and treatment to workers with reasonably steady wages; and some unions supplied unemployment pay or even, in some coalfields, pensions and medical care. Charities catered for the sick, orphans, and blind; for prostitutes and drunkards; for the homeless and destitute; for single young men and women in the dangerous moral world of cities; and for mothers and their infants. Local authorities developed their own responses, through infant welfare clinics, wash houses and baths, or morally improving libraries and museums. The poor law was only one part of a wider pattern of provision which shaped the debate on welfare policy in the early twentieth century as the poor law came under intense scrutiny. Principle came to the forefront and social policy moved to the centre of political debate.[30]

As it happened, the Royal Commission was deeply divided with two separate reports setting out fundamentally different solutions. The Liberal government eventually ignored both sets of proposals, and provided a new set of initiatives and institutions. The spate of legislation on social policy had no precedent since the 1830s (see Table 16.2), and established a new approach to social questions.

The immediate context for the renewed debate on welfare policy was the challenge to other elements of the mid-Victorian consensus: free trade and taxation. The pressures on local taxation threatened the settlement of 1834, for it would be difficult to reform the poor law within the existing funding regime. Free trade was challenged by Joseph Chamberlain who promised that tariff reform would both create full employment and provide finance for old age pensions. Social reform was, in part, a Liberal attempt to find an alternative, free trade fiscal and social policy. Both the tariff reformers and social reformers were responding to a change in the electorate, a need to appeal to working-class voters who were threatening to defect to the Labour party. On this view, welfare reforms came about, at least in part, through pressure from below. However, the process was far from a straightforward response to working-class demands.

Britain was still far from being a fully democratic society. Women could not vote in parliamentary elections, though they could vote in local elections if they were the head of a household and paid rates, and they could serve on school boards and Boards of Guardians. The male electorate was not based upon the principle of one man one vote. Particular entitlements were rewarded with a vote, so that some men had several votes and others were excluded if they accepted relief from the Board of Guardians, except for medical treatment. Men who were not independent could not vote, such as living-in servants, lodgers whose rental for unfurnished rooms was less than £10 a year, and sons living at home who did not have a room of their own. A measure of stability was required, for property was to be occupied for a year in order to be registered as a voter. The large number of working men who changed addresses were therefore disenfranchised. In effect, the franchise was based upon a patriarchal assumption that the male head of household, if he occupied property and stayed for a reasonable length of time, should have a vote which represented

TABLE 16.2. *Liberal welfare reforms, 1906–14*

Education (Provision of Meals) Act 1906
Permitted local education authorities to provide meals at public elementary schools. They could finance this by private contributions, charges to parents, or, as a last resort, a rate not exceeding $\frac{1}{2}d$. in the pound. Parents who did not pay were not to suffer loss of civil rights.

Workmen's Compensation Act 1906
Granted workers a definite right of compensation against their employer on the occurrence of an accident.

Education (Administrative Provisions) Act 1907
Local education authorities were to provide for medical inspection of children, and to make arrangements for attending to the health and physical condition of children in public elementary schools (i.e. school medical service).

Children Act 1908
Consolidated legislation on protection of infant life and cruelty; extended it to cover negligence. Offence to allow children to beg or smoke. Imprisonment was abolished and remand homes created; separate juvenile courts were established.

Old age pensions, 1908
Paid to everyone over the age of 70 whose income did not exceed 10s. a week—this 'thrift clause' meant that the elderly with their own savings, earnings, or occupational pension were penalized. The pensions were financed from general taxation.

Labour Exchanges Act 1909
Empowered the Board of Trade to establish labour exchanges. No person was required to accept an appointment. Service was free for those unemployed or under notice to leave a job; those seeking to change jobs paid a fee.

Housing and Town Planning Act 1909
Permitted urban authorities to plan extensions to the built-up area.

Trade Boards Act 1909
Established boards to fix wages in certain trades where wages were low: tailoring, paper boxes, lace, chains making.

National Insurance Act, Part I, 1911
This provided health insurance. Workers over the age of 16 earning less than £160 a year and all manual workers, whatever their income, were compelled to join the scheme. They paid 4d. a week, the employers 3d., and the government about 2d. For this, the insured person received medical attendance by a general practitioner; sickness benefit of 10s. per week to insured men and 7s. 6d. to insured women for 13 weeks, and then 5s. for the next 13 weeks; disability benefit of 5s. a week when sick benefit ran out; maternity benefit of 30s. paid directly to an insured man's wife who would receive a further 30s. if she was also a contributor; treatment in a sanatorium for tuberculosis.

TABLE 16.2. *Continued*

National Insurance Act, Part II, 1911
Workers in building, shipbuilding, mechanical engineering, iron founding, construction of vehicles and sawmilling were compelled to be insured against unemployment. The workmen paid $2\frac{1}{2}d$. a week, the employer $2\frac{1}{2}d$., and the government 12s. 3d. This would provide a benefit of 7s. a week for a maximum of 15 weeks a year.

Coal Mines (Minimum Wage Act) 1912
Passed after the national miners' strike of 1912; established a minimum wage for all underground workers.

Mental Deficiency Act 1913
Made it the duty of local education authorities to discover all mentally deficient children aged 7 to 16; in 1914 granted powers to provide special education.

---

both himself and his household. As a result, at least 4.5 m men did not have the vote in 1910. Although some historians argue that this electoral system was not biased against poorer men, the various provisions do suggest exclusion of the unskilled. In Tower Hamlets, only 35.7 per cent of adult males had the vote, and in Liverpool 49.8 per cent. By contrast, enfranchisement was high in suburbs and retirement towns. By 1914, only eighty-nine constituencies, electing ninety-five MPs, had a predominantly working-class electorate.[31]

Many workers were sceptical of the involvement of the state in their lives. Although the poor law had become less repellent, the taint of pauperism and the harshness which separated elderly couples in the workhouse were still resented. The provision of elementary education and enforcement of attendance led to tensions with unskilled workers. The police threatened the street life of working-class districts. Slum clearance schemes demolished low-rent property. Compulsory vaccination of children caused resentment. Opposition was not only from the lower reaches of the working class, for better-paid or skilled men were dubious about the incursion of the state. As we have seen, these men had their own, autonomous, institutions such as friendly societies which were suspicious of state welfare paid for by regressive taxes which fell upon the workers. It followed that state welfare should be rejected in favour of higher wages allowing men to remain free of the state. The radical critique of state spending as wasteful continued to exert a hold on many skilled artisans.

The hostility of friendly societies and craft unions started to change when they saw benefits from state welfare. From about 1900, friendly societies started to face financial strains as contributions became inadequate. The welfare funds of trade unions were not separated from the strike funds which might either limit industrial action to protect welfare benefits or erode benefits at a time of strike action. The position of the friendly societies and trade unions would be stabilized if they could secure a preferential status in state insurance schemes. Above all, unions representing unskilled men took a different attitude, for their members were more susceptible to poverty and less able to afford subscriptions. They saw the attractions of state pensions or medical services on two conditions: that working-class representation in the Commons was increased; and that welfare was financed from redistributive taxation. During the 1890s, the approach of the Trades Union Congress shifted and these policies were taken over by the new Labour Representation Committee and party. In 1907, Labour introduced an Unemployed Workmen's Bill which aimed to extend the Unemployed Workmen's Act of 1905 to organize public works schemes and to give the right to work to any man who was registered as unemployed.[32]

Labour members of parliament faced a dilemma in their response to the Liberal welfare reforms. School meals, school medical inspection, and non-contributory old age pensions financed from a higher income tax were in part responses to pressure from working-class groups. The National Insurance scheme of 1911 was a different matter. The precise form of the insurance schemes did not arise directly from working-class pressure so much as from a Liberal attempt to contain Labour's distinctive welfare schemes. It rested on flat-rate contributions from workers supported by a flat-rate contribution from employers and a modest subvention from the state. The burden of flat-rate contributions fell most upon men who were excluded from the electorate, and benefited better-off members of the working class who were already paying contributions to friendly societies and trade unions. The state was 'topping up' their existing schemes rather than redistributing from rich to poor. The risk pool was narrow and exclusive. Contributory insurance was cheaper and more politically appealing to the Liberal government, for it limited the demand for tax-based schemes which might alienate middle-class voters, and appealed to the better-off workers who were more likely to be Liberal voters. The Labour party was split in its response. Should contributory insurance be opposed as a burden upon workers and a capitalist stratagem; or should it be supported as offering some benefits? The Liberals were largely successful, for Ramsay MacDonald reluctantly supported the measures rejected by the party conference. Rather than welfare reforms arising directly from the pressure of newly enfranchised workers, the Liberal insurance schemes arose from an attempt to retain the allegiance of men who had the vote under the third Reform Act. The Liberal measures were a pre-emptive strike against the Conservatives and tariff reform and against Labour's more redistributive approach. Although the Labour party by the First World War was demanding a 'national minimum' based upon a minimum wage and a comprehensive and universal state medical service, the welfare schemes of the Liberals more realistically reflected a franchise which excluded many unskilled workers.[33]

Pressure for welfare provision came just as much from employers as from their workers. The Birmingham Chamber of Commerce advocated labour exchanges in 1905 and social insurance in 1907, stressing concern for 'the future industrial efficiency of this country'; it urged that the 'bona fide unemployed' were 'assets of the nation' and should be separated from 'the unemployable'. The Chamber rejected the Labour party's policy as a threat to 'independence and self-reliance'. In many ways, its sentiments continued the approach of the Goschen and Chamberlain circulars, with a greater willingness for direct state action to support efficient workers. Such sentiments were not shared by all employers. Charles Macara, a leading figure in the cotton industry, launched the Employers' Parliamentary Association to oppose the insurance schemes. The crucial issue was where the incidence of employers' contribution would fall. The government assured employers that it could be passed to consumers, or that improvements in productivity meant that insurance would 'pay as a business proposition'. However, export industries, such as cotton, could not easily pass on the cost, and some employers, such as railway companies, had their own welfare schemes and saw state welfare as a threat. Neverthless, most employers were anxious to secure a productive workforce and if they could pass on the cost, they might be more favourably disposed to state intervention.[34]

Until the end of the nineteenth century, most retirement was a result of infirmity. In 1881 73.6 per cent of men aged over 65 worked; by 1931 the proportion had dropped to 47.9 per cent. A new pattern of retirement emerged even before the coming of old age pensions; workers were more likely to retire before disability, partly as a response to employers' concern for efficiency and partly as a result of a change in their self-perception. Old age pensions appealed to some employers as a way of encouraging the displacement of older workers. However, pressure from employers was not the only or even main reason for the change. Old age pensions also appealed to trade unions as a way of reducing pressure on the labour market. Initially, friendly societies were suspicious but they were under pressure as older workers secured 'disguised' pensions through sick pay. For them, a tax-funded scheme was more desirable than a contributory scheme, for few members would be able to pay pension contributions as well as maintaining their cover for sickness. In 1899, unions and friendly societies joined in support of a tax-funded state pension through the National Committee of Organized Labour for Promoting Old Age Pensions for All. The government saw the attraction of old age pensions as a way of removing the elderly from the poor law. In the opinion of the Liberals, it would also encourage self-sufficiency by making thrift more sensible and realistic.[35]

Business interests were not consulted in any depth on the shape of the welfare reforms. However, their general attitude did shape the context for policy. Industrial employers were, on the whole, not hostile to state welfare and most were content to pass welfare issues outside the firm. Most businesses did not have the administrative capacity that would allow the state to incorporate employers' schemes into their own welfare policies; existing capacity was found elsewhere, above all in friendly societies and trade unions. The state was not 'captured' by class or sectional interests. Rather, policies emerged from and were shaped by the organizational capacities of state and non-state bodies.[36] The poor law meant that the state was already deeply involved in the provision of welfare. The central state was seen as a force for economy and efficiency in the existing welfare system, quite unlike in the United States where the involvement of the federal government in Civil War pensions entailed corruption and patronage, and reduced pressure for more state intervention. In Britain, powerful executive and administrative bureaucracies seemed largely immune from corruption or patronage: the civil service claimed to have a powerful ethos of independence. In the United States, the federal bureaucracy was very small, and lacked continuity and independence. British civil servants and politicians were more confident about devising schemes to 'sell' to business and labour interests—in the process working within the available capacities of existing institutions, and accepting that public spending and taxation were fair and legitimate. Political parties and the nature of democratization were also different. In the United States, the franchise was extended earlier and parties used patronage to win elections. In Britain, parties needed to appeal to successive new groups of electors with programmes.[37]

The Royal Commission on Labour responded to the growth of unskilled unions and labour militancy by arguing for recognition of trade unions as a means of securing stability. The strategy was pursued by the Labour Department of the Board of Trade, where civil servants such as Herbert Llewellyn Smith helped to develop a system of arbitration and conciliation, and was continued by David Lloyd George in response to the threatened national strike on the railways in 1907. Lloyd George was anxious to side-step pressure for expensive, tax-financed reforms. After the constitutional crisis of the People's Budget, he could not afford another scheme like OAPs. Hence the decision in 1911 to shift to contributory insurance schemes. His aim was to build upon the administrative capacity of unions and friendly societies, making them part of the state provision of welfare. His appeal to German models of social insurance did not indicate a shared hostility towards unions; rather, contributory insurance offered both Bismarck and Lloyd George an alternative means of finance.[38]

The strategy of labour relations and the incorporation of friendly societies and unions into state welfare may be viewed as a cynical attempt to exploit the potential of working-class institutions to contain conflict. A modified version of this argument suggests that union leaders allied with employers against the interests of the rank and file, trading workers' control of the shop floor for recognition.[39] But is this correct? Policies might emerge from co-operation between civil servants and union officials, acting against the wishes of employers and the rank and file. A good example is the use of the new labour exchanges to decasualize the waterfront. Certainly, many rank-and-file workers opposed decasualization, but so did many waterfront employers. The employers had good reason to be concerned, for the union leaders wanted decasualization in order to secure a closed shop. The alliance was in fact between the union leaders and civil servants who were anxious to create an orderly labour market, against employers and the rank and file of dockers.[40]

An important theme in Liberal welfare legislation was the care and protection of children. Clearly, the introduction of maternity benefit in 1911 and the control of mental defectives in 1913 were part of a debate about the standard of the population. Children were seen as a national asset, and various programmes emerged at the end of the nineteenth century to improve maternal education and infant welfare (see Chapter 10). The Malthusian fear of overpopulation gave way to a realization that 'numbers are of importance. In the competition and conflict of civilizations it is the mass of the nations that tells.'[41] Attitudes towards the family and motherhood changed. Major-General Maurice, who was in charge of army recruitment in the Boer War, raised concerns about the standards of the population, and he quoted with approval the view of the Kaiser that 'for the raising of a virile race . . . it is essential that the attention of the mothers of a land should be mainly devoted to the three Ks—Kuche, Kirche, Kinder'.[42]

One approach was to educate mothers, with the state intervening if parents were failing. The Poor Law Act of 1899 allowed children to be removed from unsatisfactory parents; alternatively, parents could be helped in their care for children by the provision of school meals (1906), school medical inspection (1907), and maternity insurance (1911). In 1902, midwives were obliged to have training and in 1907 all births were notified so that health visitors could be sent to the family. Voluntary societies were established to teach working-class women their maternal duties. The sanctity of the family was overridden by a realization that the next generation was vital to the future of the state. Many commentators felt that infant mortality was the product of the mother's ignorance and neglect. Maternity was given a heightened dignity, and at the same time a greater role was given to professional, male over amateur, female management of birth and infants. In 1914, Herbert Samuel (as President of the Local Government Board) produced a memorandum advocating a 'complete scheme' for maternity and child welfare, with the Treasury paying half the cost. Samuel explained his approach:

it is the duty of the community . . . to relieve motherhood of its burdens, to spread the knowledge of mothercraft . . . to make medical aid available when it is needed, to watch over the health of the infant. And since this is the duty of the community, it is also the duty of the State. . . . the mother can be helped and can be taught by the State.[43]

This ideology placed mothers on a pedestal, and laid them open to correction and exhortation by the state.

The eugenicists feared that the 'healthy, careful and thrifty are having smaller families than the unhealthy, careless and thriftless'. They argued that the children of the less fit could not be raised up by character building or environmental improvement, for they were inescapably inferior. In the eugenicists' view, class was synonymous with intelligence so that the decline in the birth rate of the middle class was full of dire consequences. 'The mentally better stock in the nation is not reproducing itself at the same rate as it did of old, the less able, and the less energetic, are more fertile than the better stocks.'[44] The state should intervene to encourage the fit to breed, and to sterilize the unfit, remove mental defectives from society, and control immigration. It was an exclusively genetic or biological account of evolution, which was promulgated by the Eugenics Education Society, the National Eugenic Laboratory, the National Council of Public Morals, the Immigration Reform Association, and the National Birth Rate Commission.

Such concerns raise the question of the connection between biology and society. Darwin's theory of evolution rested upon the notion of the survival of the fittest, which was based, in part, on Malthus. Malthus argued that state intervention to support the poor merely allowed the population to grow beyond its ability to be sustained. Such a position was rephrased by Darwin's evolutionary theories, for intervention might permit the survival of the unfit and prevent the operation of natural selection. Darwin's theory could therefore be used to justify extreme individualism. However, the concept of evolution did not simply provide support for unmitigated competition and individualism. In *Social Evolution* (1894), Benjamin Kidd argued that progress up the evolutionary scale meant an increase in altruism. He believed that group solidarity was important, so that the moral imperative to consider the welfare of others had a scientific rationale. T. H. Green and L. T. Hobhouse took a similar stance, arguing that evolution led to the dominance of the rational mind, with mutual dependence between individual self-improvement and social reform. Patrick Geddes argued in *Cities in Evolution* that man was the maker and administrator of geographic space and urban life, and was therefore a creative, conscious actor. Hence improvement of city life would lead to 'evolution rather than the deterioration of others'. Biological theories could therefore be used to justify public intervention.[45]

The direct influence of the eugenics movement was not great, for the Liberal government took an environmental approach. Although mental testing was introduced into schools, it was used to select able working-class children for secondary education. The eugenics movement could lead to policies designed to allow ability to flourish rather than to destroy the unfit. As we saw in Chapter 11, the campaign for eugenics was marginalized by a stress on preventive medicine and environmental intervention. Evolution and concerns for the future of the race were important, without necessarily leading to eugenics.

Despite the concern for children and maternity, mothers received few direct benefits. Adult male workers were the main beneficiaries of state welfare and priority was given to male breadwinners. Male unionists vigorously opposed family allowances paid to mothers as a threat to a 'family wage'. The distinctiveness of Britain is highlighted by a comparison with the United States and France where state welfare was initially based on the needs of mothers. In the USA, women's groups had more power and male unions were weak. In Britain, male unions were stronger and they were represented in political parties which were competing for their allegiance as the franchise was widened. In France, women were weaker and family allowances rested on social Catholicism and a feeling that the decline in the birth rate made support of children a collective responsibility. The policy was supported by employers to hold down wage demands and trade unions were too weak to block the proposal. The development of welfare policies in France followed a 'parental' logic, that is to redistribute the cost of dependent children across society. By contrast, the British welfare system was highly gendered, following a 'male breadwinner' logic right up to William Beveridge's famous report of 1942.[46]

The Liberal reforms were more than a response to increased knowledge and understanding of poverty and social insecurity. A line is often drawn from Charles Booth's massive survey of the *Life and Labour of the People of London* and B. S. Rowntree's *Poverty: A Study of Town Life* (1901) to social reform, on the assumption that they indicated an intolerable problem demanding action. In fact, Booth's approach did not mark a significant break, and Rowntree was somewhat disingenuous in arguing that his study of poverty found similar results of about 30 per cent of the working class living in poverty. More interestingly, the responses of Booth and Rowntree were sharply divergent. Booth took a relaxed attitude towards the poverty he discovered; the whole point of his investigation was to refute socialist criticisms. Booth did not claim that 30 per cent of the population was in absolute need, but that they could do with more of most things. The real problem lay with the members of classes A and B. Class A consisted of semi-criminal loafers who should be 'harried out of existence'. Class B was 'a deposit of those who . . . are incapable of better work', whose members should be placed in labour colonies where they would be taught the virtues of hard work. The consequence would be jobs and better wages for irregularly employed members of Class C who were 'the most proper field for charitable assistance'. Booth was still thinking in terms of moral failure rather than the impersonal failings of a market economy. Booth's work indicated continuity between the 1860s and 1880s rather than a major change in attitudes.[47]

The real break in attitudes came in the late 1890s, as exemplified by Rowntree. He was still concerned with character but in a muted way with a greater emphasis on structural problems. He found that many families fell below the poverty line—the income for mere subsistence—at various points in their life. Primary poverty was caused by low wages; in 'secondary' poverty, income was above the basic threshold but money was spent on other items than basic necessities—medicine for a sick child, or union and friendly society subscriptions, as well as drink and gambling. His approach forms part of an intellectual shift, along with the Webbs' *Industrial Democracy* of 1899 and William Beveridge's *Unemployment: A Problem of Industry* of 1909. Despite the major policy disagreements of the Webbs and Beveridge, their analysis of poverty had common features when set against the views of the COS. These older views did not disappear, but they faced a new challenge after the turn of the century.[48]

How is the change to be explained? One influence was the marginalist revolution in economics associated with W. S. Jevons and Alfred Marshall with its assumption that wages were determined by the marginal return. But in certain circumstances, the wage paid to labour did not amount to the marginal return, for some employers did not pay the full cost of their workers who might be 'sweated' or exploited, so passing costs to other employers and to society as a whole in terms of poverty and illness. Public intervention was justified to ensure that the full costs of employment fell on those who derived the benefits. The idea of 'efficiency wages' was also developed, in order to encourage workers to increase their productivity.[49]

The issue of unemployment and the labour market was central to policy debate from about 1900. Increasingly, attention turned to imperfections in the market which allowed an individual employer to pay a wage below the benefit he received, and below the income which the worker needed to maintain efficiency. Moral failings were no longer central. How should these imperfections be removed? Beveridge denied the possibility of unemployment arising from a lack of demand. The problem was poor organization and lack of information on where jobs existed such as in the London docks where men looked for work at many different hiring stands without information on which had work on any day. Beveridge's answer was to reform the organization of the market by the creation of labour exchanges, allowing regular employees to be directed where work was needed. He assumed that the men no longer seeking casual labour would find permanent work, for he believed that the economy was naturally in a state of equilibrium. At most, unemployment would be short term, and unemployment insurance would tide people over between jobs. Furthermore, regularly employed workers would no longer need the supplementary earnings of their wives. If minimum wages were imposed in the sweated trades, employers would no longer be able to pay below the marginal return of the worker. A major explanation of poverty was, therefore, a matter of the organization of industry and the labour market.[50]

The confidence of Beveridge that reform of the labour market would end the problem of underemployment and low wages was criticized by some members of the Liberal and Labour parties. Beveridge's strategy, implemented in the creation of labour exchanges in 1910 and unemployment insurance in 1911, assumed that jobs would be available for all by removing institutional imperfections. Hobson and Chiozza Money disagreed. The few rich people with large incomes could not consume everything they received, so that there was over-saving at the top; the savings could not be invested at home because the market was inadequate as a result of underconsumption by the many poorer people. Consequently, savings went abroad. The solution was a massive redistribution of income from rich to poor. The discovery of poverty therefore led to a concern for the economic and social consequences of overseas investment and a debate over the principles of taxation.[51]

The British scheme of labour exchanges and unemployment insurance was shaped by existing institutions and policies. Employers paid a flat-rate contribution for all their workers into a national pool to provide benefits for short-term unemployment. The scheme did not seek to change the behaviour of employers, for they did not get any remission of contributions if they kept their workers in employment. By contrast, the American scheme of 1935 did aim to change the behaviour of individual employers: they paid their contributions into reserves for individual industries or companies, and were excused payments if their workers did not make claims. In other words, the state acted to encourage the habits of 'good' employers.[52]

Although the debate on social policy moved on from a concern with individual moral failure, character remained an important feature. How far could individual will or character surmount social problems, and what was the precise relationship between the state and the individual? These issues were crucial to the Liberal reforms, and an understanding of how far they marked a shift from laissez-faire to collectivism. A. V. Dicey, an opponent of the reforms, argued that there was a fundamental break and he complained that 'the doctrine of laissez faire had already lost its popular authority' by 1900. When Dicey analysed the Liberal welfare reforms in 1914 he believed that the trend towards collectivism had been carried still further. Old age pensions were, he claimed, a new form of outdoor relief. Insurance, he argued, should be a matter of individual choice and he feared that unemployment insurance offered a guarantee by the state of the right to work. As for school meals, Dicey was horrified: 'Why a man who first neglects his duty as a father and then defrauds the State should retain his full political rights is a question easier to ask than to answer.'[53] Dicey regretted the shift to what he saw as collectivism. Beatrice and Sidney Webb welcomed it. They detected new principles of curative treatment, and believed that the state should control people.[54]

In fact, Dicey misunderstood the philosophical basis of the Liberal reforms. The Liberal government rejected the Webbs' recommendations contained in the minority report of the Royal Commission on the Poor Law, and Beatrice expressed her deep misgivings about the direction of policy:

> Doling out weekly allowances . . . is a most unscientific state aid . . . What the government shirk is the extension of treatment and disciplinary supervision . . . No attempt is made to secure an advance in conduct in return for an increased income . . . The only moral advantage of insurance was its voluntary character; when that is superseded by compulsory contributions all the moral characteristics vanish . . . I cannot dismiss my rooted prejudice to relief instead of treatment . . . The issue is fairly joined—complete state responsibility with a view of prevention, or partial state responsibility by a new form of relieving destitution unconnected with the poor law.[55]

The Webbs wanted a compulsory use of labour exchanges to replace the free market. Hiring and firing would be illegal other than through the exchanges; redundant workers would be compulsorily retrained; and the unemployable would be sent to detention centres. The labour market would be run by a central department of the state. On the other hand, insurance would be voluntary, offering a test of character for 'any grant from the community to the individual . . . ought to be conditional on better conduct'. Medical inspection and treatment would be compulsory, with ill health considered 'as a public nuisance'. The Webbs' approach was based upon an institutional approach to collectivism and gave little weight to the individual. 'The perfect and fitting development of each individual', remarked Sidney in *Fabian Essays*, 'is not necessarily the utmost and highest cultivation of his own personality, but the filling in the best possible way, of his humble function in the great social machine.' Priority was given to the corporate group. The citizen was to be improved 'whether he likes it or not'. It was to many people a chilling prospect, leading one leading Liberal to remark that he was 'rather horrified at Mrs Webb's zeal for disciplining people'.[56]

The Webbs' approach to welfare reform stood at one pole of the debate and may be labelled 'mechanical reform'. At the opposite pole stood Bernard and Helen Bosanquet who were associated with the Charity Organization Society and with the majority report of the Royal Commission on the Poor Law. Bernard stressed the primacy of the will over circumstances, claiming that the individual could mould the external environment. Character was the key to social reform, and he complained of the 'inadequacy with which our social reformers conceive the power of character as a material agent'. The correct social policy was apparent: 'only give scope to character and it will unfailingly pull us through'. The Bosanquets therefore believed that it was wrong to approach social problems through material conditions for the important consideration was individual acts of will. Their approach therefore rested on 'moral regeneration', and nothing should be allowed to blunt the individual will. Bosanquet's approach led to a shift in the policies of the Charity Organization

Society. Rather than separating the deserving from the undeserving poor, the issue was whether people in social difficulties were 'unhelpable' or 'helpable'. Once the 'helpable' had been discovered, assistance might come not only from organized charity but also from state agencies—a widening of the COS's earlier approach. The Bosanquets differed radically from the Webbs who doubted whether the presence or absence of will explained the plight of the poor. Their attitude to the state was also fundamentally different. In Bosanquet's philosophy, liberty meant conformity to the 'general will' embodied in laws. Since the state was the realization of the freedom of its members, the better life would be degraded if it went beyond the general will in the way proposed by the Webbs.[57]

The Webbs and the Bosanquets represented two views of the state and character in the minority and majority reports of the Royal Commission on the Poor Laws and Relief of Distress. A third voice was that of Leonard Hobhouse, and was much closer to the spirit of the Liberal reforms. He agreed with the Webbs that it was necessary to consider material conditions; he also accepted the Bosanquets' position that 'to try to form character by coercion is to destroy it in the making'. He disagreed both with the Webbs' priority of the state over the individual, and with the Bosanquets' view that the state was the realization of freedom. Instead, he gave priority to the individual: the role of the state was to remove the material conditions preventing the emergence of character. Individuals were not to be merely 'passive recipients' of welfare; they were also to be 'practical contributors'. Moral freedom and change from below were at the centre of Hobhouse's view of social reform, and he believed that 'the heart of Liberalism is the understanding that progress is not a matter of mechanical contrivance, but of the liberation of living spiritual energy'. The state would remove those material conditions which were too great for the will of an individual to overcome, so allowing the will and freedom of each member of society to develop. It was

the function of the State to secure the conditions upon which mind and character may develop themselves . . . to secure conditions upon which its citizens are able to win by their own efforts all that is necessary to a full civic efficiency . . . It is for the State to take care that the economic conditions are such that the normal man who is not defective in mind or body or will can by useful labour feed, house, and clothe himself and his family . . . .[58]

Here was the fundamental aim of the Liberal welfare reforms. This approach may be termed 'moral reform'.

The Liberal social reforms side-stepped reform of the poor law, not only because of the connection with the major (and highly technical) issue of local taxation, but also because the competing ideologies of the majority and minority reports were equally unacceptable. The Liberal government found it easier to steer a middle course. This was true of the labour market, where exchanges were voluntary without any direction of workers or curative treatment. The state would locate those places in the economy where the market was not working properly, in order to preserve and enhance its operation. Dicey denounced the new institutions as a breach with laissez-faire, but he fundamentally misunderstood the thrust of the Liberal reforms. 'I do not want to see impaired the vigour of competition', stressed Churchill, 'but we can do much to mitigate the consequences of failure. We want to draw a line below which we will not allow persons to live and labour, yet above which they may compete with all the strength of their manhood.' Compulsory insurance and old age pensions accorded with the view of character outlined by Hobhouse. 'You do not make a man self-reliant by crushing him under a steam-roller,' commented Churchill. He then proceeded to distance himself from the Webbs: 'Nothing in our plans will relieve people from the need of making every exertion to help themselves, but, on the contrary, we consider that we shall greatly stimulate their efforts by giving them for the first time a practical assurance that those efforts will be crowned with success.' The provision of a modest pension would encourage people to save; a small state subsidy to insurance would offer success to many workers who failed to keep up contributions to friendly societies. Thrift and character would be developed.[59]

The Liberal reforms offered an escape from the mounting problems of local taxation by shifting some of the costs of unemployment, old age, and medical relief from the poor law to central government and then to insurance contributions. The shift towards insurance reduced the problem of alienating middle-class income tax payers but created another problem of interest group politics. The insurance scheme affected friendly societies which provided sick benefit and the doctors who provided their medical treatment. It also had implications for industrial insurance companies selling life insurance; and for trade unions which supplied unemployment benefit. The insurance scheme immediately led these bodies to demand that their interests be protected. Social reform was based upon co-operation between these various interest groups and the state, and was essentially conservative in building upon the existing friendly societies, insurance companies, and trade unions which became 'approved societies' to administer the insurance programme. Beatrice Webb preferred direct control by a state bureaucracy. She missed the point of the Liberal strategy, which was to create a moral consensus between different groups. Above all, the Liberals wished to avoid the creation of a large state bureaucracy by turning to the friendly societies and trade unions. It was less a policy designed to incorporate and control these working-class organizations than to shackle the state by leaving the implementation of policy to self-governing bodies accountable to their members. There was to be a minimum of direct contact between the state and the citizen. 'The Scheme', the government explained in 1911, 'is so worked that the burden of mismanagement and maladministration would fall on the workmen themselves . . . .. Once they realise that . . . they will take the surest and shortest way to discourage it'.[60]

Lloyd George wanted British social insurance to be more self-governing and less bureaucratic than its German counterpart. However, the complex negotiations between the government and the various interests led to a different outcome. The government intended that the approved societies should be 'subject to the absolute control of the members, and with provision for the elections of all committees, representatives and officers by the members'.[61] The industrial insurance companies did not fit this description, and neither did they provide sick insurance. However, they feared that their life insurance business might be eroded by friendly societies in close contact with households; if they could themselves become approved societies, they would be able to sell their life policies. The campaign of the insurance companies succeeded and the clause requiring approved societies to be self-governing was set aside. As a result, Labour had little reason to support the devolved operation of the insurance scheme now that it involved commercial considerations. In any case, Labour preferred redistributive, tax-funded welfare. Again, a contrast with the United States brings out the distinctive feature of the British welfare system. In the United States, the medical profession and insurance companies resisted any moves to include health within the social security system.[62] In Britain, the rank and file of the medical professional accepted the terms offered by Lloyd George; and insurance companies clamoured to be admitted to the insurance system in order to protect their interests.

The social policies of new Liberalism had a clear underlying motivation. It aimed 'To foster economic independence of the individual and the integrity of the family, to encourage industry and thrift, to promote the institutions of self-help and peaceful collective bargaining, these were the underlying objectives of all the supposedly collectivist legislation of the period'.[63] In a sense, the Liberal reforms were not a major departure from Victorian morality so much as a realization that a deterrent poor relief was not enough to create self-sufficient, thrifty, competitive individuals.

War and Depression

The Liberal governments of 1906 to 1914 embarked on a significant programme of reform and laid the basis of an 'insurance state'. Many of the schemes had barely started before the outbreak of the First World War. As we will see, the government was forced by the pressure of circumstances to take tighter control over the economy in the second half of the war, and then abandoned most of the controls at the end of the war. Was a similar pattern found in social policy? According to Andrzejewski, the higher the level of participation in the military effort, the greater the need to secure the consent of the population, and hence the greater the likelihood of increased spending on welfare.[64] Clearly, experience from the Boer War onwards led to a desire to protect the health of mothers and children, and the First World War might be expected to strengthen the case for maternalist social policies. In 1918, the provision of welfare services for pregnant and nursing women, and children up to school age, was systematized.[65] Similarly, government controls over the labour market during the war speeded up the decasualization of the workforce. But many historians argue that the ambitious programme of post-war reconstruction was soon defeated, either in response to the need for economies in government spending with the onset of depression or because Lloyd George's coalition was taken over by 'hard-faced men who look as if they had done very well out of the war'. In this interpretation, the war marked a lost opportunity for social change.[66]

Philip Abrams claimed that the programme of social reform was already in serious trouble before the slump and the dominance of the right: the government was looking to return to 1914 and a free market; and the machinery of government was not capable of carrying through reform. It is true that some of the ministries could not carry their case against the Treasury; and the new Liberals who had driven change before the war were a minority within the coalition. Some of the more radical reforms, such as co-ordinating the existing institutions of health care, were not implemented in the face of opposition. As a result, the new Ministry of Health of 1918 continued the existing poor law system. The extension of unemployment insurance was also difficult: only an additional 200,000 workers were covered by the Act of 1916. Education plans were cut back. Neither was the programme for 'homes fit for heroes' completed.[67]

Nevertheless, the overall level of social spending increased as a proportion of gross national product. In 1913, central government spending on social services was 4.1 per cent of GNP; in 1921, it was 10.1 per cent and the cuts only reduced the level to 8.4 per cent in 1924, with a further rise to 11.3 per cent in 1938.[68] Of course, a large part of the increase in spending was the result of the depression and the need to support the long-term unemployed, but the increase in transfer payments was considerable. The criticism of the coalition government for 'failing' to introduce reform and for cutting spending with the 'Geddes axe' neglects how much spending increased, and the difficulties faced by the government at the end of the war. A more realistic way of considering the impact of the First World War on social policy is to analyse how the strains of war and the 'shock' of the trans-war period placed pressure on the existing institutions, so forcing changes in policy which threatened the basis of the Liberal welfare reforms.

Before the war, voluntary or charitable bodies were crucial components in the 'mixed economy of welfare', and they continued to be important between the wars. Their role was apparent in the care of wounded veterans. Although widows and dependants of men killed in the war, as well as disabled soldiers, received pensions, the cost was a much smaller proportion of British state spending than in Germany. In the later 1920s 20 per cent of annual spending in Germany went on war pensions, compared with 7 per cent in Britain. Traditionally, care for ex-soldiers rested with charities connected with the armed forces, and the pattern continued after the First World War. Deborah Cohen argues that these charities assisted social reconciliation more successfully than in Germany with its greater reliance on state aid—though there were many other reasons why British soldiers were not disaffected in the same way as their German counterparts.[69]

Many in the philanthropic world did see their role between the wars as working with the state, complementing the more impersonal state services through personal involvement. State co-operation with voluntary bodies such as the Church of England Children's Society continued and was extended. As the Prince of Wales pointed out, unemployment offered 'a national opportunity for voluntary social service'.[70] The tradition of settlement houses and boys' clubs was transferred to the depressed areas. The British Legion offered financial and personal support to members. The National Birthday Trust Fund helped to reduce infant mortality in the Rhondda valleys. The National Council for Social Services established education centres in the depressed areas, and its New Estates Committee aimed to provide community centres in the large council estates of the 1930s. In 1934, Elizabeth Macadam characterized these bodies as the 'new philanthropy' which 'combined statutory and voluntary social service'.[71]

However, voluntarism was also under threat. Many of the voluntary bodies were now working within the orbit of the state, and the balance within the mixed economy of welfare was shifting towards public initiatives. The NEC, for example, was a small addition to the huge public investment in housing, and the charities that played a considerable role in social housing before the war were marginalized. Above all, the voluntary hospitals were facing serious financial difficulties. During the war, they came under pressure as they coped with the wounded. After the war, they were in straitened circumstances. In 1921, a committee on the finance of voluntary hospitals recommended a subvention of £ 1m from the state; a grant of £ 500,000 was offered, and permanent support or tax relief on donations were refused.[72] Increasingly, they relied on means-tested payments, with contribution schemes and private wards for better-off patients. Not surprisingly, many patients saw tax funding of the hospitals as desirable. The consultants shared this belief, for the limits of voluntarism meant that they were not able to adopt the latest advances in treatment.

Problems were not only afflicting the voluntary sector: the poor law was facing financial difficulties. As we have noted, the costs of local government were outstripping local revenue by the opening of the twentieth century. Although old age pensions and unemployment insurance removed some pressure, the problem was far from solved. Above all, the rise of mass unemployment after the war meant that many workers who were not covered by insurance as a result of their inability to pay contributions turned to the poor law. The extension of the franchise and the removal of pauper disqualification led to fear that the poor law might fall into the hands of the beneficiaries of relief, or even of socialists. The Guardians in Poplar provided a warning. Lansbury was now within the Labour party, campaigning against the poor law and its injustices, refusing to apply the strict means test, allowing the Poplar union to run into debt, and eventually turning the Guardians into 'martyrs' by being imprisoned. In some coalfields, the Guardians offered generous relief to the families of strikers. Although the court of appeal had ruled that relief could not be paid to any able-bodied men when employment was available, it could be paid to their families and to men when destitution meant that they were no longer able-bodied. Guardians could therefore pay relief to wives to support the family of strikers, not least in the coal dispute of 1926. In some districts, Guardians took a much less sympathetic attitude: Lichfield tried to remove all relief to miners' dependants on the grounds that there was work for them, only to be stopped by the Ministry.[73]

The solution favoured by the Conservative government was to contain local democratic pressures which threatened to subvert the poor law. In 1926, the government took powers to suspend any Guardians who ran up a deficit. Audit was further tightened in 1927, and in 1929 the unions were abolished and their powers handed to county and borough councils who were considered to be more responsible. The aim was to dilute the democratic threat of the pauper vote, but the new Public Assistance Committees of the local councils still responded to local concerns. In 1934, the process of transferring power from elected politicians susceptible to pressure from the beneficiaries of relief was taken further with the creation of the Unemployment Assistance Board, an appointed body. This could be seen either as a final onslaught on the 'dangers' of Poplarism by taking relief out of politics; or as a sign of the government's desire to distribute resources more equitably around the country and to remove wide disparities of relief. In fact, these interpretations are complementary: the change allowed more central government finance and redistribution between prosperous and depressed areas, at the expense of local autonomy.

Local authority finance was under strain. The revenue of depressed districts was reduced, and they faced the largest demands on limited resources. In an attempt to win support from industrialists, Churchill partially 'derated' industry in 1929 so that the depressed industries were not forced to pay high levels of local taxation. A national business rate was introduced and grants were paid to each local authority according to various criteria, such as the level of unemployment or the number of children under the age of 5. The aim was to equalize the resources of local authorities, and at the same time remove the autonomy of profligate councils. Again, the policy aimed to combine greater central control with a transfer of resources. The changes in local government finance meant that local industrialists had less need to be concerned about the cost of local government, and the shift in company structure also weakened the role of business elites in local affairs. National politics were now much more important in terms of tariff policy, rationalization, or wage bargaining, than local bases of power. Local councils in the large industrial centres largely fell into the hands of small traders or, increasingly in the 1930s, of Labour. In London, for example, Herbert Morrison was able to extend social policies. However, the Labour party did not necessarily see local government as the way forward: it was more interested in using the power of the central state. Morrison realized that many social and economic problems were regional, involving the distribution of industry and housing, and the provision of transport or electricity: the existing local authorities were inappropriate.[74]

These issues were to be of particular importance for health services. After 1929, the poor law hospitals were passed to the Public Assistance Committees or to the local authorities, and local advisory boards could be created to co-ordinate the relationship between local authority and voluntary hospitals. The proposal did not work. One of the few areas with effective co-ordination was Manchester, where the driving force was the university and specialists in the hospitals, rather than the local authority and philanthropists.[75] Although some local authorities were developing a wide range of health services by 1939, it remained to be seen whether they would provide the basis of reform after the Second World War.

The approved societies were another important element in the pre-1914 system of welfare. The Liberal government opposed a highly centralized, bureaucratic system of welfare which was nevertheless what emerged after the Second World War. As we have seen, the government's scheme was modified in 1911 with the extension of approved society status to commercial insurance companies which were not democratically accountable to their members, and in 1925 Labour pointed out that the democratic ambition of the scheme was a dead letter. One solution was to nationalize the insurance companies or to remove their approved society status. Of course, Labour was suspicious of the entire principle of contributory insurance but criticism of the commercial approved societies was not confined to Labour, for Beveridge was a fierce opponent. For their part, the Conservative governments and many officials saw the virtues of approved societies as a useful device to contain the demands of the public for improved welfare benefits. The government could present itself as responsible, stopping the societies from spending too much on new initiatives. They were under tight control from the government actuary and the Controller of the Health Service Division of the Ministry of Health: the government paid its contribution to the societies, and then decided how much each could pay in additional benefits. Apparently technical, apolitical decisions determined the operation of the societies, without a right of democratic appeal. The Controller was explicit in 1934: 'the Health Insurance scheme is highly decentralized and the "buffer" Approved Societies divert much criticism from the Government.' The autonomy of the societies was therefore more apparent than real, and many members were losing interest in the rituals and sociability of the societies. What was the point of self-governing bodies if their autonomy was threatened by officials? A centralized system would also be more equitable. After all, the members of different approved societies within one street had different benefits, largely for the healthiest members of society, and without any co-ordination with local authority health services. In the words of the minority report of the Royal Commission on National Health Insurance in 1926, 'the object of a "national" health insurance system must presumably be, not to supply cream to the fat and skim milk to the lean, but good milk to all insured persons'.[76]

What happened to the principle of actuarially sound, limited insurance? Between the wars, the trends ran in different directions, for the contributory principle was extended to pensions and was threatened in unemployment insurance. The Treasury was never happy with the non-contributory nature of old age pensions and its fears were confirmed as the cost mounted from £8.1 m in 1908–9 to £12.3 m in 1912–13, and threatened to grow ever higher. Not surprisingly, the Treasury argued for a shift to contributory funding in order to contain this demand. The war led to renewed demands with the formation of the National Conference on Old Age Pensions in 1916, urging an increase in the pension and an end to the 'thrift' clause which denied pensions to those with some income from their savings or friendly societies. Despite the Treasury's hostility to tax-funded, non-contributory pensions, the committee appointed to consider these demands found poverty amongst pensioners, and the government had little option except to increase pensions.

In the early 1920s, the Treasury started to fight back. In 1925, pensions were introduced for widows and orphans, a compulsory scheme financed by the contributions of male breadwinners. Contributory pensions were also introduced for those aged 65 to 70, with a supplement for those aged over 70. The scheme contained more radical demands from Labour and shifted the balance between redistributive taxation and insurance contributions, so blocking the dangerously redistributive potential of pensions. Instead of posing a threat to private property, pensions now formed part of 'populist capitalism'. The scheme met the demands of the pensioners by removing the thrift disqualification. The contributory scheme offered a basic pension, at the level afforded by the lowest-paid workers; better-off workers could top up the state pension without a loss of entitlement. The non-contributory pension was marginalized, and those who had no other entitlement were in serious difficulties. Of course, the change was not welcomed by Labour; and the scheme also departed from equal rights for women whose entitlement was now linked to a male breadwinner. Pressure continued in the 1930s with demands for a higher pension conditional on retirement, and for an extension of benefits to spinsters. But concessions were resisted by the Treasury. The reforms of 1925 created the basis of the pension system as it existed after the Second World War: the proposals of Beveridge were essentially to combine the schemes of 1908 and 1925 into a single contributory pension, and to make it available to everyone.[77]

Pensions therefore moved a considerable way from tax-funded redistribution to contributory insurance. Maintenance of contributions proved much more difficult in the case of unemployment insurance as a result of high unemployment in the 1920s and 1930s. Of course, the labour movement was doubtful of the contributory principle: skilled workers with an exclusive risk pool might be able to afford better terms; and unskilled workers argued that the insurance scheme was not redistributive between rich and poor. At the end of the war, the government had not prepared its plans to extend unemployment insurance, and the immediate response was the 'out of work donation'. A new principle was introduced: relief without contribution. The scheme was costly, and was abandoned after two years. In 1920, the government tried to revert to the principle of 1911 by extending contributory insurance to all workers except in agriculture and domestic service. But unemployment soared shortly after the Act was implemented and the fund ran into deficit. Many workers were thrown out of work before they were able to pay enough contributions to secure benefits, and had no alternative except the poor law. In 1921, the contributory principle was breached: the unemployed could claim 'uncovenanted benefits'. As a result, two principles were operating: benefit according to need; and benefit according to contribution. 'Uncovenanted', 'extended', or 'transitional' benefits continued throughout the inter-war period. These supposedly temporary concessions brought the entire basis of welfare policy into dispute. The payment of relief was in constant turmoil, involving a prolonged struggle between the unemployed and the national exchequer, between voters and taxpayers, and between rival conceptions of social welfare.[78]

The Treasury viewed the problem of unemployment as largely one of wage rigidity; it also wished to make the unemployment insurance scheme more self-sufficient. For its part, the TUC maintained its opposition to contributory insurance and argued for a right to work or the payment of benefits from general taxation. The response of industrial employers varied. Some feared that higher contributions would make their costs higher and price them out of export markets. They wished to return to a strict interpretation of the principles of 1911, leaving those who had not paid contributions to a deterrent poor law. Others, especially in the 'sheltered' industries, favoured insurance schemes for each industrial sector so that they could offer more generous benefits without subsidizing the declining industries. This approach was welcomed by Beveridge.[79]

In 1922, extended benefit was made conditional on 'genuinely seeking whole-time employment'; in practice, the main effect was to exclude married women. A means test was also introduced so that benefit was removed from applicants with some other household income above 13s. a week. The minority Labour government ended the means test, raised the level of benefit, and paid 'uncovenanted benefit' as a legal right, provided that thirty weeks' contributions had been paid in the previous two years. Here was a major breach in the actuarial basis of contributory insurance. The committee appointed by the new Conservative government in 1925 recommended the abolition of extended benefit and the creation of a 'standard' benefit for everyone who paid thirty contributions a year, without limit by the rule of one week's benefit for six weeks' contributions. Until economic recovery allowed the unemployed to meet this requirement, 'transitional benefit' should be offered to anyone who paid eight contributions in the previous two years or thirty at any time. These recommendations were implemented in 1927; in fact, transitional benefits remained in place for seven years. Although some attempt was made to limit demands by requiring all claimants for benefits to show that they were 'genuinely seeking work', the actuarial principles of 1911 had not been restored. In 1930 the Labour government abolished the genuinely seeking work test and made the Treasury responsible for transitional benefits. The outcome was a shift from poor relief and local rates to transitional benefits and national taxes. The resulting deficit in the unemployment insurance fund contributed to the fall of the government in 1931.

Beveridge was concerned at the retreat from 1911 and feared the result of unlimited benefits would be wage demands and rigidities. He felt that the changes prevented more thorough reform. He wrote to Churchill in 1930:

The trouble with the insurance system today is not merely or mainly the maintenance of people [who are] unemployable, but the fact that with its flat rate of contributions for an unlimited benefit, it subsidises the casual and disorganized industries . . . at the expense of other industries . . . All unemployment policies of 1909 which aimed at diminishing unemployment . . . have been neglected in favour of extension of benefit.

His concern was the need for structural reform of the labour market. In Beveridge's view, the unemployed should be classified into three groups. Men with a realistic chance of employment should be covered by contributory insurance according to the principles of 1911, with contributions adjusted for each industry. Trades with a persistently high level of dismissals could be decasualized by the government. Workers who used up their benefit with little prospect of regaining their jobs would be relieved as a matter of discretion: they would be retrained or sent to penal labour colonies. Beveridge was, in other words, adopting a position closer to the minority report of 1909.[80]

The immediate response of the national government in 1931 was to restore the actuarial basis of unemployment insurance. It cut the level of benefit by 10 per cent; imposed a time limit of twenty-six weeks on insured benefits; and introduced a means test for transitional benefits. Means testing led to resentment against intrusive inspection and against making adult men partly dependent on their children and wives. Married women were disqualified, unless they could show that they had a reasonable chance of insurable employment and that their prospect of employment was not reduced by marriage. In effect, they were largely excluded from relief, with serious consequences in mill towns where the family income assumed two wages. Relief also varied between PACs. In 1934, insured workers and the long-term unemployed were separated into two new bodies. The Unemployment Insurance Statutory Committee, under Beveridge's chairmanship, was to look after insured workers. The experience forced Beveridge to adjust his views. He found that malingerers were not common, that many workers were willing to pay more for better cover, and that many white-collar workers wished to be included. He was also brought up against the administrative complexities and anomalies of relief. Why was the unemployment benefit twice the level of sick pay? What should be done in the poorest-paid trades where benefit for large families was higher than wages? At the same time, relief of the long-term unemployed was passed to the Unemployment Assistance Board which could be interpreted as an attempt to remove anomalies and improve conditions in the least generous areas, or as a ploy to control the remaining discretion of generous authorities.[81] In any event, the generous areas did not surrender and the government had to concede a right to claim on either the local PAC scale or the national UAB scale, whichever was the higher.

The result was complexity. Civil servants feared that 'scroungers' were claiming benefit rather than seeking work. In reality, refusal of relief led to poverty; and the real problem was not malingering so much as a loss of dignity and low wages for men with large families. Welfare was confused and divided. The result was a gradual shift towards a more centralized system which was less accountable to local interests and members. The aim of the new Liberals was largely rejected—a change in emphasis which caused concern not least to Beveridge.

The result of these developments was a shift towards more bureaucratic systems and a reduction in the role of women in the shaping and running of social policy. In the nineteenth century, many policy initiatives emerged from the charitable sector which offered women an unpaid profession. The most prominent women had a national role in advising on policies: Octavia Hill, Helen Bosanquet, and Beatrice Webb served on the Royal Commission on the Poor Laws. But with the emergence of council housing, management became a male and technocratic initiative. When women were employed by some local authorities in the 1930s, it was as lower-grade staff. Similarly, the social case-work approach of the COS led women to be employed by local authorities as social workers. They moved, as Jane Lewis remarks, from unpaid influence to 'paid oblivion'.[82] Whether the policies adopted also neglected the interests of women is a controversial issue to which we will return.

How are developments between the wars to be summarized? David Vincent views the story as one of containment of the democratic promise of 1918. But care is needed with this argument. Social policies were costly, and there were limits to what the taxpayer could be expected to pay. The history of pensions and unemployment insurance could be read as an attempt by the Treasury and Cabinet to balance the costs of welfare against the acceptable limits of taxation. Criticism of the Treasury often portrays officials as limiting the redistributive potential of democracy, without considering the real dangers of allowing expenditure to rise. Welfare spending did not fall; whatever the miseries of the means test, the principle of contributions was not imposed on the unemployed. The boundaries of state action were extended, and in one important case more power was given to local authorities: the construction of local authority housing. Although the more ambitious post-war scheme was rejected, a major and expensive public housing programme remained. The poor no longer had a stark choice between the workhouse and destitution, but they were obliged to contribute to their own support where possible. Local relief was considered unwise with the extension of the franchise and the end of pauper disqualification; instead, relief was to be in the hands of the central government with minimal parliamentary supervision. Vincent suggests that only the elderly gained; otherwise the poor were excluded from society. But is his account too critical? The poor might now obtain a council house; the level of welfare spending had increased since 1914; there were better local services for health care and maternity. Of course, the system had its faults, but it should be judged against most other countries facing depression in the 1930s. As prices fell, the real value of unemployment benefits rose; and they were also increased in 1924, 1928, and 1930. The benefits for a family of four rose in real terms by 240 per cent between 1920 and 1931. Was this really a story of containment and defeat? The Treasury had a genuine concern about cost, and could not exceed the limits of what was politically feasible without a revolt by taxpayers. Thane points out that the aims of the government in the 1930s were to stimulate economic growth within a free enterprise economy, while maintaining social order. These aims might be compatible through raising efficiency but were also in tension if the cost of welfare was too high and wages were held up.[83] Clearly, there was mounting criticism: contradictory principles and overlapping institutions left gaps in coverage and anomalies in the level of benefits, so that by the outbreak of the Second World War, there were demands for consolidation and reform.

The Creation of the Welfare State

In 1941, William Beveridge was appointed chairman of an interdepartmental inquiry to co-ordinate the various existing programmes of social insurance. He was under no illusion about the reasons for his appointment: he was being sidelined by Ernest Bevin, the Minister of Labour. Beveridge was demanding immediate and complete control over the labour market, in opposition to Bevin's more cautious and conciliatory line. But Beveridge's disappointment was to become a huge opportunity, for his report on *Social Insurance and Allied Services* was transformed from a technical inquiry into a call for post-war reform. In dramatic terms, he offered security from 'the cradle to the grave', and declared war on the 'five giants' of want, ignorance, squalor, disease, and idleness. The report was greeted with scepticism by Churchill, who was concerned at the distraction from the war effort; with deep alarm by commercial insurance companies who feared a loss of business and the abolition of approved societies; and by foreboding within Whitehall which feared that the cost would drive up taxes and hinder reconstruction.[84] However, its popular reception was enthusiastic and stimulated a searching debate. After the war, a welfare state was constructed and Beveridge's report is usually given pride of place in its genesis. How far was the report a break with earlier thinking on welfare, or was it mainly a summing up of earlier trends? How far did it provide the basis for the policies implemented after the war?

Many problems had been identified before the war, and a large element of Beveridge's report was administrative reform. There were seven departments dealing with benefits for different needs as well as the local authority committees providing means-tested public assistance and a range of health services. There were different methods of finance through the rates, general taxes, and insurance contributions. The level of benefits varied between unemployment and sick pay; different approved societies paid different additional benefits; and some groups were not effectively covered. The war gave these concerns a new urgency and stimulated interest in social reform. The focus shifted from long-term unemployment. Work was no longer a problem; the issue was rather the relief of poverty. The experiences of bombing in 1940 and mass evacuation showed the defects of the existing system of hospitals, and exposed child poverty. The pressures of war created a sense of social solidarity, weakening Beveridge's earlier fears that generous benefits might undermine incentives and lead to malingering. Rather, social reform would maintain morale and secure the support of organized labour for the war effort.[85]

Beveridge's report built upon his thinking since his involvement in the creation of labour exchanges and unemployment insurance, and his more recent experience since 1934. A central principle of his report was universalism—a single insurance scheme to cover all insured risks. The idea of 'all in' insurance was proposed by the

Anderson Committee of 1923–4, but collapsed in the face of mass unemployment. Beveridge supported 'all in' insurance in 1924, arguing for a single contributory flat-rate premium to cover health, unemployment, old age, industrial accidents, widows' benefits, and orphans. In 1942, he extended the argument: a single Social Security Board should cover all forms of insurance; it should cover the entire population and offer standard benefits for a flat rate of contribution. The population would be divided into categories—employees, the self-employed, housewives, those below working age, and those incapable of work. They would receive seven types of benefit: family allowances, old age pensions, disability benefit, unemployment benefit, funeral expenses, loss grants for self-employed, and grants for housewives. As a temporary measure, Beveridge proposed means-tested 'national assistance'. Comprehensive contributory insurance meant that any residual assistance could be offered on strict conditions, and the concern for disciplinary treatment remained.

The contributory principle remained central as it had in 1908 when he opposed non-contributory old age pensions as a penalty for thrift. Non-contributory benefits paid out of general taxation were servile; in an advanced industrial economy, people should be able to pay for their own welfare. His ambition was 'self-governing pluralism' with social welfare supporting active citizenship. As he remarked in 1942,

The state should offer security for service and contribution. The state in organizing security should not stifle initiative, opportunity, responsibility; in establishing a national minimum, it should leave room and encouragement for voluntary action by each individual to provide more than a minimum for himself and his family.

Social welfare should be contractual and not 'giving to everybody something for nothing'. Universal contributory benefits should cover subsistence, and encourage individuals 'to win for themselves something above the national minimum.' His approach was that of an Edwardian new Liberal, assuming that the state would provide the foundation upon which individuals could construct independence and develop personal responsibility. But universalism and contributions were in conflict with the provision of an adequate minimum of support. His definition of the minimum was indeed minimal, in order to encourage private saving and to maintain a substantial gap between wages and benefits. The level of benefits was set by the flat-rate contribution afforded by the lowest-paid worker, below subsistence level.[86]

A universal, comprehensive, and contributory insurance scheme could only work on the assumption of full employment. In 1909, Beveridge accepted as axiomatic that supply and demand would remain in balance, and long-term unemployment would not be a problem. The depression of the 1930s showed that assumption was false. In the report of 1942 and in *Full Employment in a Free Society* of 1944, he tried to show how unemployment could be abolished. Initially, his approach owed less to Keynes and demand management than democratic planning of production. His thinking on full employment in 1942 was 'essentially a socialist ... conception'. In 1944, he was more willing to support Keynesian demand management. Above all, full employment was necessary for the extension of insurance to the whole population and to the financial stability of the scheme. The availability of jobs for everyone also meant that compulsion would be needed only for the few people who failed to find work. The better-off could 'top up' state benefits; the poorest could not and they therefore relied on tax-funded national assistance.[87]

The report has been criticized by feminists for continuing many of the patriarchal assumptions of male breadwinner welfare. Beveridge took for granted the norm of a male-headed household, assuming that most women would marry and that their main duty was to raise children. Criticism of these assumptions from a later perspective is easy. However, at the time many women saw an improvement over inadequate treatment by the existing system. Although a single woman in employment had the same rights as a man, they were lost on marriage; divorced or separated women, and spinsters caring for relatives, only received public assistance. Hence much of the burden of poverty and unemployment between the wars was carried by women. Whatever his patriarchal assumptions, Beveridge's report offered women much more than in the past. He proposed that women should be dealt with in five ways. Employed single women would have the same benefits as men. Married women would be covered by a 'housewives' policy' paid for by their husbands' contributions, pensions at 60, and domestic help when ill. Employed married women could choose between the housewives' policy or their own contributions as an employed person, with a lower benefit to reflect the fact they were housed by their husband. Beveridge wished to improve the conditions of housewives and mothers, within the traditional expectation that they had 'vital work to do in ensuring the adequate continuance of the British race and British ideals in the world'. Women's groups were critical. The Married Women's Association argued they should be full contributors apart from their husbands; the National Council of Women felt that women employees, both married and single, should have the same benefits as men. But Beveridge felt that he was reflecting social reality: most women were dependent on their husbands, and the needs of married women were lower than those of single women. Most women shared the assumptions of the 'male breadwinner' system of welfare, and they did gain from the extension of their benefits.[88]

The Beveridge report endorsed one of the major demands of the women's movement: family allowances paid to the wife. His support for the proposal went back to the publication of Eleanor Rathbone's *The Disinherited Family*, and he immediately introduced family allowances when he was Director at the London School of Economics. He shared Rathbone's hope that allowances would end the problem of child poverty in large families, but their analysis then diverged. Rathbone expected that allowances would reduce the birth rate by raising expectations; Beveridge hoped they would increase births. At this point, his support for family allowances rested on a fear that birth control had solved the Malthusian threat of overpopulation at the expense of other dangers: an ageing population, deterioration of the race, and the swamping of the 'advanced' races. In the 1930s, he was less concerned with population and more with poverty. Although male trade unionists continued to fear that 'Family Allowances will tend to dig at the roots of a virile Trade Unionsim', the TUC gave its reluctant support.[89]

Many of the proposals were implemented in the final stages of the war and by the Attlee government. A new Ministry of National Insurance was created in 1944, and the Family Allowances Act was introduced by the wartime coalition in 1945. In 1946, legislation was passed to reform both pensions and national insurance, complemented by the creation of national assistance in 1948. But perhaps the most striking change was in health. The National Health Act of 1946 took the hospitals into state control and made general practitioner services available to all, free of charge at the point of delivery. The National Health Service started in 1948.

The health care system faced widespread criticism before the war. Health insurance did not cover hospital care, and excluded non-working mothers and pre-school children. General practitioners complained that their payments were low, and medical independence was circumscribed by the approved societies. Insured patients felt they received second-class treatment compared with paying patients—who in turn resented the costs of private insurance or fees. Consultants in the voluntary hospitals complained of the lack of funding. The voluntary and public hospitals were not co-ordinated with each other, or with the various health services provided by the local authorities. These glaring problems of inefficiency and poor co-ordination were exposed by the pressures of war, and the creation of the Emergency Hospitals Scheme. Action seemed essential, and universalism was likely to be accepted. Indeed, the basic principles were laid down by the report on health services in 1920: a comprehensive, free, and equal service offering the best care to all.[90]

Nevertheless, the administrative structure of the medical service and its finance were highly contentious. Bitter conflict soon arose, despite the basic agreement on the problems facing the service. By 1939, the more progressive local authorities were running a wide range of services, and one approach was to make them the agents of change. After all, they were running the school medical service (1906), tuberculosis sanatoria (1911), infant and maternity clinics (1918), poor law hospitals (1929), and cancer clinics (1939). The Ministry of Health had long-standing relations with these authorities, and initially favoured such an approach. In 1944, the government suggested a system based on a health centre for primary care in each locality, with a district hospital run by a regional board. However, there were serious drawbacks. The medical officers of health were seen as conservative and lacking in the ability to run a larger service. Local authorities were also divided and hostile. The large urban authorities feared that they would lose power to the county councils. Doctors were alarmed, for localism would mean a loss of professional autonomy. General practitioners preferred to remain self-employed. Similarly, consultants in the voluntary hospitals were in favour of co-ordination, but not under the control of local authorities.

As a result, the local authorities retained their existing preventive and domiciliary services when hospitals—both public and voluntary—were nationalized. This solution cut through the animosities between local authorities, which were in any case facing other major tasks of reconstruction. It was more acceptable to the doctors, particularly as the minister, Aneurin Bevan, ceded the power of administering the NHS to them. The ministry appointed fourteen regional hospital boards in England and Wales and five in Scotland to rationalize the service; below them hospital management committees, similarly appointed by the minister, ran the hospitals. In England and Wales, the teaching hospitals remained separate with their own boards of governors, and in voluntary hospitals consultants were able to continue with their private practices. The hospital service lacked close democratic control, and to a very large extent was run by the medical profession. Meanwhile, the general practitioners retained their independence, despite Bevan's initial posturing. Their services were run by their own councils, with the practitioners receiving fees as self-employed contractors. Co-ordination with other local services was absent.

Despite the shortcomings, Bevan's achievement was to create a free and equal service for the whole population. Unlike in the social security services covered by Beveridge, contributions were reduced in importance. In 1938/9, the cost of health services in England and Wales was £66.0 m, with 17.0 per cent from social security contributions, 4.5 per cent from central taxes, 61.1 per cent from local taxes, and 17.4 per cent from voluntary contributions. The initial government proposals of 1944 would have raised the total cost to £132.0m, with 27.0 per cent from social security contributions, 36.6 per cent from central taxes, and 36.4 per cent from local taxes. In 1945, the new approach meant that the cost was expected to be £145.0 m, with 24.6 per cent from social security, 71.2 per cent from central taxes, and only 4.1 per cent from local taxes.[91]

The welfare state is seen by some historians as a sign of a wartime consensus. Others have their doubts, suggesting that 'national consensus was an artificially manufactured myth'. There was general agreement on the past failings of social policy, and a convergence on the main policies that were needed. The prudence of the Treasury, the wariness of civil servants, and the caution of Churchill were largely overcome. Although divisions remained, there was sufficient overlap and blurring to allow co-operation. Lowe suggests that there were two main views: the reluctant collectivists, including Beveridge and Keynes as well as moderate Conservatives, and the democratic socialists, who included many of the leading figures in the post-war government. The reluctant collectivists accepted the virtues of the free market as the best way of ensuring individual initiative and political freedom, but admitted that state intervention was needed to remove the flaws in the market. The democratic socialists were more critical, and wished to replace the free market in order to create a just and equal society. In practice, these democratic socialists saw the difficulties of their task. Equally, some of the reluctant collectivists become less reluctant. The two approaches could blur and overlap, agreeing on policies to rectify the social problems of capitalism despite their ideological divergence. The coalition's White Paper on full employment in 1944, for example, drew on both strands to agree on a commitment to full employment. A third position was marginalized: Hayek's outright commitment to a free market which Churchill attempted to utilize in 1945. When agreement re-emerged after 1947, it was largely the result of a mutual retreat from divergent positions. The Conservatives realized that their defeat in 1945 was in large part the result of ignoring social reform. Meanwhile, the economic crises of 1947 forced Labour to reconsider. As Rodney Lowe points out, the resulting consensus was not a positive commitment to shared policies, but a negative sense of what could not be done.[92]

This debate over consensus raises another question: what was the social basis of support for reform? The Conservatives' realization that they could not roll back the welfare state suggests that it was more than a response to the needs of the poor, for there was also a shift in the attitudes of the middle class. The reforms to social insurance and the NHS brought them within the system and gave them considerable benefits. The most obvious was the abolition of school fees, but it applied equally to other policies. Risk categories are not the same as social class. Although industrial workers are more liable to unemployment and accident, everyone is liable to illness, old age, and the costs of raising children. As well as redistribution from rich to poor, there are transfers over the life cycle, between healthy and sick, young and old, fit and disabled, employed and unemployed. Better-off people are more able to cope with these risks and are more likely to favour an exclusive risk pool through their own efforts. Poorer members of society are more likely to favour an inclusive risk pool which redistributes between high and low risk groups, above all when the system is financed by taxation. Of course, the division is not straightforward. Many white-collar workers were no better paid than skilled manual workers, and might not be able to cope with risk through their own devices. Indeed, less well-paid members of the middle class paying for their own medical treatment or pension might well be in a worse position than members of the working class covered by state insurance. Peter Baldwin argues that the emergence of a solidaristic welfare system owed much to the realization by many members of the middle class that risk and class were not coterminous, and that even they could gain from an inclusive risk pool. Indeed, studies in the 1950s and 1960s indicated that when tax breaks are taken into account the middle classes were amongst the largest beneficiaries of the welfare state. The choice between private and public provision did not necessarily matter to the better-off middle class, who might have used their resources to purchase their own welfare; the choice did matter to poorer families. By locking the middle classes into the welfare state, universalism created more support for the care of the poor. Middle-class acceptance of an inclusive or solidaristic form of welfare was partly a matter of self-interest, and of a realization that existing provision was inefficient and inadequate. Partly it was the result of a sense of social solidarity during wartime. Partly it reflected acceptance of the legitimacy of the state and taxation.[93]

Despite the stress on contributions and the ambition of full employment, there was still a major call on general taxation to cover the cost of pensions for those who had not paid contributions and to support the health service. Although health was not part of Beveridge's remit, he did suggest the creation of a free national health service. Not surprisingly, the Treasury became alarmed that Beveridge's proposals would raise the costs of welfare about threefold, with the prospect of continued increases. Beveridge pared the costs and reduced the level of benefits, so exposing the tensions between contributions and adequate benefits. Nevertheless, the Treasury remained concerned and some recent historians have reiterated their alarm, most notably Correlli Barnett. In his opinion, the welfare state undermined enterprise, diverted investment from industry and reconstruction, and drove up taxation with a consequent loss of incentives. The possible danger that high welfare spending and taxation would harm incentives was a common complaint, and one to which Labour was sensitive. It did not, however, develop a positive case in support of spending on welfare as leading to efficiency and higher productivity. Indeed, the government's Investment Programme Committee tried to contain the cost of welfare. Priority was given to housing and the IPC concentrated its cuts on capital spending on health. In 1951, new housing took 19.6 per cent of gross domestic fixed capital formation, education 3.1 per cent, and health services only 0.8 per cent. No new general hospital was built by the Attlee government, and the programme in 1949 was only a quarter of what had been anticipated before the war. Between 1938/9 and 1952/3, capital expenditure in hospitals fell by two-thirds in real terms. Welfare spending was not high compared with other European countries, and the countries spending large amounts on social welfare grew faster than those countries spending less. The post-war welfare state was austere.[94]

The criticism of the British welfare state could be rephrased: the problem was less the level of spending than what it was spent on and how it was funded. By the late 1950s and early 1960s a common Conservative complaint was that the welfare state was too dependent on general taxation. Despite Beveridge's hopes, national assistance expanded rather than declined with the result, so the critics argued, that high levels of taxation blunted incentives, with a transfer of resources from the general taxpayer to the employer. Would employers use their workforce more efficiently if they were obliged to pay more of the cost through larger contributions or a payroll tax, so encouraging them to switch to more capital-intensive production? The way the money was spent also differed. A lower proportion of spending went to workers who were temporarily sick or unemployed, but normally active in the labour market. More money went to people who were outside or marginal to the labour market. In other countries, the health service was in part financed from contributions from those in work; in Britain, it was available free to everyone, and was paid out of direct taxation.[95]

The welfare system in Britain in 1951 was far removed from the new poor law. Despite the survival of flat-rate contributions and benefits in the national insurance system rather than redistribution, Labour was pursuing a strategy of inclusion and fairness. Above all, the aim was to reduce insecurity and defeat poverty. Such a strategy did not necessarily mean that the gap between rich and poor was closed. The poor had a safety net; at the same time, better-off families gained from education and health care.[96] The emergence of the welfare state was linked with a desire to plan the economy and to provide full employment—ambitions far removed from 1851 when the government limited itself to providing the framework for the economy to function through free trade and stable money.

NOTES

1. For example, note the subtitle of Gilbert's study of the introduction of national insurance, *The Origins of the Welfare State*, or the title of Fraser's general history of social policy, *The Evolution of the British Welfare State*.
2. Middleton, *Government versus the Market*, tables 3.1 and 3.2, 90–1.
3. For example, Smith, 'Charity, self-interest and welfare'; Smith, 'Some issues concerning families and their property in rural England'; Laslett, 'Family, kinship and collectivity'.
4. For example, Miliband, *Capitalist Democracy* or Gough, *Political Economy of the Welfare State*.
5. Foucault, *Discipline and Punish*.
6. For example, Skocpol, *Protecting Soldiers and Mothers* and Orloff and Skocpol, 'Why not equal protection?'
7. Johnson, 'Risk, redistribution and social welfare'.
8. See Daunton, *Progress and Poverty*, 492–3.
9. Levitt and Smout, *State*, 152–3, 173–4, 177.
10. Ferguson, *Scottish Social Welfare*, ch. 11.
11. Rose, 'Allowance', 609, 618; Ashford, 'Urban poor law', 133, 138.
12. Rose, 'Crisis of poor relief', 64.

13. Thane, 'Old people and their families', 118–22; Lees, 'Survival of the unfit', 68–9, 72, 82–3, 87, 88.
14. Rose, 'Crisis of poor relief', 54–5.
15. Rose, 'Rochdale Man', 195, 199–201.
16. Hodgkinson, *Origins of the National Health Service*, ch. 14; Abel-Smith, *Hospitals*, 69–76.
17. Webb and Webb, *English Poor Law Policy*, 115–23; Abel-Smith, *Hospitals*, 84–5, 119–29.
18. Webb and Webb, *English Poor Law Policy*, 264.
19. Webb and Webb, *English Poor Law Policy*, 207–9; Hobson, *Social Problem*, 201.
20. Abel-Smith, *Hospitals*, 90–4, 106–7; Hodgkinson, *Origins of the National Health Service*, 215.
21. Abel-Smith, *Hospitals*, 89, 125, 130–2, 200–2, 206.
22. Ibid., 200.
23. Styles, 'Evolution'; Feldman, 'Migration', 200–1 and *Englishmen and Jews*, 289–90.
24. On COS see Stedman Jones, *Outcast London*, part III; Rose, *English Poor Law*, 222–34.
25. Harris, *Unemployment*, 75–6, 90; Brown, *Labour and Unemployment*.
26. Ryan, 'Politics and relief', 163–5.
27. Crowther, *Workhouse System*, 57; Ashforth, 'Urban poor law', 135.
28. *Local Government Board, 29th Annual Report, 1899–1900*, 362.
29. Webb and Webb, *English Poor Law Policy*, ch. 5, 274–7.
30. Harris, 'Transition to high politics', 63.
31. Davis and Tanner, 'Borough franchise', 312, 314, 317–18, 321, 326; Matthew, McKibbin, and Kay, 'Franchise factor', 725–9, 733.
32. Duffy, 'New unionism'; Thane, 'Working class and state "welfare"'.
33. Marwick, 'Labour party and the welfare state'; Clarke, 'Edwardians', 52.
34. Hay, 'Employers and social policy', 440, 444, 454.
35. Macnicol, *Politics of Retirement*, 23, 126–31, 134; Thane, *Old Age in English History*, 216–18, 280, 286.
36. Skocpol and Amenta, 'States and social policies'; Skocpol and Amenta, 'Did capitalists shape social security?', 574.
37. For this general approach, see Ikenberry and Skocpol, 'Expanding state benefits'.
38. Hennock, *British Social Reform and German Precedents*, 208–9
39. Price, *Masters, Unions and Men*, 201, 207.
40. Phillips and Whiteside, *Casual Labour*; for the alternative view, see Holton, *British Syndicalism*.
41. Samuel, preface to Llewelyn Davies, *Maternity*.
42. Maurice, 'The nation's health', 50–1.
43. In preface to Llewelyn Davies, *Maternity*, unnumbered page; see also Davin, 'Imperialism'.
44. Szreter, *Fertility*, 227.
45. Crook, *Benjamin Kidd*, 57–60; Collini, *Liberalism and Sociology*, 26–9, Geddes, *Cities in Evolution* 75, 388–92, 400–2.
46. Skocpol, *Protecting Soldiers and Mothers*; Orloff and Skocpol, 'Why not equal protection?'; Pederson, *Family Dependence and the Origins of the Welfare State*.
47. Hennock, 'Poverty and social theory', 89; Brown, 'Charles Booth and labour colonies'.
48. Hennock, 'Poverty and social theory'.

49. Tawney, *The Establishment of Minimum Rates*; Ensor, 'Case for a legal minimum wage'.
50. Beveridge, *Unemployment*.
51. Hobson, *Imperialism*; Chiozza Money, *Riches and Poverty*.
52. See Ikenberry and Skocpol, 'Expanding social benefits', 400–1.
53. Dicey, *Lectures*, XXXV, XXXVII, XXXVIII.
54. Webb and Webb *English Poor Law Policy*, 268.
55. Webb, *Diary*, iii. 151–2.
56. McBriar, *Edwardian Mixed Doubles*, 158; *Fabian Essays*, 58; Webb, Diary, iii, 45, 77, 100, 118, 151–3, 158–9; Beveridge, *Power and Influence*, 66.
57. Clarke, *Liberals and Social Democrats*, 14–15; McBriar, *Edwardian Mixed Doubles*, 6–7, 57, 84, 121, 122, 285, 323–4, 340–1, 359, 362, 368, 369, 378; Collini, 'Hobhouse', 92.
58. Hobhouse, *Liberalism*, 54, 60, 63, 66, 69, 76.
59. Churchill. *Liberalism and the Social Problem*, 82, 376.
60. Hennock, *German Precedents*, 191.
61. Ibid. 189–196.
62. Ikenberry and Skocpol, 'Expanding social benefits', 397.
63. Phillips and Whiteside, *Casual Labour*, 108.
64. Andrzejewski, *Military Organization and Society*.
65. Quoted Dwork, *War is Good for Babies*, 213.
66. Keynes, *Economic Consequences of the Peace*, 91; Abrams, 'Failure of social reform', 45–6, 62; see also Marwick, *The Deluge*, 350–3.
67. Lowe, 'Erosion', 270–86, Abel-Smith, *Hospitals*, ch. 18; Crowther, *British Social Policy*, 33; Simon, *Politics of Educational Reform*, 25, 27, 50; Swenarton, *Homes Fit for Heroes*; for a good general account, see Morgan, *Consensus and Disunity*, chapter on 'Priorities and Policies: Social Reform', 80–108.
68. Peacock and Wiseman, *Growth of Public Expenditure*, 184–91.
69. Cohen, *War Come Home*, 7.
70. Quoted in Finlayson, *Citizen, State, and Social Welfare*, 325.
71. Ibid., ch. 3; Hayburn, 'Voluntary occupational centre movement', 157; Macadam, *New Philanthropy*, 67–71, 210–3; Olechnowicz, *Working-Class Housing*, 165–171; Harris, 'Voluntary action and unemployment'; Harris, 'Government and charity'.
72. Thane, *Foundations*, 192; Daunton, 'Payment and participation', 191–3.
73. Ryan, 'Poor law in 1926', 361–2, 363, 371, 375; Branson, *Poplarism*, 58, 114, 116, 119; Webb and Webb, *English Poor Law History*, ii. 834–45; Thane, *Foundations*, 186; Crowther, *Workhouse System*, 78, 79, 103–6.
74. Daunton, 'Payment and participation', 201–4.
75. Pickstone, *Medicine and Industrial Society*, 272, 278–83.
76. Daunton, 'Payment and participation', 182–6; Whiteside, 'Private agencies for public purposes', 186.
77. Macnicol, *Politics of Retirement*, 162, 203; Thane, *Old Age in English History*.
78. Whiteside, *Bad Times*, 72–85; Gilbert, *British Social Policy*, 162–75; Garside, *British Unemployment*, 31–83; Whiteside, 'Welfare legislation', 861, 866, 867; Harris, *William Beveridge*, 352.
79. Whiteside, *Bad Times*, 72–7.

80. Harris, *William Beveridge*, 353–6.

81. Ibid. 360; Vincent, *Poor Citizens*, 62.

82. Prochaska, *Women and Philanthropy*; Lewis, 'Women, social work and social welfare', 204–6, 210, 219–20.

83. Thane, *Foundations*, 173, 174, 217; Vincent, *Poor Citizens*, 206.

84. Harris, *William Beveridge*, 420–6.

85. Ibid. 378–9, 381–2.

86. Beveridge, *Social Insurance and Allied Services*, 6–7, 170; Harris, *William Beveridge*, 346; Harris, 'Beveridge's social and political thought'.

87. On inter-war thinking, see Harris, *William Beveridge*, and on his thinking on full employment, 142, 346–61, 391, 417–18, 428–41.

88. Harris, *William Beveridge*, 402–7; Lowe, *Welfare State*, 33–6; Thane, 'Women in the British Labour party', 361, 373; Pederson, *Family Dependence*, 290–1, 294, 339, 354–6.

89. Harris, *William Beveridge*, 341–6, 390; Pedersen, *Family Dependence*, 289, 294.

90. Lowe, *Welfare State*, 167, 170–83; Webster, *National Health Service*, 3–5.

91. Webster, *National Health Service*, 23.

92. Addison, *Road to 1945*; Jeffreys, 'British politics'; Harris, 'Political values', 238–9, 256–7; Lowe, 'Second World War', 159, 161, 166–9, 180–1; Lowe, *Welfare State*, 16–27.

93. Baldwin, *Politics of Social Solidarity*, 10–31, 296–8.

94. Harris, *William Beveridge*, 407–12; Macnicol, *Politics of Retirement*, 289, 354, 398; Barnett, *Audit of War*, 239–42; Tomlinson, *Democratic Socialism*, 259–62; Chick, *Industrial Policy in Britain*, 31–4; Tomlinson, *Democratic Socialism*, 248; Harris, 'Enterprise and welfare', 44–5.

95. Harris, 'Enterprise and the welfare state', 43–4, 46–51; Daunton, *Just Taxes*, 311–3.

96. Tomlinson, *Democratic Socialism*, 265–70.

FURTHER READING

Abel-Smith, B., *The Hospitals, 1800–1948: A Study in Social Administration in England and Wales* (1964)

Abrams, P., 'The failure of social reform 1918–20', *Past and Present*, 24 (1963)

Addison, P., *The Road to 1945: British Politics and the Second World War* (1975)

Anderson, O., *Rights and Wrongs in Mid-Victorian England* (1988)

Andrzejewski, S., *Military Organization and Society* (1954)

Ashforth, D., 'Settlement and removal in urban areas: Bradford, 1834–71', in M. E. Rose (ed.), *The Poor and the City* (1985)

Baldwin, P., *The Politics of Social Solidarity: Class Bases of the European Welfare State 1875–1975* (Cambridge, 1990)

Barnett, C., *Audit of War: The Illusion and Reality of Britain as a Great Nation* (1986)

Beveridge, W., *Unemployment: A Problem of Industry* (1909)

—— *Social Insurance and Allied Services* (1942)

Brand, J. L., *Doctors and the State: The British Medical Profession and Government Action in Public Health, 1870–1912* (1965)

Branson, N., *Poplarism, 1919–25: George Lansbury and the Councillors' Revolt* (1979)

Briggs, E., and Deacon, A., 'The creation of the Unemployment Assistance Board', *Policy and Politics*, 11 (1973)

Brown, J., 'Charles Booth and labour colonies, 1889–1905', *Economic History Review*, 21 (1968)

—— *Labour and Unemployment, 1900–14* (Newton Abbot, 1971)

Burrow, J., *Evolution and Society: A Study in Victorian Social Theory* (Cambridge, 1966)

Chick, M., *Industrial Policy in Britain 1945–1951: Economic Planning, Nationalisation and the Labour Governments* (Cambridge, 1998)

Chiozza Money, L., *Riches and Poverty* (1910)

Churchill, W. S., *Liberalism and the Social Problem* (1909)

Clarke, P. F., *Liberals and Social Democrats* (Cambridge, 1978)

—— 'The Edwardians and the constitution', in D. Reed (ed.), *Edwardian England* (1982)

Cohen, D., *The War Come Home: Disabled Veterans in Britain and Germany, 1914–1939* (Berkeley, 2000)

Collini, S., 'Hobhouse, Bosanquet and the state', *Past and Present*, 72 (1976)

—— *Liberalism and Sociology: L. T. Hobhouse and Political Argument in England 1880–1914* (Cambridge, 1979)

Coplon, M., 'The new poor law and the struggle for union changeability', *International Review of Social History*, 23 (1972)

Crook, D. P., *Benjamin Kidd: Portrait of a Social Darwinist* (1984)

Crowther, M. A., *The Workhouse System, 1834–1929: The History of an English Social Institution* (1981)

—— 'Family responsibility and state responsibility in Britain before the welfare state', *Historical Journal*, 25 (1982)

—— *British Social Policy 1914–1939* (1988)

Daunton, M., *Progress and Poverty: An Economic and Social History of Britain, 1700–1850* (Oxford, 1995)

—— 'Payment and participation: welfare and state formation in Britain, 1900–51', *Past and Present*, 150 (1996)

—— *Just Taxes: The Politics of Taxation in Britain, 1914–79* (Cambridge, 2002)

Davidson, R., 'The Board of Trade and industrial relations, 1896–1914', *Historical Journal*, 21 (1978)

Davin, A., 'Imperialism and motherhood', *History Workshop*, 5 (1978)

Davis, J., and Tanner, D., 'The borough franchise after 1867', *Historical Research*, 69 (1996)

Deacon, A., *In Search of the Scrounger: The Administration of Unemployment Insurance in Britain 1920–31* (1976)

—— 'Concession and coercion: the politics of unemployment insurance in the 1920s', in A. Briggs and J. Saville (eds.), *Essays in Labour History 1918–39* (1977)

—— and Briggs, E., 'Local democracy and central policy: the issue of pauper votes in the 1920s', *Policy and Politics*, 2 (1974)

Dicey, A. V., *Lectures and the Relation between Law and Public Opinion in England during the Nineteenth Century* (1914)

Duffy, A. E. P., 'New unionism in Britain, 1889–90: a reappraisal', *Economic History Review*, 2 (1961–2)

Dwork, D., *War is Good for Babies and Other Young Children: A History of the Infant and Child Welfare Movement in England 1898–1918* (1987)

Eder, N. R., *National Health Insurance and the Medical Profession in Britain 1913–39* (New York, 1982)

Feldman, D., *Englishmen and Jews: Social Relations and Political Culture, 1840–1914* (New Haven, 1994)

—— 'Migration', in M. Daunton (ed.), *The Cambridge Urban History of Britain*, iii: *1840–1950* (Cambridge, 2000)

Ferguson, T., *Scottish Social Welfare, 1864–1914* (1958)

Finlayson, G., *Citizen, State, and Social Welfare in Britain 1830–1990* (Oxford, 1994)

Foucault, M., *Discipline and Punish: The Birth of the Prison* (Harmondsworth, 1979)

Fox, D. M., *Health Policies, Health Politics? The British and American Experience 1911–65* (Princeton, 1986)

Fraser, D. (ed.), *The New Poor Law in the Nineteenth Century* (1976)

Garside, W. R., 'Juvenile employment and public policy between the wars', *Economic History Review*, 30 (1977)

—— 'Unemployment and the school leaving age in interwar Britain', *International Review of Social History*, 26 (1981)

—— *British Unemployment, 1919–1939: A Study in Public Policy* (Cambridge, 1990)

Geddes, P., *Cities in Evolution: An introduction to the Town Planning Movement and to the Study of Civics* (1915)

Gilbert, B. B., *The Evolution of National Insurance: The Origins of the Welfare State* (1966)

—— 'Winston Churchill versus the Webbs: the origins of British unemployment insurance', *American Historical Review*, 71 (1966)

—— *British Social Policy, 1914–1939* (1970)

Gough, I., *Political Economy of the Welfare State* (1979)

Halliday, R. J., 'Social Darwinism: a definition', *Victorian Studies* (1971)

Harris, B., 'Voluntary action and unemployment: charity in the south Wales coalfield between the wars', in E. Aerts and B. Eichengreen (eds.), *Unemployment and Underemployment in Historical Perspective* (Leuven, 1990)

—— 'Government and charity in the depressed mining areas of England and Wales, 1928–30', in J. Barry and C. Jones (eds.), *Medicine and Charity in Western Europe before the Welfare State* (1991)

Harris, J., *Unemployment and Politics: A Study in English Social Policy, 1886–1914* (Oxford, 1972)

—— *William Beveridge: A Biography* (Oxford, 1977)

—— 'Enterprise and the welfare state: a comparative perspective', in T. Gourvish and A. O'Day (eds.), *Britain since 1945* (Basingstoke, 1991)

—— 'The transition to high politics in English social policy, 1880–1914', in M. Bentley and J. Stevenson (eds.), *High and Low Politics in Modern Britain* (Oxford, 1983)

—— 'Political values and the debate on state welfare, 1940–45', in H. Smith (ed.), *War and Social Change* (Manchester, 1986)

—— 'Beveridge's social and political thought', in J. Hills, J. Ditch, and H. Glennerster (eds.), *Beveridge and Social Security: An International Perspective* (Oxford, 1994)

Hay, J. R., 'Employers and social policy in Britain: the evolution of welfare legislation, 1905–14', Social History, 4 (1977)

—— The Development of the British Welfare State, 1880–1975 (1978)

—— 'The British business community, social insurance and the German example', in W. J. Mommsen (ed.). The Emergence of the Welfare State in Britain and Germany (1981)

Hayburn, R. H. C., 'The voluntary occupational centre movement, 1932–39', Journal of Contemporary History, 3 (1971)

Hennock, E. P., 'The origins of British national insurance and the German precedent, 1880–1914', in W. J. Mommsen (ed.) Emergence of the Welfare State in Britain and Germany (1981)

—— British Social Reform and German Precedents: The Case of Social Insurance, 1880–1914 (Oxford, 1987)

—— 'Poverty and social theory in England: the experience of the 1880s', Social History, 1 (1976)

Hobhouse, L. T., 'Liberalism and other writings', in J. Meadowcraft (ed.), Cambridge Texts in the History of Political Thought (Cambridge, 1994)

Hobson, J. A., Imperialism: A Study (1902)

—— The Social Problem (1901)

Hodgkinson, R., The Origins of the National Health Service: The Medical Services of the New Poor Law, 1834–71 (1967)

Holton, B., British Syndicatlism, 1900–14: Myths and Realities (1976)

Honigsbaum, F., The Division of British Medicine, 1911–68 (1980)

Ikenberry, S. J., and Skocpol, T., 'Expanding social benefits: the role of social security', Political Science Quarterly, 102 (1987)

Jeffreys, K., 'British politics and social policy during the Second World War', Historical Journal, 30 (1987)

Johnson, P., Saving and Spending: The Working-Class Economy in Britain, 1870–1939 (Oxford, 1985)

—— 'Risk, redistribution and social welfare in Britain from the poor law to Beveridge', in M. Daunton (ed.), Charity, Self-Interest and Welfare in the English Past (1996)

Keynes, J. M., Economic Consequences of the Peace (1919)

Kidd, A. J., 'Charity organization and the unemployed in Manchester, c.1870–1914', Social History, 9 (1984)

Koven, S., and Michel, S. (eds.) Mothers of a New World: Maternalist Politics and the Origins of the Welfare States (1993)

Lambert, R., 'A Victorian national health service: state vaccination, 1858–71', Historical Journal, 5 (1962)

Laslett, P., 'Family, kinship and collectivities as systems of support in pre-industrial Europe: a consideration of the "nuclear hardship" hypothesis', Continuity and Change, 3 (1988)

Lees, L. H., 'The survival of the unfit: welfare policies and family maintenance in nineteenth-century London', in P. Mandler (ed.), The Uses of Charity: The Poor on Relief in the Nineteenth-Century Metropolis (Philadelphia, 1990)

—— The Solidarities of Strangers: The English Poor Laws and the People, 1700–1948 (Cambridge, 1998)

Levitt, I., 'The Scottish poor law and unemployment, 1890–1929', in T. C. Smout (ed.), *The Search for Wealth and Stability* (1979)

—— and Smout, T. C., *The State of the Scottish Working-Class in 1843* (Edinburgh, 1979)

Lewis, J., 'Women, social work and social welfare', in M. Daunton (ed.) *Charity, Self-Interest and Welfare in the English Past* (1996)

—— *The Politics of Motherhood: Child and Maternal Welfare in England, 1900–39* (1980)

Llewelyn Davies, M., *Maternity: Letters from Working Women Collected by the Women's Co-operative Guild* (1915, Virago edition, 1978)

Lowe, R., 'The Ministry of Labour 1916–24: a graveyard of social reform?', *Public Administration*, 52 (1974)

—— 'The erosion of state intervention in Britain, 1917–24', *Economic History Review*, 31 (1978)

—— *Adjusting to Democracy: The Role of the Ministry of Labour in British Politics, 1916–39* (Oxford, 1986)

—— 'The Second World War, consensus, and the foundation of the welfare state', *Twentieth Century British History*, 1 (1990)

—— J. 'A prophet dishonoured in his own country? The rejection of Beveridge in Britain, 1945–70', in J. Hills, J. Ditch, and H. Glennerster (eds.), *Beveridge and Social Security* (Oxford, 1994)

—— *The Welfare State in Britain since 1945* (2nd edn., Basingstoke, 1999)

Macadam, E., *The New Philanthropy: A Study of the Relations between the Statutory and Voluntary Social Services* (1934)

McBriar, A. M., *An Edwardian Mixed Doubles: The Bosanquets versus the Webbs: A Study in British Social Policy, 1890–1929* (Oxford, 1987)

McKibbin, R., *The Ideologies of Class: Social Relations in Britain, 1880–1950* (Oxford, 1990)

MacLeod, R. M., 'Law, medicine and public opinion: the resistance to compulsory health legislation, 1870–1907', *Public Law*, 12 (1967)

—— 'The frustration of state medicine, 1830–1900', *Medical History* (1967)

Macnicol, J., *The Movement for Family Allowances 1918–45* (1981)

—— *The Politics of Retirement in Britain, 1878–1948* (Cambridge, 1998)

Marwick, A., 'The Labour party and the welfare state in Britain, 1900–48', *American Historical Review*, 73 (1967–8)

—— *The Deluge: British Society and the First World War* (1965)

Matthew, H. C. G., McKibbin, R. I., and Kay, J. A., 'The franchise factor in the rise of the Labour party', *English Historical Review*, 91 (1976)

Maurice, J. F., 'The nation's health: a soldier's study', *Contemporary Review* (1903)

Middleton, R., *Government versus the Market: The Growth of the Public Sector, Economic Management and British Economic Performance c.1890–1979* (Cheltenham, 1996)

Miliband, R., *Capitalist Democracy in Britain* (1982)

Mitchison, R., 'The making of the Scottish old poor law', *Past and Present*, 63 (1974)

Morgan, K. O., *Consensus and Disunity: The Lloyd George Coalition Government, 1918–22* (Oxford, 1979)

Olechnowicz, A., *Working-Class Housing between the Wars: The Becontree Estate* (Oxford, 1997)

O'Neill, J. E., 'Finding a policy for the sick poor', *Victorian Studies*, 7 (1964)

Orloff, A. S., and Skocpol, T., 'Why not equal protection? Explaining the politics of public social spending in Britain, 1900–11, and the United States, 1880–1920', *American Sociological Review*, 49 (1984)

Peacock, A., and Wiseman, J., *The Growth of Public Expenditure in the United Kingdom* (1960)

Pederson, S., *Family Dependence and the Origins of the Welfare State: Britain and France, 1914–1945* (Cambridge, 1993)

Pelling, H., 'The working class and the origins of the welfare state', in H. Pelling, *Popular Politics and Society in Late Victorian Britain: Essays* (1968)

Phillips, G., and Whiteside, N., *Casual Labour: The Unemployment Question in the Port Transport Industry, 1880–1970* (Oxford, 1985)

Pickstone, J., *Medicine and Industrial Society: A History of Hospital Development in Manchester and its Region, 1752–1946* (Manchester, 1985)

Price, R., *Masters, Unions and Men: Work Control in Building and the Price of Labour, 1830–1914* (Cambridge, 1990)

Prochaska, F. K., *Women and Philanthropy in Nineteenth-Century England* (Oxford, 1980)

Rivett, G., *The Development of the London Hospital System, 1823–1982* (1986)

Rose, M. E., 'The allowance system under the new poor law', *Economic History Review*, 19 (1966)

—— (ed.), *The Poor and the City: The English Poor Law in its Urban Context, 1834–1914* (1985)

—— 'The crisis of poor relief in England, 1850–90', in W. J. Mommsen (ed.), *The Emergence of the Welfare State in Britain and Germany 1850–1950* (1981)

—— *The English Poor Law, 1780–1930* (Newton Abbot, 1971)

—— 'Rochdale Man and the Stalybridge riot', in A. P. Donajgrodski (ed.), *Social Control in Nineteenth-Century Britain* (1977)

Ryan, P., 'Politics and relief: East London unions in the late nineteenth and early twentieth centuries', in M. E. Rose (ed.) *The Poor and the City* (Leicester, 1985)

—— 'The poor law in 1926', in M. Morris (ed.), *The General Strike* (Harmondsworth, 1976)

Simon, B., *The Politics of Educational Reform 1920–40* (1974)

Skocpol, T. *Protecting Soldiers and Mothers: The Political Origins of Social Policy in the United States* (Cambridge, Mass., 1992)

—— and Amenta, E., 'States and social policies', *Annual Review of Sociology*, 12 (1986)

—— —— 'Did capitalists shape social security?', *American Sociological Review*, 50 (1985)

Smith, R. M., 'Charity, self-interest and welfare', in M. Daunton (ed.), *Charity, Self-Interest and Welfare in the English Past* (1996)

—— 'Some issues concerning families and their property in rural England, 1250–1800', in R. M. Smith (ed.), *Land, Kinship and Life Cycle* (Cambridge, 1984)

Soloway, R. A., *Birth Control and the Population Question in England, 1877–1930* (Chapel Hill, 1982)

Styles, P., 'The evolution of the law of settlement', *University of Birmingham Historical Journal*, 9 (1963–4)

Swenarton, M., *Homes Fit for Heroes: The Politics and Architecture of Early State Housing in Britain* (1981)

Szreter, S., *Fertility, Class and Gender in Britain, 1860–1940* (Cambridge, 1996)

Tawney, R. H., *The Establishment of Minimum Rates in the Tailoring Industry under the Trade Boards Act of 1909* (1915)

Thane, P., 'The working class and state "welfare" in Britain, 1880–1914', *Historical Journal*, 27 (1984)

—— (ed.), *The Origins of British Social Policy* (1978)

—— 'Women and the poor law in Victorian and Edwardian England', *History Workshop Journal*, 6 (1978)

—— 'Women in the British Labour party and the construction of state welfare, 1906–39', in S. Koven and S. Michel (eds.) *Mothers of a New World: Maternalist Politics and the Origins of Welfare States* (1993)

—— *The Foundations of the Welfare State* (1982)

—— 'Old people and their families in the English past', in M. Daunton (ed.), *Charity, Self-Interest and Welfare in the English Past* (1996)

—— *Old Age in English History: Past Experiences, Present Issues* (Oxford, 2000)

Tomlinson, J., *Democratic Socialism and Economic Policy: The Attlee Years, 1945–51* (Cambridge, 1997)

Vincent, D., *Poor Citizens: The State and the Poor in Twentieth-Century Britain* (1991)

Webb, B., *The Diary of Beatrice Webb, iii: 1905–23: The Power to Alter Things*, ed. N. Mackenzie (1984)

Webb, S., and Webb, B., *English Poor Law Policy* (1910)

—— —— *English Poor Law History*, 2 vols. (1927–9)

Webster, C., *The National Health Service: A Political History* (Oxford, 1998)

Whiteside, N., 'Welfare legislation and the unions during the First World War', *Historical Journal*, 23 (1980)

—— 'Industrial welfare and labour regulation in Britain at the time of the First World War', *International Review of Social History*, 25 (1980)

—— 'Private agencies for public purposes: some new perspectives on policy making in health insurance between the wars', *Journal of Social Policy*, 51 (1983)

—— *Bad Times: Unemployment in British Social and Political History* (1991)

....

CHAPTER 17

Managing the Economy

In 1930, Winston Churchill reflected on the change in the nature of politics during a career that had taken him from involvement in new Liberal social reforms before the First World War to Chancellor of the Exchequer in the Conservative government of 1924–9. Only since the First World War, he suggested, had economic issues intruded into politics.[1] Perhaps he was exaggerating the change, for the election of 1906 was fought on an economic issue and he had himself abandoned the Conservative party in opposition to tariff reform. Welfare reform had an economic dimension, as his own speeches made clear: the reform of the labour market and creation of an efficient capitalist system.

Nevertheless, Churchill did have a point. Before the First World War, the government left the economy to the free play of the market, which was itself shaped by state action. At home, protection and monopolies were removed; overseas, the British government used its influence to encourage other nation-states to reduce tariff barriers. The government took steps to prevent new forms of monopoly in the network and utility industries from exploiting consumers. These industries needed government action to operate; and they were regulated or even taken into public ownership. Banks and the money supply were controlled by the Bank Charter Act of 1844 and by the gold standard. The tax system did not alter the balance between groups and interests; and a legal framework was laid down for trade unions and friendly societies. The state was therefore active in shaping the market and its institutions.

These discussions of the nature of the market were cast in terms of morality and character. The political culture of free trade embodied normative assumptions about how the economy should function. In industrial relations, recognition of trade unions was a means of creating stability and harmony in class relations. The Bank Charter Act rested on the moral assumption that tight credit would purge the economy of speculative excess. Similarly, the law on bankruptcy and credit made assumptions about the virtues of risk and the vices of speculation. Furthermore, the tax system was not used to shape the economy, though it did contain assumptions about thrift and the role of incentives. The government was therefore deeply involved in setting the context for economic life; what it did not attempt was to influence the total level of activity.

Once the basic legislative and institutional structures were laid down, the Bank rate and level of money supply were not used to influence the level of activity or prices in the economy. Labour relations, free trade, and the gold standard 'represented the exclusion of "economics" from "politics"'. The result was, in the words of Ross McKibbin, 'a viable class-neutral state' which did not side with either labour or capital, and stood back to allow them to resolve their own conflicts.[2] On this view, the government could no more determine the level of activity in the economy than it could alter the weather.

At first sight, the Liberal government of 1906–14 marked a change by embarking on an extensive programme of social reform. But it still did not aim to change the total level of activity in the economy. By contrast, the general election of 1929 marked a change in the tenor of political debate. The ability of the state to end unemployment was at the centre of politics. Churchill's erstwhile colleague in the pre-war social reforms, David Lloyd George, now believed that the government could restore prosperity. The Liberal manifesto made a bold claim:

If the nation entrusts the Liberal Party . . . with the responsibilities of Government, we are ready with schemes of work which we can put immediately into operation . . . The work put in hand will reduce the terrible figures of the workless in the course of a single year to normal proportions, and will, when completed, enrich the nation and equip it for competing successfully.[3]

Keynes was involved in these schemes for public works and an active policy of state spending. In the event, the Conservative government lost the election not to the Liberals but to a minority Labour administration. The new approach did not convince everyone—above all the Treasury.

Churchill's experience as Chancellor allowed him to define, with his usual force, the existing conventions of economy policy as seen by the Treasury:

The classical doctrines of economics have for nearly a century found their citadels in the Treasury and the Bank of England. In their pristine vigour these doctrines comprise among others the following tenets: Free imports . . . Ruthless direct taxation for the repayment of debt . . . Rigorous economy in all forms of expenditure . . . Stern assertion of the rights of the creditor, national or private, and full and effectual discharge of all liabilities. Profound distrust of State-stimulated industry . . . or of State borrowing. . . . Absolute reliance upon private enterprise . . .[4]

Most of these principles would have been familiar to Gladstone. For his part, Churchill played with heretical approaches to economic policy during his own time at the Treasury. Although he defended free trade against tariff reformers in the Conservative party and returned to the gold standard, he feared that placing too much emphasis on repaying the national debt would weaken the competitiveness of British industry. For this reason, he was willing to use somewhat devious methods to maintain the appearance of a balanced budget while actually spending more money than the government was receiving. But his flirtation with unorthodox finance was tentative. The belief in rigorous economy, the discharge of liabilities, and the distrust of state-stimulated industry and employment remained in the ascendant. These assumptions were summed up in the concept of the 'balanced budget', the belief that the state should never spend more than it received.

During the Labour government of 1929–31, Oswald Mosley picked up the approach of Lloyd George and the Liberals, arguing for a programme of public works. When his schemes were rejected, Mosley abandoned Labour and created the New party before forming the British Union of Fascists.[5] When the Labour government collapsed and a new National government was formed, the Chancellor, Neville Chamberlain, remained firmly committed to the need to balance the budget. Although Keynes continued to argue for public expenditure and public works, and a large number of economists wrote to The Times urging a shift in policy, the National government and the Treasury remained suspicious.

The history of economic policy in the 1930s and 1940s was initially written as a battle between Keynes and the Treasury. On this account, ignorance was in the ascendant and Keynes's solution of loan-financed public works was rejected as a result of dogmatic blindness. Civil servants at the Treasury, leading politicians, and economists outside Keynes's Cambridge disciples appeared to be misguided and perverse. The Second World War brought Keynes into the Treasury with a group of young economists who developed the national income accounts which informed the budget of 1941. Ignorance was in retreat and a Keynesian revolution was under way which resolved the problems of the depression of the 1930s and delivered full employment. This interpretation was the product of a historical moment, reflecting both the hegemony of Keynesian economists in the 1950s and 1960s, and the closure of the official papers which allowed Keynes's forceful account to dominate. The depression of the 1930s was therefore interpreted as an unnecessary product of the triumph of ignorance over wisdom.

This account faced a challenge as the attractions of Keynesian policies became less apparent in the 1970s. By the late 1970s, monetarism was to the fore, and the fiscal discipline of the 1930s seemed more appealing to Conservative politicians. Historical understanding of the 1930s was influenced by the changing economic and political context of the 1970s and 1980s, so that it was now Keynes who was attacked. Perhaps, it now seemed, the Treasury was wise to maintain balanced budgets and to avoid 'feather-bedding' decaying industries. Of course, not everyone in the 1980s accepted the Thatcherite agenda, but the ideological ground had shifted. The picture was also changed by the opening of government papers so that historians had access to the thinking of the Treasury. In the words of one historian, 'the Keynesian condemnation of interwar policy-makers has been both misdirected and myopically over-confident'.[6] The Treasury was concerned with administrative practicality and political pragmatism; it had an analytical model of the economy and its own carefully considered response to the economic problems of the 1930s. There was more than a division between rigid Treasury orthodoxy (or error) and a Keynesian alternative (or truth).

The Treasury versus Keynes

The Treasury view should be understood in three interconnected ways. First, it rested on a number of theoretical propositions drawn from classical and neo-classical economics. Keynes came to the realization that the policies he had been advocating since the late 1920s would not be accepted until the theoretical underpinnings of the Treasury were undermined. Second, it drew on the Gladstonian conventions of state finance. Third, it rested on immediate political contingencies. Together, these formed a formidable barrier against Keynes's heterodoxy.

The Treasury view assumed that the economy is normally in equilibrium, with resources fully utilized and demand and supply in balance; any deviation was short term and self-correcting. By the end of the nineteenth century, unemployment was less readily blamed on the moral failings of workers but the basic assumption remained that work was available. As we have seen, Beveridge's analysis of unemployment assumed that labour exchanges would provide information to dockers to find work anywhere on the waterfront rather than turning up at hiring stands where work might not be available. Once dockers had knowledge of the demand for labour, the curse of casual underemployment would be lifted. Beveridge did not entertain the possibility that full employment of some dockers would mean unemployment for others: if workers had knowledge of the existence of jobs, everyone could be employed. Markets would clear and all resources would find their use.[7]

Keynes's ideas were also criticized by R. G. Hawtrey who used the quantity theory of money to explain the economic problems of the 1920s. In his view, the supply of money set the level of prices, with income and employment determined by productivity and thrift. The trade cycle was a monetary phenomenon, and it followed that the government should rely on monetary policies rather than increasing public spending. However, his analysis was not welcomed by his colleagues or the Bank in the 1920s, for it implied that the main reason for depression was the pursuit of high interest rates to return to gold. In his view, the Bank should have reduced interest rates and denuded its gold reserves. He argued that an expansion in credit and a reduction in Bank rate would be as effective as public works in creating employment. Only after the abandonment of gold in 1931 did the Treasury accept the thrust of Hawtrey's argument.[8]

Hawtrey was more in tune with general thinking in the Treasury in the 1920s when he argued that a policy of financing public works from 'genuine savings' would merely shift private expenditure into the hands of the state without increasing the total volume of employment. Here was the basic proposition of the Treasury view: spending on public works would 'crowd out' private investment. In 1921, Stanley Baldwin defined the Treasury view: 'Money taken for government purposes is money taken from trade and borrowing will thus tend to depress trade and increase unemployment.' As Churchill put it with more panache, 'It is to be hoped that we shall not let ourselves be drawn by panic or electioneering into unsound schemes to cure unemployment, and divert national credit and savings from the fertile channels of private enterprise to State undertakings fomented mainly for political purposes.' In the Treasury's view, Keynes's policy of public works would make matters worse. High labour costs and welfare benefits were already encouraging consumption and reducing savings. The result of higher spending on public works would merely lead to 'the transference of labour and capital from exports to internal development works'. The only way to prevent crowding out was by expanding credit. This would avoid diverting money away from private enterprise. But as Hawtrey put it, resorting to credit expansion in order to finance public works 'is to burn down the house for the sake of the roast pig', that is, destroying the economy for short-term gains. Since the Liberals denied that their scheme would cause inflation, it followed that there would be crowding out of domestic investment. This outcome was not necessarily harmful, for he noted that investment overseas might even be desirable to encourage more exports as was believed to have happened before the war. What Hawtrey did admit was that loan-financed public works might be sensible in 'exceptional circumstances', when investors could not find a profitable use for their funds and held them as idle balances. The Treasury was therefore more flexible than its critics allowed.[9]

Keynes argued that the Treasury's belief that the economy was naturally in equilibrium at full employment rested on Say's law that supply created its own demand. This law relied on the proposition that creating goods produced the income to purchase them, on condition that prices and wages were flexible. A monopolistic railway or gas company might charge too much for their services, so upsetting the balance between demand and supply; or high wages might force up the price of commodities and choke off demand. Hence the power of monopolies needed to be controlled in order to ensure that prices were responsive to competition. Wages should also follow prices. Markets would clear at full employment, on condition that they were allowed to function without hindrance.

Of course, income received for producing goods was not necessarily consumed at once. The recipient might decide to save which was seen to be desirable for the individual and also for society as a whole. A high level of savings would allow a high level of investment; and the rich who saved more of their income were therefore beneficial for the economy. Keynes himself accepted the orthodox view in 1924: 'A supply of *new* capital . . . can only come into existence in so far as those who have claims on the community's flow of income are willing to *defer* their claims, ie out of savings. . . .'[10] These theoretical assumptions were closely connected with a second set of ideas—the Gladstonian conventions of the Treasury in managing the finances of the state. The Treasury's approach to policy rested on management of the government's finances rather than an attempt to manage the economy as a whole. The Treasury's pre-eminence was challenged during the First World War by the pressure of military necessity; at the end of the First World War, it regained and extended its hold on government spending. In 1919, the permanent secretary of the Treasury, Warren Fisher, was also made head of the civil service. The Treasury feared that any relaxation of balanced budgets would tempt politicians into extravagance. The insistence on balanced budgets therefore provided a way of limiting politicians' freedom to succumb to the temptation of spending in order to secure votes, or of accepting the plans of spending departments. The argument was political as much as economic: the concept of the balanced budget constrained profligate and inherently self-seeking politicians. Keynes assumed that public works could be turned on and off over the cycle at the discretion of the government; the Treasury was more sceptical (or realistic), fearing that expenditure was more likely to increase under the pressure of spending departments and their clients.[11] In 1933 Richard Hopkins at the Treasury explained the political reasons for rejecting Keynes's demand for a budget deficit:

If the Budget were unbalanced by £50 millions to take a shilling off the Income Tax, the process would not stop there. If once expenditure can be incurred without the unpleasant necessity of imposing taxation to cover it it would become impossible for the Chancellor of the Exchequer or the Government or the House of Commons to control public expenditure, especially if borrowing for current expenditure was advocated as the road to prosperity. . . . Keynes and Co., whilst agreeing that normal Budgets must be balanced to prevent disaster, say that this is the one psychological year when a concatenation of circumstances has arisen to justify deliberately unbalancing the Budget. But can anyone suppose that once a precedent of this kind was set, people would remember the special arguments adduced to justify it?[12]

Of course, such hostility could be used as an ideological case against Labour's policy of a shift in the balance between private and public spending. But the Treasury did have a shrewd sense of the need to present the state as neutral between interests. Many later economists saw the force of the Treasury's concern: if the constraint of the balanced budget were overturned and no new rules were put in its place, how was the limit of government spending to be set?

The Treasury's approach rested on the financial needs of the state rather than responsibility for the economy as a whole. Its strategy was 'facilitative'.[13] In the words of Peter Clarke, 'it saw itself as the national housekeeper, not the national breadwinner' in ensuring that the books balanced.[14] The case for sound finance was much more than an acceptance of the special interests of the City; it was principled and with the interests of the state in mind.[15] The Chancellor and his leading officials assessed the condition of the economy in order to estimate the likely income from taxes, and then compared their revenue with anticipated expenditure. They did not attempt to use taxes or the level of spending to influence the economy in the short term, or to manipulate the level of demand. Their concern with the impact of taxes and the budget was much more general: a desire to maintain balance and equity between interests. The aim was to ensure that the government used its resources efficiently. Each budget should provide a sum for the redemption of the national debt, and any surplus left at the end of the year should be directed to that purpose. The budget should never allow for a deficit for unbalanced budgets were feared as inflationary. Taxation was seen as a burden and should therefore be kept as low as possible, limited to the essential services of the government. If the Treasury were seen as flirting with heretical doctrines, foreign money might flee Britain. Of course, the government would need to borrow for capital projects or in times of national emergency; financial confidence in the British government as a result of balanced budgets and debt redemption meant that funds were readily available at a low interest rate. The Treasury gave priority to the credit of the government and financial stability over unemployment—and their concern was not mere obscurantism. The Treasury felt that Keynes ignored or underplayed the need to maintain confidence at home and abroad, and to secure the support of different, conflicting interests.

In the Treasury's view, financial rigour was at the heart of national security, and it was also considered to make excellent economic sense. The Treasury believed that individuals were better able to use their money in the most efficient way, whereas the government was more likely to be wasteful and inefficient. These views continued after the First World War. As one Treasury official explained, financial policy since the end of the war had three aims: to balance the budget out of revenue; to reduce the debt; and to cut public expenditure so as to reduce taxation.[16] The government needed to cut its spending or it would starve industry of capital and hinder the process of recovery. At the same time it should maintain debt redemption in order to return money to private individuals. This stress on the balanced budget and tax cuts might lead to the idea that the Treasury rolled back the state and imposed severe economies. In fact, the level of spending remained stable at a higher level than before the First World War. Between 1924 and 1937, the elasticity of government expenditure relative to growth of GDP at current prices was 1.60, compared with 1.21 between 1960 and 1976.[17] Indeed, the balanced budget might have been an issue of presentation, for the treatment of income and expenditure was a matter of accounting practice which could be adjusted by politicians and civil servants. An estimate of the budget on a standardized basis shows that there was in fact a deficit in 1930/1, 1931/2, and 1932/3, and again in 1937/8 and 1938/9.[18] Of course, the deficit was not large and the Treasury believed that deliberate and open acceptance of a deficit was politically dangerous.

One way of reading financial policy between the wars is as a political balancing act to preserve consent to an unprecedented level of spending, as well as restraining politicians from following their own short-term electoral calculations. The revenue from these higher taxes increasingly went to welfare, and the increase in public spending helps to explain the particular British response to the depression. Margaret Weir and Theda Skocpol point out that the response of the Labour party in 1929–31 was shaped by the existing nature of welfare provision. The introduction of unemployment insurance in 1911 meant that Labour politicians concentrated their energies on the terms and conditions of relief for unemployment rather than on public works schemes. Indeed, the deficit on the insurance fund was crucial to the downfall of the Labour government in 1931. The contrast with Sweden is striking: that country had no unemployment benefits, but an Unemployment Commission was set up in 1914 which provided relief work after the war. The institutional structure allowed public works and political debate concentrated on this issue. Similarly, the United States did not have insurance against unemployment prior to the onset of the depression so that the initial response in the New Deal was to provide public works much as in Britain in the cotton famine of the 1860s.[19] Rather than criticising the British state for its inadequate response to the depression and its failure to adopt schemes to create employment, we could point to the early development of relief for unemployed workers.

The Treasury view rested on theoretical assumptions and long-held administrative practices. But Treasury officials were also concerned about immediate political contingencies and the need to preserve legitimacy and trust in the state. One abiding principle in the second half of the nineteenth century was that Treasury policies should be politically neutral.[20] This ambition often complemented, though sometimes challenged, the electoral calculations of their political masters. The rejection of public works might not make political sense when unemployment was exceptionally high with an immediate threat to social cohesion. A desire to redeem the national debt might be an excellent long-term ambition, but the Treasury might temper its enthusiasm in the short term if high levels of taxation threatened political revolt.

The Treasury view was developed in response to the Unemployed Grants Committee which provided money for useful work after the war. The government adopted similar policies before the First World War in response to the cotton famine of the 1860s and in the Unemployed Workmen's Act of 1905. In each case, the aim was to respond to a serious social problem rather than to use public spending to stimulate the economy. It was also realized that if steps were not taken to assist deserving men, the integrity of the deterrent poor law might be threatened. The Treasury was critical of the policy in the early 1920s fearing that welfare spending on public works or the construction of council housing might threaten the financial stability of the government, reducing its ability to apply taxes to the reduction of the debt. The Treasury was particularly concerned by the Liberal proposal of 1929 to spend an additional £251 m on public works over two years.

In fact, the central government was responsible for very few public works. In 1929–32, gross domestic fixed capital formation by the central government was 3.4 per cent of GDP compared with 26.5 per cent by local government.[21] The central government was dependent on the localities, and Hubert Henderson pointed out in 1933 that 'all that the Government can do is to bribe and to harry'. The Treasury was concerned with practicalities. Could the Liberals' public work scheme be implemented in Britain's decentralized system, or would it require a more centralized state? The financial relationship between local and central government was already a matter of tension after the reforms of 1929. The Treasury was not alone in its concerns, and hostility to public works might more accurately be termed a 'Whitehall view'.[22]

The Treasury was not only constructing an argument against public works and deficit finance. Officials also developed their own analytical model and proposed an alternative solution. The experience of the 1920s taught them that their minimalist view of the Treasury's role was not entirely appropriate. The old idea that the economy was self-acting, and that the Treasury could leave adjustments to be made by an automatic, self-correcting system, no longer seemed to apply. Prosperity had not been automatically restored, and the actions of the Treasury did indeed have economic consequences. By the end of the 1920s, the Treasury was therefore tackling the question of how the economy worked, and what it should do. It was moving to a supportive role.[23] Keynes was one influence but so was the Treasury's own realization of the inflexibilities in the economy, and the need to respond to both the Liberal manifesto of 1929 and the election of a Labour government. Of course, the crisis of 1931 meant that the self-acting model collapsed, and the Treasury was obliged to take more control.

In the Treasury's opinion in the run-up to the election of 1929, public works were irrelevant and might even make matters worse. The real problem, it seemed, was not a lack of investment; it was uncompetitiveness. In theory, the gold standard entailed a reduction of prices and hence wages in order to maintain a fixed exchange rate. But the Treasury admitted that the policy was not working. By 1929, the Treasury shifted from its earlier scepticism towards Keynes's claim that money wages were not falling in line with prices, and admitted that they were indeed 'sticky'. Consequently, interest rates were not working as expected in reducing prices and forcing down wages and costs. The Treasury therefore accepted that Keynes's diagnosis was right, but without accepting Keynes's solution—public works. The Treasury took a different line. Costs of production were too high and workers were the authors of their own problems which would be solved by a wage cut. The result would be to solve most of the problem of unemployment—but organized workers preferred their existing wages at the cost of the unemployed. However, the Treasury tempered its view. Perhaps the answer was less a cut in real wages than an increase in efficiency. It admitted that improved organization and efficiency were needed.[24]

Unlike Keynes, the Treasury had a greater awareness of political and institutional constraints, and continued to express concern that public spending might make British industry less competitive. They accused the Liberals of economic confusion in 1929. Their programme rested on preserving the gold standard and free trade. Would the increase in domestic demand created by public works merely result in more imports and a worsening trade deficit? The Treasury argued that the programme would do nothing to solve the difficulties of the export industries where unemployment was concentrated. As Hopkins pointed out, public works 'would concentrate employment in a marked degree upon individual trades . . . and while increasing employment and profit making there would be little or nothing for the depressed basic trades'. The Treasury did not see either demand or industry as homogeneous, insisting that they should be broken down into their constituent parts.[25] As the Treasury commented to the Committee on Finance and Industry, 'Keynes . . . lives in a world of abstractions. He speaks of "Industry", "Profits", "Losses", "Price Level" as if they were realities. In fact, we have no such thing as "Industry". What we have is a series of different industries . . .'[26] Advice given to the Treasury by Sidney Chapman, an economist at the Board of Trade, and by Henry Clay to the Bank of England took the same line. Industries supplied particular markets and could not be instantly adjusted. Any solution to the problem of lack of demand and unemployment therefore rested on allocating spending. As Clay pointed out, 'the spending that we have to stimulate, if we wish to relieve unemployment, is largely spending by overseas customers'.[27] This was somewhat defeatist: by stressing rigidities, these advisers were not allowing for the possibilities of change. Although Keynes assumed rigidity of wages, he assumed flexibility in the organization of industry.

The Treasury response was more concerned with structural weakness, and felt that recovery would take place with an improvement in business profitability as a result of a modest rise in prices. The relationship between costs and prices was no longer being adjusted by a fall in money wages, so a new mechanism was needed. If wages were 'sticky', the solution was a modest rise in prices to reduce real wages on the assumption that wage rates would not follow. Profits would therefore rise. At the same time, industry should be forced to be more efficient. In 1929, one Treasury official argued for 'a bold industrial concentration policy' to overcome the problems of poor industrial organization. Industrial rationalization and support of prices through restrictive agreements and monopolistic practices would increase profitability. Richard Hopkins, a senior Treasury official, argued that the real need was to make British industry more competitive so that unemployment would be reduced through what has been called 'deflation-induced rationalization'.[28]

In the 1930s, the Treasury was more willing to accept some role for public works. In 1930, the Labour government's White Paper promised 'immediate employment by pressing forward development work of public utility'. Henderson was involved in drafting this document as well as the Liberal manifesto of 1929, and he went on to argue from his new position as a Treasury adviser that public works offered a 'means of facilitating a large readjustment of the national economy'. Public works could assist the structural change desired by the Treasury. The crowding-out argument had less force; public works might create the environment needed to escape from the rigidities stressed by Chapman and Clay. In joining the Treasury, Henderson distanced himself from the more unorthodox views of Keynes; at the same time Richard Hopkins moved from the more orthodox Treasury position. Both men were willing to support sound public works schemes, while remaining sceptical about the larger claims of recovery. The case for public works was stronger in 1937 when recovery came to a halt. As we noted, Hawtrey accepted that public works might be necessary if business failed to respond to low interest rates, and that public works might be justified in exceptional circumstances. Indeed, the Bank of England was doubtful from the early 1930s whether cheap money was an adequate response. As Clay remarked, 'it does not follow, because credit restrictions will check a boom, that credit expansion must create a boom.'[29] The Bank was therefore sympathetic to the case for public works. The main difficulty blocking change was now the political complexion of the National government.

Of course, the danger of the Treasury's policy on industrial rationalization was that restrictive agreements might allow prices to rise and profits to recover at the expense of the consumer. The Treasury presided over an erosion of the free market that it had so carefully guarded, and the lack of competition both from abroad and at home did not provide the incentive for efficiency. A recovery strategy based on support for prices and profits might be counter-productive, establishing the basis for the low-effort equilibrium of post-war Britain. In focusing on price support as a means of reducing real wages and increasing profits, the Treasury was ruling out an explicit attack on wages. A political deal was struck after the First World War that the gains made by labour in wages, hours, and welfare benefits would be retained—a deal which politicians were reluctant to reopen. Critics in the United States felt that the British government made a choice to abandon the gold standard rather than to cut wages in order to maintain fixed exchange rates, and that this helped explain the collapse of the world economy.[30]

The Treasury view was based on more than outmoded theory and ignorance. The Treasury had its own policies which were not without credibility; it had a clear sense of administrative and political realities; and it was far from rigid and inflexible in the face of changing circumstances. The Treasury view should be rescued from the caricature of Keynes. It went some way to meet Keynes's points, accepting the case for rigidity of wages, admitting that the mechanism of interest rates was 'jammed', and coming to accept that public works had some virtue. Keynes accepted the rigidities in wages, and tried to work around them; the Treasury was more concerned to reduce costs. These decisions were not a monolithic Treasury view versus the insights of Keynes. As Peter Clarke argues, 'the options constituted a matter of finely calibrated judgement rather than doctrinaire polarization of opinion'.[31]

Despite the shifts in the position of the Treasury, Keynes realized that his argument for public works and deficit finance would not be fully accepted without an intellectual onslaught on existing theories. In *We Can Conquer Unemployment*, the Treasury's assumption that any public spending would crowd out private investment was rejected:

There is no fixed fund of employment . . . . In special circumstances like the present, private investment may not be forthcoming on a sufficient scale; and yet there may be work waiting to be done which is either outside the sphere of private enterprise, or which private enterprise unassisted cannot be expected to undertake . . . . If State enterprise is invoked in directions in which it will not conflict with or displace private enterprise, it has no less effect in increasing employment than that of any other enterprise. Indeed, having as a prime consideration the provision of employment, it can be so chosen that a maximum of employment is provided for a given expenditure.[32]

This claim was limited, for it did not argue that public works could increase employment and stimulate recovery; it was essentially relief work. Neither did it offer a theoretical foundation for rejecting crowding out. Even when the Treasury moderated its opposition to public works, it still did not admit that deficit finance could increase the total level of activity in the economy. If progress were to be made in securing acceptance for unbalanced budgets, refuting the Treasury case was a necessary condition. In order to achieve this task, Keynes moved from political advocacy to the intellectual endeavour of overturning the assumptions of classical economics.[33]

Keynes's approach was that of an 'imperfectionist'. Unlike the Treasury, he stressed obstructions which prevented markets from 'clearing'. Such an approach was not far distant from Beveridge in 1909, who similarly pointed to imperfect information which prevented the labour market from clearing. Beveridge's solution was to ensure that information was available; what he did not accept was the possibility of long-term disequilibrium and persistent unemployment. Although Keynes had a stronger sense of the imperfections and rigidities in the economy than did Beveridge, he did not at first challenge the assumption that the economy would naturally tend to equilibrium. In the 1930s he took a further step. In his *General Theory*, Keynes challenged the theoretical assumptions of the Treasury view and classical economics. Above all, he attacked Say's law. Not all income was spent on the consumption of output, and the gap must be filled by investment in order to maintain full employment. Keynes argued that there could be a deficiency in 'effective demand', with a fall in output and in incomes so that savings and investment could reach a point of equilibrium below the level of full employment. In the classical model, savings from consumption led to investment, so that the economy remained in equilibrium: the dog of savings wagged a tail labelled investment. Keynes reversed the proposition, and questioned the belief that savings were always moral and prudent. In his economics, a dog called investment wagged a tail labelled savings; and the amount of investment depended on the level of demand in the economy.[34]

The level of 'effective demand' might be too low to use all resources. Much depended on the psychology of consumers, investors, and industrialists. Different people had a different propensity to consume. At times of uncertainty, caution about the future might make people less likely either to spend or to invest, and they might opt for keeping cash in hand. Similarly, industrialists would only invest if they expected to sell their output and make a decent profit. An industrialist would not invest in a new factory just because savings were available; the crucial consideration from their point of view was whether there was demand for their goods. Hence the problem was more than rigidities preventing a swift return to the natural state of equilibrium at full employment; the economy could be stuck below the level of full employment of resources as a result of its own processes, and would not automatically adjust. Of course, if demand were high, an industrialist would invest and so utilize savings which would otherwise be idle. The way to move from underemployment of resources to prosperity was to boost effective demand with government spending: a budget deficit could fill the gap and push the economy back to equilibrium. Thus a budget deficit and public works spending would not 'crowd out' private investment; it would increase the level of demand and raise the level of investment. A major prop of his argument was the notion of the 'multiplier', the name given by Keynes to Richard Kahn's idea of 1931. The impact of public works would not be limited to the sum actually spent by the government and the creation of primary employment, for it would also create secondary employment. Such was the benefit from secondary employment that the government would be justified in undertaking completely useless initiatives. Keynes seized on the argument as a demonstration that public works provided more employment at less cost than the Treasury assumed.[35]

Keynes's new model provided the basis for macroeconomics in the next generation. Keynes did not overturn a monolithic established position, for economics in the 1930s consisted of a multitude of voices. He drew on various elements in this literature in an attempt to create a new orthodoxy in response to intellectual uncertainty which left economists without a clear, formal model of the economy. The model that came to dominate after the war as 'Keynesian economics' was, in fact, both more and less than the contents of the *General Theory*.[36]

These considerations are of great importance for an understanding of the intellectual history of macroeconomics, though less for the development of policy in the 1930s. Cabinet discussions in the 1930s were more concerned with the empire than with issues of balanced budgets and deficits. Policy debates were considerably more complicated than a division between Keynes and the Treasury, for there were other radical visions of the economic future. The policies of the National government can hardly be defined as orthodox or conservative in view of its rejection of free trade, its abandonment of gold and adoption of an active domestic monetary policy, and its involvement in the affairs of industry. For its part, Labour remained outside the National government and developed its own policies. This thinking informed Labour's manifesto of 1945 and its policies in government up to 1951 which were far from being inspired by Keynes who was suspicious of Labour's stress on planning. Keynes's policies were treated with considerable caution by Labour as an attempt to mend capitalism and preserve the market, rather than to create a new socialist society. The difference was apparent during the war when Keynes's proposals for managing the economy were only partially adopted. Indeed, planning was high on the agenda in the 1930s and 1940s, and not only on the left. At one extreme, planning could imply something on the lines of Soviet Russia: the replacement of the market and price mechanism by controls. But it could take other forms, from democratic socialism through to industrial self-government or corporatism which connected with the interest of the Treasury in rationalization. Keynes's economics could be read not only as a response to the Treasury view and classical economics but equally as an argument in favour of the market and individual choice against planning.

Planning

Out of the welter of modern politics, out of the economic storms of our period, one idea is crystallising in the minds of most intelligent people—that planning of some kind has become necessary . . . . The real issue that has to be fought out in England during the second third of the twentieth century is the aim of that planning and in whose interests are the plans to be made.[37]

This comment by Ellen Wilkinson, the MP for the depressed shipbuilding town of Jarrow, and her co-author points to a common response to the economic problems of the 1930s: the market had failed and needed to be replaced or supplemented by planning. The sentiment was not only found on the left. T. E. Gregory remarked in 1933 'that whilst Socialists necessarily are planners, not all planners are Socialists'.[38] Socialists saw planning as a way of replacing or at least limiting the market; equally, planning might be seen as a way of preventing socialism and rescuing capitalism from its left-wing critics. Although these different groups of planners might agree that the National government was failing, they were not allies in any other respect.

Another way of characterizing the debates on economic policy in the 1930s and 1940s is to ask: what were the limits of the market? Keynes was concerned with the overall level of demand, and preferred to leave the allocation of resources to the market. Others were more inclined to intervene, but in very different and contested ways. Planning could entail the allocation of resources by means other than the market; it could mean a greater role for trade associations, supported by the state. The exact nature of the government's role varied, but essentially involved microeconomic management of supply rather than macroeconomic management of demand. Should the state take over the role of planning itself; should it act as an umpire, allowing industry and labour to discuss plans; or should it entirely cede the task to industry? Planning was a contested and divisive notion in the 1930s and 1940s.

In 1937, one Conservative MP remarked that planning offered 'the only way in which capitalism can be strengthened and rejuvenated'.[39] Clearly, his definition meant something rather different from Stalin's five-year plan. Many Conservatives and industrialists adopted a form of 'capitalist planning' in the hands of trade associations or boards. Different structures were proposed for these institutions. They might represent only businesses or they might include representatives of labour; the wider process of negotiation over the economy as a whole might be undertaken through parliament or by a new body. This approach has been termed 'corporatism', a somewhat misleading term with its connotations of contemporary developments in fascist Italy.

A number of models already existed. The coal-owners' associations, for example, devised schemes to allocate output and control prices. Such bodies could lead to the notion of 'industrial self-government' by an extension of cartels and trade associations to fix prices and output quotas. 'Capitalist planning' or 'self-determination' by business organizations would make government intervention unnecessary.[40] These ideas were developed by two pressure groups.

Political and Economic Planning was formed in 1931, bringing together economists and leading businessmen. Its aim was to develop 'capitalist planning' as an alternative to socialism and laissez-faire, designed to 'counter the growing tendency to conclude that capitalism is incapable of large-scale planning, and thus hold back an eventually serious swing towards whole-hog Socialism'. PEP criticized public works schemes designed to cure unemployment, arguing that unemployment was a symptom of economic difficulties. PEP stressed the role of industry in solving its own dilemmas. Who should do the planning? PEP proposed 'industrial self-government' through industrial associations, co-ordinated by a national industrial council representing the associations. Although consumers and labour would be represented in consultative bodies, the government was merely to create the legislative framework for self-government and then to refrain from intervention. In the opinion of Arthur Salter, 'with such institutional regulation and control, organised and directed from inside the economic system and not externally imposed, the present defects of the system can be sufficiently remedied to make it work and still leave room for private enterprise and the stimulus of self government'.[41]

A similar approach was advocated by the Industrial Reorganization League established by Harold Macmillan. In his opinion, the depression arose from the saturation of the market as a result of mass production made possible by new technology, and of competition leading to falling prices. The solution was to plan output to meet effective demand. His solution was 'orderly capitalism' overseen by industrial councils who would come together in an 'industrial parliament'. 'The whole intention of the policy . . . is to achieve planning through self-government as an alternative to bureaucracy'.[42] Many leading industrialists supported Macmillan's scheme.

The League and PEP were in general agreement, proposing slightly different versions of industrial government in two bills presented to parliament in 1933. The ambition was to permit an industrial association to create a corporation in any trade where the majority of firms reached agreement. The corporation would then have power to close uneconomic factories, license existing firms, and control entry; it would establish marketing boards and central research facilities; and it would plan production to meet demand. Such schemes seemed to be in line with Treasury thinking on rationalization. The proposal was supported by many Conservatives, with some support from Liberals who saw similarities with their Industrial Inquiry of 1928. However, other Liberals were sceptical. *The Economist* pointed out that the scheme would tackle 'the paradox of Poverty in the midst of Plenty' by the curious means of limiting plenty. In 1940, *The Economist* castigated Conservative industrial policy for proposing an 'orderly organization of industry, each ruled feudally from above by the business firms already established in it', with 'high profits and low turnover'. Was this really the way to rejuvenate industry?[43]

Labour was firmly opposed to the scheme. Privately planned capitalism would be 'plainly anti-social'. The scheme gave little role to workers and unions. PEP gave employers the right to decide on the exact role for workers, who would be limited to discussion of material conditions. Macmillan was willing to offer unions some representation on conciliation committees, and to appoint TUC members to the national economic council. But many capitalist planners felt that any role for workers in the process of planning would threaten the principle of private ownership. The bill therefore excluded labour from any body governing industries. Michael Zvegintzov of ICI and a supporter of PEP saw the problem clearly:

this Bill gives *statutory* powers to an Industry Board, which is composed entirely of 'masters', who are thus given hereafter complete authority. In other words, the conception that 'masters' and 'men' used to be allowed to tussle or cooperate with each other, while the State 'kept the ring' is now replaced by one in which the State definitely acknowledges and confirms the 'masters' as *complete* controllers of industry. You will see, I think, the psychological implications of this.[44]

Not surprisingly, most unions were deeply sceptical. The Economic Committee of the General Council of the TUC devised its own proposals which had many similarities with PEP and the League; the crucial difference was union representation on a national industrial council. Many industrialists were not convinced by capitalist planning, let alone its socialist counterpart. They feared that planning was less a defence against socialism designed to preserve capitalism than an opening for any future socialist government to seize control, or for other interest groups to demand representation. Lionel Robbins shared their concern. 'Nothing but intellectual confusion', he asserted, 'can result from a failure to realise that Planning and Socialism are fundamentally the same.'[45] The FBI was wary of moving beyond existing voluntary schemes to devolved statutory powers which could only come with a political price.

Critics of capitalist planning saw that the main beneficiaries would be dominant firms who would be able to exclude newcomers. Industrial self-government rested, as one cynic remarked, on the 'amazing doctrine' that 'an industry belongs to those already in it'. The leading industrial economist, P. Sargent Florence, felt that parliamentary supporters of the bill were naive in assuming it would create efficiency rather than high prices and profits. And the arch-opponent of socialist planning, Friedrich von Hayek, was no less hostile to capitalist planning than to socialism: any attempt by industry to plan would lead to 'concentration on maximum monopoly profits rather than on making the best use of the available factors'. He doubted that rationalization would lead to efficiency.[46]

Despite these reservations and criticisms, the National government was sympathetic and the Conservative party set up a committee to report on 'the future relations between the state and industry'. Although the report rejected laissez-faire, it did not recommend state control over industry nor the devolution of powers to industrial bodies. Compulsion would be seen as an attack on individual enterprise, which was politically dangerous; the answer was to encourage voluntary agreements and to rely on intermediaries such as the Import Duties Advisory Committee or the Coal Mines Reorganization Commission.[47]

The government was still going too far for some. Walter Runciman, a National Liberal at the Board of Trade, denied the claim of advocates of the scheme that the state was devolving its powers to industrial corporations. Parliament would scarcely cede its powers to industrial associations without showing an interest in prices and profits, so that the result would be constant intervention rather than self-government. What would happen if a corporation collapsed? Did devolution mean that the government should not intervene in voluntary schemes in order to protect the public?[48] Even the initiators of the campaign for industrial self-government had second thoughts. PEP expressed concern that the government was handing over public money without 'any commensurate concessions'. It turned away from industrial self-government to the dissemination of expert opinion and support for Keynes's policy of public works and deficit finance. For his part, Macmillan moved from industrial self-government to argue that planning needed 'a strong government organizing and co-ordinating it'. He turned to the Next Five Years Group which sought a middle way between socialism and fascism. Each industry would adopt industrial self-government and would be concerned for welfare and employment, but would concentrate on issues beyond the range of any single industry. Although some historians see this as a sign of a progressive consensus, in reality its links to 'capitalist planning' meant it differed from Labour's position. Indeed, it could be rejected as a device to prevent socialism. As Harold Laski remarked, 'Germany and Italy have shown us what happens to a society when the State seeks to plan without altering the essential foundations of economic power'.[49] In fact, there were significant differences from corporatism in continental Europe. The National government in Britain had no intention of using the power of the state to attack labour or to run industry. Macmillan was an opponent of fascism and turned to Keynes; he was, after all, the publisher of the *General Theory*. The emphasis on planning was being tempered by an interest in demand management.

Labour rejected the ideas of planning developed within the National government as a cover for retrenchment and monopoly; for its part, the Labour party turned to socialist planning after 1931 as a 'scientific' alternative to the failures both of free-market capitalism, and the inadequate policies of the first and second Labour governments. But deciding how to plan was a difficult matter and led to deep divides within the party. At one extreme were the totalitarian planners or Gosplanners who wished to replace the market with a command economy. They were represented by the Socialist League whose motion was passed by the Labour conference in 1933, stating that the party's aim was 'to eliminate all private enterprise as quickly as possible'. It was all or nothing. Not surprisingly, the party leadership was wary. As

Herbert Morrison pointed out in 1934, 'in formulating political and economic policies we have to consider not only what we want; we have to consider what we can persuade the country to accept.' The Gosplanners were countered by a democratic or liberal-socialist position developed by a group of young economists around Dalton and the New Fabian Research Bureau. These 'thermostatters' rejected the totalitarian view and public ownership, moving instead to a mixed economy of private and public enterprise. Planning should improve the performance of the economy less through ownership of industry than through a variety of policy tools to create stability and economic growth. Their approach rested on a consensual, tripartite view of planning between government, unions, and trade associations which entailed the maintenance of free collective bargaining and parliamentary sovereignty. This approach left a number of questions in the air.[50]

How should the nationalized industries be run, and how should the remaining private sector be planned? Morrison proposed that nationalized industries should not be run directly by ministers or civil servants but as autonomous public corporations with boards appointed for their experience and with freedom to pursue their own policies for efficiency. As he put it, 'the high moral purpose of Socialism does not and must not prevent the Socialist in public affairs carrying a sound business head on his shoulders'. By pursuing efficiency, the boards would necessarily create full employment and economic growth. Not surprisingly, the left argued that the result was that the structure of power within industry remained unchanged; and they doubted that technocratic management could deliver social justice.[51]

In the case of private industry, the democratic socialists proposed a National Investments Board. The left gave the NIB a much more powerful role, essentially replacing the banks and controlling investment in fulfilment of a national plan drawn up by a Supreme Planning Authority. The moderates were cautious: in their proposals, the NIB would be an autonomous body of financial experts which could provide oversight of investment decisions, less through direct control than by licensing new public issues. Unlike the banks and City, experts could look to long-term growth rather than short-term gain. The moderates were somewhat vague about the need for a powerful central planning authority to establish a clear plan; their aim was rather to encourage large companies to behave rationally and to pursue long-term growth. Indeed, the liberal socialists were wary about replacing the market and the price mechanism, for they shared some of the concerns of Hayek that allocation of resources by administrative procedures was likely to be both inefficient and a threat to liberty. Libertarian economists argued that planners failed to appreciate the way that market prices produced complex information about consumer choice and the efficient use of resources. If the planners allocated resources, how would they know that consumers were receiving the maximum utility? The planners might distort consumer preference, so undermining individual decisions and leading to the misallocation of resources. Planners responded that they could mimic the market or gather information in different ways. The democratic socialists were willing to give a role to the price mechanism and some of their allies parted company with them on this point. Dalton felt that market pricing in a socialist society was an oxymoron of 'laissez faire socialism'. Morrison was similarly sceptical, remarking that 'it was pedantic to think consumers' preference important so long as there was great poverty'. There were similar doubts about following the democratic socialists in incorporating Keynes's proposals for demand management; the left feared that Keynes was offering no more than a means of rescuing capitalism rather than replacing it.[52]

Planning offered the Labour party an idea to distance itself from the failures of Ramsay MacDonald and to offer a solution to the depression, but did it mean the end of private enterprise and the market as the source of decisions—or piecemeal intervention and general guidance to a largely private economy? The party went into the election of 1935 deeply divided. The more extreme case was marginalized as the immediate crisis of 1931 faded and the moderate position was more widely adopted. But ambivalence and contradictions remained. Although democratic socialists admitted that planning would misallocate resources and accepted a role for the price mechanism, they were not comfortable with endorsing the market as an equitable allocative device. Neither were they entirely sure about the profit motive. The party came to an uneasy agreement on a reformist programme by the Second World War, with many issues left ambiguous in the interests of electoral success. Of course, the experience of running the war gave new force to the case for physical planning. When the party took power in 1945, the advocates of these competing strands had their opportunity to shape post-war reconstruction.

From War to Reconstruction: The Economics of the Attlee Administration

By the outbreak of war, Keynes's ideas had some purchase. Both the capitalist planners and the moderate socialist planners admitted some role for demand management, without abandoning an interest in industrial self-government or physical planning. Similarly, Treasury officials accepted elements of Keynes's analysis.[53] Nevertheless, Keynes's approach was not fully accepted. During the war, Keynes himself came into the inner circles of the Treasury and played a major role in negotiating the post-war financial settlement. But did this mean that his approach to the domestic economy was now fully accepted by the government?

Keynes adapted his case for demand management to the new circumstances of the war. The war created a new need to reduce demand in order to prevent inflationary pressures. He set out his ideas in *How to Pay for the War*, with its proposals to remove the 'inflationary gap' between available goods and demand by means of taxes and 'deferred pay'. This approach required national income accounts which were used by Kingsley Woods in his budget of 1941. The same year, James Meade set out the means of preventing general unemployment by controlling aggregate demand over the trade cycle. Despite these changes, a Keynesian revolution was still far from assured.[54]

Keynes's proposals were seen as emergency wartime measures rather than permanent and they were resisted in various quarters. The trade unions were wary of deferred pay which they felt might never be returned. Many members of the Labour movement still preferred direct control and planning as a more just solution to the problems of shortages. Keynes argued that the removal of the inflationary gap would obviate the need for direct controls and rationing: the amount of goods would tally with effective demand and consumers could be left to make their own choices. But would this be socially just in the absence of administrative procedures to ensure that everyone had their fair share of basic food and commodities? Neither was the Treasury enthusiastic. In a misunderstanding of Keynes's intentions, some officials saw management of demand as an unacceptable intrusion into liberty. For his part, Hopkins felt that Meade and his colleagues were 'misleading, academic and dangerous'. Could the budget really be balanced over the trade cycle—or would public spending simply rise in the downturn without falling back in the upturn? Nevertheless, something had changed. Whatever the remaining doubts and resistance, the commitment of Churchill's wartime coalition government to 'the maintenance of a high and stable level of employment after the war' was striking after the defeatism of 1929.[55] Would this be achieved by demand management or intervention on the side of supply?

Labour's manifesto of 1945 was ambiguous. It committed a Labour government to 'plan from the ground up', but through a mixture of macroeconomic management and physical controls. Hence the National Investment Board would both plan the direction of investment and influence the timing of public spending for macroeconomic management. The manifesto noted that much could be achieved by means of 'a high and constant purchasing power', but also pointed out that slumps in uncontrolled private industry were certain to be so severe that nationalization would be needed. In the event, the balance fell more on the side of physical controls than Keynesian macroeconomic management of demand. The problem of the manifesto and Labour's policies after its victory in 1945 was that the theoretical issues of how to replace price signals and the market by planning were not resolved. The task was much easier in the war when military success was the paramount need. But how were resources to be allocated in peace? As Noel Thompson points out, the issue was evaded through a 'ploy of simplification by analogy' with the task undertaken by the housewife in her weekly budget. The highly complex issue of how to judge consumer preferences was avoided.[56]

The debate continued. Despite his association with the younger economists in the 1930s, the incoming Chancellor, Hugh Dalton, did not really understand Keynes and vacillated between the Gosplanners and the thermostatters. He preferred to contain inflationary pressures by controls and calls for increased production rather than by demand management or changes in the interest rate. The government emphasized the supply side of the economy, given the urgent need to increase production for the export drive which was vital to restoring Britain's external economic position. Planning was linked with modernization, a task not suitable to Keynesian management of aggregate demand. Instead, domestic demand was held down by rationing and controls. Hence wartime controls were preserved. Import controls were retained and even extended. Building licences were used to direct resources to council housing and to the depressed regions. The government was therefore committed to physical planning, which still left many unsettled questions from before the war.[57]

An important feature of Labour's thinking before the war, and a key element in its manifesto in 1945, was the establishment of a National Investment Board. Although the government nationalized the Bank of England and introduced a Capital Issue Committee to control new issues, it did not go so far as the creation of an NIB.[58] Shortages of labour and materials seemed more pressing, and the economy could be shaped through physical controls. Dalton could also influence investment in other ways, through the nationalized industries and by using differential profits tax in the private sector. Cheap money seemed to make more sense as a financial strategy. Dalton was less interested in the use of monetary policy to control inflation than the fact that low interest rates reduced the cost both of servicing the national debt and of borrowing. The rigid adherence to cheap money meant that Labour had no sense of how to use monetary policy to manage the economy; and the failure of institutional reform meant that the Bank of England regained its power, regardless of nationalization.[59] Such an approach left a number of questions. Could nationalized industries be trusted to make rational decisions in the interests of society as a whole; could the government influence private firms to act in the national interest as well as in the interest of their own shareholders; and how was the price mechanism to be used in allocating resources?

Nationalization was an important feature of policy, arising mainly from earlier trends in regulation of utilities and the need to resolve the difficulties of sectors facing long-term decline such as coal and the railways, as well as from an ideological commitment to public ownership in the case of road transport and steel. However, nationalization was not adopted in any major manufacturing industry. Cotton was one possible candidate but nothing was done. Although the cotton industry was obviously of great importance for Lancashire, it was not vital to the success of the economy in the same way as coal, electricity, or steel. Neither would nationalization in itself secure export markets without other action against foreign producers; nationalization might even disrupt the export drive.[60] Indeed, Labour also embarked on denationalization at the end of the war, returning state capacity in the arms industry to the private sector.[61]

What form should the nationalized industries take? Should each industry be in the hands of a single body, or should there be an element of competition or at least of decentralization? The choice was shaped by the assumption that large-scale production was more efficient and that public ownership would both allow effective co-ordination and protect the consumer. Competition was, on the whole, seen as wasteful. State concerns were therefore monopolies, and the government opted for public corporations rather than the Post Office model of direct control. The public corporation model seemed to work well in the case of the BBC, Central Electricity Board, and London Passenger Transport Board between the wars. But it was still possible to insert an element of competition through a decentralized structure. For example, each coalfield could have its own divisional board under the general supervision of a national board. Morrison saw the possibility of 'socialist competition'. This did not mean actual competition through differential prices; a single national price was set, and low-cost areas cross-subsidized high-cost areas. In the case of electricity, the structure was more centralized: all generation was in the hands of a central board and the regional boards merely handled distribution without the ability to purchase power from the lowest-cost power stations.

Although Morrison believed that the public corporations 'must regard themselves as the high custodians of the public interest', there were a number of difficulties. Despite its arm's-length approach, the government was seen as responsible for the nationalized industries. It also wished to co-ordinate the decisions of the nationalized industries in order to plan the economy but might not be able to impose its wishes. Rather than allowing rational planning, the new public corporations might create interest groups to resist the wishes of the government. Were the boards too powerful and self-interested? Hugh Gaitskell as Minister of Fuel and Power wanted the electricity industry to set prices to reduce peak demand, whereas the industry itself wished to maximize sales. The electricity board got its own way on this issue, and in 1951 turned the government's proposed reduction in investment into an increase. Even Morrison had his doubts, pointing out that 'We ought to take a fairly early opportunity to review the powers of the government to control socialised industries. It is of great advantage to have brought the public utility services and certain basic industries under the control of public boards . . . but the government has a wider viewpoint of the public interest than the boards, and I am far from happy that we are in a position to exercise the control in wide issues of policy which the national economy requires.' Douglas Jay was also concerned about the government's approach of creating public monopolies. Was the government's insistence that no private firm could exist in a sector a threat to liberty? Might the absence of competition lead to complacency and a failure to meet consumer demand? Gaitskell's experience with the electricity industry no doubt contributed to his doubts on clause IV of the Labour party constitution which pledged the party to nationalization. The revisionist position was most clearly set out in Tony Crosland's *The Future of Socialism*: 'public-monopoly nationalisation . . . no longer seems the panacea that it used to.'[62]

How was the output of nationalized industries to be priced in the absence of competition? An intense, technical debate started among leading economists with some favouring marginal cost pricing (the consumer paid the cost of producing the final item as the best measure of its value to them) and others calling for average cost pricing (dividing the cost of production by the total output). On the whole, the government accepted average cost pricing, but modified it. In the coal industry, for example, high-cost pits were subsidized by low-cost producers; and the government's concern for price stability meant that coal prices were amongst the lowest in Europe. Similarly, electricity prices were set at a low level which did not reflect the cost of producing at times of peak demand. When a committee recommended in 1951 an increase in the price of coal and a greater use of the price mechanism, the government ignored the proposal and opted for administrative restrictions on demand and appeals to the conscience of consumers. The government was reluctant to use the price mechanism effectively in distributing resources.[63] It continued rationing, and even extended it to goods that had not been rationed during the war. Many basic goods were subsidized in order to hold down costs to the poor, and the expenditure on subsidies rose from 4.2 per cent of central government spending in 1944 to 16.9 per cent in 1948.[64] Similarly, the price of basic 'utility' goods was held down and exempted from the purchase tax whereas luxury goods paid as much as 100 per cent. Critics complained that the result was to distort consumer preference and to create difficulties for industry. Exports were more likely to be in higher-quality goods than in basic utility items, but industrialists lacked a sufficiently large home market to allow them to cut costs and introduce new lines.

A related point was the role of competition, which was very limited. At home, competition was absent in the monopolistic public utilities and in the private sector agreements were endemic. Entry by new concerns was difficult. Externally, competition was contained by import controls, tariffs, and dollar restrictions. Large-scale monopolistic concerns in the public sector and in private industry could be viewed in two ways. On the one hand, they could lead to efficiency through mass production and the avoidance of waste; on the other, large concerns could lead to monopoly profits so that competition might be desirable. As Harold Wilson put it, 'competition is the public's natural safeguard in any industry which continues on the basis of private enterprise'. Both sides could agree that private firms should not be allowed to adopt 'anti-social' restrictive practices, and Labour's manifesto of 1945 attacked 'bureaucratically-run private monopolies' and promised that 'anti-social restrictive practices will be prohibited'. The concern was entirely understandable, for 23 per cent of gross manufacturing output in 1935 was in the hands of the largest 100 concerns, and 25–30 per cent of manufacturing output was covered by restrictive agreements. The Board of Trade and Economic Section feared that cartels led to inefficiency, allowing industrialists to charge high prices for low turnover and poor productivity. However, the record of the government in tackling these issues was less than convincing. The Monopolies and Restrictive Practices Act of 1948 had few real powers. The Act created an independent tribunal—the Monopolies and Restrictive Practices Commission—to consider monopolistic production with the power to ban practices found to be against the public interest. By 1951, only two reports were produced on minor trades. Indeed, the proportion of gross manufacturing output covered by restrictive agreements actually rose to 50–60 per cent in 1956. Neither was action taken against resale price maintenance despite a special report by the Commission recommending an end to the practice. Although some large retailers were eager to see the end of RPM, and some industrialists were frustrated by agreements covering their own inputs, the FBI was reluctant to encourage government action. Many industrialists feared a return to destructive competition in any future recession and remained loyal to the agreements negotiated in the 1930s. Above all, they were opposed to American pressure to end international cartels. The charter of the putative International Trade Organization initially proposed a ban on international cartels and referral of complaints to the ITO; the British government managed to weaken the ban, and referred complaints to national bodies. Industrialists and retailers who might wish to use the Monopolies and Restrictive Practices Commission were therefore reluctant to encourage an active policy which would affect international agreements. For its part, the government was dependent on trade associations to operate physical controls and so had little room for action against their restrictive practices.[65]

The bulk of industry remained in private hands, so that Labour's ambitions to plan the economy depended on its ability to secure compliance from the private sector, and on its opportunity to utilize various controls over resources and finance in order to modernize the economy, improve productivity, reduce costs, and increase output. Morrison was adamant that the government should 'put this problem of increased productivity first among the current problems to which planning must help to find the answer'. Ministers in Attlee's administration had considerable wartime experience, for they had served in the Board of Trade, Ministry of Supply, and Ministry of Aircraft Production. After the war, they applied some of the lessons they had learned. At the Board of Trade, a Production Efficiency Unit and Special Research Unit were created to apply operational research and standardization. The

Department of Scientific and Industrial Research was given more funding, and a new National Research and Development Council was set up. The government believed that economies of scale would lead to improved productivity, and followed through the wartime proposals of industrial boards with the Industrial Development and Organization Act of 1947 and Development Councils with power to impose a levy for research and development. In fact, only a few sectors implemented the scheme. The Anglo-American Council on Productivity was a further initiative to implement American business practice. Productivity was a matter of improved management and human relations as well as investment in machinery, and the government accordingly funded the British Institute of Management in 1946 and stressed the need for co-operation between workers and employers through Joint Productivity Councils. The practical impact of these initiatives was slight.[66]

Planning was less effective than Labour hoped. Its ability to control even the nationalized industries was limited, and in the private sector it attempted to create consensus through tripartite bodies such as the National Production Advisory Council. These bodies were consultative, with the government merely setting out its ambitions. Consensus was difficult to achieve. The national employers' associations might pay lip service to tripartism, but they were reluctant to admit a voice to unions and often resisted the government's modernization schemes. In part, industrialists' scepticism reflected their concern that 'Americanization' and mass production were inappropriate. Their hostility also reflected suspicion towards the intentions of the government, given Labour's ambivalence to private industry. Labour's ideological and social base was in the trade unions and the non-industrial middle class, and the party had little appreciation of the private sector. Industrial employers were seen as an essentially hostile force, and the unions were resistant to any threat to voluntary wage bargaining or independent action. They were dubious of the human relations approach; a policy of working with a progressive industrial management in pursuit of improved productivity would imply a major ideological shift. The unions were suspicious of employers and continued 'adversarial bargaining'. The Labour government was committed to free collective bargaining, and backed off wartime manpower planning or schemes to control wages which threatened to politicize the wage bargain. The government was therefore limited by a system of tripartism which offered little more than a talking shop. In any case, the government was wary of making the tripartite bodies more powerful and so threatening the sovereignty of parliament.[67]

A number of historians have criticized the post-war Labour government for devoting its activities to building a new Jerusalem rather than reconstructing the economy.[68] At the time, Douglas Jay denied that the government ignored the productive base of the economy for expensive welfare schemes; it was, he claimed, 'almost the reverse of the truth'.[69] He had a point, for the post-war welfare state was somewhat austere and the government was clearly anxious to improve the economy. Whether its policies succeeded is a different matter.

In the opinion of some historians, there was a clear shift in policy with the budget of 1947, and the easing of the worst shortages allowed controls to be dismantled from 1948. On this view, the government realized that planning was failing, so compelling Labour towards Keynesian policies in response to the fuel and convertibility crises of 1947. The outcome, in the opinion of Noel Thompson, was 'a Keynesian socialist conception of planning' which stressed control over the macroeconomy rather than the direct allocation of resources.[70] The shift was marked by the replacement of Dalton at the Treasury and Morrison at the Ministry of Economic Affairs by Cripps, who saw the virtue of fiscal and monetary measures. Consequently, the Treasury regained its dominance with a move from planning to Keynesian demand management which was appealing now that it strengthened their case for a reduction in public spending. The Cabinet set up a Controls and Efficiency Committee which concluded that controls resulted in inefficiency and lack of flexibility. Meade urged that the gap between supply and demand should be measured in terms of income and expenditure rather than by physical measures, and the change was implemented with the creation of the Central Economic Planning Staff and the Investment Programmes Committee which monitored departmental spending plans in terms of finance or income and expenditure, and tried to time investment in response to the trade cycle. On this view, physical planning gave way to demand management and adjustment of the national income. Table 17.1 shows that rationing was reduced by 1951, and a lower proportion of imports and raw materials was subject to controls. But was the shift away from planning in fact so marked?[71]

Despite the reduction in the proportion of goods subject to controls, the figures in Table 17.1 suggests that the economy was still subject to considerable direct, physical regulation. Indeed, Cripps felt that the use of demand management would not make planning redundant so much as increase its effectiveness. The CEPS and IPC tried to shape the economy through the allocation of funds and through quotas for steel. They tried to balance the needs of housing, education, and defence

TABLE 17.1. *Level of controls in the British economy, 1946–51 (%)*

	1946	1948	1951
Consumers' expenditure subject to rationing	28	31	10
Imports controlled	96	91	54
Industrial raw materials controlled	94	81	41
Price-controlled goods/consumers' expenditure	48	49	40

Source: Tomlinson, 'Supply side', 11.

with the claims of nationalized and private industry, with obvious political tensions between ministers over spending priorities. Hence high levels of investment in housing and in education limited other spending, above all on health. Investment in rail and roads was cut and the government adopted a policy of repair rather than modernization. Its priority was to push resources into sectors which could help the balance of payments, most strikingly in oil refining. The government may be accused of responding to immediate problems rather than developing a long-term strategy but the immediate problems were huge, and investment in housing was not unreasonable. Planning remained an ambition. Harold Wilson did not admit the defeat of physical planning, and he suggested in 1949 that the government should introduce permanent economic controls. He drew a distinction between two forms of control. The government should sweep away controls which were merely a 'hang-over from the wartime administration . . . limiting competition between those firms and preventing the entry of often enterprising, progressive, efficient firms from outside'. On the other hand, the government would 'maintain as a permanent part of our policy those controls . . . which are necessary to keep the economy on an even keel, and to maintain full employment'. Hence the government announced that its legislative programme for 1950 would secure permanent 'powers to regulate production, distribution and consumption and to control prices' in the Economic Planning and Full Employment Bill. Although the government was shifting to a concern for consumer choice, and was more willing to use demand management, physical controls and tripartism continued.[72]

Planning was not abandoned, but its effectiveness was limited. The nationalized industries were difficult to control, and the private sector even more so as a result of reliance on trade associations. A Labour government was obviously wary of intervening in the realm of trade unions, so planning of manpower and of wages was rejected. The unions were equally wary of any threat to free collective bargaining. Labour was heavily reliant on exhortation and rhetoric, using tripartite bodies to seek consensus rather than to impose its will.

The Attlee government was clearly concerned with economic modernization and did not embark on high welfare expenditure at the expense of the productive economy. Nevertheless, it was deeply committed to ensuring that the economy was more socially just than in the past. Hence Labour's concern about the role of the market and price mechanism, and its desire to limit inequality of income and wealth. Social justice was felt to be compatible with a more productive economy, and ethics and efficiency were allied rather than opposed. At its most ambitious, Labour was embarking on an attempt to change human personality and motivation. Its aim was expressed in *Labour Believes in Britain* which argued that the public needed to be taught 'a higher conception of social ideas and values and . . . the personal obligations of duty and service'. The war indicated that men and women were driven by a just cause and not only by money. Labour hoped to recreate the same sense of commitment after the war. Planning was not only about modernization; it was intended to complement redistributive taxation in creating equality and capturing socially created wealth for the community. As a result, democracy and freedom would be extended, contrary to Hayek's fear that planning meant a loss of liberty on a road to serfdom. As in the war, all 'useful' people should be united against the useless. The aim was to allow everyone to realize their full potential and not simply to provide more goods. Attlee remarked in 1940 that the Labour party was more than an economic doctrine or class domination. Labour's ambitions were high, even utopian:

First, we believe that inequality of opportunity and gross inequality of wealth are both morally unjust and economically crippling. We have set out, therefore, to establish equality of opportunity for all and to abolish extremes of wealth and poverty. Second, we believe that the economic destinies of the people should not be dictated by a privileged minority of owners. We have set out, therefore, to place economic power in the hands of the nation. Third, we believe that capitalism has, through inefficiency and unemployment, wasted the capacity to produce that the machine has put in our hands. We have set out, therefore, to enlarge the productive power of the nation, to banish mass unemployment, and so to raise the standard of life of the people. Fourth, we believe that only by creating a flourishing and sensible democracy, as virile in industry as in the council chamber and Parliament, can we enhance human dignity and individual freedom.

The problem was that many people wanted more material goods, and the ability to get on with their own lives in the way they pleased. Labour was not in touch with these sentiments.[73]

NOTES

1. Quoted in Clarke, *Keynesian Revolution*, 28, from Churchill, 'Parliamentary government and the economic problem', 174.
2. McKibbin, *Ideologies*, 27–31.
3. Quoted in Middleton, *Towards the Managed Economy*, 145.
4. Quoted ibid, 176.
5. Skidelsky, *Mosley*; Skidelsky, *Politicians and the Slump*.
6. Middleton, *Towards the Managed Economy*, 2.
7. See chs. 12 and 16.
8. See Peden, 'Treasury view', 168; and Howson and Winch, *Economic Advisory Council*, 27; Clarke, *Keynesian Revolution*, 146–7.
9. Peden, 'Treasury view', 169, 171, 172; Clarke, *Keynesian Revolution*, 48–50 , 61; Hansard, 5th ser. 227, 15 Apr. 1929, col. 54; Clarke, 'Treasury's analytical model', 187.
10. Keynes, *Collected Writings*, xiii. 19–23, cited in Peden, 'Treasury view', 170.
11. Peden, 'Treasury view', 180–1; Middleton, 'Treasury in the 1930s', 50, 56–62.

12. Quoted in Middleton, 'Treasury in the 1930s', 59–60.
13. Booth, 'Britain in the 1930s', 501.
14. Clarke, 'Treasury's analytical model', 173.
15. See Clarke, *Keynesian Revolution*, 27, 47, 69.
16. Niemeyer quoted ibid. 31.
17. Middleton, 'Treasury in the 1930s', 50.
18. Ibid., table 1.
19. Weir and Skocpol, 'State structures', 122–3.
20. Middleton, *Towards the Managed Economy*, 6–7.
21. Middleton, 'Treasury in the 1930s', 66 and table 2.
22. Peden, 'Treasury view', 174–5.
23. Clarke, 'Treasury's analytical model', 174; Booth, 'Britain in the 1930s', 501.
24. Clarke, 'Treasury's analytical model', 179, 180, 186, 190; Peden, 'Treasury view', 170; Clarke, *Keynesian Revolution*, 6–7.
25. Middleton, *Towards the Managed Economy*, 154–5.
26. Clarke, 'Treasury's analytical model', 191.
27. Quoted ibid. 192.
28. Quoted ibid. 180; Booth, 'Britain in the 1930s', 510; Peden, 'Treasury view', 176.
29. Clarke, 'Treasury's analytical model', 194–201.
30. Booth, 'Britain in the 1930s', 511–12, 517.
31. Clarke, 'Treasury's analytical model', 193.
32. Keynes, *We Can Conquer Unemployment*, 54, quoted in Middleton, *Towards a Managed Economy*, 147.
33. Clarke, *Keynesian Revolution*, 69.
34. Ibid. 246.
35. Skidelsky, *John Maynard Keynes*, ii. 448–52, 471; Clarke, *Keynesian Revolution*, 246–9, 252–5, 289–90.
36. Laidler, *Fabricating the Keynesian Revolution*.
37. Wilkinson and Conze, *Why Fascism?*, 235 quoted in Ritschel, *Politics of Planning*, 49.
38. Quoted in Ritschel, *Politics of Planning*, 144.
39. C. U. Peat quoted in Ritschel, 'Corporatist economy?', 42.
40. Ibid. 44.
41. Quoted ibid. 44–6; Ritschel, *Politics of Planning*, 162.
42. Ritschel, 'Corporatist economy?', 46–7.
43. Ibid. 47, 48–9; *The Economist*, 15 June, 140, quoted in Tomlinson, *Government and the Enterprise*, 135.
44. Ibid. 51.
45. Ritschel, *Politics of Planning*, 207.
46. Ibid. 204–7.
47. Ibid. 223–7.
48. Ritschel, 'Corporatist economy?', 59.
49. Ibid. 63–4; Ritschel, *Politics of Planning*, 228–9, 235, 249–64, 270, 323–4; Marwick, 'Middle opinion'.

50. Tomlinson, 'Planning'; Ritschel, *Politics of Planning*, ch. 3, 101, 105, 107, 109; Toye, 'Gosplanners versus thermostatters'.
51. Ritschel, *Politics of Planning*, 110, 117.
52. Durbin, *New Jerusalems*, 281; Ritschel, *Politics of Planning*, 108, 113–14, 115, 117, 126–39; Tomlinson, *Democratic Socialism*, 126–9.
53. Ritschel, *Politics of Planning*, ch. 8 and conclusion; Peden, 'Richard Hopkins', 295.
54. Booth, 'Keynesian revolution', 107–8.
55. Peden, 'Richard Hopkins', 281; Booth, 'Keynesian revolution', 112, 107–8; Toye, 'How to pay for the war', 256, 260–1, 278–81.
56. Thompson, *Political Economy and the Labour Party*, 141.
57. Toye, *Labour Party and the Planned Economy*, 187–93, 215–16, 236.
58. Tomlinson, 'Whatever happened to the NIB?'
59. Howson, ' "Socialist" monetary policy'.
60. Singleton, 'Debating'.
61. Edgerton, 'British arms industry'; Edgerton, 'Whatever happened to the British warfare state?', 111.
62. Chick, *Industrial Policy*, 83–5, 90, 92, 95, 96, 99–100, 102; Tomlinson, 'Missed opportunity?', 109.
63. Chick, *Industrial Policy*, 105–6.
64. Ibid. 11–12.
65. Mercer, 'Anti-monopoly policy', 55, 57, 60; Mercer, *Constructing a Competitive Order*, 172–3; Mercer, 'Monopolies and Restrictive Practices Commission', 84.
66. Tomlinson, 'Supply side', 2, 3–4, 16–17; Tomlinson, 'Productivity policy', 37, 46–7, 49–50, 54.
67. Tomlinson, 'Supply side', Tomlinson, 'Iron quadrilateral'; Tomlinson, 'Missed opportunity'; Tiratsoo and Tomlinson, *Industrial Efficiency*.
68. Above all Barnett, *Audit of War*, ch. 1, especially 11–38.
69. Quoted in Tomlinson, 'Supply side', 6.
70. Thompson, *Political Economy and the Labour Party*, 142.
71. Booth, 'Keynesian revolution', 121; Tomlinson, 'Keynesian revolution', 259; Chick, *Industrial Policy*, 6–11, 198.
72. Rollings, 'Reichstag method', 15, 21, 27; Toye, *Labour Party and the Planned Economy*, 224; Chick, *Industrial Policy*, 16–17, 24–5, 42–4, 202; Tomlinson, 'Supply side', 6–8, 10–11.
73. Francis, 'Economics and ethics', 225, 243; Fielding, 'Labourism in the 1940s', 143, 145, 146, 147.

FURTHER READING

Barnett, C., *The Audit of War: The Illusion and Reality of Britain as a Great Nation* (1986)
Booth, A., 'The "Keynesian revolution" in economic policy making', *Economic History Review*, 36 (1983)
—— 'Defining a "Keynesian revolution" ', *Economic History Review*, 37 (1984)
—— 'Economic advice at the centre of British government, 1939–1941', *Historical Journal*, 29 (1986)

—— 'Britain in the 1930s: a managed economy?', *Economic History Review*, 40 (1987)

Chick, M., *Industrial Policy in Britain 1945–51: Economic Planning, Nationalisation and the Labour Governments* (Cambridge, 1998)

Churchill, W. S., 'Parliamentary government and the economic problem', in W. S. Churchill, *Thoughts and Adventures* (1932)

Clarke, P., *The Keynesian Revolution in the Making, 1924–1936* (Oxford, 1988)

—— 'The Treasury's analytical model of the British economy between the wars', in M. O. Furner and B. Supple (eds.), *The State and Economic Knowledge: The American and British Experiences* (Cambridge, 1990)

Durbin, E., *New Jerusalems: The Labour Party and the Economics of Democratic Socialism* (1985)

Edgerton, D., 'Public ownership and the British arms industry 1920–50', in R. Millward and J. Singleton (eds.), *The Political Economy of Nationalisation in Britain, 1920–50* (Cambrdige, 1995)

—— 'Whatever happened to the British warfare state? The Ministry of Supply, 1945–51', in H. Mercer, N. Rollings, and J. Tomlinson (eds.), *Labour Governments and Private Industry* (Edinburgh, 1992)

Fielding, S., 'Labourism in the 1940s', *Twentieth Century British History*, 3 (1992)

Francis, M., 'Economics and ethics: the nature of Labour's socialism, 1945–51', *Twentieth Century British History*, 6 (1995)

Hancock, K. J., 'The reduction of unemployment as a problem of public policy, 1920–29', *Economic History Review*, 15 (1962)

—— 'Unemployment and the economists in the 1920s', *Economica*, NS 27 (1960)

Howson, S. K., ' "Socialist" monetary policy: monetary thought in the Labour party in the 1940s', *History of Political Economy*, 20 (1988)

—— 'Cheap money and debt management in Britain, 1932–1951', in P. L. Cottrell and D. E. Moggridge (eds.), *Money and Power* (1988)

—— 'The origins of cheaper money, 1945–47', *Economic History Review*, 40 (1987)

—— and Winch, D., *The Economic Advisory Council, 1930–39: A Study in Economic Advice during Depression and Recovery* (Cambridge, 1977)

Jones, G., and Kirby, M., *Competitiveness and the State: Government and Business in Twentieth-Century Britain* (Manchester, 1991)

Keynes, J. M., *The General Theory of Employment, Interest and Money (1936)*, in *The Collected Writings of John Maynard Keynes*, xiii (1989).

Laidler, D., *Fabricating the Keynesian Revolution: Studies of the Inter-war Literature on Money, the Cycle, and Unemployment* (Cambridge, 1999)

McKibbin, R., *The Ideologies of Class: Social Relations in Britain, 1880–1950* (Oxford, 1990)

Marwick, A., 'Middle opinion in the thirties: planning, progress and political agreement', *English Historical Review*, 79 (1964)

Mercer, H., 'Anti-monopoly policy', in H. Mercer, N. Rollings, and J. Tomlinson (eds.), *Labour Governments and Private Industry: The Experience of 1945–1951* (Edinburgh, 1992)

—— 'The Monopolies and Restrictive Practices Commission, 1949–56: a study in regulatory failure', in G. Jones and M. W. Kirby (eds.), *Competitiveness and the State: Government and Business in Twentieth-Century Britain* (Manchester, 1991)

Mercer, H., *Constructing a Competitive Order: The Hidden History of British Anti-trust Policies* (Cambridge, 1995)

—— Rollings, N., and Tomlinson, J. D. (eds.), *Labour Governments and Private Industry: The Experience of 1945–1951* (Edinburgh, 1992)

Middleton, R., 'The constant employment budget balance and British budgetary policy, 1929–39', *Economic History Review*, 34 (1981)

—— 'The Treasury and public investment: a perspective on interwar economic management', *Public Administration*, 61 (1983)

—— 'The Treasury in the 1930s: political and administrative constraints to acceptance of the "new" economics', *Oxford Economic Papers*, 34 (1982)

—— *Towards the Managed Economy: Keynes, the Treasury and the Fiscal Policy Debate of the 1930s* (1985)

Millward, R., and Singleton, J. (eds.), *The Political Economy of Rationalisation in Britain, 1920–50* (Cambridge, 1995)

Peden, G. C., 'The "Treasury view" on public works and employment in the interwar period', *Economic History Review*, 37 (1984)

—— 'Sir Richard Hopkins and the "Keynesian revolution" in employment policy, 1929–1945', *Economic History Review*, 36 (1983)

—— 'Keynes, the Treasury and unemployment in the late 1930s', *Oxford Economic Papers*, NS 32 (1980)

Ritschel, D., 'A corporatist economy in Britain? Capitalist planning for industrial self-government in the 1930s', *English Historical Review*, 106 (1991)

—— *The Politics of Planning: The Debate on Economic Planning in Britain in the 1930s* (Oxford, 1997)

Rollings, N., ' "The Reichstag method of governing"? The Attlee governments and permanent economic controls', in H. Mercer, N. Rollings, and J. Tomlinson (eds.), *Labour Governments and Private Industry* (Edinburgh, 1992)

—— 'British budgetary policy, 1945–54: a "Keynesian revolution"?', *Economic History Review*, 41 (1988)

Singleton, J., 'Debating the nationalisation of the cotton industry, 1918–50', in R. Millward and J. Singleton (eds.), *The Political Economy of Nationalisation in Britain, 1920–50* (Cambridge, 1995)

Skidelsky, R., *Oswald Mosley* (1981)

—— *Politicians and the Slump: The Labour Government of 1929–31* (1967)

—— *John Maynard Keynes: A Biography*, 3 vols. (1983–2000)

Thompson, N., 'Hobson and the Fabians: two roads to socialism in the 1920s', *History of Political Economy*, 26 (1994)

—— *Political Economy and the Labour Party: The Economics of Democratic Socialism, 1884–1995* (1996)

Tiratsoo, N., and Tomlinson, J., *Industrial Efficiency and State Intervention: Labour 1939–51* (1993)

Tomlinson, J., *Government and the Enterprise since 1900: The Changing Problem of Efficiency* (Oxford, 1994)

—— 'Productivity policy', in H. Mercer, N. Rollings, and J. Tomlinson, (eds.), *Labour Governments and Private Industry* (Edinburgh, 1992)

—— 'The failure of the Anglo-American Council on Productivity', *Business History*, 33 (1991)

—— 'Why was there never a "Keynesian revolution" in economy policy?', *Economy and Society*, 10 (1980)

—— 'A "Keynesian revolution" in economic policy making?', *Economic History Review*, 37 (1984)

—— 'Mr Attlee's supply side socialism', *Economic History Review*, NS 46 (1993)

—— 'The iron quadrilateral: political obstacles to economic reform under the Attlee government', *Journal of British Studies*, 34 (1995)

—— 'Attlee's inheritance and the financial system: or, whatever happened to the National Investment Board?', *Financial History Review*, 1 (1994)

—— 'Planning: debate and policy in the 1940s', *Twentieth Century British History*, 3 (1992)

—— 'Labour and the productivity problem, 1945–51', in G. Jones and M. Kirby (eds.), *Competitiveness and the State* (Manchester, 1991)

—— 'A missed opportunity? Labour and the productivity problem, 1945–51', in G. Jones and M. Kirby (eds.), *Competitiveness and the State* (Manchester, 1991)

—— *Democratic Socialism and Economic Policy: The Attlee Years, 1945–51* (Cambridge, 1997)

Toye, R., 'How to pay for the war', *Twentieth Century British History*, 10 (1999)

—— *The Labour Party and the Planned Economy, 1931–1951* (Woodbridge, 2003)

—— 'Gosplanners versus thermostatters: Whitehall planning debates and their political consequences, 1945–49', *Contemporary British History*, 14 (2000)

Weir, M., and Skocpol, T., 'State structures and the possibilities for "Keynesian" responses to the Great Depression in Sweden, Britain, and the United States', in P. Evans et al., *Bringing the State Back In* (Cambridge, 1985)

Wilkinson, E., and Conze, E., *Why Fascism?* (1934)

Winch, D., *Economics and Policy: A Historical Study* (1969)

....

CHAPTER 18

The Festival of Britain and British Identity

By 1951, Britain had experienced six years of war and six years of austerity—and the government felt that the nation deserved to celebrate what had been achieved through self-sacrifice and communal spirit. The Festival of Britain of 1951 provided—in the words of its director—a 'tonic to the nation', marking a shift from austerity to affluence, from reconstruction to achievement, and not coincidentally encouraging voters to reflect on the record of the Labour government. Herbert Morrison, the minister responsible for the Festival, summed up its character as 'the people giving themselves a pat on the back'. In all, 8.5 million visitors passed through the pavilions on the South Bank of the Thames, and as many as 18 million people attended events around the country—arguably a higher proportion of the population than in 1851.[1]

The initiative for the Great Exhibition came from the Royal Society of Arts, and in 1943 the Society suggested an event to commemorate its centenary in 1951. The Great Exhibition was run by a combination of private enterprise, voluntary associations, and state support; a hundred years later, the event was run by the state—a clear reflection of the shift from private enterprise and voluntary associations to collective action in the welfare state. The Great Exhibition brought together the products of Britain and the world, and inspired a series of international exhibitions or world fairs, most recently the Paris Exposition of 1937 and the New York World Fair of 1939. At the end of the war, the idea of an exhibition was taken up by the Board of Trade, with the intention of holding the first post-war international exhibition 'to demonstrate to the world the recovery of the United Kingdom from the effects of the war in the moral, cultural, spiritual and material fields'.[2] The emphasis soon shifted to a more limited national event.

In 1946, the Board of Trade organized an exhibition at the Victoria and Albert Museum—itself a production of the Great Exhibition—to show that 'Britain Can Make It'. The choice of name was significant, a conscious echo of the wartime slogan that 'Britain Can Take It'. Now, national survival depended on an export drive, a victory in markets as well as on the battlefields. The exhibition was successful, with about 500,000 visitors admiring the new domestic appliances and furniture that were, as yet, unavailable in the shops at a time of rationing and austerity. Perhaps, one wit remarked, Britain can make it—but Britain could not have it. At the close of 1947, Herbert Morrison announced a more ambitious scheme—'a national display illustrating Britain's contribution to civilisation'.[3] The notion of hosting the first post-war international exhibition—a London World Fair—gave way to a purely British festival to celebrate national identity and pride.

The most recent exhibition held in London was the British Empire Exhibition of 1924/5, whose iconic building was the Wembley Stadium completed in 1923. The exhibition showed that empire markets and products were at the heart of British economic recovery from the depression of the early 1920s. Its aim was 'to stimulate trade, to strengthen the bonds that bind the Mother Country to her Sister States and Daughter Nations, to bring all into closer touch, the one with the other, to enable all who owe allegiance to the British Flag to meet on common ground, and to learn to know each other. It is a family party, to which every member of the Empire is invited, and at which every part of the Empire is represented.'[4] Much the same themes emerged in the final Empire Exhibition at Glasgow in 1938.

By contrast, the Festival of Britain celebrated neither internationalism nor imperialism. In 1951, the British economy was still heavily protected, despite the ambition of the Americans to return to multilateralism. The Great Exhibition had not been a partisan celebration of free trade, but it had nevertheless shown how a divisive economic policy and massive economic changes could be incorporated into British identity and pride. At the time of the Great Exhibition, import duties were falling: the ratio of duties to total imports was 34.3 per cent in 1830, falling to 21.7 per cent in 1850 and 4.4 per cent in 1913. By 1938, the figure was back to 24.1 per cent—and in 1950 stood at 31.2 per cent where it remained until the 1970s.[5] Despite Bretton Woods, the Festival did not mark a turning towards internationalism. Foreign countries did not appear at the Festival, and the Britain celebrated in 1951 still had more in common with the 'insular capitalism' of the 1930s than the global economy of the second half of the nineteenth century. Imports were limited by duties and controls, and the pound was not freely convertible. The Festival looked inwards, to Britain's own identity—with foreign food banned from the cafeteria, and foreign art excluded from the Arts Council's programme of music, drama, and fine art.

Although imperial preference remained an important element in trade policy, in other respects the empire was marginalized. Before the war, the contribution of the empire to Britain's economic and political power was obvious, as a market for British exports, the source of food and raw materials, a basis of national pride, and an indication of great power status. But it was also divisive. Was it any longer possible to incorporate the dominions and colonies into an exhibition of Britain's contribution to civilization, without provoking nationalists and annoying the Americans? Should the loss of the Raj be celebrated as a sign of successful transformation to an independent democracy; or would this lead to questions over the future of other imperial possessions? Perhaps avoidance was a better choice.[6]

The Festival was a national celebration rather than an imperial or international exhibition. It turned inwards, and largely ignored ties with the rest of the world. As Lord Ismay remarked, 'We are not holding an international festival—or even a Commonwealth festival. The Festival of Britain is British in the purest sense of the word.'[7] The view of Britishness expressed at the Festival was social democratic, classless, and egalitarian, achieving unity through an acceptance of diversity and by balancing an ancient past with a modern future.[8] Multiculturalism was not yet an issue, for migration from the colonies into Britain had barely started in 1951. The first migrant ship from the West Indies—the *Empire Windrush*—arrived in 1948, and the presence of Muslims, Hindus, and Sikhs from India and Pakistan was still largely in the future. British identity seemed stable and unproblematic.

The British, so the Festival suggested, were known for their 'realism and strength, . . . independence and imagination', for inventiveness and love of freedom, toleration and resourcefulness. Despite their diversity, they were united by their modest, peaceable, domestic character, and by their sense of belonging to a place.[9] British history was portrayed as a fight for civil and religious freedom, for parliamentary government. The interpretation followed the main lines of the Victorian account of British history, and its more recent restatement by G. M. Trevelyan and Arthur Bryant during the Second World War. Up to the middle of the nineteenth century, the reading of British history was contested between Whigs and Tories, reflecting the divides of the Civil War and 'revolution' of 1688. In the mid-nineteenth century a new consensus emerged which was expressed in the work of historians, as well as in paintings and museums. British history was seen as a combination of Anglo-Saxon liberties and Norman centralization; of romantic Cavaliers and efficient Roundheads. British history and culture were seen as inclusive and integrative, unlike many other European countries where the literary canon and historical interpretations remained deeply divided between republican and monarchic, revolutionary and conservative, traditions.[10]

The theme of British history as a long march of freedom was taken up by the Festival. The future would continue the work of the past, extending democracy from merely having the vote to the emergence of a more educated and engaged citizenry, and offering real social justice for all. The classic statement of this argument was T. H. Marshall's *Citizenship and Social Class* of 1950, with its account of the successive emergence of legal citizenship with equality before the law; political citizenship with the extension of the franchise; and ultimately economic citizenship with the availability of welfare and full employment. The representation of the past was tailored to this vision of the future of social justice and equality. The industrial revolution and the Victorian period were tarnished with inequality, class divides, and imperialism. The Festival stressed what brought people together—constitutionalism and traditional customs, a sense of fair play and freedom. The notion of 'unity' reflected a desire to retain the spirit of comradeship and spirit of the war, a nostalgic longing for the common purpose in defeating an external enemy which minimized the reality of wartime divisions. The National Federation of Community Associations remarked that 'Since 1945 men and women in all kinds of neighbourhoods—new housing estates, suburbs and central areas of large cities—have sought ways by which they could preserve something of the warmth and comradeship which they knew in the war years.'[11]

These sentiments could be unexceptionable pieties; they could also provide the basis of social policies whose ideological implications were by no means shared across the political spectrum. The Festival was not an explicit celebration of Labour's policies, any more than the Great Exhibition was a partisan defence of free trade. Morrison realized that the Festival should not refer to specific policies of the Labour government, such as the National Health Service or nationalization. It was to be non-partisan, overseen by a council chaired by Lord Ismay, chief of staff in the war; members included R. A. Butler, soon to be Chancellor of the Exchequer in the incoming Conservative government, as well as cultural figures such as Kenneth Clark (director of the National Gallery), T. S. Eliot (poet and publisher), John Gielgud (the actor), and Noel Coward (singer and writer), with the king and queen agreeing to become patrons. Although the Conservatives accepted that they should support the Festival, at least by implication the message was not to their liking. It was a state venture, unlike 1851—and did not portray the products of individual firms. The Festival showed that voluntary organizations were an important element in British life, but mainly through sports and pastimes rather than at the core of economic life or the delivery of social policies. The Festival suggested that progress would be achieved through collective action and planning, which would replace the curse of individualism and the chaos of the market.

Even if the Festival did not directly celebrate Labour's policies, it expressed the sentiments of equality and inclusiveness that provided the justification for the National Health Service or nationalization. In Poplar in the East End of London, a model housing estate was built—the Lansbury estate, named after George Lansbury, a leading advocate of a generous poor law system or 'Poplarism' and the leader of the Labour party before the war. Rather like the new towns in process of construction around London and in the depressed areas, the Lansbury estate was to provide a sense of community in 'neighbourhoods', quite unlike private speculative developments or the inter-war council estates. The neighbourhood would have a range of housing for different families and classes, with schools, playing fields and parks, old people's homes, churches, a shopping centre, in order to create social life and cohesion. The minority report of the wartime commission on post-war town planning explained the thinking behind these schemes:

A strong and well-balanced industry, a healthy and well-housed population, good educational and recreational facilities. The absence of slums, of poverty and of unemployment were the necessary environment for individual freedom and a well-ordered community. The nation has not only to maintain freedom for her citizens, but to make that freedom worth enjoying.[12]

Abercrombie was a signatory of the report and his own *Greater London Plan* reflected the approach of planning preservationists and the Campaign for the Preservation of Rural England of the 1930s: a concern for the region as a whole, allowing the redevelopment of the inner city, the creation of self-contained new towns, and the maintenance of the countryside. Planning was essential. The modern efficiency of the Lansbury estate was contrasted with 'Gremlin Grange', a parody of the mock-Tudor semi-detached houses of the 1930s, with its lack of taste and avoidance of functionality.[13]

In the words of J. B. Priestley, planning in Britain was 'cosy', like a family deciding how to use its resources. Whether people really did wish to become part of cosy communities was doubtful. At the end of the war, many people considered better housing to be an urgent need—but they did not necessarily share the ambition of Labour politicians and town planners to create a sense of community and to stimulate active citizens. They were more interested in their own families and needs, in buying new consumer goods and enjoying an individual form of consumption. Indeed, there was a real danger that Labour's plans, without the fulfilment of active participation in a socialist commonwealth, would become little more than bureaucratic statism.[14] Stevenage was far from being everyone's ideal of a modern, balanced community; and many people preferred the individuality of Gremlin Grange to the efficient flats of the Lansbury estate. *Punch* satirized Labour's programme as a 'Merrie Effort' run by a 'Merrie Board', akin to the export drive and productivity effort with their plethora of commissions and planners.[15] More seriously, planner preservationists were criticized for destroying what they sought to preserve. Could modernity and tradition be so easily united if efficient agriculture meant rooting out hedgerows and using large amounts of fertilizers and pesticides? Did the reconstruction of city centres after the Blitz and slum clearance really lead to efficiency or to sterility? One response was to turn from the present to history. The vernacular landscape and history was set against progressive planning and the future.[16] The Labour government had a difficult task in steering between the needs for more housing and factories, and the preservation of the traditional aesthetic of the countryside.

In order to produce goods for export and to meet domestic demand, British industry needed to be more productive. Morrison felt that the Festival would encourage people to work harder:

Every progressive business now recognizes that men and women do not give of their best unless they are shown pretty clearly what they are working for and unless they can feel that in some sense it is their show. Yet we expect many millions of people to toil and if necessary die for their country who live in conditions where they can hardly catch the slightest glimpse of what their country and its civilization really mean.[17]

Equality and a sense of cohesiveness were both ethically desirable and efficient: Morrison's statement marked a rejection of the belief that growth and productivity came from incentives offered by high wages and profits.[18] Although the Festival was intended to mark the end of recovery and austerity, many in the Labour party remained suspicious of personal consumption and affluence, with competition between producers for market share. They preferred nationalization of utilities and basic industries which transferred ownership to the people. Consumer goods were left to private industry, and many Labour politicians saw the emergence of large concerns as efficient. There was little support for encouraging competition to reduce prices or improve quality, and to offer consumer choice. The Festival of Britain displayed a wide range of goods, with new and excitingly modern designs—but Labour remained ill at ease with the world of plenty.

The Festival celebrated modern industry, expressed in the Dome of Discovery—a gleaming futuristic building seemingly landed on the South Bank from outer space—and the Skylon—a slender tower balanced on a point whose lack of visible means of support seemed to *Punch* to encapsulate the state of the British economy. Science was integral to the Festival. The Dome of Discovery brought together intrepid adventurers and men of action with men of science who were similarly pushing into unknown areas of the physical world and outer space, showing 'British contributions to world civilization in the arts of peace'. The close connection between warfare and science was written out of the story—a striking omission in view of the wartime development of radar, aircraft, and the atomic bomb. A few years later, C. P. Snow argued that the two cultures of science and the arts were hostile, and that the dominance of a classically educated political elite led to industrial decline. His case was self-serving—a plea for more funding for science—and far from an objective account of the role of science in the British state. Indeed, the problem was less that science was marginalized by a dominant literary culture; it was rather that science seemed to offer an easy solution to deeper structural problems in the British economy. Science was positive and technocratic, a force for efficiency and prosperity and central to Britain's identity. Scientists and technicians were portrayed as crucial to Britain's economic prosperity and strategic policies; the Festival aimed to diffuse knowledge of science.[19]

The Festival was advised by the Arts Council and the Council of Industrial Design set up by the Board of Trade in 1944 to encourage function and modern design, and to assist in the rejuvenation of British industry. To complement them a Council for Architecture and a Council for Science and Technology were created. The main site at the South Bank was largely overseen by the Council of Industrial Design and the Council for Science. The Council of Industrial Design continued the theme of its earlier involvement in 'Britain Can Make It', selecting goods for their quality of design and economy, and advising on how best people might spend their money. In the words of one of its publications, 'When consumer knowledge increases still further, the minority of less satisfactory appliances will be reduced to a negligible quantity.' The aim was not only to improve the design of goods, but to educate the consumer into making sensible choices based on knowledge and discrimination.[20]

There was an air of didacticism at the Festival, both in the representation of science in the Dome and in the activities of the Arts Council. The Council was formed in 1945, emerging from the wartime Council for the Encouragement of Music and the Arts, with the intention 'to increase the accessibility of the fine arts to the public'.[21] In 1945, its first chairman—John Maynard Keynes—expressed his own ambitions for the new body, building on his long-standing assumption that economic prosperity should create a good life. 'We look forward', he remarked, 'to a time when the theatre and concert hall and art gallery will be a living element in everybody's upbringing, and regular attendance at the theatre and at concerts a part of organized education.'[22] The Labour government and the Festival organizers had a similar ambition of raising standards of taste and in the process healing class conflict. The aim was not merely to improve material standards of life, but also intellectual and artistic engagement. Morrison pointed out in 1949 that 'Socialism is not bread alone. Material security and sufficiency are not the final goals. They are means to the greater end—the education of a people more kindly, intelligent, co-operative, enterprising and rich in culture.'[23] High culture should not be seen as the exclusive preserve of a narrow elite; it should be available to all educated citizens. Indeed, popular culture was defined as second-best and inappropriate to a properly democratic and egalitarian society.[24] Many of the events of the Festival gave the population what was good for them. As Hugh Casson, one of the leading architects of the Festival, remarked, it was 'the usual charade of Hampstead wets teaching the working classes to have fun'.[25] Michael Frayn pointed out in 1963 that the workers were treated as 'the loveable but inert objects of benevolent administrators' whom he called the 'herbivores' in contrast to the carnivores of brash American entertainment and capitalism.[26] When the government renewed the charter of the BBC in 1946, Morrison believed that it had a duty to improve public taste. The

Director-General of the BBC agreed that broadcasting had the duty to 'seek the good, the beautiful and the true':

It rests on the conception of the community as a broadly based cultural pyramid slowly aspiring upwards . . . . The listener must be led from good to better by curiosity, liking, and a growth of understanding. As the standards of the education and culture of the community rise so should the programme pyramid rise as a whole.[27]

The state was consciously stepping into the shoes of the private patron, reflecting the redistribution of income and wealth after the war and, as Sir Ernest Pooley remarked, 'a democratic conviction that has steadily been growing through the years that good art is enjoyable art and should be appreciated by all and sundry, whatever their incomes may be'.[28] These 'herbivore' sentiments were not accepted by everyone. T. S. Eliot feared that 'more means worse'—a reactionary cry that only a small, cultured minority could really appreciate art. He was alarmed that politicians were making culture into an instrument of policy, in the process reducing standards, 'destroying our ancient edifices to make ready the ground upon which the barbarian nomads of the future will camp in their mechanized caravans'.[29] 'Carnivorous' Tories took a more robust and populist view: why should the herbivores preach to the people who should be allowed to enjoy themselves as they pleased, watching Hollywood movies, attending sporting events, or visiting the pub? The issue divided parties. Some Labour politicians were suspicious of foisting middle-class culture on the workers; others were eager to make the enjoyments of the rich available to all. Some Conservative politicians were hostile to American popular culture; others argued that people should have what they wished in a free market. Such divisions were apparent in the debates over the Television Act of 1954 which allowed commercial television—a measure that Labour promised to repeal if it won the next election.[30]

The Festival marked a moment of change in British culture. Up to 1950, Ross McKibbin argues that British culture had two relatively cohesive forms, which were not integrated with each other. On the one side, there was the culture of the music hall and football, of hobbies such as leek growing or pigeon racing; on the other side, the pastimes of the middle class, from whist and bridge, to golf and symphony concerts. Of course, there were exceptions, and the cinema and radio marked the beginnings of a more integrated national culture.[31] But the major change did not occur until the 1950s and, above all, the 1960s. Not only did television reach a majority of the population, but there was also the growth of a distinctive youth culture cross-cutting lines of class and income. Affluence, and changes in occupational structures, broke down the rigidities of communities in industrial districts; and the development of secondary education meant that teenagers were more likely to create their own identities than to join the adult world of work. The proliferation of goods and opportunities meant that taste and discrimination became more varied and malleable. The Festival of Britain was on the cusp of these changes—with the Labour party suspicious and uneasy of what they might mean.

In 1951, Britain was poised on the edge of an economic boom and a period of unprecedented affluence, of high employment and rising standards of living, universal health care, improvements in education, and a gradual breakdown of the solidaristic working-class communities of the heavy industrial districts. The Conservatives returned to power with the prospect that they could now implement policies of free enterprise and competition in opposition to planning and controls, as Churchill had intended in 1945 with his acceptance of F. A. Hayek's critique of Labour policies in *The Road to Serfdom*. When the Festival closed in September 1951, the new Conservative government cleared the site on the South Bank of the Thames. The Festival seemed to the new government to symbolize much of what was wrong with Britain. The Dome of Discovery and Skylon were dismantled—a sign to some commentators that the new government was rejecting the ideology of Labour. There were some changes: nationalization was halted, and road transport and steel were returned to private ownership; controls and rationing were dismantled.

The moral of the story was more complex than a rejection of Labour's ambitions. Many of the buildings were planned from the first as temporary constructions and some of the major buildings remained, such as the Festival Hall which continued as the leading London venue for orchestras subsidized by the Arts Council. Similarly, many policies of the Labour administration survived. The welfare state was popular with middle-class electors, and was confirmed and entrenched in the late 1950s. The Conservatives embarked on a programme of expansion of higher education and invested in the welfare state, with government spending remaining much higher than before the war. Denationalization was not taken any further, and a shift to competition in the private sector was muted. Personal incentives or high profits to stimulate economic growth were treated with caution: the outcome might be animosity from workers with a demand for higher wages, the onset of inflation, and a balance of payments crisis. Many of the institutional structures of the previous century still remained in place—not least the privileged legal position of trade unions and the belief of the government and employers that the best way of containing wage inflation was to work with them. In 1951, the level of competition from foreign goods and between British firms remained low. The result, in the opinion of Crafts and Broadberry, was a 'low-effort equilibrium'—a sense that modest profits and reasonable wages were possible without too much effort.[32]

The prospect of a more radical reconsideration of the existing institutional structure emerged in the 1960s and 1970s. Britain was not growing at the same rate as its European neighbours, and a period of heart-searching and reassessment started. Imperial preference gave way to the European Economic Community; the Bretton Woods system of fixed exchanges gave way to floating rates; and the compact between trade associations, unions, and the government came under immense strain. After 1979 and the election of Mrs Thatcher, many of the institutions created in the century between the Great Exhibition and the Festival of Britain were unmade. The autonomy of the great cities was eroded. Nationalization went into reverse and council houses were sold off. The City of London was deregulated and international capital mobility returned to levels not seen since before the First World War. The privileged legal status of unions was revoked, and inflation was controlled by unemployment rather than deals with the government and trade associations. Equality was now seen as a threat to efficiency; higher incomes and lower marginal tax rates were valued as incentives to growth. By the time of the next celebration of British identity at the Millennium Dome in 2000, a 'new' Labour party could claim pride in a 'new Britain' as dynamic, enterprising, cool, and multicultural.

NOTES

1. Weight, *Patriots*, 204–5; Banham and Hillier, *Tonic to the Nation*.
2. Quoted in Weight, *Patriots*, 192.
3. Ibid. 193.
4. See the website on the Exhibition at http://members.lycos.co.uk/bee1924/index2.html.
5. Broadberry, *Productivity Race*, table 9.8.
6. Weight, *Patriots*, 197–8; Conekin, *Autobiography*, 185.
7. Lord Ismay, 'Welcome to the people of all lands', *Daily Mail, Festival of Britain 1951*, 3.
8. Conekin, *Autobiography*, 26–9.
9. Ibid. 29.
10. Burrow, *Liberal Descent*; Collini, *Public Moralists*.
11. National Federation of Community Associations festival leaflet quoted at www.museum-oflondon.org.uk/archive/exhibits/festival.
12. Matless, *Landscape and Englishness*, 204.
13. For images, see the English Heritage website at http://accessibility.english-heritage.org.uk, entry on Publications/The Survey of London/Recent Work/Poplar/Lansbury Estate, last accessed on 21 July 2004; Matless, *Landscape and Englishness*, 268.
14. Fielding, ' "Don't know and don't care"'; Fielding, 'What did "the people" want?'; Fielding, 'Labourism'.
15. Matless, *Landscape and Englishness*, 272.
16. Ibid. 274.
17. An interview with the Rt. Hon. Herbert Morrison MP in *The Times Festival of Britain Supplement, May 1951: The Meaning of this Year—A Challenge to British Leadership*.
18. See Ellison, *Egalitarian Thought*; Daunton, 'Payment and participation'.

19. Weight, *Patriots*, 200; Snow, *Two Cultures*; Edgerton, *Warfare State*; Forgan, 'Festivals of science'; Conekin, *Autobiography*, 57–67; see also Cox (Director of science for the Festival), 'Science at South Kensington', *Daily Mail, Festival of Britain 1951*, 48.
20. On the Council, Conekin, *Autobiography*, 49–5; Maguire, 'Designs on reconstruction'.
21. Royal charter incorporating the Council in 1946.
22. Quoted in Conekin, *Autobiography*, 10.
23. Quoted ibid. 48.
24. Ibid. 10–13.
25. Weight, *Patriots*, 196.
26. Frayn, 'Festival of Britain', 320.
27. Weight, *Patriots*, 167–70.
28. Sir Ernest Pooley in *The London Season of the Arts Programme*, from www.museum-oflondon.org.uk/archive/exhibits/festival.
29. Quoted Weight, *Patriots*, 168–9.
30. Ibid. 240–54.
31. McKibbin, *Classes and Culture*, 527–8.
32. Broadberry and Crafts, 'British economic policy'.

FURTHER READING

Banham, M., and Hillier, B., (eds.), *Tonic to the Nation* (1976)

Broadberry, S. N., *The Productivity Race: British Manufacturing in International Perspective, 1850–1990* (Cambridge, 1990)

—— and Crafts, N. F. R., 'British economic policy and industrial performance in the early post-war period', *Business History* 38 (1996)

Burrow, J. A., *A Liberal Descent: Victorian Historians and the English Past* (Cambridge, 1981)

Collini, S., *Public Moralists: Political Thought and Intellectual Life in Britain, 1850–1930* (Oxford, 1991)

Conekin, B., *The Autobiography of a Nation: The 1951 Exhibition of Britain, Representing Britain in the Postwar World* (Manchester, 2003)

Cox, I., *The South Bank Exhibition: A Guide to the Story It Tells* (1951)

Daily Mail, Festival of Britain 1951: Preview and Guide (1951)

Daunton, M. J., 'Payment and participation: welfare and state-formation in Britain, 1900–51', *Past and Present*, 150 (1996)

Edgerton, D., *Warfare State: Britain, 1920–1970* (Cambridge, 2006)

Ellison, N., *Egalitarian Thought and Labour Politics: Retreating Visions* (1994)

Fielding, S., ' "Don't know and don't care": popular political attitudes in Labour's Britain, 1945–51', in N. Tiratsoo (ed.), *The Attlee Years* (1991)

—— 'What did "the people" want? The meaning of the 1945 general election', *Historical Journal*, 35 (1992)

—— 'Labourism in the 1940s', *Twentieth Century British History*, 3 (1992)

Forgan, S., 'Festivals of science and the two cultures: science, design and display in the Festival of Britain, 1951', *British Journal for the History of Science*, 31 (1998)

Frayn, M., 'Festival of Britain', in P. French and M. Sissons (eds.), *The Age of Austerity* (1963)

Hilton, M., *Consumerism in Twentieth-Century Britain* (Cambridge, 2004)

McKibbin, R., *Classes and Cultures in England, 1918–51* (Oxford, 1998)

Maguire, P., 'Designs on reconstruction: British business, market structures and the role of design in post-war recovery', *Journal of Design History*, 4 (1991)

Matless, D., *Landscape and Englishness* (1998)

Snow, C. P., *The Two Cultures* (Cambridge, 1993)

Weight, R., *Patriots: National Identity in Britain, 1940–2000* (2002)

INDEX